Malaysia

0 — 200 km
0 — 200 miles
N

page 312
Kudat
Kota Maruda
Pitas
Simpangan
Kota Belud
page
Kinabalu 4101
Lingkabau
Tua 314
Ranau
Klagan
Kota Kinabalu
Sandakan
Kuala Penyu
Tambunan
Pulau Labuan
Beaufor
Keningau
Kinabatangan
Lahad
Bandar Seri
page
Sabah
Kuamut
Datu
Bagawan
Lawas
276
1280
BRUNEI DARUSSALAM
Trusan
Pandawan
Miri
Limbang
Pensiangan
Sibuti
Long
Lumbis
Semporna
Niah
Pa Sia
Kelabakan
Tawau
Suai
Gunung Mulu
Ulu-Ulu
Pulau
National Park
Mensalong
Sebatik
page
Lama
Malinau
Pulau
Bintulu
299
Bario
Bemiang
Bunyu
Tubau
Tanjung
Tarakan
Oya
Lio Matoh
Ambalat
Igan
Sebauh
Bonganlongit
Mantadau
Celebes
Mukah
Belaga
Tanjungselor
Sea
Dalat
Balingian
2499
Longlemuat
Sibu
Nanga Merit
Kiampanjang
Sarikei
Kanowit
Sarawak
Kapit
Rejang
Tanjungredeb
page
Saratok
Datahdian
Kongkemul
278
Metulang
2053
Kuching
Simunjan
Betong
Muarabu
Domaring
Bau
Sri Aman
Brahim
Manesi
Sepinang
Lubok Antu
G. Liangpran
Muarawahau
ma
2240
Putussibau
Borneo
Sangkulirang
Baraikarangan

PHILIPPINES

Malaysian States

0 — 200 km
0 — 200 miles

I A

Sabah

BRUNEI
DARUSSALAM

Sarawak

I N D O N E S I A

INSIGHT GUIDES

MALAYSIA

APA PUBLICATIONS L

Part of the Langenscheidt Publishing Group

ABOUT THIS BOOK

INSIGHT GUIDE
Malaysia

Editorial
Project Editor
Francis Dorai
Editorial Director
Brian Bell

Distribution
UK & Ireland
GeoCenter International Ltd
Meridian House, Churchill Way West
Basingstoke, Hampshire RG21 6YR
Fax: (44) 1256-817988

United States
Langenscheidt Publishers, Inc.
36–36 33rd Street 4th Floor
Long Island City, NY 11106
Fax: (1 718) 784-0640

Australia
Universal Publishers
1 Waterloo Road
Macquarie Park, NSW 2113
Fax: (61 2) 9888-9074

New Zealand
Hema Maps New Zealand Ltd (HNZ)
Unit D, 24 Ra ORA Drive
East Tamaki, Auckland
Fax: (64 9) 273-6479

Worldwide
Apa Publications GmbH & Co.
Verlag KG (Singapore branch)
38 Joo Koon Road, Singapore 628990
Tel: (65) 6865-1600; Fax: (65) 6861-6438

Printing
Insight Print Services (Pte) Ltd
38 Joo Koon Road, Singapore 628990
Tel: (65) 6865-1600; Fax: (65) 6861-6438

©2007 Apa Publications GmbH & Co.
Verlag KG (Singapore branch)
All Rights Reserved
First Edition 1972
Eighteenth Edition 2000
Updated 2007

CONTACTING THE EDITORS
We would appreciate it if readers
would alert us to errors or out-
dated information by writing to:
Insight Guides, P.O. Box 7910,
London SE1 1WE, England.
Fax: (44 20) 7403-0290.
insight@apaguide.co.uk

www.insightguides.com
In North America:
www.insighttravelguides.com

The first Insight Guide pioneered the use of creative
full-colour photography in travel
guides in 1970. Since then, we
have expanded our range to
cater for our readers' need not
only for reliable information
about their chosen destination
but also for a real understanding
of that destination. To achieve
this, our guides rely heavily
on the authority of locally
based writers and
photographers.

How to use this book
The book is carefully
structured to convey an
understanding of Malaysia and
its culture, and to guide readers
through its diverse range of
sights and attractions:

◆ The **Features** section, with a
yellow colour bar, covers the
country's history and culture in
authoritative essays.

◆ The main **Places** section, with
a blue bar, is a complete guide
to all the sights and
areas worth visiting.
Places of special inter-
est are cross-refer-
enced by numbers or
letters to specially
commissioned full-
colour maps.

♦ The **Travel Tips** listings, with an orange bar, provides information on travel, hotels, restaurants and other practical aspects of the country. Information can be located using the index printed on the back cover flap.

The contributors

Apart from the usual tourist stomping grounds, this new 18th edition covers exciting new sights in Malaysia. Supervised by Singapore-based managing editor **Francis Dorai**, the book was completely restructured, building on the earlier edition put together by **Jessamym Cheam-Gwynne**.

Updating the history chapters and writing new essays on contemporary politics and religion was **Desmond Tate**, author of several books on Malaysian history. Malaysian Nature Society managing editor **Gail Saari** revised the environment chapter. Practising architect **Puvan J. Selvanathan** wrote the piece on architecture. **Wendy Moore** wrote the Insight On picture stories and the arts and crafts essay.

In the Places section, Peninsular Malaysia was updated by Kuala Lumpur-based freelance journalist **Siew-Lyn Wong**, who also wrote the piece on adventure sports and the new Travel Tips section. The Sabah and Sarawak sections were updated by **Wendy Hutton** and **Jill Gocher**. New photography was provided by **HBL Network, Arthur Teng, R. Mohd Noh** and **Jill Gocher**.

This guide was updated in 2007 under the supervision of **Low Jat Leng** at Insight Guides' Singapore office. **Fong Peng Khuan**, a veteran of the tourism industry, updated the Peninsular Malaysia chapters. The Sabah and Sarawak sections were handled by Southeast Asia expert **Wendy Hutton**, who also covered the Travel Tips section along with travel writer **David Bowden**. **Siew-Lyn Wong** also contributed to the update.

This edition retains material from previous editions, largely the work of writers like **Star Black, Harold Stephens, Sharifah Hamzah, Marcus Brooke, Susan Amy, Joseph Yogerst** and **Jeremy Cheam**. The copy was edited by **Tim Harrison** and indexed by **Hilary Cooper**.

Map Legend

— ·· —	International Boundary
— — —	State Boundary
⊖	Border Crossing
—•—•—	National Park/Reserve
— — —	Ferry Route
✈ ✈	Airport: International/ Regional
🚌	Bus Station
P	Parking
❶	Tourist Information
✉	Post Office
🏛 † ⛪	Church/Ruins
†	Monastery
☾	Mosque
✡	Synagogue
🏰 🏚	Castle/Ruins
∴	Archaeological Site
∩	Cave
⚲	Statue/Monument
★	Place of Interest

The main places of interest in the Places section are coordinated by number with a full-colour map (e.g. ❶), and a symbol at the top of every right-hand page tells you where to find the map.

INSIGHT GUIDE
Malaysia

CONTENTS

Maps

Introduction

History

Features

A note on place names

It's not unusual for the same place to be called a variety of names in multicultural Malaysia. Some places are routinely referred to by their English names, others by their Malay ones. Rather than follow a rigid system of using English place names followed by their Malay equivalents in brackets, we have adopted the name most commonly used by locals first. Sometimes, therefore, it's English first and at other times Malay.

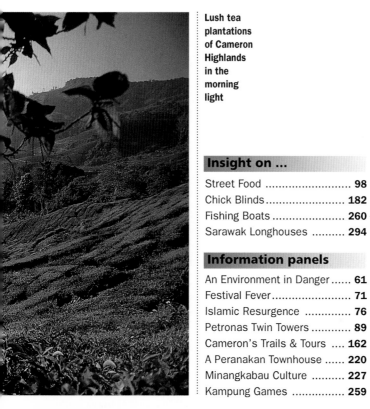

Lush tea plantations of Cameron Highlands in the morning light

Places

THE BEST OF MALAYSIA

The unique attractions of Malaysia, dynamic culture, fabulous markets,
sun-soaked beaches, breathtaking nature… here, at a glance,
are our recommendations, plus some tips that even Malaysians won't always know

ABOVE: Gunung Mulu National Park's Lang Cave.

MALAYSIA FOR FAMILIES

● **Kuala Lumpur City Centre.** Frolic in KLCC Park's wading pool and playground; for indoor edutainment, **Petrosains**' interactive science exhibits and **Aquaria** KLCC's 5,000 marine and land creatures beckon. *Pages 140–2*
● **Genting Highlands (Pahang).** Its outdoor and indoor theme parks are surefire hits with children; over 60 rides, a 4D movie theatre, a skydiving wind tunnel and more. Lots of shopping and dining options for the rest of the family. *Pages 165–6*
● **Ma' Daerah Turtle Sanctuary (Terengganu).**

Be volunteers for a weekend; moniter green turtle landings, collect turtle eggs, assist in hatchery work, and learn about conservation at the same time. *Page 251*
● **Sepilok Orang-utan Rehabilitation Sanctuary (Sabah).** The largest orang-utan sanctuary in the world. See Borneo's adorable young apes feed and learn to live in the rainforest. *Pages 334–5*
● **Sea walking (Sabah).** Put on a special helmet, sink a couple of metres to the seabed, and breathe fresh air as you walk around a reef looking for Nemo. *Page 316*

ONLY IN MALAYSIA

● **Petronas Twin Towers (Kuala Lumpur).** The world's tallest twin buildings are a sight to behold. **Suria** KLCC mall within offers great shopping. *Pages 140–2*
● **Hill stations.** English colonials found reprieve from the heat on **Frasers' Hill** and **Cameron Highlands** in Pahang (*pages 160–5*) and **Bukit Bendara** in Penang (*pages 194–5*); so can you.
● **Palatial townhouses. Cheong Fatt Tze Mansion** in Penang (*page 190*) and the **Baba Nyonya Heritage Museum** in Melaka

(*pages 220 & 221*) are stunning showpieces that blend Chinese, Malay and Victorian architectural styles.
● **Gunung Mulu National Park (Sarawak).** Vast caves with beautiful stalagmites and stalactites amid a lush rainforest. *Pages 113, 298–302*
● **Longhouses (Sarawak).** Discover traditional tribal life on a longhouse visit. *Pages 292–3, 294–5*
● **Mount Kinabalu (Sabah).** Watch the sunrise from the peak of one of the highest mountains in Southeast Asia. *Pages 320–5*

LEFT: Genting's outdoor theme park has plenty of kid-friendly amusement rides.

BEST SHOPPING EXPERIENCES

● **Bukit Bintang (Kuala Lumpur).** Glitzy malls galore offering brand-name goods, local designs, computers and gadgets. *Pages 143–4*

● **Central Market (Kuala Lumpur).** Get Malaysian and Southeast Asian souvenirs, from ikat fabrics to Kelantanese silverware, here. *Page 134*

● **Royal Selangor Pewter.** Take home unique, refined pewter gifts available at RSP's visitor centre in KL's Setapak Jaya suburb (*page 389*) and in stores in major cities.

● **Main Bazaar (Kuching, Sarawak).** Shops filled with curios and antiques alongside old-style shops and sellers of edible birds' nests and fresh Sarawak pepper on this kilometre-long, river-facing strip. *Page 279*

ABOVE: Endau-Rompin National Park is home to the Wagler's pit viper and other unique wildlife.

ABOVE: Kuala Lumpur's glitzy Bukit Bintang.

TOP HISTORICAL SIGHTS

● **Sultan Abdul Samad Building (Kuala Lumpur).** Neo-Saracenic-style colonial building with copper domes and arched colonnades. *Page 135*

● **Lembah Bujang Archaeological Museum (Kedah).** Remains of millennium-old *candi* (temples) indicate early Buddhist and Hindu influences. *Page 201*

● **Dutch architecture (Melaka).** The brick-red **Stadhuys**, **Christ Church** and **GPO** in the Town Square date back over 300 years ago. *Pages 217–8*

● **Niah Caves (Sarawak).** Where a 25,000-year-old skull and ancient rock paintings were found. *Pages 302–3*

BEST NATURAL ATTRACTIONS

● **Endau-Rompin National Park (Johor/Pahang).** Unique plant life (including 71 palm species) and animals in this second-largest national park. Challenging trails and beautiful cascades. *Pages 234–5*

● **Taman Negara (Pahang).** Said to be the oldest rainforest in the world. Go on jungle trails, observe nocturnal wildlife from animal hides or even ascend the mighty Gunung Tahan. *Pages 267–70*

● **Bako National Park (Sarawak).** Sarawak's smallest national park is full of fascinating plants and animals, plus a lovely little beach. *Pages 284–6*

● **Kinabalu Park (Sabah).** From hot springs to rare orchids, buttercups to pitcher plants, this huge park around Mt Kinabalu has everything. *Page 321*

● **Kinabatangan River (Sabah).** The best place in Southeast Asia for viewing wildlife, including endemic proboscis monkeys, orang-utans, Borneo pygmy elephants and brilliant birds. *Page 336*

RIGHT: the grand Sultan Abdul Samad Building is one of the most photographed structures in Malaysia.

ABOVE: Pulau Pangkor Laut's powder-white beach, Emerald Bay.

BEST BEACHES AND ISLANDS

● **Pulau Pangkor Laut (Perak).** Privately owned island with the exclusive Pangkor Laut Resort. Luxury chalets on stilts over the sea. *Page 175*
● **Pulau Langkawi (Kedah).** Fine beaches, first-class resorts, historical attractions and nature excursions – everything you'd want for a tropical holiday. *Pages 204–9*
● **East coast beaches.** A powder-white, 240-km (150-mile) stretch from Kemaman all the way to Kuala Besut. Gorgeous views make a drive on the coastal road truly memorable. *Page 250*
● **Pulau Redang (Terengganu).** Offers some of the best diving in Malaysia with a rich marine ecology and amazing visibility. *Pages 255–6*

● **Pulau Perhentian (Terengganu).** Perhentian's twin isles have shallow waters for snorkelling, pristine beaches for sunbathing, and a relaxed air for an idyllic vacation. *Pages 256–7*
● **Pulau Sipadan (Sabah).** Probably Malaysia's most famous island and certainly its only oceanic isle, Sipadan is deservedly rated one of the world's top dive sites. *Page 340*
●**Tunku Abdul Rahman Park (Sabah).** A marine park with five islands, each with glorious beaches, coral reefs and crystal-clear waters. *Pages 316–7*

BELOW: the fishing's good in Malaysia's waters.

BEST PLACES OF WORSHIP

● **Masjid Sultan Salahuddin Abdul Aziz (Selangor).** The Blue Mosque radiates an imposing aura with its spectacular blue-and-white dome and four towering minarets. *Page 149*
● **Sri Subramaniar Swamy Temple (Selangor).** The colourful annual Thaipusam procession from Kuala Lumpur culminates at this temple complex in the limestone Batu Caves.

ABOVE: Kek Lok Si Temple has an eclectic mix of architectural styles.

The world's largest statue of Lord Murugan (43 metres/140 ft) stands at the foot of the outcrop. *Pages 152–3*
● **Kek Lok Si Temple (Penang).** One of the most important Buddhist temples in Southeast Asia. Fine views from its seven-tier pagoda sporting Chinese, Thai and Burmese architectural styles. *Pages 193–4*

BEST EATS

● **Street food.** Kuala Lumpur's streets brim with good eats in night markets, Chinese coffee shops and *mamak* (Indian Muslim) stalls. To sample the best street food in the capital, head to **Jalan Alor** *(page 144)*, **Petaling Street** *(page 137)*, **Jalan Tuanku Abdul Rahman/Jalan Masjid India** *(page 139)* and **Kampung Baru** *(page 142)*.

● **Eat regional.** Each region offers its unique cuisine and signature dishes. Don't miss Penang and Melaka's Peranakan cuisine, prepared with a fusion of Malay and Chinese ingredients and cooking styles; Ipoh's *kway teow* (flat rice noodles); the east coast's *nasi dagang* (coconut rice with tuna curry); spicy Sarawak laksa and more. *Pages 93–7, 374–83*

ABOVE: *mee rebus*, a popular Malay noodle dish found at hawker stalls.

ABOVE: Always a hive of activity, Siti Khadijah Market offers glimpses of local life in Kota Bharu.

BEST MARKETS

● **Kampung Baru Sunday Market (Kuala Lumpur).** A night market with all things Malay, from textiles to silverware to food. *Page 142*
● **Petaling Street Bazaar (Kuala Lumpur).** Bustling night market offers copies of everything – handbags, watches, T-shirts and more. The food here is excellent. *Page 137*
● **Siti Khadijah Market (Kota Bharu, Kelantan).** This fresh-produce market makes for an unforgettable experience with its colours, smells and noise. *Page 257*
● **Gaya Street Fair (Kota Kinabalu, Sabah).** Sunday morning market with food, clothing, orchids, trinkets and treasures, as well as local families on outings. *Page 315*
● **Kota Belud** *tamu* **(Sabah).** Sunday morning market interesting for its mix of tribal people as it is for the huge range of produce. *Page 318*

MONEY-SAVING TIPS

● **Domestic flights.** Book internal airfares with AirAsia (www.airasia.com), Fly Asian Xpress (www.flyasianxpress.com) and Berjaya Air (www.berjaya-air.com) in advance to get excellent rates.
● **Cash is king.** Note that credit card payments incur a 3 percent surcharge. Cash payments get you better prices too.

● **The art of bargaining.** Goods in smaller shops and markets most likely have prices that can be bargained down. Bargaining is also a great way to interact with locals. Start by knocking 50 percent off the price, then increase to the amount you are prepared to pay as you haggle. Throw in a few local phrases like "Boleh kurang?" (Can you reduce the price?) or "Mahal sangat!" (Too expensive!). If you do not want to pay the "final price", walk away. If your offered price is indeed acceptable, the seller is likely to call you back. If he doesn't, you know you have gone too low. The first and last customers of the day usually get good prices.

A PALETTE OF IMAGES

Blending millennia-old rainforests with high-tech skyscrapers,
Malaysia will astound the most jaded of travellers

Selamat Datang ke Malaysia – "Welcome to Malaysia" – is perhaps the first sign you'll see walking past the cool steel and glass corridors of the gleaming Kuala Lumpur International Airport (KLIA). It is a sentiment that will be warmly echoed by the smiling Malay, Indian or Chinese taxi driver who takes you from the airport into the booming capital of Kuala Lumpur. Even if you enter Malaysia by road and arrive first at a small Malay *kampung* (village), this same friendly greeting will be warmly offered.

Over the centuries, Malaysia has been open to millions of visitors from all over the globe, and its people have changed, absorbed and adapted customs and traditions from far-flung countries to suit the Malaysian way of life.

What is the most accurate image of the country? Travel brochures depict a romantic land of beaches with coconut palms, lost idyllic islands and amazing coral reefs. Somerset Maugham's short stories paint vivid pictures of colonial bungalows set in rubber plantations, while naturalist Alfred Russel Wallace's *Malay Archipelago* conjures up pictures of ancient jungles, screaming with monkeys and orang-utans, and brimming with butterflies. Yet, given the publicity Malaysia has enjoyed in recent years (thanks partly to the strident proclamations of its former prime minister Dr Mahathir Mohamad), the media would have us believe that the country is grooming itself to become the next Asian metropolis with big-ticket projects like the Petronas Twin Towers, Kuala Lumpur International Airport and the Multimedia Super Corridor IT project. These images are far from contradictory; indeed, Malaysia combines, album-like, every one of these visions – and more.

In Malaysia, you may find yourself in many incongruously different scenarios: from bopping at a ritzy Kuala Lumpur nightclub and visiting Malay *kampung* on the east coast to tramping millennia-old rainforests in Pahang and visiting tribes once known for their headhunting exploits in Borneo. And, there's adventure too, everything from climbing to the clouds on Mount Kinabalu to scuba diving at world-famous Sipadan island.

Some of the country's secrets will be unlocked from the pages of this guide; others are waiting to be discovered. You will find those idyllic beaches and islands, those rubber plantations (with the *punkah wallah* replaced by air-conditioning) and you will, if you venture out, find yourself in age-old jungles. But, no matter how strange the sights are to you, there is an innate sense of being in a land that welcomes you – Malaysia beckons, as it has done for countless centuries. ❏

PRECEDING PAGES: a *gasing*, or top spinner from Kelantan; ancient burial poles of Sarawak. **LEFT:** KL's Petronas Towers lays claim to fame as the world's tallest twin buildings.

Decisive Dates

THE EARLY CENTURIES

c.40,000 BC Earliest known habitation at Niah Caves, Sarawak. Remains of a palaeolithic stone-tool workshop at Kota Tampan, Perak, could be even older.

c.2,500 BC Proto-Malays spread south from Yunnan area in China.

c.300 BC Earliest signs of Bronze and Iron Age cultures in Malaysia.

c.200 BC Start of trade with India and China.

100 BC–AD 200 Emergence of trading kingdoms in the Isthmus of Kra.

AD 500–1000 Development of Hindu-Buddhist trading kingdoms in Kedah's Bujang Valley, northern Perak and Santubong, Sarawak.

1303 Terengganu Stone records introduction of Islam to the Malay Peninsula.

THE RISE OF MELAKA

c.1400 Founding of Melaka by Parameswara.

1409 Chinese Admiral Cheng Ho arrives in Melaka.

1411 Parameswara converts to Islam and travels to China to meet the Ming Emperor.

1446 Melaka expands under Sultan Muzaffar Shah.

c.1456–98 Tun Perak serves as prime minister under four sultans and Melaka becomes biggest empire in Southeast Asia.

1511 Melaka falls to the Portuguese.

1512 Melaka's deposed sultan sets up new capital in Riau-Lingga which later becomes Sultanate of Johor.

1528 Sultan Muzaffar Shah starts the Perak Kingdom.

1641 The Dutch take Melaka from the Portuguese; start of Dutch dominance in the area.

1699 Assassination of Sultan Mahmud of Johor.

1699–1819 Empire of Johor, mostly at Riau, under Bendahara line.

1699–1784 Period of Minangkabau-Bugis struggle for domination of the Straits of Melaka.

1726 First sultan of Terengganu Kingdom installed.

1784 Death of Raja Haji at Melaka; Dutch break Bugis power in area.

1786 The British occupy Penang.

1812 Death of Sultan Mahmud Shah, last ruler of united Johor-Riau Kingdom.

COLONIAL MALAYA

1819 British occupy Singapore.

1824 Anglo-Dutch Treaty carves up Malay world into colonial spheres: Dutch cede Melaka to British and keeps Riau.

1826 Singapore, Melaka, Penang and Province Wellesley become Straits Settlements under British control.

1831–32 Melaka Malays rebel against British in Naning War.

1840s Tin rush attracts an influx of Chinese tin miners to the western coast of the peninsula.

1841 James Brooke established as Rajah of Sarawak.

1846 British annex the island of Labuan.

1858–68 Civil war in Pahang.

1867–74 Selangor civil war.

1874 Pangkor Treaty signals start of British intervention in Perak, Selangor and Negeri Sembilan.

1875–76 Perak War signals uprising against British after introduction of controversial tax and subsequent murder of British Resident.

1881 British North Borneo Chartered Company establishes a centre in North Borneo, now Sabah.

1891–95 Pahang Rebellion.

1895–1905 Mat Salleh Rebellion. The introduction of new taxes had earlier created general discontent, and Mat Salleh gathers many supporters in his revolt against the North Borneo Company.

1896 Federated Malay States (FMS) are created.

1909 Treaty of Bangkok transfers four northern Malay states from Thai sovereignty to British control.

1914 Johor brought under British control.

1914–18 World War I.

1920–41 British adopt decentralisation policy in FMS; early signs of a Malay nationalism against British rule begin to surface.

MALAYA, MERDEKA, MALAYSIA

1941–45 Japanese conquest and occupation.

1945 British reoccupy Malaysia.

1946 Malayan Union scheme introduced but is opposed; formation of United Malay National Organisation (UMNO); Sarawak and British North Borneo become Crown colonies.

1948 Malayan Union scheme abandoned; Federation of Malaya inaugurated.

1948–60 Communist uprising – The Emergency.

1952 Municipal elections in Kuala Lumpur; UMNO and Malayan Chinese Association (MCA) parties cooperate.

1953 Alliance coalition comprising UMNO, MCA and Malayan Indian Congress (MIC) formed.

1955 First general elections in the peninsula; landslide win for the Alliance.

1956 Tunku Abdul Rahman leads Merdeka Mission to London to negotiate for independence.

1957 Malaya becomes independent, and the Union Jack is lowered for the last time.

1960 The state of emergency ends.

POST-INDEPENDENCE

1961 Tunku proposes a political association – called Malaysia – that would include Malaya, Singapore, North Borneo, Sarawak and Brunei.

1963 Creation of Malaysia without Brunei.

1963–66 Confrontation with Indonesia. In 1966, Indonesia's Sukarno is ousted; new Indonesian government led by Suharto ends confrontation. Philippines drops its claim on Sabah and recognises Malaysia.

1965 Singapore leaves Malaysia and becomes an independent nation.

1969 Riots in the wake of the general elections on 13 May are the result of racial tension between Malays and Chinese. Violent outbreaks, mainly in Kuala Lumpur, in which hundreds are killed.

1970 New Economic Policy (NEP) established to encourage fairer distribution of wealth among races.

1981 Malaysia's fourth prime minister, Dato' Seri Dr Mahathir Mohamad, takes office.

1983 Constitutional crisis involving the position of Malaysia's hereditary rulers.

1987 UMNO racked by power struggle between Mahathir Mohamad and Tengku Razaleigh Hamzah; "Operation Lallang" carried out by the Mahathir administration results in detention of prominent opposition politicians, trade unionists, educators and community leaders.

1988 UMNO *Baru* (New UMNO) is formed by Mahathir.

PRECEDING PAGES: Selangor royalty, circa 1874.

LEFT: Sultan Abu Bakar of Johor.

RIGHT: prime minister, Abdullah Ahmad Badawi.

1989 Semangat '46, led by Tengku Razaleigh Hamzah, registered as a new political party. The Communist Party of Malaysia abandons its 41-year armed struggle to overthrow the Malaysian government.

1990 General elections – the ruling coalition retains its two-third majority in Parliament.

1990s National car project, Proton, leads the move to transform Malaysia into fully-developed nation.

1997 Petronas Twin Towers completed. During the Asian financial crisis, currency control laws are imposed to stop the free fall of the ringgit.

1998 Kuala Lumpur is first Asian city to host the Commonwealth Games. Deputy Prime Minister Anwar Ibrahim is dismissed and arrested. *Reformasi* move-

ment demonstrations in support of Anwar create political crisis.

1999 Anwar Ibrahim jailed six years for corruption and further tried for sodomy. Ruling coalition retains two-third majority in snap general elections, but the opposition PAS (Islamic party) takes Terengganu and Kelantan.

2000 Anwar sentenced to additional six years' jail.

2003 Malaysia's longest-serving prime minister Mahathir Mohamad retires. He is replaced by his deputy Datuk Seri Abdullah Ahmad Badawi.

2004 In a ringing endorsement for the moderate and consensus-seeking Badawi, the ruling Barisan coalition wins the elections by a landslide victory, with PAS-controlled Terengganu returned to the government.

2005 Ringgit unpegged from the US dollar. ❑

BEGINNINGS

Malaysia's ancient history is shrouded in myth, but its ideal position as a port brought rapid development. And with trade came mighty empires

Gentle, young and growing – Malaysia is all this. But peel away the surface layer of modernity, and the kaleidoscope of Malaysia's history unfolds. The beginnings of human settlement go back at least as far as 40,000 years, with a diverse cast of Malays, Ibans and Bidayuhs, Kadazandusuns and Muruts, Chinese, Indians, Europeans and other races. And the land's rich architectural history has borne an abundance of megaliths, ancient inscriptions, traces of Buddhist temples, abandoned forts, medieval mosques, and neo-classical colonial buildings.

Prehistoric Malaysia

The story of human habitation in Malaysia is enveloped in shadows as deep as those cast by the equatorial rainforest. What we know is pieced together from archaeological discoveries and ancient Indian, Chinese and Arab texts. However, these origins are still rife with unexplained mysteries and are hotly debated.

A *Homo sapiens* skull discovered in Sarawak's Niah Caves, and believed to date from 25,000 years ago, provides one of the earliest evidence of human life in Malaysia. In the Malay Peninsula, the discovery of a stone-tool workshop in Kota Tampan, Perak, dates back to 34,000 years ago or even earlier, while the earliest skeletal remains found are at least 10,000 years old. The evidence indicates that these people were Mesolithic (Middle Stone Age) hunters and shifting cultivators. They lived in rock shelters and caves in the limestone hills of the peninsula and used stone implements for cutting and grinding, as well as for hunting wild animals. These people may have been the ancestors of the Negrito aborigines (Orang Asli) or of their successors, the Senoi.

Around 2,500 BC, the Proto-Malays, spreading south from Yunnan in China, made their way to the Malay Peninsula and the islands beyond. These were the Neolithic people, their

implements more sophisticated than those of the Negritos or Senoi. As well as hunters, they were also cultivators and sailors and thus lived a more settled life. Eventually they forced the Negritos and Senoi into the hills and jungles of the interior of the peninsula.

Much later, around 300 BC, a new wave of

immigrants, also of Malay stock pushed the Proto-Malays inland. Called Deutero-Malays by anthropologists, these were Iron Age and Bronze Age people, who used metal for their weapons and tools. The Deutero-Malays are in fact the direct ancestors of today's Malays in the peninsula and the archipelago.

Through trade, the early inhabitants of the Malay Peninsula were exposed to older civilisations. The peninsula's location (including the Isthmus of Kra above it) interrupted direct sailing on the main sea route between east and west and the area was affected by nature's arrangement of alternating monsoons – southwesterly followed by northeasterly. These factors made

LEFT: ancient megalith at Negeri Sembilan.
RIGHT: Orang Asli family, the original inhabitants.

it the natural meeting point for Indian and Chinese traders to exchange their wares. These foreign traders also came to buy the produce of the region itself, such as gold – the Malay Peninsula was known to early geographers as "the Golden Chersonese" – aromatic woods, spices, and as far as the Chinese were concerned, birds' nests, highly prized for making revitalising soups.

The first of these Indian and Chinese trading voyages are believed to have taken place in prehistoric times and by the beginning of the Christian era, the trade routes were already well established. Convenient ports of call soon

The Indian period

Some settlements eventually grew to become kingdoms in which various features of Indian culture were adopted. The local rulers were known as *rajah*, and Brahmin rituals dominated royal courts. Even today, this early Indian influence can still be seen. Many Malay words are derived from Sanskrit, and some Malay social customs, especially wedding rites, reflect Hindu customs. So deep was this impact on local Malay society that the 1,500 years of Malaysian history between the arrival of the first Indians and the coming of Islam is called the Hindu or Indian period.

sprung up, which would later become the nuclei for other minor states.

Trade grew with China and India. But the Chinese traders kept to themselves largely and were more interested in trade, thereby making little impression on local Malay culture. But a good number of the Indian traders settled down and integrated with the local inhabitants. As a result, many settlements along the straits were influenced by Indian ideas and resulted in many local Malays becoming Hindus or Buddhists. These new converts built temples, traces of which are still visible in the Bujang Valley, Kedah, and Santubong in Sarawak; both sites date back to 5th century BC.

The fame and fortunes of the Indianised kingdoms of the region depended entirely on their success in dominating the trade routes passing by their shores. Monopoly was the name of the game, and the port-kingdom which could secure the widest control over international and local trade by attracting foreign traders to its harbour was the winner, and thereby evolved into a maritime empire.

The first of these empires was Funan, based on the Mekong Delta. Next was Sri Vijaya, which from its base at Palembang in Sumatra, dominated the trade of the Straits of Melaka for the best part of a thousand years. In the 14th century, it was the turn of the great Javanese empire of Majapahit to control the trade of the region. Then at the dawn of the 15th century came Melaka, the first maritime power to be based on the Malay Peninsula itself. It is with Melaka that the story of Malaysia truly begins .

The *Sejarah Melayu* (*Malay Annals*) was written in the early 1600s. Part historical fact and part legend, the text traces the transformation of a small coastal village into this famous trading empire. According to the *Malay Annals*, it all began on the island of Tumasek (now Singapore) at the tip of the

RAPID DEVELOPMENT

Parameswara founded Melaka with just a handful of followers; within just two years, the population had reached 2,000.

Taking a cue from this good omen, Parameswara decided to build a settlement on the site. As he happened to be standing near a melaka tree, he decided that the settlement should bear the name of that tree. The great port and kingdom of Melaka (or Malacca) came into being.

Parameswara and his followers cleared the land around it, planted rice and orchards, and exploited the rich tin deposits inland. News of the settlement's wealth spread, which soon began to attract passing traders.

Malay Peninsula, which at the time was ruled by a Palembang prince with the Hindu title of *Parameswara*. When Javanese forces attacked Tumasek, Parameswara and his followers were compelled to flee northward to Muar in Johor on the peninsula.

One day, when Parameswara was out hunting near the coast, one of his hounds was kicked by a white mousedeer. The king, always appreciative of valour, exclaimed, "This is a good place! Even the mousedeer are full of fight!"

LEFT: 9th-century Hindu temple in the Bujang Valley, Kedah, reflects the influence of Indian traders.
ABOVE: Melaka was once a bustling trading port.

Chinese protection

At this time, the Ming Emperor of China was sending out large fleets of ships to expand trade with Southeast Asia and beyond. In 1409, one of his most famous admirals, Cheng Ho, called at Melaka. He recognised Parameswara as its legitimate ruler, and at Parameswara's request, placed the new port under China's protection. In 1411, Cheng Ho took Parameswara back with him to China – a trip which confirmed Parameswara's status as a sovereign ruler owing fealty to China alone. These moves were very important for Melaka's survival, for the new port-state was under constant threat of Siamese attack.

Melaka was ideally placed as a port and emporium. It had an ideal position on the Straits of Melaka, astride the great east-west maritime trade route. It also had a fine harbour free of mangrove swamps and deep enough for the ships of the day, with waters sheltered from storms by the island of Sumatra.

Melaka's harbour soon became crowded with ships of all kinds, the streets of the city alive with merchants from all parts of Asia. Its bazaar was crammed with exotic goods: silks, brocades,

ARABIC ARRIVAL

Muslim traders brought Arabic script to Melaka – the Malay version is called *Jawi* – which replaced the ancient Indian script Melakans had used before.

well as settling disagreements among the sailors and merchants in his group.

The first Muslims in Southeast Asia were Arab traders, who can be traced back as early as the 11th century. Marco Polo, the great Italian traveller, discovered a Muslim kingdom in North Sumatra at the end of the 13th century. From North Sumatra, Islam was introduced into Melaka which by the early 15th century had become a fully-fledged Muslim sultanate. Muslim Indian traders played a major role in this conversion and it was through trade that Islam spread to the other parts of the Malaysian/Indonesian world. At the same time, Islam became established wherever Melaka's own power as a maritime empire expanded. By the end of the 15th century, Melaka's empire included all the states of the Malay Peninsula and those on the east coast of Sumatra.

The other states' conversion to Islam was a total revolution for the Malays. Islam brought with it new ideas about government and encouraged literacy by reading the Koran and other Islamic texts. Being a missionary religion with a message for each individual, Islam gradually had a great impact on the values and outlook of ordinary people. At the same time, however, the Malays managed to retain or merge much of their pre-Islamic customs with the new religion.

Mighty power

Over a period of some 20 years, Melaka rose from obscurity to become one of the most powerful states in Southeast Asia. Its population at the zenith of its might was 40,000 – mainly Malays, but also including a large number of Javanese and other settlers from the region, as well as Indian and Chinese traders.

The city was located at the mouth of a river and was divided into two halves. The sultan's palace and the Malay *kampung* were south of the river, while on the north bank the houses and stores of the merchants provided the cosmopolitan bustle of the city. The two halves were linked by a bridge, on which, like the bridges of many medieval European cities, a number of merchants built their shops.

The palace was the centre of life. Peasants, traders and noblemen had the right to present their petitions to the sultans, in his *balai*, or

and porcelain from China; cloth, glassware and jewels from India; jade and diamonds from Burma; pepper, sandalwood, ebony and rice from the islands of the Malaysian/Indonesian archipelago, and tin, gold and other produce from Melaka's own hinterland.

An important reason for Melaka's success was its ability to ensure the safety of the traders who called there. Melaka's rulers commanded the allegiance of the Orang Laut, or sea gypsies, who managed to curb the pirate menace in the Straits of Melaka. In Melaka itself, *shahbandars* or harbourmasters, were appointed, each representing a particular community of traders. He watched over the daily affairs as

audience hall. The sultan would sit on a raised platform, surrounded by richly embroidered cushions and flanked by his ministers, two or three steps below him.

The ruler's power was, in theory, absolute and the biggest crime was *derhaka* or disloyalty to him. This concept is well illustrated by the famous tale of Hang Tuah and Hang Jebat, two of the Sultan's most famous warriors, who were also good friends of one another. In an act of treachery intended to please a capricious sultan, Hang Tuah murdered his old friend Hang Jebat. The killer was regarded at the time to have acted correctly; loyalty to the ruler, right

Shapers of Melaka

Parameswara died in 1414, leaving behind him a prosperous trading port. When his grandson, Sri Maharaja, died in 1444, there was a power struggle in the court between Malay chiefs and their supporters who defended Hindu tradition, and a rival group of Malay chiefs who, with the backing of Indian Muslim merchants, favoured Islam. It centred on two rivals as heirs to the throne. In the end the Muslim party won.

Muzaffar Shah, the new ruler, declared Islam the state religion. An able man remembered for his code of laws, his reign saw the emergence of Tun Perak, who was to become the leading

or wrong, came above all else. The *Sejarah Melayu* is full of tales of Melakans who would sooner have killed their friends or relatives, or suffered in silence, than to have shown disloyalty to the sultan.

In his administration, the ruler was assisted by a *bendahara* (chief minister), a *temenggung* (chief of police), and a *laksamana* (admiral). Below them were the various titled nobles. The royalty, common people and traders abided by this system. Apparently, it worked for Melaka.

LEFT: Indian Muslim traders played a crucial role in the expansion of Islam.
ABOVE: a Dutch-built bridge over the Melaka River.

ROYAL PREROGATIVE

The power of the sultan and the royal family was emphasised by a series of special privileges and prohibitions. No commoner could wear yellow, the colour of royalty. White umbrellas were to be used only by rulers, and yellow umbrellas only by princes. And only royalty was allowed to wear gold anklets.

There were also strict rules on language, with special words reserved for royalty and denied to commoners. For example, the everyday Malay word for "to eat" was *makan*; the act of taking sustenance became *santap* when applied to royalty. And while commoners would merely sleep (*tidor*), a tired royal would regally *beradu*.

figure in Melakan politics for 42 years. He became the new *bendahara* in 1456, and in that year repelled a Siamese invasion.

During the reign of Sultan Mansor Shah, who succeeded Muzaffar Shah, Melaka reached the peak of its glory. Its expansion is largely attributed to Tun Perak's efforts, who built a formidable fighting force. He also honoured brave warriors with the title of *Hang*, or captain, including the bearers of such famous names in Melaka's history as Hang Tuah and Hang Jebat. Tun Perak's expeditions led to the conquest of most of the peninsular states as well as those on the Sumatran shore opposite.

Sultan Mansur Shah was succeeded by Sultan Alauddin Riayat Shah. He was probably the strongest and most efficient of Melaka's rulers and took a direct and active part in the administration, including – so the *Sejarah Melayu* tells us – walking the streets at night to check the enforcement of law and order. But his direct methods upset some of his high officials who felt that their own powers were being undermined, and made him many jealous enemies. After a reign of only 12 years, he died in mysterious circumstances, probably poisoned. Alauddin's successor, Sultan Mahmud, was a man of different mould. He was destined to lose Melaka to the Portuguese.

The invasion of the "Franks"

The 15th century was Portugal's age of discovery. The Portuguese had two basic reasons for their voyages of expansion to the far corners of the world. One was to continue their crusade against Islam, for had they not just liberated their own homeland from the Muslims? The second was to grab a slice of the lucrative trade in spices from Southeast Asia. Since that trade was virtually monopolised by Muslims, their two objectives conveniently merged into one. And there was also the fabled Christian kingdom of Prester John, believed to lie in Abyssinia which, if found, could prove a useful ally.

Spices were the most important commodity in the trade between Europe and Asia. Portugal wanted to divert the trade route via the Red Sea and the Mediterranean, which was monopolised by Muslim traders, to a new route around Africa's Cape of Good Hope. Melaka was one of their targets, as it was the collecting point for spices from the Moluccas (the Spice Islands). As the Portuguese writer, Barbosa, put it, "Whoever is Lord in Melaka has his hand on the throat of Venice", which was the European terminal and mart for spices at the time.

The Portuguese first arrived in Melaka in 1509. They sought permission to establish a trading post, but were rebuffed by Tun Mutahir, the *bendahara*, who – backed by the Indian Muslim traders – attempted to seize the Portuguese and their vessels. Warned by a Melakan woman, the Portuguese – whom the Malays had nicknamed the "Franks" – escaped, leaving 20 of their number behind. These men were taken prisoners, giving the Portuguese a good excuse to return in force. This took place in 1511, when a large Portuguese fleet, led by Alfonso D'Albuquerque, the architect of Portuguese expansion in Asia, attacked Melaka. The Portuguese concentrated their onslaught on the bridge over the river, where the Melakan defenders put up a courageous resistance. Even Sultan Mahmud and his son were in the thick of battle, riding on caparisoned elephants. Most foreign traders, however, were either apathetic or supported the Portuguese.

On 24 August 1511, Melaka fell and the sultan and his followers fled into the country. Melaka had lost its independence, and under a string of foreign rulers, it never regained its former days of glory.

D'Albuquerque set up a Portuguese administration and built a fort, calling it A' Famosa ("The Famous"). Within its formidable walls, a medieval Portuguese-style city developed, with a town hall, offices and homes for the Portuguese civil servants, while locals and other workers lived outside the walls of the town.

The Portuguese set about restoring Melaka to its former status as the leading emporium in the region, a title it formerly enjoyed under its Malay rulers. They also tried to make Melaka a great centre

FORMIDABLE FORTRESS

The A' Famosa fort, built by D'Albuquerque in the early 1500s, was so solidly constructed that no enemy managed to breach its walls for over 130 years.

fending off attacks from their Malay neighbours on all sides. In many cases, *A Famosa* proved to be the only saving factor. As for the attempts to proselytise, Catholicism did not appeal to the local population – least of all to the Muslims – and the Europeans' arrogance did not go down particularly well either.

Meanwhile, following his flight from Melaka, Sultan Mahmud had settled in Bintang in the Riau Archipelago. He made two unsuccessful attacks on Melaka, and died in 1528. His elder

for Catholic missionary work among the local population. St Francis Xavier, the well-known Catholic missionary, stayed in Melaka three times whilst spreading the Christian gospel.

But the Portuguese did not succeed in either direction. They attempted to obtain a monopoly of the spice trade by requiring all ships using the straits to obtain passes from them, and by imposing arbitrary duties at the port of Melaka. But such actions aroused strong anti-Portuguese feelings, and they found themselves

LEFT: the Portuguese first arrived in Melaka in 1509.
ABOVE: Alfonso D'Albuquerque led the Portuguese conquest of Melaka in 1511.

son established himself in Perak, while his younger son started a new sultanate in Johor, from where he too continued to harass Melaka periodically. Meanwhile, in North Sumatra, Aceh, with a growing monopoly over pepper, became an important local power. It launched attacks on its main rivals in the area – Melaka, Johor and other Malay states. This three-cornered contest for control over the trade of the Straits of Melaka dragged on throughout most the 16th century.

Later developments in Europe led to the arrival of the Dutch and the English in Southeast Asian waters. In 1594, the port of Lisbon, now the spice mart of Europe, was closed to

Dutch and English merchants, compelling them to go direct to the source of the spices and collect them for themselves. The Dutch trading companies combined to form the United East India Company (VOC) in 1602. The VOC's interests were primarily focused on the Moluccas. However, they considered control of Melaka necessary to complete their own monopoly over the spice and local trade of the region,

In 1640, after blockading the port of Melaka and bombarding A' Famosa, the Dutch encircled the town. As the siege continued, the Portuguese garrison and the people trapped in the fort began to starve and were forced to eat

whatever came into sight – rats, dogs, cats and snakes. It was reported that a mother even ate her dead child. The acute hunger was aggravated by diseases such as malaria, typhoid and cholera. Finally, in 1641, after a seven-month siege, the Dutch forces stormed into A' Famosa and fought on to victory.

The Dutch were much more powerful and efficient than the Portuguese and were able to establish a much more effective monopoly over the trade of the region, particularly in spices, which they rigidly enforced. Since they made Batavia (now Jakarta) their headquarters, Melaka declined in importance as a trading centre. But it was useful as a base from which to control the local trade (such as tin and pepper) of the Straits of Melaka.

The Malay world

Meanwhile, Johore and the other Malay states of the peninsula continued very much as they had always done, in spite of the Portuguese and then the Dutch presence in Melaka. The main effect of the European presence was to reduce the scope of their trade. The Dutch capture of Melaka put paid to the triangular contest for control of the straits between the Portuguese, the Acehnese and the Johoreans, because the trade of both Aceh and Johore suffered as a result of the Dutch monopoly. Johore was further weakened by a disastrous war with Jambi, one of its former vassals in Sumatra in the 1670s, and at the end of the century, the last of its rulers directly descended from the sultans of Melaka was assassinated.

The pattern of a triangular contest to control the trade of the Straits of Melaka was repeated during the 18th century, but the players were newcomers – the Bugis, traditional seafarers and mercenary warriors from Celebes; the Minangkabau, based on the Sumatran state of Siak; and the Dutch themselves in Melaka.

By the 1780s the Dutch had come out on top, but by this time Bugis "underkings" were in effective control of the Johor sultanate and had established an independent sultanate of their own in Selangor. The Minangkabau settlers in the hinterland of Melaka had also established an independent state of their own in the form of a federation called Negeri Sembilan (The Nine States). Of the rest of the peninsula states, Perak, Terengganu and Pahang still owed allegiance to the sultans of Johor but in practice ran their own affairs. In the north, Kelantan and Kedah had fallen within the orbit of the Thais of Bangkok.

As for what is today Malaysian Borneo, Sarawak was a province of the sultanate of Brunei, while Sabah was divided between Brunei and the Sultanate of Sulu, which dominated the northeastern part of the domain.

Such was the state of affairs when the British appeared on the scene in the form of Francis Light and founded a settlement on Penang Island in 1786. ❑

LEFT: A' Famosa fort in Melaka still stands today.
RIGHT: a 17th-century Italian map of the peninsula.

GOLFO DI SIAM

SIAM

STRETTO DI MALLACCA

MALACCA

Along
Claio
Pulo Cara
Pulo Panjag
Pulo Ubi
Ligor
I. Ligor
Bondelon
Wanting
Cabo Patane
P. Coffin
Tuaro
S.P. Rou
Pinaca
Pendaon
P. Boulon
Singor
Keidab
P. Iado
Queda
o Vechio
Patane
F. Secco
F. Kedautan
Pulo Ridang
P. Pisang
Torano
F. Serga
Poncian
Baman
Kedaor
Pulo Capes
Bazuas
Soengei Boroas
Salom
gri
Lago di Diamanti delli Olandesi
P. Sambila
F. Bossot
F. Dongon
P. Barbala
Eil
I. del Aqua
P. Iara
Soengei Pao
F. Palang
Pontigoran
P. Verella
Parri
Casang
Brama
Porto Besan
Peira
Solongor F.
Pulo Pracelar
Tingoran
Pahang
P. Timon
P. Pisang
P. Laor
P. Aru
C. Rachardo
Malacca
Djohor
Sincapoor
Passir
P. Tingi
di S. Ama
di Loque
Behaell
P. Medang
I. Pedrus
Barro
Quecilor
Lanta Detana
C. Romania
Utiel I.
Gol. di Tempesta
Cincel
Boere
Pita
I. Naos
I. Pantou
Stretto di Sincaporea
Brancalis
Pisang
Sialqua
Carimon Saban
Bintan
Cincon
Balahan
Sickerban
Camper
Domines
P. Boby
P. Batou
Passaman
Aceu
Pontanaca
Lingen
Gelgote
Equinox
Priaman
Cafatenga
Padang
Drop
Andragari
Trogie Olandesi
Sojo
Liz
Fratelli
Tellekan
Speriamo
Tutou
Bil
Manacabo
Saleda
Baros
Indrapour
Remtapou
Lamby
Telombuan
ISOLA BANCA
Cocos
I. Willems
Mochomocho
Lomanin
Salecar
La 1.ᵃ Punta
Bana
Pietra di Guvin
Bantal
Palambam
La 2.ᵃ Punta
La P.ᵐᵃ Punta
Nasson I.
Lamang
Cattoun
F.S. Giouani
Mosquiten
I. Cocos
3 Monti
Apee
F.S. Clara
I. Tartaruga
Pepeolen
F. Dolce
I. Bassa
Monte Sillebar
met Recif
Fort Martebourg
Dampin
Cabo Triste
Goudan
Sillebar
Tanjon Tiande
ISOLE
Pongon
Pisang I.
Engano I.

Petten I.

tona For
na

da

COLONIAL MALAYA

Malaya's position as a trading nation continued to attract the attentions of Europe's imperial powers, eager to exploit its wealth

The British first arrived in Southeast Asia in the early 17th century. But finding their trading opportunities stymied by their more powerful Dutch trading rivals, the British had concentrated their efforts on India instead.

The English East India Company (EIC) had, by parliamentary charter, been granted monopoly rights over all British trade with India and beyond. In the 200 years since their first unsuccessful forays into the region, the EIC had developed a very profitable trade with China, exchanging Bengal opium for Chinese tea. A base along the way would protect the trade and serve as collecting centre for straits produce.

Doing deals

The first step in the formation of the Straits Settlements occurred in 1785 when the Sultan of Kedah allowed the EIC to establish a base on the island of Penang. The sultan saw this as his chance to obtain protection against Siam, his northern enemy, and was prepared to grant trading rights to the British in exchange.

Captain Francis Light, who had negotiated the agreement on behalf of the EIC, landed in Penang in 1786 and raised the Union Jack on the sparsely populated, jungle-smothered island. But Light's agreement with the Sultan of Kedah was based on false pretences. The sultan wanted British protection against his enemies but it soon became obvious that the EIC had no intention of providing this. The angry sultan assembled his ships to recapture Penang, but Light attacked first and destroyed the fleet. The resulting treaty guaranteed the sultan $6,000 a year, in return for which the EIC got Penang.

Penang was declared a free port, attracting merchant vessels from all over the east-west trade route. The population grew rapidly and Light followed the Malay and Dutch practice of appointing several *kapitan* – community leaders with authority to hear all minor crimes committed by members of their representative

communities. For major crimes, Light himself tried offenders with his rough and ready sense of justice. Penang prospered, but not as greatly as the EIC had hoped, for it proved to be a little too far up the Straits of Melaka to be a focal point of regional trade.

The second of the British settlements in the

straits was Singapore, occupied when the EIC's representative, Stamford Raffles, landed there in 1819. Raffles was a great imperialist and champion of free trade – which suited British commercial interests – and he was alarmed at Dutch attempts to restore their monopoly over regional trade. So Singapore was designed as a regional bastion of free trade, as well as a useful port of call on the China trade route. The territory was fully secured by treaty in 1824.

The last of the three main British settlements in the straits was Melaka itself. The British had already occupied Dutch-controlled Melaka on two occasions during the French Revolutionary and Napoleonic wars. The French had occu-

---

LEFT: James Brooke, first "White Rajah" of Sarawak.
RIGHT: Francis Light monument in Penang.

pied Holland, and the British were concerned that Melaka too might fall to them. The onset of peace saw the Dutch returning to Melaka in 1816, but only for a few years. In 1824, under the terms of the Anglo-Dutch Treaty of that year, which settled conflicting British and Dutch interests in the region, the British acquired Melaka in exchange for their Sumatran settlement of Bencoolen.

In 1826 Penang, Singapore and Melaka came together under one administration based in Singapore, and given the collective name of the Straits Settlements (SS). Singapore soon emerged as the most important. With its free port status and strategic position, Singapore became the new emporium, its harbour crowded with ships of all nations. By the 1850s, it was the leading port in the region and its trade further increased after the opening of the Suez Canal in 1869. Singapore soon became one of the greatest ports in the world.

Strictly speaking, the SS were concerned only with trade, and the British tried to stay out of the peninsula's other affairs. But this official policy of non-intervention was broken on a few occasions, generally in order to protect British trade from Thai interference in the northern Malay states.

ROGUISH RAFFLES

The way in which Stamford Raffles acquired Singapore was as devious as Light's dealings with the Sultan of Kedah over Penang. He took advantage of a succession dispute to the Johor throne, supporting the claim of Tengku Hussain against his rival in Riau who was actually in power but was unwilling to recognise the British. In the end, Hussain became recognised as Sultan of Johor while his rival became the Sultan of Riau. In return, Hussain, and the ruler of mainland Johor granted the British permission to set up their trading post in Singapore. The British gained full possession of Singapore by another treaty between the same parties in 1824.

British intervention

But there were murmurs of dissent from the merchants of the Straits Settlements. Many were growing restless with the policy of non-intervention. The Chinese had started to plant pepper in the neighbouring Malay states of Johor, and tapioca in Melaka and Negeri Sembilan. Prosperous straits merchants wanted similar opportunities for investment. But the biggest attraction was tin.

The Malay Peninsula had always been rich in tin, its ore mined and traded for centuries. In the mid-19th century, with the rise of the canning industry, demand for the metal shot up. SS merchants with money invested in the new mines of Selangor, Perak and Negeri Sembilan now campaigned for British intervention in these states to safeguard their interests.

The tin rush brought with it widespread unrest. Malay chiefs blessed with rich tin deposits in their domains became rich and powerful magnates whom the sultans could no longer control. Conflicting ambitions led to disputes and civil war. Even the Chinese miners who flocked into the tin districts were themselves divided between rival secret societies that constantly fought one

LOCAL GOVERNMENT?

The Straits Settlements were the responsibility of the British government in India until 1867; from then on they came under direct control from London.

nese miners of Larut on his ship off Pangkor Island. This resulted, in January 1874, in the signing of the Pangkor engagement, which settled a dispute over the throne of Perak, and imposed a British "Resident" on the new sultan whose advice had to "be asked and acted upon on all questions other than those touching Malay religion and custom". By August, Clarke had made a similar agreement with Selangor, and soon after that with Sungai Ujong, the largest of the Negeri Sembilan states.

another. These uncertainties threatened investments, and caused a drop in tin exports just as world demand began to exceed supply. The troubles also threatened to overflow into the SS. Meanwhile, British officials feared that if they did not intervene in these states, investors would seek assistance from a rival imperialist power, such as France or Germany.

A new governor, Andrew Clarke, was sent to sort out the situation. First, he met the Malay chiefs of Perak and the leaders of the rival Chi-

---

FAR LEFT: Stamford Raffles, founder of Singapore.
LEFT: painting of early 19th-century Penang.
ABOVE: British officials pose for the camera.

The residential system

Under the new system in these states, British residents were appointed only "to advise" the rulers on how to improve the administration of their states. However, control would ultimately rest with the resident, and the success of the system very much depended on how each resident exercised his power.

J. W. W. Birch was the first resident in Perak. Intolerant and tactless, with little regard for local customs and impatient for change, his proposed reforms of taxation and the banning of debt slavery threatened to undermine the social fabric of the state. The reforms were naturally opposed by the Perak chiefs and by the sultan himself. In response, in 1875 the governor ordered the state to be placed under the direct rule of British officials. Birch's attempt to put this new command into effect cost him his life. He was killed at Pasir Salak, a village on the Perak River.

Birch's eventual successor was Hugh Low, who took a different approach and laid the foundations for the effective working of the residential system. One of his innovations was the setting up of a state council. Its members included the

THE BIG PAYBACK

Debt slavery – mortgaging yourself to your creditors in return for financial help – was common practice in 19th-century Malaya. In bad times, it was the only way a peasant could raise finances.

port of the *Yam Tuan Besar* or head of the Negeri Sembilan federation and resorted to arms, but were easily defeated by superior British musketry. In the end the progress brought about by the residential system in Sungai Ujong finally won over the Yam Tuan and the heads of the other states of the Negeri Sembilan Federation. In 1895, they were joined by Sungai Ujong in one reunited state with a British resident and the Yam Tuan as their head.

Exaggerated reports of great mineral wealth

resident, the sultan, major chiefs and one or two Chinese leaders who discussed the government's policies. The council provided a useful sounding board for public opinion, but the resident was the real policy maker. The format of the Perak State Council was adopted by the other states which came under the residential system. Low also succeeded in ending debt slavery in Perak, but by gradual means which avoided hardship.

Residential progress

In Selangor, things went a little more smoothly. In Sungai Ujong, the Malays were divided. Those who opposed British rule got the sup-

in Pahang awakened British interest in the state. In 1887, Pahang's ruler, Sultan Ahmad, was persuaded to accept a British agent, but the first agent, Hugh Clifford, found the sultan and his chiefs unwilling to relinquish their rights. The atmosphere grew tense, and when the following year a British subject was murdered in Pekan, the state capital, the British used this as an excuse to force the sultan to accept a British resident. But many of the Pahang chiefs resented the new regime because of their loss of power and income. In 1891, a number of them rebelled against the British presence, led by Dato' Bahaman of Semantan (Temerloh). Though the British were far too strong to be defeated, the rebellion took four years to quell.

In 1896, Selangor, Perak, Negeri Sembilan and Pahang were brought together as the Federated Malay states (FMS), with its capital at Kuala Lumpur. A British resident-general was appointed with jurisdiction over the four states. The purpose of this move was to ensure uniformity in administration, promote faster economic development, and to help the richer members (i.e. Perak and Selangor) assist the poorer ones, especially Pahang. The creation of the FMS made for more efficient government and served the business and commercial interests of the colonial regime.

and Perlis in the north of the Malay Peninsula recognised the general overlordship of Siam. This was demonstrated by the sending of the *Bunga Mas* (golden flowers) to Bangkok.

British strike deal with Siam

However, Thai power over these states was vague and fluctuating. In 1909, the British made a treaty with Siam. This gave to Britain whatever rights and power Siam possessed in these states, so that they now became British protectorates under British advisors with similar status to the British residents in the FMS.

This change was made without consulting

The rulers agreed to the federation thinking that, by joining together, they would exercise more control over the residents and regain their lost authority. Unfortunately, this did not happen. Instead, the resident-general now exercised real power, which he used without reference to the residents or the rulers. In effect, "federation" centralised power in the hands of British officials, who ran the show almost by themselves.

Meanwhile, Kelantan, Terengganu, Kedah

the Malay rulers concerned, which caused a lot of resentment. In fact, these states had run their own affairs quite satisfactorily, and British interference was unpopular. In Kedah, a treaty defining the role of the British advisor was not signed until 1923 because of the hard bargaining to win Malay acceptance of the British presence. In Kelantan (1916) and Trengganu (1928), there were popular anti-British uprisings which were put down by force. Finally, in the south, Johor – the most progressive of all the Malay states – was pressured into accepting a British advisor in 1914. British control was complete, and the Malay Peninsula was divided into three separate parts – the Straits

FAR LEFT: Hugh Low, who laid the foundations of the Residential System. **LEFT:** Sultan Abdullah of Perak. **ABOVE:** Frank Swettenham, the Resident of Selangor. **RIGHT:** *Bunga Mas* tribute to appease the Siamese.

Settlements (SS), Federated Malay States (FMS) and the Non-Federated Malay States (FMS).

The Malay Peninsula had just undergone rapid change. Meanwhile, the territory of Sabah (called British North Borneo) and the "White Rajah" state of Sarawak, had been enjoying developments of their own.

The first "White Rajah" of Sarawak, James Brooke, was an Englishman born in India. As a young man, he had served with the East India Company's army in Burma and when his father died in 1835, leaving

> ### BUOYANT EXPORT
> By 1920, the rubber tree was the mainstay of Malaya's economy – the country provided over 50 percent of the world's rubber.

crushed and in return for Brooke's help, Rajah Muda Hashim awarded him control of the province. In 1841, Brooke, aged 38, was installed as Rajah of Sarawak.

With the help of local chiefs, Brooke set out to establish law and order. This meant overcoming Iban and Malay warriors who lived by piracy. He won, because he had the help of British warships against which Iban and Malay *perahu* (boats) were helpless. Brooke did not introduce new laws, but used existing customs and consulted with the chiefs.

Brooke a sum of money, he used it to buy a schooner and organise an expedition to explore Borneo and the Celebes.

Brooke's lucky break

Stopping off at Singapore on his way, Brooke was asked by the governor to deliver a message to the Malay governor of Sarawak, a province of Brunei confined to the area around Kuching. When Brooke arrived in Kuching in 1839, he found the Rajah Muda Hashim, a relative of the Sultan of Brunei, trying to put down a rebellion against Sarawak's governor. On returning a year later, Brooke decided to help the Rajah Muda Hashim. The rebellion was

Brooke was always short of money, but he refused to introduce foreign capital; he believed that government should be in the interests of the Sarawakians, and not of outside business interests. Under his rule, more territories were brought under Sarawak's control. In 1857, a Chinese revolt nearly overthrew him, but it was quickly suppressed. In 1863, he retired to England where he died five years later.

Brooke's nephew, Charles Brooke, became the second rajah. A better administrator than his uncle, he brought Sarawak out of debt, reduced head-hunting, expanded trade, and brought greater prosperity. He died, at the age of 87, in 1917.

Meanwhile, sovereignty over North Borneo (present-day Sabah) was acquired from the sultans of Brunei and Sulu in 1877 by Overbeck, the Austrian consul-general in Hong Kong, and Alfred and Edward Dent, prominent Hong Kong businessmen. In 1881, Overbeck withdrew and the Dents formed the British North Borneo Company under a royal charter.

The North Borneo Company, like the Brookes in Sarawak, faced considerable opposition to the imposition of its rule. The most serious resistance came from Mat Salleh, a Sulu chief, who rose up in revolt in 1895. The introduction of new taxes had created general discontent, and Mat Salleh gathered many supporters. In 1900, Mat Salleh was killed, but the rebellion was not quelled until five years later.

Material wealth

Throughout the entire colonial period, tin and rubber were Malaysia's main exports. It was these that engendered the development and great social changes that the region enjoyed.

Tin rose in importance in the mid 19th century because of the invention of the tin can, the rise of the canning industry and other new uses for tin plate. This created an ever-increasing demand for Malayan tin on the world market. By 1904, the peninsula was producing more than half the world's tin supply. Besides the political repercussions on the Malay States, this also led to a huge influx of Chinese immigrants.

Until the 1900s, tin mining was mainly in Chinese hands. The introduction of tin-dredging in 1912 enabled Europeans to gain an upper hand in the industry, as they had the technology and capital which the Chinese did not.

Rubber arrived in Malaya as a foreign plant but grew to become the mainstay of its economy. Rubber seeds were transported from Brazil to London's Kew Gardens for experimentation as an Asian crop in the 1870s. Some of the seeds were sent to Malaya where they were planted in Singapore and elsewhere. The millions of rubber trees in Malaysia today all stem from these original seedlings.

However, no one took rubber seriously until H.N. Ridley became director of the Singapore Botanical Gardens in 1888. Ridley had no doubts about the future of rubber but his attempts to persuade coffee planters to experiment with this strange new crop were initially unsuccessful. However, at the end of the 19th century, the price of coffee collapsed. The birth of the motor-car industry and the consequent demand for rubber tyres triggered the rush to farm the plant. Many fortunes were made in the great rubber-boom which followed.

Migrant Indian labour was brought in to work the rubber estates, while many Malays became smallholders. The industry went through gluts and slumps, but remained the mainstay of the Malaysian economy right up to the 1970s.

Revenue from tin and rubber was used to build up the country's infrastructure and social amenities. Attention was focused on the tin mines and rubber estates at the expense of the less profitable areas, which remained neglected. In particular, development and social change were noticeably slower in Sabah and Sarawak, although rubber was still very important to both their economies. As the tin and rubber industries boomed, Malaysia's plural society developed. By the 1930s, the population of Malaya (excluding Singapore) was about 4 million, comprising 49 percent Malays, 34 percent Chinese and smaller groups of Indians, European expatriates and other races. ❑

LEFT: Sarawak's Ibans with their *perahu*, or small boats, were no match for the British warships.
RIGHT: tapping latex, the raw material of rubber.

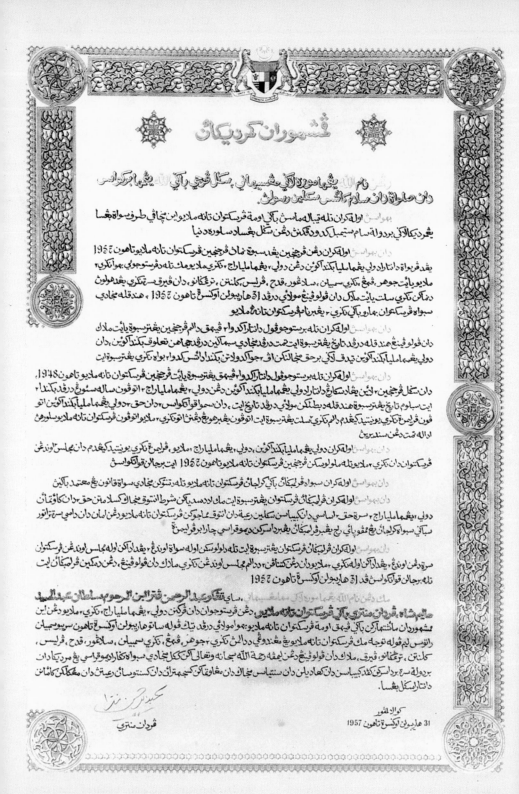

ڤمشهوران کمرديکاءن

دڠن نام الله يڠ مها ڤموره لاڬي مها مڠاسيهاني، سڬالا ڤوجي باڬي الله يڠ مها بركواس دان صلوات دان سلام اتس رسولڽ مليه مكلين مسلين ورسوله.

بهاوسڽ اوله کران تله تيباله ماسڽ باڬي اومت ڤرسکتوان تانه ملايو اين منچاڤي طرف يڠ بهاڬيا...

...ملايو تاهون ١٩٥٧...

کوالا لومڤور
٣١ هاري بولن اوڬوست تاهون ١٩٥٧

تونکو عبدالرحمن ڤوترا

ڤردان منتري

MALAYA, MERDEKA, MALAYSIA

After a period of peace and prosperity, World War II shattered the colonial calm.
For good or bad, Malaysia would never be the same again

Between 1900 and 1941, British rule in Malaya was stable, their subject peoples contented, and the economy basically sound and expanding. In many ways, British Malaya was a showcase of benevolent imperialism. The British referred to Malaya during this period as a land without politics.

This, of course, was not quite true. The British had brought into being a multi-racial society, the contradictions of which were steadily mounting – even if they had not yet reached crisis point. Issues which would one day have to be faced, included the rights of the Malays and other indigenous peoples in their own country, and the position of the Chinese and Indians, the two major immigrant groups, who were beginning to regard Malaya as their permanent home. British policy was to stick to the principle that Malaya was the land of the Malays, and that Sabah and Sarawak were also the lands of their indigenous peoples. This was acceptable when there were no pressures, economic or political. But rising nationalism, the threat of international communism, and the impact of the Great Depression of 1929–33 increasingly threatened the Pax Britannica.

The Japanese Occupation

But what finally ended the deceptive calm was the sudden extension of World War II – raging in Europe since 1939 – to Southeast Asia. In December 1941, Japan launched her attack on the Western colonial powers which she believed were out to strangle her. Within 9 weeks, Japanese forces had overrun the whole of Malaya. Their victory destroyed the comfortable colonial world and ended for ever the unchallenged supremacy of British rule. Things could never be the same again.

The writing on the wall had come in 1931 when the Japanese army unilaterally annexed Manchuria, and became the dominant force in

LEFT: the Malay Proclamation of Independence, 1957.
RIGHT: a Japanese Occupation newspaper reports on Japan's successful invasion, 1943.

Tokyo. The next move came in 1937, with the attempt to bring China under Japanese control. But China proved unconquerable, and the growing Japanese need for strategic raw materials such as oil and rubber made Southeast Asia the target, especially the British and Dutch possessions where these materials abounded

but were denied them by the Western powers. In early 1941, the Japanese took advantage of France's defeat to occupy French Indo-China. It was clear that Malaya would be next.

Among the many reasons advanced for Britain's humiliating failure to defend Malaya – poor strategies, untrained troops, guns pointing in the wrong direction, etc. – the most telling is British weakness in the air. Effective airpower would have crippled the Japanese invasion. Instead, it was Japanese airpower that triumphed; by sinking two capital British warships in the first week of the invasion, the British were crippled.

The Japanese Occupation caused great hardship among the peoples of Malaya. The Japanese arrived with persuasive propaganda about a "Co-prosperity Sphere" and "Asia for Asians". But they had won a great battle, not the war, so were unable to put these promises into effect. Instead, they were obliged to rule with an iron fist to control the resentment of a population suffering from shortages of food and essential goods, high inflation and low incomes.

The Japanese were especially wary of the Chinese, most of whom were hostile towards

NEW NATIONALISM

The end of World War II saw conspicuous growth in political self-determinism, now summed up by the fashionable slogan: *Malaysia Boleh!* (Malaysia Can Do It!)

ority before the white man. Those working in the administration, in public utilities and wherever else assumed the responsibilities once held by their European masters, and gained a new self-confidence and self-respect. This was the beginning of the spirit of *Malaysia Boleh!* (*see page 47*). As a result, when the Japanese were finally defeated by the Western powers, Malayans had a new attitude and new outlook. They were no longer prepared to go back to the way things were before World War II.

them because of "the China incident". The brunt of Japanese brutality was directed against the Chinese, tens of thousands of whom were executed or imprisoned. Europeans (except for nationalities who were neutral or Japanese allies in the war) ended up living under atrocious conditions in detention camps. Some were sent, along with thousands of Indian labourers and a good many Malays, to work on the notorious "Death Railway" – constructed to provide a rail link between Thailand and Burma. Conditions there were even worse, and many died.

Despite the terrible suffering, the Japanese Occupation did have an important plus side. It liberated Malayans from their sense of inferi-

Peace and a fresh start

The Japanese Occupation ended as swiftly as it had begun with the dropping of atomic bombs on the Japanese cities of Hiroshima and Nagasaki in early August 1945. The war finally ended in Malaya in September, when British and Australian forces landed in Malaya and Borneo – in fact the liberation of Borneo had already begun – and re-established British authority. The British received a warm welcome; their return promised relief from the hardships of the Japanese occupation. But everyone agreed, including the British themselves, that the political situation had changed and that British rule could not last for ever.

In fact, the British had already decided to form the FMS, the non-FMS, Penang and Melaka – but not Singapore – into a single state to be called the Malayan Union. The union would have a central government headed by a (British) governor and the former Malay States would cease to exist, their rulers simply remaining as heads of Islam.

At the same time a common citizenship was created, including long-term Chinese and Indian residents as well as the Malays. In short, Malay sovereignty was to be transferred to the British Crown, turning Malaya into a colony and destroying Malay political pre-eminence. A British envoy came to Malaya, and after using a lot of pressure, got all the Malay rulers to accept the scheme.

However, this proposal was strongly opposed, especially by the Malays, who felt that they were being sold down the river. In March 1946, representatives of 41 Malay associations met in Kuala Lumpur to form a national movement to oppose it. This led to the birth of the United Malay National Organisation (UMNO) led by Dato' Onn Jaafar. UMNO demanded the repeal of the union. Although the British inaugurated the union in 1946, Malay opposition was so strong that after negotiations with the Malay rulers and UMNO it was replaced by the Federation of Malaya, which included all the Malay States and Penang and Melaka as members. The new federation came into being on 1 February 1948.

The Malays accepted the federation because it preserved the sovereignty of the rulers and restored state rights. Because the citizenship terms for Chinese and Indian Malaysians were not so generous as before, it was more grudgingly accepted by those communities.

Meanwhile, in 1946, Sarawak and North Borneo became crown colonies. The cost of post-war reconstruction was beyond the resources of the Brooke government and of the British North Borneo Company. In Sabah, the change was accepted without protest, but in Sarawak there was serious opposition, particularly from the Malays who feared they would lose their privileged position without the Brookes. The climax of this opposition came in 1949 when the new British governor was

assassinated in Sibu. This action was too extreme for most Malays, and the movement gradually lost momentum and faded away.

The Emergency

During the Japanese occupation, guerrilla groups which were mainly Chinese, lived in the jungles and organised resistance against the invaders. The most important group was the Malayan Communist Party (MCP) whose guerrillas called themselves the Malayan Peoples' Anti-Japanese Army (MPAJA). Their aim, once the war was over, was to expel the British and set up a communist republic in Malaya.

When the MPAJA was disbanded after the war, the MCP believed that they could overthrow British rule by stirring up mass unrest, particularly through the trade union movement. Communists began infiltrating the unions and succeeded in organising a series of strikes among dockworkers, tin miners and rubber plantation labourers demanding better living conditions. This alarmed the colonial authorities and laws were passed to bring the trade unions under stricter control. This was probably the main reason for the MCP's decision in 1948 to abandon its non-violent strategy and to resort to armed insurrection instead. Under its new leader, Chin Peng, the MCP was reorganised and

LEFT: Japanese leaders surrender their swords in 1945.
RIGHT: a Communist caricature.

all its activities moved underground. After a spate of attacks on European miners and planters, the government proclaimed a national state of emergency in June 1948. "The Emergency" became the official name for the communist insurrection which lasted 12 years, so called, it is said, to escape inconvenient insurance requirements connected with acts of rebellion – a matter of some importance to rubber and tin companies whose property was being attacked and destroyed by the insurgents.

From their secret jungle bases, the communists caused widespread confusion. They would also coerce food and supplies from Chinese

COMMUNIST TACTICS

For a guerrilla army, the Communist Malayan Peoples' Anti-British Army (MPABA) was a well-organised fighting force. They grouped themselves into regiments and lived in jungle camps. These camps, well-screened from the air, with effective escape routes and well-organised living quarters, could often accommodate 300 men. From these bases, the communists would attack rubber estates and tin mines in order to disrupt the colonial economy. High wire fences were put up around tin mines and rubber estates to keep the communists out, but travel was particularly risky because of the danger of ambush lurking at every corner.

squatters in remote areas, and attempt to indoctrinate them. But clamping down on guerrilla activity was made especially hard by the lack of coordination between the various security forces. However, the tide began to turn with the appointment of General Sir Harold Briggs as Director of Operations in 1949. Briggs, a veteran of the World War II Burma campaign against the Japanese, was responsible for the basic strategies which overcame the MCP revolt. He set up war executive committees which coordinated military and civil operations, and created 500 new villages to re-house squatters in less remote areas. This cut off the main source of the communists' food supply. As anticipated, the insurgents attacked the new settlements, but the security forces, now fighting on their own ground, were too strong for them. These forces were soon able to concentrate on jungle operations to destroy the communists and their camps.

In 1953, areas from which the communists had been eliminated were declared "white areas". Food restrictions and curfews in them were relaxed, inducing fuller local co-operation with the government. By 1954, a large number of the communist guerrillas had been eliminated. Many more surrendered later, and the few remaining guerrillas retreated deep into the jungle. The state of emergency officially ended on 31 July 1960.

Malayan nationalism

A major factor that enabled the quelling of the communist revolt was that it was largely a Chinese affair – few Malays or Indians were involved. At the same time, the British saw the need to meet the growing demand for national independence. If they had not done this, many Malayan nationalists might have made common cause with the rebels to oust the British.

Stirrings of a Malayan nationalism were felt throughout the country soon after World War II. The problem was how to unite the three main races in the peninsula in a common struggle for independence from the British. The first step was taken in 1951, when the Malayan Chinese Association (MCA) formed a political partnership with UMNO. The Malayan Indian Congress (MIC) followed suit in 1954, and the political coalition called the Alliance came into being, which played a major role in the struggle for independence.

Elections were held for the Federal Legislative Council for the first time in 1955, and the Alliance won 80 percent of the votes cast. Tunku Abdul Rahman, UMNO's leader, became Malaya's first chief minister. A district officer in Kedah before the war, he took a law degree at the University of Cambridge and soon after entered politics. He took over the leadership of UMNO in 1951.

In 1955, the Alliance government offered an amnesty to the MCP and invited Chin Peng to Baling, Kedah, for talks to end the Emergency.

POLITICAL PEDIGREE

It could be argued that Tunku Abdul Rahman, Malaya's first chief minister, was born to lead – his father was Sultan of Kedah.

based on a memorandum submitted by the Alliance, was accepted by the Malay rulers, and the British and Malayan governments.

Malaya became a constitutional monarchy, with the king selected from among the nine Malay rulers every five years. Parliament consisted of a fully elected lower house and a senate of nominated members. Executive power lay mainly in the hands of the lower house. Each state had its own fully-elected state assembly. Malaya became an independent state at midnight on 30 August 1957.

The talks failed and Chin Peng went back into the jungle. The Alliance now concentrated on bringing about national unity in Malaya's multi-racial society. One move was the creation of a national system of education which catered for the needs of Malays, Chinese and Indians alike.

In 1956, Tunku led a delegation to London to negotiate the terms for independence. As a result, a commission of Commonwealth legal experts, headed by Lord Reid, was appointed to draw up a constitution. The draft document,

LEFT: a British jungle patrol to flush out communists.
ABOVE: Tunku Abdul Rahman gives the *Merdeka* salute, declaring Independence in 1957.

The formation of Malaysia

In 1961, Tunku proposed the formation of Malaysia, a wider federation which would include the territories of Malaya, Singapore, British North Borneo (Sabah), Sarawak and Brunei. In Singapore, opinion was sharply divided over the merits of the plan; Brunei decided in the end to stay away. A commission of Malayan and British members investigated the reaction of the inhabitants of Sabah and Sarawak and found that the majority of people there were in favour of the plan. Therefore, the British and Malayan governments set 31 August 1963 as the date on which Malaysia would be established.

But Indonesia condemned the whole scheme as a neo-colonialist plot, and in January 1963 announced a policy of "Confrontation" against Malaysia. Meanwhile, the Philippines also opposed the creation of Malaysia, claiming that North Borneo belonged to them. Confrontation took the form of armed Indonesian incursions across the borders of Sarawak and North Borneo. Indonesia and the Philippines both repudiated a United Nations survey which confirmed that the Borneo territories wanted to be a part of Malaysia.

EARTHY ORIGINS

In local dialect, the Malay people have traditionally been referred to as *Bumiputras*, which translated means "sons of the soil".

Meanwhile, political differences had surfaced between Malaysia and Singapore. On 9 August 1965, Singapore left the Federation and became an independent state.

When Malaysia was formed, its population stood at 10.4 million – Malays forming 47 percent; Chinese 34 percent; Indians, 9 percent; Dayaks, 4 percent; Kadazans, 2 percent; other indigenous groups, 3 percent and foreign immigrants, 2 percent. Turning this medley of peoples into one nation was not an easy feat. Under colonial rule, economic roles tended to

Territorial disputes

When the Federation of Malaysia was officially inaugurated on 16 September 1963, Indonesia and the Philippines severed diplomatic ties with Malaysia; Indonesia intensified its attacks along the borders of Sarawak and British North Borneo (now renamed Sabah) and Indonesian troops made landings in Peninsular Malaysia to carry out acts of sabotage. But they were quickly foiled by the security forces.

In 1966, Sukarno was ousted from power and the new Indonesian regime wanted to end confrontation – negotiations settled the conflict. The Philippines also dropped its claim on Sabah and recognised Malaysia.

be identified with specific ethnic groups. In particular, the Chinese resented the Malays' greater political power, while the Malays feared the greater economic strength of the Chinese. The simmering racial tension erupted on 13 May 1969 in the wake of the general elections. Communal riots broke out, mainly in the capital, Kuala Lumpur, killing hundreds of people and destroying a considerable amount of property. As a result, the constitution was suspended and a Department of National Unity was set up to formulate a national ideology and social programmes. Finally, a statement of ideological principles, the *Rukunegara*, was produced to guide the national polity.

The 13 May incident represented a watershed in Malaysian politics, as the government was forced to formulate new economic and political strategies to restore long-term national stability. The riots would also spawn the New Economic Policy (NEP) and the formation of the Barisan Nasional (BN) or National Front.

The BN was the work of Tun Abdul Razak, successor to Tunku Abdul Rahman who resigned a month after the riots. Tun Razak reorganised the Alliance, incorporating every political party except the Democratic Action Party (DAP) and some smaller parties. In 1974, the BN won a landslide majority, and won again in 1978.

Economic policy

Although the nation's new constitution gave the Malays considerable political power, their participation in the country's trade and commerce was minimal. Despite accounting for over half of the country's population, the Malays owned only 2 percent of corporate equity. The Chinese, on the other hand, practically ran the economy, holding prominent positions as bankers, brokers and businessmen.

In 1970, the New Economic Policy (NEP) was launched to encourage a fairer distribution of wealth among the races. This involved setting up corporations and share-ownership schemes to elicit greater Malay participation in the economy. Racial quotas, scholarships and subsidies were introduced to raise the Malay stake in the economy to 30 percent. However, the plan was to achieve this by increasing the size of the pie, and not at the expense of the non-Malays. Therefore, everybody would benefit.

The NEP was inevitably deemed unfair by many non-Malay critics who felt that the Malays already had too many privileges and that "positive" discrimination on the basis of race and not merit would seriously undermine the economic, political and cultural position of non-Malays in Malaysian society.

In any event, the business acumen of the Chinese has kept them prosperous. Twenty years later, however, the Malay, or *bumiputra* stake has reached only 20 percent, the majority of which is owned by big *bumiputra* investment

companies. In 1991, the old policy was replaced by the New Development Policy (NDP), a more liberal strategy which uses incentives rather than quotas, and sets no deadline for the 30 percent *bumiputra* ownership target.

The boom years

When Malaya became independent in 1957, the economy was almost completely dependent on exports of tin, rubber, palm oil and tea. Therefore, in the early 1970s, the government launched an ambitious crusade to transform Malaysia from its agro-mining foundation to a mixed economy with a strong manufacturing

sector. By the end of the 1970s, substantial progress had been made. Light industries had been formed and were now saturating the local market. The country was poised to make an industrial leap to becoming an exporter of manufactured goods and in concentrating on heavier industry. The 1970s also witnessed the harvesting of newly-found offshore oil and natural gas reserves in the South China Sea, giving a spectacular boost to the economy.

This impressive economic performance was brought about by a series of Malaysian Five-Year Plans. However, much of the credit for the country's rapid economic progress since 1981 must go to one man: Dr Mahathir Mohamad. ❑

LEFT: Tun Razak (with cane) succeeded Tengku Abdul Rahman as PM. **RIGHT:** Islam figures strongly in Malaysian politics; prayer time in KL's Jamek Mosque.

CONTEMPORARY MALAYSIA

Under the leadership of Dr Mahathir Mohamad, Malaysia became one of the stronger economies of Asia. But at what price to political freedom?

The appointment of Mahathir Mohamad as Malaysia's fourth prime minister in 1981 marked the start of a new era in the nation's politics. It was an era that lasted over two decades until his retirement in 2003 – one of the longest terms of political leadership in Southeast Asia – and left behind an indelible stamp; half the country has grown up knowing only Mahathir's tough leadership style.

The Mahathir era marked a break with the past. Unlike his three predecessors, Mahathir was not only a commoner, but also the first Malaysian prime minister to have received all of his education locally and not in Britain. He was also much younger on taking office, a member of the post-World War II generation of students who fought for national independence.

Right from the start, Mahathir was a stormy petrel in UMNO politics. He was expelled from the party in 1969 for criticising what he saw as then prime minister Tunku Abdul Rahman's failure to protect Malay political interests. His comeback began in the 1970s. Re-admitted into UMNO, in 1974 he took his first ministerial post (Education) and the following year was re-elected to the Supreme Council to became the party's vice-president. In 1978, he was appointed deputy prime minister under Hussein Onn.

Radical reforms

One of Mahathir's first acts on assuming office in 1981 was to make all government servants clock in for work – a harbinger of the no-nonsense style of government he aimed to promote. Since that day, there has hardly been a dull moment. Mahathir's initial priorities were to shake the Malaysian, and more particularly, the Malay mindset out of its colonial mould, to make Malaysians more self-reliant, and to raise their self-esteem. He also wanted to establish Malaysia as a power to be noticed and taken heed of. All this is conveniently summed up by

LEFT: Malaysia's hosting of the 1998 Commonwealth Games was a high point. **RIGHT:** much of its economic success is due to its manufacturing expertise.

the now fashionable slogan, *Malaysia Boleh!* (Malaysia Can Do It!).

To achieve these aims Mahathir resorted to shock tactics. One of them was to jolt Malaysians out of their reverential attitude towards all things Western, and particularly British. In 1982 came his "Buy British Last" campaign. This

was ostensibly in retaliation for the British government's action in raising university fees for foreign students, but in reality it was designed as a slap in the face for Malaysians brought up to believe that "British is Best". He also urged Malaysians to adopt a "Look East" policy, and singled out Japan as a role model of hardwork and efficiency that Malaysia should emulate.

Mahathir also commissioned numerous civil engineering projects, building roads, bridges, and, most spectacularly, skyscrapers. While each has its own merits, these high-profile schemes also served collectively to demonstrate to the world what can be done when a Malaysian puts his mind to something.

In the same vein, he encouraged Malaysians to make their mark in the world arena as individuals, by going for world-class exploits. By the turn of the 21st century, Malaysians had climbed Mount Everest, taken part in international safaris and even sailed solo around the world, charting a new course on the way. The successful hosting of the Commonwealth Games in Kuala Lumpur in 1998, a triumph of both individual and collective Malaysian effort, seems to have marked the apogee of Mahathir's grandiose mega schemes.

Another of Mahathir's efforts on the global stage was to project himself as a world leader, at least in the eyes of his countrymen. He certainly succeeded in making Malaysia heard as a champion of the Third World and as cheerleader for the countries of the undeveloped "South" in their attempts to secure a better deal from the wealthy industrialised "North".

Mahathir's strident criticism of Western values and policies had been good for Malaysian pride throughout his leadership, however much it had irritated people in the West.

Mahathiresque economics

Nevertheless, the most important of Mahathir's initiatives laid in economic policy and affairs.

ENGINEER OF SUCCESS

Former prime minister Mahathir Mohamad's obsessive love of ambitious mega projects has seen Malaysia trumping the world in many aspects of civil engineering. The 7-km (4½-mile) long bridge linking Penang Island to the mainland is Asia's longest; Kuala Lumpur Tower was the world's third highest when built, and the Petronas Twin Towers, completed in 1998, are the world's tallest pair of buildings. Kuala Lumpur also lays claim to one of the world's highest flagpoles at Dataran Merdeka (Independence Square). The country has also constructed one of the most sophisticated airports in the world, the Kuala Lumpur International Airport (KLIA).

After only a couple of years in power, the Mahathir administration was confronted with a major global trade recession; but it proved its mettle and was able to ride the storm. Assimilating the new trend away from government control over national economies towards liberalisation and the free market, Mahathir launched a thoroughgoing privatisation programme of his own, tagging it with another catchy slogan, "Malaysia Inc." – i.e. the entire nation as a commercial enterprise involving everybody.

After its inception early in 1983, when the programme was widely publicised, a whole series of government institutions and agencies were gradually privatised, including power and water supplies, telecommunications, postal services, the railway, the national airline, and the construction of toll highways.

Boom time

Privatisation proved highly successful; the country was brought out of recession, and the government divested much of its heavy burden of expenditure on basic services. Foreign capital poured in, business boomed, the property market expanded, and the stock market soared.

At the same time, another major thrust with

> **BOUNCING BACK**
>
> Among its many economic achievements, Malaysia is the largest producer of condoms and surgical rubber gloves in the world.

ufacture were projects by the government-owned Heavy Industries Corporation of Malaysia (HICOM; now known as DRB-HICOM).

Other giant infrastructural projects included the 848-km (527-mile) North-South Expressway (NSE); ocean ports at Pasir Gudang, Port Klang and Lumut; the huge natural gas plant at Bintulu, and the controversial Bakun Dam. Most ambitious of all was the attempt to catch the wave of the future by making Malaysia a frontrunner in information technology through its Multimedia Super Corridor, a

image-building implications was the fostering of heavy industry along with a massive broadening of the infrastructure. First came the creation of a local automobile manufacturing industry, which in 1985 produced the Proton Saga, the first locally manufactured car and the first to be made and designed in Southeast Asia (with help from Mitsubishi of Japan). Today, Proton vehicles not only dominate the domestic market but are also exported to various countries. This and ventures into iron and steel man-

new international hub of IT centred in the Klang Valley where the capital sits. Low labour costs have also enabled Malaysia to become a world leader in electronic goods and microchips.

By the early 1990s, locally manufactured products had become the country's greatest export earner, leaving the traditional export of raw materials far behind. Malaysia had also become one of the fastest growing economies in Asia, with one of the highest GDPs in the region.

Much credit must go to the innovative thinking and bold entrepreneurial moves that Mahathir promoted. But providence has played its part, not least the discovery in the 1960s of substantial natural gas and oil reserves off Malaysian shores.

LEFT: KL's National Stadium was erected for the 1998 Commonwealth Games. **ABOVE:** Symbols of success, Malaysian-built Proton car and country flag.

Vision 2020 and the future

All this material progress found philosophic expression in another typical Mahathir contribution – "Vision 2020" (*Wawasan 2020*), a statement setting out the targets that the nation should achieve by 2020. Though primarily economic – i.e. the achievement of Newly Industrialised Country (NIC) status by that date – the "vision" also incorporated the goals of creating a common and unified Malaysian identity to replace the various communal identities – Chinese, Indian, Malay and so on – that stand for "Malaysian" today. Mahathir also hoped to establish an educated society based on spiritual values.

However, the achievements of the Mahathir era were suddenly placed in serious jeopardy by the Asian financial crisis of 1997. Over the next 18 months, the Kuala Lumpur stock market index fell by 80 percent, precipitating a political crisis on top of economic problems.

Benevolent dictator?

The political crisis centred on the sudden dismissal in September 1998 of Anwar Ibrahim, the deputy prime minister, and his subsequent arrest, trial and imprisonment on charges of corruption and homosexuality. The vicious manner in which this was carried out and the perceived unfairness

POLITICS IN SABAH AND SARAWAK

In Sarawak, the ruling coalition – led by the Parti Pesaka Bumiputera Bersatu Sarawak (PBB) – has been in power for over a quarter-century. In Sabah, the Malay/Muslim ruling coalition is dominated by UMNO (of Peninsular Malaysia) – a result of political developments in the 1990s.

Politics in Sabah and Sarawak have little relevance to the peninsula, and vice versa. However, Sabah's and Sarawak's support for the Barisan National (BN), the ruling coalition in the federal parliament, is vital. Without it, the BN could lose its majority and its control over constitutional change. So the federal government's policy towards these political parties has been highly flexible, subject to their

unquestionable loyalty to the BN. Kuala Lumpur has never tolerated any chief minister in either state showing signs of independence. Hence, the ousting of Kalong Ningkan, Sarawak's first chief minister, in 1966; the eclipse of Dato Mustapha Harun, Sabah's first head of state, in 1976; and the downfall of Pairin Kitingan, the chief minister of Sabah, in 1992. The BN hasn't yet found the need to establish a presence in Sarawak, but the strong opposition to federal influences in Sabah resulted in UMNO making a base there in 1992. With Kuala Lumpur's financial backing and carefully redrawn constituency boundaries, UMNO and its local allies have ruled the roost ever since.

of the court proceedings evoked an outburst of protest on a scale not witnessed since independence. More than anything else, these events put in high relief the most prominent political trend manifest during the Mahathir era – the steady growth of authoritarian government.

Mahathir's long tenure showed that he was a shrewd political operator, but his success had been largely achieved by gathering power into his own hands and using it to maintain his own position. During his office, the constitution was amended almost beyond recognition, the fundamental rights which it originally enshrined were strangled by various escape clauses and qualifications. The prerogatives of the monarchy was also reduced – in a manner that enhanced the power of the prime minister.

Amendments to parliamentary procedure have robbed the legislature of much of its authority. The independence of the judiciary was emasculated, a process that began in 1988 with the removal of its head. Draconian legislation (the Internal Security Act) today allows detention without trial, muzzles the press and restricts access to official information.

Nevertheless, the Barisan Nasional (BN), the name of the ruling coalition, has romped home in each of the previous national general elections. A deep-rooted desire for security and stability, and fear of communal unrest and disorder form the glue which binds many Malaysians to the present regime – feelings more firmly entrenched amongst the Chinese and Indians in the peninsula than amongst the Malays.

However, the Anwar affair, as well as the perceived corruption of the ruling coalition with its "money politics" has seen the Malay-dominated areas turn to the main opposition party PAS (Islamic party). Having lost Kelantan state to PAS in the 1990 election, the ruling party was dealt a second blow in 1999, when Terengganu too came under the PAS fold. The politics of Sabah and Sarawak, however, is another thing. (*see box opposite*).

Riding on pro-Anwar sentiment, the opposition parties attempted a coalition in order to challenge the ruling party but this fizzled out in 2001. Then a year later, Mahathir made a shock announcement that he would retire, naming his deputy Abdullah Badawi as successor.

LEFT: ex-PM Dr Mahathir at a signing ceremony.
RIGHT: On his way to court, ex-DPM Anwar Ibrahim.

A different leadership style

Since assuming power in October 2003, Abdullah Badawi has shown himself to be the people's prime minister. He overhauled the civil service, dealt with corruption, and ended Mahathir-era economic policies and mega projects. The latter manoeuvre has invoked the chagrin of the former prime minister, who has since 2005 vociferously taken Abdullah to task in public.

The people responded to Abdullah's policies and moderate government style by voting overwhelmingly for the Barisan coalition in the 2004 elections, which were the first with Abdullah as prime minister. A major victory was the

return of Terengganu to the Barisan fold, while the Kelantan seat was only narrowly lost.

Abdullah's administration centres on "Islam Hadhari" (translated from Arabic as "civilisational Islam"), a set of principles based on moderate Islam. In 2006, he unveiled the Ninth Malaysia Plan (2006–2010), which outlined the country's aim to become an inclusive and technologically progressive developed nation. Billions of ringgit would be allocated to narrow the economic gap between urban and rural areas. The plan identified biotechnology as a new source of wealth creation, and called for the modernisation of the agricultural sector, which had previously been sidelined by Mahathir's mega projects . ❏

THE LIVING WORLD

From lush rainforests to the coral reefs that fringe its shores, Malaysia has
some of the most important – and fragile – environments on earth

The Indo-Malayan rainforests are the oldest in the world, making those in Africa and South America seem adolescent in comparison. While creeping icecaps were swelling and shrinking across the northern hemisphere, the Indo-Malayan jungles lay undisturbed – for an estimated 130 million years. As a result many diverse species of animal and plant life evolved, with a large number of these occurring nowhere else in the world.

Amazing biodiversity

Rainforests on the Malaysian peninsula and in the Malaysian states of Sabah and Sarawak on the island of Borneo continue to excite a great deal of scientific interest. But those visiting for only a few days, or even weeks, will miss most of the rare flora and fauna; scientists can spend entire lifetimes at work here. Optimists believe that the plants and animals yet to be investigated may hold cures for many human diseases.

The biodiversity is truly staggering. It is estimated that over 15,000 flowering plant species (9 percent of the world's total) and 185,000 animal species (16 percent of the world's total) are found in Malaysia. The flowering plants include some 2,000 types of trees, including 200 different palms, and 3,000 species of orchids, the most exotic of flowers. The 50-hectare (125-acre) Forest Research Institute of Malaysia (FRIM) contains more tree species than exist in the whole of North America. The world's largest flower, the *Rafflesia*, is unique to the region (*see box right*). Carnivorous pitcher plants can be seen, most abundantly on the slopes of Mount Kinabalu in Sabah but also on the peninsula, waiting for careless insects to drop in and drown. Another record-breaker is the towering *Tualang tree*, tallest of all tropical trees. It can reach up to 80 metres (260 ft) in height and over 3 metres (10 ft) in girth.

The rainforests also hold hundreds of thousands of animal species, many of which are unique to the region. Almost 300 species of mammals live here including tigers, elephants, rhinoceros (though sadly their numbers are greatly diminished), black and white tapirs, civet cats (*musang*), leopards, honey bears, and

RAFFLESIA

The *Rafflesia* sp. is the largest flower in the world, measuring up to 1 metre (3½ ft) in diameter when in full bloom. Rafflesia can be found in forests on the Main Range in Peninsular Malaysia as well as in Sabah and Sarawak. There are seven species altogether, *R. arnoldii* being the largest.

A parasite by nature, the plant lives by infecting the roots of a woody climber, *Tetrastigma* sp. The flower takes many months to develop, and the open bloom – which lasts for only a few days – looks like dead meat, crawling with maggots when it starts to rot. It emits a similar odour, thereby attracting flies for pollination.

PRECEDING PAGES: *Rafflesia*, the world's largest flower. **LEFT:** orang-utan, or "man of the forest" in Malay, hanging onto the jungles of Borneo. **RIGHT:** one of Malaysia's myriad butterflies rests on a hibiscus.

two kinds of deer – the *sambar*, and the barking deer (*kijang*) with its dog-like call. Malaysia is also home to the cat-sized mousedeer (*kancil*), which is technically not a deer at all, the scaly anteater (*pangolin*), the badger-like *binturong* with its prehensile tail, and many kinds of gibbons and monkeys including the quaint loris with its sad eyes and lethargic manner. Borneo is also home to the extraordinary orang-utan ("forest man" in Malay).

Whether you venture into the jungle or not, you are sure to see some of the estimated 736 species of birds (11 of which are endemic) and quite a few of the 150,000 species of invertebrates. Alfred Russel Wallace, the celebrated Victorian naturalist who spent more than ten years in the Malay Archipelago, had a particular fondness for insects of all sorts and often described himself as "trembling with excitement" upon the discovery of a new type. The country is also home to over 1,000 species of butterfly, and an estimated 12,000 different species of moth.

Shades of green

About three-quarters of Malaysia is covered in trees (about 50 percent forest and 25 percent rubber and oil-palm plantations.). The green

cover begins at the edge of the sea and climbs to the highest mountain peaks. Along the coastline, there are extensive areas of mud swamps, peat swamps, and mangroves. Behind the mangroves are lowland dipterocarp forests, which extend to an altitude of 600 metres (2,000 ft) and where some forest giants attain heights of 80 metres (262 ft), with the first branches 20 metres (65 ft) above ground. Much of these forests, particularly on the peninsula, have been logged or replaced by plantations. Timber is one of Malaysia's main exports – comprising 10 percent of its earnings – and efforts are being made to control logging so that the country's fertile jungles will assure the industry a green future.

The next level of forest is mostly oak and chestnut. Above 1,500 metres (5,000 ft) it becomes a kind of never-never land with elfin woodlands of small gnarled trees covered in folds of hanging mosses and lichen.

With growing awareness of the importance of conservation, the government has set aside 12.5 million hectares (30 million acres) as Permanent Forest Estate, to be managed sustainably, and an additional 1.2 million hectares (3 million acres) as National Parks, Game Reserves and Wildlife Sanctuaries. There is room for hope that the Malaysian jungle will be allowed to flourish and retain some of its great biodiversity.

In this regard, the Wildlife Department has evolved from an office that mostly oversaw the issuance of hunting licences, into an organisation that actively enforces preservation of wildlife and habitats, though at present the department remains handicapped by a lack of resources and manpower. Poaching is still a problem, as there are markets both locally and abroad for the parts of wild animals, especially as traditional remedies and aphrodisiacs.

MALAYSIAN MAJESTY

The beautiful Rajah Brooke's Birdwing, with its emerald markings on jet-black wings, is Malaysia's national butterfly.

Lush vegetation

A smooth highway unrolls through green hills. Rubber trees flash by in never-ending even rows, and tin mines appear where plantations leave off. Freshly-planted oil palms cover the land in a patchwork of deep green against cleared red earth. In northern and coastal areas, fields are rich with stalks of golden rice.

As far as the eye can see the lush green vegetation of the tropics smothers the landscape. Yet, contrary to its looks, Malaysia is not suited to intensive agriculture. Unlike the Nile River Basin or the Ganges Valley, where seasonal rains flooding the land bring new fertile soil, the torrential downpours in Malaysia wash away the thin but valuable topsoil, leaving only red mud and filling the rivers with silt.

Erosion is one of Malaysia's oldest problems. Geologists believe that the Malay Peninsula and Borneo were once a single rugged landmass running the length of the Indonesian and Malay archipelago. Over millennia the sun, wind and

LEFT: the sculptural form of the strangling fig.
RIGHT: buffaloes working the rice fields.

torrential rains have reduced the mountains to hillocks and outcrops. Precious soils were washed into the sea, and land became cut off by subsidence and erosion.

Despite the shifting landscape and annual monsoon rain, Malaysia's early settlers were basically food growers. As far back as AD 500, crops such as sugar cane, bananas, pepper and coconuts were grown for export, while rice was introduced over 1,000 years ago. Traditionally both men and women were involved in rice cultivation – the staple food and prime

source of income for rural Malaysians. The tempo of kampung life has quickened with the introduction of double cropping, using hybrids which yield a second crop every year. Although it is not as prevalent as it once was, the rubber tree, originally from Brazil, was initially viewed with great scepticism, and even some scorn, by the planters.

The man inspired to bring the rubber tree to Malaysia was H. N. Ridley, director of the botanical gardens in Singapore, where some of the first trees were planted. "Rubber Ridley", as the planters called him, was convinced that his crop had great possibilities and he journeyed around the country with seeds in his pockets, looking for anyone he could convince to plant them. It was a farsighted and lonely crusade until John Dunlop invented the tyre and Henry Ford put the automobile on the assembly line.

Agricultural expansion

To this day the rubber tapper continues to set out before dawn to collect the cups of latex that make up nearly half of the world's rubber supply, but he stops short of the old estate boundaries to view a field planted with oil palms.

The Malaysian government encourages farmers to diversify their crops by growing coconut, coffee, tea, fruits, nuts, spices – and oil palm.

pled with the discovery of large tin deposits in the early 19th century, led to new settlements springing up from a few prospectors' shacks and growing into large cities like Kuala Lumpur and Ipoh. The industry gave the British the revenue to build roads and railways through the jungle, and it also introduced Chinese settlers to Malaysian soil.

The all-male mining townships were rough and risky. Malaria and cholera thrived in the intense heat and wiped out thousands. Those who survived did so under a constant threat of tiger attacks, recorded at one time as a daily occurrence. Thousands more perished in

The first commercial planting of oil palm started in Malaysia in 1917, but development was slow until the 1950s, when the government embarked on a massive commodities diversification programme. Many estates replaced rubber with oil palm and opened up new land for its cultivation. The area planted with oil palm increased from 54,000 hectares (130,000 acres) in 1960 to almost 3 million hectares (7.4 million acres) in 2002. Today, Malaysia is easily the world's largest producer of palm oil, accounting for about half of the world's output.

For over a century, tin and rubber were the two main pillars of the Malaysian economy. The growth in industrial demand for tin, cou-

Chinese secret-society feuds. Others made fortunes; for decades, the Chinese held a virtual monopoly on the tin-mining industry.

By 1883, Malaysia had become the largest producer of tin in the world, and by the end of the 19th century, it was supplying about 55 percent of the world's tin supply. Today, it is still a significant player, contributing about 30 percent of the world's output.

Tides upon the sea

For three months of the year, fishing people on Malaysia's east coast store away their nets, dock and repair their boats, move their fishing huts far up the beach and settle down in the shelter of their wooden houses to wait for the winds to change. During the rainy season, time is spent in more leisurely pursuits: repairing fishing nets, making a trip to the city or even embarking on a pilgrimage to Mecca if the year's trade has been prosperous. When the winds drop, they will again venture out to sea in search of the wide variety of fish and other seafood for the nation's markets. This pattern of life has characterised Malaysia's eastern shore for centuries.

TRADING CENTRE

Business in 16th-century Melaka was conducted in 84 languages. Small wonder that Malay contains words adopted from Arabic, Chinese, Sanskrit, Persian, Portuguese, Dutch and English.

Six hundred years ago, spices were literally worth their weight in gold, and it was the Moluccas, with their cherished aromatic produce, that set Asian maritime kingdoms against one another and sparked off the European Age of Discovery in the 15th and 16th centuries. In time, the spice trade to Europe became so lucrative that a vessel loaded with spices from the Far East could make enough profit to pay the cost of the voyage, including the value of the ship, 10 times over. "Melaka is the rich-

Almost entirely surrounded by water, Malaysia has always been where the monsoons meet, where the tides of the Indian Ocean and the South China Sea flow together into the Straits of Melaka. Seafaring merchants, explorers, adventurers and pirates stopped along the coasts to wait for the tradewinds to blow their way and carry them onward on their journey. As Malaysia was midway between China, India and the Moluccas (Spice Islands), some of its ports became major entrepots.

LEFT: the rubber industry was once a significant contributor to the economy. **ABOVE:** cruising around the islands that dot Malaysia's coast.

est seaport in the world with the greatest number of merchants and abundance of shipping that can be found in the whole world," wrote one Portuguese sailor in the 16th century.

Ocean bounty

Piracy was once widespread and for centuries sailors trembled at the thought of passing unarmed through Malaysian waters. The most formidable pirate bands were the Lanun from Mindanao in Philippines who would sometimes recruit Borneo head-hunting warriors. While the captains pillaged the cargoes, the crew collected war trophies. Today, piracy has been largely eradicated, although there are still sporadic episodes, especially in the seas off Sabah.

Above water, a steady stream of oil tankers and cargo vessels ply the Straits of Melaka, transporting crude oil and natural gas instead of silks, spices and porcelain. The recent increase in offshore oil exploration and mining has greatly enhanced the value of sea territory with the result that the nations of the region are involved in a number of sovereignty disputes.

On the other hand, progress has been made among ASEAN nations to address cross-boundary problems, including pollution of the Straits of Melaka and air pollution from forest fires. It is hoped that these efforts and a growing

rounded by coral reefs, and Malaysia is known for its great diversity of coral species, and for the marine life that inhabits them.

To protect these unique and biologically important ecosystems, Malaysia has gazetted 38 of its coral islands as protected areas. Some of the more important are Perhentian, Redang, Kapas and Tioman on the east coast of the peninsula, and Langkawi and Pangkor on the west. Consistently voted as one of the world's best dive sites, Pulau Sipadan in Sabah is Malaysia's only oceanic island. Also worth visiting in Sabah are the Tunku Abdul Rahman Park and the Semporna and Lankayan islands.

awareness of its uniquely rich environmental heritage will enable Malaysia and its neighbours to manage their natural resources wisely.

Underwater treasures

Malaysian seas today hold untold riches from ships wrecked by storms or plundered by pirates. Rumours still circulate of hidden treasures buried in caves on islands off the east coast of the peninsula.

Whether or not there are secret treasure troves loaded with gold and precious jewels, there are certainly other underwater treasures – the beautiful and varied marine life of the Malaysian waters. Much of the coast is sur-

Four species of giant sea turtles, including the endangered Leatherback, lay their eggs on Malaysian shores, while offshore the *dugong*, or sea-cow, can occasionally be found.

Until recently, the seas were thought of only as a source of food, but today there is growing interest in underwater discovery. Numerous scuba-diving and marine clubs are springing up as interest in the sport grows. Malaysia is reaping new profits from its long stretches of beach and coral-fringed islands as tourists flock to these places for recreation. ❏

ABOVE: Good visibility and a thriving underwater life make for some excellent diving in Malaysia.

An Environment in Danger

Malaysia is one of the world's 12 mega diversity areas. Many plants and animals are found nowhere else in the world and the majority most likely have yet to be identified and named. Tropical forests, the most biologically diverse ecosystems on earth, cover approximately 46 percent of the land. In addition, Malaysia is blessed with a variety of other ecosystem types, including mangrove and peat swamps, mountain ranges, coral reefs, limestone habitats, and caves.

Whether Malaysia can maintain its unique natural heritage will depend on its ability to balance environmental conservation with economic development and a fast-growing population. Malaysia's population has doubled in the past 30 years and is expected to double again by 2025, with some major urban areas experiencing up to 5 percent growth annually. Squatter settlements have mushroomed and in many cases intruded into forested reserves. As such illegal settlements are not usually serviced by the cities' infrastructure, this leads to open burning or dumping of wastes into rivers.

As the country has progressed, there has been competition for land use for agriculture, mining, industry, timber and development. Decisions about land conversion are based exclusively on economic rates of return on investment. This contributed to massive deforestation for tin mining in the early 1900s, for agriculture and land development schemes in the 1960s and 1970s, and for urban and industrial development in the 1980s and 1990s. Rubber and oil palm are two major cash crops, occupying 15 percent and 12 percent, respectively, of the total land area in Peninsular Malaysia. Oil palm cultivation is the main reason for the loss of lowland forests, and the amount of land under oil palm cultivation was increased by 10 percent annually from 1970 to 1992.

Another major money earner is timber. In response to international consumer pressure, there is a declared objective to implement sustainable-yield harvesting, and Malaysia's furniture-making industry is being promoted so that more money can be made from fewer logs. Nevertheless, the authorities find it difficult to police the

RIGHT: lorries laden with tropical timber – sometimes illegally gotten – are a familiar sight on interior roads.

vast, densely-forested areas involved, so excessive logging continues.

As Malaysia continues its transition from an economy based on commodities to an industrialised one, future threats to the environment are likely to be from industrial pollution. During the early industrial phase of the 1970s, palm oil and rubber processing resulted in the discharge of large amounts of organic effluents into Malaysia's water. With growing industrialisation, the Department of Environment (DOE) has identified the chemical, food and beverage, textile, metal finishing, and animal husbandry industries as additional contributors of pollution. According to DOE's 2004 Malaysia Envi-

ronment Quality Report, of 120 river basins monitored for water quality, nine were categorised as highly polluted and 53 as slightly polluted.

Air pollution has also increased, with the Klang Valley experiencing hazy skies for months on end during the dry season, caused by smoke from the burning of forests in neighbouring Indonesia.

Malaysians have, over the years, suffered the effects of various environmental disasters, from landslides and floods to a tsunami and contagious-disease epidemics. These have begun to drive home the importance of nature's role in preserving the quality of human life. Changes in attitude and policy are clearly perceptible; one hopes that Malaysians care enough to preserve their beautiful land. ❏

THE PEOPLE

Aborigines, Malays, Indians, Europeans, Chinese – these are just some of the many and diverse peoples that have given Malaysia its unique character

The traveller in Malaysia will be fascinated by the obvious multi-culturalism of the country: there are Malays, Chinese, Indians and Eurasians; as well as large tribal communities like the Kadazandusuns of Sabah and the Iban of Sarawak. And given the melting pot of ethnicities, there is a sizeable mixed-race population as well.

The population stands at over 26 million today, with 83 percent living in Peninsular Malaysia, 9 percent in Sarawak and the remaining 8 percent in Sabah. The distribution of population is grossly unequal when one considers that most people are found in the peninsula, which at 131,587 sq km (50,800 sq miles) is considerably smaller than Sarawak (124,967 sq km/48,250 sq miles) and Sabah (72,500 sq km/27,900 sq miles) put together.

The Orang Asli were the original inhabitants of the peninsula. Then came the Malays, who built upon traditions of the soil and ocean and embraced influences from elsewhere as well. With its rich resources and strategic location, the peninsula also attracted others – Indians, Chinese and Europeans. The result is a Malaysia with a rich culture and diverse traditions.

Orang Asli

The Malay term Orang Asli means "original people" and covers three more or less distinct groups and a score or more of separate tribes. Of the estimated 98,000 Orang Asli, 89 percent live in rural areas, many of which are on the fringes of towns, selling forest produce such as bamboo, and wild fruit and vegetables to the townspeople. The British were perhaps the first to group the Orang Asli together, using the term *sakai* or debt-slave to define them. Their origins still remain something of a mystery; what is known is that the main groups vary from one another racially, culturally and linguistically.

Undoubtedly, the oldest inhabitants of the

Malaysian Peninsula are the Negritos, arriving in the Malay Peninsula at least 10,000 years ago. Numbering around 2,000, they are mostly dark-skinned and frizzy-haired, their features, though unique, are similar to the peoples of Papua New Guinea or East Africa. The Negritos mostly inhabit the northeast and northwest

of the peninsula, and are the only truly nomadic of the Orang Asli tribes. Practising little or no cultivation, the Negrito tribes pride themselves on their mobility. However, like other tribes, some Negritos have left the forest and sought education and jobs in the city.

The largest group, numbering around 40,000, is the Senoi – thought to share a common ancestry with the hill peoples of northern Cambodia and Vietnam – arrived in the Malay Peninsula between 6,000 and 8,000 years ago. Most of the tribes are shifting cultivators, moving from a settlement when the land is exhausted. Many Senoi in the Cameron Highlands have become wage-earners, working on

---

PRECEDING PAGES: snapshots on a longhouse wall.
LEFT: the new breed of high-tech workers.
RIGHT: inside a makeshift Orang Asli home.

the highland tea estates. Others have headed for the bright city lights, getting jobs as varied as civil servants and taxi drivers.

The last group of Orang Asli, the Proto Malays or Aboriginal Malays, were the last to arrive – from the Indonesian island of Sumatra – around 4,000 years ago. Many of this group also have a distinct resemblance to the Malays; indeed modern Malays have a common ancestry with many of them.

Malays

The Malays, long linked to the land as *bumiputra*, or sons of the soil, are known for being

duced to raise the Malay stake in the economy.

Rural Malays today still cherish the simplicity of the uncluttered, outdoor life, nurturing a provincial conformity laid down centuries ago. Malay *kampung* are peaceful enclaves, with wooden houses propped up on stilts above courtyards shaded by coconut palms, banana and papaya trees. The village mosque calls the faithful to prayer several times a day, often interrupting evening television programmes that are now a part of everyday family life.

Kampung youth and children may favour shorts and blue jeans but the daily dress code is still the comfortable cotton *sarung*. Rolled

generous and hospitable with an easy smile and a well-developed sense of humour – traits perhaps of a people who have had the good fortune to live peacefully in a land abundant year-round with food.

As a whole, Malays comprise 54 percent of Malaysia's population. Historically, as *bumiputra* or "sons of the soil", the Malays have always wielded political authority. However, when the status quo of the Malays was threatened in the 1969 elections, culminating in bloody racial riots, the New Economic Policy (NEP) was set in place to protect the interests of the *bumiputra*. Racial quotas, scholarships and business and housing subsidies were intro-

HOME CLEAN HOME

In Malay homes, be it a humble *kampung* dwelling or a high-rise condominium in the suburbs of Kuala Lumpur, traditional customs hold sway.

The most noticeable hallmark of a Malay home is cleanliness, a trait considered next to godliness. It is said that the brighter the house, the more blessings God will bestow upon those who dwell within its walls. In *kampung* homes, a basin of water is always placed at the bottom of the entrance stairs. This is to allow for the washing of feet before entering. As in practically all Asian cultures, to tread into someone's home wearing any form of footwear is unacceptable.

expertly at the waist, and topped off with either a batik shirt or T-shirt, this airy garment is especially indispensable among older Malays. On special occasions, the traditional and comfortable *baju kurung*, a long-skirted suit usually made of colourful silk, is worn by women, while men don their *baju melayu*, a loose pantsuit worn with a short sarong, topped with a black velvet fez known as a *songkok*.

> **THE BIRTH OF ISLAM**
>
> The earliest record of Islam on the Malay Peninsula is an inscription in Terengganu dating from 1303, prescribing penalties for those not observing the faith's moral code.

The inherent talents of the Malays, however, find outlets far from the countryside. Malay businessmen and civil servants in the cities wear Western-style clothes, drive cars, speak English fluently, and carry mobile phones. Urban youths pick up the latest in street fashion from the US and display their new togs in shopping malls. Hard rock and heavy metal is popular, as is the electric guitar. The amplified sounds of the instrument can even be heard blaring from isolated *kampung* houses.

Although the rift between the *kampung* and the city has widened over the years, it does not threaten the strong unity the Malays derive from a common faith. The laws of Islam immediately set a Malay apart from fellow Malaysians. Intermarriage between races is uncommon, though Muslim foreigners are accepted, keeping the Malay-Muslim cultural identity distinctly separate.

Muslim women, especially, stand out from other ethnic Malaysians mainly because of their dress codes. Recently, an increasing number of Malay women have chosen to wear the veil, or *tudung*, a garment of modesty. Despite this seemingly strict dress code and traditional Islamic laws (which, for example, allows polygymy), Muslim women in Malaysia are given an increasing amount of employment and property rights; many run their own businesses and have high-profile jobs.

Indians

Indians began visiting Malaysia 2,000 years ago, following rumours of fortune in a land their ancestors knew as Suvarnadvipa, the fabled "golden peninsula". Tamil blood even flows through the royal lineage dating back to

13th-century Melaka, where the first sultanate was found. But it was not until the 19th century that Indians arrived and stayed in large numbers, employed mainly as rubber tappers or other plantation labourers. Most came from south India, and about 80 percent were Tamil, with small numbers of Sikh, Bengali, Keralan, Telugu and Parsi. Malaysian Indians still maintain strong home ties with their former villages, sometimes even taking wives from there and bringing them to live in Malaysia.

Today, Indians (mostly concentrated in the states of Selangor, Perak and Penang) make up less than 10 percent of the population of Malaysia, yet they own less than one percent of the country's corporate wealth. It has been estimated that four out of five Indians, mostly Tamils, are still manual labourers on plantations, a situation that has been explained as a legacy of colonial Malaysia.

However, as the country gains in economic prosperity, other Indian communities are increasingly well-represented in the various professions. Several programmes have been initiated to raise the Indian share of Malaysia's wealth but the general consensus is that the eco-

LEFT: friendly Malays, also known as *bumiputera* or sons of the soil. **RIGHT:** Indians are a minority race.

nomic restructuring plans of the NEP have generally overlooked the Indians.

Indian Muslims are also a significant part of the Indian community. When they arrived in Malaysia, many opened restaurants, textile shops and other successful businesses, and some of them married Malay women.

Southern Indians have brought a rich cultural influence and colour to Malaysian life. Bright silk saris, fiery Indian cuisine, Tamil movies with their song-and-dance scenes, and the indomitable

> ### EARLY ARRIVALS
>
> Chinese Ming admiral, Cheng Ho, first visited Melaka in 1403; many Chinese traders afterwards followed his example and set up warehouses for trade there.

tants:... they are the only people from whom a revenue may be raised without expense and extraordinary effort by the government."

It was for both fortune and adventure that the Chinese first headed for *Nanyang*, the South Seas. From the 13th century onwards, the Chinese were frequent traders in the Indonesian and Malay archipelago. However, the majority of the Chinese arrived in the 19th century during the Manchu dynasty when problems were rife in China. An edict was issued banning Chinese

prevalence of the Hindu faith that continues to absorb change have all become part of Malaysia.

Chinese

The Chinese population makes up 25 percent of the country's total, yet their presence and control of major industries such as rubber and tin and the commercial sector would seem to make their numbers far greater. They can be found in any trading centre, from Kuala Lumpur to the smallest isolated shop far up the Rejang River in Sarawak. In 1794, Francis Light, founder of Georgetown, Penang, was so impressed by the hardy Chinese that he wrote: "The Chinese constitute the most valuable part of our inhabi-

from travelling abroad, but a number risked their lives and escaped. These later Chinese immigrants were organised under clan associations (*kongsi*) and secret societies, which often engaged in rival warfare. The new settlers took on many of the toughest jobs in tin mining, road and railway construction; but they also played as hard as they worked, and opium and gambling were popular pastimes.

Rather than integrating with Malay culture, the Chinese community has put its own traditional stamp on the land. Officially, all Chinese must learn Malay, but at home, Mandarin and local dialects prevail. Younger generations, however, are more caught up in modern Western lifestyles.

There is a strong belief in self-help and industriousness among the Chinese, but close family and clan ties are also priorities. The Chinese in Malaysia are defined by their history of hardship and pioneering, as well as the three important Chinese code of ethics: Confucianism, Taoism and Buddhism. Even if converted to Islam or Christianity, this background is deep-rooted and many of the associated festivals are regularly celebrated.

Even among modern Malaysian Chinese, the belief in symbolism is prevalent. Jade is worn by the majority of Malaysian Chinese for aesthetic reasons as well as for its evil-warding powers. *Feng shui* (literally, "wind, water") is the Chinese belief system based on geomantic omens. The numeral 8 is extremely coveted for house numbers and car licence plates, as it sounds like the Cantonese character for "prosper"; meanwhile, the number 4 is carefully avoided, as it sounds like "death".

Peranakans

The Peranakan culture was first established when Chinese trade missions established a port in Melaka in the early 1400s. Inter-cultural relationships and marriages were forged between traders and local Malay women, as well as between Melaka's sultans and the Chinese Ming emperors. In 1460, Sultan Mansor Shah married Ming Princess Hang Li Poh, who brought with her 500 "youths of noble birth", and many handmaidens and settled around Bukit Cina (Chinese Hill).

Subsequent generations of Chinese-Malays were known as Straits Chinese, or Peranakan, which in Malay means "born here". When the Dutch colonists moved out in the early 1800s, more Chinese immigrants moved in, thus diluting Malay blood in the Peranakans, so that later generations were almost completely Chinese. However, this did not alter the Straits Chinese identity, which combines the best of Malay and Chinese cultures. This colourful balance encompasses Malay dress such as the *sarung kebaya*, a unique bi-cultural cuisine, and a spoken language of mixed Malay, Chinese and some English colloquialisms.

Peranakan culture reached its height in the 19th century, and though Melaka was the Peranakan centre, large communities also flourished in Penang and Singapore. Today's Peranakans are proud of their heritage and consider themselves different from the other Chinese, although they are counted as part of the community.

Eurasians

When the Sultanate of Melaka fell to Portuguese invaders in 1511, the new rulers sought to establish control by encouraging the Portuguese soldiers to marry local Melakan women. As can be expected, a strong Eurasian community grew up with loyalty to Portugal

through its ties of blood and the Catholic faith.

Nearly 500 years after their arrival, there is still widespread evidence of the Portuguese legacy. Eurasians in Melaka, as well as in other towns in Malaysia, bear such Portuguese surnames as Sequiera, Pinto, Dias, D'Silva and D'Souza, and still cherish the traditions of their European lineage. They are proud of their unique Eurasian cuisine, and some still continue to speak *Cristao*, a medieval dialect from southeastern Portugal. The language has long since died out in Europe, but is still used in some parts of Malaysia. Descendants of cross-cultural marriages in the 19th and 20th century are equally proud of their English or Dutch heritage.

LEFT: the Chinese are well known for their business acumen and industriousness. **RIGHT:** a Peranakan bride getting dressed for her big day.

The people of Sabah and Sarawak

The two easternmost states of Sabah and Sarawak, situated in the north of the island of Borneo, have the most diverse racial groups of all Malaysia. Most of them are of Mongoloid extract and moved here from Kalimantan (Indonesian Borneo).

In Sabah, the largest group comprises the Kadazandusun tribes, followed by the Murut, Bajau and Rungus, and Bisaya, Suluk, Lundayeh and Kedayan in smaller numbers.

In Sarawak there is also a great diversity of peoples and languages: the Dayak include Ibans, who make up the majority of the Sarawak population, and the Bidayuh or land Dayaks. The Melanau are also a large community, and then there are many tribes lumped together under the name of Orang Ulu. This term, meaning "interior people", has become somewhat derogatory in the sense that it denotes a primitive and ignorant people – most tribes prefer to be known by their own names. The Orang Ulu group includes the nomadic Punan and Penan, the highly structured Kayan and Kenyah communities, and the Kajang, Kelabit, Lun Bawang and Bisaya. Even these names house several different tribes who have their own special names. ❑

MYTHS AND TRADITIONS

Borneo has been known as a land of head-hunters, a term which seems to conjure up a cruel and aggressive people. Contrary to this misconception, the people of Sarawak are a gentle, law-abiding people and in the days of head-hunting, taking the heads of one's enemies only occurred when the community suffered some plague. The heads of enemies were thought to bring protection from danger and sickness. Taking a head was also a way of proving one's manhood. Only the heads of warriors were coveted, and the women and children of the enemy eventually became integrated into the victor's community. Today, head-hunting is outlawed, and the skulls seen hanging in longhouses are those that have been inherited by families.

Tattoos are another cultural tradition in Borneo, and both men and women sport elaborate designs on their bodies. Worn both for protection and decoration, each tattoo is designed to suit the wearer. These days, however, tattoos are becoming more of a fashion statement for young urban Iban.

In the past many tribes also placed long weights or simple wooden plugs in the ears of children in order to stretch the earlobe. Women wore the heaviest ones so that their lobes eventually stretched down to their chests. Such lobes are still considered a sign of great beauty by traditional tribespeople, although this practice has now died out.

Festival Fever

Malaysia's multi-cultural population makes for a heady mix of festivals. Not only are all the major religious events celebrated, there are also dozens of other secular happenings around the country – from music festivals to Formula One racing. Most religious festivals are calculated on the lunar calendar and their dates vary each year, so check with Tourism Malaysia (tel: 1300-885 050 within Malaysia; www.tourism.gov.my) first.

If you don't know any locals, the big religious celebrations can be a non-event for tourists as most of the action happens in the home. If you get an invitation, take it up, as it is the only way to really experience these events. Enquire at tourism offices about homestays and families who invite tourists to participate in their celebrations.

Here are just a few of the major events:

January–March

● During the **Chinese New Year**, which culminates in the festival of *Chap Goh Mei*, houses and shops are decorated, lion dances are performed and worshippers throng temples. Kuala Lumpur's Petaling Street night market before the New Year is not to be missed.
● **Thaipusam**, a spectacular Hindu festival where penitents pierce their bodies with hooks and shoulder huge yokes, draws up to a million people at Selangor's Batu Caves; also held in Penang.
● **Le Tour de Langkawi**, Malaysia's answer to the classic Tour de France, a gruelling bike race.

April–June

● The world's top drivers compete on the high-tech tracks of the Sepang International Circuit during the **Petronas Malaysian F1 Grand Prix**.
● **Sabah Fest** is an annual two-week get-together for the state's 30 ethnic groups, culminating in the two-day Harvest Festival celebrations.
● **Gawai**, Sarawak's biggest event, is a celebration of the rice harvest, with dancing, feasting and bountiful toasting with *tuak* (rice wine).

July–September

● Excellent bargains are up for grabs nationwide during the annual **Malaysia Mega Sale Carnival**.
● **National Day**, the commemoration of Independence, is held every 31 August with pomp and parades, in a different location each year.
● **World Rainforest Music Festival**, at the Sarawak Cultural Village, Damai, brings together the best of world music and indigenous beats.
● The **Mooncake Festival**, also known as the Lantern Festival, marks an ancient Chinese peasant victory over Mongolian warlords. Special cakes are eaten and children celebrate with lantern processions.

October–December

● **Deepavali**, the Hindu Festival of Lights, is a family affair to celebrate the triumph of good over evil. Tiny oil lamps flicker all night long in Hindu homes.

● **Mount Kinabalu International Climbathon**, the toughest mountain race in the world, attracts the best mountain runners every year.
● **Christmas** is best enjoyed in Melaka, especially in the Portuguese Settlement, where the Eurasian Catholic minority celebrates in exuberant style.

Variable Dates

● **Hari Raya Haji** marks the completion of each year's pilgrimage to Mecca.
● **Hari Raya Aidilfitri** celebrations at the end of the Muslim fasting month of Ramadan include special food, prayers, and a month-long open house when families and friends visit each other and enjoy a spectacular array of cakes and snacks. ❏

LEFT: An Iban of Sarawak in traditional dress.
RIGHT: the lion dance is a vibrant highlight of the Chinese New Year celebrations.

RELIGION

*Malaysians have long enjoyed a harmonious atmosphere of religious tolerance.
But recent outpourings of Islamic extremism could presage future strife*

For anyone wanting a crash course in comparative religion, Malaysia is the place to come. From animism to the latest revivalist movement, Malaysia is home to all the world's major beliefs and a host of minor ones besides. Religion is found everywhere – in mosques, temples and churches, in the perpetual round of religious festivals, in diverse rites of passage, and in a multitude of everyday sights and sounds.

Each faith tends to identify with a specific ethnic group. Every Malay is a Muslim, but there are also Indian Muslims, Sarawak Muslims (Melanau) and Sabah Muslims (Bajau and Orang Sungai), as well as small but significant groups of Chinese, Kadazandusun, Murut and other converts. Buddhism is allied to the Thais and the Chinese, while most Chinese who are not Buddhists are Confucians, Taoists and/or ancestor-worshippers. Hinduism is the preserve of the Hindus, and Sikhism of the Sikhs. Only Christianity is truly multi-ethnic, embracing small minorities of Indians and Chinese in the peninsula and rather larger groups of Ibans, Bidayuhs, Kedayans, Kadazandusuns and Muruts in Sarawak and Sabah. Folk religion holds sway among many in these Bornean states. In the interior of the peninsula, small clusters of Orang Asli (aborigines) still cling to their ancient animism.

Religious tolerance

This great variety of faiths within the compass of a small nation is hardly surprising, given the rich ethnic mix that Malaysia enjoys. What is more surprising is that the followers of these different creeds – some of whom are at daggers drawn with one another elsewhere – live here in relative peace and harmony.

Although Islam is the official religion and Muslims account for over half the total population, the constitution guarantees the free pur-

suit of all other beliefs. Religious friction rarely arises. If it does, it is easily controlled by a combination of effective monitoring by government, and of a lively awareness among people at large of its destructive and antisocial consequences. In any case, ethnic interaction, particularly in urban areas – at the workplace,

in shops and offices, in the arts, on the sportsfield, and on social occasions – contributes towards mutual understanding and tolerance.

One advantage of a land with many different creeds is a prolificacy of public holidays. All the major religious festivals are treated as national holidays, and a list of minor ones at state level adds to the score.

This happy state of affairs has given rise to the peculiarly Malaysian "open house". Guests don't have to be followers of the particular religion whose sacred feast is being celebrated. Operating at all social levels, at its pinnacle, the homes of royalty and political leaders are thrown open to everybody, including tourists.

PRECEDING PAGES: Kayan girls of Sarawak.
LEFT: Impish schoolgirls sporting *tudung* (Muslim headwrap). **RIGHT:** a more liberal Muslim sister.

Islamic Resurgence

Islamic resurgence in Malaysia forms part of a global Muslim phenomenon which has emerged since the end of World War II. In general, its proponents say that it is a movement to restore Islamic civilisation to its former prominence, and to re-establish an alternative world social order to the existing one dominated by the individualistic and materialistic values of the West. The ultimate goal of this re-ordering of Islamic society is the creation of Islamic polities, whose government and administration are based on the *Koran* and the *Sunnah*

(i.e. the words, deeds and actions of The Prophet).

Since the early 1970s, there has been a conscious attempt to establish an Islamic identity in law, medicine, education, economy, and ultimately to set up an Islamic state. From the purely religious point of view, this is all well and good. But in Malaysia's plural society, Islamic resurgence poses problems both for Muslims (especially the Malays) themselves, and for non-Muslims who make up almost half the country's population.

For the Malays, the growing trend of Islamic resurgence has deepened the rifts already existing between fundamentalists and moderate Muslims, politically expressed in the rivalry between the fundamentalist Pan-Malay(si)an Islamic Party

(PAS) and the United Malays National Organisation or UMNO, the party of the moderates. A foretaste of what life might be like in an Islamic state is provided by Kelantan, where PAS forms the state government and imposes strict regulations regarding the consumption of alcohol, dress codes and forms of entertainment, including traditional ones. However, the rights of non-Muslims in the state have been equally strictly respected.

Tensions caused by stricter interpretations of Islamic rules have been sharpened by UMNO's identification with a rising Malay middle class wed to capitalism and urban living, as opposed to PAS's stand for a pristine Islam rooted in a rural society. For non-Muslims, the spectre of Islamic rule, with all the implications this holds, has reinforced their support for the ruling coalition, the Barisan Nasional (BN), of which UMNO itself is the leading member.

The successful Iranian Revolution of 1979, as the first successful Islamic revolution in modern times, gave an enormous fillip to Islamic resurgence everywhere, including Malaysia, and aggravated existing tensions. The summary dismissal in late 1998 of Anwar Ibrahim, the deputy prime minister, himself a prominent champion of Islamic values, seemed also to have alienated many Malaysians, especially Malays, from the BN. This gave further impetus to the Islamic resurgence movement. Over the years, PAS has managed to collect an average of almost one-fifth of the total votes cast in most general elections and made large gains in the 1999 elections.

Aware of the dangers of extremism in a multi-racial society, BN has met mounting Islamic resurgence with a policy of adoption and assimilation. Existing Islamic institutions have been strengthened and new ones added, including Islamic banks, schools and an international Islamic university, a system of separate *syariah* courts with judicial autonomy, and greater media coverage on Islamic issues.

Abdullah Badawi, who took over as prime minister in 2003, is an Islamic scholar by training. He has offered a moderate alternative to Islamic extremism, advocating "Islam Hadhari". Translated from Arabic as "civilisational Islam", this set of principles stresses economic and technological development, social justice and tolerance for other religions. Abdullah's governance and BN's strategies have proved quite efficacious. In the 2004 general elections, BN succeeded in winning back the Terengganu seat that was previously lost to PAS.❑

LEFT: Islamic not just in manner but in dress – Kelantan schoolboys in traditional garb.

The reward for queueing long hours to gain entry is the chance to greet the VIP in person and to partake of the fare always provided.

Another revelation for the visitor from abroad is the devoutness of the adherents of all faiths. Religion is a living force in Malaysia. At prayer times mosques and temples are packed and the large congregations in churches must be the envy of any parish priest in the West. Hindu and Chinese devotees perform their penance in their thousands. The faithful participate in

> **BEAUTY FATWA**
>
> Although Malaysia's Islamic law is generally moderate, in 1997 *ulamas* (muslim theologians) in Selangor placed a *fatwa* banning beauty contests in the state.

not make Malaysia an Islamic state, because government is not based on Islamic law. But it does mean that Islam has the full backing, financial and otherwise, of the state. Left to fend for themselves, other religions are all the more conscious of their dependence on their own efforts to survive and flourish.

As for the administration of Islam itself, each of the 9 Malay rulers is the religious as well as political head of his state, while in states not headed by Malay royalty – such as Sabah and Sarawak – the

ABOVE: Islamic calligraphy outside a KL mosque.

religious parades and processions in the tens of thousands. Religious devotions are observed with equal zeal at home.

Of course, not all Malaysians take their religion so seriously. But religious faith is real and palpable and forms an important element in determining public values to a degree rarely found in modern Western society.

The role of Islam

This great religious fervour is probably a consequence, at least in part, of Islam's position as the official religion. Islam's official status does

King of Malaysia fills the gap. Maintaining the Malay rulers in this traditional role – acting at federal level collectively through the Conference of Rulers, with the king as their chairman – helps solve a major dilemma; reconciling Islam's dogma of the unity of the religious and the secular with modern Western pragmatism, which keeps the two distinctly apart. The arrangement also facilitates the acceptance by the Muslim majority of secular laws for secular affairs, while domestic religious issues (such as property rights, marriage and divorce, etc.) remain under the jurisdiction of the Islamic *syariah* courts. By the same token, the Islamic courts hold no jurisdiction over non-Muslims, so that the system safeguards the interests of other creeds as well.

Despite its obvious pre-eminence today, Islam was a late arrival in Malaysia, long preceded by Hinduism, Buddhism and animism. The Malay conversion to Islam was only effectively completed some 500 years ago, during the days of the Melaka sultanate. Before that, Malays had been Hindus, Buddhists or animists (or all three rolled into one). But unlike the aristocratic forms of Hinduism and Buddhism which it replaced, Islam is a religion of the people, with a message of salvation for everyone. Propagated by generations of Arab and Indian-

sist of Malaysian Thais and smaller Burmese and Sinhalese groups.

The main difference between the two seems to be one of sophistication. The Theravada School is much simpler, more abstract and claims to be much closer to the original teachings and way of life of the Buddha. The Mahayana School, having absorbed other influences in the lands where it flourishes (such as in China itself) acknowledges a number of deities, the most famous in Malaysia being the Goddess Kuan Yin. The Mahayana School also has far more complicated rituals and observances.

Chinese Buddhists have been long established

Muslim missionaries, the new faith gained an unshakeable hold over the Malays. It is probably the single most important factor that saved Malay society from disintegration under the pressures of the industrial imperialism of the West in modern times.

Malaysian Buddhists

Next to Islam, in terms of numbers, comes Buddhism, forming just under a fifth of the total Malaysian population. Buddhists fall into one of two main schools, the Mahayana and Theravada (Hinayana). The Mahayana (Great Path) School is the Buddhism of the Chinese, while Theravada (Little Path) Buddhists con-

in Malaysia, being virtually synonymous with Chinese settlement in the country. Their earliest contact probably goes back to the days of the Sri Vijayan Empire during the 9th century AD, when its capital, Palembang in Sumatra, was a great centre for Buddhist studies. But Chinese Buddhism only achieved a permanent presence when the Chinese began to establish themselves as a community in Melaka. Most Chinese Buddhists today are the descendants of the droves of Chinese immigrants who arrived during the 19th century and the first half of the 20th.

Chinese Buddhists are far more numerous than their Thai counterparts. It has been reckoned – though no one has actually taken a count

– that there are at least 3,000 Chinese Buddhist temples, societies and organisations in Malaysia, all of which run their own affairs, although most are also members of the Malaysian Buddhist Association. Thai Buddhists arrived on the scene much later, namely during the late 18th century when their political influence penetrated deepest into the Malay Peninsula. As a result, they are mostly concentrated in the peninsula's northern states where their legacy lies in some of the most beautiful temples to be found anywhere. Apart from the Thais, there is a community of Burmese Buddhists in Penang, and one of Sinhalese

pounded with traditional ancestor worship into an intricate web of ideas, beliefs and ritual that is best described simply as "Chinese Religion".

Wherever the Chinese went, they took their "religion" with them as an integral part of their culture. Today, Chinese religious traditions reveal themselves in ubiquitous household altars, in little shrines along the roadside, in giant joss sticks smouldering at temple thresholds, and in little prayer slips and red paper banners serving a multiplicity of purposes; keeping evil spirits at bay, seeking a cure for an illness, and paying respect to the dear departed.

As with Buddhist organisations, Chinese

Buddhists, whose impressive headquarters forms a prominent landmark in Kuala Lumpur.

Chinese religion

The line between Chinese philosophy and religion has always been a tenuous one. The thoughts of Confucius and the mysticism of the Taoists have been dominant influences in the evolution of the Chinese world view. Down the centuries, these influences have become com-

temples are run autonomously by local associations, although most of them also are members of the umbrella Buddhist, Confucian and Taoist Association of Malaysia. Altogether, about one tenth of all Malaysians come under the category of Chinese religion.

Hindus and Sikhs

Hinduism goes back to the dawn of history, when it came with the first Indian traders to Malaysian shores. The new religion created a cultural revolution. It transformed Malay headmen into kings who absorbed Hindu beliefs and cosmology and adopted Hindu traditions of government without losing their own identity as

FAR LEFT: a Chinese house altar with offerings.
LEFT: Thai-inspired image of the Buddha.
ABOVE: a Hindu devotee carrying sacrificial *kavadi* during the festival of Thaipusam.

Malays. This Hindu period, which lasted for 1,500 years before it was replaced by Islam, has left its traces in Malay language and literature, in Malay art forms such as the shadow play (*wayang kulit*) and in such traditions as the *bersanding* ceremony, when the bridal couple sit in state during a Malay wedding.

However, the Hinduism of the past has very little to do with today's Malaysian Hindus. Now numbering around one million, they are the descendants of Indian immigrants who over the last 200 years came to work as contract labourers, with a seasoning of English-educated clerks, apothecaries, shopkeepers and mer-

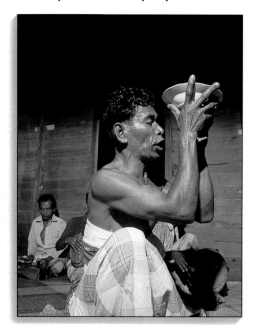

chants who laid the foundations of a modern Indian middle-class. Hindu temples in Malaysia are managed by local committees, following closely the traditions of their place of origin in India. Temples in the towns are more sophisticated affairs, supported by wealthier members of the community.

The 50,000 Sikhs in Malaysia are the representatives of a Hindu sect which became a religion. It was founded in 15th-century India by Guru Nanak who, influenced by Islam, converted his pantheist Hindu followers into monotheists. The Sikh presence in Malaysia is a direct result of British recruitment of members of this famous warrior community to provide the core of the new police forces in the country. Sikhs nowadays are prominent in business and the professions, and despite their small numbers, are found in all the main centres in the land, including Sarawak and Sabah.

Christianity

The first Christians in Malaysia were the Portuguese conquerors of Melaka in 1511, whose descendants from inter-marriage with local women still live there, forming a distinct group of their own. The Dutch, who followed a century later, made no attempt to convert their subjects and so the great period of Christian proselytisation came in the 19th century with the British. Official British policy was not to interfere with other people's beliefs, but Western Christian missionaries were given a free hand to spread their religion, which they did primarily by founding English-medium schools. Christian missionary activity got a second wind after World War II, led by small Christian revivalist churches, many from the USA.

Today, there are over two million Christians in Malaysia, two-thirds of them in Sabah and Sarawak. The three main Christian divisions are all present, but Orthodox Christians constitute only a handful. Roman Catholics, of whom the first were the Portuguese, form the largest group, about two-fifths of the whole. The Protestants are represented by Anglicans – a legacy of British colonialism – Methodists and Presbyterians, largely American-dominated, and smaller groups amongst which the Baptists are the most prominent. ❏

SPIRITS IN THE TREES

In traditional Malay society, the *bomoh* (witch doctor) is a respected spiritual expert, often called upon to use *ilmu* (knowledge) and herbal potions to heal illnesses, especially those caused by *hantu* (spirits). Primitive animism, which peoples every article of creation with resident spirits, is practised by a tiny, dwindling group of Orang Asli (aborigines), living in the remoter areas of the peninsula's interior.

The folk religions of the indigenous peoples of Sarawak and Sabah are more sophisticated, and feature ingenious theories about the origins of life. Their deities are often imbued with very human foibles.

LEFT: a *bomoh* seeking help from the spiritual world.
RIGHT: St. George's Church in Georgetown, Penang.

ARCHITECTURE

From traditional homes to the shining splendour of the world's tallest skyscraper,
Malaysia's buildings reflect both its colourful past and its hopes for the future

I t is said that the spirit of a society is embodied in its architecture, and Malaysia, a champion and torch-bearer for developing nations the world over, has taken this sentiment to heart. As a result, the evolution of vernacular and modern architecture on the Malay Peninsula and in the Borneo states of Sabah and Sarawak ably documents not only the history of the land, but also the essence of its various indigenous and immigrant peoples.

The evolution has been guided by historical markers, the colours of which are strong even today: the first ocean-canoeing Polynesians from the Pacific; Indian and Arabic traders from the West; the era of the wealthy sultans; the European influence; imported Chinese and Indian cultures; the elation of Independence; and the path to globalisation.

City of dreams

The architectural journey begins at the US$6 billion-plus, ultra-modern Kuala Lumpur International Airport (KLIA). When craning to view the skylights 40 metres (130 ft) above you, the grandeur of the project becomes apparent. As all architects agree, design is in the details, and KLIA bags the prize in every category: from the conical columns-cum-air-conditioning vents and returns; the inspired "forest-canopy" effect lighting; and the highly contrived but suprisingly effective "forests" within the satellite building. International flights are usually routed through the satellite, involving an electric shuttle journey into the main terminal for your encounter with Malaysian immigration.

The show continues along the 88-km (55-mile) journey as an autobahn-standard highway snakes its way into the capital. Kuala Lumpur rears into view, as any city sporting the world's tallest twin buildings might, with as much drama as surprise. The highway links directly

with the inner ring-road and the Golden Triangle in the most built-up part of the city. Among a drab offering of 1970s international styles and post-modern aspirants, the elegant Tabung Haji (or Pilgrim's Fund) "hourglass" building draws the eye, but then, out of the concrete forest, rise the Petronas Twin Towers.

The towers brought Kuala Lumpur the kind of instant charisma once promised to puny boys in the advertisements at the back of comic-books – no more would this former tin-mining outpost have sand kicked in its face! During office hours, visitors can ascend to the Sky-bridge on the 42nd floor for expansive views of the city. Entrance is free but you'll be encouraged to part with your foreign exchange in the vast shopping mall "podium" from which the monument rises. Also at the towers is the impressive home of the Malaysian Philharmonic Orchestra, the Dewan Filharmonik Petronas which, on a per-seat basis, is the most expensive concert hall ever constructed.

PRECEDING PAGES: Kuala Lumpur's National Stadium. **LEFT:** Minangkabau-inspired architecture, Negeri Sembilan. **RIGHT:** Kuala Lumpur International Airport.

Colonial past

Stepping outside brings you back to the real Kuala Lumpur, with the standard architectural hang-ups of any insecure city. Eagle-eyes will spot many high-rises with pitched-roofs: a contemporary vernacular that captures domestic Malaysian sensibilities, and couples them with the country's reach-for-the-sky aspirations. Lower your view, and head toward the tallest flagpole in the world (it's even in the record books). Located in the *Padang*, upon which cricket is still played, the Malaysian flag flies over the centre of the former British administrative headquarters of Malaya. As with all colonial planning, the adage "God, King and Country" are literally represented by St Mary's Cathedral, the Sultan Abdul Samad Building and the Royal Selangor Club. Of the three, it is the club which has changed the most architecturally: its mock-Tudor facade has undergone numerous face-lifts and extensions over the years. On the other hand, the conspiratorial chattering of the lawyers who frequent its Long Bar has probably altered little since the distant days of Governor Swettenham.

The legacy of Victorian society can be seen along every trunk-road out of the city, in the form of estates of linked-terraced houses. These

THE MALAY KAMPUNG HOUSE

Once out of the urban centres, which are dominated by the ethnic Chinese, the *kampung* (villages) are characterised by a simplistic vernacular architecture representative of the ethnic Malay lifestyle. The basic elements are a single-level wooden structure, raised off the ground with wooden or bamboo walls and a thatched roof; these have evolved to incorporate many decorative influences from Indonesia and Thailand (in the south and north of the peninsula, respectively), and also from Indian and Arab traders.

There are four acknowledged styles of Malay house – Perak, Melaka, Kedah and East Coast. The styles are primarily differentiated by roof shapes, geometric patterning of the wall panels, fenestration and layout. Generally, the climate-friendly design accommodates a verandah, a sleeping area, the main living room and a kitchen at the back. The windows are shuttered and set at a low height to allow occupants to look out when seated. There are several practicalities to the design: the raised floor protects against floods and fauna, and also against heat gain from the ground by circulating air beneath the structure; the steep roofs shed water quickly, their deep eaves shade windows and the thatch dampens the sound of beating rain – while the high interior disperses warm air effectively.

have become the preferred dwelling-type of a burgeoning middle-class. Built to government order, such developments grow in strict regimen; you'll see various stages of completion in sequence on the same site. Sub-contractors move from ground-beams up, until the homes are completed.

An imaginary line joins the Twin Towers to the airport, known as the Multi-media Super-Corridor (MSC). Planned as a "global-gateway" for everything "cyber", the MSC has suffered from an over-liberal planning brief. The result is a mish-mash of architectural styles that spectacularly fails to match the political coherence of Malaysia's policy on new technologies. MEASAT (the Malaysian Satellite Broadcasting company) managed a low-rise brick-motif gesture with a Vegas-esque signboard, while Microsoft and all the others who took advantage of the everything-exempt sweeteners to take up space, are planning sheds that appear to import their aesthetic from Nebraska.

Ancient origins

An hour or so south of Kuala Lumpur sits Melaka, founded around 1400 by fleeing Sumatran Prince Parameswara. He laid the foundations for what was to become a centre of teaching and trade in the thriving Southeast Asia of the 15th century. The Melaka Cultural Museum is housed in an 1895 replica of the timber-framed palace of the third sultan, Mansur Shah, which was originally destroyed by the Portuguese during their 130-year rule. The Portuguese's architectural artefacts in Melaka are the most significant – including the formidable *A Famosa* fort of 1512.

In 1641, control of Melaka was wrested by the Dutch, who set about building a regional trade hub, the administration of which was housed within the Stadhuys. This 1650s town hall, together with the Christ Church of 1753 (the ceiling beams of which are formed from single trees with no joints), represent probably the most complete examples of 17th-century colonial Dutch architecture in the region.

Commerce with the Dutch saw the growth of Johor as an urban centre. However, the architectural character of the city was defined later, in the 17th and 18th century with the influx of

Minangkabau and Bugis immigrants from Sumatra and Sulawesi respectively. The ordered and highly artistic Minangkabau later headed north – their tall, sweeping roof-style is found throughout the state of Negeri Sembilan (adjacent to Melaka). The Bugis, however, a feared warrior race, stayed in Johor, establishing a distinctive vernacular of ornate timberwork and design. Modern Johor has suffered from its proximity to Singapore. Having assumed the role of a black-market border-town, its grandiose "floating-city" schemes have resulted in urban erosion and negligible architectural worth.

THE STRAITS ECLECTIC STYLE

The favoured building-type in the Straits Settlements (from Penang down to Singapore) was the "shophouse", a double-storey unit with a lower level business floor and a verandah to keep pedestrians sheltered from the sun or rain, while upstairs the family maintained a residence. The style evolved from buildings favoured in mainland China, but Malay, Indian, Arab and Peranakan (Straits-born Chinese) flavourings have created lively and colourful variations on every street facade. This building-type has since matured into the most ubiquitous commercial architectural form on the peninsula – new shophouse developments climb six storeys or more.

LEFT: KL skyline with the green expanse of the *padang* as focus. **RIGHT:** Dutch architecture, Melaka

Kampung life

Island-life encounters along the east coast are far more inviting. Although the journey from Johor up to Terengganu takes in a number of vast hotel resorts, you'll also see scattered fishing communities with their beach-huts and stilt-raised shelters nestling in quiet coves and on the shore above the cobalt surf. The traditional thatched roof and walls, however, have given way to utilitarian zinc sheeting and planks.

Although not as dominant as the west coast colonial settlements, the east displays every evolutionary variant of the Malay *kampung* (village) house.

Crossing to the east coast involves a trek over a highland spine featuring architecture both wholly indigenous and imported. Taman Negara National Park occupies tens of thousands of hectares between the coasts and is home to the Orang Asli, or "original people". Their transient settlements are driven by their nomadic lifestyle – simple shelters of bound leaves and flexible supports adjacent to a hearth for cooking and warmth, all built using materials from the jungle.

The cultivated contrast of the colonial Cameron Highlands hill resort offers the peculiar charm of an English country village surrounded by verdant tapestries of lush tea

plantations. Die-hard archaeologists could circuitously route themselves via the state of Kedah in the northeast corner and find in the Bujang Valley remnants of the 9–11th-century *candi* (temples) of the Malay Peninsula's Hindu-Buddhist period.

The quiet reflection of such an experience offers a delicate preamble to the bustling urban centre of Penang which attracted the most dynamic influences of British and Chinese architecture. The British contribution is apparent in the urban planning, wide boulevards, sea esplanade and imposing administrative buildings; the East India Company literally ran the island from 1786 onwards, and a great deal of capital was invested in its power base. Building conventions and by-laws took root here which set a precedent for almost every other high-street in Malaya.

Travelling back to Kuala Lumpur via Ipoh reveals another important architectural phase fuelled by wealth (primarily from tin-mining) and independence in the 1960s. Self-determination brought with it an architectural self-actualisation that resulted in forms unmatched ever since in integrity or detail. The cantilevered free-forms of amoebic car-porches were perfectly in tune with the swinging culture that borrowed the very shiniest from the West and cultivated home-grown heroes such as the legendary actor P. Ramlee. In the light of contemporary attempts at seeking a distinct Malaysian architectural identity – the current common approach being to slap a suitably Islamic motif on a pre-packaged curtain wall system – the 1960s remain a beacon of light.

Over in the states of Sabah and Sarawak, 1,000 km (620 miles) over the South China Sea on the island of Borneo, the longhouse (see *pages 294–5*) is the typical indigenous building. The basic construction follows the lines of a *kampung* house, but is extended to provide dwellings for many families – and sometimes an entire village. While the layout remains simple, including a "street" formed either between facing rows of living units or on their perimeter, the social organisation is highly complex; where, when and how units are allocated are based on hierarchy, and define cultural rituals of welcoming visitors, marriage, childbearing and security. ❑

LEFT: a Malay *kampung* house on stilts for ventilation.

Petronas Twin Towers

The 88-storey Petronas Twin Towers stand 452 metres (1,480 ft) tall as the focal point of the Kuala Lumpur City Centre development. When first commissioned, the towers were the subject of much contention. Many may quibble on points of political motives, white elephants, Other People's Money and absolute irrelevance – but there is no denying the extraordinary power of such monumental architecture. On par with Gustav Eiffel's tower heralding the advantages of steel-construction, or the dramatic urban planning of Christopher Wren's St Paul's rising goliath-like over a shanty 17th-century London, the spirit of the Twin Towers is historic and "millennial". Considering that the local content (both in terms of expertise and materials) is minimal, the fact that they were built in Malaysia at all is testimony to the power of globalisation and how projects of any nature and size will be developed in years to come the world over.

Architecturally, the towers are practically faultless: the American architect Cesar Pelli delivered a Gotham-esque vision shinily clad in about 85,000 sq metres (280,000 sq ft) of imported European stainless steel. Executed with the simple, almost fascistic clarity of vision of all great monuments, scores of imported consultants laboured for just under – a remarkably short – four years to deliver the Kuala Lumpur skyline an attention-wrenching silhouette. When pushed into providing a link with local sensibilities, some rather contrived sketches reveal an 8-pointed star superimposed on eight semi-circles which together yield a tenuous Islamic floorplate geometry, giving face to Asian Values.

The path to realisation was fraught with having to achieve as many "world-firsts" as possible – the Malaysian rally-cry that screams "*Malaysia Boleh!*" ("Malaysia can do it!") could permit an attitude of no less. Some of these included the blistering construction schedule of two daily 12-hour shifts utilising over 2,000 workers at any given time; the double-level skybridge on the 42nd level, which is one of the highest in the world at 170 metres (560 ft) and took 4 weeks to lift into place; and the highest number of "double-deck" lifts to be contained in a building ever, running at speeds of 5 metres (16 ft) per second – it takes

only a minute to go from the basement to the top.

When completed in 1998, the towers held the status of being the world's tallest buildings. The record height was disputed by the incumbent Sears Tower in Chicago; the latter wasn't quite ready to step off its podium. However, Malaysians insisted that the towers were the final word on the matter. To cap it all, literally, and somewhat controversially, were the two 75-metre (246-ft) stainless-steel spikes that sat atop the 88th level, which, arguably, gave the buildings the winning edge over Sears Tower. Such unbecoming squabbling was put to rest when Malaysia declared that it was never the original intention to construct the tallest buildings

in the world – it was just a "happy coincidence". Even then, the record was held only briefly; in 2003, Taipei 101 tower in Taipei overtook the Petronas Twin Towers as the world's tallest building. Still, Malaysia can stake its claim to the world's tallest *twin* buildings.

Visitors can ascend to the skybridge (open Tues–Sun 9am–5pm; tel: 03-2331 1769) on the 41st and 42nd floors for views of the city. Free tickets (only 1,300 a day) are issued at the information desk on the ground floor of Tower 2 from 8.30am onwards. Sean Connery and Catherine Zeta-Jones had access to the top when they filmed the 1999 movie *Entrapment*, but if you want to get to the higher floors, you had best ask the Prime Minister. ❑

RIGHT: the stunning Kuala Lumpur City Centre.

CUISINE

*Malaysia's many peoples have retained their own culinary traditions. The result
is a deliciously diverse national menu – and a playground for the tastebuds*

Malaysia has been blessed with reliable weather and a lush landscape: tropical jungles, verdant rice paddies, endless coconut groves and teeming coral reefs submerged in emerald seas. These gifts of nature, and the ethnic complexity of Malaysia's population, combine to provide the country with flavours to thrill the palate.

This hedonistic encounter extends not only to multicultural tastes, aromas, colours and textures, but also to the vast spectrum of dining experiences available in Malaysia. Eating establishments range from dusty roadside stalls and noisy Chinese coffee shops, to smart air-conditioned restaurants and Western-style fast-food joints. The choices are infinite.

Village fare

For centuries, Malays lived in *kampung* (villages) close to rivers and coasts, enjoying the natural abundance of food. Traditional meals consisted of rice, fish, vegetables, and chilli sauces (*sambal*), while fresh herbs and coconut milk added fragrance and richness. However, until the 20th century, travel across the jungle-covered country was limited and regional styles of cooking prevailed. The northern states of Kedah, Kelantan, Perlis and Terengganu, for instance, have incorporated sour tamarind (*asam*), limes and fiery chillies in their cuisine because of the influence of neighbouring Thailand. One of the best known northern dishes is *nasi ulam*, a dish consisting of rice, finely sliced raw herbs and vegetables, a spicy chilli-coconut sauce, grilled fish and other cooked side dishes.

Indonesian influences are evident in various Malaysian states. In Johor in the far south, Javanese food was assimilated into Malay cooking over the past few centuries. In the central state of Negeri Sembilan, Minangkabau settlers from West Sumatra brought with them their rich, spicy dishes cooked in coconut milk. A perfect example is *rendang* – a semi-dry coconut-based curry which needs hours of gentle simmering, melding beef with fresh herbs like lemon grass, turmeric and ginger, and spices such as coriander, nutmeg and cloves. The result is pure ambrosia.

SATAY

Satay is possibly the world's most popular Malay food, but whatever else you've tasted in your own country, nothing can prepare you for the real thing. Marinated bite-sized pieces of beef, mutton or chicken (and pork if sold by Chinese) are skewered onto thin, bamboo sticks, and barbecued over a charcoal fire. The sizzling satay is served with thick, spicy peanut gravy, chunks of raw onion and cucumber, and *ketupat* – compressed squares of rice. Leave the remaining bamboo sticks on the table, as the "bill" is settled by counting the total number of sticks left. For the adventurous, there are even satay variations of tripe, intestines, or crispy chicken skin.

PRECEDING PAGES: rice is the focus in this spread of fiery but flavoursome Malay fare.
LEFT: local produce on sale at a Kota Bharu market.
RIGHT: charcoal-grilled *satay*.

Despite differing regional styles, Malay food is, in general, heavily seasoned. Chillies are an everyday pick-me-up, either in dishes or as a blended *sambal* side-dish. The key to almost any Malay dish, however, is the *rempah* – a pounded paste of onions, garlic, chillies, fresh turmeric, and galangal (*langkuas*). The rempah is stir-fried in hot oil in a *kuali* (Chinese wok) and patiently stirred to prevent sticking and to release its tantalising aromas; it is said that this process is the make or break of the whole dish. A subtle seafood flavour is often added in the form of dried shrimps, dried anchovies (*ikan bilis*) or a pungent shrimp paste (*belacan*).

Rice and noodles

Mouthwatering as they may sound, Malay recipes are lost without the simple, indispensable staple: rice (*nasi*). Rice dishes take many forms: *nasi minyak* (flavoured with spices like cardamom and cinnamon), *nasi tomato* (with tomatoes for a hint of sourness), *nasi goreng* (stir-fried with meat, eggs and chillies), and entire meals consisting of rice and side dishes: *nasi padang* (of Indonesian influence), *nasi kandar* (famous in Penang), and *nasi dagang* and *nasi ulam* (in Kelantan and Terengganu). Another popular rice dish is *nasi lemak*. The name means "rich rice" – a savoury rice cooked

MILDER MALAYSIAN

The keynote of any Malaysian dish is chilli – and often lots of it. For milder tastes, the selection at hawker stalls and in Chinese coffee shops presents a mind-boggling selection. Among the more popular fare, **wantan mee** are thin, fresh egg noodles either served in a broth or tossed in a chilli and oil-and-soy-sauce dressing, and topped with roast pork slices and prawn and pork dumplings. Another popular noodle dish is **Ipoh kway teow**. As the name suggests, this soupy dish gained fame in the town of Ipoh, Perak. Smooth, translucent strips of rice noodles are served in a prawn and pork broth and garnished with bean sprouts, shredded chicken and prawns. Ipoh boasts the most

delicate *kway teow* and fattest bean sprouts, supposedly because of the soft water which flows down from the surrounding limestone hills.

Char kway teow is another classic Malaysian-Chinese noodle dish: stir-fried flat rice noodles, garlic, prawns, cockles, bean sprouts, eggs, chilli paste, and lashings of thick, dark soy sauce for a hint of sweetness. Finally there is **chicken rice**, which no gourmand should miss. There are several variations, but the most popular is the Hainanese style, where whole chickens are simmered in chicken stock so that each slice is moist and tender, and served with delicious rice cooked in chicken stock instead of water.

not in water, but gently steamed in coconut milk till every drop of the liquid richness has been absorbed. The rice is then served with a fiery *sambal*, cucumber for coolness, small crispy fried fish, and a fried egg or omelette.

When you tire of rice, try noodles. Chinese immigrants introduced noodles to Malay cuisine and they are now an indispensable part of Malay cuisine: *mee* (a spaghetti-like yellow wheat noodle), *kway teow* (flat strips of smooth rice noodle), and *mee hoon* (thin rice vermicelli) – all can either be stir-fried (*goreng*), served in a light soup, or in speciality dishes such as *mee siam* (mee hoon in a red, spicy, and sour soup), and *mee rebus* (mee in a thick, brown spicy gravy). Chinese immigrants also brought with them the cooking styles of their mainland regions; Cantonese, Hokkien, Teochew, Hakka, and Hainanese predominate.

You are what you eat

Symbolism plays an important part in Chinese cuisine. There is a belief that parts of the animal are supposed to strengthen the corresponding part in the human body. Hence, eating pig's brain soup will increase concentration and alertness, braised beef tendons will boost tired legs, and so on.

Symbolic meaning also comes from the names of foods. For example, a kind of seaweed that looks exactly like black hair is called *fatt choy*, meaning hair vegetable; an unappetising pronunciation, but one phonetically identical to the Chinese characters meaning "to prosper". This weed is often stewed with dried oysters (*hou si*), which sounds like "good business". Not surprisingly, this dish is a standard inclusion on annual Chinese New Year menus, as are prawns (*ha*), which symbolise happiness.

Restaurant Chinese food in Malaysia is considerably more traditional and less novel. Dainty Cantonese *dim sum*, spicy Szechuan food, crispy Peking duck, shark's fin and other Chinese classics are available and cooked to high standards. Although many authentic mainland dishes still remain intact, some so-called Chinese food in Malaysia would baffle any mainland Chinese, just as "chop suey" and "egg rolls" confound many non-American Chinese.

LEFT: *mee rebus*, Malay-style noodles smothered in spicy gravy. **RIGHT:** for chicken rice, whole chickens are simmered in stock for extra flavour.

Go Indian

Although Indians make up only about 10 percent of the population, Indian stalls and restaurants proliferate. The majority of Indians are Tamils from the south Indian state of Tamil Nadu, whose food is hot and spicy and served with rice. But there are also northern Indian restaurants, dishing up milder fare with delicious breads like *naan* and *poori*. In addition, there are eateries run by Indian Muslims, who observe strict Muslim dietary laws.

Eating at one of the many south Indian "banana leaf curry" restaurants in Malaysia, you will experience one of the heartiest and

most colourful culinary spreads around. The banana leaf itself is not eaten, but acts as a natural, disposable green plate from which spicy dry *mysore* mutton, fried fish, chicken curry, red curried crabs, and a variety of spiced vegetables and pickles are eaten. The meal is often accompanied by fresh yoghurt to cool the palate, and cups of thin, spicy soup (*rasam*) to aid digestion. The meal is strongly seasoned with the dried spices used by Indians for thousands of years: chillies, cardamom, cloves, cumin, fenugreek, cinnamon, fennel and mustard seeds, to name just a few of the aromatics used. Fresh lime juice is almost always available to top it all off.

Malaysians would stand firm on the claim that India's greatest culinary contribution to Malaysia is the multi-layered, feather-light *roti canai* (flattened bread) – a flaky fried bread made of wheat flour, *ghee* (clarified butter) and a touch of milk for lightness. A stretchy dough is kneaded, rolled into balls, then dramatically tossed repeatedly into the air; the resulting dough is paper thin, and is folded and fried on a griddle to yield a crisp, flaky pancake. A popular breakfast item, *canai* can also be eaten at any time of

> **PRECISION CUISINE**
>
> Nothing in traditional Peranakan cooking is large or clumsy; every bite has to be equal in size, and measure approximately 2 centimetres (1 inch) in length.

the day. When visiting Indian hawker stalls, don't forget to try Indian *mee goreng* (fried yellow noodles), which are similar to the Malay version, but with slightly different spices, and Indian *rojak*, deep-fried fritters and vegetables served with a sweet, hot sauce.

Peranakan cuisine

Peranakan food is a bi-cultural cuisine unique to Malaysia and its island neighbour, Singapore. It is a food of love, conceived by the interracial marriage of early Chinese immigrants and native Malays, resulting in the Peranakan, or Straits-born Chinese culture. These Nyonya women combined the best of both cuisines, pro-

ducing delectable dishes for their Baba men.

Peranakan food subtly merges typical Chinese ingredients such as pork, soy sauce and preserved soya beans with Malay spices, *rempah* ingredients and the ever-present coconut milk and/or tamarind juice. Being non-Muslim, Peranakan pork dishes are everyday fare. Some favourites are *babi asam* (a tamarind-based pork curry), and pork satay, with pineapple-enhanced peanut sauce.

Duck, traditionally not consumed by Malays, is popular in Peranakan kitchens, where it is braised whole, or made into a curry or sour soup (*itek sio*). Chicken is also commonly used, transformed into varied dishes such as chicken *kapitan* (chicken in spicy coconut milk) and *enchee kabin* (fried chicken with a tangy dip).

Much like Malay cuisine, Peranakan food evolved differently in different parts of the peninsula. *Laksa*, a classic Nyonya dish, comes in two varieties: Melakan cooks favour *laksa lemak* (also called curry laksa) which consists of noodles, prawns and other toppings bathed in a *lemak* (rich) spicy coconut soup. Then there is *asam laksa*, a famous speciality of Penang Nyonyas. This variety, with distinct Thai influences comprises noodles in a clear, fish-based soup, topped with raw cucumber and onion rings, pineapple chunks and mint sprigs.

Not only is Peranakan food delicious, it is also painstakingly prepared. Despite the many servants of old-style Peranakan homes, young Nyonya women traditionally spent hours in the kitchen mastering the precise culinary skills that would please their would-be Baba husbands. Under the watchful eye of elder Nonya women, the girls would practise pounding *rempah*, and slicing and chopping everything in the correct manner.

Eurasian and colonial

Malaysia's other ethnically complex cuisine is Eurasian food. The mecca of this type of cooking is undoubtedly Melaka, which fell to Portuguese invaders in 1511. Although Portuguese rule ended in 1641, and Dutch sovereignty some 150 years later, three centuries of mixed marriages resulted in modern-day Catholic descendants of Portuguese, Dutch, Malay, Javanese and Indian ancestry.

Eurasian cuisine is typically multicultural: Malay herbs enliven Chinese cuts of pork, further enhanced by Indian mustard seeds and chillies. A famous dish is devil curry, a fire-and-brimstone name for a spicy dish based on a Goanese vindaloo, further pepped up with vinegar, mustard and chillies. Similarly, English dishes such as stews and roasts are transformed with the simple addition of soy or oyster sauce, green chillies, or sour tamarind juice.

Undoubtedly, though, the highlight of any Eurasian kitchen wafts through the air in the form of warm, buttery, baking aromas. Eurasian cakes are sinfully delectable – rich fruit cakes, and the infamous *sugee* cake: a rich yellow cake made with heaps of only the best churned butter (traditionally imported in a can), sugar, vanilla, and a mixture of wheat flour and gritty *sugee* (semolina). The result is a decadent tea treat favoured highly by most Eurasians.

Related to Eurasian cooking is colonial food – British dishes that were originally cooked by a hired help (almost always Hainanese Chinese). These cooks slipped Chinese seasonings such as soy sauce and oyster sauce into sedate English food, resulting in tastier roasts, and famous chicken and pork chops slathered with peas, onions and a gravy seasoned with garlic and soy sauce. The altered dishes met with little protest and have remained till today, in older hotels and locally-run Western restaurants across Malaysia.

Food from the jungle

Traditional Borneo food is hard to find outside the longhouses and remote villages. Rice is the staple, although some tribes still adhere to diets based on boiled sago palm and tapioca root. Raw meats and fish are preserved by smoking, or curing in salt. Jungle vegetables like bamboo shoots and fern tips are regular accompaniments, as are lashings of lime and chilli.

Nowadays, what is typical food in Sabah and Sarawak is in fact a Chinese- and Malay-influenced cuisine. From the Chinese immigrants this century, Borneo food has adopted ingredients like soy sauce, and stir-frying and other cooking methods; from the Malays, chillies, dried shrimp, and prawn paste (*belacan*). Using these ingredients, vegetables, jungle animals such as wild boar, and seafood from the coast and rivers are deliciously braised and stir-fried.

Stranger jungle fare can be found even on the peninsula. For those with adventurous spirits and strong stomachs, jungle-food restaurants can be found in many states. Johor, for example, boasts popular Chinese restaurants serving bullfrog, wild-boar, snake, flying fox, civet cat and a host of seasonal "chef specials", which should be tasted first before being identified if they are to be enjoyed. Although the meats used may turn Western stomachs, the cooking is imaginative and the dishes usually tasty. ❏

LOCAL EATING HABITS

To be completely immersed in the whole Malay culinary experience, it is imperative to try at least once the traditional Malay way of eating, still practised in the average Malay home – with your fingers. It may look simple, but it is a skill to be mastered. Using only the tips of the fingers on the right hand (the left hand is considered unclean and never used), any Malay can pick, tear, and scoop with complete deftness.

Increasingly, however, outside the home many Malays use a spoon in the right hand, which is brought to the mouth, and a fork in the left, used mainly for manoeuvring food onto the spoon.

LEFT: in "banana leaf restaurants", food is served on a natural, disposable green "plate". **RIGHT:** a sampling of spices and herbs used in Peranakan cooking.

HAWKER FOOD AND OUTDOOR EATS

The best of Malaysia's food isn't served at fancy restaurants but at stalls set up by the roadside, in hawker centres, or in street-side coffee shops

Patronised by rich and poor alike, hawker stalls are found all over Malaysia, from urban sites beside busy highways, to idyllic seaside locations. Feeding and slaking the thirst of the nation is a round-the-clock affair: Malaysians, as a rule, live to eat and not the other way around. With such low prices who'd be bothered to cook, and as most hawkers specialise in only a few dishes, they have perfected their culinary skills to a degree where most people would prefer to eat out than in. Basic tables and stools are provided on-site. Hawkers will often ask if you want to *makan* – "eat there", or *bungkus* – "take-away".

WHERE TO EAT

Each state has its own famous outdoor eating centre. In Kuala Lumpur (KL), head for Chinatown's famed Petaling Street night market (*above*) for Chinese specialities. For Malay food don't miss the Saturday night market in Kampung Bahru. After dark in Penang, Gurney Drive offers an array of multi-ethnic treats by the sea. In Kota Bharu, have breakfast upstairs in the Central Market, and dinner at the car park, which turns into a night-time eating centre, offering mouth-watering Kelantanese delicacies. Melaka's best-known hawker scene is at the Glutton's Corner opposite the Mahkota Parade shopping centre.

▽ NASI LEMAK
Malaysia's favourite breakfast consists of rice cooked in coconut milk, served with egg, cucumber, anchovies and a spicy *sambal* sauce.

▽ SNACK TIME
A variety of sweet and savoury snacks, go by the generic name of *kuih*. These stalls proliferate during the Muslim fasting month of *Ramadan*.

▽ MORNING TEA
On KL's Jalan Tun Tan Siew Sin, office workers enjoy mid-morning snacks of banana-leaf-wrapped savouries, cakes and tarts.

△ PENANG TREAT
At Georgetown's Esplanade, hawkers prepare *rojak pasembur*, deep-fried seafood and tofu smothered in peanut sauce.

▷ KL BREAKFAST
KL's Masjid India area is popular for *roti canai* with *dhal* or lentil gravy, and accompanied by *teh tarik*, a sweet strong tea.

ROTI CANAI BREAKFAST

Walk through any Malaysian town mid-morning, and the most crowded eateries will usually be those serving *roti canai*. Its English description, an unleavened pancake served with dhal, just doesn't do it justice. It is deliciously light, flaky and crisp, the perfect vehicle to soak up spicy sauces and curries.

Most cooks show off their skills at the front of their shops; it takes years of practice to swing out the dough until it is paper thin. The theatrical flourishes when tossing the *roti* may appear excessive, but are needed to keep the pancake as light and flaky as possible.

A speciality of Indian-Muslim cooks, the origins of *roti canai* are obscure, and like many Malaysian favourites, it has evolved over generations into a strictly localised dish.

△ CHINESE BREAD
Deep-fried *yu char kway*, a Chinese snack, on sale near Georgetown's Campbell Street market, Penang.

△ SATAY
Marinated morsels of meat are grilled over a charcoal brazier for *satay*, a popular after-dark snack and the unofficial "national" dish.

▷ INDIAN PANCAKE
Roti canai is best eaten with your hands. Just tear off a flaky portion, and dip it into a saucer of *dhal* or lentil curry.

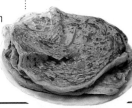

ARTS AND CRAFTS

Malaysia has always been proud of its rich craft tradition. Now a new breed
of artists are pushing back the boundaries of contemporary Asian art

From prehistoric cave murals to cutting-edge contemporary oil painting, the story of Malaysian art spans over 2,000 years of creativity; traditional crafts, which still survive on the Malay Peninsula's east coast and in the longhouses of Sarawak, could well have been around for even longer. Located at the heart of Southeast Asia, at the meeting of the ancient trade routes, Malaysian culture has always been heavily influenced by external influences; its arts and crafts a reflection of this cross-cultural interweaving.

Prehistoric art

Over two millennia ago, unknown artists painted abstract designs, human figures and animals on the walls of a cave near Ipoh, Perak. Meanwhile, across the South China Sea in Sarawak, artisans in the Niah Caves were also painting over 100 depictions of human figures and boats, in murals which stretch over 50 linear metres (165 linear ft). Cave paintings are rare in Malaysia and for many years scholars wondered who these artisans were, and what the drawings meant. Later discoveries of contemporary Orang Asli cave drawings in Perak, in Sarawak and in Sabah, suggest that the prehistoric artists were probably the ancestors of the more recent Orang Asli cave painters, and that the murals depicted the cultural and religious aspects of the original prehistoric painters' lives.

Malaysian crafts date back to the earliest human settlement. A Palaeolithic workshop for making crude stone chopping tools, excavated at Kota Tampan, Perak, dates to 38,000 years ago, while sophisticated flaked stone tools from Sabah's Tingkayu region can be traced back some 28,000 years.

Around 2,000 BC, during the Neolithic era, pottery and polished stone tools appeared. Wooden paddles and anvil stones were proba-

bly used to produce some of the pottery, including sophisticated three-colour urns from the Niah Caves. This production method is still used today by Sarawak's Iban peoples.

In the remote highlands of Bario in Sarawak, and in the lowland wetlands near Santubong, there are some unusual rock carvings where

figures and spiral designs have been engraved into boulders. The only stone carvings in Peninsular Malaysia are a group of carved megalithic stones at Pengkalan Kempas in Negeri Sembilan. This group of three stones, of unknown origin and age, are one of Malaysia's greatest archaeological mysteries as they depict Hindu-type phallic symbols along with the Islamic script for Allah (God). Scholars are divided as to whether the carvings were done at the same time, or whether the Allah inscription was done later to sanctify a pagan site. Stone foundations of buildings and temples found in Kedah's Bujang Valley apparently supported a wooden infrastructure which has long since perished.

PRECEDING PAGES: an oversized Malaysian kite or *wau*.
LEFT: fine art of handpainted batik. RIGHT: megaliths in Negeri Sembilan testify to early artistic leanings.

Wood-carving is a popular craft in Sarawak, where the Kajang people still carve wooden burial poles, or *klirieng*, to house jars containing ashes of deceased chiefs. The oldest surviving pole is 200 years old, but the tradition is believed to date back many centuries more. Other wood-carving traditions survive with the Mah Meri of Pulau Carey, Selangor, who carve legendary figures believed to be the spirits of their ancestors, and the Jah Hut of Pahang, who also sculpt their legends in wood. The Iban of Sarawak carve spectacular hornbill sculptures, while the upriver Kenyah carve mythical dog-god ancestors.

Examples of his work still exist and show how upper-class houses were constructed using no nails, with beautifully carved panels of floral patterns and verses from the Koran.

Metalwork and jewellery

From the first century AD, Indian and Chinese travellers told of legendary Malay kingdoms like Langkasuka and Chi Tu (Red Earth Land). They would describe ancient courts where rulers wore fabulous gold jewellery and dressed in "rose-coloured cloth" – possibly the first-known reference to Malay handwoven *songket*. It is hard to separate reality from fiction in these

Carving comeback

In the peninsula, wood-carving is undergoing something of a revival. There is a new interest in the old craft, and today Malay wood-carvings not only adorn the walls of museums, but decorate the foyers of banks, businesses and government offices, including that of the prime minister. Some of the finest antique wood-carvings can be seen on the panelling, pillars, windows and doors of the nation's oldest royal palaces, which were all built of wood. Encik Long of Besut, Terengganu, was a celebrated master carver, and during four decades of his century-long life he was the principal builder for the Raja of Besut.

fabled accounts, but by the time of the Melakan Sultanate in the 14th century, artisans and craftspeople were an integral part of the royal court. Many lived and worked in the villages beside the palace. Sultans, chiefs, nobles, and their wives and families were the moneyed class, and silversmiths and goldsmiths, silk-weavers, and wood carvers depended on royal patronage for their existence.

A royal wedding was the ultimate event and every artisan was involved in preparing the trousseau and the ceremonial items needed for such a prestigious affair. However, when the courts became more westernised, rulers started buying imported jewellery, clothing, and artefacts. The habit of betel-nut chewing went out of fashion, for instance, rendering obsolete the silver items used in its preparation, and forcing many artisans to hang up their tools. Similarly, many traditional arts and crafts are in danger of extinction.

Fortunately, however, in the predominantly Malay-populated regions of the peninsula's east coast, craftsmen and women have preserved their age-old practices. Today, silverworking, silk-weaving and wood-carving are all experiencing a huge revival. For example, silversmiths still thrive in Kota Bharu, despite having vanished elsewhere. These days, jewellery and functional pieces like fruit bowls, tea-sets and spoons are popular, and although past fashions called for different artefacts, the designs and techniques employed are the same. In Islam, it is taboo to use anthropomorphic figures, and many of the patterns are therefore inspired by flowers, branches and even clouds.

Early silverware is often of exceptional craftsmanship and some pieces, like the earliest surviving example – a royal Johorean betel-set from the early-18th century – employ a painstaking technique that is seldom seen these days. Probably the most fascinating of all the old pieces are leaf-shaped modesty discs which until the 19th century were the only clothing worn by little Malay girls.

In the 1800s, the Straits Chinese of Melaka and Penang, also known as Peranakan – whose ancestors were early Chinese traders who intermarried with local women – borrowed heavily from Malay silver and gold traditions to create their own craft, which is distinguishable from traditional Malay work by its designs which often feature birds and flowers.

Fabrics and weaving

Silk brocades, known as *kain songket*, have always been the favoured textiles for royal occasions, and these elegant woven cloths are still the preferred wear, not only for courtly occasions but for government functions. They are most often used as traditional bridal wear, when both the bride and groom are dressed in sumptuous brocade outfits. At a Kelantanese

weaver's showroom, a pale mauve colour is still sold only to royalty, and there are certain designs which are even now the prerogative of the traditional ruler.

Weavers are usually women who have learnt the craft from their mothers and grandmothers. The very best weavers worked for the palace, like the grandmother of one of Terengganu's top weavers, who was picked from two thousand local artisans of her day to become the sultan's head weaver. Like most other time-honoured crafts, *songket* weaving is practised in

Terengganu and Kelantan, and the techniques and looms used are the same as in the old days. Woven on a simple four-posted loom, the brocade consists of a coloured silk background with a floating weft of gold and silver threads. A distinctive part of every length is the *kepala*, a centre panel with a particularly elaborate pattern. The names of the designs echo the Malay fascination with nature and the countryside: one is known as "bamboo shoots", another "the tail feathers of a cock". Traditionally, nobles would design their own *songket* patterns. This legacy lives on today as a Terengganu prince, Tengku Ismail Tengku Su, continues to create new designs at his well-known workshop. Related to

FAR LEFT: Sarawakian burial pole. LEFT: traditional dress made of rich songket. RIGHT: a songket weaver.

the *kain songket* is *tekat*, an ancient craft of gold embroidery on rich, dark velvet. This luxurious material is popular among Malays for home furnishings, wall hangings, cushions and even bedroom slippers.

From Sarawak hails *ikat*, a unique woven fabric with a tie-dyed warp. Iban textiles serve many ritual purposes: newly-born babies are wrapped in them to ward off evil influences and in the past, trophy heads from headhunting expeditions were even draped with *ikat* cloths.

> **CLASSY CLOTH**
>
> Batik derives from the Malay word *tik*, meaning "to drip". It is thought that batik replaced tattooing as a mark of status in Malay culture.

Batik

Batik cloth is often used to symbolise Malaysia. The national airline uses it for its uniforms, batik shirts are *de rigueur* as men's formal attire and are even compulsory dress at the nation's only casino. It is also worn as sarongs and used for the fashionable and traditional women's dress known as *baju kurung*. But batik-making is not a traditional Malay craft: it was introduced from Indonesia in the 1930s. However, although it is of recent origin, there is no denying that batik-making is now the nation's most popular craft.

Using a wax-resistant technique, the patterns are stamped onto lengths of cloth using a print-ing block made from zinc strips bent into the desired shaped, and dipped in molten wax. However, the biggest success story is of hand-painted batiks, where the designs are drawn on the cloth using a *canting*, a "pen" filled with liquid wax, with the dyes then painted on with brushes. This latter method means that more colours can be used than with the vat-dyeing method, and the freehand designs are only limited by the artisan's imagination. Batik workshops are now opening up all over Malaysia, but the majority of craftspeople are based on the east coast of the peninsula.

Pottery and other crafts

Beside the Perak River, opposite the royal town of Kuala Kangsar, is the village of Sayong, renowned throughout Malaysia for the manufacture of *Labu Sayong*. Literally "Sayong Pumpkins", these gourd-shaped pottery water vessels keep liquids cool in even the hottest weather. The women of Sayong are the potters, and have been for more generations than they can remember. The pots are made in moulds from local clay, and then finished on the wheel where they are incised with freehand designs. After drying in the sun they are fired in small brick kilns. Both terracotta and black-coloured wares are made, with the latter obtaining their distinct colour from being buried in rice husks while they are still hot from the kiln.

In Sabah and Sarawak, the indigenous peoples are renowned for their skill in weaving baskets and hats. The nomadic Penan weave fine black and white baskets from split rattan. To find the best materials they often have to walk a day's journey deep into the forest, then they dry, split, and finally colour the rattan with dye made of forest leaves.

Making mats from *nipah* palm or *pandanus* leaves is a more down-to-earth craft, though one that still requires great skill. Throughout the country, woven mats are an essential part of daily life, used on the floor in *kampung* houses, on beds, on the beach, in mosques, for drying food under the sun, and anywhere else that a convenient, light covering might be needed. Weaving begins at the centre of the mat and moves outwards, using dyes to produce simple criss-cross patterns. More professional weavers (mostly women) fashion hexagonal boxes of nipah palm leaves. In Sabah and Sarawak, floral and even pictorial stories are part of the woven mat's design.

Contemporary art

When the British colonial era introduced industrially-made goods, it was inevitable that traditional arts and crafts would go into decline. At this same time, however, new arts were being introduced like oil painting and watercolours. At first, Malaysian artists emulated Western styles, but after independence a new group of artists came into their own, creating their own brand of abstraction more in line with Islam.

Hoy Cheong's epic series on immigration, Ahmad Zakii Anuar's smoke-blurred portraits and Lee Joo For's bonding of Eastern and Western visual language, to name but a few. Some of the new breed trained overseas, bringing a fresh angle to local traditions. During the 1960s and 1970s, artists were keen to distance themselves from local motifs in order to look "modern". However, after more than four decades of independence, Malaysian artists have come of age, and have rediscovered their roots while continuing the Malaysian tradition of blending both local and foreign influences. The result is a style uniquely their own. ❏

Three of the best known of this group are Latiff Mohidin, who uses indigenous motifs and the environment as inspiration; Syed Amad Jamal, who champions abstract expressionism; and, most famous of all, Ibrahim Hussein, whose linear abstracts can be seen at his gallery/workshop in Langkawi.

In the economic boom of the late 1980s and 1990s, a new breed of artists emerged whose works sold as fast as they were being produced: Rafiee Ghani's colourful "roomscapes", Wong

FAR LEFT: pumpkin-shaped pottery of Sayong, Perak.
ABOVE: an example of Rafiee Ghani's "roomscape".
RIGHT: contemporary Malaysian painter, Rafiee Ghani.

RAFIEE GHANI'S WORLD OF COLOURS

Kedah-born and Kelantanese-raised Rafiee, one of Malaysia's hottest new artists, combines European style with tropical Malaysian colours and patterns. His signature "roomscapes" are of everyday objects infused with extraordinary light and colour, bold and spontaneous in the tradition of Van Gogh and Matisse. While his oils celebrate everyday life, much of his inspiration is derived from his travels in Europe, Asia and Australia. Rafiee's big break came in 1993 with the success of his "Room of Flowers" exhibition, and he has exhibited widely ever since. His work can be seen at Rusli Hashim Gallery of Fine Art in the Crowne Plaza Mutiara Hotel shopping arcade in Kuala Lumpur.

ADVENTURE SPORTS

Forest-clad mountains, giant caves, roaring rivers and deep oceans make
Malaysia a challenging destination for the thrill seeker

Drenched in rain and sweat, too tired to pluck off yet another leech, you make the decision to slide the rest of the way down the almost vertical slope of soft clay. Through the drizzle, the welcome sight of smooth large boulders can be barely made out, beyond which is the source of the roar audible for the last hour: a 30-metre (100-ft) high waterfall, thundering down in fine spray.

This is adventure indeed, a 3-day trek in the rugged interior of a tropical rainforest. Malaysia's highland forests are also the source of swift, bubbling headwaters that run into massive river systems, offering superb rafting and kayaking. Some of these streams seep through the porous limestone massifs, forming huge cave systems waiting to be explored and mapped. Their tiny entrances are often masked by thick foliage – which is also why few cliff faces are available for rock-climbing. Those that are suitable, however, are excellent.

Outdoor pursuits

Malaysia's rainforests offer all manner of challenges to both body and mind; but this is largely ignored by its populace. Trekking is popular among boy-scouts and university students, but Malaysians are generally not fond of the outdoors. Blame it on the rain, blame it on the sun. Blame it on the mosquitos and the leeches, the sweat and the dirt. To the urban Malaysian, leisure means a family picnic in a carefully-landscaped park or at one of the easily-accessible beaches or waterfalls near town. Rural folk spend their free time on traditional art forms such as *wau*-flying (kite-flying) and top-spinning. And for the indigenous people, these challenges *are* part of daily life.

Yet adventure sport is slowly gaining ground among younger, more affluent Malaysians, whose exposure to western trends comes as a

result of time spent abroad, at an overseas university or travelling. Sometimes, the interest is driven by Malaysia's expatriate community. The exception would be scuba diving, which, due to the heavy promotion of Malaysia's underwater attractions for tourism, is enjoying a massive growth in popularity.

For other adventure sports, however, the infrastructure is nascent, expertise is scarce, and sites undeveloped. Taking up these activities is also very expensive, as much of the equipment has to be imported – which is why they are largely limited to middle-income, city-dwelling 30-somethings. Nonetheless, there are clubs for kayaking, a mountaineering association (whose members were the force behind Malaysia's successful 1997 Mount Everest ascent), rock-climbing, as well as jungle-trekking and caving (under the Malaysian Nature Society Selangor branch). These are all, however, based in Kuala Lumpur.

Multi-sport expedition racing is gaining some

PRECEDING PAGES: windsurfing on the wide open South China Sea, off the peninsula's east coast. **LEFT:** whitewater action at one of several rivers in Sabah. **RIGHT:** the majestic Gunung Kinabalu.

interest. In the early 1990s, the punishing Raid Gauloises, the so-called Holy Grail of expedition racing, was held in the spectacular mountain, jungle and cave terrain of Mulu, Sarawak. Each team had to have an obligatory local participant. Then in 1998, a local team became the first Asian team to complete the other big international expedition race, the Eco-Challenge, going on to finish another three in subsequent years. The team leader, Chan Yuen-Li, now organises short adventure races under the Eco-X label.

> **RAINY DAYS**
>
> Highland rivers can swell to Grade 5 rapids after a downpour. In some areas, "dry season" means that it only rains in the afternoon instead of all day.

Probably the greatest difficulty faced by rainforest-based adventure sports proponents in Malaysia is the humidity, which can reach close to 100 percent in the forest. Dehydration is another problem because of the heat. Luckily there is always an icy-cold river close at hand. In some areas, fortification is necessary against the threat of tropical diseases such as malaria.

The most challenging jungle-trekking is to be found in the country's mountainous interiors. In the peninsula, these concentrate in the backbone of Banjaran Titiwangsa (Main Range); in Sabah, the Crocker Range; and in Sarawak, the northern Mulu area. Countless routes can be taken, whether in the Livingstonian quest for

waterfalls, or to scale a mountain, or simply to experience the many ecosystems that make up the rainforest. Hundreds of kilometres of trails wind through protected park areas, mainly serving conservation objectives. Other trails have been trammelled for generations by the indigenous people who still travel on foot to their remote villages. In wilder country, it is the animal trails along the steep ridges that form some kind of pathway through the thorny rattan- and liana-strewn undergrowth.

Many of the longer trails involve ascending to mountain tops, such as the 7-day hike to Gunung Tahan (2,200 metres/7,000 ft) in Taman Negara, and the 4-day ascent to Gunung Mulu (2,400 metres/7,900 ft). The popular overnight trail up the country's highest peak, Gunung Kinabalu (4,100 metres/13,400 ft) is relatively civilised, if stamina-sapping. Exciting country lies in the largely unvisited northern tracts of Banjaran Titiwangsa in the peninsula's Belum area, steep hilly terrain full of hidden waterfalls, and in Sabah's Maliau Basin, termed East Malaysia's last frontier.

Trekking is often a wet experience on muddy trails and across numerous rivers, sometimes by boulder-hopping. However, hot-footing it with a backpack is the best way to experience the amazing jungle, and have a chance to encounter the extremely elusive tropical wildlife. And because the Orang Asli and natives make the best jungle guides, it provides a chance to learn about remarkable and fast-disappearing ways of life.

Climbing the walls

Rock-climbing has long been popular among tiny pockets of enthusiasts. But the sport's best shot in the arm came in the early 1990s when, in line with world trends, Malaysia saw the advent of sport-climbing, which is more accessible than traditional climbing. The other factor was that climbing was part of the government's *Rakan Muda* youth programmes, prompting the growth of artificial climbing walls. In 1999, the first indoor climbing gym opened in Kuala Lumpur, the brainchild of Chan of the Eco-Challenge fame, also Malaysia's pioneer and foremost rock-climber.

All of Peninsular Malaysia's rock-climbing

surfaces is limestone, characterised by steep overhanging rock and often stalactites, which make routes tough (at least 6A French grade; climbing grades range from 3 to 9A). The cliffs are also high, usually 100 metres (300 ft), so paths have to be established from the ground up.

The most frequently visited rock-climbing spots around the capital are Batu Caves and Bukit Takun near Templer's Park. The former is easy to access and has moderately challenging routes. Takun is a more traditional rock face,

TOUGH GOING

Malaysia makes for challenging climbs. Rock faces are always steep, cliffs are often high, and dense vegetation makes some faces almost impossible to scale.

water-level fluctuations, depending on rain; dry floors are often thick with guano. There are spectacular traverses, squeezes and stretches of tough ropework. There is plenty of clambering around massive stalagmites and crossing narrow bridges of fretted rock. No one knows how much more of Mulu remains to be discovered, and foreign caving groups come in on surveying expeditions virtually every year.

North of Gunung Mulu National Park is Gunung Buda National Park, covering 6,235

which involves a bit of a clamber through thick undergrowth to reach. However, both offer several interesting routes. The highest grade of climb locally is 7C.

Cave adventures

Superlatives abound when it comes to the caving haven of Mulu – largest, longest, most decorated. Mulu's giant caves offer superb adventure and technical caving opportunities. Most of the area's 200 km (124 miles) of surveyed passages are wet, with large and sudden

hectares (15,400 acres), described by American caving expeditionists as "a literal garden of Eden complete with fruits, serpents and an eternity of virgin passage". It is truly one of the most spectacular areas for caving in the world, among its wonders is the deepest vertical drop in Southeast Asia (140 metres/460 ft), accessible through challenging ropework amid thundering waterfalls. Another cave houses the region's greatest vertical relief at 465 metres (1,500 ft).

If pre-arranged, equipment and guides can be hired at the Gunung Mulu National Park headquarters. There are no caving clubs, but the Malaysian Nature Society (tel: 03-2287 9422; www.mns.org.my) has a caving group.

LEFT: rock-climbing near Batu Caves, Selangor.
ABOVE: inside a cavern in Sarawak's Mulu Caves

On your bike

While old timber trails in the interior sometimes give hikers access to undisturbed forest, they are more popular with mountain bikers. There are no clubs as such, but various groups comprising mainly friends spend weekends exploring oil palm and rubber plantations, as well as secondary forest near towns. These provide everything from fairly simple trails to challenging hilly terrain, and the vegetation makes for much cooler riding than on the road.

CAPITAL WHEELS

Specialist mountain bike shops are centred in Kuala Lumpur, and sell a range of bikes and accessories. They are also a good place to find out about biking groups.

Wider and flatter jungle trails can actually also make good, if tough, riding – with their root-covered paths, numerous river crossings and breathtaking views. The Headhunters' Trail in Mulu, Sarawak, is one such trail, while another good trail is the dirt road on the border of Taman Negara which leads from Jerantut to the Kuala Tahan *kampung*, opposite the park headquarters.

Aerial sports

Flying microlight or ultralight aircraft is almost prohibitively expensive to take up in Malaysia, but instruction is available. A good start is the 20-minute introductory training lesson, where students are accompanied by licensed pilots.

In Malaysia, microlights are allowed to fly at a maximum height of 150 metres (500 ft), with a 5-km (3-mile) radius from the point of take-off. "Cowboy" operators abound, so check if the outfit is licensed by the Department of Civil Aviation (DCA) Malaysia, whether the instructor has certification and that a logbook is maintained.

Lessons to fly parachutes and winged aircraft are offered by the Experimental Aircraft Association of Malaysia (www.ultralight.bizland.com). The outfit operates from the Nusajaya Flight Park in Johor state, located just off the Second Link to Singapore.

Lessons cost around RM285 per hour, and the flight course takes in mangrove swamps, rivers and rubber plantations, spectacular both in the early morning – when flying is best – and at sunset. Getting a licence for the powered paraglider and powered parachute requires three and six hours respectively, while a student pilot's licence for winged aircraft requires 30 hours of flight training.

Like microlighting, skyjumping is offered by only a handful of operators in Malaysia. One operator uses the Segamat Country Club, a golf course in Johor, for student jumps. The 2-day course includes ground training, and static jumps must be completed before freefalling is allowed. Equipment can be rented and jumps are charged according to height. Tandem skyjumping with an instructor is also available.

Whitewater action

Malaysia's many rivers offer good whitewater experiences. One of the top sites is the spectacular Padas Gorge in Sabah. Tour operators usually offer rafting experiences on 8- to 10-seater inflatable rafts with river guides. Generally, whitewater tour operators are well-organised, experienced and provide safety equipment, a briefing, sometimes insurance, and lunch. Kiulu River, closer to Kota Kinabalu, offers a softer advernture.

Two rivers in Perak, about two hours north of Kuala Lumpur, have become centres for nice-and-easy kayaking and rafting, with up to Grade 3 rapids. Sungai Sungkai near the town of Sungkai and Sungai Kampar near Gopeng are set in rustic, rural landscapes of lush plantations and Malay and indigenous Orang Asli villages. More adventuresome multi-day destinations include Sungai Nenggiri in Kelantan, and Sungai Endau in the Endau-Rompin Park.

The big blue

Scuba-diving is the fastest-growing adventure sport in the country. Malaysia's precious coral islands offer a multitude of stunning possibilities, and with the gazetting of many sites as marine parks, tourists are flocking to them as snorkellers, and, increasingly, divers.

Almost every diveable Malaysian destination has operators offering tours, full equipment rental and dive instruction in PADI, NAUI and/or

Sabah, off whose coast is the region's premier dive destination, Sipadan. The island also has the country's only dedicated sports-diving hyperbaric chamber; others are in navy bases in Kuantan, Melaka and Lumut. Close to Sipadan is the muck-diving haven at Mabul, popular with underwater photographers for its exotic life unique to the silt, while hammerhead and manta ray enthusiasts head for Layang Layang, situated in the South China Sea, 300 km (186 miles) west of Kota Kinabalu.

Malaysia's reefs and marine life are among the world's richest and most diverse. Each dive destination, and sometimes dive spot, is char-

SSI. Besides resort-based facilities which accept walk-in trade, scheduled dive trips are offered by operators in Kuala Lumpur, Kuala Terengganu, Pulau Tioman and Kota Kinabalu.

While there are internationally rated dive centres, at the other end of the scale are operators who are not registered with dive agencies, or are lax about medical and safety equipment such as buoyancy compressors. The Malaysian Sports Diving Association is trying to set local standards and make insurance mandatory. The most developed facilities and services are in

acterised by endemics, from odd macro life in Kapalai to pelagics in Tenggol, coral-wreathed wrecks in Labuan, to the huge diversity of marine life in Redang. Nitrox or technical diving is also becoming popular. Likewise photography, with some operators renting out underwater cameras too.

Other seasports, while popular, do not enjoy such enthusiastic patronage. You'll find windsurfing at beach resorts, while sailing has a small, mainly-expatriate following among members of yacht clubs. Incredibly, there is a surfing group who head regularly to the east coast to take on what must be mere ripples compared to the surf in Bali and Hawaii. ❏

LEFT: paragliding panoramas.
ABOVE: be prepared for encounters with sharks.

PLACES

*A detailed guide to the entire country, with principal sites
clearly cross-referenced by number to the maps*

The visitor's first impression of Malaysia when flying into Kuala Lumpur typifies the country. The view from the aircraft window is of a sweeping agrarian landscape, a deep green carpet of oil palm plantations; but then the plane touches down at an avant-garde international airport, one of the most advanced in the world.

Malaysia is a land of surprising contradictions: picturesque fishing villages and opulent hotels share the same sandy beach; cosy colonial resorts nestle on hillsides that host spirit-worshipping tribal ceremonies, while dense tropical forests are penetrated by the strains of karaoke. Throw in the cultural pastiche that is the Malaysian people, and the result is an irresistible combination of charm and adventure that is still just a glimpse of the "real" Malaysia.

Situated right in the middle of Southeast Asia, with a total land area of 329,000 sq. km (127,000 sq. miles), Malaysia is about the size of Japan, and has a population of over 26 million. The country's infrastructure is well set-up for tourism and consequently, it is fairly easy and very safe to travel anywhere in the country.

Peninsular Malaysia juts out from the southern-most part of the Asian continent. The most developed part of the country is the west coast, dissected from the more traditional and rural east coast by a chain of mountains. Then, about 640 km (400 miles) of ocean – the South China Sea – separates the peninsula from the east Malaysian states of Sabah and Sarawak on the island of Borneo. With its own diverse ethnic tribes, lifestyles and the rich natural heritage, at times, this part of Malaysia seems almost a different country.

Geography has left an indelible stamp on today's Malaysia. The monsoons were what brought disparate cultures to her shores, bringing the religions that now hold sway, influencing architecture and even the model of government. The changing of the winds still affect the important fisheries industry, but for the tourist, it now signifies merely wet and less wet times to visit the country.

Since independence in 1957, Malaysia has faced a series of economic and political pitfalls. Each time it has emerged with the same clear-eyed determination to succeed. From an almost total dependence on raw commodities like rubber and tin, to a broad manufacturing base, Malaysia is now looking beyond that into 21st century global citizenship with hi-tech industries as its vanguard.

But Malaysia's soul is still very much in its *kampung* (villages) and its small town heartlands; in its rainforest and marine heritage; in its religious foundations; and in its cultural roots. And while the quest continues, all these have found some form in a unique Malaysian identity. ❑

PRECEDING PAGES: the majestic Batang Ai river in Sarawak; Pulau Manukan in Sabah's Tunku Abdul Rahman Park; Sultan Abu Bakar Mosque in Johor Bahru **LEFT:** picture-perfect Pulau Tioman, where the musical *South Pacific* was filmed.

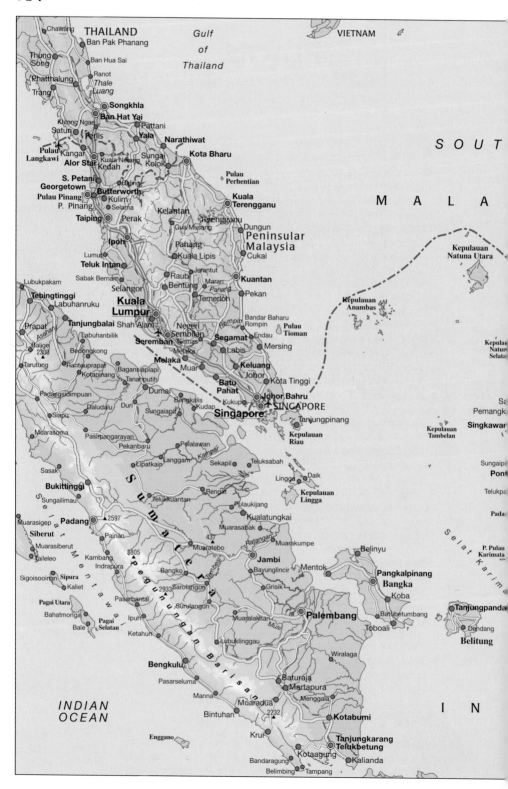

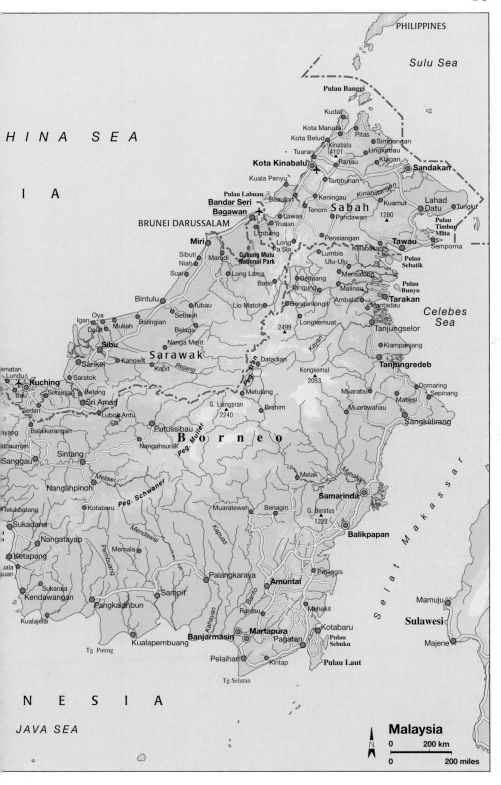

PHILIPPINES

Sulu Sea

HINA SEA

Pulau Banggi

Kudat

Kota Maruda
Kota Belud   Pitas
                                        Simpangan
              G. Kinabalu   Lingkabau
         Tuaran   4101
Kota Kinabalu   Ranau   Klagan

Kuala Penyu   Tambunan   **Sandakan**

I A   Pulau Labuan   Kinabatangan
              Beaufort   Keningau   Kuamut   Lahad
Bandar Seri   Tenom   **Sabah**   Datu   Tungku
Bagawan   Lawas   1280
                    Trusan   Pandawan
BRUNEI DARUSSALAM   Limbang   Pulau
                    Long   Pensiangan   Timbun
Miri   Pa Sia   **Tawau**   Mata
    Sibuti   Marudi   Lumbis   Kelabakan   Semporna
    Niah   Gunung Mulu   Ulu-Ulu   Pulau
    Suai   **National Park**   Long Lama   Sebatik
                    Bario   Benuang   Mensalong
Bintulu   Tangung   Malinau   Pulau
                                        Bunyu
         Tubau   Lio Matoh   Bonganlongit   Ambalat   **Tarakan**
Igan   Oya   Sebauh   Mantadau   Celebes
Dalat   Mukah   Balingian   2499   Longkemuat   Sea
    Belaga   Tanjungselor
Sibu   Nanga Merit   Kiampanjang
    Sarikei   Kanowit   **Sarawak**   Datadian   **Tanjungredeb**
matan   Saratok   Kapit   Rejang
Lundu   **Kuching**   Kongkemul   Domaring
Bau   Simunjan   Betong   Metulang   2053   Muarabu   Sepinang
Serian   **Sri Aman**   Brahim   Mahesi
    Lubok Antu   G. Liangpran   Muarawahau
ayang   Balaikarangan   2240   Sangkulirang
ahauman   **Putussibau**   **B o r n e o**
Sanggau   Sintang   Nangahsurak   Peg. Muller
         Melawi   Melak   Mahakam
Nangahpinoh   Peg. Schwaner
Telukbatang   Kotabaru   Muarateweh   Benagin   **Samarinda**
Sukadana   G. Beratus
Nangatayap   Mendawai   1223   **Balikpapan**
Ketapang   Memala   Kapuas
uala   Sukaraja   Palangkaraya   Petangis
juan   Kendawangan   Sampit   **Amuntai**
    Pangkalanbun   Rantau   Mehakit   Kotabaru   Mamuju
Kualajelai   Barito   Pulau   **Sulawesi**
    Kualapembuang   **Banjarmasin**   **Martapura**   Sebuku
Tg Puting   Pagatan   Majene
    Pelaihari   Kintap   **Pulau Laut**
         Tg Selatan

N E S I A

JAVA SEA   **Malaysia**
                              N   0   200 km
                                   0   200 miles

KUALA LUMPUR AND ENVIRONS

Young, vibrant and bursting with energy, Malaysia's capital is the epitome of a modern Asian city

First-timers expecting to see shanty towns, a populace in Oriental dress, and other "quaint" aspects of Asia, are in for a severe dose of disillusion when they actually reach Kuala Lumpur. What they get instead are skyscrapers of contemporary design, gleaming European and Japanese cars, sober-suited executives, and brand names from Marks & Spencer to Louis Vuitton.

It might have taken some time, but Kuala Lumpur has finally emerged from the shadows of its Asian rivals Bangkok and Singapore. A veritable force today, the capital spearheads the country's economic growth and entices with the trappings of city life. It is the centre of everything: business, trade, finance, politics, arts, fashion, trends – in short, it all starts here. You feel it in the air, the mad pace of life, in the traffic-choked streets, the crowded malls, and the incessant beat of techno in the discos. And you feel it when at last you reach your hotel, peel off your dusty shoes and wash the grime from your face.

The capital sits in the Klang River Valley, referred to as the Klang Valley, an area of townships and large industrial estates linked by a network of highways. The Klang Valley is the hub of development, the economic magnet that draws in Malaysians hungry for money, experience, and a taste of big city life.

In the city, tourists like to head to the pockets of colonialism and old Asia, but cannot escape the thrust of modernity. They try to frame a picture of the old Mughal-style mosque with their camera, but it is impossible to exclude the metallic light rail tracks in the background. Even in a Chinatown wet market, a chicken-seller on a stool is consulting his stockbroker on his mobile phone.

The "real" thing does exist, in the *kampung* just outside the Klang Valley. For while "kampung" translates literally as "village", in city terms, it also carries connotations of being rural, rustic, almost backward. The Klang Valley is forward-looking, technologically bonded, and even Western in outlook. But to many, it is also just a place to *cari makan*, to "earn a living". It is certainly not home, for home is still the *kampung* – where the heart is.

And so, during the major festive occasions of Hari Raya Puasa and Chinese New Year, hundreds of thousands *balik kampung*, returning home to their villages or towns.

This annual exodus sees the highways deserted, hawker stalls closed, while the city's parks echo to the *caw caw* of crows. After the holidays, you can almost hear the machine grinding up again, and before long, it is throbbing once more with noise, chaos, and life.❑

PRECEDING PAGES: the glittering Kuala Lumpur city skyline.
LEFT: Jalan Petaling night market all lit up for the Chinese New Year.

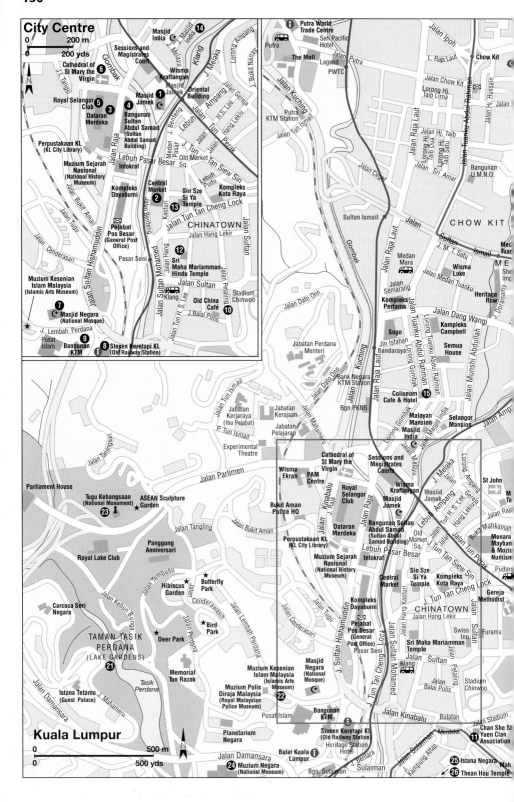

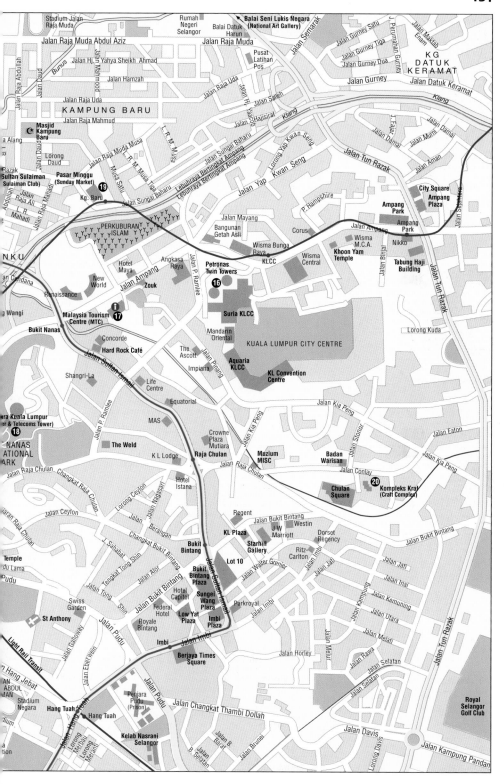

KUALA LUMPUR

From colonial mansions and the bustle of Chinatown to the modern magnificence of the Twin Towers, Kuala Lumpur represents the true essence of today's Malaysia

Map on pages 130–31

Kuala Lumpur

A mining outpost 150 years ago, a dynamic Asian city today, Kuala Lumpur is the capital of Malaysia and home to about 1.6 million people. With its constant facelifts and ever-rising skyline, Kuala Lumpur – or KL, as it is popularly known – embodies the aspirations of a nation working hard to carve its niche in an era of globalisation.

In KL, the East-West and old-new juxtapositions are most apparent. Stately old mansions of eclectic styles, traditional mosques and Hindu temples are squeezed between concrete high-rises and steel-and-chrome office blocks. Trendy 30-somethings trade pleasantries with traditionally garbed shopkeepers. *Feng shui* and Islamic values blend in global deal-making, just as a fortune teller is consulted in the face of leading-edge technological innovation. With its variety of sights, food and shops, cosmopolitan Kuala Lumpur has something for every visitor.

Bare beginnings

Miners and traders first came upriver to where the Klang and Gombak rivers converge in search of tin. The Gombak estuary was the highest point upstream that the miners could land their supplies for prospecting tin in Ampang, a few kilometres further inland. They named the settlement Kuala Lumpur, which means "muddy estuary" in Malay. By the 1860s, the landing place had become a flourishing village.

Fierce rivalries over mining claims and water rights led to gang clashes and bitter feuds. Finally, the predominantly Chinese settlement was put under the leadership of Yap Ah Loy, the *kapitan cina* (Chinese headman). The *kapitan* warred against crime, built a prison and quelled revolts. Under his supervision, KL grew into a thriving township.

Then Frank Swettenham, the British resident of Selangor, moved his administration to KL. Brick buildings were introduced and street by street, the wooden shanties were pulled down. In 1886, the country's first railway line connected KL to the coastal town of Klang.

As the state capital of Selangor, KL was the centre of administration and trade. In 1946, it was established as the headquarters of the Federation of Malaya, with its development intensifying after independence in 1957. But KL truly came of age in 1974, when it became a unit of its own called Wilayah Persekutuan (Federal Territory). Today, it is the business hub and commercial centre of the whole of Malaysia.

Historic heart

KL's central attractions are close enough to cover on foot. To reach the sights that are a little further away, hop into a taxi, commuter train or LRT (Light Rapid Transit) – but walking may be quicker during the

LEFT: the striking Islamic-inspired Dayabumi Complex. **BELOW:** the Mughal-style Jamek Mosque.

Malaysia's tallest flagpole stands at the Independence Square.

BELOW:
traditional Malay brocade at the Central Market.

traffic-choked peak hours. Alternatively, many city tours cover the main sights in KL as well as its surroundings. You can book a local tour or hire a taxi for the day (negotiate the price before you set off) and explore the city on your own.

A good starting point is in the historic centre at **Masjid Jamek ❶** (Jamek Mosque; open Sat–Thur 8.30am–12.30pm and 2.30–4pm, Fri 8.30–11am and 2.30–4pm; tel: 03-2691 2829), standing proudly at the confluence of the Gombak and Klang rivers, where the first miners landed. This elegant structure, adapted from a Mughal mosque in northern India by architect A.B. Hubback and built in 1909, is an oasis of serenity once you enter the palm tree-filled grounds through the *sahn* (walled courtyard).

Close to the river confluence, bordered by Lebuh Pasar Besar and Medan Pasar, is the Old Market Square or **Medan Pasar Lama**, the business and social centre for the early settlers. The original demarcations of the square have disappeared due to urban renewal. Look out for a clock tower; this was built to mark the coronation of England's King George VI in 1937.

Around the market square are double- and triple-storey shophouses, ubiquitously found in the city's historic parts. These have designs that are typical in many parts of Southeast Asia where immigrants from southern China settled. They extend 30–60 metres (100–200 ft) to the back, with the ground level used for business, while upstairs is where the proprietor's family lives. The newer three-storey shophouses, built in 1906–7, incorporate Western decorative details like fluted pilasters and ornate window frames and fanlights.

The original market on Medan Pasar was moved south to the place now occupied by **Central Market ❷**, or Pasar Seni (open daily 10am–10pm; tel: 03-2274 9966), on Jalan Hang Kasturi. A former fruit-and-vegetable market, this Art Deco showpiece was saved from demolition by conservation-minded architects, who eventually won an award for their restoration and renovation efforts. It is now one of the city's most popular tourist stops, with art exhibitions, performances, restaurants, and souvenir shops purveying everything from batik scarfs to portraits done on the spot. Along the side of Central Market is Jalan Hang Kasturi, a pedestrian mall where other pre-war buildings have been turned into souvenir shops.

Colonial core

To the west of the river confluence is the colonial core, distinguished architecturally by domes, minarets and large arches of the neo-Saracenic style. This style was developed in India and combines features of Islamic architecture with Gothic elements.

At the heart is the **Dataran Merdeka ❸** (Independence Square). Originally called the Padang (Malay for "field"), this parade ground was renamed to commemorate Malaysia's independence. It was here, at midnight on 30 August 1957, that Britain's Union Jack was lowered and the flag of the newly independent Malaya was flown for the first time on 31 August.

Today, Dataran Merdeka is an occasional venue for the National Day parade. It is also a popular one for cultural events such as the colourful parade that kicks off Colours of Malaysia (*Citrawarna Malay-*

sia), a month-long tourism event that promotes Malaysian culture and food. Every Saturday evening, the adjacent road, Jalan Raja, is closed to traffic and is abuzz with people enjoying the breeze and the bright lights. The groomed field of the square, however, is off-limits to the public. Casting a 95-metre (310-ft) high shadow on the green is one of the tallest flagpoles in the world.

Map on pages 130–31

Opposite the green is the imposing **Sultan Abdul Samad Building ④** (Bangunan Sultan Abdul Samad). This former colonial administrative centre now houses the High Court. Built between 1894 and 1897, it was the first of the neo-Saracenic buildings introduced by the chief architect, A.C. Norman. Particularly pretty when it is all lit up at night, the building is constructed of red bricks, with three Mughal-inspired domes covered in copper, surrounded on all sides by wide and shady verandahs. The architectural style was something new in the Federated Malay States then. It went on to be reproduced in a number of buildings, including the Old Federated Malay States Survey Office buildings that now house the **Sessions and Magistrates Courts**, located to the north of the Sultan Abdul Samad Building.

Fountain detail from the Independence Square.

The Dataran Merdeka is flanked on one side by the mock-Tudor-style **Royal Selangor Club ⑤**, built in 1884. Formerly nicknamed the Spotted Dog, a derisive allusion to the club's emblem of a running leopard, it is the oldest membership club in Malaysia and the nexus of late 19th-century European social life in KL. Today, lawyers and businessmen prop up the long bar where the British once sat over their *stengah* (literally "half", meaning half a peck of liquor).

To the north of the square is the neo-Gothic **Cathedral of St Mary the Virgin ⑥** (open daily 7am–3pm; tel: 03-2692 8672). An earlier structure, consecrated in 1887, was destroyed by fire, and the current building was

BELOW: the Mughal-inspired Sultan Abdul Samad Building.

constructed in 1922 on the site of the Royal Selangor Club's former horse stables. The church has some interesting features, including stained-glass windows honouring colonial planters and depicting crops such as rubber and oil palm, which were the agricultural mainstays of the economy.

At the southern end of Dataran Merdeka, the **Muzium Sejarah Nasional** (National History Museum; open daily 9am–6pm; free; tel: 03-2694 4590; www.jmm.gov.my) continues the neo-Saracenic architectural tradition. It houses exhibits dating from the country's prehistory to the independence period. Next door is the **Kuala Lumpur City Library**, or Perpustakaan Kuala Lumpur (open Mon 2–6.45pm, Tues–Sat 9.30am–6.45pm, Sun 11am–5pm; free; tel: 03-2692 6204). The empty building beside it is the former home of the library, bearing the sign **Pustaka Peringatan Kuala Lumpur** (Kuala Lumpur Memorial Library). It is striking in being the only neo-Renaissance-style building in the area.

KL's neo-Saracenic architectural stretch is capped by the Kuala Lumpur Railway Station and Bangunan KTM. En route to these from the colonial district on Jalan Sultan Hishamuddin is the **Kompleks Dayabumi** (Dayabumi Complex) with its filigree-like Islamic-design arches. It is most impressive at night when it is flood-lit. At its base is the **Pejabat Pos Besar** (General Post Office; tel: 03-2274 1122).

A pedestrian tunnel south of the Kompleks Dayabumi leads to the **Masjid Negara** (National Mosque; open Mon–Thur 10am–noon and 2–4pm, Fri for Muslims attending prayers only, Sat, Sun and holidays 9am–noon and 2–6.30pm; tel: 03-2693 7784) on Jalan Perdana, completed in 1965. This is the first local mosque to depart from the neo-Saracenic style, and is arguably a watershed in Malaysia's architectural history. The jagged 18 points of the star-shaped roof represent the 13 states of Malaysia and the five pillars of Islam. The mosque represents national unity as well, for non-Muslims donated generously towards its building fund.

Further south along Jalan Sultan Hishamuddin, the old **Stesen Keretapi Kuala Lumpur** (Kuala Lumpur Railway Station; tel: 03-2274 7410) stands with magnificent turrets, spires, minarets and arches. The station was constructed in 1911 to the standards applied to Victorian public buildings all over the empire. Its construction was once held up because the roof did not meet the specification that it supported one metre of snow! Now, only the intra-city KTM commuter and the Eastern & Oriental Express trains stop here; all interstate and city trains stop at the ultra-modern KL Sentral Station in Brickfields, near the National Museum. Opposite and connected by an underpass to the old railway station is the **Bangunan KTM** (KTM Building), headquarters of Malaysian Railways, featuring a pastiche of architectural elements, from Mughal-style minarets to large Gothic-style windows and ancient Greek columns.

Chinatown

To the east of the historic heart lies Kuala Lumpur's Chinatown, whose main streets are Jalan Sultan, Jalan Tun H.S. Lee and Jalan Petaling. It is a paradise for the inveterate shopper and connoisseur of exotic oddities. Chinese apothecaries display their herbs and medicines in porcelain pots and beneath glass counters; there are

BELOW: the interiors of the Modernist-style National Mosque.

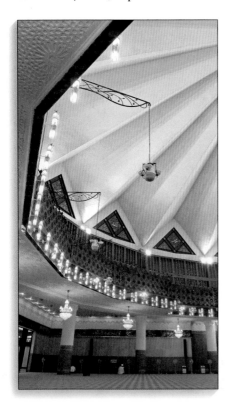

ewellers and goldsmiths, casket and basket makers, dry goods stores, pet shops, erbalists, frame makers and haberdashers. Modernisation wields its hand in air onditioning and contemporary decor, but there is still plenty to experience.

The term "Chinatown" is often used interchangeably with **Jalan Petaling ⑩**, ite of the famous night market. Better known as Petaling Street, this section of own sees action from dawn. The **Petaling Street Market** (main entrance on alan Hang Lekir next to Hotel Malaya), a fresh-produce market, is the place to ind Chinese housewives haggling for fresh chicken slaughtered on the spot, reens of all kinds, and chrysanthemums for their altars. Be warned, though – ne smells are something else.

treet bazaar

As the city wakes up, stalls begin to line both sides of the road and pedestrians igzag from coffee shop to fruit stall and back, impervious to the heavy traffic. At midday, office executives begin to fill the eateries. Chinatown is reputedly where the best Chinese street food can be found, from all sorts of noodles to pork bs soup (*bak kut teh*) and roasted meat snacks. There is dim sum from 6am, nooncakes for the autumnal Mooncake Festival, and bittersweet herbal brews cure all sorts of ailments at the roadside medicinal drinks stalls.

Petaling Street assumes a festive air from 5pm. A section of the street closes traffic for the *pasar malam* (night market), where the stalls, restrained all ay at the kerbs, take over the road. They are soon joined by twice as many talls, all erected at lightning speed. Here you can find all the "genuine" copies f brand-name watches and T-shirts, as well as DVDs of movies that haven't ven made it to the local cinemas yet. There are also precious stones, antiques

At the junction of Jalan Petaling and Jalan Hang Lekir is a stall (open daily 10.30am–10pm) selling air mata kucing, a sweet drink of dried longan fruit – it's a must-try.

BELOW: candy stall in Petaling Street.

Tea appreciation at Purple Cane Tea House. Tapping the table with bent index and middle fingers after your cup is filled is a way of thanking the person serving you the tea.

BELOW: details on Sri Maha Mari-amman Temple's gateway tower.

and household goods for sale. Browse at leisure and shop around; when you are read to buy, remember to bargain.

During the day, respite from the crowds and heat can be found in the interior of the **Chan She Shu Yuen Clan Association** ⓫ (open daily 8am–5pm; tel: 03 2678 1461), at the southern end of Jalan Petaling. Serving the needs of Chinese bearing the surname Chan (as well as Chen and Tan, which are spelling variations of Chan), this clanhouse was constructed in 1906. The building is deco rated with elaborate glazed ceramic tiles and ornamentation, and intricate wa paintings depicting mythological and historical tales.

Multicultural colours

Off Petaling Street behind the Traffic Police Headquarters is a little street calle **Jalan Balai Polis**, which has a row of beautifully refurbished pre-war shop houses. Besides cafés and bookshops, there is the **Old China Café** (open dail 11am–10.30pm; tel: 03-2072 5915), a restaurant-cum-antique shop. It was for merly the headquarters of the Selangor and Federal Territory Laundry Associ ation, a trade guild that flourished in the pre-washing-machine days. It has charming 1930s ambience, with elements such as the *pintu pagar* (swing doors and pulley-drawn lights well preserved. The café serves Peranakan cuisine, pre pared with a fusion of Malay and Chinese ingredients and cooking styles uniqu to Malaysia's Straits Chinese community. Along Jalan Balai Polis and Jala Panggung, several tea houses offer the chance to learn about the ancient Chines art of serving and drinking tea. A popular tea house is **Purple Cane Tea Hous** (open daily 11am–8pm; tel: 03-2072 1349) at 9 Jalan Panggung.

Head north on Jalan Panggung, turn left at Jalan Sultan and then right alon Jalan Tun H.S. Lee. On the left is one of KL's mos famous Hindu temples, the **Sri Maha Mariamma Temple** ⓬ (open daily 6am–9pm; tel: 03-2078 3467 Its tower gateway is decorated with an explosion c colourful gods entangled in an arresting design c south Indian origin. Built in 1873, it occupies a important place in Hindu religious life. This is th starting point for the annual Thaipusam pilgrimag of penance to the Batu Caves temple just outside KI (*see pages 152–3*). On other days, women and chil dren sell strings of fragrant jasmine on the pavement and a man in a traditional *dhoti* sarong watches ove shoes on a rack for those have entered the templ courtyard. Devotees emerge from prayers, their fore heads smeared with sacred white ash.

Continue on Jalan Tun H.S. Lee past the intersec tion with Jalan Tun Tan Cheng Lock. Almost com pletely hidden behind a group of pre-war shophouse is the **Sin Sze Si Ya Temple** ⓭ (open daily 7am–5pm tel: 03-2072 9593), accessed through a narrow, ornat gateway with a red sign against an image of a pair c dragons. This temple was built by Yap Ah Loy, a *kap itan* (headman) of the Chinese community, in 186 to honour the deities Sin Sze Si Ya and Si Sze Ya. Th former was a *kapitan* Yap had once served under, an the latter was Yap's loyal lieutenant; both died in bat tle before Yap did. In keeping with the Chinese prac tice of ancestor worship, they were accordingl eified. After his death in 1885, Yap Ah Loy was also enshrined in the temple, n a side altar which also holds a photograph of him.

ndian and Muslim flavours

orth of the river confluence, and centred on the pedestrianised **Jalan Masjid ndia** ⓰ and the roads leading off it, is a chaotic, crowded and noisy yet colourl district known for its very visible Indian Muslim flavour and specialty shops. his is an excellent place to shop for Indian textiles, saris and jewellery, and to observe local life. Look out for a small crowd gathered in one spot and you ay find a snake charmer, or a medicine man proclaiming the miracle attributes f his wares. After six every evening, portable kitchens with tables and chairs ke over the street under the stars, offering tasty, spicy food.

Parallel to Jalan Masjid India is **Jalan Tuanku Abdul Rahman**, named after the rst king, or *yang di-pertuan agong*, of the Federation of Malaysia. It was once L's main shopping area, earning itself the moniker "Golden Mile". Tradesmen om the Indian subcontinent, in particular, dominated the street in the early 20th entury. Some family businesses here are several generations old, still thriving espite stiff competition from the city's mega malls. Every Saturday night, a *pasar alam* (night market) is set up along **Lorong Tuanku Abdul Rahman**, off Jalan uanku Abdul Rahman, with stalls offering a wide array of goods and snacks.

The area's most written-about place is the **Coliseum Café and Hotel** ⓯ (open aily 8am–10pm; tel: 03-2692 6270) at 98–100 Jalan Tuanku Abdul Rahman. Still rving customers after almost 80 years, its bar was once the favourite watering ole for planters, journalists and government officials. The decor has changed lit- e since those days and its steaks continue to attract attention for their quality and

Map
on pages
130–31

TIP

A traditional colonial-era non-alcoholic drink found throughout the former British empire is a "gunner", made of equal parts ginger ale and ginger beer, with a dash of Angostura bitters. It is a refreshing thirst-quencher. Order one at the Coliseum Café.

BELOW: shopping for fabrics in Jalan Masjid India.

affordable prices. Next door to this establishment is one of the country's firs cinemas, the **Coliseum Cinema**, a neoclassical structure built in 1920 to show case "the highest type of films", as a 1921 daily put it, to a targeted patronage c Europeans. Today, Malay, Indonesian and Tamil films are shown here.

The northernmost stretch of Jalan Tuanku Abdul Rahman runs from Jala Dang Wangi up to Jalan Ipoh, through an area known as **Chow Kit**. In the day Chow Kit is a popular place to buy household items and fresh produce, but a night, it is taken over by drug addicts and prostitutes. The area is sleazy, an tourist safety cannot be guaranteed here; beware of pickpockets.

At the other end of Chow Kit stands the 40-storey-high **Putra World Trad Centre** (tel: 03-4043 3399), which houses government offices like th Ministry of Tourism and **Tourism Malaysia**, a concert hall and a convention an exhibition complex. The **Seri Pacific Hotel** stands beside it, with elevators o the outside of the building, affording an interesting view of the area. Acros the road is a modern shopping centre, **The Mall**, and **The Legend Hotel**.

Tall towers

The **Golden Triangle** is the city's main commercial and financial district. I three points are roughly at the Klang–Gombak river confluence in the west, th junction of Jalan Yap Kwan Seng and Jalan Tun Razak in the northeast, and th junction of Jalan Imbi and Jalan Pudu in the southeast. Most of the high-rise here house large corporations, MNCs, banks, and government-linked companie

At the heart of the Golden Triangle is the city's most eye-catching landmar the **Petronas Twin Towers** ⓰, on Jalan Ampang. Currently holding the recor for the world's tallest pair of buildings, the glass-and-steel towers soar some 45

etres (1,480 ft) to reach 88 storeys. Designed by American architect Cesar elli, they combine Islamic patterns with state-of-the-art engineering techniques *see page 89*). You can make a trip up to the double-deck **skybridge** (open ues–Sun 9am–5pm; free; tel: 03-2331 1769) on the 41st and 42nd floors for anoramic views of the city. Only 1,300 tickets are issued a day from 8.30am nwards at the information desk in Tower 2.

Tower 1 is occupied by the national petroleum company Petronas and Tower is taken up by various multinational companies. The towers anchor the 40-ectare (100-acre) **Kuala Lumpur City Centre** (KLCC; www.klcc.com.my). t the base of the towers is the ultra-modern **Suria KLCC** mall (open daily 0am–10pm; tel: 03-2382 3359; www.suriaklcc.com.my). Other than shop-ing, the mall offers a few attractions worth visiting, including **Petrosains** open Tues–Sun 9.30am–5.30pm; entrance fee; tel: 03-2331 8787), a terrific nteractive museum about science and the oil and gas industry; and **Galeri etronas** on level 3 (open Tues–Sun 10am–8pm; free; tel: 03-2331 7770; ww.galeripetronas.com), which showcases contemporary and traditional art.

Dewan Filharmonik Petronas (Petronas Philharmonic Hall; open Mon–Sat 0am–6pm; box office tel: 03-2051 7007; www.malaysianphilharmonic.com), ocated on the ground floor of Tower 2, is an intimate venue fashioned after 19th-entury European concert halls. It is home to the Malaysian Philharmonic Orches-a and hosts a varied concert season featuring international and local performers.

KLCC also includes the huge **Kuala Lumpur Convention Centre** (open daily am–5pm; tel: 03-2333 2888; www.klccconventioncentre.com) as well as the LCC **Park** where the whole family can enjoy watching synchronised foun-ains and frolic in the playground and the wading pool. The **Aquaria KLCC**

Map on pages 130–31

Children can have hours of fun with the interactive exhibits at Petrosains museum.

BELOW: Underwater tunnel at Aquaria KLCC.

(open daily 11am–8pm; entrance fee; tel: 03-2333 1888; www.klaquaria.com
an impressive aquarium with over 5,000 types of aquatic and land creature
from 150 different species, is both fascinating and educational.

Jalan Ampang mansions

Jalan Ampang, which runs along the front of KLCC, is the main artery throug
the Golden Triangle. In the late 19th and early 20th century, the road was but
trail cut through forest and swampland, leading about 5 km (3 miles) to the ti
mines upstream. As the city began to grow, rich Chinese miners and busines
men built their ostentatious mansions – some have survived to the present
along this road. Fashioned after the bungalows of British India, many of then
are being conserved, particularly at the upper end of Jalan Ampang past Jala
Tun Razak, where there are now embassies and consulates.

One of the best preserved of these mansions is the **Malaysia Tourism
Centre ⑰** (open Mon–Fri 7.30am–5.30pm, tourist info desk open daily 7am
10pm; tel: 03-2163 3667; www.mtc.gov.my), a one-stop visitor centre an
theatre complex at the Jalan Sultan Ismail junction. Built in 1935 by the wealth
Chinese tin mogul and rubber planter Eu Tong Sen, the villa served as the wa
office for the British army, and later, the Japanese army. Following Malaya
independence in 1957, it saw the first sitting of the new nation's parliament.
was also the scene for installation ceremonies for Malaysia's kings. In the lat
1980s, it was refurbished and commissioned for its present use.

West of KLCC lies the **Menara Kuala Lumpur ⑱** (open 9am–10pm; entranc
fee; tel: 03-2020 5444; www.menarakl.com.my), also known as the KL Towe
This 421-metre (1,380-ft) structure, designed with Islamic architectural feature
has an observation platform that reveals KL's su
rounding hills. It also has souvenir shops and resta
rants, including a revolving one. Below it is the **Buk
Nanas Forest Recreational Park** (open daily 7am
6pm; free), a 10-hectare (25-acre) lowland rainfore
with well-marked trails and a children's playground

Saturday's Sunday Market

For yet more *pasar malam* (night market) shoppin
head for **Kampung Baru** off Jalan Raja Abdullah ne
Jalan Ampang. Literally meaning "new village", Kam
pung Baru came into being in 1889. Even though bric
houses have now replaced many of the original woode
houses here, Kampung Baru has stubbornly remaine
a Malay village while the city around it grew.

The **Pasar Minggu ⑲** (Sunday Market) here spring
to life on Saturday evening around 6pm, and lasts unt
the wee hours of Sunday morning. The *pasar* is we
worth a visit for its exclusively Malay offering
Songkok (fez), prayer books, Islamic calligraphy an
batik sarongs are on sale at the stalls, as are all kinds
handicrafts, such as earthenware pots (*labu*), Kelai
tanese silverware and *songket* (Malay brocade) fro
Terengganu. There is a huge variety of Malay foo
from the ubiquitous satay and *nasi lemak* (coconut ric
to *bubur* (rice porridge) and spicy regional delight
Nearby on Jalan Tun Razak is the **Istana Buday**
(National Theatre; open daily 9am–4.30pm; tel: 0

TIP

The Golden Triangle
is also where you'll
find KL's great
nightlife. The hot
spots are along Jalan
Sultan Ismail, as well
as the roads off it:
Jalan P. Ramlee, Jalan
Kia Peng, and the
Asian Heritage Row
on Jalan Doraisamy.

BELOW: the
Malaysia Tourism
Centre occupies a
historic French-
style building.

)25 5932; www.istanabudaya.gov.my), a modern complex for musicals, plays and
her performances. Designed by Malaysian architect Muhammad Kamar Ya'akub,
e theatre building is fashioned after a traditonal *wau* (kite) in flight. The roof is
spired by the *sirih junjung*, which are betel leaves arrayed in a particular man-
r for use in traditional Malay ceremonies. The **National Library**, or Perpus-
kaan Negara (open Tues–Sat 10am–7pm, Sun 10am–6pm; tel: 03-2687 1700),
down the same road. Shaped like a *tengkolok*, the Malay male headgear, it is
laid with blue tiles to resemble the rich texture of *songket*, the gold-threaded
aterial from which the headgear is usually made.

A sampling of local art can be found in the galleries of the **Balai Seni Lukis
egara** (National Art Gallery; open daily 10am–6pm; tel: 03-4025 4990;
ww.artgallery.gov.my) in Jalan Temerloh. On the first Saturday of each month,
owds gather at **Laman Seni** (Kuala Lumpur Arts Market; open 8am–5pm)
the grounds of the art gallery. More a carnival-like fair than an arts and crafts
arket, it has affordable art pieces, cheap food and lots of chaos.

Map on pages 130–31

The National Theatre is fashioned after a wau *(traditional kite).*

igh life

he apex of consumerism in KL is the **Bukit Bintang** area, with large shopping
alls, expensive stores, high-class restaurants, international hotels and party-till-
u-drop nightlife. It is centred on the 1-km (½-mile) long **Bintang Walk**, a
oad landscaped boulevard that begins at the Westin hotel at the Jalan Bukit
intang intersection with Jalan Raja Chulan and stretches all the way to the
t 10 mall on Jalan Sultan Ismail. KL's answer to Paris' Avenue des Champs-
lysées, Bintang Walk is lined with sidewalk cafés, boutiques and live music
tablishments, popular with families and the young set.

BELOW: choosing prayer beads in Kampung Baru. **LEFT:** Bukit Nanas has well-marked nature trails.

The indoor Cosmo's World theme park at Berjaya Times Square.

BELOW: Bukit Bintang cross junction with Berjaya Times Square on the left.

Bukit Bintang's main draw is no doubt the shopping offered by its many malls. The rabbit warren of **Sungei Wang Plaza** (tel: 03-2144 9988) and the adjacent **Bukit Bintang Plaza** (tel: 03-2148 7411) offer more than 600 shops; **Low Ya Plaza** (tel: 03-2162 1176) and **Imbi Plaza** concentrate on computers and soft wares; the upmarket **Starhill Gallery** (tel: 03-2148 1000) has designer wear and fashionable eateries; **Lot 10** (tel: 03-2141 0500) houses chic boutiques; and the huge **Berjaya Times Square** (tel: 1300 888 988) in nearby Jalan Imbi has 900 retail outlets, 65 dining outlets, an indoor theme park and nine mega screens.

Street food and fine dining

On one side of Jalan Bukit Bintang is **Jalan Alor**, a street lined with Chinese coffee shops, which becomes KL's street food central when temporary hawker stalls take over the road at night. Among the fare offered are Chinese noodles, satay and grilled seafood. There is more good food along **Tengkat Tong Shin** which runs parallel to Jalan Alor. Tengkat Tong Shin has enjoyed renewed popularity in recent years with the influx of backpacker hotels, cafés and pubs that also spill over to adjoining **Changkat Bukit Bintang**.

Changkat Bukit Bintang is part of the area known as Bukit Ceylon (Ceylon Hill), long a trendy nightlife venue with fine-dining restaurants and fashionable bars. Many of these occupy charming old-style bungalows that have been artfully renovated to attract the city's chi chi crowd.

Arts and crafts

Near Bukit Bintang on Jalan Conlay, off Jalan Raja Chulan, is **Komplek Kraf Kuala Lumpur** ⑳ (Kuala Lumpur Craft Complex; open daily 9am–7pm;

free; www.kraftangan.gov.my; tel: 03-2162 7459). It has a collection of shops offering traditional and contemporary crafts, including handwoven textiles, woodwork, batik, basketwork, pewter and pottery. There are also demonstrations of *songket* cloth weaving, batik printing, and silver and copper tooling. The building at the back houses a small craft museum (open daily 9am–5.30pm; entrance fee) and a cafeteria. In one corner is the **Artists' Colony**, a cluster of 22 huts housing new and established artists who work and sell their art here.

Opposite the Craft Complex, on Jalan Stonor, is a bungalow that dates from 1925. It houses the **Badan Warisan Malaysia** (Heritage of Malaysia Trust; open Mon–Sat 10am–5.30pm; tel: 03-2144 9273; www.badanwarisan.org.my), a non-governmental organisation advocating architectural conservation. On its grounds is a stunning traditional Malay timber house, the **Rumah Penghulu Abu Seman**, from the northern state of Kedah (tours Mon–Sat at 11am and 3pm; fee). This finely crafted structure was dismantled and relocated to KL, where it was restored as a showpiece. Originally constructed by Penghulu Abu Seman bin Nayan, a village chief, the house has three main sections that were built at different periods between the mid-1920s and the early 1930s.

A garden retreat

Southwest of the city centre is the city's green lung and largest park, **Taman Tasik Perdana ㉑** (Lake Gardens; open daily 24 hours). The gardens comprise 104 hectares (257 acres) of lawns, trees, landscaped gardens and undulating hills, at the heart of which is the lake, Tasik Perdana. Early in the morning and in the evening, joggers run past picnickers, senior citizens perform *tai chi* routines and lovers rendezvous here. It is also a great place to watch KL families at play.

Map on pages 130–31

Rumah Penghulu Abu Seman, an old Malay house, on the grounds of Badan Warisan Malaysia.

BELOW: a batik artist shows his craft at the Craft Complex. **LEFT:** street food in Jalan Alor.

The Tugu Kebangsaan in the Lake Gardens is a tribute to those who died in the communist insurgency of the 1950s.

BELOW: the Butterfly Park has over 6,000 butterflies and moths.

From 10am–5.30pm daily (except lunchtime), a free shuttle bus, which starts at the boathouse, does a 10-minute circuit of the gardens past key attractions, stopping wherever passengers wish to alight. The shuttle runs only when there are enough passengers, and does not follow a timetable. If you are walking around and the bus happens to pass by, you can flag it down.

Surrounding the lake are various attractions. The **Islamic Arts Museum ㉒**, or Muzium Kesenian Islam Malaysia (open Tues–Sun 10am–6pm; entrance fee; tel: 03-2274 2020; www.iamm.org.my) lies on Jalan Lembah Perdana. It has a collection of spectacular crafts from all over the Islamic world and fine models of the world's best-known mosques. The **Planetarium** (open Tues–Sun 9.30am–4.15pm; entrance fee; tel: 03-2273 5484) sits close by in a landscaped garden. It features a 36-cm (14-inch) telescope and the Arianne IV space engine used to launch Malaysia's first satellite, the Measat I. The **Bird Park** (open daily 9am–6pm; entrance fee; tel: 03-2272 1010) and the **Butterfly Park** (open daily 9am–5pm; entrance fee; tel: 03-2693 4799) house local and foreign species in pretty, forested enclosures. Other attractions include an orchid garden (open daily 9am–6pm; entrance fee on weekends and holidays) and a deer park (open Mon–Thur 10am–noon and 2–6pm, Fri 10am–noon and 3–6pm, Sat–Sun 10am–6pm; free).

Fallen heroes

On another hill opposite the gardens stands the **Tugu Kebangsaan ㉓** (National Monument), which commemorates those who died in the struggle against the communist insurgency in the 1950s. The monument is modelled after Washington D.C.'s famous Iwo Jima Monument, and the galleries at its base record the names of the units who fought, including British, Australian and Malay troops.

The **Cenotaph** nearby was erected by the British to commemorate the soldiers who died in World Wars I and II. At the base of the hill is the ASEAN **Sculpture Garden**, featuring works by artists from Southeast Asian countries. Down the road is the **Parliament House**, which is not open to the public.

At the eastern edge of the Lake Gardens, bounded by Jalan Damansara and Jalan Mahameru, is the delightful **Carcosa Seri Negara** (tel: 03-2295 0888; www.ghmhotels.com), built in 1896. It was once the British resident Frank Swettenham's official residence and is now a luxury hotel. Try the delicious curry tiffin lunch at Gulai House (Sun only noon–2.30pm) or the high tea (daily 3–6pm) at the Drawing Room. But even if you don't have a meal here, walk through the lobby and public spaces which still have their old-world charm intact, and imagine the grand balls that took place here during the colonial times.

The **Muzium Negara ㉔** (National Museum; open daily 9am–6pm; entrance fee; tel: 03-2282 6255; www.jmm.gov.my), nearby on Jalan Damansara, is modelled after Kedah's Balai Besar, a 19th-century Thai-influenced audience hall for sultans. It has galleries on local material culture, natural history, and arts and crafts.

Beyond the city centre

Jalan Damansara joins Jalan Istana, named for the **Istana Negara ㉕** (National Palace), the official residence of the *yang di-pertuan agong* (king). The country has a new *agong* every five years, the position rotated among its sultans. The palace was a wealthy Chinese businessman's townhouse before it was converted into a palace in 1926. Typical of colonial-era mansions, it has large balconies and gardens; not so typical are its golden domes. The grounds are not open to the public, but the main entrance is a popular photography spot.

Further south off Jalan Syed Putra is the massive and visually stunning **Thean Hou Temple** ㉖ (open daily 9am–9pm; tel: 03-2274 7088) on Persiaran Endah. Built in 1985 with millions contributed by wealthy Chinese, the temple is dedicated to three deities: Thean Hou (Heavenly Mother), Goddess Swei Mei (Goddess of the Waterfront) and Kuan Yin (Goddess of Mercy). The views from this hilltop temple are great, and restaurants here provide refreshments.

Across Jalan Syed Putra is **Brickfields**, a lovely old neighbourhood that was originally a brick-manufacturing centre. Its distinct Indian character is most evident in the shops and restaurants along Jalan Tun Sambanthan and Jalan Sultan Abdul Samad. These offer everything from Bollywood VCDs and statues of Hindu deities to fiery meals on banana leaves.

Jalan Syed Putra leads to the suburb of Mid Valley City, comprising offices, condominiums, hotels and the up-sized **Mid Valley Megamall** (tel: 03-2938 3333). North of Mid Valley City is **Bangsar**, which has some of the most expensive real estate in KL. Its two main entertainment areas, Bangsar Baru and the Bangsar Shopping Centre, are dense with chic bars, clubs and eateries filled by the fashionable set. About 5 km (3 miles) northwest of Bangsar is the suburb of **Sri Hartamas**. Like Bangsar, this upscale area is chock-a-block with restaurants and bars that literally buzz on weekends. ❑

TIP

The Museum Garden Shop on the National Museum's grounds sells Kelantanese coconut craft and ceramics from Kedah. It also has a range of Asian knick-knacks.

LEFT: have a fiery banana leaf meal in Brickfields.
BELOW: a royal guard at the National Palace.

SELANGOR

Map on page 150

*The area of Selangor around Kuala Lumpur is the developed hub
of Malaysia's industrial economy. But beyond the hinterland, the
landscape yields to limestone cliffs, caverns and jungle trails*

Heading west from **Kuala Lumpur ❶** on the Federal Highway, the massive Moorish-style arches of the million-ringgit **Kota Darul Ehsan** announce that you are departing the Federal Territory and entering the state of Selangor. According to the Tourism Malaysia brochure, this marble *pintu gerbang*, flanked by ancient Selangor canons, was commissioned in 1974 and opened in 1982"to mark the sacrifice" made by the Sultan of Selangor in ceding Kuala Lumpur to the Federal Government as the national capital.

More than two decades later, more land has been ceded for the administrative capital, **Putrajaya**, the intended heart of the ambitious information technology-driven Multimedia Super Corridor (MSC), which runs through Selangor. Putrajaya hosts government offices, foreign embassies, the prime minister's palatial residence, convention facilities and shopping malls. At its southern end is the 10,000-hectare (24,710-acre) **Kuala Lumpur International Airport** (KLIA), one of Asia's largest airports: so large, in fact, that it has a Formula One racing circuit running within its perimeter. Near Putrajaya is **Cyberjaya**, the MSC's dedicated "intelligent" city for multimedia companies.

Mining roots

Like Kuala Lumpur and Perak, Selangor grew rich on tin, prompting power struggles and civil wars in the 19th century. Selangor's original Minangkabau settlers were displaced by the Bugis, who established the present sultanate at Kuala Selangor. In 1894, Selangor was among the first four states in the British Federated Malay States (FMS) which later became Malaya and then Malaysia.

Before reaching the state capital **Shah Alam ❷**, the busy Federal Highway goes through the huge residential city of **Petaling Jaya** (PJ), whose population commutes daily into Kuala Lumpur. Shah Alam was built in 1963 and is more of a quiet suburb than administrative centre, with large houses, tree-lined boulevards, and numerous roundabouts. It is also a centre for heavy industries, including Proton, the national car project developed with Mitsubishi of Japan. There are a lot of Protons on Malaysia's roads; the company commands about two-thirds of the local car market, due mainly to high duties imposed on foreign models.

The Sultan of Selangor resides on a hilltop in Istana Bukit Kayangan. The jewel in the crown is the **Masjid Sultan Salahuddin Abdul Aziz Shah** (open Mon–Fri 9am–5pm; closed during Fri prayers; tel: 03-5519 9988). Known also as the Blue Mosque, it features some of the Islamic world's tallest minarets and largest domes. Its worship hall is bigger than London's St Paul's Cathedral, and can accommodate 16,000 worshippers.

LEFT: lush forests in Kuala Selangor Nature Park offer nature trails.
BELOW: the Blue Mosque.

TIP

Near Putrajaya on the old highway to Kuala Lumpur is a small town called Kajang, which claims to offer the best satay in Malaysia. And many KL-ites agree.

Seafood capital

At the western end of the Federal Highway, **Klang ❸**, the former state capital, conceals a colourful and violent past. Given its commanding position near the mouth of the Klang River, it was obvious that whoever possessed the town controlled the lucrative tin trade. Klang became a centre of fighting during the Selangor Civil War of the 1870s. Raja Mahdi, one of the chief protagonists, built his fort on the hill where the neoclassical municipal offices now stand.

Across the bridge on Jalan Tepi Sungai in the old town is a former warehouse for tin called the **Gedung Raja Abdullah**, built in 1857 by Raja Abdullah, one of Mahdi's principal opponents in the civil war. The warehouse exemplifies traditional Malay workmanship and has been converted into a tin museum (open daily 9am–4pm; tel: 03-5519 7604), bringing Klang's exciting past to life.

Klang is linked to KL by the KTM Komuter train system which ends in **Port Klang ❹** (Pelabuhan Klang). Eight kilometres (5 miles) by road from Klang, it is best known for its wonderful seafood restaurants at Pandamaran. The major seaport for Kuala Lumpur and the Klang Valley, it is one of the fastest growing container ports in Southeast Asia. This is also the base for local cruise ship companies, as well as port-of-call for ships from Singapore and other foreign lines. Packages from a 3 day/2 night duration cover destinations such as Singapore, Melaka, Penang and Langkawi, as well as Phuket in Thailand.

For shorter trips, boats and ferries from the port go out to the various islands in the Klang River delta, a favourite spot with weekend anglers. Two hours away through monotonous mangrove scenery is **Pulau Ketam** (Crab Island), probably the last Chinese fishing village on stilts in the state. Unfortunately, cleanliness is not its strong point, although it offers cheap and excellent seafood.

BELOW:
Pulau Ketam's
seafood bonanza.

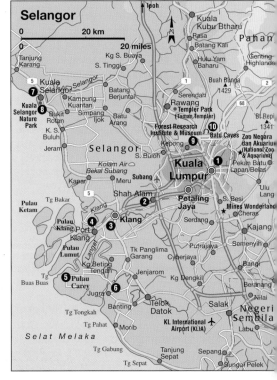

Head south for about 17 km (11 miles) to get to **Pulau Carey** ❺, home to the most famous of indigenous craftsmen, the Mah Meri Orang Asli traditional wood-carvers. The Sungai Bumbun Mah Meri tribe is best known for its dream-inspired spirit masks and unique *Moyang Tenong Jerat Harimau* tiger sculpture. Turn right at Teluk Panglima Garang, then right again to enter the Golden Hope estate road, and finally left at the fork. The tiny shop opposite the house of the leading woodcarver, Pion Anak Bumbon, is also the woodcarving centre. The designs are documented in a voluminous research text which doubles as both a "bible" of authenticity and a sort of sales catalogue for the unique craft. Large carvings can take as long as three months to complete and cost upwards of RM300.

Historic Selangor

The road south from Pulau Carey leads via Jenjarom to yet another old Selangor capital, **Jugra** ❻, which, unlike Klang, is completely out of the development limelight. On the hill overlooking the village and estuary are the graves of Selangor royalty and noblemen. The ruins of some old government buildings can be seen below. Standing amid the paddy fields are the abandoned palace, built in the 1800s, and the equally elaborate mosque where the sultan used to pray. Both are fine examples of late 19th/early 20th-century architecture.

Bird sanctuary

About 45 km (28 miles) north of Klang is the pretty, peaceful town of **Kuala Selangor** ❼ on the Sungai Selangor estuary. This was the 18th-century base of the state's Bugis rulers whose mausoleums are now a tourist attraction. The fort was built by the Dutch in the futile attempt to control the tin trade, and it still stands at

Map
on page
150

TIP

If not venturing to Pulau Carey, you may like to know that Mah Meri craft can also be bought in Cameron Highlands (*see Hill Stations, page 161*).

BELOW: Mah Meri woodcarving, Pulau Carey.

A Dutch cannon on Bukit Melawati.

BELOW: the Sri Subramaniar Swamy Temple inside the Batu Caves.

Bukit Melawati, complete with cannons that point out to sea. Today, however, they are merely iron sentinels to the **Kuala Selangor Nature Park** (visitors' centre open daily 9am–6pm; entrance fee; tel: 03-3289 2294) at the foot of the hill.

Protecting the area's coastal mangroves, and therefore its fisheries industry, the park is a joint project between the Malaysian Nature Society (MNS) and the state government. Some 160 species of birds have been recorded here, and an estimated 100,000 birds pass through during their annual migrations south. Artificial ponds that blend in beautifully with the surroundings attract the birds, surrounded by nature trails and observation hides – don't forget your binoculars. A pioneering attempt to breed endangered milky storks is undertaken here in a large aviary. The park has chalet and hostel accommodation as well.

There are several interesting Chinese fishing villages around Kuala Selangor. At **Pasir Penambang**, salted fish and fishballs are prepared in seafood processing warehouses (visitors are welcome), and there are some great seafood restaurants with lovely river views.

Further upriver about 9 km (5½ miles) from Kuala Selangor is **Kampung Kuantan**. When night falls, lights "come on" along the river. This is one of the few places in the world with such a large colony of synchronously flashing fireflies, or *kelip-kelip* (literally "twinkle"). Book a river cruise for this spectacular sight at the jetty on Jalan Rawang (daily 8–10.30pm, ticket office opens 7pm).

A limestone shrine

One of the most amazing sights in Malaysia is Thaipusam, the Hindu festival of penance associated with Lord Murugan, which occurs in January or February. The most sacred temple for this festival is the **Sri Subramaniar Swamy Temple** at the **Batu Caves** (open daily 8am–9pm), about 15 km (9 miles) north of Kuala Lumpur. This is the final destination for the rippling sea of devotees who follow the procession from the Sri Maha Mariamman Temple in Kuala Lumpur and painstakingly climb the 272 concrete steps that lead up to the cave. As repentance for past sins and to demonstrate their vows, many devotees carry large wooden and metal structures called *kavadi*. Some of these can weigh over 20 kg (44 lb) and are supported by long, thin spikes pinned into the body. Others fall into a trance and have their backs, chests, cheeks or tongues pierced to atone for misdeeds or as a purification ritual. Those who have had a request granted by Murugan carry milk in jugs up to the temple to bathe his statue.

On other days, the temple is peaceful. The excellent audio tour (daily 9.30am–5.30pm) is highly recommended; the booking office is just after the car park. The well-researched recording, complete with sound effects and a map, covers some 27 sites and explains the caves' history and Hindu mythology.

The limestone massif's main cavern, known as the **Temple** (or Cathedral) **Cave**, is a huge vault pierced by stalactites that point downwards 6 metres (20 ft). Eerie shafts of light streak down from gaps in the ceiling high above. At the base of the Temple Cave, to the left of the steps, are two smaller caves with beautiful art (both open daily 6am–9pm; entrance fee).

One houses the **Gallery of Indian Art**, which has brightly coloured, almost garish wall paintings of Hindu myths. The other cave features **Velluvar Kottam**, which contains colourful clay figurines. The gold-painted statue of Murugan at the foot of the outcrop is the world's largest, standing at 43 metres (140 ft).

Batu Caves is also popular with adventure sports enthusiasts. There are about another 20 caves within the massif, and the **Dark Caves**, open only to MNS tours (tel: 03-2287 9422), has narrow passages where you could encounter bats and creepy crawlies. The other side of the cliff is popular with rock climbers, as is **Bukit Takun** located further north along the old trunk road (Route 1).

Tamed jungles

The Takun area is also home to several parks, offering easy tracks, and pools and waterfalls for swimming. Among them is the popular Templer Park (Taman Templer), and scenic Hutan Lipur Kancing (Kancing Forest Reserve). But better trails wind through the 1,528 hectares (3,776 acres) of the **Forest Research Institute and Museum (FRIM)** ⑩ (open daily 7am–7pm; entrance fee; tel: 03-6279 7575; www.frim.gov.my) at Kepong, about 7 km (4¼ miles) west of Batu Caves. The country's top forest research facility, FRIM has experimental plantations, arboreta and an excellent forestry museum. A key attraction here is the 30-metre (100-ft) high canopy walkway, which commands magnificent views of the forest.

Malaysia's wildlife is on show at the **Zoo Negara dan Akuarium** (National Zoo and Aquarium; open daily 9am–5pm; entrance fee; tel: 03-4108 3422), 13 km (8 miles) from Kuala Lumpur by way of Jalan Genting Klang. Its collection includes a nice display of birds, reptiles such as pythons, *seladang* (the world's largest wild buffalo), tapirs, crocodiles, tigers, and of course, the orang-utan. ❑

Map on page 150

Going on the canopy walkway at FRIM can be an unnerving yet thrilling experience.

BELOW: a canopy of Kapur trees at FRIM.

THE NORTHWESTERN PENINSULA

This is an area of immense variety, spliced in the middle by a mountainous jungled backbone, Banjaran Titiwangsa

Heading north out of Kuala Lumpur is like heading through the country's so-called first wave of development – this is the land of tin and rubber, and, nearer the Thai border, rice. Global demand and phenomenally high prices for the first two natural resources were behind the peninsula's rapid growth from the late 19th century till the middle of the 20th century.

Perak's Kinta River Valley was once the tin capital of the world. Now, a daisy-chain of huge mining ponds sit in silence amid deserts of stark, bleached sand and the odd tin dredge made of wood; but life is returning to this seeming desolation. The lakes have evolved into a wetland habitat, attracting many species of both native and migrant bird, some never seen here before. Elsewhere, the concrete and metal of industrial parks are testament to the new manufacturing industries, so vital to the state's continued economic progress.

Some former mining towns remain frozen in time – Papan, Batu Gajah, Pusing. Others retain their charming old-world core but have continued to build on that early prosperity, and are thriving – Ipoh, Kuala Kangsar, Taiping.

However, while many rubber plantations have been supplanted by the more lucrative oil palm, visitors will still pass through acres of this early fortune-maker, thanks to a new rubberwood furniture industry utilising fast-growing, high-yield strains. In the irrigated plains of Kedah and Perlis, paddy covers much of the land in this, the country's largest rice-growing area.

Limestone is another feature of the north. Large outcrops dripping with vegetation dot Perak and Perlis, and make up the entire islands of the Langkawi archipelago. Swathed in mist at dawn, the limestone hills are inspiration for any number of Chinese brush paintings, while the earliest evidence of prehistoric human civilisation in the country can be found among the caves.

On the isles, it is always holiday time. Penang continues to bewitch with its plethora of heritage buildings, temples, cluttered lively city streets, and golden beaches. More long sandy beaches beckon at Langkawi, still sleepily enwrapped in legend; likewise Pangkor, still following the rhythms of the sea, as it has throughout the ages. ❏

PRECEDING PAGES: rows of terraced vegetable plots in the highland resort of Cameron Highlands.
LEFT: palms reign supreme on Langkawi's beaches.

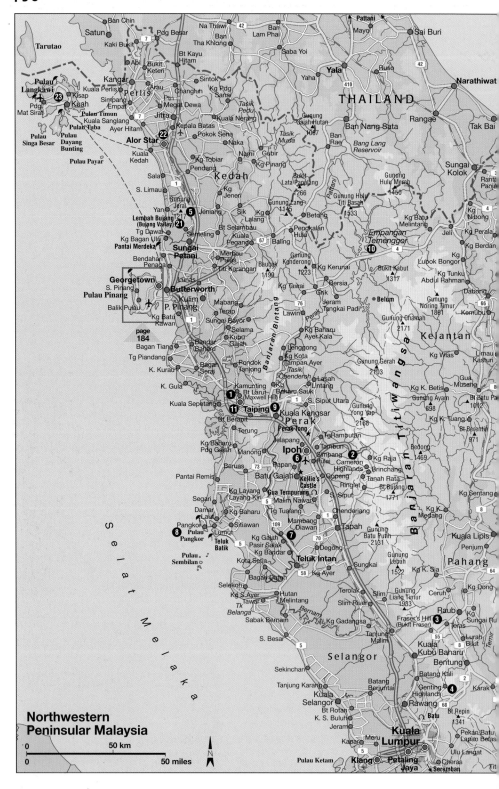

Northwestern
Peninsular Malaysia

THAILAND

Pattani
Mayo
Sai Buri
Na Thawi
Ban
Lam Phai
Ban
Tha Khlong
Saba Yoi
Yala
Yaha
Ruso
Narathiwat
Rangae
Tak Bai
Ban Nang Sata
Sungai
Kolok
Ranta
Panja

Ban Chin
Satun
Pdg Besar
Kaki Bukit
Bt Kayu
Hitam
Bukit
Keteri
Kangar
Arau
Changlun
Kg Pdg
Sanai
Sintok
Kuala Perlis
Kisap
Simpang
Empat
Ptn
Megat Dewa
Tasik
Pedu
Kuala Nerang
Gunung
Gajah Hutan
Ban
Rae
Bang Lang
Reservoir
Gunung
Hulu Merah
Titi Basah

Tarutao
Pulau
Langkawi
Kuah
Pdg
Mat Sirat
Pulau Timun
Kuala Sanglang
Pulau Tuba
Ayer Hitam
Jitra
Kepala Batas
Pokok Sena
Naka
Nami
Gubir
Bukit
Lata Papulang
Gunung Hulu
Titi Basah

Pulau
Singa Besar
Pulau
Dayang
Bunting
Pulau Payar
Alor Star
Kuala
Kedah
Sala
S. Limau
Pendang
Kedah
Kg Tobiar
Kg Pinang
Tasik
Muda
Betong
Kg Batu
Melintang
Kg
Nibong
Kg
Perala

Gunung
Jerai
Yan
Lembah Bujang
(Bujang Valley)
Tg Dawai
Kg Bagan Ulu
Pantai Merdeka
Bendahari
Penaga
Kg
Jeneri
Jeniang
Sik
Kg
Lalang
Bt Selambau
Semeling
Kuala
Pegang
Baling
Pengkalan
Hulu
Empangan
Temenggor
Kg Berdan
Lubok Bongor
Kg Tunku
Abdul Rahman
Kelantan

Georgetown
Pulau Pinang
S. Pinang
Balik Pulau
Butterworth
Kulim
Mabang
P. Pinang
Terap
Kg Batu
Kawan
page
184
Bagan Tiang
Tg Piandang
K. Kurau
K. Gula
Kuala Sepetang
Selama
Sungai Bayor
Kubu
Gajah
Bandar
Baharu
Pondok
Tanjong
Bagan
Serai
Kamunting
Bt Larut
Maxwell Hill
Kg
Baharu Sauk
Kg Baharu
Ayek Kala
Lawin
Jeram
Tangkai Padi
Gunung Chamah
2171
Gunung
Noring Timur
1861
Kemubu
Dabong
Limau
Kasturi
Gua
Musang
Kg K. Betis
Gunung Ayam
698
Bt Batu Pa
1012
Kg K. Tuang

Merbau
Pulos
Titi Karangan
Baubak
1198
Gunung
Kenderong
Kg Kerunai
Bukit Kabut
1317
Bersia
Chik
Belum
Kg Tawai
Lenggong
Kg Kota
Tampan Ayer
Tasik
Chenderoh
Lasah
Gunung Gerah
2703

Selat Melaka

Taiping
Bt Beraph
Terung
Kg Baharu
Pdg Gajah
Manong
Beruas
Pantai Remis
Segari
Damar
Lalu
Pangkor
Pulau
Pangkor
Teluk
Batik
Pulau
Sembilan
Kuala Kangsar
Perak
Perak Tong
Jelapang
Ipoh
Papan
Batu Gajah
Kellie's
Castle
Gua Tempurung
Malim Nawar
Kg Baharu
Tg Tualang
Mambang
Diawan
Kg Gajah
Pasir Salak
Kg Bandar
Kota Setia
Bagan Datoh
Selekoh
Kg S. Ayer
Tawar
Tk
Belanga
Sabak Bernam
S. Besar
Simpang
Pulai
Gopeng
Ringlet
S. Siput
Chenderiang
Tapah
Degong
Teluk Intan
Sungkai
Terolak
Slim
Slim River
Kg Gadangsa
Tanjung
Malim
Kg Ayer
Bt Berentin
971
Bedong
1469
Kg Raja
Cameron
Highlands
Brinchang
Tanah Rata
Bt Bujang
1771
Kg Sentang
Kg K.
Medang
Kuala Lipis
Penjum
Pahang
Kg K. Sia
Kg Dong
Raub
Kg
Sungai Ru
Teras
Fraser's Hill
(Bukit Fraser)
Lurah
Bilut
Gunung
Yong Yap
2168
TgRambutan
Tambun
Gunung
Batu Putih
2131
Gunung
Lebah
1522
Gunung
Liang Timur
1993
55

Sungai
Sekinchan
Tanjung Karang
Kuala
Selangor
Bt Rotan
K. S. Buluh
Jeram
Meru
Kapar
Pulau Ketam
Klang
Petaling
Jaya
Kuala
Lumpur
Ulu Langat
Cheras
Seremban
Pekan Batu
Lapan Belas
Selangor
Batang
Beriuntai
Kuala
Kubu Baharu
Bentung
Batang Kali
Genting
Highlands
Rawang
Batu
Bt Repin
1341
Karak

0   50 km
0   50 miles
N

Banjaran Bintang

Banjaran Titiwangsa

HILL STATIONS

Map on page 158

With their temperate climates and tranquil gardens, the high hill stations of central Malaysia are as popular with tourists today as they were with the British colonialists before them

The insufferable heat drove them to the hills. Once there, they pushed back the jungle and created little pockets of England with rose gardens and mock-Tudor bungalows; from that point on, life in the colonies assumed a more bearable aspect for the British. Today for much the same reason – cooler climes, those little snapshots of Englishness – tourists flock to the former hill stations of Maxwell Hill, Cameron Highlands and Fraser's Hill. Some of the buildings have been taken over by multinationals as hillside retreats, others are now hotels, while yet more new high-rise developments attempt to emulate their colonial predecessors – with varying degrees of success.

Restful retreat

The oldest hill station, and the one least touched by time, is **Bukit Larut ❶** (Maxwell Hill) in Perak. Rising over 1,000 metres (3,280 ft) above the serene Lake Gardens of Taiping, it is largely responsible for Taiping being the wettest place in the peninsula. This is a peaceful hill resort; there are no golf courses or fancy restaurants, only gardens, jungle walks and a badminton court. The attraction for visitors is the cool air and the fine vistas: clouds over the Straits of Melaka, thick mist-laden jungles and the Lake Gardens below.

Large bungalows, complete with fireplaces, sit at different elevations of this hill. (For bookings, call tel: 05-807 7241.) The road up the hill was constructed during World War II with the "help" of Japanese prisoners-of-war. Before that, anyone who wished to reach the top had to hike three hours or go by pony or sedan chair. At one time, the trail was used by porters carrying heavy loads of fragrant tea downhill. Now the tea plantations are no more, leaving only the **Tea Garden House**, midway up, with its view of Taiping and the Lake Gardens. A handful of labourers keep the jungle at bay and the lush gardens neatly manicured.

Access to the hill is denied to private vehicles. Instead, government-owned Land Rovers (tel: 05-807 7241) serve as mountain taxis departing every hour between 7am and 6pm. They take eight persons seated, and two standing at the back, hanging grimly on to the top bar. The one-lane road is steep and narrow; at sharp bends the jungle suddenly parts to reveal the green land below divided into a pattern of roads and fields.

The air becomes brisk, and the sun is lost in mist and clouds. The 12-km (7½-mile) journey takes 40 minutes, and you are deposited at the front step of your bungalow. At the foot of the hill sits a war cemetery of Commonwealth soldiers who died in the Japanese invasion. Nearby is a large freshwater swimming pool fed by a waterfall.

BELOW: mist-shrouded Cameron Highlands.

TIP

If you are in good
physical shape,
explore the Cameron
hills on a bicycle.
Bicycles are available
for hire at the
goldsmith, Kedai
Emas Loon Hing,
on the main road in
Brinchang.

BELOW:
harvesting tea in
Cameron Highlands.

The tea highlands

Crewcut tea bush rows lend the rolling hills of **Cameron Highlands ➋** a soft green glow in the dewy early light. Vast tea plantations distinguish this most developed of Malaysia's hill stations, which peaks at 2,030 metres (6,660 ft).

Although Camerons, as it is called, is actually part of Pahang, it can be reached via Tapah or Simpang Pulai in Perak. From Tapah and Ipoh, there are regular buses to Tanah Rata, Camerons' main town, between 8am and 6pm. Taxis can also be chartered. Tapah is also on the train route, and there are express buses from Kuala Lumpur and Penang that go all the way to Brinchang.

If you are driving, turn off at the old trunk road just north of Tapah that leads via Chenderiang to the gorgeous **Lata Kinjang**, a towering 850-metre (2,790 ft) multi-step waterfall visible from the North-South Expressway. There are picnic spots, gardens and a spray-misted suspension bridge here. Orang Asli guides who live at the foot of the falls can guide you to other cascades and to their durian fruit orchards in the forest for a fee, but you need permission from the Forestry Department in Tapah to enter the area, which is a forest reserve.

From Tapah, the Camerons road twists its way uphill for 90 km (60 miles) through a dense forest of coniferous trees, thick ferns, and clusters of bamboo that add the touch of a Chinese scroll painting. The hairpin bends on this road can make the journey uncomfortable; if you are prone to motion sickness, avoid eating too much or take travel sickness pills before ascending. Camerons is particularly well known for its tree ferns and wild orchids. While you're travelling up, you will pass Orang Asli on motorbikes or on foot, carrying butterfly nets, on their way to their villages which dot the hills.

Ringlet is the first and rather ugly little settlement at the 45 km (30 miles)

marker. Push on, and 4 km (2½ miles) later you will reach the **Sultan Abu Bakar Lake** (Tasik Sultan Abu Bakar), an artificial body of water formed by the damming of Sungai Bertam for Camerons' hydroelectric scheme, which is one of the country's oldest. Perched on a bluff above the lake is the first Tudor-style hotel, which offers sweeping views of the valley.

The road from Simpang Pulai makes for an easier climb to Camerons as it is wider and less winding. From the North-South Expressway, turn off at the Simpang Pulai exit and follow the signposts. You will pass Kampung Raja and Tringkap before reaching Brinchang, the highest town in Cameron Highlands.

Vegetables and inns

Farmlands begin before Sultan Abu Bakar Lake, the cultivated terraces that have earned Camerons the nickname of vegetable capital of the peninsula. There are also nurseries which supply roses, carnations and chrysanthemums to domestic and overseas markets. An interesting trend among these growers is the move towards organic farming, thanks to pressure against pesticide use. About 15 km (9 miles) further on lies **Tanah Rata**, the principal township, a bustling tourist centre with hotels, shops and restaurants.

Cameron Highlands is home to many rare species of butterfly.

Discovered by William Cameron, a government surveyor on a mapping expedition in 1885, "this fine plateau with gentle slopes shut in by the mountains" was unknown even to the locals in the lowlands. After 1931, tea planters, then farmers, claimed the plateau, and built a road to carry their produce to market.

Today, Tanah Rata is popular with Malaysian families, college students, retirees and diplomats alike. Boy scouts with knapsacks on their backs thumb rides up the winding hills, while Singaporean tourists lounge on colonial-style verandahs, munching fresh strawberries and cream. To some, arriving from the tropical lowlands, it seems somewhat incongruous to arrive at Tanah Rata and find logfires lit every night, and Devonshire tea and English breakfast on menus. But the local steamboat soup dish is also popular, and among the Chinese hotels are several very good Indian restaurants, serving simple snacks and meals that agree well with the climate here.

BELOW: a temperate haven in the tropics.

Check out the excellent Yung Seng souvenir shop at No. 23 on the main road, which has beautiful native craft, including the wonderful Mah Meri masks of Selangor, and Temiar fishing traps, as well as crafts from other Southeast Asian countries.

En route to Brinchang is the **Cameron Highlands Resort** (www.cameronhighlandsresort.com), a deluxe boutique hotel with a spa offering treatments that draw on the restorative properties of tea. It is located opposite an authentic replica of an English inn, **The Smokehouse Hotel** (www.thesmokehouse.com.my), which has a well-kept garden and ivy-covered walls of stone. Inside the cosy living rooms are stuffed chintz settees and old photographs, clocks, and other characterful remnants of the British colonial era. The 13 suites are equally charming. Behind the inn is one of the country's oldest golf courses, which survived tigers, vegetable farmers and World War II to become the 18-hole course it is today. A pavilion with a bar and a restaurant overlooks the golf course.

Cameron's Trails and Tours

I n 1967, while on holiday in Cameron Highlands, the American Thai-silk entrepreneur Jim Thompson went out for an evening stroll along one of the highlands' many trails. He was never seen again.

Even today, spirit-world, wild-animal and conspiracy theories surround the disappearance of the highlands' most famous missing person. Somehow this has added weight to the otherwise standard precautions requiring visitors to tell someone which trail they are taking and to stick to the paths.

Most Cameron Highlands maps include walking trails. The roads themselves make good walks, and there is a paved walkway all the way from Tanah Rata to Brinchang. A fairly easy and popular trek at Tanah Rata is the 1-hour **Robinson Descent** (Path 9) which starts at the falls and goes downhill to the power station – the last stretch is fairly steep

though. The longer and flatter **Boh Road** trail (Path 9A) branches off to the left at the top of Path 9 and leads to the Farlie Boh Tea Estate road near Habu. Another easy route is **Parit Falls** (Path 4), a flat 20-minute stroll from the Garden Inn hotel to Taman Sedia, known for the KMH Strawberry Farm.

All these trails join up with the circular **Gunung Beremban** track (Path 8 from Robinson Falls and Path 3 from Parit Falls). The trek is steep and you need to cross some streams. It takes about 3 hours to reach the 1,800-metre (5,900-ft) peak, but the sunsets and sunrises are great – bring a tent and warm clothes if you intend to camp out. Path 3 actually ends in Brinchang at the golf course, or joins Path 2, to go past the hilltop Sam Po Buddhist temple into town. The Beremban track splinters at various parts, so ensure you take the path you really want to take, or you could end up somewhere else.

There is a trail that leads north from Brinchang up to **Gunung Brinchang** (Path 1). It is a long 4-hour trek, though a fairly easy one, but can be wet and slippery after rain. Keep your eyes open for pitcher plants in this damp and fern-rich mossy forest.

There are several interesting tours out of Brinchang and Tanah Rata that go off the beaten track but require minimum numbers. Golden Highlands Adventure Holidays (3900 Tanah Rata, Main Bus Station; tel: 05-490 1880/1/2; goldenadventure.cameronhigh lands.com) specialises in nature interpretation. Its programmes include treks to the highland cloud or mossy forests at Gunung Brinchang (half-day) and Gunung Irau (2 day/1 night), tours to Semai Orang Asli villages, and the jewel in the crown, a Rafflesia tour, which is run only when guides encounter a patch where this rare parasite, the world's largest flower is, or is close to, blooming.

Other tour companies offer a half-day jungle trekking tour that takes in a waterfall, and an all-day tour that covers a tea plantation, a visit to an Orang Asli village, and picturesque cave waterfalls. Contact CS Travels & Tours (47 Jalan Besar, Tanah Rata; tel: 05-491 1200; www.cstravel.com.my) or Titiwangsa Tours & Travel (36 Jalan Besar Brinchang; tel: 05-491 1755; www.titiwangsatours.com).   ❑

LEFT: the carnivorous pitcher plant.

More accommodation is available along this stretch of road before you hit **Brinchang**. This once-pretty area is now populated with modern high-rise developments, a scene compounded further by tacky attractions such as Cactus Valley, the Rose Centre and Butterfly Farm. The town is also at the tail-end of the new Simpang Pulai road that links to Ipoh.

Just beyond Brinchang is the **Kea Farm area**, the heartland of vegetable farms and nurseries. Here farmers set up roadside stalls to sell produce from wild honey and asparagus to strawberries and tomatoes.

The prettiest tea estate in Cameron Highlands is the **Sungai Palas Tea Estate**, located further north from Brinchang. The oldest tea factory is the one built in 1929 in the **Farlie Tea Estate** near Habu, where the original processing technology is still used. The most accessible plantation to photograph is the **Bharat Tea Estate** near Tanah Rata, which has a teahouse as well but no tours. The first two estates belong to the local giant Boh Tea, which operates a chain of "tea cafés" in cities as well as at both their highland tea estates.

The new **Sungai Palas Tea Centre** (open Tues–Sun 9am–4.30pm; tel: 05-496 2096; free) in the Sungai Palas Tea Estate is worth a stop. Visitors can learn about the history of the Boh tea plantations and the tea manufacturing process. At its **Tea'ria** souvenir and tea shop, you can savour teas and sandwiches while enjoying elevated views of the surrounding area.

From the Sungai Palas Tea Estate, a steep road winds 6 km (4 miles) up to Gunung Brinchang, Camerons' highest point, and panoramic views of the forested valley. This also makes quite a nice – if long – early morning walk that takes in vegetable farms, the bird-filled forest near the top, and the colourful periwinkles growing freely among the tea bushes.

Map on page 158

TIP

Try Boh's flavoured teas at Tea'ria. These are blended with local fruit such as lychee, and spices such as cinnamon and ginger. The tea shop also has a wide range of beautifully packaged products including instant mix iced teas.

BELOW: the mock-Tudor Smokehouse Hotel in the Cameron hills.

Creepers and moss clinging to a mammoth tree trunk on Fraser's Hill.

BELOW: tee off in Fraser's Hill, Selangor.

Tea in the garden

Much quieter is **Fraser's Hill ❸** (Bukit Fraser) in Selangor, although its past is more colourful. The hill resort is named after Louis James Fraser, an elusive English adventurer, who had long disappeared when the hill station was built in 1910. He apparently ran a notorious gambling and opium den here for local miners and planters, as well as a mule train, and later, a transport service in the lowlands.

The 1,500-metre (5,000-ft) high resort is scattered over seven hills on which sit a series of English greystone bungalows, surrounded by neat English gardens blooming with roses and hollyhocks. The tiny town centre around the clock tower has some rather disastrous newer additions, and there are also high-rise hotels which fail to blend with the landscape.

A better bet is to go with the economical if run-down bungalows, now state-run. The prettiest and most expensive accommodation is **The Smokehouse Hotel** (www.thesmokehouse.com.my), a replica of the Camerons outlet, where you can also enjoy Devonshire tea or apple pie in the lovely garden. The road to the inn leads on to Jeriau Waterfall, once a pretty picnic spot, but now permanently silted, the result of resort development years ago.

Because of its proximity to Kuala Lumpur, Fraser's is crowded on weekends, but there are enough walks and trails to take you away from the madding crowd. The ring road around the 9-hole golf course makes a pleasant two-hour walk, and brings you past the old bungalows and newer resorts. The picturesque golf course (open daily 8am–7pm; tel: 09-362 2122) was carved out of an old tin mine, and is one of the few public courses in the country.

There are also eight jungle trails of varying lengths, which are well marked and easy to follow. The most popular is the ½-hour **Bishop's Trail**, while the scenic **Hemmant Trail** skirts the golf course. Fit trekkers will appreciate the challenging 6-km (4-mile) **Pine Hill Trail**, which leads 1,450 metres (4,750 ft) up to breathtaking views. Fraser's trails run through montane forests, where trees are generally shorter than in the lowlands, growing up to only 30 metres (100 ft) tall, and are usually coated with lichens, ferns and orchids. Dominant species are oaks, laurels, tree ferns and conifers. Scientists have found over 30 species of plants that live only in these hills. On your treks, you may chance to encounter birdwatching groups who are drawn to the forests by the estimated 275 local and migratory species.

If you have your own transport, there are good drives around the area, such as the second loop that goes past the holiday bungalows of multinational corporations. Driving is the best way to get to Fraser's. From the base of the hill, it is a 45-minute drive up a one-way road. Midway up the hill is the **Gap**, which was a rest stop for mule and bullock cart transporters in the old days. It was named the Gap as it was literally a gap between the boundaries of the Selangor and Pahang states.

The original winding road is now used only for descending traffic. It was along this century-old road from Kuala Kubu Bharu that British High Commissioner Sir Henry Gurney was ambushed and killed by communist guerilllas in 1951.

By bus, it is an hour's journey from Kuala Lumpur (100 km/60 miles) to the town of Kuala Kubu Bharu, from where you take a second bus ride for another 1½ hours to get to the top.

Gamblers' paradise

Newer hill resorts are popular, but lack the charm of the three "oldies". A definite study in contrast is **Genting Highlands ❹**, 2,000 metres (6,600 ft) above sea level. Just one convenient hour from Kuala Lumpur, it is actually visible from the capital, a city of pleasure shrouded in mist, on top of Banjaran Titiwangsa (Main Range), the mountain range that runs down the centre of the peninsula.

Genting is the Las Vegas of Malaysia, a rambling complex of hotels, theme parks and a casino, the country's sole gambling den. And it is something people either love or loathe. Amid lush surroundings, the complex is entirely artificial, giant boulders included, and it is possible to not surface for sunshine the whole time you are there. Genting just never goes to sleep.

The whole development comes under **Genting Highlands Resorts** (tel: 03-2718 1118; www.genting.com.my), owned by businessman Lim Goh Tong, who mooted the idea for the resort, spending seven years alone to build the steep road.

Genting's casino is one of the largest in the world and offers the gamut of games, both Western and traditional Chinese like *tai sai*. There are also rows of slot machines and computerised racing. A shirt and tie is compulsory for men, or you can opt for a batik shirt, the Malaysian formal wear, which can be rented at the door. In accordance with Islamic law, a sign over the casino entrance warns that Muslims are forbidden to try their luck here.

Accommodation is plentiful and affordable; there are over 7,000 rooms

Map on page 158

Batik shirts are considered formal wear and will allow men entry into the Gentings' casino.

BELOW:
Genting Highlands theme park.

Spice Garden restaurant in Genting Highlands Resort serves Indian and Middle Eastern fare.

BELOW: Orang Asli child.
RIGHT: jungles of Sungai Teroi.

available at five hotels, and a wide range of food is served at over 90 food outlets. Together, the outdoor and indoor theme parks offer more than 60 rides. The former, set around an artificial lake, has rollercoasters, boat rides and a monorail. The indoor theme park houses rides and a 4D movie theatre. There are also two theatres which feature international magic acts or cabaret dinner shows, and famous singers often make appearances. Save your jungle shoes for the other hill stations, but bring along your umbrella and windcheater as it gets wet and chilly here.

Things are a little less manic 10 km (6 miles) down the hill at the **Awana Golf and Country Club** (www.awana.com.my), which has an 18-hole golf course and panoramic views. Awana and Genting Highlands resorts are linked by a skyway, a cable car system covering the 3½-km (2-mile) journey in 11 minutes (daily 24 hours). If it is not misty, the scenery on this short ride is quite spectacular, with montane vegetation spread out beneath. Free shuttle bus services transport passengers from the hotels to the skyway stations.

Express buses from Kuala Lumpur's Puduraya Bus Station, KL Sentral Station and KLIA run daily to the cable car complex at the foot of the hill. The ticket price covers the cable car ride. A special taxi stand at Puduraya also services Genting.

To drive to Genting from Kuala Lumpur, head northeast to reach the Karak Highway. Drive for about half an hour before you see a multi-storey rest stop on your right, marking the turn-off to Genting Highlands. From here, it is a 15-minute drive up a winding road to the main resort.

Aboriginal treasures

Genting can also be accessed via the considerably more pleasant old Pahang Road through Gombak. At Gombak, you might want to pop into **Pak Ali's House** (Rumah Pak Ali) for a quick look at a traditional Sumatran-style house.

About 15 km (9 miles) down the old Pahang Road is the excellent **Orang Asli Museum**, or Muzium Orang Asli (open Sat–Thur 9am–5pm; tel: 03-6189 2122; free). Sitting on a hill at an Orang Asli settlement, it provides a fascinating insight on the Malaysian peninsula's aboriginal peoples. A good range of exhibits such as old photographs, artefacts, handicraft, and tools and implements used in daily life, make this museum well worth a visit.

Another hill station is **Gunung Jerai 5**, Kedah's highest peak. The 1,217-metre (3,993-ft) high limestone massif has commanding views of the surrounding rice plains and the Main Range. On the other side, you can see across the Straits of Melaka into Penang, and even as far as Langkawi island. Part of the **Sungai Teroi Forest Recreation Park** (Hutan Rekreasi Sungai Teroi), which has some forest trails, the hill is also home to a forestry museum. At its peak sits the pretty **Gunung Jerai Resort** (tel: 04-423 4345).

Jerai is accessed from Sungai Petani or Gurun from the North-South Expressway. Turn off at Guar Chempedak. If you don't have your own transport, jeeps can ferry you up the 13-km (8-mile) winding road between 9am and 5pm. Alternatively, if you are energetic enough, a mountain track goes right up to the peak. ❑

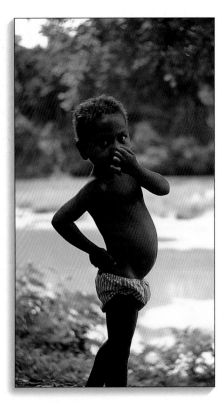

PERAK

It was once the wealthy tin-mining centre of Malaysia. Now the home of the country's longest-surviving sultanate, Perak woos the tourist dollar to its beaches

Map on page 158

Perak state was once one of the world's most important sources of tin ore. In Bahasa Malaysia, *perak* actually means "silver" – it was the "silver" of the tin revolution that lined the state's coffers, making it one of the wealthiest states in the land. The accompanying feuds and power struggles prompted greater British intervention in the whole country, eventually shifting the centre of power from the old capitals along the Perak River to the tin-rich areas of Larut and Kinta.

When the bottom fell out of the industry in the 1980s, entire towns shut down. However, thanks to industrialisation and the rapid pace of development in the country, the state's limestone hills are now feeding huge cement factories.

The town that tin built

The Kinta Valley remains Perak's leading district, and its main city, **Ipoh ❻**, the most prosperous of its settlements. Beginning as a tin mining field in the 1870s, Ipoh developed into a hub for road, rail and river transportation. Its name comes from the *epau (antiaris toxicaria)* tree, whose poisonous sap is used for the darts of aboriginal blowpipes. When Ipoh took over as the state capital from Taiping in 1937, it was the best-planned town in the peninsula, with broad, regularly laid-out streets.

Nestled in the craggy bosom of limestone outcrops and the more distant hills of the Main Range, Ipoh is one of Malaysia's largest cities with a population of over half a million. Its **Old Town** on the west side is where you'll find the *Padang* (Town Green), the epitome of every Malaysian town with a colonial past. Surrounded by the Royal Ipoh Club, court houses, municipal library and the stately **St Michael's Institution**, it is the scene of important matches, school athletic meets, and parades. Near the **Masjid Negeri** (State Mosque) and the Clock Tower, is the Moorish **Stesen Keretapi Ipoh** (Ipoh Railway Station), whose silver dome, graceful arches, and interminable colonnades, bear a striking resemblance to the Kuala Lumpur Railway Station.

East of the river lies the **D.R. Seenivasagam Park** (Taman D.R. Seenivasagam) which, typical of most public parks in Ipoh, hosts large dawn gatherings of *tai chi* practitioners. Here, groups faithfully go through all forms of the martial art, some using words and fans too.

On Jalan Panglima Bukit Gantang Wahab is the **Muzium Darul Ridzuan** (Darul Ridzuan Museum; open daily 9am–5pm, except Fri noon–3pm; free; tel: 05-253 1437). The century-old mansion used to be the residence of Malay chieftains and British officials, but now showcases the state's history, Ipoh's development and the story of tin mining.

LEFT: the stately Ubudiah Mosque. **BELOW:** one of many temples embedded in the rockface around Ipoh.

Grand mansions in huge grounds still sit along **Jalan Sultan Azlan Shah**, commonly referred to by its old name, Tiger Lane. Also along this road is the **Geology Museum**, or Muzium Geologi (open daily 8am– 4.30pm; free; tel: 05-540 6000). It has over 600 examples of minerals, an exhibition on tin ore, including one of the best examples of cassiterite in the world, and a fine collection of precious stones, rock specimens and minerals.

About 15 minutes' drive east of town is **Tambun**. Among its attractions are the **Lost World of Tambun** (open Mon, Wed–Fri 11am–6pm, Sat–Sun 10am–6pm; entrance fee; tel: 05 542 8888; www.sunway.com.my), a popular water theme park located on Persiaran Lagun Sunway 1, with amusement rides, hot springs and a man-made beach. Tambun also has the **National Stud Farm**, where thoroughbred race horses are raised, and the **Tambun Caves** with Neolithic-period rock paintings depicting human and animal motifs.

Succulent pomelo, very similar in taste and texture to the grapefruit, is found everywhere in Ipoh.

Temples in the rock

Ipoh's undisputed top attractions are its cave temples. The naturally hollowed insides of the Kinta Valley's limestone formations, so reminiscent of southern China, have served as homes for ancient peoples as well as hideouts for bandits.

They are also spiritually significant for both Buddhists and Hindus. Devotees have built entrances to these temples that range from the simple to the ostentatious; sometimes entire buildings complete with red-tiled pagoda roofs "grow" out from the rock. Walking into the dimly lit interiors, with their altars, the smell of incense and the occasional echoes of bats and swallows, can make for a heady experience for the uninitiated.

BELOW: colourful paintings from the cave walls of Perak Tong temple.

The largest of the rock temples, **Sam Poh Tong** (open daily 8am–4.30pm; free)

Map on page 158

s 5 km (3 miles) south of Ipoh in Gunung Rapat, on the old trunk road near a line of stalls selling pomelos and local biscuits. The temple dates back to the 1890s when a passing monk found the cave and made it his home and meditation base for 20 years until his death. Today, a group of monks and nuns reside in the temple.

Statues of Buddha are dotted everywhere, even among the stalagmites and stalactites. A stiff climb up 264 steps leads to a panorama of Ipoh and its surroundings. Of renown is the temple's pond of small tortoises; visitors can buy spinach to feed them. Tortoises are Chinese symbols of longevity.

Close by is the **Gua Kek Lok Tong**, known also as the Brass Temple after its gleaming statues. You can walk through the cave to the back where its dog's teeth of limestone formations frame a peaceful green valley of ponds and hills.

Another famous cave shrine is the **Perak Tong** (open daily 8am–6pm; free), 5 km (4 miles) north of town on Jalan Kuala Kangsar, the old trunk road. Traditional Chinese paintings adorn the walls and relate traditional folk tales and legends. Built in 1926 by a Buddhist priest from China, the temple has more than 40 statues of Buddha, the central figure rising 13 metres (40 ft) high.

On the same limestone massif as Sam Poh Tong is a giant Mercedes Benz logo, presented to the city by the German manufacturer in thanks for the huge purchases by rich miners.

Caves and castles

The prettiest view of Ipoh's limestone hills is just past the city as you head south on the North-South Expressway. Unfortunately, this gives way briefly to blasted rock, precious material for the country's development, before coming to the imposing Gunung Tempurung limestone massif. One of the show caves, **Gua Tempurung** (open 9am–5pm), just 24 km (15 miles) from Ipoh, can be accessed from the Gopeng interchange and 2 km (1 mile) down the old trunk road south. The turn-off is at the pretty Kampung Gunung Mesah.

BELOW: Buddhist statues (left) crowd a shrine in Sam Poh Tong, and (right) the temple exterior.

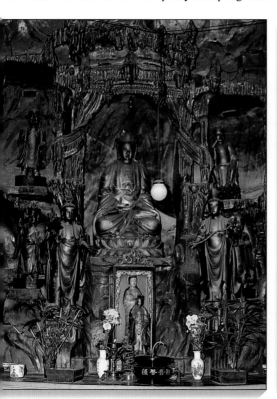

Look hard enough in the countryside of Perak and you may spot abandoned wooden tin dredges, a sight from yester-year when tin was king in Perak.

Used variously by tin miners and communists on the run, the 1.9-km (1-mile) long river passageway is now accessible via an illuminated walkway. The concrete pathway climbs up to the 180 metre by 120 metre (540 ft by 360 ft) Alam Cavern, the biggest of the five chambers, and also passes through interesting formations such as gigantic stalagmites and flowstones dating back to 8,000 BC.

Tours run from a 40-minute basic trip to the 4-hour grand tour, which involves a river stint. There are morning and afternoon sessions for the longer tours, and guides will bring in a minimum of two. Weekends and public holidays can be crowded with tour buses, after which graffiti appears on the walls, to be painstakingly cleaned off by management. Camping is allowed on site.

The old trunk road in Perak goes through mainly flat and open land, offering vistas of deserted mining pools over the bleached scars of tin tailings and glimpses of the wooden *palong* (tin dredges). An incongruity among these ruins is that of a Scottish mansion, about 5 km (3 miles) from Batu Gajah, half an hour from Ipoh. **Kellie's Castle** (open daily 9am–6.30pm; entrance fee; tel: 05-366 8198) was built by William Kellie-Smith, a rubber plantation owner who made his fortune in Malaya. Smith brought in Tamil workers from southern India to build the house in 1915, which was meant to remind him of home. But he died while visiting Lisbon and his widow sold the estate, halting work on the dream house in 1926. His ghost is said to haunt the mansion. At a Hindu temple just down the road, Smith is commemorated amid a cluster of rooftop statues.

Historic river valley

For centuries before the tin boom, Sungai Perak provided the only access to the state's interior. The river valley stretches from the royal town of Kuala Kangsar,

Map on page 158

ɔ the coastal village of Beting Beras Basah, near the town of Bagan Datoh. The ɪain area of Malay settlement, this was also the scene of some of the most dra ɪatic events in Perak's history. Now good roads run along either side of the ɪanana tree-lined banks, through villages which were once the homes of the ɪate's greatest heroes.

Perak is the only state whose royal house can claim direct descent from the sul ɪns of Melaka. Throughout the valley, there are about 20 tombs of Perak's sul ɪns, all carefully marked and cared for by the villagers. Some of the graves have ɪecome *keramat* (shrines) visited by humble folk in search of blessings or favours. ɪ is also a tradition that a newly installed Sultan of Perak must pay his respects ɪ every shrine, travelling by boat, before he can truly be accepted as ruler.

Some of these graves can be found in one of the country's most important ɪites, which saw the first local uprising against British colonialists. Now a well ɪrganised tourism complex, **Pasir Salak** ❼ (open Sat–Thur 9am–4.30pm; ɪntrance fee; tel: 05-631 1462) was where the state's first British resident, James ɪirch, was assassinated in 1875 while bathing in the river. The local ringlead ɪrs, Dato' Sagar and Dato' Maharajalela were executed. Today, there are memo ɪials at the complex to both the British and local heroes.

The complex is a beautiful collection of original and reconstructed buildings ɪf historic value blended into a peaceful kampung. Of particular note is the ɪrchitecture, which has elements of Perak's *rumah kutai* (old houses) – two ɪriginals sit in the compound. The historical tunnel, which is also the informa ɪon centre, features a diorama giving a good overview of the country's history. ɪ resort to the left of the complex offers a Malay *kampung* (village) homestay ɪxperience, with river-view chalets and, for large groups, a traditional wel ɪoming ceremony performed by the *kampung* folk.

To get to Pasir Salak, which is 70 km (40 miles) ɪrom Ipoh, head south on the old trunk road towards ɪampung Gajah through Bota or Batu Gajah. The ɪourney there passes Bota Kanan, which has a ɪatchery for river terrapins, the *labu* (traditional ɪottery) area of Pulau Tiga, and fruit orchards, ɪarticularly of the pungent *durian*. There are also ɪany delightful villages in the area, where traditional ɪerak-style houses are still found.

ɪsland in the sun

ɪf you can't make it to the beaches of the peninsula's ɪast coast, **Pulau Pangkor** ❽, off the coast of Perak, ɪs pleasant. The well-signposted road there from Ipoh ɪoes through Sitiawan to Lumut, the principal base ɪor the Royal Malaysian Navy.

Pangkor is a smaller, less developed version of ɪangkawi, and is popular with locals and tourists. ɪublic holidays find it packed and prices doubled, but ɪff-peak, the taxi drivers play draughts, and the isle is ɪnveloped in a lovely lazy atmosphere.

There are many versions to the origin of the island's ɪame; one is that Pangkor derived from the Thai "pang ɪoh", meaning "beautiful island". Like so much of ɪalaysia, the isle's place names are legend-inspired. ʰhe northern **Pantai Puteri Dewi** (Beach of the Fairy ɪrincess) is named after a princess who flung herself

A Hindu shrine near Kellie's Castle, erected for the plantation workers has, among the figures of animals and gods, a man in a green suit and topee hat – could this be an image of the castle's architect, Kellie Smith?

BELOW: rock inscribed with the coat-of-arms of the Dutch East India Company in Pangkor.

TIP

Teluk Intan, the chief
town of Lower Perak,
has an unusual claim
to fame. The
century-old clock
tower has its own
Tower of Pisa-style tilt.

BELOW: salted fish
being sun-dried
in Pangkor.

off a cliff when she learned that her suitor had died in battle. However, for the Malaysian schoolchild, Pangkor is better known for the historic treaty signed there in 1874, granting the British entry into the Malay states for the first time. From Lumut, ferries run to the Pangkor jetty every 15 minutes from 6.30am–7pm. The fast ferry takes about 20 minutes, while the slower ones take twice as long. For more information, call the Lumut Tourist Services Centre at tel: 05-683 2400.

The beach resort stretch is on the western side of the island, and has great sunset views. The only means there from the jetty is by taxi-vans at government-fixed rates. However, the closest beach, **Pasir Bogak**, is only 20 minutes' walk away. The most established of the beaches, Pasir Bogak is by no means the prettiest, but it does make a good base from which to explore the island by rented bicycle or motorcycle. Cyclists should note, though, that the island is pretty hilly. Pasir Bogak has plenty of accommodation and places to eat.

North of Pasir Bogak is the prettier **Teluk Nipah**, packed with virtually identical backpacker accommodation. There are some souvenir shops and good Chinese seafood restaurants here. Don't be surprised to see a hornbill or two sitting on an electricity pole outside your resort. In the adjacent beach, **Coral Bay**, is a hawker centre. As with Teluk Nipah, the waters here are lovely, and great for snorkelling. Just before Teluk Nipah is **Teluk Ketapang**, where turtles sometimes come ashore to lay eggs.

Heading north again through rainforest, the road cuts inland at a narrow point of the island. The left branch goes to the upmarket Pangkor Island Beach Resort on the lovely Beach of the Beautiful Princess, more popularly called Golden Sands. There is a nine-hole golf course in the hotel's grounds. The beach and hotel facilities are open to day visitors for a fee.

Head out through more rainforest, and the lovely kampung-style Teluk Dalam Resort spreads out before you. Just before the road reaches the fishing villages on the east coast, there is a jungle trek to Pasir Bogak that climbs **Bukit Pangkor**, offering good views.

Tourists and traditions

Little has changed in the eastern villages of **Kampung Sungai Pinang Kecil** (better known as SPK, also a ferry stop) and **Kampung Telok Kechil**, with their quaint tiny wooden houses on stilts over the water. Despite tourism being well-established, the island's economy is dependent mainly on the sea. The villages are therefore alive with activity when the bright yellow boats leave and return from their night stints. To reach any of the jetties, just head right through the courtyard and what looks like someone's living room – ingeniously-converted warehouses! At SPK, drop in at the famous **Hai Sap Hei satay fish factory**, where sea produce is dried, packed and sold.

South of the island in the middle of a *kampung* sit the remains of a Dutch fort, **Kota Belanda**, built over 300 years ago in an attempt to control Perak's tin trade and to fight the tyranny of piracy in the Straits of Melaka. Reconstructed by the National Museum in 1973, features of the original building still survive such as the Dutch East India coat-of-arms chiselled on a boulder close to the fort. Later adventurers have added their own graffiti. On a large rock opposite the fort is the remains of a drawing of a tiger mauling a boy. The drawing has been crudely etched in and the child is believed to be the son of a Dutch dignitary who disappeared mysteriously in the forest.

Map on page 158

Smart resorts

Off the coast of Pasir Bogak is **Pulau Pangkor Laut**, a privately owned island with the exclusive patrons-only **Pangkor Laut Resort** (www.pangkorlaut resort.com). Apart from beachfront and hillside villas, the resort offers villas on stilts over the sea, as well as spa treatments and a full range of amenities. The resort also has its own ferry from Lumut. Pulau Pangkor Laut's most famous feature is Emerald Bay, a gorgeous beach with powdery white sand and clear waters.

Lumut is a well-developed jumping-off point for Pangkor, with tourist information, money-changers, car-parks, and food. It is busiest during the Pesta Laut (Sea Festival) in August, a popular local attraction. Pangkor can also be crowded at this time and during the Malaysian school and public holidays. Because Lumut sits on the Dinding River, it has no beach, but it does have some good accommodation, and is a quiet, pleasant getaway.

Often, locals don't even cross to Pangkor, but head for **Teluk Batik**, a public beach 5 km (3 miles) from Lumut packed with food stalls, seafront A-frame accommodation for backpackers, and classier hotels on the headland and inland. At **Teluk Rubiah**, several kilometres south, is another stretch of sandy beach.

Golden dome, royal town

Perak's royal capital, **Kuala Kangsar ❾**, is a lovely garden town about 35 km (20 miles) north of Ipoh across the Perak River. Within walking distance of the

BELOW: gorgeous Emerald Bay, Pangkor Laut

town's attractions is the quiet Government Rest House on Jalan Istana, which overlooks the river. It also has a charming little museum.

Follow Jalan Istana past the Old Residency to reach Bukit Chandan, where the huge golden dome of the century-old **Masjid Ubudiah** (Ubudiah Mosque) gleams. Its striking and symmetrical domes and minarets make it one of the most photographed Muslim buildings in the country; if it is reminiscent of Kuala Lumpur's Moorish architecture, it is because it had the same architect.

Beyond the mosque, the road circles the Sultan of Perak's palace, the Saracenic style **Istana Iskandariah**. Next to it is the smaller but more dignified and charming **Istana Kenangan** (tel: 05-776 5500; open daily 9am–5pm; free). Its name translates as the Palace of Memories and the original construction was in accordance with Malay tradition, without a single nail or architectural plans. The building, a beautiful example of Perak architecture, is now a **royal museum** with an interesting collection of mementos and photographs of the Perak royal family. All displays are in Bahasa Malaysia, although guided tours are sometimes available.

The **Sultan Azlan Shah Gallery** (open Tues–Sun 10am–5pm; entrance fee; tel 05-777 5362) is nearby on Jalan Istana. Housed in Istana Hulu, a former palace built in 1903 in Art Deco style, the gallery pays tribute to the current sultan of Perak, Sultan Azlan Shah, with an exhibition of his personal effects and achievements.

Kuala Kangsar is also home to one of the pioneer batch of rubber trees that arrived here in the 1870s as seeds from Brazil and eventually took over the country. One of these first trees is found near the agricultural office in town. Though some plantation owners have switched to oil palm because of higher revenues, others are cashing in on rubberwood, an important new commodity for Malaysia's booming furniture industry.

BELOW:
Istana Kenangan
in Kuala Kangsar.

Close by is the **Malay College Kuala Kangsar** (MCKK). Founded in 1904 as residential school for the sons of the Malay aristocracy, it is now the seedbed or a good cross-section of Malaysia's political establishment.

On the outskirts of Kuala Kangsar, about 20 km (30 miles) along the poh–Enggor road, is the pottery district of **Sayong**, also once the home of sulans. Turn off at the bridge and turn left again to get to Kampung Kepala Benang, the original potter's village, and you will be greeted by scores of vases, shtrays and ornaments drying in the sun all along this dirt road. The most amous of the traditional designs is the black *labu*, gourd-shaped water pitchrs with broad bases and tall narrow spouts that keep cold water really cold.

Waterfall haven

from the highlands of the Main Range spring the waters of Sungai Perak, the econd-largest river in the peninsula. The river's flow is controlled by Malaysia's argest dam, 150 km (95 miles) upstream from Kuala Kangsar on the Temengor River tributary. Once a "black area", where armed forces fought the comunists, the region is still largely covered by thick mountainous jungle, and orms the northernmost part of the wildlife corridor stretching through Taman egara and Endau-Rompin. It has one of the best remaining populations of arge mammals in the country, including endangered species such as the tiger, umatran rhino and Malayan bear.

Cutting through the area is the spectacular East-West Highway to Kota Bharu, robably the only public place you'd see a road sign warning of elephants rossing. The road bypasses the picturesque **Empangan Temenggor** ⑩ Temenggor Dam), covering 15,200 hectares (37,560 acres), where there is a esort and houseboats for fishermen.

The jungles of Temenggor south of the highway are lowly opening up to nature enthusiasts due to the ttention brought to it by the Malaysian Nature Sociey (MNS). North of Temenggor across the highway the lush, mountainous **Royal Belum Forest**, a state ark. Access to Belum is still restricted, and a permit, hich takes 2–3 weeks to process, is required from e Perak State Park Corporation (tel: 05-791 4543).

Temenggor is dotted with numerous beautiful towring waterfalls accessible through steep, rugged terin across swift rivers, on ridges used by the Orang sli to collect rattan, that follow trails left by animals uch as deer or elephants. Among the area's popular ites are the seven-step thundering **Kerteh Waterfall**, here the lucky could catch sight of the giant Raffleia bloom, and the eight-step **Kelaweh Waterfall**, ith a lovely campsite at its spray-misted base.

Animals are difficult to spot, but there are plenty of resh hoof-prints and droppings on the ground and law-marks on trees. Trails are flanked by tall hill ipterocarp trees, medicinal plants and shrubs underoot, and of course, the thorny rattan that grabs at leeves and flesh. The leech-phobic would do well to tay away. The dryer months are traditionally in the rst half of the year, but "dry" is a relative term here.

Tour guides arrange entry permits but the District ffice might sometimes require a meeting with for-

Map on page 158

Sayong is well known as a centre for these characteristic gourd-shaped pottery.

BELOW: Temenggor is dotted with pretty waterfalls like this.

eigners. All groups are guided by the Orang Asli, who comprise the peaceabl and friendly Temiar and Jahai peoples, and a tour usually includes a night at thei thatched hut villages and a little *bersewang* (traditional dance) performance

The jumping-off point to Temenggor is **Grik**, one and a half hour's driv from Kuala Kangsar on a scenic and winding road. Serenely shrouded in mis in the early morning, the town has basic accommodation, including a govern ment resthouse, and lots of eateries, though serving local food only. During th communist warfare years, Grik was the compulsory check-in point for the day time-use only East-West Highway.

Town of everlasting peace

South of Grik is **Taiping** ⓫, the former state capital. The town with the heav iest rainfall in the peninsula has one of its loveliest names: "everlasting peace in Chinese. The name derives from the ending of the bloody struggles betwee rival Chinese mining factions in Larut after the Treaty of Pangkor was signed

The beautiful **Lake Gardens** (Taman Tasik), fringed by old raintrees, wer established at an abandoned tin mine on the edge of the town in the 1890s, lon before the word ecology was in use. In the grounds is a nine-hole golf course an the rustic 50-hectare (120-acre) **Taiping Zoo & Night Safari** (open dail 8.30am–6pm and 8–11pm; entrance fee; tel: 05-807 2057; www.zootaiping gov.my). A road leads to Bukit Larut (Maxwell Hill), Malaysia's oldest hi station (*see Hill Stations, page 159*).

The entrance to the gardens is marked by a number of architectural gem including the colonial town hall and the government offices. The **Pera Museum**, or Muzium Perak (open daily 9am–5pm except Fri noon–2.45pm

There is so much rain in Taiping that its residents place bets on what time it will fall. The bookie's office is a downtown hawker centre with a zinc roof and a digital clock put in by the punters.

BELOW: the Lake Gardens of Taiping.

ee; tel: 05-807 2057; www.jmm.gov.my), housed in a venerable Victorian
uilding, is the oldest in the country. Its collections include excellent natural
istory, ceramic and ethnology displays. The **Ling Nam Temple** is the oldest
hinese temple in Perak, and within it there is a model of a boat dedicated to the
hinese emperor who built the first canal in China.

1angrove magic

aiping was also the terminus for the country's first railway line, – now disused
which ended in Kuala Sepetang (Port Weld) on the coast. The road there
asses the old fort of **Kota Ngah Ibrahim**, named after the Malay territorial
ief of Larut who grew rich through the tin trade, but was unable to control the
rbulent Chinese factions producing the wealth.

The road also leads to the 40,000-hectare (98,900-acre) **Matang Mangrove**
orest (Hutan Baleau Matang), which has a park (open daily 8am–7pm; free;
l: 05-858 1762) with a boardwalk going through a sustainably managed man-
ove forest, which has been harvested for charcoal for nearly 100 years. The
aditional charcoal kilns make an interesting visit as do the fishing villages, but
u might need to find a guide for this. Enquire at Taiping.

A portion of the mangrove swamp further north near Bagan Serai is the 8,200-
ctare (20,260-acre) **Kuala Gula Bird Sanctuary**, where many rare species
ed and nest. Between August and December, migratory birds stop here en
ute south to Australia. The sanctuary is also home to otters, monkeys, and
e ridge-back dolphin. There is limited and basic accommodation here. For
formation and bookings, contact the Wildlife Department (tel: 05-243 6645)
the Kuala Gula Conservation Centre (tel: 05-890 2207). ❑

*Despite its name,
Kuala Gula Bird
Sanctuary is also
home to monkeys and
other small animals.*

BELOW: gnarled
buttress roots of
the fig tree.

HE PERAK MAN

he "Perak Man" is the peninsula's oldest skeleton,
dating from 11,000 years ago. He was discovered
ried in a cave in the Lenggong vicinity near Grik together
th remnants of burial paraphernalia such as stone tools,
ellfish and meat offerings, by prominent archaeologist
Zuraina Majid, who had also uncovered the country's
dest stone tools nearby, potentially dating back 100,000
ars. The "Perak Man" is thought to be an ancestor of the
grito Orang Asli people, a small hunter-gatherer tribe
garded as the oldest inhabitants in the peninsula.

The Lenggong stone tools in Kota Tampan were also
scovered intact. Anvils, stone hammers and tools in
rious stages of being made – complete with flakes and
ips – suggest that the site was a tool factory. It was
andoned all those years ago when a volcanic eruption
ewed clouds of ash that buried everything – the same
uption that created Lake Toba in Sumatra. Stone tool
ctories have also been excavated in Tingkayu, Sabah,
d Kubang Pasu, Kedah.

The "Perak Man" skeleton and the stone implements
e exhibited in the Lenggong Archaeological Museum
en daily 9am–5pm except Fri 12.15–2.45pm; free; tel:
-767 9700/9963; www.jmm.gov.my) in Kota Tampan.

CHICK BLINDS: OLD FASHIONED URBAN ART

Malaysian streets are always vivid and colourful, but when shopkeepers lower their chick blinds, the street fronts take on a whole new look

Made of split bamboo or thin wooden rods laced with twine, these sun blinds, known as *bidai* in Malay, serve a dual purpose.

Not only do they shade the colonnaded verandah in front of the shop, known as the "five-foot-way"; they also provide the shopkeeper with the perfect canvas to advertise his goods and services, giving every street a distinct and vibrant character.

With the advent of modern, Western-style shopping malls, some pundits have predicted the demise of the shophouse, and with it the chick blind. This may be true in some Malaysian cities, but in most smaller towns, rows of traditional shophouses prevail and their useful and colourful awnings are still prolific, and as popular as ever.

SIX CENTURIES OF HISTORY

Chick blinds have a long and colourful history. When the notorious Mongol leader Tamerlane and his "Golden Horde" sacked the Indian city of Delhi in 1398, it was noted that the tent openings of the much-feared conquerors were covered with blinds made of thin wands lined with rose-coloured silk. Indeed, the name is thought to derive from the Mongol word *tchik*.

Malaysia's chick blinds first appeared on the front of colonial bungalows in the 19th century, and were most probably introduced as a tropical architectural element from British India. Traditionally, the blinds were painted in black and white stripes, and lined with navy-blue muslin, which is the preferred backing fabric on urban chick blinds even today.

▷ **SARONGS FOR SALE**
In Kuala Terengganu, a Malay woman and child leave a shop through the "door" of its chick blind, which advertises "Rajah Brand" men's sarongs.

△ **FUNKY ROLEX**
The world's best-known watches honour a jewellery shop's blind in Taiping, Perak, a town where streets of traditional shophouses still survive.

△ **NOON GLARE**
Hawkers sell tropical *duku* fruit in front of a wall of chick blinds in the main street of Bagan Serai, Perak.

◁ **SPIDER SARONGS**
Men's *pelikat* sarongs come in a variety of brands, including *Chop Laba Laba*, or "Spider Brand".

"FIVE-FOOT-WAY" SHOPS

The long colonnaded space, known as the "five-foot-way", or *kaki lima* in Malay, which fronts all traditional rows of shophouses is said to have originated in a directive by Sir Stamford Raffles, founder of Singapore.

Raffles decreed that all urban buildings should have "a verandah of a certain depth, open to all sides as a continuous and open passage on each side of the street", so people could walk comfortably along, sheltered from the fierce heat of an equatorial sun or a monsoon downpour. However, it wasn't long before hawkers began exploiting these shaded spaces and the "five-foot-way" shop came into being.

Some are merely extensions of the shops behind, or additional display spaces for already crammed premises, but others are individual, cupboard-sized establishments often known as Mamak shops, because they are run by Indian-Muslim Malaysians, colloquially known as Mamak. These miniature shops still survive in many of Malaysia's rural towns.

STOMACH PILLS
"Chi-Kit" pills, a Chinese remedy for stomach ailments, are advertised in this chick blind at a Taiping Chinese pharmacy.

ANONYMOUS ART
In Taiping, songbirds in bamboo cages share hanging space with a chick blind advertising a popular brand of milk powder.

▷ **BRIDAL TAILOR**
In Kuala Kangsar, Perak, a tailor advertises his speciality – Western-style wedding attire. Some artworks, like this one here, are painted to the client's specification; others, like those advertising brand-name goods, recur in many towns.

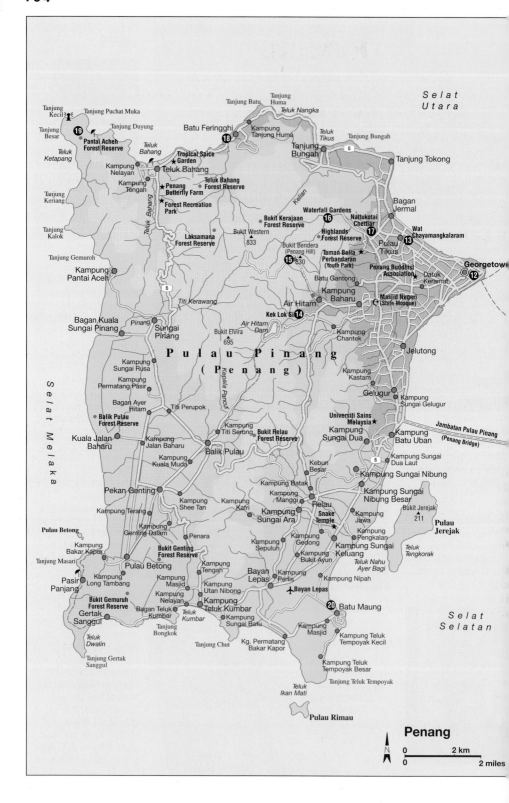

Tanjung
Kecil
1 **19**
Tanjung Puchat Muka
Tanjung Besar
Pantai Acheh
Forest Reserve
Teluk Ketapang
Teluk Bahang
Kampung Nelayan
Tanjung Keriang
Kampung Tengah
Tanjung Kalok
Tanjung Gemuroh
Kampung Pantai Aceh
Tanjung Duyung
Tanjung Batu
Tanjung Huma
Teluk Nangka
Batu Feringghi
18 Kampung Tanjung Huma
Teluk Tikus
Tanjung Bungah
Tanjung Bungah
Tanjung Tokong
Teluk Bahang
Tropical Spice Garden
Teluk Bahang
Penang Butterfly Farm
Teluk Bahang Forest Reserve
Forest Recreation Park
Laksamana Forest Reserve
Bukit Western
833
Bukit Kerajaan Forest Reserve
16 Waterfall Gardens
Highlands Forest Reserve
Nattukotai Chettiar
17
Wat Chayamangkalaram
13
Bagan Jermal
Pulau Tikus
Georgetown
12
Datuk Keramat
Bukit Bendera (Penang Hill)
15 830
Taman Belia Perbandaran (Youth Park)
Penang Buddhist Association
Bukit Elvira 695
Air Hitam Dam
Kek Lok Si **14**
Batu Gantong
Masjid Negeri (State Mosque)
Kampung Baharu
Kampung Chantek
P u l a u   P i n a n g
(P e n a n g)
Kampung Kastam
Jelutong
Bagan Kuala Sungai Pinang
Pinang
Sungai Pinang
Kampung Sungai Rusa
Kampung Permatang Pasir
Bagan Ayer Hitam
Balik Pulau Forest Reserve
Kuala Jalan Baharu
Kampung Jalan Baharu
Titi Perupok
Kampung Kuala Muda
Kampung Titi Serong
Balik Pulau
Bukit Relau Forest Reserve
Kebun Besar
Geluger
Kampung Sungai Geluger
Universiti Sains Malaysia
Kampung Sungai Dua
Kampung Batu Uban
Jambatan Pulau Pinang (Penang Bridge)
Kampung Sungai Dua Laut
Kampung Sungai Nibung
Pekan Genting
Kampung Shee Tan
Kampung Terang
Kampung Genting Dalam
Penara
Kampung Kafri
Kampung Batak
Kampung Manggol
Relau
Kampung Sungai Ara
Snake Temple
Kampung Sungai Nibung Besar
Bukit Jerejak 211
Pulau Jerejak
Kampung Jawa
Kampung Pengkalan
Kampung Sungai Keluang
Teluk Tengkorak
Pulau Betong
Kampung Bakar Kapor
Tanjung Masari
Pasir Panjang
Kampung Long Tambang
Bukit Genting Forest Reserve
Pulau Betong
Kampung Tengah
Kampung Sepuluh
Kampung Gedong
Kampung Bukit Ayun
Teluk Nahu Ayer Bagi
Bukit Gemuruh Forest Reserve
Gertak Sanggul
Kampung Nelayan
Bagan Teluk Kumbar
Teluk Dwalin
Kampung Masjid
Kampung Teluk Kumbar
Teluk Kumbar
Tanjung Bongkok
Bayan Lepas
Kampung Perlis
Kampung Utan Nibong
Kampung Sungai Batu
Kampung Nipah
Bayan Lepas
20 Batu Maung
Kampung Masjid
Tanjung Chut
Kg. Permatang Bakar Kapor
Kampung Teluk Tempoyak Kecil
Kampung Teluk Tempoyak Besar
Tanjung Teluk Tempoyak
Tanjung Gertak Sanggul
Teluk Ikan Mati
Pulau Rimau

S e l a t
U t a r a

S e l a t
M e l a k a

Kepala Pancur

Kelian

S e l a t
S e l a t a n

Penang

N
0   2 km
0   2 miles

PENANG

Map on page 184

A rich heritage and a mystic, spiritual core – as well as fine beaches and wonderful food – make the island state of Penang a perennial favourite among visitors to Malaysia

Temples shrouded in incense smoke and palm-fringed beaches have been attracting curious visitors to **Penang** for several hundred years. One of the most famous islands in Asia, Penang is also perhaps the best-known tourist destination in Malaysia.

Throughout history, Penang has changed names like the seasons. Early Malays called it Pulau Ka Satu, or Single Island. Later it appeared on sailing charts as Pulau Pinang, or Island of the Betel Nut Palm. The British renamed it Prince of Wales' Island, and finally, with Malaysia's independence, it became Pulau Pinang once again. But romance, sustained by tourist brochure copywriters, is hard to dispel: Penang is also the Pearl of the Orient, Gateway to the East, and the Isle of Temples.

The trade

From the mainland, the 7-km (4-mile) **Penang Bridge** (Jambatan Pulau Pinang) offers exhilarating views of the harbour and the jagged skyline of condominiums and office blocks set against the hilly centre.

A very different aspect would have greeted English trader and adventurer Captain Francis Light in the 18th century, but he saw the advantages of having the island – then under Kedah – as a station for Britain's East India Company. Light saw Penang as a base to replenish company ships on their long haul to China in the flourishing tea and opium trade, and serve as a headquarters to further British interests in Southeast Asia.

Light, fluent in Thai and Malay, and a familiar figure in the Kedah court, persuaded the sultan to trade Penang for British protection against threatening Thai and Bugis enemies. But the British did not honour the agreement, and going to war only saw Kedah lose more land to the Empire – this time on the mainland, named Seberang Prai by the Malays.

To encourage trade and commerce, the British made the island state a free port; no taxes were levied on either imports or exports. This strategy worked and in eight years, the population increased to 8,000, comprising many immigrant races – Chinese, Indians and Bugis, among others.

Today, the state of Pulau Pinang or Penang as everyone calls it, comprises Seberang Prai (or Butterworth as it was formerly known) on the mainland and Penang island, linked by both the bridge and ferry services. The ferries carry both passengers and vehicles; ferrying your car over costs the same as the bridge toll and you pay at the Seberang Prai side. The ferry terminus at the Seberang Prai is linked to bus, taxi and railway stations – the transport goes all the way to Thailand.

BELOW: travelling salesman in Georgetown.

The clock tower opposite Fort Cornwallis in Georgetown was a gift from a Chinese millionaire to celebrate Queen Victoria's Diamond Jubilee in 1897.

Different faces

Like most cities of Asia that juxtapose the glass and concrete of the new with the tile and teak of the old, Penang has several dimensions. You can arrive by ferry, be transported by trishaw to a Chinese hotel on Lebuh Chulia in the heart of Chinatown, eat at the outdoor food stalls, visit the waterfront villages, and after two weeks, leave Penang having never stepped into anything built after World War II. But another visitor can have cocktails at the poolside overlooking the sea while getting a golden tan, dine in a gourmet restaurant, and never brush shoulders with a Chowrasta Market butcher in town.

Vibrant **Georgetown** ⓬ is the heart of Penang. Named by the British after King George III, it is unmistakably Chinese, its narrow streets congested with pedestrians, vehicles, signboards and temples. The best way to experience it is on foot, or you could hire a trishaw for the day – but bargain first. By trishaw, the city passes by in a kaleidoscope of changing colours, and even in the rain, the driver zips you into a plastic covering, and pedals slowly through the wet streets. At night, there is a special romance about riding in the glow of neon signs and blinking lights.

An excellent route that takes in the main sights is the signposted Heritage Trail – ask for a map from any of the travel agencies near the **Clock Tower** Ⓐ. The trail starts at **Fort Cornwallis** Ⓑ (Kota Cornwallis), the place from which probably the most costly cannon ball in history was shot. When Francis Light was clearing land for his settlement, the thick undergrowth proved arduous work for the sepoys, Indians employed as soldiers by the British and other European powers. To motivate the disgruntled sepoys, Light loaded a cannon with silver dollars and fired it into the jungle – this prompted them all to work to retrieve the coins; and before long the land was cleared and the first camp established.

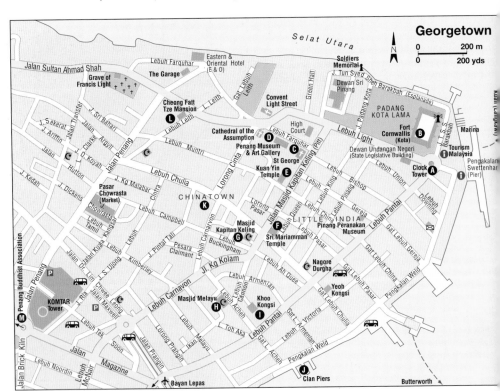

Magical cannon

Originally a wooden structure, Fort Cornwallis was rebuilt with convict labour in the early 1800s. Today, the old fort's precincts have been converted into a public park and playground. Its ramparts are still guarded by old cannon, the most venerable and famous of which is Seri Rambai, presented by the Dutch to the Sultan of Johor in 1606. Seven years later, it was captured by the Achehnese and taken to Acheh, where it remained for almost 200 years. The cannon was then sent to Kuala Selangor in the quest of a Bugis alliance. After the British bombarded Kuala Selangor in 1871, the cannon was brought to Penang. Like most ancient cannon, Seri Rambai is attributed with magical powers; it is believed that women desiring children will have their wish fulfilled if they place flowers in the cannon's barrel and offer prayers.

Next to Fort Cornwallis lies the *padang* (town green) and the Esplanade (Jalan Tun Syed Sheh Barakbah). The handsome 19th-century colonial **State Legislative Building** (Dewan Undangan Negeri) stands at one end of the Padang; at the other, near the entrance to Fort Cornwallis, traffic circles the Clock Tower, which was presented to Penang by a rich Chinese *towkay* (businessman), Cheah Chin Gok, in commemoration of Queen Victoria's Diamond Jubilee. The dignified **St George's Church** ◉, built in 1818 on nearby Lebuh Farquhar, is the oldest Anglican church in Southeast Asia. Francis Light lies buried in the frangipani-shaded cemetery down the road, along with other notables of old Penang, many of whom succumbed early in life to the rigours of the tropics.

At the **Penang State Museum and Art Gallery** ◉ (open Sat–Thur 9am–5pm; free; tel: 04-261 3144) on the same side of the street as St George's Church, visitors can peer into a Chinese bridal chamber created in the lavish style of the 19th

Maps:
Area 184
City 186

TIP

Public buses cover the whole the island but follow no timetable. Bus terminals are at Lebuh Victoria and Jalan Dr Lim Chwee Leong. Fares are low and you can go around the island in one day with an early start.

BELOW: colonial State Legislative Building.

Dragon figurine at Penang's Kuan Yin Temple, dedicated to the Buddhist Goddess of Mercy.

century, or see a bejewelled *keris*, the dagger Malays used for protection. The gallery displays work by local artists, including batik, oils, graphics and Chinese ink drawings. Further east along Lebuh Farquhar stands Georgetown's oldest hotel, the **E&O Hotel** (www.e-o-hotel.com), which once played host to luminaries such as Rita Hayworth and Somerset Maugham. Built in 1887 by the Armenian Sarkies brothers, the property is one of Asia's grandest hotels.

Houses of worship

Three of the state's oldest worship houses are in the Jalan Masjid Kapitan Keling area. Along that road is Penang's oldest Buddhist temple, the **Kuan Yin Temple** ❸ (open daily), which is the most humbel and crowded. The temple belongs to the people in the street – the noodle hawkers, trishaw riders, and workers building cupboards, repairing bicycles or selling sundry goods. A Buddhist deity who refused to enter Nirvana so long as there was injustice on earth, Kuan Yin typically personifies mercy. She is ever-present on Chinese altars, whether Taoist, Buddhist or Confucian, and is perhaps the most beloved divinity.

Jalan Masjid Kapitan Keling leads into the tiny **Little India** where saris, garlands, and jewellery deck the stores, and the spicy scent of curry wafts through the air. Indian merchants arrived in Penang with the British, as did Indian convicts, who built the first roads and filled in the swamps on which the town now stands. Assimilated into local society, it is not surprising to find their descendants fluent in Tamil as well as in Bahasa Malaysia, English and some Hokkien.

In Lebuh Queen sits the **Sri Mariamman Temple** ❹ (open daily), which was built in 1883 and boasts an ornate South Indian gateway. However, many Indians who came to Penang were Muslim, and the state has a large Indian-Muslim population, whose delicious *nasi kandar* rice and scorching-hot curry dishes are relished by all Malaysians. Their oldest place of worship, and the state's oldest mosque is on Jalan Masjid Kapitan Keling. The Moorish-style mosque, **Masjid Kapitan Keling** ❺ (open daily), which dates from 1800, is named after the Indian-Muslim merchant headman, or *Kapitan Keling*, Caudeer Mohudeen. Head into Lebuh Armenian, which is flanked by early 19th-century shophouses originally belonging to Malays and Sumatrans. **No. 120 Lebuh Armenian** was the Penang headquarters of the Tongmenghui, the political party of the Chinese leader Dr Sun Yat-sen. It was set up in 1910, a year before the Manchu rule was toppled in China. An octagonal minaret at the end of the road marks the entrance to the **Masjid Melayu** ❻ (open daily), also known as Acheen Street Mosque, which is a mixture of Egyptian and Javanese styles.

Narrow alleyways off the bustling roads lead to quiet rows of Chinese homes with carved lintels and elaborate doorways. The mansion on Gat Lebuh Gereja (Church Street) built by millionaire Chung Keng Kwee is now the **Pinang Peranakan Museum** (open daily 9am–6pm; entrance fee; tel: 04-264 2929). Inside the temple is a lifelike bronze statue of Chung in the robes of a Chinese mandarin. Chung made his fortune from the tin mines in Larut, Perak, and was one of the leaders of the Chinese factions in the Larut Wars of the 1860s.

King of the clanhouses

In Georgetown, many Chinese guild halls honour both ancestors and outstanding members. Among these are the Yap Kongsi on Lebuh Armenian and the Cheah Kongsi on Gat Lebuh Armenian.

The most elaborate clanhouse is the **Khoo Kongsi** ❶ (open daily 9am–5pm; entrance fee; tel: 04-261 4609; www.khookongsi.com.my) at the junction of Jalan Masjid Kapitan Keling and Lebuh Acheh. Designed to capture the splendour of an imperial palace, it has a seven-tiered pavilion, "dragon" pillars and hand-painted walls engraved with the Khoo rose emblem. The original design was so ambitious that conservative Khoo clansmen cautioned against it, lest the emperor of China be offended. After eight years, the building was completed in 1902; but on the first night after it was finished, the roof mysteriously caught fire. Clan members interpreted this as a sign that even the deities considered the Khoo Kongsi too palatial for a clan house. The Khoos rebuilt it on a more modest scale. Following a massive renovation by 16 Chinese artisans using traditional Chinese materials, the clanhouse has been restored to its former splendour.

At Georgetown's waterfront near the ferry terminus, entire villages belong to clans. These are the **Clan Piers** ❷, comprising wooden houses perched on stilts over the sea, which in the pre-condominium era, were the most outstanding feature to greet visitors who travelled to the island by ferry. Each of the six villages has its own temple, and houses just one clan, except for one "mixed" village. Therefore, on Lim's Pier, you'll find only members of the Lim family, while Tan's Pier is the sole property of the Tan clan. Nearly all but the Chews have abandoned the fishing trade, but all the houses are occupied, and no one minds if a visitor strolls along the plankwalks.

Map on page 186

Kongsi are Chinese associations, each made up of individuals from the same dialect group and from the same part of China. They look after kin in Penang, hold ancestral records and have altars for ancestral worship.

BELOW: the ornate entrance of a Georgetown clanhouse.

THE CHINESE CLANHOUSES

Chinese immigrants arriving in Malaysia in the 19th century fell under the protection and control of clan associations, whose functions were not unlike those of medieval European guilds: to promote the interests of their members and provide help to those in distress. You'll find the ancestral halls or *kongsi* of associations such as the Khoo, Ong, Tan and Chung clans scattered all over Georgetown.

Many of these clan houses are beautiful pieces of traditional Chinese architecture and house important antiques and artwork. But there is concern about their future, as well as the shophouses in their vicinity, due to the abolition of the Rent Control Act in 2000. The Act limits the rent that owners can charge tenants, but it is feared that its abolition will see owners looking to maximise profits by re-developing the land, or selling it off for money-raking high-rises. The non-profit Penang Heritage Trust (www.pht.org.my) is lobbying hard to save these important buildings.

At the community level, clans are taking steps to preserve their heritage. The Khoos, for instance, owners of the Khoo Kongsi clan house (*see above*) have turned the buildings around their *kongsi* into a cultural and heritage village, with souvenir and retail shops and budget accommodation.

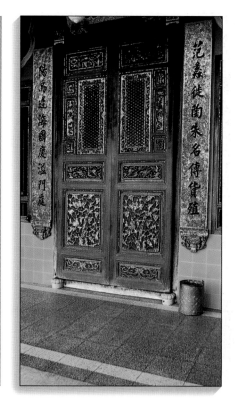

Wooden clogs like these are more charming as wall hangings than foot wear. Find them in Penang's Chinatown.

BELOW: rooftop patterns of Chinatown.
RIGHT: Chinese opera in action.

Backpacker alley

The hotch-potch of streets and alleys of **Chinatown** Ⓚ are home to over 8,000 examples of 19th-century and early 20th-century buildings. At dawn, goods are unloaded at century-old shophouses, the lorries blocking half the already-narrow road. In the coffee shops, old men exchange daily news over cups of coffee with bread and *kaya* (coconut jam). For shopaholics, there are antiques and curios galore, as well as more contemporary items such as leather goods and batik. Second-hand bookstores are treasure-troves of old tomes, as well as the latest paperback bestsellers left behind by backpackers in Lebuh Chulia.

The tiny old Chinese hotels have held out against time, and are some of the best places to soak up Chinatown's old-world atmosphere. You may catch sight of a funeral procession through the streets, complete with drums and gongs and mourners. In the afternoon, a lion dance may be staged to bring luck to a new sundry goods shop – a noisy affair with more drums and gongs.

The hotels are supported by cafés offering Western food, tours, bicycles for hire and money-changers. The backpacker row extends to Lebuh Leith, on which enterprising entrepreneurs have turned a row of heritage buildings into trendy restaurants and pubs. Here also is the carefully restored late 19th-century **Cheong Fatt Tze Mansion** Ⓛ, which has a unique blend of Eastern and Western architectural styles (guided tours daily 11am and 3pm; entrance fee; tel: 04-262 0006; www.cheongfatttzemansion.com). Originally built by craftsmen from China's Guangdong province, this grand courtyard house was sensitively restored and won a UNESCO Asia Pacific heritage award for conservation in 2000. The owner also operates a boutique hotel on the premises (*see Accommodation, page 360*).

There are lots of small and friendly pubs in Georgetown. Many are located in The Garage on Jalan Penang, and on Gurney Drive and Lebuh Leith. Some of these keep a "family album" of snapshots showing just about every traveller who has ever walked in and bought a drink. They provide jukeboxes for dancing, games machines for entertainment and barmaids for conversation.

Jalan Penang (better known as Penang Road), the old shopping area, ends in the towering air-conditioned KOMTAR shopping complex at the top of a bus station, which also houses a tourist information centre and the Tourism Malaysia office. Take a lift up its circular tower for a bird's eye view of the city (entrance fee).

Take a walk through **Pasar Chowrasta** (Chowrasta Market), between Jalan Chowrasta and Lebuh Tamil. A wet market with the customary wet market pong, it has a section facing Penang Road that offers the Penang specialities of local biscuits and preserved nutmeg and mango prepared in a wide variety of styles. On Lebuh Tamil is the row of *nasi kandar* (mixed curry rice) stalls whose food is reputed to be the best in the country.

Food is Penang's favourite export to the rest of the country. Here, hawker centres commandeer every corner, the most famous of which (and you pay the price for it) is on the seaside **Gurney Drive** stretch, open in the evenings. However, wander into the **Pulau Tikus** area behind Jalan Burma, and you pay far less for food that is perhaps twice as good. Pulau Tikus is also the heartland of the *Baba-Nyonya*, descendants of Chinese immigrants who married into and absorbed Malay culture, including wearing batik sarongs and the adoption of local spices and coconut milk in their unique style of cooking. Also known as Peranakan or Straits Chinese, these communities are predominant in the British Straits Settlements states of Penang, Melaka and Singapore.

Map on page 186

TIP

Along Jalan Penang and the streets off it are shops offering everything from batik souvenirs to leather goods to antiques and curios.

BELOW: *kacang puteh* or nuts vendor in Pulau Tikus market.

Temples of incense

The eve of Chinese New Year at the **Penang Buddhist Association**  (open daily) on Jalan Anson is a more formal affair compared to the mad rush of devotees at other temples. Association members busily arrange bright flowers, fruits and coloured cakes on a large, shiny table of blackwood imported from Canton. Enthroned on the high altars are six white marble statues of Lord Buddha and his disciples. Crystal chandeliers from Czechoslovakia hang overhead, and the walls are decorated with paintings depicting Buddha's path to enlightenment. A teenage girl patiently leads her dignified grandfather across the wide marble floor, where a seated congregation chants praises to Lord Buddha.

As temple bells tinkle, the chanting rises to usher in the new year. Outside the front door, beggars sit quietly chatting amongst themselves. They know benevolence is a precept of the Chinese New Year and they receive it passively.

Ordinarily, the large, luminous hallway that dominates the Chinese Buddhist Association is the most serene sanctuary in Penang. The building, completed in 1929, reflects the desire of a Buddhist priest who wanted to indoctrinate his followers with orthodox rites and ceremonies. Joss-stick hawkers or paper-money burners are not found here. Prayers are considered the essence of Buddhist worship, and the association cherishes the simplicity inherent in its Buddhist faith.

The variety of Buddhist worship in Penang is so striking it makes every temple a new experience. One can enter the gigantic meditation hall at **Wat Chayamangkalaram**  (open daily 6am–5.30pm) and find a workman polishing the left cheek of 32-metre (100-ft) long Reclining Buddha. The *wat*, on Lorong Burma, is a Thai Buddhist monastery. Gigantic *naga* serpents, mystical creatures that link earth to heaven, form the balustrades at the entrance,

Be prepared to get soaking wet if you visit Wat Chayamangkalaram in April, during the Thai Songkran festival. Mischief-makers hurl water-filled plastic bags on passers-by on the pretext of "purifying" them.

BELOW: the Thai-inspired Wat Chayamangkalaram.

while fierce-visaged giants tower over the doorways in the role of otherworldly bodyguards. Inside is an impressive gold-plated reclining Buddha, while the walls are covered with thousands of Buddha images.

Another form of Buddhist worship can be seen in the **Dharmmikarama Burmese Buddhist Temple** (open daily 5am–6pm) on the other side of the road. An 8.3-metre (27-ft) tall standing Buddha with a haughty yet serene expression is worshipped here. Another shrine is surrounded with a moat over which "heavenly" bridges fly. On either side are Buddha images. Little shops in the shaded walkways sell little pink and green lotus flower-shaped candles to worshippers, who leave the lighted candles reverentially in front of the shrines.

Maps:
Area 184
City 186

Inspired by a vision

Penang's loftiest temple sits on a hilltop at Air Itam, 6 km (4 miles) from the Buddhist Association. **Kek Lok Si ⑭** (open daily 9am–6pm), the largest Buddhist temple complex in Malaysia and one of the largest in the region, owes its existence to Beow Lean, a Chinese Buddhist priest from Fujian province in China who arrived in 1887 as the resident priest of the Kuan Yin Temple in Lebuh Pitt. Impressed by the religious fervour of Penang's Buddhists, he founded a monastery on a hilly site reminiscent of Fujian. A good time to visit is the Chinese New Year period in January/February, when the temple is beautifully adorned with hundreds of lanterns.

The main buildings were completed in 1904. The seven-tier great Pagoda of Ten Thousand Buddhas (entrance fee), erected in 1930, is dedicated to all manifestations of the Buddha, hence its name. Its walls are decorated with 10,000 alabaster and bronze Buddha images, and it is renowned for having three

Naga, or serpent guardian at Wat Chayamangkalaram.

BELOW: joss stick offerings at Kek Lok Si temple.

TIP

The sidewalk stalls on the steps leading up to Kek Lok Si are good spots for buying cheap souvenirs such as Buddhist paraphernalia, old coins and windchimes.

architectural styles: a Chinese base, a Thai middle section and a Burmese top.

The Kek Lok Si complex is split into three sections spread over Crane Hill. The three "Halls of the Great" honour Kuan Yin, Goddess of Mercy; the Laughing Buddha, who spreads prosperity and happiness; and Gautama Buddha, founder of the faith. It is here that the monks pass their hour in prayer. The Tower of Sacred Books on the topmost tier houses a library of Buddhist scriptures and Sutra, many of which were presented by the Qing dynasty emperor Guang Xu. An edict from the same emperor, cemented into a wall of this block, grants imperial approval to the establishment of the temple.

A 3-km (2-mile) road from Kek Lok Si winds its way up to the **Air Itam Dam** (open daily 6am–6pm), with an 18-hectare (45-acre) lake reflecting the lush green foliage of the surrounding jungle. The dam is popular with walkers and joggers in the early morning and late evening for its cool air and steep road.

Hill with a view

Jalan Air Itam also leads to **Bukit Bendera** (Penang Hill), established as a quiet getaway in 1897. This 830-metre (2,720-ft) high hill station was saved about 80 years later from large-scale commercialisation by public petition, a rare people-power victory. The best part of the experience is the 30-minute ride to the summit in the Swiss-modelled funicular railway (open daily Mon–Fri 6.30am– 9.30pm, Sat–Sun until 11.45pm; entrance fee). With lower temperatures, the summit makes for a lovely respite from the tropical heat, and provides good vantage for views of Penang island and the Straits of Melaka. On the hilltop, there are also gardens, a bird park (entrance fee), holiday bungalows and a tea kiosk where refreshments are available. Go on a walk on the 1.7-km (2.2-mile) long

BELOW: the funicular railway at Penang Hill.
RIGHT: the Kek Lok Si Temple.

Canopy Walkway (8.30am–5.30pm; free), a suspension bridge from which you can see the tops of trees and even chance upon small animals in the forest.

You can also hike up Penang Hill on any one of the three trails that start from the Waterfall Gardens , also known as the Penang Botanic Gardens (open daily 5am–8pm; free; tel: 04-227 0428), on Jalan Kebun Bunga. If you aren't so keen on the idea of a hot, sweaty trek, you'll enjoy strolling through the gardens. This mature and beautifully cultivated showcase of tropical plants is about 2 km (1 mile) from Pulau Tikus, with waterfalls that start over a hundred metres above the gardens and cascade through the greenery. On holidays, families round up relatives for a picnic lunch by the stream, while barefoot children romp on the rocks or play follow-the-tourist. Benches are scattered throughout the gardens and provide pleasant resting spots in the shade.

Nearby, atop a hill and reached only by a long flight of steps, is the Hindu temple of Nattukotai Chettiar (open daily). A good time to visit is 5–5.30pm, when a simple ceremony of bathing and unveiling the main statue takes place. Every January, this becomes the centre for the Hindu festival of penance, Thaipusam. After a period of fasting, devotees carry devotional *kavadi* structures made of metal, and pierce their flesh with skewers. Many consider the processions here more dramatic and interesting than the one in Selangor's Batu Caves. Certainly, more coconuts are smashed in Georgetown's streets, including by non-Hindus, who see no harm in amassing some good luck too.

Ferringhi beach

Penang's holiday beaches are in the north, from Tanjung Bungah to Batu Ferringhi and Teluk Bahang. The road up from Jalan Tanjung Tokong follows the curve of the land, twisting up and around a hill, or skirting the fringe of the sea. Rocky headlands divide the shoreline into small bays and coves, each with a different character and charm. The beaches are popular for swimming, sunbathing and aquatic sports.

The northern beaches are self-contained; there is little need for visitors to venture to town. Accommodation choices range from apartments for longer-stay guests to beachside places for backpackers, and a bus station, post office, clinic, grocery shops and souvenir outlets. At night, the naked bulbs and blaring music of a *pasar malam* (night market) add to the bustle. Car and bicycle hire is available, and most hotels have a free shuttle service to Georgetown; there are plenty of taxis too.

Activities are centred around Batu Ferringhi. This is where several famous luxury hotels are located, including Shangri-La's Rasa Sayang Resort & Spa (www.shangri-la.com) at the start of the stretch. However, small inns and motels are plentiful too, as well as accommodation offered by villagers. Likewise, the whole range of eateries can be found here, from air-conditioned steak and seafood restaurants to hawker stalls under winking fairy lights.

Yahong Art Gallery (open daily 9.30am–10pm; tel: 04-881 1251), at 58D Batu Ferringhi, has some of the finest arts, crafts and antiques of Malaysia and China. It is also the home of Chuah Thean Teng, the internationally acclaimed father of Malaysian batik art. His sons are

Watch out for pesky monkeys in Penang's Waterfall Gardens, some of which can be aggressive. Feeding them is discouraged but the notice is often disregarded.

BELOW: Batu Ferringhi beach.

Cocoa pods are cultivated in Penang. Look out for the bright orange papaya-like fruits.

all talented artists too, and their works are on display and for sale in the gallery.

Some 6 km (4 miles) further down the coast is the fine **Teluk Bahang** beach. En route you'll find the **Tropical Spice Garden** (open daily 9am–6pm; entrance fee; tel: 04-881 1797; www.tropicalspicegarden.com), a quiet haven of flora and foliage set on a hill slope with a tea house and souvenirs galore.

On Jalan Teluk Bahang, there are souvenir shops and a batik factory. Further along is the **Penang Butterfly Farm** (open daily 9am–5.30pm; entrance fee; tel: 04-885 1253; www.butterfly-insect.com), where large varieties of butterflies and unusual insects are bred. A couple of minutes down the road are the **Forest Recreation Park and Museum** (open daily 9am–5pm; entrance fee), which is good for a picnic, and the **Tropical Fruit Farm** (open daily 8.30am– 6pm; entrance fee; tel: 04-866 5168; www.tropicalfruits.com.my). For more trekking and resort-free beaches, head towards the northwestern tip of the island to the Penang National Park at **Pantai Aceh Forest Reserve** ⑲ (open daily 8.30am–6.30pm; free), where there are trails to Muka Head, a favourite boy-scout camping-spot. At the fishing village at the entrance of the forest reserve, you can arrange for a boat to pick you up. The road to Balik Pulau goes down the west coast and around the island. Here, a different Penang begins: an agrarian world, quiet, peaceful and thinly populated.

Round the island

BELOW:
Giant moth, Penang Butterfly Farm.

As much as the port is Chinese, so is the countryside Malay. The winding and sometimes mountainous round-island road runs for 74 km (46 miles), a journey you can cover in air-conditioned buses with guides (book through hotels and tour agencies) or rented chauffeured cars with or without guides.

The road through the rolling hills offers striking views of the island dropping to the sea far below. Dense, damp jungles are interspersed with the plantations of pepper, clove and nutmeg that lured Arab, Spanish, Portuguese and other Western traders to this part of the world long ago. When in season, nets are spread out below the durian trees in the orchards, to prevent damage to the fruit, which drops when ripe. Visitors throng the temporary roadside stalls, savouring the pungent flesh or haggling over prices.

At Titi Kerawang, there are waterfalls and a serene view of the Indian Ocean. The natural freshwater pool is filled from the waterfalls, and is suitable for bathing, although a big water pipeline mars the scenery.

Kampungs and footprints

As you head south, the scenery gives way to flat land. Several small roads branch off to the coast, usually the commercial link between a fishing village and the trunk road. It was in small villages such as these that the few Malays lived when Francis Light established the first settlement. Although updated with bricks, the *kampung* (village) houses look much the same today as they did 100 years ago. If you have your own transport, it is worthwhile turning off into the coconut tree-lined paths to explore a village. Malays are proud of their homes, and many have pretty courtyards planted with flowers and fruit trees. The smiles are inevitably warm, with locals always ready to make your acquaintance.

As you head to the east coast, bustling urbanity starts to rear its head. Turn off to **Batu Maung** ⑳, about 3 km (2 miles) from the Bayan Lepas Airport, and you will reach a shrine built around an 85-cm (33-inch) footprint in stone, believed to be that of Admiral Cheng Ho, the Chinese Columbus. The well-kept shrine sits in

Map on page 184

Admiral Cheng Ho's "footprint" appears in the myths of other cultures as well. Malay folklore has it as the giant Gedembai's footprint, while Indians believe it belongs to Hanuman, the great monkey god.

BELOW: Malay *kampung* house.

Map on page 184

At the Snake Temple, pit vipers are venerated by the Chinese because of their kinship to the mythical dragons of Chinese folklore.

BELOW: Cheng Ho's footprint, Batu Maung.
RIGHT: sunset at Batu Ferringhi.

a beautiful Chinese garden that overlooks the jetty and fishing boats of the village.

It is believed that Cheng Ho called at this spot on one of his seven voyages to Southeast Asia. On Pulau Langkawi, 96 km (60 miles) further north, is a similar footprint. The two are believed to be a pair, and anyone who lights incense sticks and places them in the urns at the shrine will enjoy good luck and great fortune.

There are a couple of large restaurants here which are famous for their seafood. Walk down from the shrine past the eatery next door, and you'll come to a garden of incongruous statues, ranging from mythical Indian and Chinese gods, to Snow White and the Seven Dwarfs, and the Statue of Liberty. The garden is neglected, which is sad, for the choice and juxtapositioning of these figures is an ironically accurate summary of Malaysian life.

Silicon and sleepy snakes

If you take the right fork from Batu Maung to go north, you will pass behind the airport and cut through the **Bayan Lepas Free Trade Zone**, the Silicon Valley of Malaysia. The huge area is the home of high-technology industries, ranging from microchip-manufacturing multinationals such as Dell and Intel, to success-hungry export-orientated local giants.

These factories have now completely hemmed in the Temple of Azure Cloud, more popularly known as the **Snake Temple** (open daily 9am–6pm; free). Here, venomous pit vipers, doped perhaps by the incense, lie coiled around everything: altars, incense burners, candlesticks, vases, tables, underfoot and overhead. However, the air of mystery surrounding the temple, and the reason why the reptiles would congregate here has vanished, together with the lush jungle behind it; today the temple is now just another commercial attraction.

A highway runs the length of the east coast from here to Georgetown. This is built on reclaimed land, and Penangites joke about how this has changed the shape of the island; before it resembled a tortoise, whereas now it looks more like a rather pregnant one.

More microchips

The mainland section of Penang state is nearly twice as large as the island, a thriving industrial area built around Seberang Prai (Butterworth) that has become one of the world's leading producers of microchips, disk drives and other computer parts. Both sides of the North-South Expressway and the approach to the Penang Bridge are covered with sprawling high-tech factories. East of Seberang Prai, the **Penang Bird Park** (open daily 9am–7pm; entrance fee; tel: 04-399 1899), on Jalan Todak, has over 200 species of tropical birds from around the world housed in specially designed homes, including a huge walk-in aviary and geodesic domes.

Another patch of green is the 37-hectare (92-acre) **Bukit Mertajam Recreational Park**, about 18 km (11 miles) from the Penang Bridge. It has numerous walking trails for trekkers and rest huts when you tire. Near its entrance is the stark-white **St Anne's Church**, a well-preserved 19th-century colonial relic. Its annual candlelight procession on the Feast of St Anne's from 21 to 30 July draws some 80,000 pilgrims from as far as Europe and Australia. ❏

KEDAH AND PERLIS

Map on page 158

The most traditionally Malay of the northern states, Kedah and Perlis offer the modern traveller ancient Hindu settlements, lush mountain parks and the carefree resort isle of Langkawi

I t beckoned, a bluish-grey mass which towered in the distance, and so civilisation took root in the land. At 1,200 metres (3,900 ft), Gunung Jerai in the state of Kedah served as a lodestar to early merchant voyagers; it was at its ɔot that one of the peninsula's first known kingdoms established itself.

But Kedah's position at the crossroads of Southeast Asian trade also exposed to constant danger. Initially controlled by the great trading empires of Funan ɪ Vietnam, and then Sri Vijaya in Sumatra, Kedah later became part of the lelaka sultanate. Until the beginning of the 19th century, Kedah's rulers were ɪmarkably successful in preserving their independence. However, despite havɪg put their faith in British power (and losing Penang in the process), Kedah fell ɔ the Thais, and Perlis had to be given up as well. Both states were transferred ɔ British suzerainty in 1909, but the mainly Malay population somehow manɟed to maintain their way of life, unlike other peninsula states.

ᴨcient temples

ɪnlike the sailors of old from across the Bay of Bengal, modern-day travellers ɔpproach **Gunung Jerai** (*see page 166*) on the North-South Expressway ɪrough **Sungai Petani**, Kedah's second-largest town and the country's fastest-ɪowing. Close by is one of the largest archaeological ᴋtes in the country, dating back to the 5th century.

After over a century of digging, archaeological finds ɔm the edges of villages, riverbanks and the foot of ɪngled hills point to many more treasures in the ʰhole area between the **Lembah Bujang ㉑** (Bujang alley) and **Sungai Muda**. One of the earliest Hindu ᴇttlements in Southeast Asia, it also had an earlier ᴜddhist phase, and possibly even a prehistoric Malay ᴇttlement before that. About 10 ancient *candi* (tem-les) have been excavated and restored, the largest ɪd best-preserved being the **Candi Bukit Batu ᴀhat** (Temple of the Hill of Chiselled Stone). Inscrip-ɔns in Sanskrit, porcelain pieces from China, Indian ᴇads, and glassware from the Middle East point to ᴇ site's importance as an international entrepot.

The **Muzium dan Taman Arkeologi Lembah ᴜjang**, or Lembah Bujang Archaeological Park and ᴀuseum (open daily 8am–4.15pm; free; tel: 04-457)05; www.jmm.gov.my), showcases important finds ɔm the area, and has a display of photographs and ᴀodels. Pretty landscaped paths lead to the four closest ᴇstored temples. Guided tours must be pre-arranged. ɔ get there, exit the North-South Expressway at Sun-ᴀi Petani and head towards Bedong, turning left to the ᴅlage of Merbok and the museum. Otherwise, catch a ᴋxi or bus from Sungai Petani to Merbok, 30 km (19 ᴅiles) away, from where you walk to the museum.

LEFT: Langkawi fishermen heading home.
BELOW: neolithic stone tool from Bujang.

*In the predominantly
Malay-Muslim states
of Kedah and Perlis,
men wearing the
songkok (fez) on
Friday prayer days
are a common sight.*

Beyond Merbok, the road winds prettily on and eventually turns south to Tanjung Dawai, a postcard-perfect fishing village on the Muda Estuary. A ferry (but not for cars) crosses the estuary to Pantai Merdeka, a popular beach which can also be reached 40 km (25 miles) from Penang by road.

Sungai Petani is also the jumping-off point on the spectacular East-West Highway to the peninsula's east coast. The road goes via Baling, overlooked by a spectacular limestone massif, and Grik in Perak, an important post during the communist threat of the 1960s.

The rice capital

To get to the state capital of Alor Star, head north from Sungai Petani on the highway. Here the country flattens out, and depending on the season, oceans of rippling green or gold or brown fallow ground merge with the distant cloud-flecked hills of the Main Range. This is the country's Rice Bowl, producing half the locally grown rice. There are biannual harvests, thanks to the massive Muda Irrigation Project, which covers 127,000 hectares (300,000 acres). This is one of the few schemes financed by the World Bank which has fulfilled the aims of its sponsors and provided adequate returns. A much older irrigation canal actually runs alongside the old main road from Gunung Jerai to Alor Star. Built in the 19th century by Wan Mat Saman, the then *menteri besar* (chief minister), the canal is perfectly straight throughout its long length, a feat achieved by aligning kerosene-fuelled flares.

Alor Star ㉒ generally serves as a springboard to the holiday isle of Langkawi, but it does have some fine architecture along the main road, Jalan Pekan. The large **Zahir Mosque** (Masjid Zahir), built in 1912, has the graceful colonnades and domes of Moorish tradition. Opposite it is the **Muzium**

BELOW: sun-ripened rice paddy fields in Kedah state.

)i-Raja, or Royal Museum (open daily 10am–6pm, except Fri noon–3pm; ree; tel: 04-732 7937), a former palace interesting for its layout as well as its oyal family displays, including Sultan Abdul Halim's African animal trophies.

Sacred orchestra

Next to the museum is the Thai-style **Balai Besar** (Great Hall), built in 1898. Jsed as an audience hall by Kedah's sultans of old to receive public petitions and lear grievances, it is today the site of ceremonial and state functions. The **Balai Nobat** nearby plays a unique function: it houses the instruments (*nobat*) of Kedah's oyal orchestra. Comprising a horn, three drums and a gong, only four such orchestras exist in Malaysia today, the others being in Terengganu, Selangor and Johor.

Kedah's *nobat* is reputedly the oldest, a gift from Melaka's last sultan, and considered sacred and an important part of the state regalia: no Kedah sultan is considered a legitimate ruler if he has not been installed to the accompaniment of the *nobat*. The orchestra also plays on other state occasions when the sultan is present, and may be heard daily during the Muslim fasting month. Permission to see the *nobat* may be obtained at the State Economic Planning Office (tel: 04-700 7113).

Further down Lebuhraya Darul Aman, near the stadium, is the State Museum, or **Muzium Negeri** (open daily 10am–6pm, except Fri noon–3pm; free; tel:)4-733 1162). This is another Thai-style building, with collections that include Chinese ceramics as well as exhibits from the Bujang Valley.

Outside the capital

The highway north of Alor Star ends in **Bukit Kayu Hitam**, the exit point to Thailand. There is an uninteresting duty-free emporium there, and a market

Map on page 158

BELOW: Crown of Kedah monument in the capital, Alor Star.

that is popular with locals. About 1½ hours' drive east of the capital is **Pedu Lake** (Tasik Pedu), a dammed lake retreat in peaceful surroundings that attract anglers. The road there goes through tiny wooden settlements among rolling oil palm and rubber plantations.

Malay-style seafood is best at the small fishing village of **Kuala Kedah**, 11 km (7 miles) west of Alor Star. The local *ikan panggang* (barbecued fish) and chilli crab are favourites, as is the Thai-influenced noodle dish of laksa.

On the other side of the river is the well-preserved **Kota Kuala Kedah Historical Complex** (tel: 04-731 2322; www.jmm.gov.my), whose fort was originally built in 1611 for protection against the Portuguese, Achehnese, Bugis and Siamese who attacked from the sea. In the midst of Kuala Kedah's wooden warehouses and fish market is a modern jetty (tel: 04-762 1201), serving Langkawi's holiday-makers. (For information on ferry links, see page 205.)

Malaysia's smallest state

Ikan bawal or pomfret from Kedah's coastal waters

BELOW: Kuala Perlis is the jumping-off point for Langkawi.

Perlis, Malaysia's smallest state, is really an extension of the Kedah plain, but the scenery is even more rustic, the peaceful atmosphere more lulling. Unlike Kedah, stark, limestone outcrops stand like sentinels over the flat rice fields. Spectacular and mysterious, many contain subterranean caves, with flora and fauna unique to limestone habitats. The vegetation here is also more similar to Thailand's, with the canopy turning a golden autumnal brown during the marked dry season.

About 15 minutes' drive from **Kangar**, the capital of Perlis, is **Kuala Perlis**, another jumping-off point to Langkawi. It is a busy but not particularly attractive fishing village, although there are some excellent seafood restaurants.

While the North-South Expressway ignores Perlis completely, the railway line goes through **Arau**, the royal town. The Malaysian railway system meets its Thai counterpart 50 km (30 miles) north at **Padang Besar**, which has a market that comes alive at weekends. You can also cross into Thailand by road via Padang Besar, but a more spectacular drive is west through the hills to **Kaki Bukit** (literally "the foot of the hill"), a former tin-mining outpost comprising a charming wooden Chinese village. A must-see is the **Perlis State Park** (tel: 04-977 6626; entrance fee), close to the Thai border, with good trails threading through the country's only semi-deciduous forest. Within the park is **Gua Kelam**, a former mining tunnel, which has a well-lit 370-metre (1,210-ft) walkway. The road from the park goes to Satun in Thailand.

Legendary isle

Once upon a time, **Pulau Langkawi** was a sleepy island believed to be under a spell cast by a legendary princess, Mahsuri, who lived in the 14th century and was unfairly executed for adultery. It is largely through the efforts of Kedah-born former Prime Minister Mahathir that it has been elevated to the status of major tourist destination. Malaysia's Father of Independence, Tunku Abdul Rahman, was of the Kedah royal family and many political leaders are northerners, including current Prime Minister Abdullah Badawi.

A beautiful limestone cliff and forest archipelago of some 100 islands, some of which are mere rocks

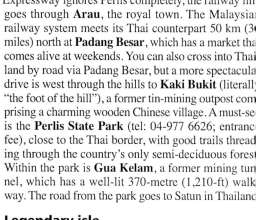

...at vanish at high tide, Langkawi is being marketed as a modern-day legend. ...erries service the main island from Kuala Perlis between 6am and 6pm at ...ourly intervals (40 minutes); from Kuala Kedah every 75 minutes between ...am and 6.30pm (1 hour); and once a day from Penang at 8am (2½ hours). ...oats also go to Satun in Thailand four times a day. During the monsoon months ...f July to September, seas can be choppy, and services may be cancelled. ...Malaysia Airlines operates daily flights from Alor Star, Penang and Kuala ...umpur, while AirAsia has daily flights from the latter two cities.

Maps:
Area 158
Island 206

...ax-free shopping

...angkawi's duty-free status has succeeded in injecting life into the island. From the ...tty to the main town, **Kuah ❶**, nearly every shop is crammed with chocolates, ...lectronic items and household goods. Not all items are a bargain, but alcohol and ...igarettes are exempt from Malaysia's heavy "sin" taxes on Langkawi; however, ...isitors are only allowed to bring out 1 litre of alcohol and a carton of cigarettes ...fter a minimum stay of 72 hours. The old market is a good place to buy Indone- ...ian batik while trendy craft shops offer hand-painted fabrics and Asian curios.

Perlis is the only Malaysian state whose royal leader is known as Rajah rather than Sultan.

Yet more shops sit on the reclaimed land which starts right next to the jetty. ...lere you'll see an enormous statue of an eagle; among the many interpretations ...f its name, Langkawi is thought to derive from the word *helang*, Bahasa ...Malaysia for "eagle". The statue of the majestic creature about to soar is a pow- ...rful allegory, one might say, for the tremendous success of the island resort. ...There are hotels and good seafood restaurants in Kuah, but the more enjoyable ...ption is to stay at one of the island's many beach resorts, only to head into town ...r a spot of shopping and sightseeing, and to sign up for tours with tour agencies.

LEFT: a Langkawi resort at sunset. **BELOW:** a fisherman waits for a bite.

TIP

There are convenient ferry services (2½ hours) between Kuah in Langkawi and the jetty in Georgetown, Penang. Alternatively, organised day tours are offered by travel agents in Penang.

Coves, coral and caves

Langkawi has good roads that go round the island. Cars and motorbikes can be hired at the jetty, in town or Pantai Cenang, the most popular beach. Alternatively, book yourself into a half-day guided tour with any tour agency at Kuah. Most visitors head for **Pantai Cenang** in the southwest, an hour from Kuah by bus and less by taxi. The beach here is lined with places to stay, while opposite are restaurants, souvenir shops, and yet more accommodation. There is something for every budget, from the luxury **Meritus Pelangi Beach Resort** (www.pelangibeachresort.com) and **Casa del Mar** (www.casadelmar-langkawi. com), to A-frame huts and rooms in well-tended gardens.

The road leads south past the coconut-tree-lined and more upmarket **Pantai Tengah** , and ends at **Awana Porto Malai Resort** (www.awana. com.my) in **Teluk Baru**. En route to Pantai Tengah is **Underwater World Langkawi** (open daily 10am–8pm; entrance fee; tel: 04-955 6100), which showcases over 5,000 marine and freshwater creatures. One highlight is

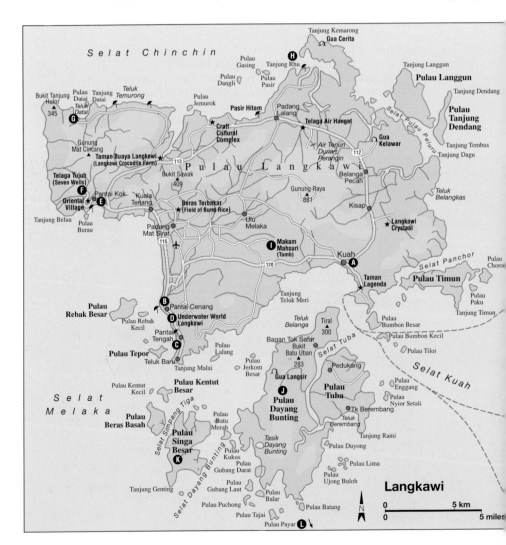

Map on page 206

5-metre (50-ft) glass tunnel within a giant saltwater tank with larger species ich as sharks, stingrays and turtles.

At the upper end of Cenang is **Laman Padi**, the rice museum (open daily im–6pm; entrance fee; tel: 04-959 4312), with surroundings of lush rice paddies id displays on the history of rice cultivation. The road goes past the airport and **antai Kok ❸**, formerly one of the island's most beautiful beaches but now the ibject of a misguided reclamation project. Further on is the pretty beach of **Burau ay** with two resorts at either end. Behind, the jagged peaks of the 708-metre *,320-ft) high **Gunung Mat Cincang** provide a dramatic backdrop to the rather .cky **Oriental Village** shopping complex (open daily 10am–10pm), which is orth visiting only to get on the **Langkawi Cable Car** (open daily 10am–8pm; itrance fee; tel: 04-959 4225). The 20-minute, 2.2-km (1.4-mile) ride brings you ▸ the top of Gunung Mat Cincang for 360-degree views of the Andaman Sea.

Telaga Tujuh ❻ (Seven Wells), a waterfall intercepted by seven pools, is ►cated further from the Oriental Village. Legend has it that mountain fairies ►me to these pools to bathe but vanish at the sight of humans. Note that the ►ols and falls have reduced water in the dry season from November to April.

Langkawi villager weaving nipah palms for roof thatching.

ocks and resorts

he Mat Cincang formation is the oldest rock in the peninsula, and a good look at ►e sedimentary structure can be had at the end of the road at **Teluk Datai ❼** in the ►rth. This is the location of the exclusive resort, **The Datai** (www.ghmhotels. ►m), an award-winning Balinese-influenced retreat with a golf course and private ►ach, as well as the multi-award winning luxury resort, **The Andaman** (www. ►mhotels.com). Two exclusive properties, **The Tanjung Rhu** (www.tanjung

BELOW:
the pool at The Andaman resort sits in the middle of lush rainforest.

rhu.com.my) and the **Four Seasons Resort** (www.fourseasons.com/langkawi) are found on the secluded northern beach nestled among mangrove forests a **Tanjung Rhu** . They both have well-known spas, gracious service and a ful range of facilities and amenities. Their white sandy beaches on Langkawi's north ern cape offer scenic sunsets against a backdrop of mountains rainforest. Gua **Cerita** (Cave of Legends) across the straits, accessed by hired boat from the Tanjung Rhu jetty, is a cave attraction with ancient writings on its walls.

Outside the glitzy tourist beaches, Langkawi's predominantly Malay popu lation of 43,000 maintain their peaceful agrarian lifestyle in much the same way they did before their home was catapulted into the limelight. The olde *kampung* (village) folk do not participate in the tourism industry – hotel staff are overwhelmingly from the mainland – and visitors are generally ignored.

From Tanjung Rhu, continue along the road to Kuah for about 5 km (3 miles) to reach the 14-tier **Durian Perangin Waterfalls** (Air Terjun Durian Peran gin), whose pools, unlike Telaga Tujuh's, never run dry, and make for refresh ing dips. Back on the main road, another turning to the left goes to **Barn Tha** (tel: 04-966 6699) in Kampung Belanga Pecah, a unique Thai restaurant with live performances, set in the midst of a mangrove swamp. It is accessed by boat or via a 450-metre (1,480-ft) wooden walkway raised above the swamp

Amid the mangrove swamps in the northeast also lies **Kilim Nature Park** sprawling some 10,000 hectares (24,210 acres). It has beautiful limestone landscape and views of wildlife such as eagles, hornbills and macaques, and is best experi enced on a boat tour along the Kilim River. On the tour, you can visit the 60-metre (200-ft) deep **Gua Kelawar** (Bat Cave), populated by fruit bats and weird-shaped stalactites and stalagmites. Arrange a tour with your resort or a local tour agency

TIP

Tanjung Rhu is probably the last place you can get *mee gulung*, a Langkawi speciality dish on the verge of extinction due to the high cost of *udang galah* (tiger prawns).

BELOW: Durian Perangin waterfalls.

LEGENDARY PLACE NAMES

Langkawi's legends are legion and often more interesting than the places they celebrate. The "main" tale concerns Mahsuri, accused of adultery by the jealous chief's wife. At her execution, white blood spurted out confirming her innocence. Before she died, Mahsuri laid a curse upon the island's next seven generations.

Immediately after, the Thais attacked Langkawi, and the villagers at **Padang Mat Sirat** burned their rice fields rather than let it fall into Siamese hands – few grains remain at **Beras Terbakar** (Field of Burnt Rice).

A Romeo and Juliet-type legend is behind several other place names. A union between a couple was refused by the girl's parents, and in a family feud, pots and pans were thrown at **Belanga Pecah** (broken pots). The gravy jug landed at **Kuah** (gravy), while jugs of boiling water formed the **Telaga Air Hangat** hot springs. The fighting ended when the two fathers were transformed into mountains – **Gunung Raya** and **Gunung Mat Cincang**.

Tasik Dayang Bunting got its name after a Kedah princess, forbidden to marry her lover, fell pregnant after drinking from the lake. The angry king banished her to the island where she drowned herself in the lake and became a rock.

Langkawi's islands

From Kuah, head west to go inland for 12 km (7 miles) to reach **Makam Mahsuri ❶**, or Mahsuri's Tomb (open daily 8am–6pm; entrance fee), which honours this local heroine. The tomb and the surrounds are constructed from Langkawi marble that is mined commercially on the island. When you return to Cenang, take the southern coastal road, Jalan Bukit Malut, to enjoy some spectacular views.

Langkawi's maze of islands is full of secret channels, narrows, inlets and bays. Shadowed cliffs, topped by dense virgin jungle, reach up to 600 metres (2,000 ft) and drop abruptly into the sea. Three are inhabited by sea gypsies. **Pulau Dayang Bunting ❶**, the second-largest island, has a unique, deep fresh- and salt-water lake, Tasik Dayang Bunting, whose waters are good for swimming and believed to aid conception. (The island's name translates as "Island of the Pregnant Maiden".) Next to it is **Pulau Singa Besar ❸**, a bird and animal sanctuary with a boardwalk that meanders along a mangrove coastline. Sun-soakers can also enjoy gorgeous beaches on some of the other islands such as **Pulau Bras Basah**. Boats from Tanjung Rhu, Pantai Cenang and Kuah tour these islands in about 4 hours. The Royal Langkawi Yacht Club (tel: 04-966 4078) at Kuah also organises sunset tours.

Marine life is richest at **Pulau Payar ❶**, a marine park, one hour by boat from the main island. While underwater visibility is rarely more than 3 metres (10 ft), it has lots of life, including baby sharks that come right up to shore, encouraged by hand-feeding visitors, and colourful soft coral blooms on wrecks in deeper waters. Book with dive operators on the main island, or if you're interested in snorkelling and a picnic, any boat operator. There are also dive sites at the neighbouring islets of Segantang, Kaca and Lembu. ❑

Map on page 206

In Mawat village is the tomb of Princess Mahsuri, who was falsely accused of adultery, and executed.

BELOW: legendary lake in Pulau Dayang Bunting.

THE SOUTHERN PENINSULA

*Village and city, ancient and modern – the contradictions are
more obvious in the south than elsewhere*

Standing as it does today at the silted rivermouth, it is barely
conceivable that tiny Melaka (Malacca) once ruled world
trade, and was responsible for the spread of Islam throughout
the Malay Peninsula. Although the world still congregates at
Melaka, these days it is to gawp at its ruins and relics, and to ride
in its riverboats, while the main trade with local merchants is in
cheap souvenirs and T-shirts.

Melaka is the undisputed top tourist draw of the southern stretch
of the peninsula's west coast. To keep the tourists coming, and coming back, the state takes great pains to keep its artefacts dusted, and
monuments spruced up. The authorities have also "developed" newer
attractions in other parts of the states, particularly in Ayer Keroh.

It was under the benign rule of Melaka that the people of the neighbouring Negeri Sembilan were able to remain true to the traditions
and customs of their native Sumatra; this is most visible today in
their architecture, notably the large sweeping roofs reminiscent of
buffalo horns. Like Melaka and Johor, the rural parts of the state
comprise clusters of charming *kampung* with neat front yards,
orchards bursting with local fruit, and a lovely lazy air.

But Negeri Sembilan is no backwater. The state is setting itself up
to tap the land and labour needs of the fast-developing Klang Valley.
The imminent arrival of the new national nucleus of government and
IT industries, and the new aviation hub of Sepang, right on the Selan-
gor-Negeri Sembilan border, offers further opportunities for the state.

South of Negeri Sembilan is the state of Johor, which has vast tracts
of rubber, oil palm and pineapple plantations. It may be a prime agricultural producer, but the federal government's ambitions for it are
much loftier. The state, in particular its capital city Johor Bahru, has
reaped the economic benefits of its location just north of Singapore,
aided by road, rail and shipping links, and a pipeline carrying water to
the island nation (which is a point of contention that crops up whenever
there are differences between the two countries). But Malaysia has sig-
nalled it prefers to be in the driver's seat for Johor's growth. Plans are
underway to remake the southern districts into the South Johor Economic Region (also known as the Iskandar Development Region), a
metropolis and growth engine replete with mega infrastructure, a logis-
tics hub, luxury housing, a tourism-friendly waterfront city and more.

As exciting as these plans might be, Johor's towns are relatively
uninteresting, except perhaps for Muar, which bears a striking resemblance to Melaka – it was to this rivermouth port that the last Sultan
of Melaka fled from the Portuguese. Inland, however, is the Endau-
Rompin National Park (Johor), a magnificent swathe of primeval
rainforest set aside for conservation and nature-based tourism. ❏

PRECEDING PAGES: Melaka village tykes.
LEFT: harvesting oil palm at one of numerous plantations that dot Johor state.

MELAKA

The site of both the first settlement on the peninsula in the 1400s, and of the declaration of Independence in 1957, Melaka can truly be called the birthplace of Malaysia

Map on page 216

History is everywhere in **Melaka ❶** (Malacca); peeping out from odd corners, hinting truths from epitaphs, outlined in the weathered face of a fisherman. Melaka is a town with a glorious past; almost five centuries ago, a Portuguese chronicler and frequent visitor said, "Whosoever holds Malacca has Venice by the throat". However, that golden grip lasted a mere 100 years. Today Melaka is in a grip of another kind. Every weekend, you'd be hard pressed to find local car licence plates among the Singaporean vehicles that jam the narrow streets. And in recent years, certain traditional areas have fallen victim to urban mismanagement: in the quest for tourist dollars, traditional craftsmen have been evicted and several historic shophouses have been demolished or else subject to sham restoration projects – diluting somewhat Melaka's cultural and historical environment.

Glory days

In the late 1300s, Melaka was a small settlement of sea gypsies, scraping a living as fishermen and farmers. Then Parameswara arrived, a Malay prince fleeing from his own invaded domain of Palembang, Sumatra. While out hunting in the area, he encountered a tiny *kancil* (mousedeer) which managed to intimidate his dogs; he took this as a sign that this should be the site of his new capital. By the end of the 15th century, Melaka had become the centre of a great trading empire and held an undisputed claim over the southern Malay Peninsula, as well as East Sumatra opposite. From every seafaring nation they came – Persians, Arabs, Tamils, and Bengalis from the west; Javanese, Sundanese and Sulus from the archipelago; Chinese, Thais, Burmese, and Khmers – in search of profit through trade, piracy or plunder. Each in turn left something of their culture behind.

The small colony of Chinese merchants, in particular, stayed behind to found the Peranakan community, which has become one of the most striking and colourful Chinese fraternities in Malaysia today. The Baba men and Nyonya women (or Straits-born Chinese) are descendants of the Chinese pioneers who accepted the practical realities of living in a Malay community, but upheld the social and religious norms of their forefathers in Fujian.

It was also through Melaka that the Islamic faith came to Malaysia. Malays have been Muslims since the early 15th century, when rich Moorish merchants from Pasai in Sumatra settled in Melaka. From here Islam spread throughout the peninsula, and eventually to its neighbouring islands. Geography was responsible for Melaka's multicultural history. Located at the mouth of the Melaka River, astride the maritime route

LEFT: Melaka's crimson Christ Church.
BELOW: a Melakan Baba merchant.

linking the Indian Ocean with the South China Sea, it was at Melaka that the monsoon winds met. Sturdy junks from China and Japan, loaded with silk, porcelain and silver, were driven up the Straits of Melaka by the northeast monsoon. Likewise, the traders from the Indonesian archipelago, with their crafts, spices and sandalwood. At the port, their cargo was exchanged for Indian and Middle Eastern cloth, carpets, glassware, iron and jewellery. When the winds changed, the southwest monsoon assisted the same vessels to return to their homes.

Taking note of this, the West decided to assume control of the hub of this lucrative trading operation, and Melaka's golden age ended when it fell in 1511 to the Portuguese. The port was theirs for 130 years, before they were ousted by the Dutch. After 154 years, the Dutch in turn ceded Melaka to the British in 1824.

Reflections of a river

Melaka's past is contained within its 1-km (½ mile) historic centre, easily covered on foot or by a leisurely trishaw ride through the narrow streets. The best place to begin your tour is right in the town centre, near the bridge built on the site the Portuguese made their final successful assault on the town. Here you will find the helpful **Tourist Information Centre** (open daily 9am–4.30pm; tel: 06-281 4803), where you can get maps, brochures and also book the 45-minute river cruise up **Sungai Melaka**. At high tide, the boats depart hourly from 10am from the jetty behind the centre or the Heeren Street jetty on the opposite bank.

At the jetty are battered junks whose high bows and raised poop decks stir thoughts of their distant cousins who once brought Admiral Cheng Ho's dragon court entourage from China to Melaka centuries ago. These days, the labourers crossing the narrow gangplanks carry no exotic spices or silks, but instead lug the

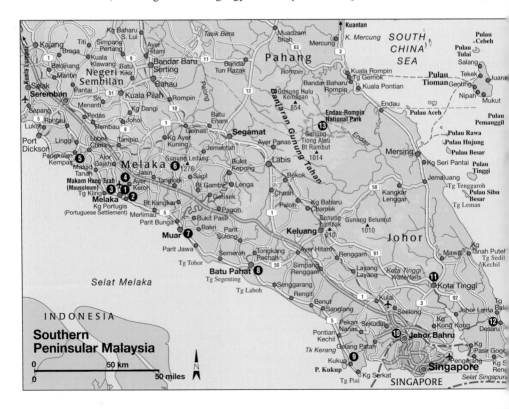

Southern Peninsular Malaysia

ulky sacks of charcoal that fire the aroma-filled kitchens of Melaka. The river cruise is quite enjoyable – if you ignore its now polluted waters – as it travels past century-old townhouses and warehouses, and ends in a traditional Malay village.

Dutch shapes

Try and get hold of a map of the Heritage Trail, which takes you through the main sights. On the east riverbank is a neat little square with a clock tower, surrounded by terracotta-red buildings and a church. They are distinctly Dutch; you almost expect to see tulips rather than tropical blooms in the flower pots.

The **Stadthuys ⓐ** (Town Hall), constructed of incredibly thick walls and massive hardwood doors supported by studded, wrought-iron hinges, served as government offices for more than 300 years. Today, it houses the **History, Ethnography & Literature Museum** (open Tues–Sun 9am–6pm; entrance fee; tel: 06-284 1934), which tells the story of the city from the time it was an ancient Malay kingdom to the present. The museum's collections include old coins and stamps, Portuguese costumes from the 16th century, and old sepia photographs of Melaka life. The Stadthuys itself is an antiquity. Erected between 1641 and 1660, it is the oldest known Dutch building still standing in Asia. The handsome General Post Office on Jalan Laksamana is also of Dutch origin, and is now the **Youth Museum** (open Wed–Sun 9am–5.30pm; entrance fee; tel: 06-282 7353), which documents the achievements of Malaysian youth.

On the embankment near the entrance to the Stadthuys is an ancient memorial whose significance has been lost in time. The stone fish with an elephant's head is believed to be a Hindu legacy predating even the Melakan sultanate. Adjacent to the Stadthuys is the fabled **Christ Church ⓑ** (tel: 06-284 8804), whose bricks

Maps:
Area 216
City 218

Dutch-built Stadthuys or Town Hall dates back to 1660.

LEFT:
European-inspired architecture.
BELOW: Melaka River.

*Two bronze statues
of St Francis Xavier
and Yajiro, a
Japanese samurai,
stand in front of the
Church of St Francis
Xavier on Jalan
Geraja. Their
encounter in
Kagoshima 458
years ago led to
the spread of
Christianity in
Japan.*

were shipped all the way from Holland. Melaka's masons then faced them with local red laterite. The church is full of old, engraved tombstones, many telling a grim tale about the hardships the early European settlers faced. The immense rafters within the nave were each carved from a single tree and above the altar a wooden crucifix hangs from the iron hoops fastened to the wall. When the church was first in use, it had no pulpit. The pastor would sit in a chair that had ropes running to the hoops. When it was time for his sermon, his sextons would winch him halfway up the wall so that the congregation could see and hear him.

Outside the church is the century-old **Tan Beng Swee Clock Tower**, presented to the town by the wealthy Tan family. The small water fountain nearby was built to commemorate the Diamond Jubilee of Queen Victoria. Four white *kancil* (mousedeer) surround the fountain – a reminder of Melaka's origins.

Formidable fortress

The only remnants of original Portuguese architecture are on the slopes of St Paul's Hill, behind the square. When the Portuguese conquered Melaka, they were determined to make it one of the mightiest strongholds in the Orient. Hundreds of slaves and captives hauled stones from demolished mosques and elaborate tombs to build the **A' Famosa** fortress.

The fortress eventually enclosed the entire hill, and withstood attacks for over 100 years, until it was finally breached in 1641 by the Dutch after an 8-month siege. However, the Dutch did not find the rich and prosperous port of the fabulous East they had expected. The city they had struggled so hard to conquer lay in near-total ruins. The Dutch lost no time putting things in order, rebuilding the city with a Dutch flavour, and repairing the fortress

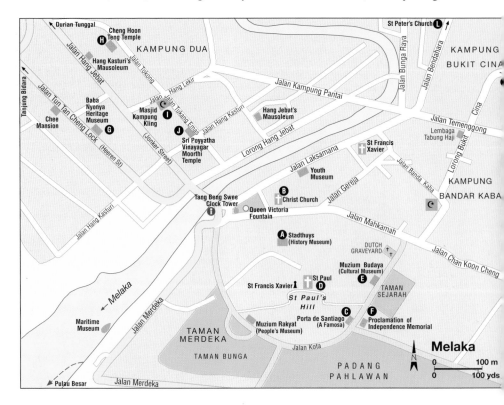

Melaka

and renaming the bastions. Melaka was soon a well-defended port once again.
Unfortunately, when the British occupied Melaka from 1824, they destroyed the fortifications to prevent the Dutch from reclaiming it. The walls and gates were badly damaged and all that was left is what stands today: the **Porta de Santiago ◉** – a gate without a wall. Recent excavations have uncovered the foundations of the Portuguese fort.

At the top of St Paul's Hill are more ruins. In 1521, a chapel, later renamed **St Paul's Church ◉**, was built by a Portuguese *fidalgo* to fulfil a vow he made on escaping death in the South China Sea. It was later taken over by the Jesuits, who completed the building and painted it white, so that it could serve as a guidepost for ships out on the Straits. The famous Jesuit missionary St Francis Xavier conducted mass in the church during his several visits to Melaka. After his death near Canton (now Guangdong), his body was shipped to and interred in St Paul's Church for some months before being taken to Goa in India.

The Dutch discontinued services in St Paul's Church when their own Christ Church was built. The engraved tombstones that line the inside walls are testament to its continued use as a place of burial thereafter.

Mahmud's palace

At the bottom of the hill is an elaborate reconstruction of Sultan Mahmud's 15th-century wooden palace as described in the *Sejarah Melayu* (Malay Annals). This is the **Muzium Budaya ◉**, or Melaka Cultural Museum (open daily 9am–5pm; entrance fee; tel: 06-282 7484), which displays aspects of Melaka's royal culture, including clothing, weapons and furniture, as well as a diorama of the court. More museums lie around the west side of St Paul's Hill.

Map on page 218

The remains of Jesuit missionary St Francis Xavier were temporarily interred in Melaka's St Paul's Church after his death in 1552.

BELOW: what is left of the Portuguese A' Famosa fort.

A Peranakan Townhouse

The front of the house is so decorative, it is like a heady visual perfume: brightly coloured tiles, wooden shutters, large gold Chinese characters on the black signboard, and those elaborate doors. It is distinctly Oriental, but the floral plaster motifs look Western. And yet the whole is unified. This is the Peranakan townhouse.

Described as Chinese Palladian, the architectural style of these buildings of the Malaysian Straits Chinese is a unique meld of Victorian, Chinese and Malay. Lining the streets of Melaka's old town, they are also found in Penang's back streets and in selected nooks of Singapore. But the Melaka buildings are among the oldest townhouses in the country, dating back to the 17th century. Those along Jalan Tan Cheng Lock are particularly elaborate because they were status symbols for their affluent owners.

The houses have two sets of doors. The main wooden doors, with their intricately carved panels, are left open during the day to let air in. The second outer set, are swinging half-doors based on the Malay *pintu pagar* (literally, fence door). On either side are large square windows with vertical bars and sometimes shutters. Above the windows are air vents, which are sometimes decorated.

A Peranakan townhouse is much longer than its entrance suggests. In fact, it can be seven times longer than it is wide. The centrepiece of the main or reception hall is usually an altar, large and beautifully carved. More likely than not, the deity among the candles and burning joss-sticks would be the white-robed Kwan Yin, goddess of mercy, flanked by tall vases of fresh chrysanthemums which are replenished daily.

Twin arched entrances lead to the sitting room. The main furniture would usually be imported blackwood furniture inlaid with mother-of-pearl and marble. These are usually set against the walls, from where portraits of ancestors in gilded frames peer down.

Behind the sitting room is the dining room and, right at the back, the huge kitchen. In between would be one or more courtyards or air wells to let light into the otherwise dark house. The courtyards serve as indoor gardens with potted plants, a fountain, and a well or large ornate jar filled with water.

The bedrooms sit upstairs at the top of a wooden staircase with balusters. The rooms and bathrooms are capacious and carry through the elements of carved lacquered wood, embroidery, and porcelain. Sometimes, the bedrooms have windows that open into the landing, complete with shutters.

Many of these houses are being restored for commercial purposes. In the process, however, many traditional tradesmen have been evicted, and the quality of the restoration work compromised for a fast buck. The best preserved are probably the Baba Nyonya Heritage Museum and the Puri Hotel on Jalan Tun Tan Cheng Lock. Others have been converted into hotels or restaurants, dishing up Nyonya food with varying degrees of success or else selling tourist trinkets. ❑

LEFT: the ancestral altar is often the focal point of a traditional Peranakan home.

The **Proclamation of Independence Memorial** ❻ (open Tues–Sun 9am–
5.30pm) is housed in the former Malacca Club House, a 1912 building which
was the centre of British colonial social life. Its displays chart Malaysia's campaign for independence, including historic documents, films and artefacts. An
obelisk outside commemorates British soldiers killed in the Naning War, a far-
cical affair in the early 1830s, which took two military expeditions over two
years to subdue Penghulu Dol Said, the defiant chief of the principality of Naning. The local hero is commemorated at his birthplace (*see page 226*).

The museums face the **Padang** (town green), which is the scene of a nightly
sound-and-light show (daily 8–9pm; entrance fee; tel: 06-286 6020) that
recounts the history of Melaka. It also serves as the "walking track" for
traditional Melaka bullock carts (RM1 per person). Beside the *padang*, a lane
flanked by handicraft stalls leads to a row of foodstalls across from the
huge Mahkota Parade shopping mall. Between the park and the river is the
Melaka Maritime Museum (open Wed–Mon 8.30am–5.30pm; entrance fee;
tel: 06-283 0926), housed in a replica of the *Flor de La Mar*, a Portuguese ship
that sank off the Melakan coast. It traces Melaka's maritime history from
the 14th century to the British colonial era and features mainly artefacts gleaned
from shipwrecks in the Straits of Melaka.

Map
on page
218

*Detail from an
ornate wall tile of a
typical Peranakan
house. Antique tiles
such as these are on
sale at Melaka's
Jonker Street.*

Antique streets

lead back to the bridge near the Town Square, and cross over to a completely different experience. The west bank has always been the main centre of Melaka's
shopping and business activities; a maze of ancient and narrow streets. **Jalan
Tun Tan Cheng Lock** – called Heeren Street by the Dutch – is named after a
leading Baba politician and architect. His family house
and the palatial townhouses of several other prominent
Chinese families line the street, flaunting Peranakan
tiles and carved wooden doors. The street is extremely
narrow so watch out for traffic; for safety, walk towards
rather than against the flow of traffic. At No. 48–50 is
the fascinating **Baba Nyonya Heritage Museum** ❼
(open Mon–Sat 9am–5pm; entrance fee; tel: 06-283
1273), where you can explore the unique interior of a
typical Peranakan house. The family which owns the
house gives guided tours and can tell fascinating stories
about some of the architecture and curios, including
blackwood tables and chairs from China and the sumptuous traditional wedding costumes.

Parallel to this road is Jalan Hang Jebat, formerly
known as **Jonker Street**, Melaka's main tourist drag.
This once-elegant street filled with quaint Peranakan
homes, age-old crafts and trades like acupuncturists,
herbalists and wooden clog makers, and Chinese clan
associations has lost some of its charm in recent years
thanks to the proliferation of tacky souvenir shops,
karaoke lounges and restaurants.

Still, if you search hard enough, you will find what
Jonker Street is most famous for – antiques. There are
heavy brass irons with receptacles for hot coals, wooden
bullock carts, ornate oil lamps, Peranakan-style furniture inlaid with mother of pearl, opium beds and altar
stands, Victorian clocks and early gramophones, brass

BELOW:
frontage of a
Peranakan-style
house.

Kuih lapis, a multi-coloured Peranakan dessert made of rice flour, coconut cream and sugar.

urns and marble statues, silver trinkets and Chinese wedding beds, as well as rare stamps and coins, and Malay *keris* (daggers).

On yet another parallel road, **Jalan Tokong**, are three of the oldest places of worship in Malaysia. **Cheng Hoon Teng Temple ❶**, or Temple of Bright Clouds (open daily; free), was founded in 1645 and is the oldest Chinese temple in Malaysia. It was originally built by a fugitive from the Manchu conquest, and was later restored by local Chinese leaders. The temple is dedicated to three deities: the main altar to Kuan Yin, the goddess of mercy, and the others to Kwan Ti (also known as Kwan Kung), the god of war who "triples" up as the patron saint of wealth and tradesmen; and Ma Choe Poh, the Queen of Heaven. Look up and you will see the carved roof, ridges and eaves elegantly decorated with Chinese mythical figures – animals, birds and flowers, of coloured glass and porcelain. Step through the massive hardwood gates, and you feel you are stepping back several centuries. Among the wood carvings and lacquerwork within is a stone inscription commemorating Admiral Cheng Ho's visit to Melaka in 1406.

Mosques and temples

Along the same road, now called Jalan Tukang Emas, is the **Masjid Kampung Kling ❶** (Kampung Kling Mosque), the town's oldest mosque, built in 1748. It sports a typical Sumatran design, with a three-tiered roof and a rather Chinese-like minaret. This style is characteristic of Melakan mosques. Another good example is the 150-year-old **Masjid Tranquerah** in Jalan Tranquerah, 2 km (1 mile) away. Its cemetery encloses the tomb of Sultan Hussain of Johor, who ceded Singapore to Sir Stamford Raffles in 1819.

Nearby is the **Sri Poyyatha Vinayagar Moorthi Temple ❶**, built in 1781 by

BELOW: Antique Peranakan silver belt.

he Hindu community of Melaka. The country's oldest Hindu temple, it is dedicated to Vinayagar or Ganesh, the Elephant God, one of the most popular deities among Malaysian devotees.

Map on page 218

A princess's legacy

There is another historical hill, a little away from the historic centre – which houses 12,000 graves. Hills are auspicious burial grounds, according to the principles of *feng shui* (Chinese geomancy), for they block evil winds and offer the spirits of the ancestors a good view over their descendants. But while most names and dates on the tombstones on **Bukit Cina** Ⓚ (China Hill) have been eroded, what remains eternal is the legacy of a Ming princess.

Sultan Mansur Shah carried on a diplomatic war of wits with the Emperor of China, which grew to be legendary. Around 1460, a Chinese ship sailed into Melaka's port. The entire interior of the vessel was delicately pinned with gold needles, and the message to the sultan read: "For every gold needle, I have a subject; if you could count their number, then you would know my power."

The sultan was impressed. He sent back a ship stuffed with bags of sago and the message: "If you can count the grains of sago on this ship you will have guessed the number of my subjects correctly, and you will know my power." This so moved the Chinese emperor that he sent his daughter Hang Li Poh, to marry the sultan. She arrived with no less than 500 ladies-in-waiting. The sultan gave them "the hill without the town" as a private residence and promised that the land they occupied would never be taken away from them. To this day, Bukit Cina belongs to Melaka's Chinese community. Several of the graves on Bukit Cina date back to the Ming dynasty and are among the oldest Chinese relics in Malaysia.

BELOW: painted temple door, Melaka.

The princess's followers built a well at the foot of the hill, whose waters soon became as legendary as her marriage contract. After Admiral Cheng Ho drank from the well, its water attained an extraordinary purity. It never dried up, even during the most severe drought, and many believed that if a visitor drank from it he would return to Melaka before he died. Now the **Perigi Rajah** (Sultan's Well) is protected by wire mesh. It has still not dried up and is as pure as ever. Many young Chinese still come to see the landmark and snap some pictures.

Head northwest from here to get to Jalan Bendahara and **St Peter's Church** Ⓛ. The Roman Catholic church was built in 1710 by the descendants of Portuguese soldiers given amnesty by the Dutch when the Portuguese garrison was forced into submission.

On Easter weekends, Melaka-born Catholics try to return to their hometown to attend the mass at St Peter's. On Good Friday itself, thousands of people – Chinese, Eurasian and Indian – take part in a candlelit procession. A life-sized statue of Christ, crowned with horns and draped in deep purple robes with gold embroidery, is solemnly borne above the devout Catholic congregation. The churchyard becomes a sea of flames from the lighted candles, accompanied by the mournful sound of hymns. After the solemnity of the mass, the crowds gather outside the church to catch up with friends, and children in their Sunday best romp around the lawns.

The Portuguese today

The legacy the Portuguese left behind is of far greater significance than mere ruins like the A Famosa fort. "I gave to each man his horse, a house, and land," wrote Alfonso d'Albuquerque in 1604, when he reported with pride to Portugal that 200 mixed marriages had taken place.

On direct orders from the king, d'Albuquerque encouraged the garrison's men to marry local women. Such intermarriages flourished and soon women were even sent out from Portugal to marry local men. The Portuguese were instructed to treat local people as equals; d'Albuquerque himself would courteously escort local women to their seats in church, as though they were members of the nobility.

Therefore, the descendants of Sequiera, Aranjo, Dias, d'Silva and d'Souza remained loyal to Portugal through blood ties and religion. After 400 years, a number of Portuguese Eurasians in Melaka still continue to speak Cristao, a medieval southeastern Portuguese dialect spoken nowhere else now.

At the **Portuguese Settlement** ❷ (Kampung Portugis), 3 km (2 miles) from Melaka's centre, near the beach, there's a community of about 2,600 Eurasians, mostly fishermen. Their unpretentious dwellings resemble Malay kampung houses with wooden walls and tin roofs, in soft hues of blue and green.

There is little of commercial tourist value here, except for the restaurants that serve Portuguese food, as well as cultural performances on Saturdays. But linger and you might just meet young boys who sing beautiful ballads in Portuguese; their sisters could well show you a dance taught by their grandmother, who was in turn taught by hers; and an old man at a fruit stall might tell tales about a secluded tunnel from St John's Fort to St Paul's Hill, in which the Portuguese hid all their treasures before the Dutch overran Melaka.

Some of the best places to meet local people are in the open-air cafés around **Portuguese Square** (Medan Portugis), which serve spicy seafood dishes and ice-cold beer.

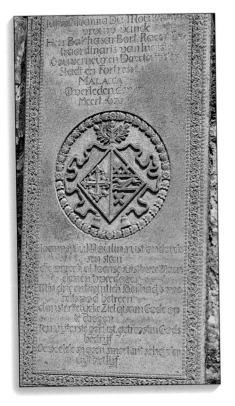

BELOW: Dutch relic from Melaka's early days.

Local customs

Each year on 29 June, at the Festa de San Pedro, the fishermen decorate their boats with bunting and sacred texts. An open-air mass is conducted and after the boats have been blessed, the evening is spent in merrymaking. Another unusual custom called Intrudu (Introductions) is celebrated on the Sunday preceding Ash Wednesday, when the residents wear fancy costumes and throw water over one another. Even those at home are not spared. The merrymakers make a point of visiting their friends at home, and drenching them with water as soon as they open their doors. To show there are no hard feelings, they are then invited in for refreshments. Later in the day, men dress up as ladies and the ladies dress as men, and go around selling cakes and fruits.

Beyond Melaka town, paddy fields stretch into the low hills and numerous side roads cut through groves of rubber and fruit trees, and past peaceful villages and compact market towns. Traditional Malay houses with curving gables, carved eaves, wide-fronted verandahs and tiled entrance steps are commonplace all the way from Tanjung Kling in the north to Merlimau in the south. The house of the Penghulu (chief) of **Kampung Merlimau** is a particularly fine specimen of this architecture, boasting delicate wood carvings and art nouveau tiles. It is sometimes open to visitors if the owners are in the mood.

Tanjung Kling, about 10 km (6 miles) from Melaka, has a resort but beach-lovers are not advised to flock to it. You'll find some resort-style condominiums here, but the sea is not very clean and is sometimes infested with jellyfish. The northern beach of Tanjung Bidara suffers similar problems. However, the seafood is generally good, particularly at Klebang Besar and further north at Pantai Kundor.

Between Tanjung Kling and Pantai Kundor is **Hang Tuah's Mausoleum ❸** (Makam Hang Tuah). Hang Tuah was a local Malay hero of legendary stature who, even till today, epitomises a subject's absolute loyalty to the ruler. He led a band of brave and noble warriors – who were also childhood friends – in the court of Sultan Mansur Shah. However, Tuah was unfairly disgraced over the sultan's consort by a jealous rival and banished from the court. His most loyal friend, Hang Jebat, went amok at this injustice and created havoc throughout the sultanate. Tuah returned, and, though torn apart by the dilemma, killed Jebat on the sultan's command. Jebat's mausoleum lies in Jalan Tukang Kuli.

This classic tale, known to every child, is at the heart of the Malay psyche. The warriors have also been immortalised in books, drama, and in 1998, Malaysia's first home-grown animated movie. Tuah's soul – some say in the form of a crocodile – is believed to reside in a well in Kampung Duyong. The waters of the well are reputed to have medicinal value, and bring good luck to those who drink at it.

Map on page 216

A Eurasian couple decked out in Portuguese costume for a cultural event.

BELOW: Portuguese descendants still speak Cristao, an antiquated dialect.

Map on page 216

Zoos and clubs

Visitors entering Melaka town from the North-South Highway may choose to come in through **Ayer Keroh ❹**, about 12 km (8 miles) from the city. At the Air Keroh Recreational Forest, 70 hectares (170 acres) of jungle have been tamed to provide walks, deer reserves, picnicking spots and camping sites.

Numerous "tourist attractions" are spread along the road, some typical, others not so typical: a butterfly park, a crocodile farm, a fish world, a tennis centre, a *feng shui* (geomancy) garden, and a huge water theme park with rides. The **Taman Mini Malaysia** (Mini Malaysia Complex; open daily 9am–6pm; entrance fee; tel: 06-231 6087), features model houses representing the traditional architecture of the various states, along with cultural and entertainment programmes. Next door is a mini-ASEAN, a similar park showcasing the architecture of the 10-member Association of Southeast Asia Nations grouping. Nearby are the **Melaka Zoo** (open daily 9am–6pm; entrance fee; tel: 06-233 2239), **Auyin Hill Resort** and **A' Famosa Resort**, with recreational and leisure facilities. Several good golf courses dot the area, a result of the huge growth in interest in the sport.

The old road to Seremban and Kuala Lumpur goes through the district of Alor Gajah and passes **Naning**, the principality whose chieftain defied the British in the 19th century. Dato' Dol Said now rests in his tomb by the roadside. Around this area are some 90 mysterious stone megaliths called *batu hidup*, translated as "living stones" because of the belief that they grow. In fact, stones like these can be found scattered throughout the neighbouring state of Negeri Sembilan as well, with a famous cluster at **Pengkalan Kempas ❺** just across the Sungai Linggi border. Some carry Islamic inscriptions, while others act as gravestones, yet others simply offer no explanation as to their origin or purpose. ❑

BELOW: a Melakan bullock cart with a creative touch.

Minangkabau of Negeri Sembilan

The sweeping, peaked-roofed "buffalo horn" architecture is the most distinguishing feature of the Minangkabau culture of **Negeri Sembilan**, Melaka's northern neighbour. It appears everywhere; in the National Museum in Kuala Lumpur, at luxury hotels fringed by swaying palms, even at a petrol station at a highway lay-by. The roofs have come to signify not just Minangkabau, but Malay and Malaysian.

It is a proud tribute to the heritage of a group of Malay settlers from west Sumatra who made their new home in the fertile valleys and hills behind Melaka, attracted by the port's success. They brought their style of architecture and, protected by the Malay sultans, continued adhering to the *adat pepatih* customs which govern laws, political organisation, traditions, and social systems.

The small principalities founded by the original settlers formed the nine *luak* or states that became the federation of Negeri Sembilan. Today, although the modern state is divided into districts, the *luak* remain. Violent clashes over tin that resulted in British intervention in the 1800s have reduced the number of *luak* to five.

Negeri Sembilan's ruler is not a sultan but a Yam Tuan Besar or Yang Di Pertuan Besar (translated as "He Who is Greatest"), who resides in Sri Menanti, 30 km (18 miles) from the administrative capital, Seremban.

Minangkabau culture and history is housed at the **Teratak Perpatih** (State Museum) within the grounds of the **Taman Seni Budaya** (Arts and Cultural Park; open Tues–Sun; free; tel: 06-763 1149) at the Seremban/Labu exit off the Kuala Lumpur-Seremban Highway. The museum's main building is a 19th-century palace from Kampung Ampang Tinggi that has been carefully reconstructed here. The museum showcases a fine display of ceremonial *keris* (daggers), Bugis and Minangkabau swords, and royal ornaments. Next door is the **Rumah Minangkabau**,

another fine piece of Minangkabau architecture. Unlike the palace's attap roof, the Rumah Minangkabau has a cover of wooden shingles. The main building has handicraft displays and weekly cultural performances such as the *tarian piring* (plate dance) and *dikir rebana* (drumming).

Green hills and landscaped gardens provide the setting for the beautiful **Museum Diraja Sri Menanti** (Royal Museum of Sri Menanti) in the royal capital. A former palace, it was built in 1903 without a single nail. The timber structure sits on 99 pillars, representing the warriors of the various *luak*. It ceased to be a royal residence in 1931, when a new palace was completed in the shape of the blue-tiled **Istana Besar** nearby.

The great, sweeping roofs of the Istana prove to be the crowning glory of the otherwise featureless state capital of Seremban. A fine contemporary use of that traditional style, the **State Legislative Assembly Building** houses various government departments. Opposite it is a gem of neo-classical architecture, the **State Library**. ❑

RIGHT: great sweeping roofs typify traditional Minangkabau architecture.

JOHOR

Its proximity to Singapore makes the state's capital and resorts a favourite with visitors from the island nation; but leave the bustle behind, and you'll find some of the most beautiful habitats on earth

Map on page 216

Beware the Causeway Clog that heads daily south from Johor Bahru, the capital of Malaysia's southernmost state, into Singapore. On weekdays, the 1-km (⅓-mile) road and rail link between the two countries is filled with thousands of Johoreans commuting to their jobs in the Lion City by bus, car, train, motorbike and on foot. The bottleneck is reversed on weekends, when Singaporeans flock to Johor to take advantage of the lower ringgit to shop, party, and relax in its waterfall, beach and island resorts. Thankfully, the building of a second bridge to the west of Johor Bahru to Singapore, called Second Link, has alleviated some of the weekend traffic jams at the causeway.

It is a symbiotic relationship extended to investments as well, fuelling Johor's development and making prices in its capital and in the Singaporeans' favourite haunts among the highest in the peninsula. Still, Johor has not lost its agricultural roots, with its hinterland covered with oil palm, rubber and pineapple plantations, fruit orchards and vegetable farms amid virgin rainforest.

Johor evolved its own identity after the fall of the Melaka sultanate to the Portuguese in the 16th century. The last ruler, Sultan Mahmud, fled to Johor and turned it into a powerful trading empire. Its old capitals along the protected reaches of the Johor River were moved to the Riau archipelago, making them more accessible to trade – and attacks. Johor not only had to fend off the Portuguese, and the Dutch, but also the Acehnese in Sumatra, and later, the Bugis, losing Singapore to the British in 1819.

A turning point

At the end of the 1800s, Johor was the fiefdom of a *temenggung*, an official of the sultan. Abu Bakar, who became *temenggung* in 1862, elevated himself to maharaja, and in 1885 was acknowledged by Britain as Sultan of Johor. Sultan Abu Bakar was educated in Singapore by English clergy. He spoke fluent English and cultivated ties with influential Europeans in the business world. Under his rule, the foundations of modern Johor were laid. In 1866, he moved his capital to Johor Bahru, transforming it into a thriving new town.

The sultan used western methods of policy-making and administration, introduced a modern bureaucracy and gave Johor the first constitution written for a Malay state. Thus he was able to defer the appointment of a British "advisor" to help him rule his state. He maintained good relations with Englishmen in Singapore and London, and was the first Malay ruler to visit England, becoming a personal friend of Queen Victoria. Johor was therefore the last Malay state in the peninsula to come under direct British control.

Johor Malays are of mainly Javanese descent, and known for *kuda kepang*, a dance set to gamelan music.

LEFT: Johor Bahru skyline across the causeway from Singapore.
BELOW: waiting for the school bus.

TIP

To get to Kukup island, register first at the Visitor Information Centre of the Pulau Kukup Johor National Park (open daily 9am–5pm; tel: 07-696 9355) opposite the bus station in Kukup town. Then hop on a boat ride from the jetty.

BELOW:
colourful Aw pottery
in Ayer Hitam.

Waterfalls and tombs

The North-South Expressway stretch from Kuala Lumpur to Singapore is a featureless, flat, ruler-straight road which encourages one to speed or doze off at the wheel. Entering the state from Melaka on the highway, a turnoff at Tangkak towards Segamat leads to **Gunung Ledang** ❻ (Mount Ophir). While popular with hikers, the mountain is often left litter-strewn. Here, Sagil Falls tumbles off the 1,276-metre (4,186-ft) peak into clear pools below. Ledang has a legend attached to it of a magical princess who finally thwarted the persistent attention of Sultan Mansur by demanding a cup of his son's blood for her hand in marriage.

The right turnoff from Tangkak goes to **Muar** ❼, a centre of furniture making and a pretty town with neo-classical government buildings, traditional Malay houses and a pleasant tree-lined walk along the river at Tanjung.

Back on the North-South Expressway, a left turnoff further south leads to **Pagoh**, home to the tombs of two Melaka sultans, and **Kampung Parit Pecah** in which stand the 99 graves of an entire village, wiped out – according to legend – by a single spear about 500 years ago. The spear was supposedly tossed by a jealous lover into the chest of a bridegroom at his wedding, removed and tossed again, eventually killing everyone, including the bride.

The highway leads on to **Ayer Hitam**, a popular stopover with coffee shops and rows of street stalls heavily laden with souvenirs, durian cakes, peanut nougat and other local produce as well as fresh and preserved fruits.

Half hidden by the stalls is the Claycraft Coffee House, where patrons sit on stoneware stools and drink out of dainty ceramic tea cups; the other half of the tables are crowded with arty relics. There is more pottery south in a village called **Machap**, including **Aw Potteries**, behind whose Minangkabau-style showroom is the studio where you can watch craftsmen at work.

From Ayer Hitam the road to the coast ends at **Batu Pahat** ❽, Johor's other Malay cultural heartland and home to one of the last few genuine *kuda kepang* troupes. The town is notorious for its floods at high tide, but also known for its cheap and good Chinese food.

A more scenic way to get to Batu Pahat is via the coastal road from Muar. The road goes through little *kampung* and orchards whose goodies are heaped upon roadside stalls during the fruiting season. It ends in **Kukup** ❾, a Chinese village raised on stilts above the water and the southernmost town of the Malay Peninsula, and indeed the Asian mainland. Hordes descend on Kukup, especially from Singapore, to eat chilli crabs. The restaurants have no fancy decor – and some do not even have walls – but they do have atmosphere and great food. Accommodation is available at the **Kukup Golf Resort** (tel: 07-696 0950) and in hotels in town and floating chalets (tel: 07-696 0027).

Just offshore is the uninhabited mangrove island of **Pulau Kukup**, a 650-hectare (1,600-acre) national park and 800-hectare (1,980-acre) wetland sanctuary. Access is by boat from Kukup town (*see margin*). Nature lovers can enjoy its unique ecosystem from its observation towers, a boardwalk and a suspension bridge.

The coastal road continues south to **Tanjung Piai**. This southernmost tip of the peninsula 90 km (56 miles) from Johor Bahru hosts good seafood restaurants and the **Tanjung Piai Johor National Park** (entrance fee; tel: 07-696 9712), a 930-hectare (2,300-acre) forest. More than half of this area is a mangrove sanctuary with diverse wildlife such as the smooth otter, dusky leaf monkey and the threatened lesser adjutant stork. Visitors may chance to observe these from a raised boardwalk running through the sanctuary. Overnight accommodation is provided by the **Tanjung Piai Resort** (tel: 07-696 9000), which has chalets on stilts, or you can camp in the park.

Abu Bakar's legacy

The best-known place in **Johor Bahru** ❿ is probably its immigration point leading to Singapore. Besides the Causeway, Johor also has a less crowded 2-km (1-mile) second link to the island nation at Tanjung Kupang as well as ferry connections at Tanjung Belungkor near Desaru (*see page 233*).

Downtown JB (as the city is known) is booming with new air-conditioned shopping malls and high-rise buildings. Remnants of old Johor can be found behind **Jalan Ibrahim** in old shophouses where Chinese and Indian traders sell everything from spices and joss sticks to tailored suits and the latest colour TVs. Scattered among the shops are cheap Chinese restaurants and Indian cafés specialising in the popular South Indian banana leaf rice and *roti canai* (Indian bread).

The State Secretariat Building, **Bangunan Sultan Ibrahim** crowns the top of Bukit Timbalan. A huge Saracen-style building with arches, columns and enclosed stone balconies, it bears a gold seal of the State of Johor on its massive front doors.

The impressive building further down the waterfront and overlooking the Johor Straits is the **Istana Besar** (Grand Palace). Formerly the residence of Sultan Abu Bakar, the stark, white structure with sweeping lawns was com-

Ice-cold lime juice is the perfect accompaniment to spicy South Indian fare served on banana leaves.

BELOW: a spice merchant in Johor Bahru.

TIP

If travelling to Kukup
from Singapore, avoid
the traffic jam on the
Causeway by taking
the Second Link. Turn
off at Gelang Patah
and follow the signs to
Pontian. From Pontian,
head south to Kukup.

missioned in 1864. It has, over the last century, hosted royalty such as the Duke of Edinburgh (Queen Victoria's son), Archduke Franz Ferdinand of Austria (whose assassination sparked World War I) and King Edward VIII of England.

Although it remains in royal hands, the palace was opened to the public in 1991 as a museum dedicated to the golden age of Johor. The **Royal Abu Bakar Museum** (open daily 10am–5pm; entrance fee; tel: 07-233 0555) is rather reminiscent of visiting the aristocratic homes of rural England, and there is no other museum in Southeast Asia quite like it.

The *dewan* (audience hall) is now a gallery detailing the history of the Johor sultanate, while the Grand Palace itself is crammed with antiques and strange knickknacks. The four-poster teak beds in the state bedrooms have British-made Corinthian-style columns dating to the 1860s. The bedrooms are still used for the lying-in-state of deceased members of the royal family. Down the hall is the opulent Reception Room, with a Baccarat crystal table and chairs. The Throne Room, with its matching gilt thrones, is used each year for investiture ceremonies on the sultan's birthday. The opulence of the Banqueting Room has to be seen to be believed.

The surrounding **Istana Gardens** has rolling parkland, immaculate lawns and several flower gardens, while just uphill from the Dewan is a Japanese garden and tea house presented by Crown Prince Hirohito on his state visit to Malaysia in 1936. Within the grounds' handicraft centre sits Mawar House, a carefully restored traditional Johor Malay house.

The next landmark along the waterfront is the **Masjid Sultan Abu Bakar** (Sultan Abu Bakar Mosque; open daily; free), completed in 1900. A bizarre blend of Italian rococo, classical Greek and traditional Muslim styles, the inte-

BELOW:
modern mosque
architecture, Johor.

Map
on page
216

ior is decorated with Corinthian columns, crystal chandeliers and Oriental car-
ets. At the front of the main hall are a fabulously ornate gilt *minbar* (pulpit) and
n ancient grandfather clock. Hawkers frequent the mosque grounds selling
rayer rugs, velour wall hangings and other souvenirs.

Much further along the waterfront is **Istana Bukit Serene**, home of the pre-
ent ruler. The huge Art Deco-style complex is off limits to the public, but you
an get a good view of the palace from Jalan Sekudai along the waterfront or
alan Straits View. Its expansive grounds contain a private air strip, a huge
atellite dish, an orchid garden and a menagerie.

Nightlife draws many customers from Singapore, attracted by cheaper drinks
nd a relatively more "liberal" atmosphere, although the JB town council
ttempts to crack down on less salubrious spots from time to time. Still, the
ity has numerous nightclubs, discos, hostess clubs and karaoke lounges.

iolf and thundering falls

ohor has the largest number of golf courses in the country. The best known
nclude the 18-hole Royal Johor Country Club, Desaru Country Club and
ofitel Palm Resort Golf and Country Club, near Senai Airport.

Many of these golf and country resorts are also in the **Kota Tinggi ⑪** area. Kota
'inggi is a small, quiet town with a loud splash. About 15 km (9 miles) northeast
f the town are its famous waterfalls (entrance fee), the bottom-most section of
/hich thunders down 36 metres (118 ft) to the polished rocks below. The entire
rea is cemented and steps lead up to the third and highest tier. Weekends find the
arge natural pools and surrounding tree-rooted slopes commandeered by the
)cals. Chalet-type accommodation and Malay hawker food is available.

From Kota Tinggi, a trunk road goes south through
uit stalls and golf resorts to the golden beaches of
)esaru ⑫, which is practically a Singapore resort.
1any Singaporean visitors travel via the ferry
etween Tanjung Belungkor, 60 km (37 miles) from
)esaru, and Changi Point in Singapore. There is a
ervice three times a day between 8.15am and 7pm
or passengers, motorcycles and bicycles only. The
ig hotels at Desaru provide transfers to the ferry
rminal for a fee.

There is a good variety of accommodation, from
otels to golf resorts and camping grounds, all sand-
iched between the beach and forest. Resorts provide
e gamut of activities from watersports to mountain
iking and racquet games. A go-kart circuit in Desaru
ttracts the young, and the **Desaru Fruit Farm** (tel:
7-822 3886; www.desaruff.com) in Sungai Cemaran,
ith 100 species of fruits, an ostrich farm and an
piary, is worth a visit.

There are also interesting side trips from Desaru.
bout half an hour away on the Kota Tinggi road is a
arnoff that goes through an oil palm plantation to
ohor Lama** (old Johor) on Sungai Johor. Once a
reat trading centre and royal capital, Johor Lama is
day a sleepy village, and only grassed-over massive
imparts remain of its old fort.

Tanjung Balau, 5 km (3 miles) from Desaru, has an
xcellent fishing museum (open 9am–6pm; entrance

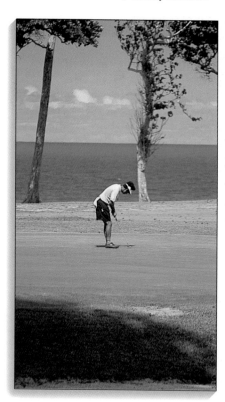

BELOW:
golf is a favourite
activity in Desaru.

fee; tel: 07-822 3687) which charts the industry's history, traditions and methods, and includes displays of traditional boats. The museum fronts a white sandy beach and chalet-type accommodation. Seafood buffs should check out the excellent Chinese-style delicacies at the fishing village of **Sungai Rengit**, 25 km (16 miles) south.

Endau-Rompin National Park in Johor is home to 71 palm species, which comprises 18 percent of Malaysia's palms – all indigenous – and more than 50 percent of its rattan varieties.

Land of palms

The road from Ayer Hitam to Mersing cuts across the state's rainforest heart, 20,000 hectares (49,000 acres) of which are the Johor section of the **Endau-Rompin National Park** . Named after the Endau and Rompin rivers, the park forms the southern end of the peninsula's wildlife corridor that stretches through Taman Negara up to Belum on the Thai border.

A conservation area developed by the Johor Park Corporation in consultation with the Malaysian Nature Society (MNS), this ancient virgin lowland forest has extensive palm species, pebbly beaches and large rivers of amazing clarity whose headwaters plunge into waterfalls. There are four campsites within the park, and chalets and dormitories at the park headquarters. Note that the park is closed during the rainy season from November to March.

The **Johor National Parks Corporation** (tel: 07-224 7471), at 475 Jalan Bukit Timbalan in Johor Bahru, rents out camping equipment and can arrange for Orang Asli guides, boat transfers from the Felda Nita jetty (25 km/16 miles from Mersing) and accommodation at the Kampung Peta park headquarters (open daily 8am–5pm). The **Johor Tourism Information Centre** (open Mon–Fri 8am–4.30pm; tel: 07-222 3591), at 2 Jalan Air Molek in Johor Bahru has comprehensive information on the park. Travel agencies in Johor Bahru, Kuantan and Kuala Lumpur run tours there as well.

The boat ride from Felda Nita takes about 2 hours; at Kampung Peta, you need to register, get your entry permit and pay park fees (including camera fees and insurance). The largest base camp is **Kuala Jasin**, km (4 miles) away, accessible on foot or by boat. Sited at the Jasin-Endau river confluence, it has great swimming areas, including a 8,000-sq. metre (78,000-sq. ft) pool. There are hornbills at dawn, and you can observe deer and monkeys from a hide.

The **Janing Ridge** trek can be accessed from Kuala Jasin: a steep climb to an amazing palm forest. The trail goes all the way to the park's star attraction, the Buaya Sangkut waterfalls, and is a 6-hour, 8 km (mile) trek. The first part treks through riparian (river) vegetation, with some waist-deep rope-aided river crossings, but the later stages involve steep stretches. Most people camp at Batu Hampar, tackling Buaya Sangkut the next morning.

En route to Batu Hampar are two base camps, Kuala Marong and Upeh Guling. **Kuala Marong** overlooks the still, clear Sungai Marong, whose waters were at one time the purest of any river studied in Malaysia. A side trail goes to **Tasik Air Biru** (Blue Lagoon), a deep shady pool that makes for a refreshing swim.

The falls at the **Upeh Guling** base camp has remarkable "bath-tub" formations at the top of rocks, probably

ormed when pebbles lodged in crevices were spun round by flowing water. There
s also a tiny island here, Pulau Jasin, which enjoys a remarkable diversity of
lants, including wild orchids and four species of the carnivorous pitcher plant.

Batu Hampar also has playful cascades and huge sun-baked boulders. From
ere, a steep ascent kicks off the section to Buaya Sangkut, and the undulating
ail goes through changing vegetation, including the peaty *kerangas* forest,
sually found only in lowlands. The umbrella palms, whose leaves reach 4
netres (12 ft) in length, just get bigger and bigger. The leaves function as roofs
or the huts at Batu Hampar, fashioned using Orang Asli techniques. Inciden-
ally, the umbrella palm leaf really does work as an umbrella in a downpour!

There is an alternative trail that climbs the final hill – this is actually part
f Janing Ridge, and therefore covered by thick palm forest, mainly the
idigenous *Livistona endauensis* fan palms.

White crocodile

t the 40-metre (130-ft) **Buaya Sangkut Falls**, seemingly static pools of water
umble down into rugged boulders, the most spectacular being the lowest of
he three-step falls. The falls, first sighted on a helicopter reconnaissance of
he park, has a charming Orang Asli legend to it, as do many of the sights.
Translating as "stuck crocodile", the reptile in question was a mythical albino
1at had died in battle with a snake, and whose carcass got caught in the falls.
he battle was over the hand of a lass of immense beauty, whose father made
 drum of the croc's skin. Unfortunately, he hung it over his daughter's bed, and
ne night, it fell and killed her. Some say the rocks at a certain point at the
/aterfall's top-most level bear a striking resemblance to a crocodile.   ❑

Map on page 216

Come nighfall, look out for fluorescent forest mushrooms in Endau Rompin National Park.

BELOW: Wagler's pit viper, Endau Rompin reserve.

THE PENINSULA'S EAST COAST

A world away from its brash western brother, the rural east coast is picture-postcard Malaysia: traditional and unhurried

If ever a mountain divided a land, the peninsula's Banjaran Titiwangsa (Main Range) has, isolating the peninsula's east coast from the progressive west coast. As such, it has retained its rich cultural identity through the ages, despite the ravages of satellite TV. And while it remains economically less advanced, it is also relatively buffered from west coast financial and environmental woes.

Embracing the states of Kelantan, Terengganu and Pahang and the eastern half of Johor, the east coast is as indisputably Malay as it is proudly rural – particularly in the staunchly Muslim north. Local dress dominates, especially among the women who are like colourful butterflies in their batik *tudung* (head-scarfs) and *baju kurung* (Malay dress). Local dialects reign, so that even west coast speakers of Bahasa Malaysia find it difficult to follow a conversation.

The economy remains rooted in fishing and rice cultivation, as it has been for generations. Traditional implements have been replaced by newer, larger, faster models, but the boats of Kelantan, for one, are still splendidly decorated. The fishing industry is celebrated in various museums, themselves fine examples of Malay architecture.

The coastline is a continuous broad beach that invites you to jump into the sea at virtually any point. Here sit peaceful, timeless villages, palms bending out over a bright blue sea, while islands beckon from the hazy horizon. The most pristine beaches of tropical paradise ilk are found on the islands. Here, the shallow waters are the clearest in the peninsula, lapping gently on white sand or crashing against giant boulders.

Underwater, the colourful landscapes are fascinating, and the diversity of life staggering. The east coast islands make up the majority of Malaysia's 38 marine parks, which protect fragile and important habitats.

As noisy as any big city is the cacophony of insect noises, bird calls and animal cries in the rainforest interiors of the east coast. Among the world's oldest ecosystems, the million-year-old forests make up conservation and tourism sites such as Taman Negara, gazetted in 1932 and the oldest national park in Malaysia, and the freshwater wetland of Bera, where the indigenous Orang Asli maintain their lifestyles closely intertwined with the ways of the land. ❑

PRECEDING PAGES: river tributary just metres away from the sun-drenched shores of Malaysia's east coast.
LEFT: teeing off at Tioman island.

240

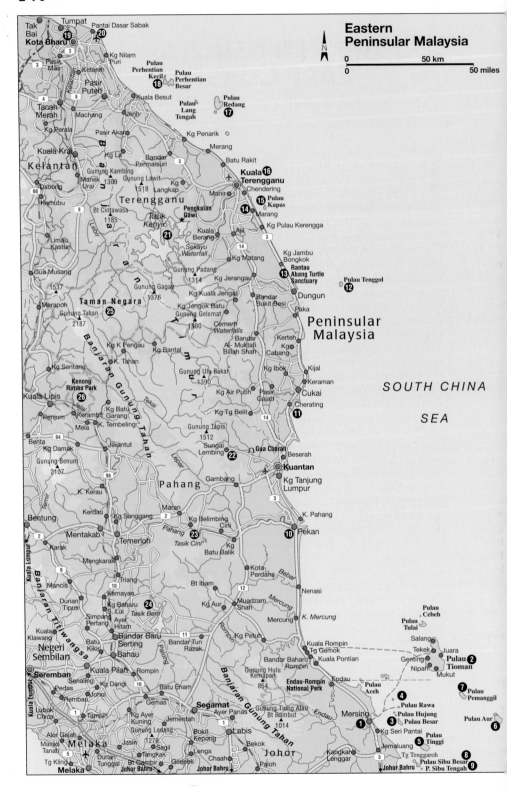

Tak Bai
Tumpat
Pantai Dasar Sabak
Kota Bharu
Kg Nilam
Puri
Pasir Mas
Keteran
Pulau Perhentian Kecil
Pulau Perhentian Besar
Pasir Puteh
Kuala Besut
Tanah Merah
Machang
Jerib
Pulau Lang Tengah
Pulau Redang
Kg Perala
Pasir Akar
Kg Penarik
Merang
Kuala Krai
Kg La
Bandar Permaisuri
Batu Rakit
Kelantan
Gunung Kambing
Gunung Lawit
Kuala Terengganu
Manek Urai 1309
1518
Langkap
Kg
Manir
Chendering
Dabong
66
Terengganu
Pulau Kapas
Kemubu
Bt Cintawasa
Pengkalan Gawi
Marang
1185
Tasik Kenyir
Kg Pulau Kerengga
Limau Kasturi
Kuala Berang
Ajil
Sekayu Waterfall
14
Kg Jambu Bongkok
Kg Matang
Gua Musang
Gunung Padang
1314
Kg Jerangau
Rantau Abang Turtle Sanctuary
Pulau Tenggol
1537
Gunung Gagau
1376
Kg Kuala Jengai
Dungun
Merapoh
Taman Negara
Kg Jengok Batu
Bandar Bukit Besi
Peninsular Malaysia
Gunung Tahan
Gunung Gelemat
1480
Paka
2187
Cemerh Waterfalls
Bandar Al-Muktafi Billah Shah
Kerteh
Kg K Pengau
Kg Bantal
Kg Cabang
Kg Sentang
K. Tahan
Kg Ibok
Kijal
Gunung Ulu Bakar
Keraman
Kenong Rimba Park
1390
Kg Air Putih
Pasir Gajah
Cukai
Kuala Lipis
Kg Tg Belit
Cherating
Penjum
Kg Batu Garang
Keramblt
K. Tembeling
Gunung Tapis
14
Mela
1512
Benta
64
Jerantut
Sungai Lembing
Gua Charah
Beserah
Kg Damak
Gunung Benum
2107
Kuantan
98
Gambang
Kg Tanjung Lumpur
K. Kerau
Bentung
Kerdau
Kg Sanggang
Maran
2
Pahang
K. Pahang
Mentakab
Temerloh
Kg Belimbing Cini
Karak
Pahang
Tasik Cini
Kg Batu Balik
Pekan
Mengkarak
9
Kota Perdana
Bebar
Triang
Bt Ibam
Mancis
10
Kemayan
12
Nenasi
Durian Tipus
Kg Baharu
Kg Aur
Muadzam Shah
Mercung
S. Lui
Tasik Bera
Simpang Pertang
Ayer Hitam
Mercung
K. Mercung
Pulau Cebeh
Kuala Klawang
Batu Kikir
11
Kg Petuh
Pulau Tulai
Salang
Negeri Sembilan
Bandar Baru Serting
Bandar Tun Razak
Kuala Rompin
Tekek
Juara
Bahau
Kuala Pontian
Genting
Pulau Tioman
Seremban
Kuala Pilah
Rompin
Bandar Baharu Rompin
Nipah
Mukut
Senaling
Kg Dangi
Gunung Hulu Kemapan
854
Pulau Pemanggil
Pedas
Johol
Batu Enam
Endau-Rompin National Park
Endau
Pulau Aceh
Rembau
Gemas
Gunung Tiong Atau
Pulau Rawa
Lubok China
1
Tampin
Kg Ayer Kuning
Jementah
Segamat
Bt Rambut
1014
Mersing
Pulau Aur
Alor Gajah
Gunung Ledang
Bukit Kepong
1
Labis
Kg Seri Pantai
Masjid Tanah
1276
Sagil
Bekok
Kangkar Lenggar
Jemaluang
Pulau Tinggi
Melaka
Durian Tunggal
Tangkak
Lenga
Chaah
Johor
Tg Tenggaroh
Pulau Sibu Besar
Tg Kling
Bt Gambir
Gersek
Paloh
Johor Bahru
P. Sibu Tengah

SOUTH CHINA SEA

MERSING AND ISLES

With long sandy beaches, unpretentious resorts, crystal-clear waters and beautiful coral reefs, these South China Sea islands achieve the difficult feat of being both popular and unspoilt

Map on page 240

Whoever planned **Mersing ❶** knew how to make the most of her views. Seen from the coast-hugging roads of this bustling fishing and jump-off port, its postcard vistas of the offshore island silhouettes have brought it considerable fame. Despite lost-looking beach-seekers at the jetty, Mersing itself retains its peaceful small-town character.

You need a car to enjoy the winding evening drives to **Kampung Sri Lalang** en route to Endau north of town (turn right just after the bridge), and through **Teluk Iskandar** on the Sekakap road (turn right at Jalan Nong Yahya opposite the hospital). There are no beaches for swimming, but lookout points and hotel rooms overlooking the sea almost make up for it.

On public holidays, Mersing's mini stadium sometimes plays host to the *kuda kepang* performance, a Javanese trance dance set to *gamelan* music and seldom seen outside Johor. Contact the **Johor Tourism Information Centre** (open Mon–Fri 8am–4.30pm; tel: 07-222 3591) at 2 Jalan Air Molek in Johor Bahru for details.

Because of its proximity to the area, Mersing is becoming a reference point for tours to the Endau-Rompin National Park (*see page 234*). More accessible and popular with locals are the recreational forests of **Gunung Belumut** and **Gunung Lambak**, inland from Mersing along Route 50. The former rises up to 1,004 metres (3,290 ft) and it takes about four hours along dense jungle tracks to reach the peak. At the base are some small waterfalls, which are easily accessible by families. Gunung Lambak is an easier climb up to 510 metres (1,670 ft) using trails of footpaths and wooden bridges. It also has pretty cascades.

However, the South China Sea islands are the prime objective of the madding crowd. Over 60 volcanic isles in crystal-clear waters make up the Johor group, six of which have tourist facilities. The Mersing jetty is also an established springboard to the popular Pahang island of Tioman. These islands are protected by their marine park status and are home to prolific and diverse marine life, much of which is endemic to the area. Some of these islands are closed during the monsoon months from November to February.

Mythical Tioman

The largest of these islands, **Pulau Tioman ❷**, is popularly believed to be named after the *burung tiong* or mynah bird. Legend says that the island was created when a dragon, which emerged from Lake Cini inland, froze into rock while waiting interminably for its mate.

There is a mention of Tioman before AD 1,000, in what was perhaps the first guide to Malaysia. Arab traders of the time noted in their "sailing directions" that Tioman offered good anchorage and freshwater

BELOW: winging it on a microlight off Mersing.

TIP

The best diving season along the east coast is from March to May when visibility is at its best. It is possible to dive right until October but from November to February all diving stops because of the monsoon. In fact many resorts close during this period.

springs. Much later, the island's twin southern peaks at Mukut (called "Ass's Ears"), were a guide to Chinese traders between the 12th and 17th century, as evidenced by shards of Ming and other pottery found on the beaches and in nearby caves. Some of the pottery now sits in a lovely little museum at Tioman's Tekek beach. It is widely believed that the waters around this crucial trading pitstop harbour many more sunken treasures in the forgotten holds of unknown wrecks.

Beach life

Tioman has been awarded duty-free status in an effort to attract Langkawi-like success, particularly with Singaporeans. At the moment, this translates mainly to the availability of cheap beer. Today, Tioman's beaches continue to attract tropical isle fans, and divers and snorkellers who have come to revel in the marine park's underwater life. The main beaches fringe the west coast, and all are lined with small chalet-type accommodation run by local Malay families. A sea-bus (speedboat) services the beaches between 8am and 6pm.

The tiny town "centre" is at **Tekek**, where you'll also find the jetty, airstrip and shops. The long beach, shaded by casuarina and coconut trees, is fronted with chalets and restaurants. Further inland on the other side of the road are *kampung*-style chalets. Despite the development, during the low season Tekek feels pretty much like the *kampung* it always was. The island's only road goes south from here to the island's one large resort, the **Berjaya Tioman Beach, Golf & Spa Resort** (www.berjayaresorts.com), which has a Ronald Fream-designed golf course. North of Tekek are the smaller beaches of **Air Batang** (better known as ABC after the original chalet operation there) and **Salang**, which also have some interesting mangrove areas.

BELOW: white-sand beaches are plentiful on Tioman.

South of Tekek are **Nipah**, a quiet chalet-only stretch, and **Mukut**, way down south at the base of the Twin Peaks, whose view of the wide expanse of blue ocean is obscured by neither islands nor passing ships. Mukut also has lots of fresh springs and a couple of waterfalls, the precious water for which the ancient mariners must have been thankful. Two other stretches on the west coast are not so pretty: Genting which sits on rocks and Paya, which has no beach to speak of, although both have plenty of accommodation.

Juara is the sole beach on the east coast, a long white stretch with relatively little tree cover, great for sun-seekers but it has no coral reefs at all. This is more of a backpackers' stretch, and can be reached from the west coast by sea-bus (2-hour journey) or by a jungle trail which starts at the jetty.

The 2- to 3-hour jungle trek across the island emerges next to the airport at Tekek, from which point you can take a sea bus back. The trail is paved in some stretches, steep in others, and climbs into thick lush forest. Another trail goes from Tekek to Batang Air and Salang.

Giant reefs

Tioman has large coral reefs on the west coast, most of which are close to shore. A feature of its marine life is its giant seafans, particularly at the top dive spot of **Pulau Tulai** or Coral Island, whose shallow waters are also popular with snorkellers. **Pulau Cebeh** provides for some fine swim-throughs, and there is cave diving just off the island while at the cliff-like rocks of Golden Reef are pretty, submerged coral gardens. **Pulau Rengis**, opposite the resort, is an accessible site with an occasional slight drift. **Pulau Jahat** is a good site south of Mukut. It is common to spot hawksbill turtles in the waters too, as well as

Map on page 240

TIP

Be careful of sandflies on Pulau Besar's beaches; the bugs are particularly nasty in the cool evenings.

BELOW: all set to dive on Tulai.

TRICKY ISLAND LOGISTICS

Getting to the isles from Mersing is possible in three types of boats – the speedboat is twice as fast as the slow boat, while the fast boats refer to the ferries. The speedboat goes to Tioman five times a day from 7am and to Rawa twice a day at noon and 5.30pm. Generally, the type of boat you take and when you leave depends on the size of the group, and your choice of resort and island. Try to book both accommodation and boat ticket beforehand, especially if your dates coincide with Malaysian and Singaporean public and school holidays. If you can rustle up enough passengers, you can charter the entire boat.

Nine big boat operators servicing all islands belong to the Persatuan Bot-bot Sewa Pelancong Daerah Mersing, or Mersing Boat Hire Association (open 8am–4.30pm; tel: 07-799 1222). Located at the jetty, they can also arrange accommodation at all the islands. Seagull is the other big operator with three ferries that depart in the morning, but only to Tioman. Then there are various small operators, some connected to the resorts, and all congregated at the jetty area. You can also check out pictures of their boats before you get on.

For more information, contact the Mersing Tourist Information Centre (METIC) at tel: 07-799 5212.

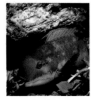

The blue parrot fish makes an audible crunching sound when it feeds on coral polyps.

groups of spiny lionfish. Walk-ins and packages are available at the seven div shops on the west coast beaches, as is full equipment rental. Instruction i offered too, and technical diving is gaining impetus here.

The 55 km (35 miles) to Tioman can be covered in an hour by schedule ferry from Mersing (try to get there in the morning), or Tanjung Gemok nea Kuala Rompin in Pahang. Boats service Genting, Tekek, ABC and Salang. A boats back to the mainland depart Tioman at 7.30am. An even quicker way t get to Tioman – with some spectacular scenery thrown in – is on board Berjay Air (tel: 03-2145 2828; www.berjaya-air.com), which flies out from Kual Lumpur's Subang Airport and Singapore's Seletar Airport.

Island cluster

Johor's islands south of Tioman are also covered in jungle and have some goo reefs; the islands are particularly popular with Singaporeans. All tour agencie offer the same 3-day/2-night package regardless of destination island: this com prises transfers, accommodation, tours (including snorkelling), and all mea including a barbeque. An all-day island-hopping trip in a 10–12 seater boat ca also be arranged. This covers a few of the nearest islands and hire of snorkellin gear, but you usually have to bring your own lunch.

The closest isle to the mainland, and the largest, is **Pulau Besar** ❸, one hou away. Pulau Besar is one of a trio of islands, including **Pulau Tengah** (a forme refugee camp for Vietnamese boat people) and **Pulau Hujung**, which are pop ular with day-trippers. However, Pulau Besar is the only one with accommoda tion, which comprises mainly basic chalet operations, and one two-star hote There is also a dive facility here. Trails from the sandy beaches lead to small plan tations and wooden *kampung*.

About the same distance from Mersing is the tin **Pulau Rawa** ❹. The island was once one of the to destinations, but it has declined in popularity some what in recent years. Rawa has only one resort, i which Johor royalty have a share, and it has dive faci ities but no divemaster. The marine life is nothing t shout about, but most visitors don't mind. They g there simply to enjoy its lovely beach – also on th island-hopping tour list – and do nothing. For th energetic, there is windsurfing, snorkelling, canoein and fishing available.

Pulau Tinggi ❺, a 40-minute trip from the main land, has a towering jungled peak, hence its nam (*tinggi* means "high"). Like Tioman's mountains, thi 650-metre (2,100-ft) giant was used as a navigation marker by Chinese mariners, and is mentioned in thei literature as the "general's hat island". There are lo of accommodation choices here, mainly budge chalets. Two islets nearby have some marine reef

Much further away are **Pulau Aur** ❻ (3–4 hours and **Pulau Pemanggil** ❼ (4–5 hours). Transport he is by chartered boat only, and is arranged through th respective resorts. Despite the distance, the islands ar very popular, particularly for fishing and diving Accommodation is plentiful but basic, and takes th form of longhouses and dormitories with commo bathrooms. The best beach at Aur is actually on

neighbouring islet, Pulau Dayang, which has a dramatic granite rock face loom-ing over the sole resort, **Dayang Island Resort**. Sea fans characterise its reefs, and experienced divers can explore a World War II Japanese wreck another 1½ hours east. The main island is hilly and good for trekking. Secluded Pemanggil has turquoise lagoons and offshore pools, and great shallow waters for snorkelling.

Map
on page
240

Deep south

Johor's southernmost pair of holiday islands is accessible from Tanjung Leman, a staging point on reclaimed land about 2 hours south of Mersing. The ferry takes half-an-hour to reach Pulau Sibu Besar and Pulau Sibu Tengah; speedboats do the journey in 20 minutes, but it's a bumpier trip.

Pulau Sibu Besar ❽ has a longer history of tourism, and therefore has more accommodation, although the bulk of it is basic. A large island, it also offers some good walks that weave through its small, forested hills. In the *kampung*, modern solar panels stand out among the traditional wooden houses – they are part of a government-subsidised power programme.

The smaller **Pulau Sibu Tengah** ❾ is being promoted as a one-island, one-resort destination, the same sales pitch as Rawa. The huge three-star **Sibu Island Resort** (www5.jaring.my/sir) sprawls over 8 hectares (20 acres) of beachfront, offering a gamut of activities including snorkelling and DIY batik.

One option is to do an all-day island-hopping tour covering these islands from Tanjung Leman. Perched near the islands are also some *kelong*, traditional fishing huts on stilts sunk deep into the ocean floor, which are open to visitors. Popular among anglers, you'd need to bring sleeping bags; food can be arranged. Enquire at the Tanjung Leman staging point. ❑

BELOW: Pulau Tinggi's peaks are among the highest in the island group.

PAHANG, TERENGGANU AND KELANTAN

Map on page 240

On the beaches of the peninsula's beautiful east coast, sun-soakers and coral-lovers mingle happily with the local folk whose families have fished its waters for generations

The Malays say the *pokok rhu* or casuarina only grows near the sound of surf. So it is these trees that flourish along the peninsula's east coast, virtually one long surf-lapping beach running through four states. Between November and February however, the *rhu* are lashed about mercilessly by angry winds which also whip up the seas – this is the monsoon season, where entire villages and even towns are inundated with water.

But this is the reality of life for generations of fishing folk who live on these beaches, their difficult but quiet existence untouched by MTV and stock market fluctuations. Even the towns seem laid back, and hold fast to age-old traditions both culturally – mainly Malay – and religiously – predominantly Islamic.

Old settlements

There is a long history of human settlement in the east coast region. Neolithic finds have been made in Sungai Pahang, while Kelantan's prehistoric finds were in interior caves. Pahang was also mentioned in Chinese texts as being a vassal of the 13th-century trading empire of Sri Vijaya, and Kelantan is thought to have been under its wing too.

Terengganu, meanwhile, was established as a cornerstone of Malay settlement. A 14th-century Islamic inscription discovered there indicates Terengganu as one of the earliest places in the peninsula to embrace Islam, before even Melaka, whose colonisation of the east coast states only happened in the 15th century. Islam has retained its strongest hold here. The Thais, who ruled Kelantan and Terengganu before British intervention, have also left their mark in the local architecture, dialect and art forms.

The east coast is linked to the west by several main routes through the spectacular Main Range: the Karak Highway (Kuala Lumpur–Kuantan), the Gua Musang Road (Kuala Lumpur–Kota Bharu), and the East–West Highway (Penang–Kota Bharu). Along the coast, Route 3 hugs the shore from Mersing all the way to Kota Bharu, a lovely drive interrupted occasionally by livestock and grinning children on bicycles. Go off the beaten track to a small fishing village, and a friendly gesture will be returned with a smile, or perhaps an invitation to tour the village where the soothing rhythms of Malay life have endured for centuries.

Kuala Rompin, near the Pahang-Johor state border, is a relatively untouched destination, mainly as a jumping-off point to the relatively undeveloped Pahang section of the **Endau-Rompin Park** (*see page 234*; enquire at Rompin's Forestry Office at

LEFT: colourful motif of a Kelantan fishing boat.
BELOW: kite maker in Kota Bharu.

TIP

If pressed for time, the inland Route 14 is the quicker link between Kuantan in Pahang state and Kuala Terengganu further north – but be forewarned that the drive is much less picturesque.

Block B, Kompleks Pejabat-Pejabat Kerajaan; tel: 09-414 5204), and to Pulau Tioman from the Tanjung Gemok jetty down south. Some travel agencies offer a four-wheel-drive tour to Jakun (Orang Asli) settlements inland at Iban (10 km/6 miles) and Kampung Aur (25 km/15 miles).

Islam, royalty and polo

At the mouth of the massive Sungai Pahang is the Pahang royal town of **Pekan ⑩**, the former state capital. The sultan's palace, the **Istana Abu Bakar**, has an enormous polo ground which doubles as what must be the flattest golf course in the world. On 24 October each year, the town is injected with festivities for the sultan's birthday celebrations.

The **Muzium Sultan Abu Bakar** (Sultan Abu Bakar Museum; open Tues–Thur, Sat–Sun 9am–12.15pm and 2.45–5pm; entrance fee; tel: 09-422 1371) has excellent displays on old Pahang, royal family memorabilia, and ancient Chinese glassware and ceramics. Nearby are a mausoleum and two handsome, white-marble mosques with a riot of golden domes. About 5 km (3 miles) from town is a silk-weaving centre at Kampung Pulau Keladi.

Kuantan, the Pahang state capital, 44 km (27 miles) north of Pekan, is not very interesting but it does have an excellent **Tourist Information Centre** (open Mon–Sat 9am–5pm; tel: 09-516 1007; www.pahangtourism.com.my) opposite the Kompleks Teruntum on Jalan Mahkota .

The town serves more as a springboard to inland attractions such as **Gua Charah** (30 km/19 miles away), **Sungai Lembing** (45 km/28 miles away), and the eight-cascade **Berkelah Waterfall** (70 km/44 miles away). Most visitors prefer to stay at the pleasant **Teluk Chempedak** beach, 1 km (½ mile) out of

BELOW: Muslim schoolgirls in *tudung* (headscarf).

own, featuring the usual eateries, pubs and both upmarket (the Hyatt Kuantan) and budget accommodation.

An alternative is to opt for one of the many beach resorts just north of Kuantan in **Beserah**. Known for its dried salted fish, a handful of Beserah's denizens still employ tough lumbering water buffaloes to transport fish from their boats on the beach to the processing areas.

Map on page 240

Fun in the sun

From the Pahang–Terengganu border, it's one long beach resort stretch all the way up to Kota Bharu. About 35 km (22 miles) from Beserah is the resort area of **Cherating** ⓫, a *kampung* (village) squeezed out of its gorgeous crescent-shaped golden beach by tourism.

Cherating was originally a backpackers' haunt, but the accommodation choices have gone upmarket and now include **Club Med Cherating** (www.clubmed.com.my) – Asia's first – on a private beach north. There are restaurants galore, souvenir shops (including DIY batik) and pubs; weekends can be one long party starting from Thursday, with the arrival of big city folk. Somehow, though, the area has avoided the claustrophobic feel of some other resort beaches, and maintains its friendly, relaxed air. A huge map at one of the two turnoffs to Cherating from the main road gives more information.

Local buses linking Kuantan and Kuala Terengganu stop on the main road, close to the beach where most of the resorts are located. Some resorts organise river trips and tours, and several travel agencies can also arrange transport to nearby islands as well as onward legs of your journey. Popular tours are to Gua Charah in Sungai Lembing (5-hour trip with a stopover in Kuantan) and Tasik Cini (7-hour

Salted fish being sun dried is a common sight along the east coast.

BELOW: the upscale Hyatt Kuantan.

trip, including a boat ride and visit to the Orang Asli village). However, minimum numbers are required, so you could end up losing out playing the waiting game.

Near Club Med at Pantai Chendor, sea turtles lay their eggs at night from May through to September. The Fisheries Department runs the **Turtle Sanctuary and Information Centre** next to the club, which is worth a visit. About 25 km (16 miles) north of Cherating is **Cukai**, a town famous for its seafood and coffee. It is the base for an excursion to **Kampung Ibok**, 11 km (7 miles) to its northwest, for a boat tour along the mangrove habitat of Sungai Yakyah to see the largest firefly colony in the east coast (tour from 7.45pm–midnight; contact mobile tel: 019-933 6458 or local tour operators).

Terengganu treasures

Cross into Terengganu and you hit oil country. The multi-million ringgit oil and natural gas industry has changed the face of Terengganu's oil stretch beyond recognition. Villages now wear whitewashed brick faces, former fishermen and farmers sport imported overalls and hard hats, and grocery shops stock German beer, Edam cheese and Japanese seaweed for the cosmopolitan mix who now calls Terengganu home. Terengganu contributes about 60 percent of Malaysia's total oil production, but 95 percent of revenues go to federal coffers. As such, fisheries remain the state's main income-earner.

The huge drilling rigs are 200 km (125 miles) offshore in the South China Sea, but giant steel structures, snaking pipelines and bullying tankers dominate the scene from Kemaman to Paka. Before and after office hours, the traffic slows to a crawl in this stretch.

Yet there are some pretty beaches. A 240-km (150-mile) long beach stretches from Kemaman to Besut; the beach at **Kijal** is particularly notable. At **Dungun** the messy industrial scenery falls away and dignified fishing villages and paddy fields reclaim the landscape. Dungun, a dreamy little seaside town and port, is a jumping-off point to **Pulau Tenggol**  a gazetted marine sanctuary 13 km (8 miles) offshore. Actually a group of islands, this destination has clear waters for diving and 20 stunning spots that feature underwater cliffs and boulders. Its deep dive profile attracts a good selection of pelagic (deep-water) marine life.

Inland from Kampung Pasir Raja is the majestic **Cemeruh Waterfalls**, 300 metres (1,000 ft) of white water thundering down a sheer rock face. To get there, you need three days through pitcher plant and palm country, across cascades and rapids. Guided tours can be arranged at Kuala Terengganu.

Ancient mariners

Twenty-two kilometres (14 miles) north of Dungun is the **Rantau Abang Turtle Sanctuary** , a 13-km (8-mile) stretch that used to be an important nesting ground for Malaysia's oldest marine creature – the sea turtle. In better times, female turtles of four species, including the 500-kg (1,000-lb) leatherback, struggled ashore to lay their eggs at night between May and September every year. But with the leatherback facing extinction and the smaller green and hawksbill turtles also at risk, turtle landings at Rantau Abang have diminished drastically and hatchings are almost non-existent. A wealth of information on turtles, including some depressing statistics, is displayed at the Fisheries Department's small information centre (open Sat–Thur 9am–11pm).

But all is not lost yet. South of Rantau Abang at Kerteh is the **Ma' Daerah Turtle Sanctuary** (tel: 09-830 5312; madaerah-turtle-sanctuary.org), a 1.7-km (1-mile) beach which still hosts nesting green turtles from April to September every year. It has a hatchery and interpretation centre, and to promote conservation awareness, the sanctuary offers a "Weekend with the Turtles" programme, during which volunteers monitor turtle landings, collect turtle eggs and help out with hatchery work. (Booking in advance and donation required; includes meals and accommodation.)

Do take note of the do's and don'ts of watching turtles. Lights and noise can scare off the females. Picking up hatchlings could tamper with the imprinting process which registers the nesting location; imprinting takes effect when they run from the beach to the sea. Shining lights at the hatchlings also distracts them – they are guided by the white breakers in the ocean. Distracting them also causes them to use up energy from the tiny yolk sack that they survive on for the 3 or 4 days it takes them to get to driftlines, out of reach of predators.

Kampung living

Just south of Kuala Terengganu is the district of Marang, dotted with picturesque villages. **Marang ⓮** beach is an old favourite of backpackers, although fancier establishments are muscling in. The inland villages, however, are just waking up to tourism. *Gula melaka*, screwpine palm sugar, is still baked in bamboo

Map on page 240

Extensive research to help turn the tide against sea turtle extinction is being conducted at the Sea Turtle Research Unit at University Pertanian Malaysia. Pledge your support in cash and kind. Visit their website at www.kustem.edu.my/ seatru

BELOW: leatherback turtle heading back to sea.

TURTLE WATCH

Nobody knows what happens between the time sea turtle hatchlings swim out into the moonlit sea and are spotted years later as juveniles, perhaps hundreds of kilometres away. Indeed, question marks surround this marine reptile: why does it swim so far away? Why does it return to the same beach to lay eggs? Why do more come up to nest some years than others?

Malaysia's Fisheries Department has been collecting data on the giant leatherback since the 1960s, artificially hatching eggs, and carrying out awareness programmes. Yet, the largest of the four species is almost extinct: there were 1,800 landings in 1956, just 210 in 1994 and by the turn of the 21st century there were less than half a dozen sightings a season. The tiny Olive Ridley is endangered, while the green and hawksbill turtles have also dwindled in numbers.

The most obvious human threat to turtles is the eating of eggs. Fisheries officers are fighting this by paying collectors for eggs which they then hatch artificially. Turtle mortality due to fishing nets and propellers is also high. Uncontrolled tourist activities can be another killer. But the pollution that affects their habitat is the hardest to monitor – plastic bags that strangle them, or pollution that kills the coral reefs and marine life on which they feed.

Chillies are central to Malay cuisine. Ask before you dig into a dish. If the food proves too fiery, downing a glass of milk instead of water will usually do the trick.

BELOW: basket and mat weaver in Terengannu.

over traditional stoves, while old ladies sit in the shade of *nipah* huts, stitching away at a new "roof" for a beach resort. Tree-climbing monkeys deftly pluck young coconuts whose sweet cool juice makes a refreshing drink. A cruise up the Marang River offers views of mangrove forest from whose banks peep monkeys, iguana and sometimes, otter.

From Marang, it is only 30 minutes and 15 minutes by boat respectively to **Pulau Kapas** ⓯ and **Pulau Gemia** for snorkelling and easy diving. En route to Kuala Terengganu, you will pass the **Masjid Tengku Tengah Zaharah**, also known as the floating mosque. Combining the modern and traditional, its serene white reflection gives an illusion of being afloat in the water.

Setting its own pace

Despite its affluence born of the state's plentiful sources of oil, enough of **Kuala Terengganu's** ⓰ old charms remain to save it from facelessness. Possibly the east coast's oldest port, the pulse of the state capital is felt most keenly in the waterfront **Pasar Payang** (Central Market) in the early morning. This is when fresh produce pours in: glistening fish by the lorry-load (the main fishing port is now in Chendering), while coconuts and *pandan* (screwpine) leaves arrive by boat from Pulau Duyung. Though less publicised than the much-photographed Central Market in Kota Bharu, this wet market is just as lively and colourful. Housed also in a concrete building, produce is sold downstairs and in the courtyard while the handicraft shops fill the first floor.

This bustle spills out into Jalan Kampong Cina, a narrow and congested crescent-shaped street lined with Chinese shophouses. This is **Chinatown**, Kuala Terengganu's original thoroughfare, where the architecture dates back to when

Terengganu was an independent state. Stroll down this street, or take a trishaw, still the most popular means of transport in downtown Kuala Terengganu. Peek into the narrow doorways – the houses seem to stretch back forever – and you might see an old lady sipping tea. The young and the trendy are moving in, though, mainly to open art and handicraft shops; this is also where many of **Pulau Redang**'s resort operators are located.

Just beyond the market in the direction of the river mouth is a broad esplanade which faces the **Istana Maziah**, the official residence of the sultan, who actually lives in another palace a few kilometres away. The Istana resembles a French country house and was built at the beginning of the century to replace an older palace destroyed by fire.

Across from the Central Market is **Pulau Duyung**, where master craftsmen once fashioned unique fishing boats with decorated fore- and main-masts, and bowsprits called *bedor*. Today, the island is famous for its custom-made yachts of local *cengal* wood for an international clientele, as well as for the annual Monsoon Cup match race in November.

Terengganu's heritage

Terenggganu's beautiful traditional Malay architecture is represented in the grounds of the **Terengganu State Museum Complex** (open daily 9am–5pm; entrance fee). Malaysia's largest museum sits on the site of the town's first settlement, and its main buildings are obscenely outsized replicas of the real thing, five well-preserved wooden houses with Islamic motifs and shades of Chinese and European architectural influence.

The excellent fisheries and seafaring open-air galleries showcase the gamut of

Map on page 240

BELOW: kite-flying is popular in the east coast.

Terengganu batik is generally more expensive than that of the northernmost state of Kelantan. The designs in the former state are finer, and involve more skilled workmanship.

boats, including two original hand-built wooden galleys used for trade in the 19th century. The museum is in Losong, which has charming kampung houses and is home to the famous Terengganu *keropok lekor*, a fishy cracker found only here and Kelantan. On the other side of the Terengganu River, at Kampung Tanjung Sabtu, is **Pura Tanjung Sabtu** (tel: 09-615 3655; www.puratanjungsabtu.com), a complex of reconstructed traditional Terengganu houses. The owner, Terengganu prince Tengku Ismail Tengku Su, is passionate about woven silk *songket* (Malay brocade), and hosts guests on homestay package deals at the complex.

Like Kuantan, Kuala Terengganu has its own beach. **Pantai Batu Buruk** is a coconut tree-fringed sandy stretch with lots of eateries – try out the local *nasi dagang* breakfast if you can stomach rice and fish curry in the morning. There is also budget accommodation and a three-star hotel here.

Arts and crafts

Though village life in Terengganu has been urbanised, many of the traditional arts it fostered are as alive as ever. Seasonal fishing and farming brought village folk leisure, and from leisure came time to devote to their arts. Folk dances, shadow plays and traditional games such as kite-flying and top-spinning were celebrated during festivals after a harvest. Many processions and rituals were related to the spirit of the rice paddy, a carry-over from ancient animistic beliefs. Today, village festivals are rarer since farmers are busy planting rice twice a year instead of once, and the Islamic doctrine discourages customs connected with spirit worship.

Chendering, 8 km (5 miles) south of town, houses some commercial handicraft centres, including the government-sponsored **Kraftangan Malaysia** craft centre (open Sun–Thur 9am–5pm), which has an apprentice programme for

BELOW: batik being sun dried in Terengannu.

weaving, stitching and brassware. Their showroom displays products from the surrounding villages. Here also is the headquarters of the **Noor Arfa Batek House** (tel: 09-617 5700; www.noor-arfa.com), the country's largest hand-drawn batik producer, where you can watch batik being made and try your hand at it too.

Map
on page
240

Jewels in the sea

Like jade in an cean of clear blue, Terengganu's islands are the most beautiful in the peninsula, and worshipped by sun-soakers and coral-lovers.

Merang, 28 km (17 miles) north of Kuala Terengganu, is the jumping-off point to **Pulau Redang** , **Pulau Lang Tengah** and **Pulau Bidong**. A range of accommodation is available on these islands, and virtually every one offers dive facilities. Visitors should book beforehand for packages with travel agents to ensure firm reservations for boat transfers, especially in the high season.

Lang Tengah is less crowded, good for easy diving and excellent snorkelling and only 30 minutes by boat from shore. Redang, two hours from shore, is famous for its great visibility and diverse dive sites, but has become very crowded. Comprising nine islands, it is also probably the peninsula's most researched island. A pleasant cross-island track through rainforest connects the pristine wide beaches of fine white sand at Pasir Panjang and Teluk Dalam. There is also a small traditional Malay fishing village on stilts where you can stop for *teh tarik* (tea) and local *kuih* (cakes).

However, diving is what has carved the island's fame. The Marine Park jetty alone has prolific marine life, including a resident Moray eel. Night dives at the submerged reefs are particularly fascinating. There is also a high chance of bumping into a member or two of the large green turtle population. In situ

Crown of thorns starfish are extremely destructive to reefs as they feed off the coral beds.

BELOW: Redang's talcum powder beaches are divine.

TIP

It doesn't matter what you wear (or don't) on the islands, but spare a thought for a vastly different culture by making sure you are decently clad when you visit a *kampung* (village).

hatching is being carried out here, as well as a research programme involving volunteers (*see Margin Note on the Sea Turtle Research Unit on page 251*).

Legend has it that two birds turned to stone and became the gorgeous **Pulau Perhentian Kecil** ⑱ and **Pulau Perhentian Besar** isles, 21 km (16 miles) from shore. *Kecil* and *besar* mean "small" and "large" respectively. The jetty is at Kuala Besut, an unspoilt fishing village where fishing boats make a dramatic show at dawn and dusk. Slow boats reach the isles in 1½ hours and operate between 9am–2pm. Speedboats take 30 minutes, but it's a bumpy ride.

Accommodation at Kuala Besut is limited, but the jetty is well serviced by buses and taxis from any major town. Boats and accommodation can be booked with travel agencies at the jetty complex. Walk-ins are common, but book beforehand during public holidays in May and August. Most resorts close during the monsoon season from November to February.

Perhentian Besar has a wider range of accommodation spread along the bay facing the smaller island, including the three-star Perhentian Island Resort. Accommodation with rock-bottom prices can still be found at Pasir Panjang on Perhentian Kechil, site of the first backpacker invasion. It has become really crowded here; the island's body-lined beach attests to its popularity. However, water remains a problem in the dry July/August period.

The traditional fishing village on Perhentian Kecil is interesting, particularly at the day's end when the villagers converge on the waterfront for a gossip surrounded by squealing children at play. The village also sells groceries and other necessities.

The diving here is more leisurely compared to Redang, and the shallower waters are good for snorkelling. There are nine dive facilities in all, each offer-

BELOW: two for the pot – a grinning lobster fisherman.

ng instruction. Gardens of soft coral – which grow to huge sizes – lots of shells, nd large boulders make for an attractive underwater playground.

Malay enclave

A few kilometres from the Thai border lies **Kota Bharu ⑲**, the cradle of Malay ulture. Although it is ruled by the opposition fundamentalist Muslim Parti Islam or PAS, Kelantan's capital is not corseted by the party's stringent policies but is, instead, vibrant with life and colour.

Kota Bharu has one of the best-known wet markets in Malaysia. The **Pasar Siti Khadijah**, also known as the Central Market (open daily 6am–6pm), on Jalan Hulu is where traders – traditionally women – sit in their colourful headscarfs and traditional *baju kurung* on raised dais among vegetables and *keropok lekor*. Upstairs is a shopping haven for east coast crafts, particularly batik and silverwork.

Just beyond the market is a cluster of museums around the old palace, **Istana Balai Besar**, which was built in 1884. Next to it is the pretty **Istana Jahar** another palace that is now the museum of royal traditions and customs. Its displays are a good introduction to traditional Kelantan life and culture; it also has an excellent weapons section. **Kampung Kraftangan**, the Handicraft Village and Craft Museum on Jalan Hilir Balai, is notable more for its traditional architecture than its contents, but nonetheless offers exhibits of batik, woodcarvings and other traditional Kelantanese crafts, as well as demonstrations by artisans. Nearby are the **Muzium Islam** (Islamic Museum), another attractive traditional wooden building, and the more modern **Istana Batu** (Royal Museum) which houses memorabilia of Kelantan's royal family.

Kota Bharu's cultural pastimes are showcased at **Gelanggang Seni**, literally

Map on page 240

TIP

All museums in Kota Bharu are open 8.30am–4.45pm, but are closed on Friday as it's a Muslim prayer day; all charge an entrance fee.

BELOW: the Central Market at Kota Bharu.

All in a day's work – monkeys trained to pluck coconuts.

the "Court of Arts" but also known as the Cultural Centre, on Jalan Mahmud Check the latest schedules at the Tourism Malaysia office (open Sun–Thu 8.30am–4.45pm; tel: 09-747 7554) in Kampung Kraftangan. Unless you are lucky enough to chance upon festivals in Kota Bharu or its surrounding villages, this is the best place to view these artforms. In a small *wakaf* (rest hut) outside the main hall, old men tune their instruments, and exponents of traditional Malay self defence, *silat*, take to the stage. On the green, the *gasing* (top) spinners are ready to spin down their prized tops onto a concrete square. From here the tops are removed with a wooden pallet onto dowels. The trick is to keep your top spinning longer than anyone else's. The drummers then beat out rhythms on the rows of colourful *rebana*, huge drums fashioned out of logs.

Wayang kulit (shadow puppet plays) and the Thai-influenced dance-theatre *mak yong*, two of the loveliest Malay artforms, were once banned from performance in the state because they are considered anti-Islam. Luckily, the *wayang kulit* troupes in Terengganu, Kedah and Perlis are alive and thriving. *Mak yong* and its sister artform *manohra*, are now revived amid renewed interest.

Surprising surroundings

Kota Bharu is surrounded by a patchwork of villages among rice paddy fields and orchards. What might seem surprising in a predominantly Muslim state is the number of Thai *wat* (temples) between Tumpat and Pasir Mas. Among them is the **Wat Photivihan**, which houses the country's largest statue of the reclining Buddha. Some villages even celebrate Thai festivals, like the Songkran water festival in April and Loy Krathong in November.

Tumpat is the terminus for the eastern railway line from Segamat. The line whisks travellers all the way to Bangkok. Head out of Kota Bharu on Route 3 to reach what is reputed to be the oldest surviving mosque in Kelantan. The 18th-century **Masjid Kampung Laut** (Kampung Laut Mosque) was originally on the banks of Sungai Kelantan but was moved out of flood's harm to Kampung Nilam Puri 10 km (6 miles) south of Kota Bharu. Built of stout chengal wood and without nails, it has a pyramidal two-tiered roof, typical of a Javanese mosque.

A great place to watch Kelantan's colourful fishing boats is at the picturesque estuary at **Pantai Dasar Sabak** ⓴, 13 km (8 miles) north of the town. The boats leave at dawn and return at about 3pm, when it is all bustle with the unloading of the catch and the washing of boats. The beach also has a 20th-century claim to fame: it was here, on 8 December 1941, that the Japanese began their brutal march south to Singapore. (The attack on Pearl Harbor was not to take place until 95 minutes later – 7 December on the other side of the dateline.)

Weekenders head for the beach facing the South China Sea, PCB or **Pantai Cahaya Bulan** (Moonlight Beach); the acronym actually used to stand for Pantai Cinta Berahi – The Beach of Passionate Love – in pre-PAS days. PCB is a handicraft haven. The gold threaded *songket*, *wau* (kites), and rows of batik hanging in the sun beckon souvenir-hunters on the 5-km (3-mile) road to the beach.

Map on page 240

BELOW: reclining Buddha of Wat Photivihan.

Kampung Games

Every Malaysian is a *kampung* kid at heart; so says Lat, Malaysia's favourite cartoonist who has a series of books contrasting the easy, down-to-earth *kampung* lifestyle with the mobile-phone and pager-punctuated life of the modern yuppie.

Despite the city-dweller's groomed image and array of gadgets, every holiday in Malaysia results in airports and highways jammed with city residents returning to their villages – *balek kampung*. Their *kampung* are their roots, and bound up in this are the traditional pastimes enjoyed there.

Throughout most of the country, **top-spinning** is a teenage game, but in the Malay *kampung* of the northeast coast, a champion spinner is the village hero. Requiring great strength to spin, tops vary from a simple wooden cylinder to fantastic streamlined discs with spindles trimmed with inlaid gold; large ones can be as big as dinner plates. With the harvest completed and all the rice stored, farmers traditionally settled down to watch and bet on the top local team. Contests feature either the endurance spinners – record times for spinning are about two hours – or the strikers who spin down 7 kg (15 lb) fighting tops faster than a speeding bullet.

Another traditional entertainment most popular in Malaysia's northeastern states, **kite-flying** was enjoyed in the 15th century. Today, great pride is still taken in the design and the hand-crafting of each aerodynamic piece of art. The paper *wau* (kite) comes in unique shapes, and bamboo pieces are often attached underneath a kite to produce a melodic humming sound (*degung*). Contests are still held for serious kite-flyers, and today, international kite festivals are held in Malaysia, drawing participants from both European and Asian countries.

Sepak takraw, a traditional *kampung* game, uses a ball about the size of a large grapefruit, made of woven rattan strips, and weighing 170 grammes (less than ½ pound). The aim of the game is to keep the ball in the air as long as possible by passing it from one player to another, using all parts of the body except for the forearms and the hands. The game requires acrobatic flexibility and practised skills, and is exhilarating to watch.

Congkak is a game requiring more wits than physical skill. Comparable to backgammon, *congkak* features a wooden boat-shaped "board" and marbles or seeds. The *congkak* board has two rows of holes in which the marbles are placed, and the object of the game is to have the most marbles to finish.

The best childhood memories come from games provided by nature. The pea-sized, red saga seeds from the large saga tree, for example, are used in a game of accuracy much like marbles. The game of pick-up-sticks is played with coconut twigs or satay skewers; chicken feathers are stuck into a flat rubber disc, and this *catek*, resembling a shuttlecock, is kept in the air while being nimbly kicked using only the instep of one's foot. Even conker-like rubber seeds are the centre of numerous, imaginative kampung games, all still fresh in the minds of almost every Malaysian. Just go ahead and ask. ❑

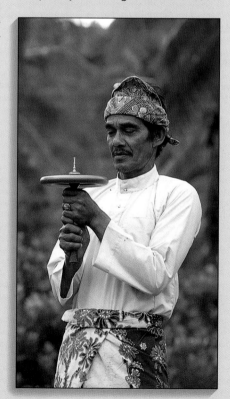

RIGHT: top-spinning is taken very seriously in the northeastern states of Malaysia.

THE BANGAU
MARITIME FIGUREHEADS

*Carved spar holders, or bangau, adorn these
colourful fishing boats, and are found only on
the Malaysian peninsula's east coast*

When engines began
replacing sails from the
1950s onwards, it was
thought that the
bangau would become
extinct. But, defying all
predictions, these
colourful objects have
been retained, because
the spars are still used
as gaffs for landing fish and for poling into shore.

In ancient times they were more than utilitarian
objects – the *bangau* also served as a repository
for the spirit of the boat, and its presence was
believed to help keep the boat safe from storms
and sea demons.

Bangau are found from the northern shores of
Kelantan – notably adorning the boats known as
perahu bauatan barat – to Terengganu in the
south, where they act as figureheads on the
curved bows of *kolek* boats.

FIGUREHEAD FASHIONS

Bangau take on various forms. Some are shaped
like birds, others of the *naga*, a legendary sea
serpent, while a few are even fashioned after
figures in traditional shadow-puppet plays. Some
prows are even shaped and painted to resemble the
garuda, a demonic birdman from
Kelantanese mythology. Were they
originally made to ward off the *naga
umbang*, a marine dragon that
according to legend lurked in the
depths of the sea? Another legendary
tale has the *garuda* residing in the
top of a huge coconut palm –
a symbolic represention of
heaven – which rises out of
the centre of the ocean.

Although the spiritual
significance of the *bangau* has
been long forgotten, the
tradition of keeping them and
the boats they adorn still
decorated, survives.

△ **PAINTED PROWS**
A naga "dragon"
adorns a prow at
Pantai Dasar
Sabak, Kelantan.

◁ **THE *ONGKAK***
Sitting opposite the
bangau, the *ongkak* often
resembles figures from the
shadow-puppet plays.

BIRD-LIKE BOAT SPIRITS

Bangau means "cattle egret" in Malay. It is thought that originally the boat fittings resembled these birds, who, while rarely seen flying over the sea, were perhaps chosen for their symbolic value due to their well-known liking for fish.

Most *bangau*, however, bear no resemblance to this bird, although bird shapes are sometimes used. Their fanciful designs probably have something to do with the strict Islamic edicts banning the portrayal of anthropomorphic figures.

At Kelantan's Pantai Baru near Bachok, a *bangau* takes on a parrot-like look (*above*), but the colours are highly imaginative.

Further south, at Penarik, Terengganu (*below*), a *bangau* keeps the long neck of its namesake but its garish blue colouring is merely for ornamentation.

△ **BEACHED BANGAUS**
One of the east coast's most enduring scenes are fleets of rainbow-coloured fishing boats lined up under the shade of coconut palms.

◁ **BOAT FIXER**
When rough monsoon seas keep boats in port, fishermen repair their craft for the next season.

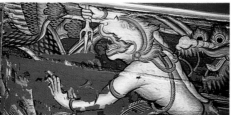

△ **DEMON DESIGN**
Trident-wielding demons were perhaps originally painted on boat hulls to scare off "sea devils".

◁ **BOAT BEACHING**
Each day at the Bachok district of Kelantan, the fishing fleet is physically hauled up onto the beach.

▷ **BLUE BANGAU**
The tuft of feathers on the head of this *bangau* could have originally mimicked the bright orange feathers which the male egret sprouts during mating season.

EASTERN INTERIOR

Inland from the east coast lies the dark green heart of Malaysia, a land of lakes and forest, of wild animals, ancient myths and the sublime beauty of Taman Negara

Map on page 240

I n the still of morning, before the first breath of wind, surreal sculptures of dead wood stand perfectly reflected in the mirror of **Tasik Kenyir ㉑**, Southeast Asia's largest artificial lake. Nineteen hills were inundated to create the 260,000-hectare (642,460-acre) lake, whose water feeds the hydroelectric power station that supplies about 8 percent of the nation's electricity.

However, the statuesque tree trunks that used to be the lake's outstanding characteristic have been removed, except in its northern fingers. Nonetheless, Kenyir's numerous tributaries continue to be an anglers' favourite, with numerous freshwater species including the *kelah* and carnivorous *toman* (snakehead).

About 14 waterfalls dot the area's 340 thickly-forested islands. The multi-tier 152-metre (500-ft) **Lasir Waterfall** is 16 km (10 miles) or 45 minutes south of the jetty by boat; and **Tembat Waterfall**, a series of five furious rapids and gorgeous giant sun-baked boulders, is an hour north. You'll find campsites on the pebble-beached **Petuang** and **Saok** rivers, which are also popular fishing spots. Otters, eagles and amphibians are common; if you are lucky, you might even spot elephants or the elusive black panther.

The road to Kenyir

The main gateway to Kenyir is the **Pengkalan Gawi** jetty, an hour from Kuala Terengganu. Buses from Kuala Terengganu go to Kuala Berang, 15 km (9 miles) from Kenyir; take a taxi for the rest of the journey. There are also overnight buses (Tasik Kenyir Express, tel: 03-4044 4276) that go direct from Kuala Lumpur (Hentian Putra) to Pengkalan Gawi.

Kenyir's visitor's centre (tel: 09-626 7788; www.ketengah.gov.my/kenyir) is located near the jetty, where day-trippers can hire fibreglass boats from the tour operators; these seat eight to 10 persons. The operators can also arrange accommodation at the resorts or budget-class, double-decker houseboats that can sleep 15 people. It is however more convenient if you book a package or day-trip with an agency in Kuala Terengganu or directly with a resort at Lake Kenyir. All resorts offer the same deal: accommodation, all meals, boat transfers, jungle-trekking, a visit to a waterfall and unlimited use of facilities.

En route to Kenyir is the picturesque seven-step **Sekayu Waterfall** (entrance fee) in a forest reserve near Kuala Berang. A 25-minute walk up a flight of steps takes you to the top, the least slippery spot for a swim. Kuala Berang was the site of the first Malay settlement in Terengganu, but nothing remains of the original dwellings. Also discovered here was Malaysia's oldest Koranic inscription. The 14th-century *Batu Bersurat* is now in the state museum.

LEFT: Orang Asli tribesman and his blowpipe.
BELOW: thundering Sekayu waterfall during the rainy season.

Towards Pahang's hinterlands

En route to Pahang's hinterlands from Kuantan, the turn-off to **Sungai Lembing** ㉒ leads to a towering limestone cliff, **Gua Charah**, whose inner cave houses a 9-metre (30-ft) long limestone statue of a reclining Buddha built by a Thai Buddhist monk. The taxing climb up to the ledge is rewarded by a great view. The cathedral-sized outer cave has thin shafts of light filtering down through cracks hundreds of metres above. There are other caves to explore but a guide is needed. On the same road is the world's second-largest and deepest tin mine, open to tours if prior arrangements are made with Pahang Consolidated Ltd. For details, enquire at Sungai Lembing.

About 16 km (10 miles) inland from Sungai Lembing is **Gunung Tapis**, a mountainous nature park with rapids, trails and fishing spots. It takes 1½-day climb to reach Gunung Tapis' peak. Contact Persona Adventure Camp (mobile tel: 012-954 9111), which has 10 chalets and a campsite, to arrange transport, trekking guides, tours and lodgings.

Mountain skyscapes

Fantastic skyscapes over islands of *pandanus* (screwpines) at sunset; boat-wide "paths" through long submerged grass; and from June to September, fragile pink waterlilies and white lotuses on immense velvet leaf carpets. This is **Tasik Cini** ㉓ (Lake Cini), a rare river-floodplain of 12 interlocking lakes about 100 km (62 miles) inland from Kuantan.

Cini is fascinating for its two main forest types – the riverine forest of massive trees and lianas overhanging the narrow Sungai Cini; and the swamp vegetation, the most prominent of which are the *pandanus*. This is also home to

BELOW:
Tasik Cini, Pahang.

monkeys and birds, including large flocks of hornbills, and kingfishers and broadbills that flash a brilliant blue across the water.

Myths and monsters

Legend has it that a lost city, probably Khmer, is believed to lie 12 metres (40 ft) below the lake's surface but Cini is probably best known for its mythical *naga*, a Loch Ness-type monster whose origins are a spiritual dragon-creature of local Orang Asli folklore. Another version tells of how two of these mythical creatures evolved to become the islands of Tioman and Daik.

The Jakun follow a traditional lifestyle, planting rice paddy and fishing; they also make fine handicrafts, now predominantly targetting tourists. Try your hand at the blowpipe at Tanjung Puput and Kampung Gumum. There is also basic accommodation and tours at the latter.

By road, Cini is off the Kuantan-Segamat Highway (Route 12), then 32 km (20 miles) from the Pahang bridge turnoff. This road goes to Kampung Gumum and the Kijang Mas Gumum Resort (tel: 09-422 1448), which has a range of accommodation, a restaurant and public toilets. A jetty here with an association of 19 boatmen (tel: 09-456 7160), offers the lake tour at a more reasonable rate than the boaters at the Tourism Complex at the Kuala Sungai Cini rivermouth (tel: 013-954 9056) which lies further down that road. Use the latter's services if you plan to access Cini by boat from Kampung Belimbing off the Karak Highway on the other side of the massive Sungai Pahang; the rate is RM50 per hour. If you want to be dropped off at your accommodation, the fare is double. All boatmen can ferry you to the campsites that dot the place or to Lake Chini Resort (tel: 09-477 8000; www.lakechini.com) which has chalets and tours.

Map on page 240

TIP

The best storehouse of tales from the rich Jakun oral tradition, is probably Tok Batin, the headman at Kampung Gumum – although the local boatmen are good sources too. You would need a translator though.

LEFT: waterlily at Cini. **BELOW:** Orang Asli blowpipes.

TIP

Club Med Cherating
usually sends
busloads of tourists to
Lake Cini on Mondays,
and weekends are
usually busy for boat
operators.

A worthwhile day trip would cover the dank, winding Sungai Cini, half the lakes, and a short jungle trek from the resort to Kampung Gumum, one of three trails in the area. A longer day trip brings you to the **Mentenang Waterfall** while an overnight option is **Gunung Cini**. Tours can be arranged from Kuantan and Cherating. Public transport runs from Kuantan and Pekan to Cini town: call the resort and they will pick you up. An express bus also goes to Cini from Kuala Lumpur's Puduraya Station.

Unfortunately, all is not well at Cini. The leafless trees at the waters' edge are the result of a bungle by authorities on a dam built in the early 1990s to regulate water fluctuations; it let in too much, and was knocked down too late, killing off large numbers of the huge *tembusu* trees. The current, British designed dyke is the third attempt to get it right. Behind the beauty of the increasingly abundant water lilies is also the ominous sign that the lake is getting shallower; the ecosystem has not found its balance yet.

Ancient lifestyles

A similar lake experience is to be had at **Tasik Bera ㉔** (Lake Bera), 1½ hour from Cini. Though the largest freshwater lake in Southeast Asia, its waters are contained in narrower "fingers" rather than the open lakes of Cini, thanks to the greater abundance of screwpine.

Bera's 26,000 hectares (64,000 acres) of wetland and swamp ecosystems are protected under the Ramsar Convention as a wetland of international importance. Like Cini, the water rises up to 3 metres (9 ft) in the wet months of September to January, blessing the rivers with fish, and making the post-monsoon months the best angling period. As the boat snakes through the narrow channels

BELOW:
view from the
East-West highway.

splash of colour in the orchids amid ferns and epiphytes catches the eye. Less obvious are the pitcher plants among the tall reed fields. Above, a hawk wings its solitary way, keeping a keen eye out for supper.

The Orang Asli of the Semelai tribe maintain their traditional lifestyles living in bamboo and bark huts, using traditional implements to trap fish and fashioning handicrafts from forest products. They also collect *minyak keruing* resin from the *keruing* tree, used for making torches, boats and perfume. Semelai homestay packages are available from the Semelai Association for Boating and Tourism (SABOT) at Tasik Bera (mobile tel: 011-912 617; tasekbera.jones.dk). Their packages include birdwatching, trekking, a lake tour and camping.

Tasik Bera's Pesona Lake Resort (tel: 09-276 2505) has rooms, dorms, campsites and covered platforms overlooking the serene waters. Three trails run around the area and there are also canoes and mountain bikes. Tasik Bera is difficult to access, but the resort does pick-ups for a fee from Temerloh and the Triang train station.

Map on page 240

Rainforest thrills

There is shuffling and grunting, but the torchlight picks out only a pair of eyes. Is it the black-and-white king of camouflage, a tapir? Or, against all odds, one of the park's remaining 40-plus Sumatran Rhino? The experience afforded by the live animal hides in **Taman Negara** ㉕ is among the attractions that have made it arguably the best-known of Malaysia's protected areas. This granddaddy, which simply translates to "National Park", sprawls over 430,000 hectares (100,000 acres) across three states, with the bulk being in Pahang. Looming over all this is the central massif of Gunung Tahan, the peninsula's highest peak.

Taman Negara offers everything from a leisurely 2 days' birdwatching to a

BELOW: Taman Negara at dawn.

2-week jungle safari, a muddy crawl through bat-infested caves to a splashy ride through Sungai Tembeling's rapids. The park's hundreds of kilometres of trails are kept cleared and well marked, and meander through fascinating lowland dipterocarp and riverine forests, climbing to stunted montane vegetation.

Birdwatching is a delight. Kingfishers, bee-eaters, fishing eagles and osprey abound, and even if you don't see them, you'd certainly hear them, in particular the hornbills' unmistakable squawk. Besides monitor lizards, the larger denizens such as elephants, black panther, *seladang* wild ox and tigers are virtually impossible to spot, so learn to identify their tracks. Nonetheless, sit quietly in the jungle, and you might be rewarded with the sight of long-tailed macaques in the treetops.

The aboriginal Batek communities are no longer a common sight around the headquarters, preferring a nomadic lifestyle deep in the forest. You might occasionally bump into them on a trail or see their temporary huts. The Batek have a natural dignity; don't be too quick to turn them into a tourist spectacle with the click of a camera. But don't be surprised if they demand a fee if you insist on clicking. The Senoi and Semak Abri tribes outside the park area, however, live more contemporary lifestyles and are more open to visitors.

Riding the Tembeling

Permits are required to enter the park and there is a fee for cameras – arrange at the Department of Wildlife and National Parks (DWNP) counter in Kuala Tembeling or at its office in Kuala Tahan (tel: 09-266 1122), or through your travel agent. Entrance to the park is usually by river from the Kuala Tembeling jetty, although a rough road also goes to the Kuala Tahan *kampung*. However, the covered 14-seater longboat ride is a great way to cover the 35-km (20-mile) journey on Sungai Tembeling. The 2-hour trip can take twice as long if the river level is low; sometimes passengers have to disembark and wade while the boatmen negotiate the shallow waters.

Kuala Tembeling is accessed from Jerantut, where express buses and the Gemas-Tumpat trains stop. From Jerantut, take a 30-minute taxi to the jetty. Tours to the park that operate from major cities and Jerantut include transfers to and from the park.

Accommodation choices range from campsites to luxurious chalets of the Mutiara Taman Negara Resort (tel: 09-266 2200; www.mutiarahotels.com). Budget accommodation is available outside the park in the village and at Nusa Camp. There is a river shuttle between the park and the *kampung*, and a riverbus run by Nusa Camp services the main jetties on Sungai Tembeling. Boats within the park must be arranged through DWNP.

At Kuala Tahan, visitors can book accommodation, arrange trips and get information and maps at either the Wildlife Department or the Tourist Information Counter at the Mutiara Taman Negara Resort. The resort and Nusa Camp have good maps and guides to the park, and provide information to non-guests as well. They also rent out camping and fishing gear if you make prior arrangements.

The park's excellent interpretation centre, squashed into the resort grounds, provides a great introduction to the park, including information on trails and rain

These banana-like fruits which grow from this tree trunk in Taman Negara look inviting but are unsafe to eat.

BELOW: jungle canopy walk at Taman Negara.

orests, and videos are screened daily. Short trails can be done yourself, or you :an hire nature interpretation guides. Guides are compulsory on the major trails, ınd guided tours are included in packages.

Walks in the wild

The most popular walk is the half-hour trek to the **canopy walkway** (open I 1am–3pm; entrance fee), a rope-and-ladder bridge among the tops of trees, ıp to 27 metres (80 ft) up. The 400-metre (1,300-ft) long walkway gives visiors a rare chance to experience the shoots, fruits and pollinating insects of the :anopy at close quarters. This trail is part of the longer loop which goes to **Tabing Hide** and **Teresek Hill** with its views of Gunung Tahan.

Another popular trek is to **Gua Telinga**, a wet, ear-shaped cave (hence its name *elinga*) where you crawl through guano beneath bats clustered on the low ceilings. The lucky could spot a cave racer, a long white snake that feeds on the bats. Fistsized toads and insects like spiders and cockroaches are plentiful too. Although they nay be unnerving to many people, all the fauna in the cave are harmless to humans.

A leisurely alternative is to glide under arches of trees up the small pretty **Sungai Tahan**, and soak in **Lata Berkoh**, a natural jungle jacuzzi formed by a ›ank of cascades. Lata Berkoh is popular with anglers, as is **Sungai Keniam**, vhich can be reached on foot or by boat. The trail to the latter, Rentis Keniam, akes in the large caves of Gua Luas, Gua Daun Menari, Gua Kepayang Kecil ınd Gua Kepayang Besar, which also boast prolific cave fauna. It's a good 2- lay trek, camping out at the caves or the popular **Kumbang Hide**.

For long-haulers, two options are the **Air Terjun Empat Tingkat** (Four-Step Waterfall) and the ultimate, **Gunung Tahan**. Each involves a 7-day trip where

Map on page 240

TIP

Mutiara Taman Negara Resort and Nusa Camp run buses (RM30 one way) daily between Kuala Lumpur (departing 8am) to Kuala Tembeling (departing 1.30pm), which are open to non-guests, but book beforehand.

BELOW: sun-baked boulders at Sungai Tahan.

Map
on page
240

TIP

The best time to fish in Taman Negara is during the drier months from February to March, and June to August; equipment can be hired. But note that fishing is not always permitted; check with the park authorities.

BELOW: Malayan Tapir.
RIGHT: face to face with pandanus plants, Lake Cini.

you need to carry your own camping gear and food. Both follow the same route along Sungai Tahan until the Teku tributary fork. There are numerous river crossings and a stretch where you have to climb 27 hills – all in 1 day.

The waterfall is a major tributary of Sungai Tahan that plunges down the eastern flanks of Gunung Tahan and Gunung Gedong. The undulating trek up to the Tahan peak, at 2,187 metres (7,175 ft), involves an exhilarating climb through montane oak and cloud forests. There is an alternative route to the peak, which takes 3 days, but it starts at Merapoh town north of Jerantut.

Other trails snake around the 36 hectares (90 acres) of forest bordering the park that belong to Nusa Camp. There are a couple of waterfalls, and the steep Bukit Warisan trek has great sunrise and sunset views of the rainforest canopy with its amazing diversity of trees.

The jungle by night

A night in an animal hide is your best chance to observe wildlife, much of which is nocturnal. These huts-on-stilts are near salt-licks, where animals come to drink. Arrive at the hides early, say around 5pm. Cooking is not allowed, so bring a packed supper, a powerful flashlight, and insect repellent, and settle down to wait. Binoculars are handy. Take turns to "watch", shining the torch every 10 minutes or so. Nosy jungle rats will help keep you awake.

As night falls, the forest comes alive with sounds and ghostly "spirits" flitting among the trees – fireflies and beetles with fluorescent wings and tails. Deer and tapir are the most common sightings, and you'll see lots of spiders and snakes moving about in the undergrowth. An alternative is to go on a night walk, where you can pick out luminous mushrooms or a slow loris, flying squirrel or civet cat.

Southwest of Taman Negara is the lesser known but no less interesting **Kenong Rimba Park** ㉖, whose specialities are birds and insects. From dawn, the 128,000-hectare (31,600-acre) park is alive with the sounds of birds, including the unique call of the white-rump shamma and the thwack of the Malayan whistle thrush smashing its breakfast of snails on a rock. You might even spot the *belalang dewa* in action grasshoppers which display locust-like behaviour in travelling in groups, decimating vegetation in one go.

A 2- to 3-hour trail loops around the park, taking in Kenong Rimba's many limestone caves and types of vegetation. There's **Gua Batu Tangga**, a huge cave believed to provide shelter for elephants. **Gua Hijau** is named after its mossy green walls, while **Batu Kajang** has folkloric connections: according to legend, it is a boat carrying a king's messenger that has been turned to stone. A more challenging route is the undulating 5-day trek to **Gua Batu Putih**, which has a delightful crystal-clear stream.

Kenong can be accessed from **Kuala Lipis**, the old Pahang capital. Kuala Lipis is also on the Segamat Tumpat train route (get off at Batu Sembilan). A 20-minute longboat ride down Sungai Jelai goes to the park at Tanjung Kiara where there are chalets and a campsite. Tours can be arranged at Kuala Lipis. For more information, contact the Kuala Lipis District Forestry Office (tel: 09-312 1273).

SARAWAK

Once, the much-feared tribes of Sarawak were after enemy heads. Nowadays, they're chasing tourist dollars

Even today, the name Borneo evokes a sense of the exotic – of adventure and a journey into the unknown. Visions of impenetrable jungle, of headhunters and jungle-dwelling tribes, of white *rajahs* (kings) and great riches refuse to fade. And yet today's Sarawak, in the heart of Borneo, is a fast-changing reality.

As loggers move ever further into the wild, deep and dark jungles become accessible, their secrets lost forever. Express boats bring once remote settlements and longhouses within reach, and trips that used to take weeks of battling fast-flowing rivers have been reduced to as many hours as powerful engines churn upriver.

While the white rajahs and headhunters are long gone, Sarawak's tradition of open hospitality continues, making Kuching Southeast Asia's friendliest city. You'll always be made welcome, whether by Chinese women offering free samples in the market, or in an Iban longhouse, where you might sit chatting with the chief over a glass of heady *tuak*, Sarawak's ubiquitous home-brewed rice wine.

While Sabah and Sarawak share a common heritage, each with a history that involved the British, their developments took different paths. Sarawak's white rajahs had great respect for their Dayak subjects and their rule took their predilections into account. Sabah grew as a trading post, with a more pragmatic and certainly less romantic attitude towards its native inhabitants. As a result, modern Sarawak retains its cultural integrity and pride in traditions.

This sprawling state makes a great introduction to Borneo. Even those with little time to spare can gain a rudimentary understanding of the country and the cultures of its people by visiting the award-winning Sarawak Cultural Centre just outside Kuching. But those with more time can look forward to some rich experiences: the enigmatic caves of Niah, with their relics of cave dwellers from 25,000 years ago; the World Heritage Site of Mulu with caves so large that their statistics astound the senses; further afield, the cool Bario Highlands, which bring contact with the warm hospitality of the Kelabits and the chance to trek through pristine jungle.

After a longboat trip upriver, visiting a longhouse, and perhaps even witnessing a longhouse celebration or *gawai,* the taste of Borneo is firmly instilled. If you are lucky enough to hear the haunting music of the *sape* and witness the dance of the hornbills, memories of Sarawak will live in the heart forever. ❑

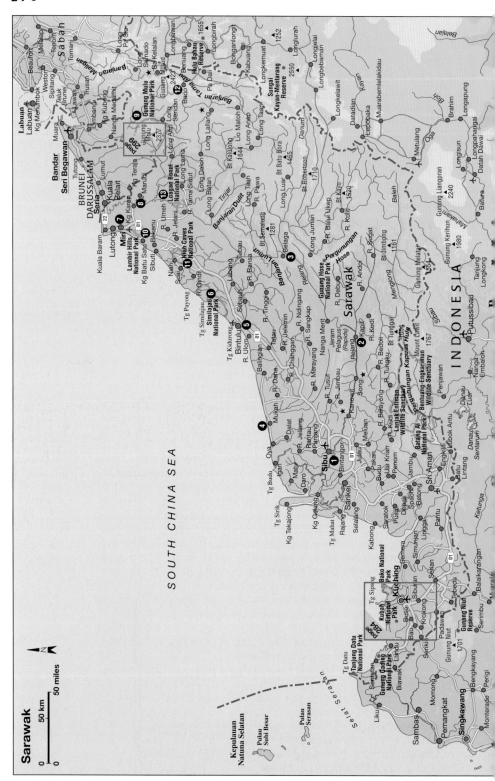

Sarawak

0 — 50 km

0 — 50 miles

SOUTH CHINA SEA

Keputauan
Natuna Selatan

Pulau
Subi Besar

Pulau
Serasan

Selat Serasan

INDONESIA

Sarawak

Page 299

Page 284

KUCHING AND THE SOUTHWEST

Maps:
Area 284
City 278

Kuching has held on to much of its original character while new development spreads further away from the old town centre. The result is one of the most charming towns in Southeast Asia

When British adventurer James Brooke made his way up the winding Sarawak River in his ship, the *Royalist*, he had little idea what was in store for him, or that in a few short years he would be ruling a whole country. It was 1839 and an uncle of the Sultan of Brunei asked Brooke to help settle disputes amongst the country's fighting factions. To the amazement of all, he managed to talk both sides into a harmonious truce. Even more incredible to the Brunei overlords was his insistence that the lives of the rebels be spared and that they be allowed to return to their villages. Thus, Brooke gained the friendship of the Dayaks, the Malays and the Chinese. In return, the Sultan agreed to Brooke's demand that he be given the title of Governor and Rajah of the Sarawak region, thus initiating the "rule of the White Rajahs" – a rule that lasted three generations and over 100 years. Brooke's admiration for the character of the Dayaks led to a long and fruitful relationship, and the novelty of the Brookes' rule became its essence: justice without favouritism.

Exploring Kuching

Winding through lowland *nipah* swamps, the Sarawak River has always been the focal point for Sarawak's capital city, **Kuching ❶**. This delightful old trading town is suffused with old memories, enhanced by the many colonial buildings that have withstood the march of progress. People are friendly and hospitable with time to stop for a chat. Amid the noisy traffic, the shophouses squeezed between the bustling markets of the Main Bazaar and the stately old buildings give the capital an elegant and dignified air. History has always seemed close to the present in Kuching and until the early 1990s, the town centre had changed little from a century ago, when pressures to modernise led to new roads and improvements to the riverfront.

Scattered around Kuching's colonial heart stand the buildings that played such an important part during the Brookes' rule. A Heritage Walk has been devised that covers many of these buildings. The best time to make an on-foot exploration is early morning, or break it up and continue after 4pm, when the heat of the day has begun to pall.

Take one of the gaily painted *tambang* – the small ferry boats leave as soon as they have sufficient passengers – from the various jetties or *pangkalan* along the Kuching Waterfront. First stop is the **Astana Ⓐ**. Built in 1870 for the newly married second Rajah, Charles Brooke, it is now the official residence of Sarawak's head of state (and therefore closed to the public). Several renovations later, it consists of three bungalows, supported by square brick pillars, with the low, spreading roof giving shade to the interior.

BELOW:
Orang Ulu woman.

Cat sculpture outside the Holiday Inn in Kuching. According to one theory, Kuching was named after the fruit 'buah mata kuching'(cat's eyes), which grows locally.

Fortified town

A little further downriver is **Fort Margherita ⓑ** (open Tues–Sun 10am–6pm; free), which holds a commanding position overlooking the town. The first of a series of forts that lined Sarawak's main rivers, Fort Margherita was built in 1879, at a calm and peaceful time. The fort was never used for its intended purpose during the Brooke era; the only time it came under attack was during a Japanese air raid in World War II. No severe damage was caused, however, and since the war, the quaint fort has been used mainly as a barracks by the police force. It also houses the surprisingly interesting **Police Museum** (open Tues–Sun 10am–6pm; free). The best time to visit is in the morning; for security reasons, you may be asked to produce a passport or ID to enter.

Back across the river is Kuching's **Square Tower ⓒ** (no formal opening times; tel: 082-426 093 for an appointment), an imaginative building built in in 1879. Its architecture harks back to the Victorian era's fascination with medieval culture. Although equipped with a real dungeon for prisoners, the tower was later used as a popular dancing hall.

Across the road from the Square Tower sits the **Court House ⓓ** – a quietly impressive colonial building built in 1874, standing stolidly beneath shading trees. Arguably the most beautiful colonial building in Kuching, the building has been converted into the **Sarawak Tourism Centre Complex**, and now houses a Visitors Information Centre (open Mon–Fri 8am–6pm, Sat, Sun and holidays 9am–3pm; tel: 082-410 942) on the ground floor, with a Lebanese restaurant on the first floor. The clock tower was added in 1883. The **Charles Brooke Memorial**, an unimposing obelisk erected in 1924, stands facing the court house. Closer scrutiny reveals four superbly crafted copper plaques depicting in

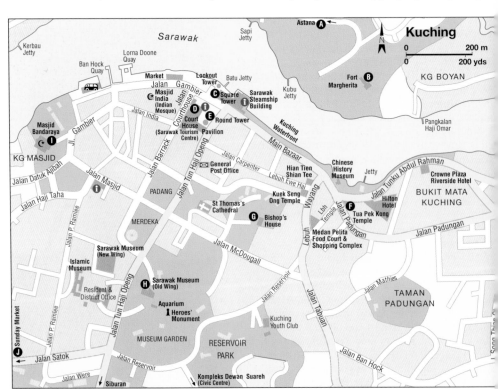

Map on page 278

turn, an Iban warrior, a Chinese courtier, a British soldier and a Malay warrior.

Next to the court house, on Jalan Tun Haji Openg, is the odd-looking **Round Tower E**, built in 1886 to house the town dispensary. Brooke seems to have had a predilection for fortifications; the Round Tower was meant to double up as a fort in times of attack. It is now occupied by the **Sarawak Handicraft Centre** (open daily 9am–5.30pm), where craftsmen and craftswomen can be seen making mats, weaving textiles, and embroidering. A good range of quality handicrafts is also on sale. Adjacent is the **Pavilion** with its elaborate frontage, now housing a new **Textile Museum** (open daily 9am–5.30pm; free; tel: 082-244 232).

Once a collection of godowns and trading stores, the old waterfront was greatly transformed in 1993 to become the **Kuching Waterfront**, a kilometre-long stretch of recreational areas, gardens, walkways, stalls and restaurants. At the beginning of the Kuching Waterfront park is the renovated **Sarawak Steamship Building**, which houses the **Kuching Waterfront Bazaar** (open daily 9am–6pm), a collection of souvenir stalls.

The **Waterfront Park** is extremely popular with locals, who can be seen here at all hours of the day and night. At the down-river end of the park, the one-time Chinese Chamber of Commerce building has been transformed into an interesting **Chinese History Museum** (open Sat–Thurs 9am–6pm; free; tel: 082-244 232). This far end of the Waterfront is dominated by the impressive white edifice of the **Hilton Hotel** – the beginning of the main upmarket hotel area.

The street facing the Waterfront, **Jalan Main Bazaar**, now forms the main tourist area – a shopping mecca not just for touristy souvenirs but with pieces to interest serious collectors. Many of the old shophouses have been taken over by travel companies, handicraft and antique stores specialising in primitive arts.

BELOW:
Fort Margherita
was named after
Charles Brooke's
wife.

Crossing the road from the end of the Waterfront one reaches Sarawak's oldest, and possibly prettiest, Chinese temple, the **Tua Pek Kong Temple** ❻. Its construction in the late 18th century marks the strong Chinese presence in Sarawak. The Chinese community trades not only in the main towns and cities but also upriver, with trade boats stocked like floating supermarkets, or with boats attached to remote longhouses, supplying goods and building up a network of trade and news wherever they go.

Naturalist Eric Mjoberg who was the first to climb Sarawak's highest mountain, Gunung Murud in 1922, was one of the more famous curators of the Sarawak Museum.

Chinese influence

Like many Malaysian towns, Kuching has its share of ornate Chinese temples. Built in 1895, the **Kuek Seng Ong Temple** on Lebuh Wayang is the traditional place of worship for Henghua fishermen, praying for good catches and a safe return from the sea. The temple is dedicated to the god Kuek Seng Ong, whose figure is placed on a sedan chair on the 22nd day of the second moon, and carried through the town's main thoroughfare.

On one side of the temple, Lebuh Ewe Hai runs into Jalan Carpenter to form the most atmospheric strip in Chinatown, with quaint shops, great food (look for the stalls set in the courtyard of a Chinese opera stage facing a temple) and traditional tradesmen.

Victorian treasure trove

BELOW: the Sarawak Museum is dedicated to the soul of Borneo.

Jalan Carpenter ends at Jalan Tun Haji Openg, which passes the impressively columned **General Post Office** (open Mon–Sat 8am–6pm, Sun 10am–1pm) built in 1931 by Vyner Brooke, the last rajah. Behind the temples and shophouses of Chinatown is one of the oldest buildings in Kuching, the sprawling

Bishop's House ⑤. It was built in 1849 by James Brooke for the Reverend Thomas Francis McDougall and his wife. With his typical astuteness, Brooke selected McDougall as the first Anglican Bishop of Kuching because he had previously been a surgeon. Nearby is **St Thomas's Cathedral**.

Map on page 278

Jalan Tun Haji Openg continues past the grassy square of Central Padang to the **Sarawak Museum ⓗ** (open daily 9am–6pm; tel: 082-244 232; free). This is perhaps the most important place of interest for the visitor. Alfred Russell Wallace, the naturalist and co-founder of the theory of evolution along with Charles Darwin, spent many months in Borneo, exploring and collecting specimens. He became a particular friend of Rajah Charles Brooke, who with Wallace's encouragement, built the museum to house a permanent exhibition of native arts and crafts, and specimens from Wallace's own extensive collection. The Brookes were steadfast in their sense of justice. They suppressed crime and established peace in the state, but wisely refrained from imposing any "civilised" versus "primitive" comparisons upon the native cultures. The Rajahs insisted upon capable curators, whose Western expertise was to serve only to illuminate the ethnological richness of Borneo and the vivid expressions of the societies it nourished. The facade of the old wing of the museum, however, betrays another influence. Its architecture was influenced by Charles Brooke's French valet, after a house in Normandy.

In the days of head-hunting, human skulls were hung from the rafters of Iban longhouses; the skulls were said to contain a powerful magic.

Spirit of Borneo

While its sense of mystery disappeared along with the marvellous old teak floors during its modernisation, the museum still invites hours of exploration. It is divided into two buildings, separated by busy Jalan Tun Haji Openg. But the museum's exhibits take you far beyond the paved streets of Kuching and into the heart and soul of Borneo.

BELOW: art on display at the museum.

One display case in the museum is devoted to the Kenyah people, who have names for 60 varieties of ancient glass beads, each one with a special value. Another houses figurines carved 2,000 years ago by the now-extinct Sru Dayaks. An entire corner has been transformed into a walk-in replica of an Iban long-house, with simulated fires, human skulls hanging from the rafters, as well as a warrior's elaborate head-dress and weaponry resting at his bedside; you almost expect him to walk in and sound the battle cry.

The Sarawak tribespeople's great love of adorn-ment is reflected in the high walls of the interior, painted with flowing designs. A museum employee found one end of a Kenyah longhouse at Long Nawang completely covered with a majestic mural celebrating "The Tree of Life" and he returned to Kuching and commissioned painters to reproduce it.

The old wing has an eclectic character that recalls a succession of spirited curators and the great diversity of Sarawak. The enthusiastic influence of scholar Tom Harrisson, who first came to explore Sarawak in the 1920s as an Oxford undergraduate (and later returned to make his home here) can be seen in many of the collections. There is a human dental plate on display that was found in the stomach of a 6-metre (20-ft)

TIP

Late afternoon on the Kuching River is best enjoyed from a *tambang*, the colourful local waterboats. Negotiate with the boatman for an hour's charter – pay no more than a few dollars – and sit back as he takes you on a leisurely ride past Kuching's bustling riverside.

crocodile. A rhinoceros horn cup that can detect poison is another item. If the drink was contaminated, the liquid bubbled to the top: since princes were always trying to poison one another, rhino horn was in high demand during the days of the dynasties.

The old museum is joined by a footbridge over the road to the new **Museum Annex** completed in 1983. Here galleries display more of this cultural treasure trove; the lifestyles and customs of the nation's various tribes are well documented, and there is a reconstruction of the Niah caves where people lived 25,000 years ago. Videos and slide-shows cover such Sarawakian topics as the Great Golden Hornbill (Sarawak is often referred to as the "Land of Hornbills"), life in the jungle, and popular tribal dances.

Continue down Jalan Barracks, past the Padang and the Central Police Station and turn left into **Jalan India Mall**, a colourful jumble of shops and small businesses, little changed from 50 years ago.

Veer left into Lebuh Market, the old market street that leads to the golden domes of decorative **Masjid Bandaraya** ❶ (Kuching Mosque), which overlooks the river. Built in 1968, it replaced the much older wooden structure built in 1852 that burned down. Retrace your steps along Lebuh Market to Jalan Gambier, where opposite the market, a spicy aroma emanates from the open sacks of spices on display. This collection of colourful shops marks what was once the main trading area. Indian Muslim traders, following the Chinese example in the 18th century, headed for Sarawak to set up textile shops and moneylending stalls; the area still exudes a faint aura of the exotic east. Across the street are a few examples of the old buildings that once lined this end of the Main Bazaar.

The **Masjid India** (Indian Mosque), in between Lebuh India and Jalan

BELOW: Kuching Mosque overlooking Sarawak River.

Gambier, was built by Indian Muslim traders in 1876. The streets around the mosque are a labyrinth of small Indian shops and spicy curry-scented restaurants. Continue the walk through this colourful area back to the Courthouse.

The popular **Sunday Market ❶**, which attracts Dayak tradesmen from the surrounding countryside, is situated on the outskirts of town at Jalan Satok. The stallholders arrive and set up market around midday on Saturday and continue until midday Sunday. All manner of strange foodstuffs – jungle produce, wild boar, bats, lizards, monkeys and turtles – are on sale here, alongside fruit, vegetables, pets, orchids and fish.

A more recent addition to the Kuching cityscape is the blue- and gold-domed **Masjid Negara** (National Mosque), an example of modern Islamic architecture which stands across the river at a newer part of town (Petra Jaya).

Maps:
Area 284
City 278

Sarawak's western beaches

Sun worshippers, beach lovers and golfers head for **Damai Beach ❷** near Santubong, just 30 minutes by road from downtown Kuching. The pioneer resort here, Holiday Inn Damai Beach, has been joined by the Holiday Inn Damai Lagoon and the Santubong Resort. As well as the various watersports offered by the resorts, an 18-hole golf course and jungle walks on Mount Santubong increase the recreational options.

For a fine introduction to Sarawak's varied cultures, visit the state's award-winning **Sarawak Cultural Village ❸** (open daily 9am–5.30pm; entrance fee; tel: 082-846 411; www.scv.com.my), adjacent to Damai Beach. Spread across 6 hectares (15 acres) of jungle at the foot of Santubong Mountain, the park has authentic dwellings of the six main cultural groups, staffed by

Temple detail from Kuching's Kuek Seng Ong temple, dedicated to protecting fishermen.

BELOW: fruit stall, Kuching.

TIP

There are traditional
dance performances
at the Sarawak
Cultural Village
at 11.30am and
4.30pm each day.
Call 082-846-411 for
more information.

BELOW:
Sarawak Cultural
Village hostess.

friendly helpers wearing the appropriate dress. The village offers demonstrations of traditional arts and crafts, as well as daily cultural shows which incorporate Iban, Kayan, Kenyah, Melanau and Malay, Chinese and Bidayuh dances.

The fishing village of **Santubong** ❹ is also worth a visit. The village dates back to the Tang and Sung dynasties (9th–13th century), when it was an important trading centre. Before reaching Santubong, you will come to the seaside village of **Buntal**, which is extremely popular for seafood, especially at night. Other beach resorts further along the coast include the Santin Holiday Beach Resort, hidden among mangroves 30 km (20 miles) west of Kuching. Tour buses leave the capital and take you to the jetty, where a boat zips you to the resort, which is inaccessible by land. There are boats to take you snorkelling and a fine beach lined with casaurina trees. With prior permission, you may be allowed to visit the green turtle sanctuary of **Pulau Satang Besar** ❺, north of Kampung Telaga Air, where precious turtle eggs are closely guarded. During the northeast monsoon season, especially December and January, the rough seas make it difficult to get there.

Sarawak's national parks

An abundance of nature can be enjoyed at the many national parks accessible from Kuching. Some parks can be enjoyed as day trips, although all deserve a longer visit. Gazetted in 1957, **Bako National Park** ❻, or Taman Negara Bako (park headquarters open daily 8am–4.15pm; entrance fee; tel: 082-248 088; www.sarawakforestry.com), was Sarawak's first, and it offers some of the best chances to see native animals in the wild. Situated on a peninsula at the mouth of the Sarawak River, Bako's relatively small area of 2,740 hectares (6,770

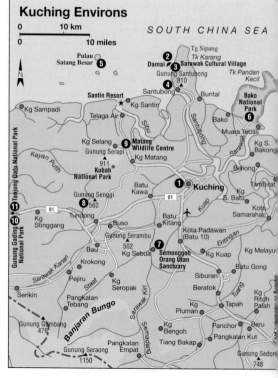

acres) is uniquely rich in both flora and fauna, offering examples of almost every vegetation group to be found in the state. Primary rainforest covers one side of the peninsula, while the other side offers a picturesque coastline of steep cliffs and sandy bays with beaches for swimming. Mud flats and sand bars support a great diversity of sea birds, as well as peculiar red crabs and mudskippers.

While it is possible to visit Bako on a day trip, the rewards are greater if you stay for one night at least – a visit of two or three nights is recommended. Some people stay for a month, relaxing in the natural environment and exploring all the park has to offer. Catch the sun setting over the coloured limestone karsts of the main beach, and enjoy the unearthly experience of walking in the luminous forest at night.

The dry plateau is home to the bizarre insect-eating flowers known as *nepenthe*s, or pitcher plants; eight species exist within the park's confines. The coastal swamp forest is a favoured retreat of Borneo's endemic proboscis, or long-nosed, monkey, the long-tailed macaque, bearded pig and sambar deer, some of which find their way down to the beaches. Within the park is a good system of well-marked paths; ask for a guide map at the Park Ranger's Office. Settle down and get ready to explore the wonders of Bako.

A magnificent plankwalk leads through a tidal mangrove forest that changes character throughout the day with the rise and fall of the sun, and the ebb and flow of the tide. Here in the early morning, when the water is low, lucky visitors may encounter the shy proboscis monkey or the silver leaf monkey, feasting on the young leaves. Tread quietly and keep your eyes wide open. The popular **Lintang Trail** leads through nearly all the vegetation types and up to the arid plateau where pitcher plants can be found among the scrub.

Map on page 284

BELOW: Orang-utan at Semonggoh.

TIP

Feeding times at the Semonggoh Orang Utan Sanctuary are from 9–9.30am and 3–3.30pm, so time your visit.

Within the park, accommodation is available at the resthouse, dormitories and chalets at the headquarters at **Teluk Assam**. A small shop supplies basic provisions which you can cook yourself, or the canteen offers a perfectly acceptable menu. Beware the cheeky long-tailed macaques which will try to find their way into your chalet kitchen or steal food right off the table in the main dining area. They are a basketful of trouble, providing high entertainment for onlookers. Book your accommodation with the National Park's desk (open Mon–Fri 8am–6pm, Sat, Sun and holidays 9am–3pm; tel: 082-248 088) at the Visitors Information Centre located in the old Court House in Kuching.

Some 22 km (14 miles) southwest of Kuching is the **Semonggoh Orang Utan Sanctuary** ❼ (open daily 8am–noon and 2–4.15pm; entrance fee) where you'll find Sarawak's first dedicated reserve for these jungle creatures. This is another must-visit excursion and a great chance for an encounter with these delightful animals. Rehabilitation for orphaned babies and adult animals who have been kept as domestic pets is an ongoing process as they are taught to climb trees, find food, make nests and otherwise survive in the wild. Semonggoh is also the home for hornbills, monkeys and Malayan sun bears.

Parks and islands

In Sarawak's southeast corner you'll find the 2,230-hectare (5,500-acre) **Kubah National Park** ❽ (park headquarters open daily 8am–12.30pm and 1.30–5.15pm; entrance fee; tel: 082-248 088; www.sarawakforestry.com), which is only 21 km (13 miles) from Kuching. Within its confines are streams, waterfalls and bathing pools. A 5–6 hour return trail leads to the park's highest peak, **Gunung Serapi,** while the most popular waterfall trail leads through dipterocarps with plankwalk sections in front of the waterfall. Kubah makes a good day trip from the capital; chalets are available for longer stays.

BELOW: sunset in Bako National Park.

The **Matang Wildlife Centre** ❾ some 14 km (9 miles) further along, is home to a number of orangutan and other local fauna which are contained in large enclosures found within the rainforest.

The little-explored western part of the state has more surprises for those who want to visit. The road west leads to **Lundu** and **Sematan**, where remote beaches – try Pandan Beach near Lundu – are only one of the attractions. Out from Sematan, a relaxed little fishing village, are several deserted islands, one of which, **Talang Talang**, is a turtle sanctuary.

More national parks can be visited in the northwest. The town of Lundu is the access point to **Gunung Gading National Park** ❿ (park headquarters open daily 8am–12.30pm and 1.30–5.15pm; entrance fee; tel: 082-248 088; www.sarawakforestry.com). Gazetted in 1983, the park covers an area of over 41,000 hectares (101,100 acres), on both sides of the Lundu River. Within the park are waterfalls and an 8-hour trail to the summit of Gunung Perigi. Giant Rafflesia blooms, growing up to a metre (3 ft), can be found in the park, and chalets are available. According to legend, Gunung Gading (Ivory Mountain) is named after a Javanese princess who used to bathe at one of its numerous waterfalls. The trails are steep but it's worth hiking them to see both Rafflesia blooms and the falls, especially Waterfall 3 and 7.

Gazetted in 1994, **Tanjung Datu National Park ⓫** (park headquarters open daily 8am–12.30pm and 1.30–5.15pm; entrance fee; tel: 082-248 088; www. sarawakforestry.com) is one of Sarawak's newest and smallest parks, covering an area of just 1,379 hectares (3,400 acres). Right at the westernmost tip of the state, the park has clear rivers and fine corraline beaches with unspoiled reefs. It is accessible by boat from Sematan and the whole journey takes around 3½ hours – but there is no accommodation available.

Batang Ai National Park (park headquarters open daily 8am–12.30pm and 2–5.15pm; entrance fee; tel: 082-248 088; www.sarawakforestry.com) and **Lanjak Entimau Wildlife Sanctuary** are favoured haunts of orang-utans, gibbons, barking deers, leaf monkeys and wild boar as well as several hundred species of birds. Both areas are located in the Sri Aman Division, north of the **Batang Ai Dam**. The Batang Ai River, a tributary of the Batang Lupar, was dammed to create Sarawak's first hydro-electric power plant, which became operational in 1985. A subject of great controversy at the time, the dam flooded over 10 longhouses belonging to the Iban and Orang Ulu, and also affected the flora and fauna in the area. During the drier times of the year, the dam is not a pretty sight as thousands of dead trees protrude from the water. The dam is fed by several tributaries where many longhouses are found.

Once past the Batang Ai dam – a 4-hour trip from Kuching – the journey to the park takes about 2 hours upriver by longboat. There are no facilities in these two reserves as yet, but Borneo Adventure (*see page 393*) has accommodation at **Nanga Sumpa** and **Wong Tibul**, on the boundary of Batang Ai National Park; excursions into the park can be arranged from there. ❑

Map on page 284

BELOW:
an Iban dancer

LONGHOUSE TOURS FROM KUCHING

A visit to a longhouse in Sarawak – mostly found in the Skrang or Batang Ai regions – is a must (*see page 294–5*). You get to see an integrated community living under one roof, and the Iban people are generally great fun and very hospitable. The Iban and most of the Orang Ulu build their dwellings near rivers, which once offered their only means of access. Today, many are accessible by road.

Visitors were previously encouraged to head out on their own, but now, unless you are invited by a longhouse host, it is advisable to use a tour operator. Many longhouses have tourist accommodation nearby, ensuring privacy for both the longhouse dwellers and visitors.

One of the best longhouse experiences is offered by Borneo Adventure (*see page 360*) at the **Rumah Along** longhouse at Nanga Sumpa, near the Batang Ai Dam some 275 km (170 miles) north of Kuching. The longhouse inhabitants have benefited from their visitors and earn a little cash without compromising their lifestyle. Sarawak's other longhouse experience is the **Hilton's Batang Ai Longhouse Resort** (*see page 381*). Opened in 1994, the upmarket resort with air conditioning and hot water features longhouse living with all the modern conveniences yet within a natural setting.

SIBU AND CENTRAL SARAWAK

Sibu is the bustling gateway to the Rejang, Malaysia's mightiest river. A trip upriver will reward you with a glimpse of the lives of the Orang Ulu and Iban peoples of the region

Map on page 276

Beyond Kuching, cosmopolitan city life fades away and the innumerable rivers that mark Sarawak's green interior become the highways to remote inland settlements. **Sibu ❶**, capital of Sarawak's third and largest district, is an easy-going and predominantly Chinese town, where the fish markets overflow with gigantic freshwater species such as carp and the much-prized *kolong,* which finds its way to the elegant dining tables of Hong Kong. Timber money has made Sibu rich and the sprawling town, abounding with glitzy hotels and karaoke bars, is home to some of Sarawak's wealthiest families. Visitors tend not to linger in Sibu – often just staying overnight after arriving from Kuching by boat, before leaving to travel upriver the next morning.

The express boat port and surrounding market area is the town's busiest spot, presided over by the imposing seven-tier pagoda that is part of the **Tua Pek Kong Temple**. From the top of the pagoda is a magnificent view of dozens of express boats lined up along the wharf, with boards in front denoting their destinations and a clock showing their departure times. The busy atmosphere lends a hint of adventure and of journeys into the unknown.

Although it is possible to take a bus from Kuching to Sibu, your bones will be considerably rattled by the time you arrive. It is far more pleasant to take the express boat, which heads down the Sarawak River, out to the South China Sea, and then up the **Rejang River** via **Sarikei**. Alternatively, there is a 40-minute flight, giving a wonderful view of the never-ending jungle with its milk-coffee rivers snaking their way through the low-lying *nipah* palm swamps. Flights to further up the Rejang River, to Kapit and Belaga, are also available.

Heading upriver

From Sibu, express boats, long and narrow, rather like wingless 747s, depart regularly. They head downstream to Sarikei and Kuching, and upriver *(ulu)* to Kapit, and also past the treacherous Pelagus Rapids to Belaga. Tourists mingle with an assortment of other passengers: Chinese merchants taking their wares to distant longhouses; river and inland officials (usually Iban) going about their business; the odd longhouse dweller returning home after a visit to the big city, or schoolchildren who attend school in Sibu but return to their family longhouses for the holidays.

Because of extensive logging, express boats now run to several of the major tributaries of the Rejang – a marvellous network that enables visitors to get around at little expense and with great ease – a situation much changed from the heady and hilarious days of Redmond O'Hanlon's explorations in *Into The Heart Of Borneo*. Other, much earlier travellers had to do it all the hard way, by hiring boats themselves.

LEFT: tributary of Sarawak's mighty Rejang River.
BELOW: semi-nomadic Penans help to transport goods.

Although expressboat prices are fixed, hire of longboats is expensive (even for locals) and heavily dependent on the water level, weather, time of day, river currents and how willing the boatman is to hurry his journey to fit your schedule. For foreigners, prices will naturally be much higher and a spot of astute but friendly bargaining is in order. Unless you take a direct express to Kapit, the express boat stops along the way at the smaller settlements of **Kanowit** and **Song**, from where local express boats can be taken to visit longhouses up these rivers.

On the river, boats and longboats, and timber tugs work their way up or glide down-river on the Rejang. Sarawak's longest river is also the natural highway for the timber industry, and you may see huge rafts stacked with logs floating downstream. Should one of these hazards become waterlogged, they present considerable danger to outboard motors; with that very danger in mind, the express boats have their undercarriage lined with steel and there is always a spare propellor shaft lashed to the roof.

Kapit – the upriver capital

The day starts early in **Kapit** ❷ as the siren call of the first express boats sound through the misty dawn. As the boats fire up their throbbing and powerful engines, passengers down their last cups of morning coffee, ready to start their journeys on the river.

To those who live far up the Rejang River, the bustling market town is the big city. Kapit has electricity 24 hours a day, shops (selling goods at considerably higher prices than back in Sibu), hotels equipped with luxuries like TV and air conditioning and fast food outlets selling fried chicken, pizza, ice cream, and other modern conveniences. As a marked contrast, the daily morning market is

BELOW:
the Rejang River in
the glow of dusk.

filled with tribal women coming to town to sell their produce, before heading off to the local provision shops to buy longhouse necessities.

Map on page 276

Only 2½ hours upriver from Sibu, and in spite of all these modern improvements, the sprawling centre still retains the atmosphere of a frontier town, bearing marks of its origins when the Brookes established it as a trading post and fort town. **Fort Sylvia**, built in 1875 by Charles Brooke, was placed strategically to prevent the movement of the Orang Ulu downstream and the Ibans moving further *ulu* or upstream, to avert more full-scale wars. Constructed solidly of *belian* or ironwood, the fort has withstood generations of floods, which in some years reached halfway up the walls. Today the fort houses the **Kapit Museum** (open Mon–Fri 9am–4pm, Sat–Sun 9am–12pm; free) with excellent ethnographic displays on the main peoples of the area.

An Iban woman weaving the pua kumbu, a traditional fabric used for ceremonial purposes.

Kapit lies in the heart of Iban country, Sarawak's largest indigenous population. Ibans were once the headhunters who gave Borneo its romantic and primitive reputation. Some understanding of their culture will help the visitor to see that they were not merely bloodthirsty in an anarchic way. To bring good fortune to the longhouse, and fame and a bride for themselves, young Iban warriors would (and some still do) set out from home to travel "the world". Status would be acquired in the form of tattoos telling of their bravery, and the heads of a few enemies brought home to imbue the longhouse with protective spirits. Only warriors of equal strength were killed, and never children, women or the old and sick. Sadly, these traditions were much misunderstood by the 19th-century writers who revelled in writing lurid stories about the headhunters of the Iban tribes.

BELOW:
Iban tattoos are heavily symbolic.

Beyond Kapit is **Belaga** ❸ – the last urban centre on the Rejang, after which it is longhouse communities all the way. Reaching Belaga means coursing

TIP

The Sarawak Tourism Board has organised a homestay programme which allows visitors to stay with selected families to sample a slice of traditional Malaysian life. Contact the board at tel: 082-240 620

through the **Pelagus Rapids**, marking the natural boundary between the Iban territory below and the Orang Ulu beyond. These rapids are the most treacherous navigable waterway in the state, and possibly in the whole of Borneo. The 2½ km (1½ miles) stretch is a series of whirlpools and waves as the river rapidly loses altitude. Many lives and boats have been lost in this maelstrom; riding the rapids atop an express boat (ready to jump off in case of trouble) provides high excitement. When the water is low – from May to August – only small longboats can struggle through, although some do try to negotiate the perils in a speedboat.

Just below the rapids is the upmarket **Regency Pelagus Resort** (tel: 084-799 050), a longhouse-style resort designed by Kuching architect, Edric Ong. The resort makes a comfortable base for excursions: to longhouses to see Iban women making high-quality *pua kumbu* or ceremonial blankets; to explore waterfalls and jungle trails; or to just laze by the pool, amid beautiful natural surroundings.

Upstream to Belaga

The real last outpost, Belaga has grown larger, due to incessant logging, but visit the town, with its few small but comfortable hotels to see just what a bazaar of the interior looks like. Some of the old wooden buildings remain, although increasingly they are replaced with ubiquitous concrete shophouses. But sit in a coffee shop, sipping on a mug of thick coffee sweetened with spoonfuls of condensed milk, and watch the passing parade of people: Kayan women wearing heavy metal decorations in their ears which have stretched to their breasts; young warriors who devote their ferocity to football rather than collecting heads; children sent down to school to learn the ways of the other world; a collection of traders, hustlers, would-be tour guides on the make, and labourers fresh from

BELOW: long boats are often the only means of travel.

the logging camps, money burning in their pockets. It's raw and primitive, with an energy you will never find in the city.

From Belaga, express boats head upstream when the water is high, but it is advisable to find a guide or an invitation before venturing afar to visit an upriver longhouse. In spite of their long traditions of hospitality to travellers on the river, most longhouse folk are just not interested in entertaining people they can't talk to and who have little to offer to their lives. Officially, foreigners wanting to head further upriver from Belaga must obtain a permit from the District Office in Kapit (tel: 084-796 322), and it is not advisable to travel near the controversial Bakun hydro-electric dam site.

Map on page 276

Sojourn with nature

Travelling northeast from Sibu along the main highway to Miri, one passes a few worthwhile stops. A good network of buses, taxis and mini buses makes it quite an easy matter to move east by public transport.

The sleepy Melanau fishing village of **Mukah** ❹ is a pleasant layover and offers a relaxed respite from jungle life. A replica of a traditional Melanau "Big House", **Lamin Dana** at Kampung Tellian just outside Mukah, offers visitors accommodation and a glimpse of Melanau lifestyle, including the fascinating process of extracting sago from thick sago palm trunks. An excursion out to sea with the fishermen is another possibility. The town is home to the enigmatic annual Kaul Festival where ancient Melanau rites appease the spirits of the sea and mark the new fishing season as well as give thanks to the fertility spirits.

The burgeoning oil town of **Bintulu** ❺ has developed out of all recognition in the past couple of decades. The old wooden bazaar has given way to new shops and hotels, as well as a deep-water port, chemical factories and a massive liquid petroleum gas (LPG) plant to exploit offshore reserves of natural gas.

About 20 km (12 miles) away from Bintulu is the **Similajau National Park** ❻ (tel: 082-391 284; www.sarawakforestry.com). Gazetted in 1976, the 7,067-hectare (17,500-acre) national park is less visited than those closer to Kuching or Miri, but its more difficult access makes it no less attractive. Opened to visitors only in 1991, the long narrow park covers a 32 km by 1.5 km area (20 miles by 1 mile) and is bordered by one of Sarawak's most beautiful stretches of unspoiled beach, with jungle trails running into the forest. Small rivers and rapids on the **Sebulong River** also make for interesting exploration. Similajau is home to saltwater crocodiles, so watch your step when walking close to river inlets. Other, less spectacular inhabitants include gibbons, banded langurs, civet cats, porcupines, wild boar and long-tailed macaques, as well as 185 species of birds, including hornbills. Green turtles come to lay their eggs on the quiet beaches between July and September.

Numerous longhouses can be visited up the Kemana River that runs into Bintulu, or up the Kakus River, reached via Tatau between Sibu and Bintulu; some are accessible by road as well. Further upriver are the Orang Ulu longhouses of the Kenyah and Penan peoples. ❏

BELOW: performing a religious ritual.

THE LONGHOUSES OF SARAWAK

A visit to an Iban longhouse offers a unique glimpse of an ancient way of life that – although changing fast – is still fascinating for outsiders

Longhouse life is a microcosm of a well-run society, where a close-knit community lives together under one roof with one chief, or *Tuai Rumah*, in charge. Within the structure, a kind of horizontal highrise, each family has its own quarters or *bilek*, where they sleep and eat. The main room is often lined with Chinese ceramic jars much prized by the Ibans. At the rear is the kitchen, where a wood fire provides the heat for cooking, adding a distinctive smokey taste to the food and a dark patina to the surroundings.

CHANGING TIMES

Times are changing in the longhouse. Walls which once held faded photographs of the Brookes and Queen Elizabeth II are now adorned with colour magazine pictures of beauty queens, racing cars and the latest pop icons. Many Dayaks have converted from spirit-sensitive animism to Christianity, and evenings once spent performing tribal chants and sacrificial ceremonies are taken up with prayer meetings. Children who once enjoyed carefree days frolicking in the longhouse and the rice fields are ensconced in schools studying Bahasa Malaysia and physics. Yet still the community spirit lives on.

▷ **LIVING OFF THE LAND**
Longhouse life is hard. Men and women spend long hours working in the fields, planting and tending their crops.

△ **ON THE VERANDAH**
Much longhouse activity takes place on the *tanju* and *ruai* – from drying cocoa beans to socialising.

▷ **COCKFIGHTING**
Cockfighting is a popular male pastime. Animistic beliefs and legendary spirits surround many of the festival cockfights.

◁ **MULTI-PURPOSE GALLERY**
Winnowing grains in the *ruai*, or gallery – the space used for everything from basket weaving to holding community celebrations.

△ **LONGHOUSE STAPLE**
Drying rice on the longhouse verandah, or *tanju*. Afterwards, the rice is stored carefully in the different family units.

◁ **TRADITIONAL SKILLS**
An Iban woman displays her handiwork in a *pua kumbu* – a ceremonial cloth used to decorate longhouse walls.

△ **IKAT WEAVING**
Preparing to dye the threads for a *pua kumbu*. Intricate pieces can use up to five or six colours, and take months to complete.

FIGHTING COCK OR SACRIFICIAL PET?

Cocks play an important part in Iban culture, and they are kept and cosseted as pets while being prepared for their first big fight. The men of the longhouse play with them regularly, engaging them in mock battles with their neighbours, but without the razor sharp spurs attached to their rear claws. Those are reserved for fighting days and can bring a lesser fighter to its death in minutes. Before the fight, the cocks are sometimes given small shots of *tuak*, rice wine, to keep them energised and slightly aggressive.

The cocks and chickens also play an important part in ceremonial issues. Chicken sacrifices are common and the occult powers of a white cockerel are highly respected, in common with many other cultures around the world.

In many ceremonies – for example, in the case of a sick or possessed person – a cock will be sacrificed, and the blood, valued for its purifying quality, sprinkled over a subject. In milder cases, the live chicken is simply waved over the subject or over the ceremony offering plates.

MIRI AND THE NORTHEAST

Map
on page
276

*Just over the border from Brunei, the oil boomtown of Miri is the
ideal spot from which to head for the magnificent Mulu caves,
or make a visit to a Sarawakian longhouse*

Located on the northwest coast near the Brunei border, **Miri ❼** became
Sarawak's original "oil town" with the establishment of the state's first oil
rig on Canada Hill in 1919. This oil rig finally ceased production in 1970,
but remains as a landmark atop the ridge overlooking the city, with a new Petroleum Science Museum adjacent.

Despite a dip in 1997, Miri regained its prominence in the oil industry when
oil giant Shell established its Asia-Pacific headquarters here in 2005. The recently
established campus of an overseas university (Curtin from Australia) has also
raised Miri's profile and added to its population. Miri has a couple of five-star
resorts near the river mouth, plus a new marina at the heart of a huge reclaimed
area known as Marina Bay, hence tempting visitors from the more austere Brunei
with a plethora of leisure, entertainment and shopping options.

For local residents, Miri is undeniably a very pleasant city to live in. Visitors
will find it worthwhile to stop here, at least overnight, en route to Lambir Hills,
Niah Caves, Gunung Mulu National Park and the Bario Highlands.

LEFT: bats take
flight in Mulu.
BELOW: fish-seller
in Miri market.

In and around Miri

Take a stroll around the heart of the old (and essentially Chinese) town close to the
river. Be sure to check out the lively local market
known as **Taman Muhibbah** (opposite the very helpful Visitors Information Centre), where the vendors are
as colourful as their produce.

The **Miri Handicraft Centre** (open daily 9am–
6pm) gives locals a chance to market their handmade
goods and imports from Indonesian Borneo. Good
buys here include beautifully woven rattan bags and
mats. You may even be lucky enough to find a few
antiques and highly treasured beads sold by a Kelabit
lady from Bario.

Miri has some excellent food, especially Chinese
and Muslim cuisines, plus plenty of cafés serving
basic Western dishes. Don't miss the fresh and relatively inexpensive seafood, best enjoyed along the
Miri River or at the coastal restaurants in Brighton
Beach and Luak Bay.

For a change from land-based activities, try scuba
diving around the reefs close to Miri. If you have time,
however, a live-aboard trip to the reefs about 4–5
hours offshore is recommended, as the waters offer
significantly better visibility.

The highway heading north towards the Sultanate
of Brunei crosses the Baram River at the Asean
Bridge, upriver from **Kuala Baram**. From there, a
ferry can take you to the duty-free island of **Labuan**.
A road also heads up the northern side of the Baram
River to the trading town of **Marudi ❽**.

*An elaborate Kenyah
headdress.*

While most visitors stop just long enough to catch the next express boat on their rush upriver to Mulu, for a taste of outback Sarawak, Marudi is worth a day or two of exploration by itself. One of the older of the Brookes' fort posts and the main supply centre or "bazaar" for the Baram region, Marudi is a fast-spreading town which retains the atmosphere of a trading post. Upriver Iban, Kenyah, Kayan and Penan tribal folk come to sell their wares to the Chinese traders of the town. A lively daily market makes a pleasant diversion and the provision shops stock everything an uplander could need – from chainsaws to chicken feed, plastic buckets to pullovers and even handicrafts. A day or two can be very pleasantly spent wandering about the town, or sitting in a local coffee shop near the express boat jetty to watch the passing parade of people and produce as boats come and go.

A visit to the Rajah Brooke's **Fort House** is almost mandatory. Erected in 1901 and overlooking the Baram River, the fort was built to control migration (and wars) up and down river. The fort burned down in the early 1990s, but has been faithfully reconstructed and turned into an interesting little museum.

From Marudi, there are flights to Gunung Mulu National Park and to Bario in the cool Kelabit Highlands, but book well in advance as seats are scarce.

Marvellous Mulu

A trip to **Gunung Mulu National Park** ❾ (entrance fee; tel: 085-433 561; www.sarawakforestry.com), together with a visit to a longhouse, are two of Sarawak's most memorable experiences. If the trip to or from Mulu follows the old **Headhunters Trail**, using forest paths and longboats, it becomes unforgettable. With the advent of several daily flights to Mulu, getting to the park

BELOW: guides
resting at "The
Pinnacles", Mulu.

ecame much faster and more efficient, but not necessarily more pleasurable, nd those with time and a love for travel still prefer to go by boat from Kuala Baram. Flying over part of the park, however, does give you a good idea of its astness and of the variety of the terrain.

Covering 53,000 hectares (130,600 acres), Mulu is Sarawak's largest park. Gazetted in 1974, it is home to a great variety of flora ranging from flowers and rchids, fungi, mosses and ferns, as well as 10 species of pitcher plants. Ten pecies of hornbills flourish within the vast park.

A number of tour operators in Miri and Kuching offer package tours, which nclude transport as well as meals and accommodation in simple lodges just utside the park boundaries. There is also accommodation within the park – he chalets at the headquarters are ideally located – while nearby, the luxurious Royal Mulu Resort comes complete with a small swimming pool. Action sports ans will find roped climbing walls, as well as canoeing and rapids shooting.

Visitors who are not on a package tour (which includes a guide) are obliged to ire a park guide. These independent travellers also pay a high price for transport y boat within the park, unless they join forces with others. Even though a trip ɔ this World Heritage Site is not necessarily cheap, it is worth every cent.

**Maps:
Area 276
Park 299**

Gunung Mulu's primary jungle contains astonishing biodiversity; every scientific expedition that has visited its forests has encountered plant and animal species previously unknown to man.

World-class caves

'or many visitors, the centre of attraction is the magnificent caves. While over 50 km (100 miles) of caves have already been surveyed, specialists estimate hat only 20 to 30 percent of this massive system has been documented. The aves are accessible by short longboat rides between the park headquarters and he various sites, and jungle plankwalks make walking easy, freeing your eyes

BELOW: hornbill at Gunung Mulu National Park.

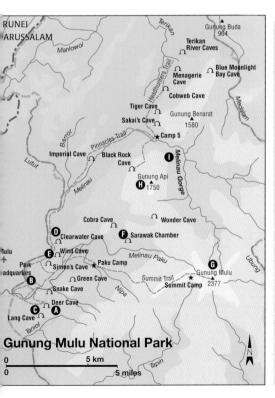

Gunung Mulu National Park

from watching your step and giving you a chance to enjoy the surroundings.

The sheer scale of these caves will please even the most discerning statisti-
cian; within their dank confines lies the world's largest natural cave chamber,
allegedly big enough to hold 16 football fields or 40 jumbo jets and to earn a
place in the Guiness Book of World Records. Clearwater Cave at 75 km (47
miles), is the longest cave in Southeast Asia.

Exploring the caves

Only four of the 25 caves so far explored are open to public viewing, but this
is plenty to gain an idea of the immensity and complexity of this cave system.
Most often visited is the **Deer Cave** Ⓐ, named after long-vanished deer. The site
is accessible by a 3-km (2-mile) plankwalk from the **Park HQ** Ⓑ, passing
through a peat swamp forest where orchids thrive and an ancient Penan burial
site. This massive hall is 2,160 metres (7,090 ft) long and 220 metres (720 ft)
deep. The plankwalk cuts a path over the mounds of guano – a tonne of which
is made each day – and leads through to the **Garden of Eden**, an enclosed valley where the vegetation has existed undisturbed for millennia.

Near the entrance to Deer Cave, you can enjoy one of the most spectacular
sights of Mulu – the nightly bats' exodus. Around 5.30pm, as the lowering sun
turns the limestone walls to gold, the first flutterings can be seen, followed by
an ever increasing number of bats circling their way out of the cave, up and over
the trees on their nightly forage for food. The dramatic spectacle (which unfortunately does not take place during rainy weather) lasts for a good 20 minutes.
Close by Deer Cave is **Lang Cave** Ⓒ, whose well-lit stalactites and stalagmites make it one of the most beautiful of all the caves.

BELOW: stunning
Lang Cave in
Gunung Mulu
National Park.

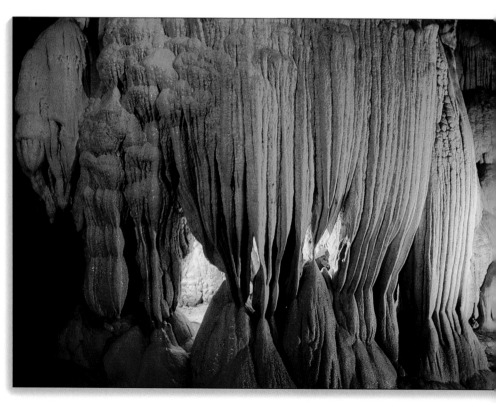

Clearwater Cave  on the way to Camp 5 is located off the main river, a 30-minute boat ride from Park HQ. The 355-metre (1,165-ft)-deep cavern is very dark inside, but with a strong torch you'll be able to see the marvellous limestone formations, and creatures including scorpions, frogs and centipedes. An exquisitely clear river flows out of the cave from under a sheer rockface, providing a popular spot for bathing. Keep an eye out for beautiful butterflies, including the iridescent green and black Rajah Brooke's Birdwing.

Just a few minutes away, and accessible via a cliff-hugging walkway, is the dramatic **Wind Cave** Ⓔ, far smaller but filled with limestone stalactites and stalagmites with plankwalks passing the most spectacular examples.

Sarawak Chamber Ⓕ, reputedly the largest cave in the world, is only accessible to scientists, museum experts and special adventure groups, much of it being extremely dangerous. Gaining access to the cavern involves a 4-hour trek through the jungle from the nearest river point, to the small entrance from where you slide into the dank inky blackness. An exciting excursion, but definitely not for the faint of heart.

Other excursions

Apart from pleasant walks along jungle trails, there are two peaks to be conquered. **Gunung Mulu** Ⓖ at 2,377 metres (7,800 ft) and **Gunung Api** Ⓗ, which at 1,750 metres (5,600 ft) is Malaysia's highest limestone mountain. The stiff ascent of both these mountains is only recommended for very experienced (and very fit) climbers.

The strange limestone spikes, known as **The Pinnacles**, on an alternative path on Gunung Api, can be tackled by anyone of reasonable fitness in about 2

Map on page 299

Caving in Mulu National Park is an unrivalled experience.

BELOW: plankwalk to Deer Cave.

to 3 days. The razor sharp peaks, some standing 45 metres (150 ft) high make a magnificent sight, almost worth the effort of ascending the mountain. The journey there begins with a satisfying longboat trip upriver from the National Park HQ, and a short stop-off to visit the Clearwater Cave. A 4-km (2½-mile) walk through lowland forest brings you to the **Melinau River Gorge** and **Camp 5** – a simple hut shelter and campsite overlooking the Melinau River, and the overnight base camp for the climb to the Pinnacles,

The steep climb, which takes 3 to 6 hours depending on fitness level, starts early morning. This allows enough time to reach the viewpoint by lunch, and to make the descent before dark. The ascent is only to be attempted with experienced guides as the limestone pinnacles are razor sharp. The rough trail passes through mossy forest where dwarfed trees are festooned with hanging moss and numerous pitcher plants, in an often misty environment.

The trip to Mulu can be combined with the **Headhunter's Trail**, either starting, or finishing at **Limbang**. The trail, used by Kayan headhunters in the 19th century is a 5- or 6-day journey through the backwoods, either entering or exiting by Camp 5, although leaving from Mulu is the easier option. You'll need a tour company or, at the very least, a guide to arrange the boat transport and longhouse accommodation along the way from Limbang (*see Travel Tips*).

Stone-age secrets

Back in Miri, there are a couple of side-trips which are the main attractions that draw most travellers to Sarawak. **Lambir Hills National Park** (park headquarters open daily 8am–12.30pm and 1.30–5.15pm; entrance fee; tel: 085-434 184; www.sarawakforestry.com), which is just south of Miri, is one of the world's most ecologically diverse park. It makes a pleasant day trip although chalets are available for longer stays. The park's highlights are waterfalls with natural swimming pools as well as a climb up **Bukit Lambir**.

Much more famous, and with more to offer, is **Niah Caves National Park** (park headquarters open daily 8am–12.30pm and 1.30–5.15pm; entrance fee; tel: 085-434 184 ; www.sarawakforestry.com), which while less dramatic than Mulu, offers visitors freedom to explore on their own; guides are also available.

The limestone caves and their past inhabitants are the attraction here. In the 1870s, animal collector and adventurer, A. Hart Everett, came across the caves – already well-known and protected by the local people – only to dismiss them as "rather dull". It was not until the 1950s that the Sarawak Museum heard of the caves being an archaeologist's gold mine. Sure enough, when the curator dug down 5 metres (16 ft), he found the skull of a young *Homo sapiens* who had lived here probably around 25,000 years ago (originally, Tom Harrisson, the museum's curator, thought that it was 40,000 years ago). The Deep Skull, as it was known, was what remained of the earliest known community of modern people in the East. It contradicted the haughty theories which insisted that humanity's true ancestor originated on the west side of the Middle East and only later "wandered" over to this part of the world.

As the archaeologists looked elsewhere, they found

aematite paintings, featuring stick figures with strange little boat-like objects.)ther discoveries revealed that people living here worked with instruments made ·om bone and shell, made pottery, cut stone adzes and carved wooden coffins or ·urial boats. Many agreed that these discoveries were as significant as the nearthing of Java Man. More recent objects, canoe-shaped coffins and paintings ·ound in the cave known as the **Painted Cave**, date from only 1,000 years ago.

When the Iron Age reached Borneo in AD 700, the Niahans were trading ·ornbill ivory and edible birds' nests for Chinese porcelain and beads. They ·ecorated enormous earthenware urns and placed them beside the graves of ·pecial men. Then in 1400, they appear to have entered a tropical Dark Age, ·hich forced them to desert the caves. They then vanished from history.

·ocal delicacy

·he Niahans may have been the forefathers of the nomadic Penan, whose elders ·ill maintain beliefs and rituals that allude to those in the pre-historic graveyards ·f the Great Caves. The Penan rediscovered the caves in the 19th century, and ·ound them to be unbelievably rich in edible birds' nests of the millions of ·wiftlets that inhabit the bowels of the Niah Caves. The glutinous saliva with ·hich they build the nests is believed to be medicinal, and makes the nests the ·nost expensive Chinese delicacy in Borneo. In the markets of Hong Kong and ·ingapore, the nests can fetch over US$1,000 per kg (2¼ lbs).

The astronomical cost is almost understandable when you learn the way in which ·he nests are collected. A typical day's work might entail scurrying up 60 metres ·200 ft) on a slender rattan ladder, scraping the nests off rock ceilings and from ·vithin deep crevices – and keeping one's balance as any fall could be fatal. You

Maps:
Area 276
Park 299

BELOW: the Niah Caves are thought to have had human inhabitants 25,000 years ago.

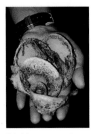

Birds' nests, made
from the hardened
saliva of swiftlets,
are treasured by the
Chinese for their
medicinal and
fortifying qualities.

could say that the high cost of nests takes a man's life insurance into consideration

Naturally, nest collectors guard their trade jealously, and pass their inherited territory on only to their sons. The hundreds of chambers, chimneys and sub-caves where the tiny swiftlets nest are divided into sectors, each privately owned. Some yield but a few hundred nests, others several thousand. The cave owners live in villages and longhouses situated in the park area, and during harvesting – normally two or three times a year, sometimes more – they bring the entire family along to help gather up the riches.

To get to the Niah Caves, you must drive or take a bus or a taxi from either Miri or Bintulu, the former being much closer. From **Batu Niah** village, a short trip along the river brings you to the **Niah Caves Visitor Centre**.

There are several small hotels at Batu Niah, but you'll have to backtrack down the river after you visit the caves – a pleasant boat trip or a 45-minute walk. It is much more convenient to stay at the government-run hostels right in the park if you plan to spend time there. The hostels are friendly and relaxed, providing cooking facilities on request, bedding, toilets and showers with hot water, and electricity. The canteen serves perfectly acceptable, freshly-cooked local food

Walking the planks

The plankwalk to the caves begins from **Pangkalan Lubang**, just across the river from the park accommodation. A museum is located right at the beginning of the walk – entry is free and the information available is useful. The 3-km (2 miles) long path is built of the mighty *belian* or ironwood, a timber so dense that it will not float. You should get to the caves in about 45 minutes if the planks are dry. Sensible shoes are preferable to sandals both for the plankwalk and the

BELOW: entrance to
the Great Cave
at Niah.

aves. Other necessities include a strong torch (with spare batteries), some waterproof clothing and a water bottle.

It is well worth stopping during the walk to absorb the atmosphere of the forest and to listen to the jungle chorus. Down one of the forks in the plankwalk, you can visit a collectors' longhouse, although they may charge you to have a look around their home.

Map on page 276

Birds and bats

At the end of the plankwalk you will arrive at a series of steps and the **Trader's Cave**, and a heap of forlorn bamboo scaffoldings where once the traders set up camp during the collecting season. The **Great Cave** is the main area for birds' nest collection – and also for another interesting substance. Besides the three species of swiftlets of which there are said to be around 4 million, there are 12 species of bats, also countable in the millions. The strong-smelling guano lines the cave floor and is collected almost as avidly as the birds' nests – for it is a rich fertiliser. In fact, you may encounter guano collectors on the plankwalk up to the caves, lugging heavy sacks on their backs on their way to Pangkalan Lubang, where it is weighed and then sent down-river to Batu Niah and to the markets beyond.

With a strong torch you will be able to pick out the creatures that inhabit the caves. Only two of the caves are open to visitors without a guide, and the second, the **Painted Cave**, can only be entered with a permit issued by the National Park Office in Kuching.

The most spectacular sight of all at Niah makes it worth taking camping equipment along. At 6pm, the swiftlets return into the caves to sleep in their nests, while the bats, being nocturnal animals, sweep past them out of the entrance of

Eight species of bat live in the Niah Caves. Most common are the horseshoe and fruit bats, but other rare residents include the bearded tomb bat and Cantor's roundleaf horseshoe bat.

LEFT: Iban tribesman.
BELOW: guano harvesters in Niah.

Map on page 276

the cave into the night. While far less spectacular than the great Mulu exodus, it is quite an experience sitting at the cave mouth, surrounded by dense, green jungle, watching the show. The reverse "shift" takes place at daybreak. It is a sight that humans must have watched and wondered at even 25,000 years ago.

Several other interesting day- or overnight trips can be arranged from Miri. **Bario ⑫** is the sleepy "capital" of Kelabit country, in the midst of the Bario Highlands. A small airstrip, one of a series across the highlands, provides access – when the weather is right – and apart from the daily flights, Bario is remote and untouched. Tom Harrisson described his wartime experiences in the region in his book *The World Within*, although there have been considerable changes since. Surrounded by pristine forest, the cool highlands are the perfect place for trekking, stopping at longhouses along the way. One of the best treks is from Bario to **Ba Kelalan**, a 3- to 4-day walk.

Warm welcome

While the culture of the Kelabits has long since given way to the mores of a fundamentalist Christianity, the Kelabits are the kindest and most hospitable people you are ever likely to encounter. The Kelabit community is split across the border between Sarawak and Kalimantan, who are little troubled with the formalities of immigration check points. Visitors are taken to an immigration checkpoint, and the simple formalities are generally ironed out with ease (or a few dollars). From Bario, and with the help of Kelabit guides, it is possible to climb **Gunung Murud**. At 2,423 metres (7,949 ft), this is the highest peak in Sarawak, and you need 5 clear days to ascend and descend the mountain, starting from Bario – a memorable experience. Kelabit guides and porters will also take you on a 6-day walk back to **Long Lallang**, from where you can fly back to the other, hectic and more hurried world. For the fit and adventurous, one of these expeditions is definitely worth experiencing.

Lawas and **Limbang** are the two forgotten parts of Sarawak, two fingers that are interspersed with the Sultanate of Brunei. **Limbang** is the starting point (or finishing point) for those following the Headhunters Trail to Mulu.

Two hours' drive from Miri, on a turnoff before reaching Niah, is **Loagan Bunut National Park ⑬**. (park headquarters open daily 8am–12.30pm and 1.30–5.15pm; entrance fee; tel: 082-248 088; www.sarawakforestry.com). Gazetted only in 1991, it centres around a mysterious lake that rises and falls with the seasons. In the dry season, the lake disappears completely, leaving a cracked lake bed and an abundant fish population that hides in the mud. The fish are easy to catch, a fact that has not escaped the local population of 32 families who are permitted to fish here, or the vast numbers of birds that visit to capitalise on all that fish.

A hilltop chalet, Mutiara Munut, has room for 24 guests, and there is also a park hostel that can accommodate 56 visitors. After arriving by car, the journey can be made into a round trip by taking a long boat and returning via the Baram River, and an express boat to Marudi, then beyond to Kuala Baram and Miri. ❑

BELOW: a soon-to-bloom fern bud.
RIGHT: copper relief of an Iban warrior.

SABAH

Stunningly beautiful, with an air of mystery, Sabah has now become home to a new breed of people seeking adventure

Today's Sabah is a far cry from the romantic days of old. As part of the mysterious Borneo, it inspired visions and wild dreams. It was a land of myth and adventure, of headhunters and strange pagan rites, and the source of buckles of "golden jade" to adorn the imperial belts of Chinese Emperors.

Sabah's ancestors spring from dozens of tribal groups, some deriving from millennia-old migrations from the north of China. Chinese traders sailed to Borneo before the days of Kublai Khan, in quest of kingfisher feathers, hornbill ivory and bezoar stones; others arrived much later, with the British, as plantation workers and farmers.

Many of today's visitors do not care about Sabah's romantic past. They are here to experience excitement and adventure, whether it is diving in unspoilt coastal waters, driving a four-wheel-drive vehicle cross-country, or scaling one of Southeast Asia's highest mountains.

Sabah has become a serious adventure destination, whose main attractions glitter bright as stars. It takes a minimum of a 10-day visit to do it any justice at all, and for most visitors, longer is better. The state offers such stellar attractions as Gunung Kinabalu (Mount Kinabalu), and Borneo's "man of the forest" at Sepilok's famous Orang-utan Rehabilitation Centre. There are primal jungle retreats, wild whitewater rafting, and river cruising to spot wild elephants or the endemic proboscis monkey. Add some of the best diving in Asia – the prime spot, Pulau Sipadan, is rated as one of the world's top five wall dives – and it's no wonder that Sabah is becoming a favoured destination.

And these are only the highlights of this varied state. For those who like to tread more softly, there are secrets to be revealed in the misty jungles and lonely plains.

Remote coral islands are the destination of green turtles, where almost every day of the year, visitors can witness these remarkable creatures laying their eggs in the clean white sands – after making their mysterious odyssey from half-way across the world, following some ancient call of nature.

Sabah may lack the longhouses and distinctive tribal communities of Sarawak, but it has remarkable natural assets, with reserves of pristine rainforest and tracts of virgin forest to explore. Places like the untouched Danum Valley exist nowhere else, and the goverment has gone to lengths to preserve this natural heritage, instilling pride in this unique environment into the hearts of the people who live here. ❑

PRECEDING PAGES: Gunung Kinabalu's dramatic rockface framed by swirling clouds.
LEFT: Bajau horsemen of Sabah, "cowboys of the east".

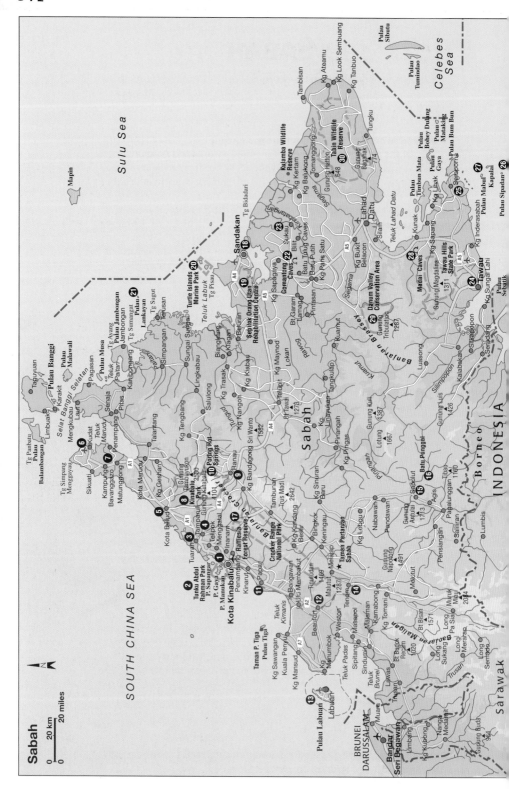

Sabah

0 ___ 20 km
0 ___ 20 miles

N

SOUTH CHINA SEA

Sulu Sea

Celebes Sea

Mapin

Pulau Sibutu
Pulau Look Sembuang
Pulau Tumindao

Tg Ateamu
Kg Ateamu
Kg Look Sembuang
Kg Tanbuo
Tambisan
Tambian

Tg Panhatu
Taguyuan
Limbuak
Pulau Banggi
Karakit
Selat Banggi Selatan
Pulau Banggi Selatan
Pulau Malawali
Pagasan
Pagasan
Pulau Musa

Tg Simpang
Menggayau
Sikuati
Kudat
Teluk
Kampung
Bavanggazo
Maruду
Penampang
Senaja
Pitas
Matunggong

Tg Ayang
Jambongan
Pulau Jambongan
Teluk
Paitan
Karubongang
Pitas
Simpangan
Terusan
Tg Sumangat
Tg Sugut
Pulau Lankayan
Pulau Lankayan
Tg Bidadari

Kota Marudu
Kg Geshan
Lingkabau
Salulong
Sungai Sungai
Beluran
Biangkungan
Nagam
Tg Pisau

Sandakan

Kg Talantang
Talantang
Kg Tengbang
Patau

Poring Hot Springs
Gunung Tambuyukon 2530
Gunung Kinabalu 4101
Kinabalu Park
Ranau
Kg Trasak
Kg Maynod
Kg Kiabau
Kg Mangoh
Sungai Sri Wanto
Lokan
Tg Trasak
B.Tawau

Kg Geshan
Kota Belud
Tempasuk
Kg Abuan
Tamparuli
Telipok
Menggatal
Inanam
Kota Kinabalu
Tunku Abdul Rahman Park
P. Sapangar
P. Mamukan
P. Gaya
Tuaran
Tamburan
Penampang
Kinarut
Papar
Kg Kiandang
Bingkor
Baru
Crocker Range National Park
Penampang Rafflesia Forest Reserve
Benoni
Bongawan
Ulu Membakut
Tuaran
Menumbok
Beaufort
Westor
Beaufort
Kuala Penyu
Taman P. Tiga
Pulau Tiga
Kg Sawangan
Teluk Kimanis
Tenghilan
Membakut
Tenom
Keningau
Nabawan
Pandawan
Pensiangan
Salirran
Agis
Sapulut
Tibab
Pagalungan
Luasong
Kalabakan

Kg Maruwu
Lotung 1667
Gunung Kuli 1357
Gunung Luis
Silimpopon
Gunung 1426
Serudong

Teluk Labuk
Turtle Islands Marine Park
Sepilok Orang Utan Rehabilitation Centre

Gomantong Caves
Batu Tulug Caves
Bilit
Bt Garam Lamag
Sukau
Batu Puteh
Kg Paris Satu
Pintasan
Segama
Kg Bukit Belacon
Kunak
Pulau Timbun Mata
Pulau Gaya
Kg Sapang

Kulamba Wildlife Reserve
Kg Kertam
Tonanggong
Gunung Hatton
Tabin Wildlife Reserve
648
Gunung Baghak
774
Tungku

Kg Balukong
Kg Maruwu
Lahad Datu
Silam
Teluk Lahad Datu

Danum Valley Conservation Area
Gunung Tribulation 1287
Kuamut
Kg Maynod

Madai Caves
Tawau Hills State Park
1371
Gunung/Magdalena
Tawau
Kg Sungai Lahi
Kg Sebatik
Kg Inderasabah
Pulau Mabul
Pulau Kapalai
Pulau Sipadan

Tingkayu
Tangkulap
Pinangas
Gunung Napodog
1287
Gunung Kuil

Teluk Labuk
Tg Bidadari

Sabah
Banjaran Brassey
Banjaran Maligan
Borneo
INDONESIA
Sarawak

Pulau Labuan
Labuan
BRUNEI DARUSSALAM
Bandar Seri Begawan
Muara
Limbang
Kg Kupong
Nanga Medamit
Lawas
Trusan
Sindumin
Sipitang
Kg Tomani
Kamabong
Kg Bisan
1571
Bt Bugok
Recam
Long Pa Sia
Long Sukang
Long Merapas
Long Semado
Long Miau
2044
Gunung Buda
964

① ② ③ ④ ⑤ ⑥ ⑦ ⑧ ⑨ ⑩ ⑪ ⑫ ⑬ ⑭ ⑮ ⑯ ⑰ ⑱ ⑲ ⑳ ㉑ ㉒ ㉓ ㉔ ㉕ ㉖ ㉗ ㉘ ㉙ ㉚

KOTA KINABALU AND THE WEST

Map on page 312

Sabah's capital is dominated by stunning vistas of the towering Gunung Kinabalu. Nearby are burgeoning new beach resorts to try before heading into the interior

The state capital on the northwest coast, **Kota Kinabalu ❶**, is a modern city with little old-world charm. Facing the west coast, it affords splendid sunsets over the offshore islands – sunsets which reflect Kota Kinabalu's history – a litany of heated passions, fights and fires before the town reached its present, easy-going ways.

The British North Borneo Chartered Company established the first settlement in 1882, on nearby **Pulau Gaya** (Gaya Island) in the bay of the present city, in line with a British colonial penchant for offshore island bases. But it was attacked and burned to the ground by the rebel Bajau, Mat Salleh in 1897. Moving to the mainland, the Chartered Company then set up Jesselton, named after the company's vice-chairman, Sir Charles Jessel. The name remained until 1967, when shortly after independence, a new Malaysian consciousness gave the settlement yet another new name.

What's in a name?

The old name for the location of Kota Kinabalu is Api Api (literally, "fire, fire"). This does not, however, commemorate bygone arson, but rather, is the name of a local mangrove tree in which the fireflies twinkle at night. For a short time, the town was called Singgah Mata ("Where the Eye Lingers"), but it is now known as Kota Kinabalu, in honour of the great mountain whose craggy peaks lend a magnificent backdrop to the city.

As a trading post, the town grew to be important enough to be bombed to ruins in 1945, in order to dislodge the Japanese from their base in this strategic position. Over the following decade, Kota Kinabalu grew into an undistinguished town, occupied with covering up the scars of World War II.

Ever since it was chosen as the site for British North Borneo's west coast base, the town has continued to encroach on the sea. Reclamation was the answer to the shortage of flat land, a process that continues as the need for this precious commodity grows. Even the "coastal highway" was pushed inland by the reclamation of huge areas of shallow sea, and one of the few remaining water villages, which was known by the generic name of Kampung Air, was demolished in 2003.

More recently, Kota Kinabalu's landscape has been changing, with the bland, uninspiring sprawl of 1950s concrete shophouses as well as stilt villages perched over the sea giving way to high-rise buildings and plush hotels.

One of the most impressive of these new buildings

BELOW: Sabahan girls in ceremonial dress.

is the gleaming tower of the **Menara Tun Mustapha** (Tun Mustapha Tower), formerly known as Sabah Foundation (Yayasan Sabah), an institution created with the timber royalties of the state. Situated to the north of the city at Likas Bay, it is one of the few "hanging" structures in the world and a 72-sided polygon that rises up some 30 storeys.

Look out for burial poles called sininggazanak at the Sabah Museum. When a Kadazan man dies without an heir, a sininggazanak – said to resemble the deceased – is built in his honour and placed on his land.

Architectural digest

To the south, the monumental **Masjid Sabah** (Sabah Mosque), on Jalan Tunku Abdul Rahman, is a fine example of contemporary Islamic architecture. The mosque's gilded dome is visible from the city, although it is located some distance from the city centre. You can visit at any time other than prayer times, but remove your shoes before entering quietly. Nearby, the **Sabah Museum** (open Sat–Thur 9am–5pm; entrance fee; tel: 088 253 199) is built in a stylised version of traditional Rungus and Murut tribal architecture. The museum has a good collection of Chinese ceramics, and the ethnological and textile sections are growing. The section on Sabah's fascinating flora and fauna helps to make sense of the bewildering variety of wildlife in the state. Also within the complex are an art gallery and a science centre with an exhibition on the oil and petroleum industry. There is also a collection of 10 life-sized traditional houses in the Traditional Village, set in the museum gardens. Each house depicts the architecture of a different ethnic group. A restaurant, coffee house, an ethno-botanical garden with an artificial lake and a souvenir shop complete the complex.

The town itself is a blend of ultramodern structures and old Chinese shophouses. Walk along **Jalan Gaya** to spot the town's few remaining traditional provision shops, where a delightful jumble of groceries, canned foods and

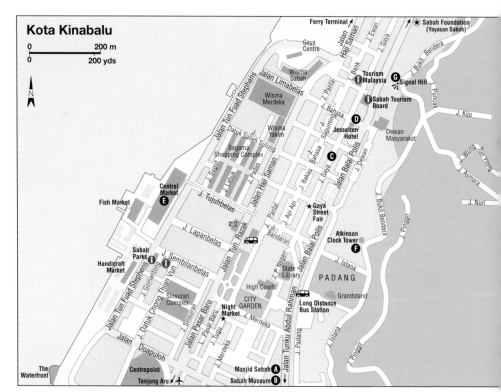

sacks of rice displayed as artfully as a film set, invite closer inspection. On Sunday mornings, there is the very popular **Gaya Street Fair** (open 8am–noon) – a city version of the traditional weekly *tamu*, which are markets that are held in venues across the state. Cheap clothes, plants, foodstuffs and, occasionally, bargain local handicrafts and antiques can be found.

Also on Gaya Street is the renovated **Jesselton Hotel** ❶ (www.jesselton hotel.com), the town's first hotel which exudes more old-world charm than it ever did before. It is a good stop for an Italian lunch or dinner, or even a stay overnight. The **Sabah Tourism Board** (open Mon–Fri 8am–5pm, Sat–Sun 9am–4pm; tel: 088-212 121; www.sabahtourism.com) on Jalan Gaya was once the main post office; its solid white-stone walls and colonial architecture make a pleasant contrast to the concrete shophouses.

The bustling **Central Market** ❸ sits midway along the waterfront, best seen early in the morning as fishermen unload their catch directly onto market tables. Kadazandusun women display their exotic range of fresh fruit and vegetables. One section specialises in tobacco and betel nut products, while yeast tablets for making the local rice wine, *tapai*, hang in strings like big, white beads. Adjacent is the **Handicraft Market** (open daily 9am–6pm) – a casual affair where handicrafts and souvenirs, mostly from the Philippines, are sold in rows of small stalls. Watch your purse as you practise your bargaining skills.

At the end of the day, Kota Kinabalu's restaurants come alive, and some of the best food in the state is served in small coffeeshops dotted around the town. As with towns in Peninsular Malaysia, night markets are ever present, selling clothes and curios, as well as local delicacies.

Few older buildings remain in town, but take note of the **Atkinson Clock**

Map on page 314

Fern tips, lightly stir-fried are a Sabahan delicacy.

BELOW: a sidewalk vendor.

Tower ⒡ at the end of the Padang. Further along Jalan Bukit Bendara, you'll reach the observatory on **Signal Hill** ⒢, which offers expansive views of the city and of the bay and islands. Situated at the eastern end of the city, the hill can be reached on foot, or by taxi or bus.

For a more contemporary view, go up to the top floor of the **Pacific Sutera** – part of the RM2.2-billion **Sutera Harbour Resort** (www.suteraharbour.com), a complex comprising two luxury hotels, golf and yacht clubs and an array of recreational facilities – at the western end of town. This vantage point offers vistas of both the sea and offshore islands and also of the golf course, across to Tanjung Aru stilt village and the city beyond, and the distant Gunung (Mount) Kinabalu.

South of town, off the airport road, is the famous **Tanjung Aru Beach**. The sea here is generally calm, the sand is clean and the coastal food stalls and restaurants offer delicious local cuisine. The huge orange-roofed complex at the tip of the cape is the popular **Shangri-la's Tanjung Aru Resort** (www.shangri-la.com).

Marine park paradise

Offshore from Kota Kinabalu, surrounded by azure waters, are the five islands of **Tunku Abdul Rahman Park** ➋, a popular destination whether for day trips or longer. The marine park headquarters is on Pulau Gaya, the largest of the islands and home to the **Gayana Resort** (located outside the park boundaries; www.gayana-resort.com), with stilted village-style accommodation. The other islands that make up the park are **Manukan**, **Mamutik**, **Sapi** and **Sulug**. Snorkelling can be enjoyed on all of these, and is best on remote Sulug. Pulau Manukan, the most developed of the islands, has chalets, a restaurant and swimming pool.

All the islands except Sulug have nature trails. Wildlife can be spotted on

occasion, sometimes closer than you'd like; watch out for the thieving macaque monkeys on Pulau Sapi. Pied hornbills and sea eagles can sometimes be seen on Pulau Gaya, and you may even spot a turtle surfacing as you swim.

You can camp on any of the islands but you must obtain a permit from the Sabah Parks office (tel: 088-212 508; www.sabahparks.org.my). Boats to the islands leave from the **Ferry Terminal**, located at the end of Jalan Haji Saman.

Maps:
Area 312
City 314

Heading north

Sabah's long west coast stretches all the way from the Sarawak border to the northern tip at **Kudat** and **Pulau Banggi** in the Sulu Sea, almost meeting the southern Philippines boundary. This area is ideally explored by car, with the freedom to stop at will. Although some areas outside the city may require a four-wheel-drive vehicle, the trunk road linking Kota Kinabalu with **Sandakan** in Sarawak and the east coast is bitumen and a cursory exploration of the state by road presents no difficulty at all.

The road north of Kota Kinabalu leads towards **Tuaran ❸**, passing en route several ceramics factories near Telipok where visitors are welcome to stop for a look and maybe make a purchase or two. At a large roundabout, you can either head north to Tuaran and a couple of beach resorts, or turn right towards **Ranau** and **Kinabalu Park**.

Bajau men, well-known for their horse riding skills, are mainly found in the Kota Belud area.

Tuaran is a small town known for its colourful Sunday *tamu*. Get there early morning to enjoy the market at its best. It is also noted for a local culinary speciality known as *Tuaran mee* – a delicious mixture of fried noodles, vegetables, egg, pork and pork crackling. Enjoy it in one of the shops on the main street before heading to the *tamu*. **Kampung Surusup** is about 15 minutes from Tuaran. There, negotiate a price with the boatmen at the jetty, who will take you by motorised canoe to visit **Kampung Penambawan** – a traditional Bajau fishing village.

About 40 minutes north of town are a couple of beach areas with luxurious resorts and golf courses. **Pantai Dalit**, a long strip of white sand backed by forested hills, is the location for the popular Shangri-la's Rasa Ria Resort (www.shangri-la.com), while on nearby **Karambunai Beach** is the plush Nexus Resort (www.nexusresort.com). In the vicinity, by a road just before Tuaran, is the **Mengkabong Water Village**, a rambling Bajau sea gypsy complex of raised stilted pathways and dozens of attap-thatched stilted huts built over an estuary. Transport around the village is by canoe, although many houses are also connected to one another by precarious-looking plank walks.

On the road leading towards Ranau is the old-world village of **Tamparuli ❹**, where the original shopping area consists of traditional wooden buildings, a sight fast fading across the country. Tamparuli is also the site of a Wednesday *tamu*. Flowing beside Tamparuli is the **Kiulu River**, a scenic area where the waters run clean. Kiulu is very popular as a scenic rafting destination, offering a more docile ride than the raging waters of the Padas River to the south.

Kota Belud ❺ is less than 1 hour's drive north from Kota Kinabalu and has two claims to fame. Firstly, it is renowned for the Bajau "cowboys", famed

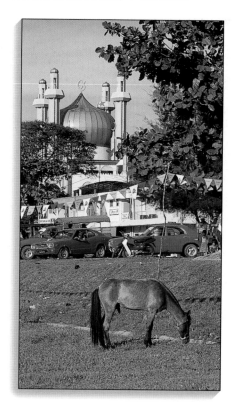

The Rungus people align their longhouses west to east, and facing Gunung Kinabalu, believing that position to be the most auspicious for good health.

for their rearing and handling of horses and buffalo. Secondly, it is the scene of one of Sabah's most colourful weekly *tamu*. Bajau and Kadazandusun women, their faces crinkled by the harsh sun, squat beside their wares – tobacco wrappers, piles of fresh vegetables or sugary doughnuts – for hours on end, constantly chewing betel nuts, which stain their gums and teeth a vivid red. There is always more on sale at the *tamu* than mundane necessities – an entire market row is devoted to the accoutrements of betel nut chewing. These women use the *tamu* not just to sell their wares, but also as a chance to catch up on the latest news and gossip.

Tourist backwater

From Kota Belud, the road heads north towards Kudat, and **Rungus** country – home to perhaps the most traditional and talented craftspeople in the state. **Kudat ❻** was the state's first capital (albeit for a mere two years), and once an important port in the trade between China and Europe. A British adventurer took advantage of this position and set up a trading post on Balembangan Island in 1763. However, this was plagued by lack of water and continual pirate raids and the area was abandoned for less troubled waters.

Today, Kudat has become the peaceful centre for the northwestern administrative district, and is also an active fishing port. Although the Kudat region has escaped the attention of tourists in the past, the traditional cultures of the Rungus and the long stretches of white sandy beaches, unspoiled and unpopulated are making it an increasingly popular destination.

The Rungus people are traditional agriculturalists, and a subgroup of the Kadazandusun tribe. Known for their excellent weaving and beadwork, the

BELOW: Rungus woman from Kudat.

Rungus live in small communities, either in longhouses or, increasingly, in single-family dwellings. The architectural style of their buildings (with their outward-leaning walls) is mirrored in the state museum in Kota Kinabalu.

The Rungus have retained their traditional spiritualistic and animist beliefs, much longer than have the other tribes of Sabah. They are also famous for the brass coils once used by women to decorate their arms. Nowadays, this practice has been discontinued – although you might still see forearm coils on older women. While the women continue to weave shoulder sashes, other woven textiles are rare; these days, people tend to wear decorated black cloth instead. Their excellent beadwork is quite visible in many of the *tamu* in the area.

Rungus life

It is possible to visit a Rungus longhouse and some have been constructed especially for visitors. Built in a green valley, **Kampung Bavanggazo** ❼, not far from the road leading to Kudat, has two purpose-built tourist longhouses where visitors will get to see Rungus women at work, weaving and making handicrafts. In the evening, enjoy a performance of Rungus dance and sample the local food and rice wine. Contact Sabah Tourism (tel: 088-212 121; www.sabahtourism. com) in Kota Kinabalu for details. At the nearby **Kampung Sumangkap**, traditional gong-making is the major activity and at **Kampung Gombizau**, villagers have taken up beekeeping and produce wax, honey and royal jelly.

There is also a large Hakka Chinese community living in Kudat, the first area to be inhabited by the Chinese in the 1880s; many of them are Christians and farmers by tradition. On the island of **Banggi**, off Sabah's northern tip, lives a small tribe long thought to be of Dusun extraction, but their dialect con-

Map
on page
312

Older Rungus women are fond of wearing long brass coils around their arms. The practice, however, is dying out with the younger women.

BELOW:
a Rungus-style
longhouse in Kudat.

tradicts this ancestry. They remain apart, living much as they have done for the last several hundred years. It is possible to visit the island, although there is no tourism infrastructure.

The ideal way to explore the Kudat region is in a four-wheel-drive vehicle, as some of the roads leading to the beaches are little more than dirt tracks. If you don't fancy staying overnight in a longhouse, then a good range of hotels are available in Kudat.

About 14 km (7 miles) before Kudat, signs direct the visitor to **Simpang Menggayau**, the northernmost point of the island of Borneo. **Kalampunian Beach**, just before the headland, is glorious, as are the beaches on the two bays of **Pantai Kelambu**, further south.

Highest mountain

Everyone in Malaysia knows about the mysterious **Gunung Kinabalu**, which, at 4,093 metres (13,428 ft), is one of the highest peaks between the Himalayas and New Guinea. The closer one journeys towards its famous jagged profile – often wreathed in feathery clouds – the better one understands the meaning it has for the local Kadazandusun people. They call it Aki Nabalu, or Revered Place of the Dead. It is believed that the spirits of the tribe's dead ancestors dwell among the forbidding peaks, and in the past no one had dared climb to the top for fear of disturbing and angering them.

In spite of the taboos and myths surrounding the mountain, Hugh Low, a young British officer, was still keen to reach the top. Climbing Gunung Kinabalu in 1851, Low was accompanied by a local chief and his guides. Struggling through the intense tangle of vegetation covering the lower slopes of the

BELOW: sure-footed Kadazandusun women porters.

mountain, Low eventually reached the summit plateau, but owing to a faulty barometer, was unable to locate the true summit. He made a second unsuccessful attempt on the summit in 1858. The honour of reaching the small peak of the summit actually ended up going to naturalist John Whitehead, who named it Low's Peak in honour of the earlier climber.

The mountain is said to still be growing, at a rate of half a centimetre a year. Relatively young, its jagged crown was sculpted by the last ice age, about 9,000 years ago. Although Kinabalu's peak is below the snow line, it grows cold enough here in December for ice to form in the rock pool at the base of the summit. Dropping away 1,800 metres (5,900 ft) straight downwards is the terrifying **Low's Gully**, its name being a typical piece of British understatement.

To get to the top, there is no need to spend days cutting through tropical rainforest, like Hugh Low did on his torturous first ascent, just to reach the granite slopes. Well-laid trails with steps and wooden rails help today's climber ascend and descend the mountain in just two days.

Accommodation is available at the park headquarters, and high on the mountain slopes. At the former, accommodation choices range from hostels to chalets, from the basic to almost grandiose. There are two restaurants (as well as a cheaper local restaurant on the main road just opposite the drive up to the park entrance), and a shop selling basic food supplies for climbers. In the administration building, on the hill to the right, just inside the park entrance, the Kinabalu Natural History Gallery has an interesting range of exhibits. There is also a range of accommodation on the eastern side of Kinabalu Park, at **Mesilau Nature Resort** (www.suterasanctuarylodges.com). On the mountain, mountain huts at Panar Laban offer cooking facilities and sleeping bag-hire, while **Laban Rata Resthouse** (www.suterasanctuarylodges.com) has a restaurant and heated rooms.

The easiest way to reach **Kinabalu Park** ❽ (open daily 7am–10pm; entrance fee; tel: 088-889 098), now designated a World Heritage Site, from Kota Kinabalu, is by mini-bus. From 7am onwards, the bus leaves for Ranau from the long-distance bus station near the Padang. The trip takes a little under 2 hours and the driver will turn off the main road to drop travellers at the park entrance.

Map
on page
312

Tips for the top

Before leaving the city, book your accommodation with **Sutera Sanctuary Lodges** (www.suterasanctuarylodges.com) at Wisma Sabah in Kota Kinabalu. Most of the year, particularly July and August and on public holidays, accommodation is tight and bookings need to be made well in advance. Alternatively, book a package tour with any of Kota Kinabalu's tour operators. Stock up on food if you want to do your own cooking, as the shop at the headquarters offers mainly noodles and chocolate. Bring a hat and gloves, as it can be extremely cold on the summit, and a waterproof garment to protect you from the frequent rainfall. If possible, leave your luggage at a hotel and take a light pack only, or use the luggage storage area at the park headquarters. A torch is also useful for the final ascent, which usually starts long before dawn.

BELOW: looking down at the world from Low's Peak.

*Hardy womenfolk
lugging firewood for
cooking.*

BELOW: granite
slabs are a sight to
behold near the
summit.

On the way to Kinabalu Park, you will pass by Tamparuli, 50 km (30 miles) north of Kinabalu (see page 317). Less than a kilometre past this town, the road begins to ascend the foothills, through landscape that is often swathed in clouds. On the left-hand side of the road as you climb — provided the weather is clear — you can catch glimpses of tiny villages, rice fields and pineapple plantations clinging to almost impossibly steep slopes. The main centre for these villages is **Nabalu**, where a *tamu* is held every Thursday. Kadazandusun women arrive early morning, their goods carried on enormous baskets on their backs. Nabalu is also a popular stop for tour buses, as it is a good place to buy genuine native handicrafts, local fruits and wild honey. You can also get a panoramic view from the top of the wooden viewing tower.

On your arrival at the park, the staff at Sutera Sanctuary Lodges will confirm your bookings, including those for the huts on the mountain. Maps, books, souvenirs and camera films are available at the souvenir store. You might choose not to climb the same day you arrive, so make yourself comfortable, acclimatise to the cool air, check out the Kinabalu Natural History Gallery and the mainly photographic display above the main restaurant, and explore the fascinating **Mountain Garden**, which houses plants from all over the park.

Peak of fitness

Although Kinabalu is an easy mountain to climb, a certain degree of fitness is required. Some regular exercise is recommended before the actual climb so that you don't come down the mountain a wreck of cramps, headaches and fatigue.

Just before the trail begins, there is a rather forbidding notice placed by the park authorities, recommending against climbs by those with the following

conditions: hypertension, diabetes, obesity, chronic asthma, heart disease, arthritis, anaemia, ulcers, hepatitis, muscular cramps and epilepsy.

Climbing 1,500 metres (4,950 ft) in one day – from the power station above the headquarters to **Panar Laban** – takes inordinate reserves of strength and zest for those who lead sedentary lives. Although experienced and intrepid climbers have climbed to the summit and back in less than 3 hours in the Kinabalu Climbathon, most people have an interest not just in getting to the top, but in fully savouring the views, and the area's flora and fauna.

After paying for a climbing permit, arrange for a local guide who will, for a fee, accompany visitors up the mountain (the guides are independent and can be found outside the registration office). Porters can also be hired at the park headquarters and will carry luggage as far as Panar Laban. Here they stop and wait for you to appear the following morning to scale the peak and later begin the descent. Fees depend on how heavy your luggage is; anything over 10 kg (22 lbs) will cost more.

On the second day, climbing from Panar Laban usually begins at 2am, although you can request your guide to start at 5am to avoid the crowds at the summit. Make sure you have a bar or two of chocolate in your pocket to provide instant energy for the climb and against the cold. You should also bring some headache tablets, as you may suffer from headaches because of the altitude.

A panoply of habitats

Passing the welcome gate at the power station (with the greeting *Selamat Mendaki* – "Happy Climbing!" written over the arch), the first steps lead down into a small, lush valley with a waterfall. After the waterfall, the climb begins, at first gently, later steeply through montane rainforest.

BELOW: Laban Rata Resthouse, Panar Laban.

All around you are some of the park's 1,500 species of orchids, clinging to mossy tree trunks and surrounded by swinging vines. Steep stairs leading ever upwards are happily spaced out between gentler paths. Small rest huts and viewpoints are positioned all the way up the trail to give the out-of-breath climber an excuse to stop and admire the view. You need not bring water, as there is pure mountain water available at all rest stops. At 1,300 metres (4,200 ft), the vegetation on either side of the trail begins to change from lowland rainforest into oak and chestnut forests of more temperate flora, like ferns and flowering plants.

Proceeding up to the next level of vegetation, one has the feeling of growing larger the higher one climbs. The trail began with huge trees towering above; now the trees have shrunk and you are almost the tallest thing in the landscape. At 2,600 metres (8,500 ft), you'll see small gnarled trees, twisted and wrinkled by the mountain air. The soil is poor here, and lichens cling desperately to the little trees.

The soil disappears altogether at 3,300 metres (10,800 ft) and the granite body of the mountain reveals itself. Only sedges, grasses and tiny alpine flowers cling to the rocky crevices where a bit of soil might remain.

Just when you thought you'd left all civilisation far below on the trail – now a hazy ribbon in the after-

Before you embark on your trek of Gunung Kinabalu, get hold of the intoductory leaflet, *Mount Kinabalu: A Guide to the Summit Trail*, published by Sabah Parks.

noon mist – you arrive at a series of huts and the resthouse where you wil spend the night.

A leisurely climb should get you here by around 2pm. At Panar Laban, you can retreat into the cosy Laban Rata Resthouse with its magnificent balcony looking up to the peak. There is a simple restaurant, as well as warm rooms and hot water. A little further up the slope is **Gunting Lagadan Hostel** (www.suter sanctuarylodges.com), which has dormitory rooms, sleeping bags for hire, and a basic kitchen equipped with cooking utensils and electricity.

Some climbers may find it hard to sleep on the mountain because of the thin air and the headaches caused by the altitude. Yet, you will need to go to sleep extra early to be able to struggle out of bed at 2am (your guide will wake you) Take a hot drink before starting the climb around 3am. Don't forget to stuff some chocolate into your pocket and bring your raincoat. Other than cameras everything else can be left at the hut for retrieval on the way down.

Rocky mountain high

Soon you will be climbing rock faces of granite in the pitch black as you hold onto the rope systems that guide the way. The steepness of the incline is difficult to gauge in the dark, though, and the granite slopes can be slippery after a night's rain. With an early start, you will be labouring up the slabs of granite with the peak in sight just as the skies begin to lighten. Here the granite rock, bared to the winds, is crumbling and broken, but at last Low's Peak arises.

Venturing a look down into the depths of Low's Gully, the view is awe-inspiring. This does indeed seem a place for spirits, for few mortals could long endure the harsh weather that sweeps away the offerings of sacrificial chickens, eggs

BELOW:
the mountain forest takes on a dream-like quality at dawn.

tobacco, betel nut, *sireh* leaves, limes and rice left here by the Kadazandusun.

The descent can be more leisurely, especially by climbers still glowing with the success of having reached the summit, but appearances can be deceptive. While it is easier on the lungs, the descent is hell to pay on the knees and in the end, can be even more painful than the climb up.

After collecting your belongings from Panar Laban, you will continue down through unique vegetation, such as pitcher plants that were probably missed on the ascent. On your arrival at the park headquarters, you can rightfully claim your badge commemorating your ascent, only for sale to those who have made it to the top.

Map on page 312

Amazing species

A guide can introduce you to Kinabalu's magnificent flora and fauna, some of it unique to the region. Among the rare plants found here is the famous Rafflesia, the largest flower in the world, which can measure up to a metre (3 ft) across, and nine species of pitcher plants. In 1858, the explorer Spencer St John chanced upon a huge specimen of the latter that contained approximately 1 gallon (4 litres) of rain water – as well as a dead rat.

The park's 750 sq km (300 sq miles) are unique in the world of flora, containing plants from almost every area on earth: the Himalayas, China, Australia, New Zealand, alpine Europe and even America. There are 1,500 species of orchid, 26 kinds of rhododendron and 60 types of oak and chestnut, as well as 80 species of fig tree. Animals found here include orang-utan, gibbons, leaf monkeys, tarsiers, pangolin (scaly anteaters), wild pig and deer. There is also a whole host of "flying" animals, some rarely found in other parts of Malaysia, including flying squirrels, colugos, snakes and lizards. Also found here – but seldom seen – is the incredibly rare clouded leopard.

The 518 species of birds include several kinds of hornbills, the scarlet sunbird, the mountain bush warbler, the pale-faced bulbul, the mountain blackeye, and the mountain's own Kinabalu Friendly Warbler. Around the area's waterfalls, look for the lovely butterflies, some as large as birds, and the less easy-to-see stick insects, well camouflaged to the human eye. You might also see squirrels, lizards, tree-shrews and bats.

BELOW: wild orchids.

Magical Mesilau

A second 5½-km (3½-mile) trail up the mountain begins in the eastern part of the park at **Mesilau**, a tougher, steeper climb that hard-core mountaineers will relish. The Mesilau trail joins the main summit trail near the rest stop at Layang Layang (accommodation at **Mesilau Nature Resort**, www.suterasanctuarylodges.com).

Mesilau is reached by road via **Kundasang** (5 km/3 miles from park headquarters), a densely packed market garden where some of the cool-climate vegetables and flowers grown on the hillslopes are sold at the stalls along the main road. Just down the road towards Mesilau, the **Kundasang War Memorial** on the right is a series of beautifully maintained courtyards and gardens honouring those who lost their lives in the infamous Death March near the end of WWII.

Stick insects in the jungles of Sabah are notoriously difficult to spot as they blend so easily against the bark of trees.

Of 2,600 Allied prisoners held by the Japanese in Sandakan, only six survived after escaping near Ranau.

Set amid wild beauty at almost 2,000 metres, Mesilau Nature Resort was built only a decade ago, and offers a range of attractive wooden chalets tucked away in the towering forest. The restaurant is set over a crystal-clear mountain stream, and the wooden deck is a great place to relax during clear weather.

Mesilau is especially noted for a hillslope where the huge *Nepenthes rajah* and other pitcher plants can always be found, along with stunning montane orchids. Before going on a guided tour to the **Nepenthes Garden**, check out the interesting information centre.

From Mesilau, the road leads to Poring via **Ranau ❾**, the main centre for the market gardens of the Kadazandusun country around Mount Kinabalu. At the weekly *tamu* in Ranau, held on the riverbank just outside town, you will see rural people dressed in a mix of traditional dress (black sarong) and Western attire.

A steaming, hot bath

At **Poring ❿**, 45 km (30 miles) to the east beyond Ranau, natural hot sulphur springs (entrance fee) will soothe those tired muscles you earned climbing the mountain. Your body soothed, you may like to check out the canopy walkway and the butterfly park.

Pleasant chalets with cooking facilities, and a couple of hostels are available, but few visitors rest long before making straight for the baths. The baths are set in park-like grounds with hibiscus bushes and frangipani trees, with the untamed jungle above and beyond. They were originally built during World War II by the Japanese, with their love of communal bathing giving them the impetus to tame

BELOW: a wreathed hornbill.

the jungle, and channel in both hot and cold water – the latter to temper the heat of mineral water.

Poring's 140 metre (460-ft) long canopy walkway strung high above the ground between giant dipterocarp trees, which literally offers a bird's-eye view of the forest, is well worth checking out. From time to time, a Rafflesia appears in the jungle areas around Poring. Near the baths is the butterfly park, filled with beautiful local species and some remarkable insects, while the **Poring Orchid Conservation Centre** has the largest collection of Sabah orchids.

In search of headhunters

Heading south from Kota Kinabalu, follow the signs from Putatan to the **Monsopiad Cultural Village** (open Mon–Sat 9am–6pm; entrance fee; tel: 088-774 337; www.monsopiad.com), a reconstructed Kadazan village in traditional style, built on the same site where the great headhunter Monsopiad lived about 300 years ago. His collection of skulls still hangs in the rafters and the centre is run by his direct descendants. Cultural shows featuring Kadazandusun dances to an authentic band are held daily (11am, 2pm and 4pm). The emphasis is on a "living museum" where Kadazandusun culture can survive and be promoted.

About 50 km (31 miles) south of Kota Kinabalu is **Papar ⑪**, situated on the mouth of the Papar River. Paddy fields surround the town and on the coast is a pleasant stretch of sand called **Pantai Manis**, or Sweet Beach. The Sunday *tamu* is a lively scene, as Kadazandusun traders bring their wares from the surrounding hills. The most interesting (and slowest) way to get to Papar is by local train; Borneo's only railway goes from Tanjung Aru near Kota Kotabalu to Beaufort and onwards to Tenom in the interior. The journey is even more memorable – albeit more expensive – on the restored wood-fired steam train known as the North Borneo Railway (www.northborneorailway.com.my). Relive the colonial days as you pass through the paddy fields on a 3½-hour return journey, enjoying a curry tiffin lunch on the way. The main highway continues on to the town of **Beaufort ⑫** and beyond to Sipitang, then to Sindumin on the Sarawak border. (Note: the rail network is scheduled to close in phases in 2007 for maintenance and will likely reopen fully in 2008.)

Beaufort is a busy highway junction, and an important stop on the railway line. It is also the staging point for whitewater rafting trips on the **Padas River** (*see page 328*) which is directly accessed by rail. Even if you don't participate you can watch rafts hurtling down the rapids from the comfort of your rail carriage.

Offshore millions

Beaufort is on the edge of a swampy peninsula with isolated fishing villages. Just offshore is **Pulau Labuan ⑬**, an international banking centre and an island that hopes to give Bermuda, Cayman and the Channel Islands a run for their money. A British naval station was established on the island in the 1870s and the Japanese forces in Borneo surrendered here in 1945, but other than those two events, little of significance transpired on the island.

After independence, Labuan was part of Sabah state

Map on page 312

TIP

Train buffs will be keen on the thrice-weekly steam train journey on the North Borneo Railway from Tanjung Aru to Papar. Built in 1896 it is powered by the last of the 60-year-old, wood-burning, British Vulcan steam engines.

BELOW: having a soak at Poring Hot Springs.

until 1984, when it was ceded to the federal government for development. Tax-free status came into effect in 1991 and the Malaysian government is keen to attract banks, insurance companies and fund management brokers to Labuan, in addition to offshore holding companies and corporate headquarters. Steps have been taken to attract business, including preferential tax laws. The island is also being developed for tourism and a number of wrecks off the coast are said to be worthwhile.

Located right at the end of Borneo's only railway, **Tenom ⑭** is the centre of Murut country and a rich agricultural centre. The Muruts or "Men of the Hills", have always lived in this region. Although many young people of the tribe have adopted the trappings of the Western civilisation creeping in from the capital, some still prefer life in remote areas. Young warriors still take their hunting dogs out for a stroll in the jungle to catch supper, hunting with a *parang* (a large, sharp knife) and a shotgun, rather than a blowpipe. Others have turned to cultivating the countryside and growing crops.

A popular festive pastime in the few remaining longhouses is jumping on the *lansaran*, a huge trampoline-like structure supported by a wooden platform. The largest can hold 40 people – perhaps the entire population of the longhouse – the basis for a wild party. The best longhouses can be found around Kamabong, south of Tenom.

Riding the raging river

Tenom is also close to the starting point for the Padas River ride, run by several tour operators out of Kota Kinabalu. After arriving at **Kampung Pangi** on the train from Beaufort, having passed through the dramatic Padas Gorge, rafters disembark, and rafts are carried to the river. There is time for a brief lesson and

donning of safety gear before taking the plunge. The 1½-hour ride is filled with thrills passing through some hefty waves, deep in the gorge, especially when the river is high. The ride finishes at **Kampung Rayoh** where lunch is served before you catch the train back to Kota Kinabalu.

Map on page 312

Tenom is also known for its **Agricultural Research Station**, 18 km (11 miles) northeast of town. The station has grown from its humble beginnings as a centre for cocoa research, to include a full-scale agri-park known as **Taman Pertanian Sabah**, or **Sabah Agricultural Park** (open Tues–Sun 9am-4.30pm; entrance fee; tel: 087-737 952). The **Tenom Orchid Centre** is also part of the park, with numerous species of orchids. Tenom's one classy hotel, the **Perkasa** (tel: 087-735 811), sits on the hill overlooking the town, although camping accommodation is available within the park.

Orchid blooms at Tenom Orchid Centre.

About 14 km (7 miles) outside of Tenom, on the Keningau road, the **Murut Cultural Centre** (open daily 8am–4pm; tel: 087-734 506) is remarkable for its massive timber buildings; the demonstration and sale of local crafts are available here. The centre is also the venue for the annual Murut Festival in May. It celebrates the culture of the group of tribes known collectively as Murut, with cultural performances, games and contests.

Some 40 km (25 miles) south of Tenom at **Batu Bunatikan Lumuyu**, close to Kampung Tomani, are Sabah's only rock carvings. Strange distorted faces and enigmatic figures are etched onto on massive boulders. These impressive paintings are thought to be crafted 1,000 years ago.

From Tenom, travel north through Keningau and Tambunan, and from there follow a rough road to Ranau and Gunung Kinabalu or follow the road over the Sinsuron Pass to Kota Kinabalu, thus completing a round trip.

BELOW: intricate Rungus bead work.

Keningau is the centre of the interior timber industry of west Sabah, with its many sawmills and log-holding depots. The town has prospered from its timber industry, and has several hotels and a sports complex.

Keningau and beyond

Driving southeast of Keningau, you come first to **Nabawan**, the last outpost of the government administration, and then to the settlement at **Sapulut ⑮**. From here, you can take a rough track to **Agis**, from where a pleasant 4-hour boat ride leads to the border and a fairly easy crossing into Kalimantan at the **Pagalunggan** checkpoint (obtain a visa first) and the traditional longhouse of **Kampung Selungai**, only half an hour away. This remote area is well worth exploring, but logging, El Niño and forest fires have taken a toll on the area in the last few years. Traditional longhouses sit along these riverbanks, where boats are built and the women engage in weaving, making intricate rattan mats and elaborate beadwork. Travellers are most welcome to stay the night, and the Muruts are renowned for their hospitality. Remember that it is polite to accept a drink when offered, as it is a host's duty to please guests with a cup of *tapai*. If you don't drink alcohol, simply touch the cup with your lips or the tips of your fingers and ask your guide to explain that you don't wish to partake of the fiery liquid. Gifts of food for the adults and toys for the

Map on page 312

children are customary, and items from your own country will be even more welcome than a product available in Kota Kinabalu.

In Sapulut, it is possible to hire a local canoe along the **Sapulut River**, for a 2–3 hour boat journey to **Batu Punggul** ⑯, a large limestone outcrop soaring 200 metres (600 ft) upwards from the encircling jungle. Local guides will show you the way to the top of Batu Punggul, a rough climb but well worth it for the spectacular view from the top. Another half-hour's walk through the forest leads to the less impressive **Batu Tinahas**, which is almost entirely obscured by the forest. This limestone massif was only recently discovered by a team from the Sabah Museum. Although not as high as Punggul, its cave and tunnel system is enormous and rivals the Gomantong Caves in east Sabah (*see page 336*).

The main road towards Kota Kinabalu shortly beyond **Tambunan** — a pleasant little town set in a picturesque valley — passes by a stone memorial on a grassy plain marking the site of Mat Salleh's last stand. Here, Sabah's most renowned hero built an underground fortress. He might have survived longer than 1900, had not a villager betrayed his location to the British forces, who promptly severed his water supply, and surrounded the fort. Mat Salleh and his followers were massacred when they emerged, ending the rebellion of a native lord who refused to pay tax to foreigners.

The route back to Kota Kinabalu from Tambunan passes by the Crocker Range National Park, with the **Rafflesia Forest Reserve** ⑰ located not far from the summit at **Sinsuron Pass**, which crosses the range at 1,649 metres (5,410 ft). The attractive **Rafflesia Information Centre** (open daily 8am-4.30pm; free) has displays on this extraordinary parasitic flower, and rangers can advise visitors if any are blooming in the 20 or so identified plots within the reserve.

BELOW: underwater hideout, Sipadan.
RIGHT: Poring's canopy walkway.

Delirious Diving

Sitting at the southern tip of the Spratly Islands, 250 km (155 miles) northwest of Kota Kinabalu, **Layang Layang** is part of the territory that is being contested by a number of countries in the region – including China, Vietnam, Indonesia and Malaysia. In the meantime, Malaysia is putting the island to good use as a tourist destination, as well as laying a claim that may become important in future negotiations.

This 7-km-by-5-km (4-mile-by-3 mile) coral atoll is as much a draw for migratory seabirds, as it is for the big game fishermen, who are attracted by the richly populated waters. Layang Layang is also the site of some of the best diving in Malaysia. Because of the distance from the the main island, the waters are particularly clear and untainted, and divers can enjoy spectacular coral walls, which drop down 2,000 metres (6,560 ft) to the coral below. Sharks and pelagic fish are common sights in these unspoiled waters, and schools of hammerhead sharks can often be seen in the months of March and April.

The island has a tiny airport, and next door is the comfortable **Layang Layang Island Resort** (www.layanglayang.com), which is dedicated to divers and has a fully-serviced dive centre, a desalination plant, rooms, a restaurant, and a swimming pool. A 45-minute flight from Kota Kinabalu covers the journey. ❑

SANDAKAN AND THE NORTHEAST

Map
on page
312

*The lively Chinese trading town of Sandakan is the tourism focus
of Sabah's east coast, and the jump off point for Sepilok
Orang-utan Rehabilitation Centre*

I n its heyday, people called the logs bobbing in the Sulu Sea "floating money".
Logs were floated down the Segama and Kinabatangan rivers from timber
concession areas near and far into the hands of Chinese entrepreneurs, who
shipped them to Japan. So prosperous was **Sandakan ⑱**, that at one time many
investors thought the town would become another Hong Kong. But the speed of
deforestation of the Sandakan region has quenched that dream. Now the logging
industry is but a shadow of its former self, and the derived wealth has been
moved to places far beyond. Sandakan – a medium sized, predominantly Chinese town and the base for tourist exploration of the east – now dervies most of
its income from palm oil.

The capital of North Borneo from 1883, Sandakan was completely razed during the bombings of World War II; the modern town was built on these ruins.
The nucleus of the original town began as a gunrunning settlement.

The gunrunners were mostly Germans, although later a Scotsman called
William Clarke Cowie ran guns for the Sultan of Sulu, setting up a camp on Pulau
Timbang which he named "Sandakan", the old Sulu name for the area. Later he
became the first managing director of the North Borneo
Chartered Company, whose main settlement was estab-
lished here on the fine harbour of Sandakan Bay.

At one time, Sandakan was a major trading centre.
Jungle products from the interior – bird's nests,
beeswax, rhinoceros horn, hornbill ivory along with
marine products like sea cucumber (*trepang*) and
pearls were valuable trade items which attracted a
cosmopolitan collection of traders from all over the
world: Europeans, Arabs, Japanese, Dusun, Javanese,
Bugis, Chinese – even Africans came to engage in the
wealth-generating business of trade.

Many visitors stay at the four-star **Sabah Hotel** (tel:
089-213 299) just outside town. Alternatively, stay at
the beautiful **Sepilok Nature Resort** (www.sepilok.
com), or at **Sepilok Jungle Resort** (www.sepilokjun
gleresort.com) rather than in the town itself.

Around town

The first Sandakan flight from Kota Kinabalu arrives
in the morning, allowing time for an exploration of
the town before heading out. An Asian breakfast can
be enjoyed in one of the Chinese *kopi tiam,* or coffee
shops, before a visit to the colourful **Sandakan
Central Market**. At its busy best in the early morning, the bustling market is an important source of local
vegetables and fresh seafood, which are exported
across the state and over to Singapore and Hong

LEFT: orang-utan at
Sepilok.
BELOW: Sandakan
was a major
logging centre.

BELOW: Sepilok is the largest of three orang-utan sanctuaries in the world.

Kong. Other town sights include the **Agnes Keith Museum** (open Sat–Thur, 9am–5pm; entrance fee; tel: 089-221 140), once the home of a famous American writer who wrote lovingly on Sabah in the 1930s and 1940s, and the adjacent **English Tea House**, a restaurant with a stunning view and even a croquet lawn.

Several Chinese temples are dotted around – the most spectacular being the huge, modern **Puu Jih Shih Buddhist Temple** on a hilltop south of town. Outside Sandakan, the **Sandakan Memorial Park** (formerly the Australian Memorial) is built on the site of a Japanese prisoner-of-war camp, and commemorates the Allied soldiers and locals who lost their lives during World War II.

Sandakan's main source of tourist fame is the **Sepilok Orang-utan Rehabilitation Centre** ⓳ (daily 8am–4.30pm, feeding times 10am and 3pm; entrance fee; tel: 089-531 180), a 20-minute drive westwards from town. In 1964, 10,000 hectares (25,000 acres) were designated a reserve for these lovable creatures. It takes but a little interaction to fall in love with these most "human" of primates. The orang-utan reportedly shares 96 percent of its genes with a human being, while its intelligence level can reach that of a six-year-old child. The centre assists orphaned orang-utans, or those who have been forced to live in captivity, to adjust gradually to jungle life and return to the wild. Instruction to the animals includes encouraging them to climb, building nests in trees (something wild orang-utans do each night) and foraging for food in the jungle. Gradually they are weaned from the milk and bananas provided, and taught to fend for themselves.

Those who stay longer than the obligatory hour-long feeding stop will find nature trails set around the park, where the stunning vegetation is the main feature, although you may spot birds, squirrels and macaques. Visit the nature centre and watch a video show on orang-utans in the wild. Adjacent to the cen-

tre are several lodges of various standards. Right next to the Sepilok Forest Reserve is the tasteful Sepilok Nature Resort, where trekking tours, birding and visits to the rehabilitation centre can be arranged. The Sepilok Jungle Resort provides a pleasant, cheaper alternative.

Map on page 312

Life of the turtle

Pulau Selingan, Pulau Bakkungan and Pulau Gulisan are the Sabah islands, which make up the trans-border **Turtle Islands Marine Park ㉑**, a 1,740-hectare (4,300-acre) tropical paradise in the Sulu Sea, about 40 km (25 miles) north of Sandakan. Green (*Chelonia mydas*) and Hawksbill turtles (*Eretmochelys imbricata*), or *sisik* as the locals call them, come here to lay eggs nearly every night of the year, but the best time to watch is between July and September. Rangers will take you out to the beaches where you can observe female turtles after they have commenced laying their eggs. Later, the eggs are scooped into plastic buckets and reburied at a nearby turtle hatchery, where they are safe from predators. Earlier in the evening, if you are lucky and a previous batch of eggs has hatched, you can witness their release and watch them begin their struggle for life as they make their way down the beach to the sanctity of the sea. Only some 3 percent of these turtles will reach maturity.

The best time to visit Turtle Islands Marine Park is between July and September when green turtles converge on the island to hatch their eggs.

Another 40 km (25 miles) due north is the exclusive and idyllic coral island known as **Pulau Lankayan ㉒**. The **Lankayan Island Dive Resort** (www.lankayan-island.com) is a tranquil place of white sand beaches that provides a wonderful escape – and utter peace. The island is particularly good for divers, with accessible wrecks to explore, and vivid marine life.

Bats galore can be seen in **Gomantong ㉒**, where some of Sabah's largest

BELOW: an endangered turtle in motion.

Map
on page
312

caves are found. These caves are also home to one million swiftlets, whose nests are collected to furnish the tables of Cantonese restaurants both in town and abroad. Collectors scale the *rotan* (cane) and bamboo ladders which hang from the cave roof up to heights of 30 metres (90 ft) above the bat guano-covered ground, to collect these treasures in the vast caves. The bats are only in evidence at dusk, as they make their nightly flight out to forage for food, just as the swiftlets return home. The huge, odorous guano pile is gradually raising the cave floor level. At one time the guano was harvested for use as fertiliser, but the cave's swift population declined so quickly that the guano now stays in an ever-mounting carpet, alive with cockroaches and other tiny cave dwellers. A wooden boardwalk makes is possible to tour the main **Simud Hitam** cave with ease. If visiting these caves, bring a flashlight and mosquito repellent. The fastidious might wish to bring a pair of disposable gloves.

River journey

An enjoyable excursion is a trip up the **Kinabatangan River**. Now one of Sabah's most popular tours, the river is dominated by tour operators who shuttle guests, by bus, to **Sukau ㉓** or **Bilit**, stopping off at the **Sepilok Orang-utan Rehabilitation Centre** as well as the **Gomantong Caves** along the way. Some tour operators, however, offer a trip upriver to Sukau, beginning from **Sandakan Bay**.

After crossing Sandakan Bay, the first stage of the journey is dominated by mangrove swamps and twisting waterways of the lowland floodplain. The occasional Orang Sungei (river people) settlement of stilted houses can be seen along the banks. Much of the original forest along the river has been replaced by oil palm, yet pockets still remain. Its role as an important wetlands area – the biggest in Malaysia – has been recognised by the WWF. The region has recently been gazetted as the **Kinabatangan Wildlife Sanctuary**.

The Kinabatangan River and its tributaries are famed for the wildlife, not least of which is the long-nosed, pot-bellied proboscis monkey. The most accessible place for close-up sightings of these unique animals is the swampy forest along the small Menanggol River, a tributary of the Kinabatangan, just upstream from Sukau. Boats leave in the afternoon (around 3.30pm to 4pm), in time to catch the monkeys as they crash through the trees, making their way to the riverside for their nightly sojourn.

Even more exciting are the wild elephants that roam the Kinabatangan area; sightings of elephants along the river are not uncommon. One of the best places to see the widest range of wildlife, including orang-utans and elephants, is at **Danau Girang**, where the famous **Uncle Tan's Jungle Camp** (www.uncletan.com) is located. The camp offers basic accommodation, boat cruises and jungle trekking.

The ox bow lakes, formed as the river has changed its slow course over the years, are exceptionally rich sources of birdlife, and you're likely to find a visit particularly rewarding. More than 100 species of bird live in these habitats, including waterfowl, snake birds and hornbills. ❑

BELOW: Gomantang Caves near Sukau.
RIGHT: Kadazandusan girls all dolled up for a concert.

TAWAU AND THE SOUTHEAST

Map
on page
312

Right in the southeast tip of Sabah, near the border with Indonesia, the regional centre of Tawau provides an access point to world-class diving and some beautiful jungle habitats

lights from Kota Kinabalu and Sandakan arrive at at a new airport about 20 km (12½ miles) north of **Tawau** ㉔, Sabah's main town of the southeast. As well as being the hub of an important timber and cocoa growing area, this busy little town has a very mixed population, where Muslim Filipinos from Mindanao and Indonesian estate workers have helped create a different atmosphere to the towns of the west coast. As well as the present timber capital of the state, Tawau is also the home of a reforestation programme situated at **Kalabakan**, where 30,000 hectares (70,000 acres) have been planted with fast-growing trees such as *Albizia facalaria*; the fastest is said to have soared 30 metres (100 ft) in just five years.

However, Tawau's real pride is the cocoa plant, which thrives in the region's rich volcanic soils, making Sabah the largest cocoa-producing state in Malaysia. Oil palm is grown, too, in huge estates that stretch mile after mile across the country. Tawau also boasts several good hotels, and the **Tawau Hills State Park**, a nature reserve where hot springs and waterfalls can be found.

Stilts and seafood

Tawau's main interest to the thousands of scuba divers who pass through each year is its proximity to **Semporna** ㉕, the gateway to Pulau Sipadan – Malaysia's only oceanic island and famous with the international diving fraternity as one of the world's five best dive sites. An hour's drive from Tawau's airport brings visitors to the small settlement, where Bajau fishermen, Suluk tribespeople, and Chinese traders lend a village atmosphere and a far-flung feel. Fringing the town are numerous settlements built on stilts over the water, an architectural style utilised by many of the newer resorts being built in the vicinity. The rich marine life around Semporna yields delicious seafood, which can be bought (often live) at the restaurant at **Dragon Inn**. Prepared by Chinese chefs in any style you wish and served with fresh, locally-grown vegetables, it is among the best seafood found in Malaysia.

Semporna's main jetty, where Dragon Inn's restaurant and chalets perch over the shallow waters, is always a hive of activity, with locals from the nearby islands coming and going in narrow wooden boats, and sleek speedboats leaving for dive resorts. Various dive companies maintain their offices on the jetty, while a couple of hotels, a souvenir shop and an air-conditioned restaurant on the Seafest jetty opposite cater to those en route for the nearby islands.

While Pulau Sipadan is the most exceptional dive site off Sabah's east coast, the jade and sapphire seas around Semporna are dotted with countless idyllic

LEFT: wild banana bloom.
BELOW: keeping sentry at Kapalai.

Moray eels can turn out to be vicious creatures if you stick your arm too far up their resting holes.

islands, surrounded by coral reefs. Unfortunately, dynamiting by fishermen has caused considerable destruction, but since the deportation of large numbers of illegal immigrants, the reefs are slowly regenerating.

The large islands of **Bodgaya** and **Bohey Dulang** to the northeast of Semporna, and several surrounding isles, have been gazetted as the **Tun Sakaran Marine Park**. As yet, facilities have not yet been developed, but the region promises to be a magnet for divers in the near future. Not far from Bodgaya, **Mataking**, the last island before the international border with the Philippines, is shared by an exclusive diving resort and the Malaysian army, which – along with navy patrols – ensures security along the entire east coast.

South of Semporna, **Pulau Sipadan** ❷❻ is Malaysia's only oceanic island. A pinnacle of limestone and coral rising up 600 metres (2,000 ft) from the floor of the Celebes Sea, it spreads out like a mushroom cap to form a 12-hectare island. The first divers to Sipadan in the 1980s slept in tents, disturbed at night only by nesting sea turtles burrowing in the sand before laying their eggs.

The stunning visibility and the incredible range of marine life – including large pelagic fish, brilliantly colourful hard and soft corals and underwater caverns – greatly impressed the late marine ecologist and diver, Jacques Cousteau. It also impressed the first foreign divers who stayed with the pioneer operator, **Borneo Divers** (tel: 088-222 226; www.borneodivers.info). Tales of schooling barracuda, mating sea turtles, huge jacks, moray eels, white-tip reef sharks and shimmering schools of exquisite reef fish soon spread. Perhaps inevitably, tiny Sipadan eventually became over-run with dive resorts and divers. In an effort to avoid environmental degradation of Sipadan and its surrounding reefs, the Malaysian government closed all resorts on the island in December 2004, per-

BELOW: snorkelling in Sipadan.

mitting divers to dive in the surrounding reefs but not land on the island. Limited day visits may be permitted in future. Most dive operators have transferred their resorts to the nearby low-lying island of **Mabul** ㉗, while **Kapalai** is occupied by a single beautiful resort perched on stilts. Both Mabul and Kapalai are renowned "muck diving" sites, great for macro life and all kinds of unusual critters that won't be seen on Sipadan.

Map on page 312

Subterranean settlements

An hour's drive from Semporna on the road to **Lahad Datu**, a turn-off leads to the **Madai Caves** ㉘, where you'll find a limestone outcrop with large caves just 2 km (1½ miles) off the main road. Outside the caves is a village that may be deserted except for a small nucleus of caretakers, but will be packed twice a year when harvesters come to gather the valuable edible nests built by swiflets in the caves.

Bring along a flashlight when exploring the caves; although sunlight filters down through crevices in the limestone roof of some caves, many of the deeper caves are pitch-black. Remains found at Madai prove that people lived in the area as long as 15,000 years ago. Further evidence of ancient settlement in the region – in this case going back some 20,000 years – can be found 18 km (11 miles) west of Madai. **Baturong** is another limestone outcrop, situated near what was once a lake known as Tingkayu, which drained away 16,000 years ago. With a guide from Lahad Datu or Kunak, you can visit this fascinating massif. The journey involves an hour's drive through cocoa and oil palm plantations to a mud volcano.

Lahad Datu is another of Sabah's "cowboy towns", known for its lawlessness. Situated close to the Sulu Islands of the Philippines, it has been, like the Semporna area, subject to occasional pirate attacks.

BELOW: aerial walkway at Danum Valley.

Map on page 312

Southwest of the town is the important **Danum Valley Conservation Area** ㉙, a 440-sq km (170-sq mile) reserve established by the Sabah Foundation for conservation and research. The inner area is totally unlogged, and has numerous walking trails through a pristine rainforest filled with waterfalls, streams and abundant wildlife. Morning starts early with the dawn chorus, as cicadas begin the chant, followed by the calls of some of the park's 270 bird species, echoed by the cries of gibbons. Hidden within this jungle paradise are rare Sumatran rhino, gibbons, mousedeer, barking deer, sambar deer, bearded pigs, giant flying squirrels and wild elephants. The conservation area houses the highly regarded **Danum Valley Field Research Centre**, which is open to day visitors. Tourists are required to stay in the charming Borneo Rainforest Lodge (tel: 088-251 634), which has a huge open lobby with a restaurant and bar looking across the Danum River to the rainforest, and comfortable stilted chalets nestled beneath trees.

Local guides, with an intimate knowledge of their subject, can take guests on nature walks; if you are lucky, they can show you how to call the different animals, and pick out a bird hidden in the jungle at a hundred paces. Many guides grew up in the region and have turned their well-honed hunting skills to better use, tracking down animals to photograph. But you'll need plenty of time and patience, standing silently, hoping to catch a glimpse. On the more remote trails, a total disregard for leeches is also an advantage during the wet months.

One of the most popular short excursions is an early morning walk to the canopy walkway, strung high between giant dipterocarps. It can be a rewarding experience to sit for an hour or so and watch for hornbills and honeyeaters, and possibly even the Asian paradise flycatcher – one of Danum's most exotic inhabitants. Night drives in an open jeep will often reveal deer, bearded pigs and other creatures, caught in the beam of the strong spotlight.

BELOW: wild elephants at Tabin.
RIGHT: waterfall in the Danum Valley.

More wildlife

Forty-eight kilometres (30 miles) to the east of Lahad Datu is the **Tabin Wildlife Reserve** ㉚ (tel: 088 261558; www.tabinwildlife.com.my). Although logging encroached on the area in the 1970s and 1980s, the re-growth has provided a home for larger mammals such as the elephant, and some orang-utans from Sepilok are now being introduced into the wild here. Comfortable chalets with fans and a restaurant are available, with nature trails for exploring the environment.

From the Tawau district, the north coast can be reached by road via Keningau (over the Crocker Range), and via Sapulut in the interior, travelling close to the Indonesian border along logging tracks passing by the **Maliau Basin**. Four-wheel-drive vehicles, which have obtained permission to carry passengers through the logging concessions, make the trip daily. The drive from Tawau to Keningau takes between 8 and 10 hours, depending on the condition of the tracks. The road north to Sandakan is easy and open, passing through mile after mile of oil palm plantations on what was once rainforest. Buses – which travel north almost to Sandakan before heading west across the Crocker Range – take 12 hours to Kota Kinabalu, and cost half the price of the airfare, although the flight takes just 40 minutes. ❑

INSIGHT GUIDES

TRAVEL TIPS

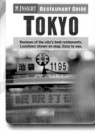

TRAVEL TIPS

TRANSPORT

GETTING THERE AND GETTING AROUND

GETTING THERE

By Air

Malaysia is connected by about 41 airlines to international destinations. The **Kuala Lumpur International Airport**, or KLIA (tel: 03-8776 4386; www.klia.com.my), located in Sepang 70 km (43 miles) from the city centre, is the key gateway in and out of Malaysia. The other main airports are in Penang, Langkawi, Johor Bahru, Kuching and Kota Kinabalu.

The **Penang International Airport** is linked by direct international flights from several Asian cities, including Bangkok and Singapore, while the **Langkawi, Kuching** and **Kota Kinabalu** airports are served by direct international flights from Singapore.

Malaysia Airlines (MAS), the national carrier (24-hour call centre tel: 03-7846 3000, toll-free within Malaysia 1300-883 000; www.malaysiaairlines.com), flies to over 100 international and domestic destinations.

Local budget airline **AirAsia** (24-hour call centre tel: 03-8775 4000, toll-free within Malaysia 1300-889 933; www.airasia.com) offers cheap fares online for both domestic and Asian destinations. A new budget long-haul airline, **AirAsia X**, is scheduled to commence flights from UK and China destinations to Kuala Lumpur from July 2007.

Malaysia Airlines flights depart from KLIA while AirAsia flights (both domestic and international) depart from the **Low Cost Carrier Terminal** (LCC-T; tel: 03-8777 8888; www.klia.com.my/LCCTerminal), located

about 20 km (12 miles) from KLIA. Feeder buses running at 20-minute intervals link the two terminals.

There is an airport tax of RM40 for international flights, which is usually built into the airfare.

Flying from the UK or US

Airlines that fly to KLIA from the UK and US include Aer Lingus, Air France, Alitalia, Austrian Airlines, EVA Air, Finnair, Iberia, Japan Airlines, KLM, Lufthansa, Malaysia Airlines and Singapore Airlines.

Passengers from the UK and EU can fly direct to KLIA in about 13 hours, though stopover flights are cheaper. Airlines that fly non-stop include EVA Air, Malaysia Airlines and Thai Airways International.

A flight from the US west coast takes about 16 hours and usually involves a connection in Japan, Taiwan or Hong Kong; the east coast route via Europe takes about 19 hours. Malaysia Airlines operates flights from New York (Newark) to KLIA via Stockholm. Note that American Airlines flies via Singapore.

By Rail

Peninsular Malaysia

Train services to and within Malaysia, operated by the **National Railways**, or KTMB (tel: 03-2267 1200; www.ktmb.com.my), are clean, cheap and reliable. Railroads link Kuala Lumpur with Thailand in the north; Singapore in the south; and the east coast of the peninsula. The rail terminal in Kuala Lumpur is **KL Sentral**.

If you are travelling from Bangkok to Kuala Lumpur, change trains in Hat Yai (southern Thailand) or Butterworth (northern Peninsular Malaysia). The express journey takes about 20 hours and costs RM150 (first class).

Airline Offices in Kuala Lumpur

Air France/KLM
Grand Plaza Park Royal,
Jalan Sultan Ismail
Tel: 03-2711 2300

Berjaya Air
6th Floor, Berjaya Times Square
1 Jalan Imbi
Tel : 03-2145 2828

EVA Airways Corporation
Suite 1205, 12th Floor, Kenanga
International, Jalan Sultan Ismail
Tel: 03-2161 7500

Japan Airlines
Suite 20.3, Level 20 Menara
Citibank, 165 Jalan Ampang
Tel: 03-2161 1740

Lufthansa
18th Floor, Kenanga
International,
Jalan Sultan Ismail
Tel: 03-2052 3428

Malaysia Airlines
Bangunan MAS,
Jalan Sultan Ismail
Tel: 03-7846 3000, toll-free within
Malaysia 1300-883 000

Northwest Airlines
8th Floor, Menara TA,
1 Jalan P. Ramlee
Tel: 03-2161 5901

Singapore Airlines
Wisma Singapore Airlines,
2–4 Jalan Dang Wangi
Tel: 03-2698 7033

Thai Airways International
Suite 30.01, 30th Floor, Wisma
Goldhill, 67 Jalan Raja Chulan
Tel: 03-2031 1900

United Airlines
2nd Floor, Bangunan MAS,
Jalan Sultan Ismail
Tel: 03-2161 1433

A less travelled route is via the east coast through the Thai town of Sungai Kolok and the town of Rantau Panjang in Kelantan, from where you can take a bus to Kota Bharu, where there are other overland options to other cities.

The express journey from Singapore's Tanjong Pagar Railway Station to Kuala Lumpur takes 8 hours and costs RM70 (first class).

To travel in style, opt for the elegant and charming luxury **Eastern and Oriental Express** (Singapore tel: 65-6392 3500; www.orient-express.com). Travelling several times a month between Singapore and Bangkok, it departs from the old railway station in Kuala Lumpur.

By Road

Peninsular Malaysia

From Singapore: The peninsula is linked to Singapore by two causeways: the **Johor–Singapore Causeway** from Woodlands (Singapore) to Johor Bahru, and the **Second Link** from Tuas (Singapore) to Tanjung Kupang. From these two points, you can connect to the North-South Expressway which runs along the west coast.

In Singapore, buses to Peninsular Malaysia depart from Beach Road (outside Golden Mile Complex), Lavender Street and Queen Street. The bus journey to Kuala Lumpur takes about 5–6 hours and costs RM30–80. While crowded and chaotic **Puduraya** is the main bus terminal for the cheaper bus services, several of the pricier operators terminate at various places in the city. These include **Aeroline** (tel: 03-6258 8800, Singapore tel: 65-6733 7010; www.aeroline.com.my; terminates at Corus Hotel on Jalan Ampang and in Petaling Jaya); **Airebus** (tel: 03-2141 7110, Singapore tel: 65-6333 1433; www.airebus.com.my; terminates at Crowne Plaza Hotel in Jalan Sultan Ismail); **Plusliner** (tel: 03-2272 1586, Singapore tel: 65-6256 5755; www.plusliner.com; terminates at the Old Railway Station); and **Transnasional** (tel: 03-2161 1864/2070 3300, Singapore tel: 65-6294 7034; www.nadi.com.my/transportation_home.asp; terminates at the Malaysian Tourist Centre on Jalan Ampang).

These companies use the more expensive VIP or Executive (24-seater) express coaches which have comfortable reclining seats, drinks and meals on board, and, on some services, individual TV screens. Cheaper non-express coaches make several stops on the way, including a 30-minute meal stop.

Malaysia Airlines operates daily

SPS coach shuttle services between Johor's Senai Airport and Copthorne Orchid Hotel (214 Dunearn Road) in Singapore for its ticket holders. Tickets are priced at RM12/S$12 (tel: 1300-883 000 for reservations). Other passengers can catch the **Causeway Link Express** coaches (about RM9) from Singapore's Kranji MRT Station to Senai Airport via the City Lounge in Johor Bahru. For more information, visit www.senaiairport.com.

If you opt for long-distance taxis, take SBS Transit bus 160 or 170, SMRT bus 950 or the Malaysian-operated Causeway Link buses to Johor Bahru and catch a taxi from there.

From Thailand: The North-South Expressway ends in **Bukit Kayu Hitam** (Kedah), the main border crossing between Malaysia and Thailand. Other border crossings are at **Padang Besar** (Perlis) and **Rantau Panjang** (Kelantan). Buses and taxis serve these points.

Buses from Thailand travel along the peninsula's west coast from Hat Yai. The journey to Kuala Lumpur takes about 9 hours and costs RM35. Many buses from Hat Yai, Bangkok and Phuket also terminate in Penang, from where you can take a local express bus. The east coast route is via Sungai Kolok (Thailand) and Kota Bharu.

Sarawak

A road goes from Pontianak in Kalimantan, Indonesia, to Kuching. This route (10 hours) is serviced by regular buses. Miri is joined by a long coastal road to Brunei's capital, Bandar Seri Begawan.

By Sea

Peninsular Malaysia

Malaysia has a number of official sea entry points: **Tanjung Belungkor** in Johor, with ferry links to Singapore; **Langkawi**, which is served by a regular ferry service from Satun in southern Thailand; **Penang**, which connects to Medan in Sumatra, Indonesia; **Melaka**, which links to Dumai in Sumatra; and **Port Klang** in Selangor, which has ferry services to Tanjung Balai in Sumatra.

Sarawak and Sabah

The sea entry points are: **Tawau** (Sabah), which connects to Nunukan and Tarakan in Kalimantan; **Labuan**, and **Limbang** and **Lawas** in Sarawak, all of which are linked to Brunei. From Kota Kinabalu, you can take a ferry to to Labuan, from where you take a boat to Brunei. From Brunei, continue by boat to Lawas and Limbang in

Sarawak. There are also boats operating between Sandakan and southern Mindanao in the Philippines.

GETTING AROUND

On Arrival

Buses and public and private taxis and limousines operate from major airports in Malaysia. Many airports, including Penang, Kuching and Kota Kinabalu, have taxi desks where you purchase a coupon; the price is fixed. Kuala Lumpur's old railway station and the KL Sentral transport hub also use a coupon system. Tolls are paid by the passenger. Elsewhere, enquire about fares at the information desk. Taxi fares from airports are higher than around town.

To and From KLIA

Taxis: Airport Limo taxis (tel: 03-8787 3030) operate 24 hours and are air-conditioned. Buy coupons from the Airport Limo counters just before you exit the international arrivals gate, or just outside the domestic arrivals gate. Tickets to the city centre cost RM67 for budget taxis, RM92 for premier taxis, and RM180 for the luxury and family-sized ones. The journey to the city centre takes 40–60 minutes, depending on traffic conditions. You need not tip the driver.

To get to KLIA, you can call the Airport Limo or take any taxi. The latter's fare comprises the meter rate plus tolls, a surcharge of RM12 and that for luggage placed in the boot. The total comes up to RM50–80. **Public Cab** (tel: 03-6259 2020) also offers a limo service to the airport that seats six. You can also book a taxi the night before for an early morning flight. Note that there is a surcharge for services from midnight to 6am.

Bus: Airport Express coaches (tel: 03-6203 3067) depart from KLIA every hour from 6.15am to 12.30am for the Duta Bus Station, and stop at major hotels en route. A ticket costs RM25. From Jalan Duta, a taxi journey to the city cost about RM15.

Coaches also go to the Chan Sow Lin LRT Station, leaving hourly 7.30am–9.30pm. From the LRT station, you can take the train into town (RM10). Tickets can be bought on the bus or at the counter before exiting the terminal (ground level).

You can request to be picked up by feeder mini buses run by the Airport Express from major hotels in Kuala Lumpur to the airport;

bookings must be made at least one day ahead (tel: 03-6203 3064).

Train: The KLIA **Ekspres** (tel: 03-2267 8000) takes you to the **Kuala Lumpur City Air Terminal** (KL CAT) at KL Sentral directly in 28 minutes. Trains run every 20 minutes from 5am to midnight, and every 15 minutes 5–9am and 4–10pm. Tickets cost RM35 one way and RM65 return.

The half-hourly KLIA **Transit** service stops at three intermediate stations – Salak Tinggi, Putrajaya and Bandar Tasik Selatan. The journey takes 35 minutes and the service hours are 5.52–1am. The one-way end-to-end fare is also RM35 but different fares apply for intermediate stops.

Tickets can be purchased from vending machines or ticket counters at KLIA and KL CAT, hotels and through appointed travel agencies.

To get to your hotel from KL Sentral, take a taxi or a connecting LRT, Monorail or KTM intra-city train. The monorail terminal is 200 metres (220 yards) away.

When departing Kuala Lumpur, Malaysia Airlines, Cathay Pacific and Royal Brunei passengers can check in at KL CAT with a valid KLIA Ekspres ticket, at least two hours before departure. A boarding pass and a claim tag for checked-in baggage will be issued. The first train departs at 5am and the last train at 1am.

From LCC-T

Take the feeder bus (5.55–12.35am) from the Low Cost Carrier Terminal (LCC-T) to KLIA and use the transport options listed above. Alternatively, the **Skybus** (www.skybus.com.my) to KL Sentral runs every 15–30 minutes from 7.15am to 12.30am. The journey takes 90 minutes and tickets (RM9) can be purchased from booths at the terminal or on board AirAsia flights. The **Airport Coach** (tel: 03-6203 3067) runs from 5am to 12.30am every 45 minutes to the Duta Bus Station (RM20) and to Chan Sow Lin LRT Station (RM10). The journey takes about 75 minutes.

Touting for Business

The airport is where you are likely to meet your first tout. Unlicensed taxi operators, called *teksi sapu* or *kereta sapu*, hang around airport, train, bus and boat terminals, and will charge a flat rate, usually higher than usual rates. They sometimes go round gathering a few passengers before they depart. Opt for a licensed cab if you can.

The LCC-T is further than KLIA but taxi tickets are cheaper. Depending on the type of car used, a taxi ride to the city centre costs RM60–150.

Sarawak and Sabah

Although Sarawak and Sabah are part of Malaysia, it is necessary for both Malaysians and foreign visitors, whether coming from other parts of Malaysia or from another country, to go through immigration and customs procedures on arrival. Foreigners need to produce their passports and Malaysians, their identification cards.

Kota Kinabalu International Airport is located 7 km (4 miles) from the city. Taxis must be paid for in advance at the airport taxi service counter; there is no bus service direct from either terminal. Budget airlines arrive at Terminal 2, near Tanjung Aru beach and about 10 minutes by taxi from Terminal 1, where all international flights arrive.

Kuching International Airport, 12 km (7 miles) from the city, has a taxi service counter in the arrival hall, where fares must be paid in advance. STC bus 12A departs from the airport every 50 minutes and takes 45 minutes to reach the city.

By Air

Travelling by air is the easiest and an affordable way to cover great distances in Malaysia. The country enjoys a thriving domestic airline market, which has ensured the affordability of air tickets.

Malaysia Airlines (MAS) has a night tourist fare which is 30 percent cheaper for travel from Kuala Lumpur to Alor Star, Penang, Kota Bharu, Johor Bahru, Kuching and Kota Kinabalu. Other discounted fares on selected routes (mainly from Johor Bahru, Kuala Lumpur, Kuching and Kota Kinabalu) include a special one-way fare (less 20 percent) if you pay 7 days in advance; a special round-trip fare (less 30 percent) if you stay between 3 and 30 days; and a group fare (less 50 percent) for travel between the peninsula and Sabah or Sarawak if you are in a group of three, pay 7 days in advance, and remain in the destination between 3 and 30 days; other restrictions apply. There is also a special rate for families. Enquire at an MAS office or visit www.malaysiaairlines.com.

Malaysia Airlines Offices

Call 1300-88 3000 (within Malaysia) or 603-7846 3000 (outside Malaysia) for enquiries or check www.malaysiaairlines.com. Note: In Kuala Lumpur, all MAS domestic flights operate out of KLIA.

Alor Star, Sultan Abdul Halim, Kedah, tel: 04-714 3202.
Bario, Bario Co-operative Society Ltd, Kelabit Highland, Baram, Sarawak, tel: 1300-883 000.
Bintulu, Syarikat Awang Radin, 4 Belaga Bazaar, Belaga, Sarawak, tel: 086-461 240.
Johor Bahru, Suite 1.1, Level 1, Menara Pelangi, Jalan Kuning, Taman Pelangi, Johor, tel: 07-331 0036.
Kota Bharu, Mezzanine Floor, Kompleks Yakin, Jalan Gajah Mati, Kelantan, tel: 09-748 3477.
Kota Kinabalu, 1st Floor, Departure Level, Kota Kinabalu International Airport, off Jalan Petagas, tel: 088-515 314.
Kuala Lumpur, Bangunan MAS, Jalan Sultan Ismail, tel: 03-7846 3000 (24 hours).
Kuala Terengganu, 13 Jalan Sultan Omar, Terengganu, tel: 09-622 9279.
Kuantan, 7 Ground Floor, Wisma Persatuan Bola Sepak Pahang, Jalan Gambut, Pahang, tel: 09-515 6030.
Kuching, Lot 215, Jalan Song Thian Cheok, Bangunan MAS, Sarawak, tel: 082-244 144.
Labuan, Level 2, Airport Terminal Building, PO Box 23, Sabah, tel: 087-431 737.
Langkawi, Langkawi International Airport, Kedah, tel: 04 955 6332.
Miri, Lot 239, Beautiful Jade Centre, Sarawak, tel: 085-417 315.
Penang, 2nd Floor, Menara KWSP, 38 Jalan Sultan Ahmad Shah, Penang, tel: 04-217 6321.
Sandakan, Ground Floor, Block 31, Sabah Building, Jalan Pelabuhan, Sabah, tel: 089-273 970.
Sibu, 61 Jalan Tuanku Osman, Sarawak, tel: 084-321 055.
Tawau, First & Second Floor, TB 319 Block 38, Jalan Haji Sahabudin, Fajar Complex, Sabah, tel: 089-761 293.

Other Airlines

Air Asia (tel: 03-8775 4000; www.airasia.com) offers low-fare, no-frills flights to most main destinations such as Penang, Langkawi, Kuching, Kota Kinabalu, Sandakan, Tawau and Kota Bharu, as well as flights between Kota Kinbabalu and Miri, Sibu, Bintulu and Kuching in Sarawak. The airline also offers a selection of holiday packages to most destinations. The airline operates out of the LCC-T at KLIA and from Terminal 2 at Kota Kinabalu International Airport. In Sarawak, AirAsia uses the same terminal as MAS.

Berjaya Air (tel: 03-2145 2828; www.berjaya-air.com) is the only airline to offer flights to Tioman, Redang and Pangkor islands. Using 48-seater Dash 7 aircrafts, Berjaya Air operates from the Sultan Abdul Aziz (Subang)

Airport in Kuala Lumpur to the two islands. The airline also offers flights from Singapore to Redang and Tioman.

Fly Asian Express (tel: 03-8775 4000; www.flyasianxpress.com), popularly known as FAX, was established in mid-2006 to take over a number of internal routes previously handled by MAS in Sarawak and Sabah. A subsidiary of AirAsia, FAX uses small Dash and Twin Otter aircrafts to service small communities. Miri is the hub for most of these flights. The FAX website uses the same simple booking facilities as AirAsia.

By Rail

The Malaysian railway system runs from Singapore through the peninsula and into Thailand in the north. Express services stop only at major towns; the others stop everywhere. Malaysian trains are comfortable and equipped with snack cars. There are air-conditioned first- and second-class coaches and bunks on the night trains. Third-class coaches are fan-cooled.

You can book seats up to 60 days ahead, and do so online. For foreign tourists (except Singaporeans), KTMB offers a **Visit Malaysia Rail Pass** for travel over a period of 5, 10 or 15 days on KTMB services in Peninsular Malaysia (and Singapore). Concessions are available for children.

For information, contact KTMB (tel: 03-2263 1111; www.ktmb.com.my).

Peninsular Malaysia

The west coast rail line goes through Kuala Lumpur to Butterworth (Penang) and joins Thailand at Padang Besar, Kedah. The Ekspres Rakyat (ER) departs every morning from Singapore to Butterworth and vice versa. Ekspres Sinaran (XSP) is the other morning service and links Kuala Lumpur and Butterworth.

The night trains are the Ekspres Senandung Malam sleepers (ESM) servicing Kuala Lumpur–Singapore and Kuala Lumpur–Butterworth, and Ekspres Langkawi (EL) servicing Kuala Lumpur–Hat Yai.

The east coast line branches off at Gemas in Johor, heads through the central forests and emerges at Tumpat in Kelantan, near the border with Thailand. Only night trains, the Ekspres Timuran (XST) Singapore–Tumpat and Ekspres Wau (XW) Kuala Lumpur–Tumpat (via Gemas) do this route.

Sabah

The only public train in Borneo operates daily from the Tanjung Aru Station in Kota Kinabalu via Beaufort to Tenom in the interior; this is one

of the world's greatest train journeys. **North Borneo Railway** (tel: 088-254 611) operates three tourist services between Tanjung Aru and Papar per week. Note, however, that at the time of writing, the railway network in Sabah is being closed in phases for maintenance; it will likely fully reopen by 2008.

By Boat

Around the peninsula, boats are the chief means of travel to the islands and in parts of the interiors. Regular ferries service the islands of Pangkor (6.30am–7pm), Penang (6am–midnight) and Langkawi (8am–6pm). Boats out to islands on the east coast generally do not follow schedules, and in the monsoon season (November–February), services may stop altogether. Note that the sea can be choppy just before and after the monsoon period and services may be cancelled.

In the northeast, services begin at 8.30–9am and stop at 2–2.30pm. Other than during public and school holidays, it is generally fine to arrive on the Perhentian Islands (from Kuala Besut) and Kapas (from Marang) without having booked your accommodation, but it is safer to pre-book accommodation and therefore boats at Redang and Tenggol (from Merang).

In the southeast, Mersing services the bulk of the Johor islands and Tioman, while Tanjung Leman is the staging point for the Sibu isles. Scheduled ferries depart Mersing only to Tioman (arrive at Mersing as early as possible) and Rawa (one service at midday). Other services can be a little confusing (see chapter on Mersing and Isles, page 241). Tioman can also be accessed from Tanjong Gemok. The Tanjung Leman boats depart daily at 11am, 1.15pm and 4.30pm.

In the interior, Taman Negara is the only destination with scheduled boats (9am and 2pm). It is generally all right to arrive at Tasik Kenyir, Kenong and Tasik Cini without booking, but arrangements for Temenggor (for Belum) and Tasik Bera must be pre-booked.

Sarawak

There are no scheduled shipping lines to Sarawak, but within the state express boats and local river craft are still the main form of transport to the interior.

There is a lot of traffic on the rivers inland throughout most of the year as roads are still few and far between and are generally in poor condition.

On the Rejang River, regular boats

run between Sibu and Kapit, and if the waters are high enough, they go on to Belaga to longhouse territory. Express boats travel to many of the smaller rivers stopping at remote longhouses along the way. Chartered boats can be fearfully expensive.

Bigger boat services operate between Kuching and Sibu – currently just one daily departure – with a 3–4-hour ride. Regular ferry services also connect Kota Kinabalu with the duty-free island of Labuan and then on to Brunei and the Sarawak divisions of Lawas and Limbang.

Cruises

Short-term cruises have been popular in the peninsula with a niche market, partly because of onboard gambling in international waters. Besides casinos, ships are usually equipped with a swimming pool, cinema, disco and karaoke. There are usually live band or cabaret-style performances, ballroom-dancing classes and other activities, and packages are full-board. The 2,000-passenger ship Virgo departs from Singapore and offers 4-day/3-night packages to Phuket/Langkawi, a 3-day/2-night Kuala Lumpur cruise to Melaka and Port Klang, and a 6-day/5-night Straits of Melaka package. Book with **Travel Malaysia** (tel: 03-2070 8667) or **Asian Overland Services** (tel: 03-425 9100, www.asianoverland.com.my), which also handles international liners.

By Road

Malaysia's interstate (outstation) buses and taxis are a fairly comfortable and convenient way of covering the country. Both the roads and public transport are better in the peninsula than in Sabah and Sarawak, but there are generally good networks linking capital cities and major towns. Sarawak's road system is pleasant enough for exploring the areas surrounding Kuching and up to the Kalimantan border. The longer drive to Miri is now relatively comfortable, thanks to the completion of much of the new Trans-Borneo highway and bridges across major rivers previously crossed by ferry.

Interstate Buses

Peninsular Malaysia

Three types of interstate buses operate in Malaysia: non-air-conditioned buses plying between the states; air-conditioned express buses connecting major towns; and non-air-conditioned buses that provide services within each state. With the exception of the express buses, the others seldom adhere to the schedule, but are frequent between 9am and 6pm.

Express buses usually connect two or three major towns, and will break the journey for a stop at a restaurant or food centre along the highway for half an hour. There are several classes of buses: the VIP or business-class coaches have the most legroom, and do not cost that much more (recommended for longer journeys).

At bus stations, you will inevitably be accosted by touts selling tickets for unlicensed operators. Tickets might be cheaper but these buses do not depart until enough passengers are rounded up; they also make numerous stops and often break down.

Different operators handle different towns – information and fares are displayed at counter windows. Outside public holidays, you don't need to purchase your ticket beforehand (bookings are rarely taken).

Plusliner (tel: 03-2272 1586; www.plusliner.com) and **Transnasional** (tel: 03-2161 1864/2070 3300; www.nadi.com.my/transportation_routes_express.asp) operate extensive networks of coach services to different destinations in Peninsular Malaysia. Their comfortable and air-conditioned coaches depart daily from Kuala Lumpur's main bus stations (*see below*). Plusliner's Nice Executive Coaches service only Penang, Ipoh and Singapore, with several departures daily from KL's old railway station (*see page 347*).

In Kuala Lumpur, north- and southbound services are found at the **Puduraya Bus Station** (tel: 03-2070 0145) on Jalan Pudu and the **old railway station**; coaches to the east coast and Tasik Kenyir depart from the **Putra Bus Station** (opposite the Putra World Trade Centre); and the interior destinations such as Kuala Lipis are serviced from **Pekeliling Bus Station** (tel: 03-4042 7988) on Jalan Pekeliling. Some north-bound buses leave from **Duta Bus Station** (tel: 03-6203 3150) on Jalan Duta.

Sarawak

There are small bus terminals in Kuching, and each bus company has its own operating area. From Kuching and southwest Sarawak, the Sarawak Transport Company can take you to Semonggoh and other points west. The distinctive green and yellow buses leave from Lebuh Jawa. Petra Jaya Transport buses go to Damai, Buntal, Santubong and Kampung Bako and leave from the bus area near the Open-Air Market.

Sabah

Buses and mini buses operate in Sabah. In Kota Kinabalu, the buses to Kinabalu Park and Kudat leave from the **Long-distance Bus Station** near the Padang. Buses to Sandakan, Lahad Datu and Tawau depart from the **City Bus Terminal** (North) in Inanam, while buses south to Beaufort and Lawas in Sarawak depart from the **Mini-bus Terminal** opposite Wawasan Plaza.

Interstate Taxis

Share taxis go to any destination and are quicker than buses. They are mostly old Mercedes Benz vehicles and some are air-conditioned. However, you have to wait until there are four passengers unless you want to pay for the whole cab – but remember, you do not have to charter the whole taxi. So turn up early and be prepared to wait. If you book a cab to yourself, the driver can pick you up from your hotel for free if you are close to town.

Note that there is a quota for the number of taxis that can ply a route. During public holidays, this quota could be full, in which case you would be asked to pay extra for non-quota taxis because the driver would not be allowed to pick up passengers on the return leg. Sometimes, if the traffic is heavy, you might have to pay more, so make sure you sort all this out with your driver first. Night journeys have a surcharge. Long-distance taxi stands are usually near the interstate bus stations. In Kuala Lumpur, the stand is at the **Puduraya Bus Station**.

City Transport

Buses and Taxis

All big towns are served by public buses and taxis. Buses usually charge according to distance except in Kuala Lumpur, where the fare is standard. Timetables are a mystery, and listings of stops and routes elusive, except for the signs on the front of each vehicle. However, bus rides are great for rubbing shoulders with the locals and the drivers are friendly towards travellers.

Taxis can be hailed at taxi stands or by the roadside. In larger cities, taxis are usually metered but in smaller towns, bargain and agree on a price before you get in.

Trishaws

Despite slowly dying out, trishaws are still used in Kota Bharu, Kuala Terengganu, Georgetown and Melaka. They are a memorable way to cover a city as their slow pace allows you to see points of interest along the way.

The bicycle is usually at the side of the carriage, except in Penang, where the two passengers sit in a sun-hooded carriage in front of the cyclist. Trishaw drivers will warn you to hold on to your bags firmly for fear of snatch thieves on motorcycles. Fix the price before you get on.

Kuala Lumpur City Transport

Taxis

Taxis in Kuala Lumpur are required by law to use meters. Fares start at RM2 for the first kilometre, with a 10-sen increase every 200 metres (220 yards). From midnight to 6am, there is a surcharge of 50 percent on the metered fare, and extra passengers (more than two) are charged 20 sen each. Surcharges also apply for bookings (RM1) and baggage placed in the boot (RM1 per piece).

Taxis of different colours belong to different companies. All have a sign on top, which, when lit, means the taxi is available. Note that there are premium taxis that have a RM4 flagfall and charge a bit more by the kilometre. There are taxi stands but you can usually wave taxis down anywhere.

Often, during peak hours, taxis will not go to places where traffic is horrendous and passengers are hard to come by on the return leg. In such cases, drivers either decline passengers or will charge a flat rate. If you have to bargain, note that fares around town start at RM5 and it should cost you no more than RM10 to go across the central city area.

KL Sentral and tourist places like Menara Kuala Lumpur enforce pre-paid coupon systems, whose fares are higher than the meter system's but are lower than flat rates.

City taxis cannot legally pick passengers up at KLIA, where a coupon system is in use, but you can take a city taxi to the airport and from the LCC-T.

Half- and full-day taxi charters to places in the Klang Valley cost RM30–35 per hour, excluding toll charges. Reliable call taxi services can be booked with **Comfort Taxi** (tel: 03-2692 2525), **Public Cab** (tel: 03-6259 2020), **Supercab** (tel: 03-2095 3399), **Sunlight Radio Taxi** (tel: 03-9057 1111) and **Selangor Radio Taxi** (tel: 03-2693 6211).

Buses

Rapid KL's **City Shuttle** buses (tel: 1800-388 228; www.rapidkl.com.my) cover most major areas in the city and provide feeder services to train (mainly LRT) stations. City Shuttle buses have a red disk on their windscreens and side windows near the front door, and they ply routes 101 to 115. The fare is RM2 for the whole day; buy a ticket on the bus on your first ride and flash it at the driver for all subsequent rides. Have exact change ready, especially during peak hours. You can also get the RM80 monthly pass for unlimited rides and a RM125 integrated LRT–Rapid KL ticket.

Services run by other bus operators are more chaotic and information is lacking, but you can get buses to outlying areas in Petaling Jaya, Shah Alam and Klang from major stops in the city, such as the Klang Bus Station, and the Bangkok Bank near Petaling Street.

The major inner city bus stops are Puduraya, Klang Bus Station, Bangkok Bank near Petaling Street, Lebuh Ampang, and the Jalan Tuanku Abdul Rahman/Jalan Ipoh intersection in Chow Kit.

Trains and Light Rail

KL's rail system consists of three types of services – the LRT which covers most of the city and inner suburbs; the semi-circular KL Monorail looping through the Golden Triangle; and the KTM Komuter for trips to the outer suburbs. The main rail terminal is **KL Sentral**, where you can get on any of these systems.

The **Light Rail Transit (LRT)** (tel: 1800-388 228; www.putralrt.com.my) has two lines which intersect at Masjid Jamek station: the Ampang/Sri Petaling line that runs from northern KL (Sentul Timur station) to Ampang in the east and Sri Petaling in the south; and the Kelana Jaya line that runs from Terminal Putra station in Gombak in northeastern KL to Petaling Jaya, ending at Kelana Jaya station in the southwest. Trains run every 7–8 minutes (every 3 minutes during peak hours) from 6am to 11.50pm (11.30pm on Sundays and holidays). Fares start at 70 sen. Monthly travel cards (RM90) can also be purchased (RM125 for integrated LRT–Rapid KL bus travel card).

The elevated **Kuala Lumpur Monorail** (tel: 03-2273 1888; www. monorail.com.my) covers central KL, from KL Sentral to Titiwangsa station. Fares are RM1.20–RM2.50 and trains run every 7–10 minutes (4–5 minutes during peak hours) from 6am to midnight. RM20 and RM50 stored-value tickets are available.

The **KTM Komuter** (tel: 03-2267 1200; www.ktmb.com.my) is an intra-city commuter train service covering greater KL. It runs two lines, namely Sentul–Port Klang and Rawang–Seremban. Fares range from RM1 to RM7.90. Tourists below the age of 30

holding the ISIC, YIEE Card or Youth Hostel Card are entitled to unlimited travel for 7 days for RM130.

Driving

Driving is the best way to see Peninsular Malaysia, which has an excellent network of trunk roads and highways. Driving is also enjoyable in Sabah and Sarawak, but you need a sturdier vehicle or even a four-wheel drive and lots more time.

An international driving licence is required except for tourists from the US, EU, Australia, New Zealand, Japan and Singapore. Car-rental firms are found in major cities and in airports.

Driving is on the left-hand side of the road. The speed limit is 50 kph (30 mph) in towns, 80 kph (50 mph) outside towns, and 110 kph (68 mph) on highways. Slow down when you go through a village, and keep left unless overtaking. The wearing of seat belts in the front is compulsory.

International traffic signs apply along with local ones. If the driver in front flashes his right indicator, he is signalling to you not to overtake. This is usually because of an oncoming vehicle or a bend in the road, or he himself might be about to overtake the vehicle in front of him. If he flashes the left indicator, this means to overtake with caution. A driver flashing his headlamps at you is claiming the right of way or indicating police ahead. At roundabouts or traffic circles, the driver on the right has the right of way, although pushing in has become the norm.

Malaysian drivers can be speed maniacs. In towns, motorcyclists can shoot out from nowhere or hog the road. Don't lose your cool; take it easy. Heavy rain can be hazardous, so switch on your lights, drive slowly and be prepared for delays as entire roads are sometimes flooded. At worst, pull over until the rain eases.

Main Routes

The North-South Expressway starts at the causeway connecting to

Singapore and runs north along the west coast to the Thai border. The old trunk road runs roughly parallel to that through small towns.

Several main routes link the east and west coasts through the Titiwangsa Range. From Kuala Lumpur, the busy Karak Highway goes to Kuantan (3 hours). A fork at Bentong heads north through Kuala Lipis to Kota Bharu on the Gua Musang road (9 hours). Kota Bharu is also linked to Penang via the East-West Highway (5 hours), and Kuala Kangsar in Perak at the Grik fork.

From Johor Bahru, the Segamat Highway goes to Kuantan (4 hours), but a more scenic and much longer route hugs the east coast from Desaru all the way to the Thai border. A parallel inland road with less traffic runs from Kuantan to Kota Bharu.

In Sabah and Sarawak, sealed roads connect major towns. Roads leading inland are often unpaved or rough, and a four-wheel drive is advisable. For day trips to Santubong, Damai, or west towards Lundu and beyond along the coast, a normal saloon car can be used. In Sabah, too, most of the main destinations along the coast are trouble free, as is the road to Kinabalu Park and north to Kudat.

Breakdown Services

The Automobile Association of Malaysia (AAM) has a prompt breakdown service for members (tel: 03-2161 0808). Rental cars may be covered by AAM services – check when you hire the vehicle.

Car Rental

Car-rental firms have branches in the main towns throughout Malaysia and at big airports. Rentals are usually based on time rather than mileage and most allow you to pick up a car from one place and drop it off at another. Credit cards are preferred.

Kuala Lumpur
Avis Rent A Car, tel: 03-9222 2558; www.avis.com
Hertz Rent A Car, tel: 03-2148 6433; www.hertz.com
Pacific Rent A Car, tel: 03-2287 4118/9; www.iprac.com

Kuching
Mayflower Car Rental, tel: 082-410 110; www.mayflowercarrental.com.my
Pronto Car Rental, tel: 082-236 889

Kota Kinabalu
Padas Jaya Rent A Car, tel: 088-239 936
Kinabalu Rent A Car, tel: 088-232 602; www.kinabalurac.com.my

ACCOMMODATION

HOTELS, RESORTS, HOMESTAYS

CHOOSING A HOTEL

Malaysia offers an abundance of accommodation choices. There are international brands, home-grown chains, resort-themed and boutique establishments, serviced apartments as well as simple resthouses and backpacker hostels. With plenty of choices around, accommodation options – even high-quality ones – remain remarkably affordable.

Hotels are rated 1 to 5 stars according to international criteria such as size, facilities, number of staff and safety. For details, visit the Malaysian Association of Hotels website (www.hotels.org.my).

Always enquire about packages, which may include a buffet or local breakfast and sometimes tours and entrance fees to attractions, with the room. If you stay more than one night, you can try bargaining for better rates. Most hotels are fine with triple-share. Hotels are required to display nett rates (including the 10 percent service and 5 percent government taxes).

At the lowest end are dormitories at RM15–40 depending on location and whether the room is air-conditioned or fan cooled. There are also the simple Chinese-run Rumah Tumpangan hotels which you can find in almost every town, and beachside Malay village-style chalets; these go from RM40 to more than RM100 and are sometimes equipped with TV, air conditioning and hot showers.

Medium-class hotels (RM100–300) come in traditional hotel blocks or chalets, and are popular with locals. The higher-end ones generally have full room facilities and services, including air conditioning, ensuite baths with hot showers, TV, IDD phones, laundry, mini bar, coffee-making facilities, room service, and a restaurant and/or coffee house. The top hotel chains and resorts come complete with the usual full room facilities and services, spas and gourmet restaurants (rooms are RM200–400; rooms in luxury hotels can be upwards of RM800). Another option in the medium to upper range are serviced apartments, which offer larger rooms and kitchenettes for longer-staying guests.

Check-in times are 1–3pm, check-out 11am–noon, with late check-out upon request. Sometimes, a 50 percent deposit is needed to secure bookings and rooms are held up to 6pm. Book in advance for stays over long weekends, Malaysian and Singaporean school holidays, public holidays – particularly Chinese New Year and Hari Raya Puasa, the Formula 1 Grand Prix period, and the super-peak months of July and August when Arab tourists flock to the country. There is usually a surcharge during these periods too. Internet rates are usually lower than walk-in or call-in rates, so check out individual hotel homepages and the Malaysian Association of Hotels website (www.hotels.org.my).

Staying in Sarawak's National Parks

Prices for national park chalets and hostels range from less than RM100 to RM200.

Bookings for Bako, Kubah, Gunung Gading national parks and the Matang Wildlife Centre can all be made at the National Park Booking Office, Visitors Information Centre, Sarawak Tourism Complex, Old Court House, Kuching, tel: 082-248 088.

In Miri, bookings for Mulu, Niah, Lambir Hills, Similajau and Loagan Bunut national parks can be made at the Visitors Information Centre, Lot 31, Jalan Melayu (close to Miri Bus Station), tel: 085-434 181; fax: 085-434 179; e-mail: vicmiri@sarawaktourism.com.

For more information, visit www.sarawakforestry.com.

Homestays

Homestays in a Sarawak longhouse or Orang Asli village are popular options in the rainforest. These are usually "tourist-friendly", but if you are lucky, your hospitable Malaysian guide might just invite you home for the real thing. Do be especially mindful that this is someone's home, and do respect local mores. Longhouse visits and stays can be arranged through tour companies; ask around first to find an interesting one.

Sarawak Fishing Village Homestays arranges stays with Malay families fluent in English, giving visitors a taste of genuine village life. Tel: 082-245 481; e-mail: gazul@tm.net.my.

In Sabah, the homestay organisation is guided by the government. Communication is sometimes a problem, both for bookings and subsequently if guests do not speak Malay. Contact Sabah Tourism (tel: 088-212 121) or look up their website www.sabahtourism.com.

PRICE CATEGORIES

Prices are for a standard double room during peak periods.

$$$$	more than RM400
$$$	RM200–400
$$	RM100–200
$	less than RM100

ACCOMMODATION LISTINGS

KUALA LUMPUR AND ENVIRONS

KUALA LUMPUR

Kuala Lumpur's budget hotels are mainly located in the Chinatown and Jalan Tuanku Abdul Rahman areas, while the medium-class and luxury accommodation is in the business and shopping areas along Jalan Sultan Ismail and Jalan Bukit Bintang.

The Ascott
9 Jalan Pinang
Tel: 03-2142 6868
Fax: 03-2142 9888
www.the-ascott.com
Located across KLCC, the Ascott, a cross between a hotel and an apartment, has splendid views of the city from its rooftop pool. Offerings range from studio to three-bedroom apartments, all with fully equipped kitchens, personalised service and facilities that cater to families and business folk. Within walking distance of a wide array of eateries. $$$$

Carcosa Seri Negara
Taman Tasik Perdana,
Persiaran Mahameru
Tel: 03-2282 1888
Fax: 03-2282 6868
www.ghmhotels.com
This former British resident's home offers colonial splendour in its extravagant 13 suites. Also has butler service, a grand restaurant overlooking huge landscaped gardens, and a bar. Not to be missed are high tea and curry tiffin on the terrace. $$$$

JW Marriott
183 Jalan Bukit Bintang
Tel: 03-2715 9000
Fax: 03-2715 7013
www.marriott.com
Centrally located hotel with a fabulous spa and the well-known Shook! restaurant with four kitchens – Japanese, Italian, Chinese and grills. It's part of the Starhill Gallery complex; guests can use the Starhill's spa

and health facilities, as well as charge their dining expenses at the mall's Feast Village to their rooms. $$$$

Mandarin Oriental
Kuala Lumpur City Centre
Tel: 03-2380 8888
Fax: 03-2380 8833
www.mandarinoriental.com
Set within KLCC which features the world's tallest twin buildings, this hotel has 643 luxurious rooms and executive apartments, six restaurants including a grill and bar, a fusion Japanese restaurant and a Cantonese restaurant specialising in seafood. Its Thalgo Marine Spa provides relaxing diversion. $$$$

The Regent
160 Jalan Bukit Bintang
Tel: 03-2141 8000
Fax: 03-2142 1441
www.regenthotels.com
One of KL's more elegant hotels situated in bustling Bukit Bintang and well-known for its service and opulence. Its 468 rooms are tastefully furnished and come with huge bathtubs and nature-based L'Occitane toiletries. Classical music welcomes you in the stylish lounge, while the gym has Roman baths. $$$$

The Ritz-Carlton
168 Jalan Imbi
Tel: 03-2142 8000
Fax: 03-2143 8080
www.ritzcarlton.com/hotels/kuala_lumpur
A business hotel, but family friendly too. It has one of the city's best personalised butler services, along with charming touches like chilled aromatherapy towels and butler-drawn baths. The high tea spread is sinful, but you can work it out at the 24-hour fitness centre. Indulge in outdoor spa baths and therapies at its Spa Village. $$$$

Shangri-La Hotel
11 Jalan Sultan Ismail
Tel: 03-2032 2388
Fax: 03-2070 1514
www.shangri-la.com/kualalumpur

This hotel has lovely gardens, a pool area nestled among skyscrapers, a large fully equipped gym and capacious rooms. Its restaurants are popular on weekends, so bookings are advised. Party-goers will relish its location just across the night clubs of Jalan Sultan Ismail. The KL Tower and the lush Bukit Nanas Forest Recreational Park are right behind. $$$$

Sheraton Imperial
Jalan Sultan Ismail
Tel: 03-2717 9900
Fax: 03-2717 9999
www.starwoodhotels.com
Part of Starwood's "luxury collection", this plush modern hotel sits within walking distance of the Jalan Sultan Ismail entertainment stretch, and right next to the swish Asian Heritage Row. The monorail is a 6-minute walk away. Polished timber, Italian marble and original art pieces feature significantly throughout the hotel, but the rooms may be a little below international standard. Despite being positioned as a business hotel, the rooms and suites are extremely kid-friendly. $$$$

Concorde Hotel
Jalan Sultan Ismail
Tel: 03-2144 2200
Fax: 03-2144 1628
www.concorde.net
Central, busy hotel close to nightlife and trendy eateries. It has 673 rooms, and a newly renovated coffee shop and lounge that attracts spill-over weekend crowds from the adjoining Hard Rock Café. Better rooms in the Premier wing. $$$

Corus Hotel
Jalan Ampang
Tel: 03-2161 8888
Fax: 03-2161 2393
www.corushotelkl.com
Some of its 378 rooms and its swimming pool have grand views of KLCC. This business hotel offers in-room broadband Internet

access and a wide range of secretarial services. $$$

Crowne Plaza Mutiara
Jalan Sultan Ismail
Tel: 03-2148 2322
Fax: 03-2144 2157
www.crowneplaza.com
563-room hotel within walking distance of Bukit Bintang. Spacious rooms, luxurious rain shower; fine dining in a popular Indochinese restaurant, and good family buffets at the Planter's Inn. $$$

Federal Hotel
35 Jalan Bukit Bintang
Tel: 03-2148 9166
Fax: 03-2148 2877
www.fhihotels.com
This hotel has 450 rooms, a revolving lounge, decent Chinese restaurant, full-window café that is great for people-watching, Latin-inspired supper club, and an 18-lane bowling alley. $$$

Hilton Kuala Lumpur
3 Jalan Stesen Sentral
Tel: 03-2264 2264
Fax: 03-2264 2266
www.kuala-lumpur.hilton.com
Each of its bright and airy rooms comes with floor-to-ceiling windows with views of the city, luxurious beds, a rain shower and 107-cm (42-inch) plasma TV (and another TV in the bathroom). Other features include a free-form pool, a multi-restaurant enclave, and the Zeta Bar, a favourite of KL's who's who. $$$

Hotel Equatorial KL
Jalan Sultan Ismail
Tel: 03-2161 7777
Fax: 03-2161 9020
www.equatorial.com/kul
Pleasant, functional and comfortable rooms, with amenities geared towards business travellers. Its food and beverage outlets are among the city's most favoured, particularly for high tea and Japanese fare. A shuttle goes daily to its pretty sister resort in Bangi, whose facilities can be used with or without a room for a day rate. $$$

Hotel Maya
138 Jalan Ampang
Tel: 03-2711 8866
Fax: 03-2711 9966
www.hotelmaya.com.my
This home-grown boutique hotel has rustic timber flooring and floor-to-ceiling glass panels looking out to either the Twin Towers or KL Tower. Its guests-only Sky Lounge provides views of both. The food outlets are excellent; in particular, try the *sosaku* (creative) Japanese cuisine – which blends continental and Asian flavours. **$$$**

Hotel Nikko
165 Jalan Ampang
Tel: 03-2161 1111
Fax: 03-2161 1112
www.hotelnikko.com.my
A five-star hotel with 470 rooms, a gym, spa, pool with a spacious sundeck, and a complimentary shuttle service to KLCC and Bintang Walk. Its Benkay Japanese restaurant, which has a Zen ambience, is famous for the freshest seasonal Japanese delicacies. **$$$**

Boulevard Hotel
Mid Valley City,
Lingkaran Syed Putra
Tel: 03-2295 8000
Fax: 03-2287 8551
www.blvhotel.com
This modern business hotel is located in the Mid Valley development, which boasts two enormous malls, so it is great for shopaholics. The rooms are large, filled with classy furniture, a flat-screen TV and beautiful artworks. It's a short drive to KL Sentral and Bangsar, and the KTM Komuter train station is within walking distance. With complimentary shuttles to the Bangsar LRT station. **$$–$$$**

Le Meridien
2 Jalan Stesen Sentral
Tel: 03-2263 7888
Fax: 03-2263 7222
www.lemeridien.com
A swanky establishment with contemporary decor, Jim Thompson upholstery, luxurious marble-clad bathrooms, and a lovely landscaped pool area. Like the rooms, the restaurants have great views of the city.

Located within the rail transport hub, so access to and from the airport or any other part of town is easy. **$$$**

Pacific Regency Hotel Apartments
Menara PanGlobal, Jalan Punchak, off Jalan P. Ramlee
Tel: 03-2332 7777
Fax: 03-2031 2492
www.pacific-regency.com
Longer-staying tourists will appreciate this serviced apartment located opposite the KL Tower. Choose from studios and two-bedroom, family-style units, all with fully equipped kitchenettes and free wireless broadband access. Has a range of fine-dining and casual eateries. The chic rooftop Luna Bar is one of the city's top hang-out places. **$$$**

Parkroyal
Jalan Sultan Ismail
Tel: 03-2147 0088
Fax: 03-2141 5524
www.parkroyalhotels.com
This 348-room hotel, close to the Bukit Bintang shopping district, offers contemporary-style rooms and suites with the usual mod cons, including broadband Internet access. Good restaurants and bars. **$$$**

Hotel Istana
73 Jalan Raja Chulan
Tel: 03-2141 9988
Fax: 03-2141 0111
www.hotelistana.com.my
Right in the heart of the Golden Triangle, this ornately decorated hotel has 516 rooms, an Italian restaurant, a lounge overlooking a garden and a health centre. **$$$**

Renaissance Hotel
Corner Jalan Sultan Ismail
Jalan Ampang
Tel: 03-2162 2233
Fax: 03-2163 1122
www.renaissance-kul.com
The Renaissance tries to capture European splendour with a plush decor of black marble and crystal chandeliers, but targets the business sector. It has two wings, the fancier West Wing and the more modest East Wing. The rooms are large, though a little worn, but beds are comfortable. **$$$**

Seri Pacific Kuala Lumpur
Jalan Putra
Tel: 03-4042 5555
Fax: 03-4041 7236
www.seripacific.com
Previously the Pan Pacific, this oldish hotel opposite the Mall and next to the Putra World Trade Centre has all-glass elevators on the exterior providing good views of the city. It has 554 rooms, and is busy during conventions. **$$$**

Swiss Garden Hotel
117 Jalan Pudu
Tel: 03-2141 3333
Fax: 03-2141 5555
www.swissgarden.com
Situated on the busy Jalan Pudu, within walking distance of Puduraya and Bukit Bintang but without being in the thick of it. This is a small but pleasant hotel, with 306 rooms and a Chinese restaurant that serves good dim sum. Has a complimentary shuttle service to major shopping complexes. **$$$**

Bintang Warisan Hotel
Jalan Bukit Bintang
Tel: 03-2148 8111
Fax: 03-2148 2333
www.bintangwarisan.com
Located in the heart of Bukit Bintang with surprisingly good facilities once the rather cluttered lobby is negotiated. The location is superb and double-glazed windows keep the noise out. **$$**

Hotel Capitol
Off Jalan Bukit Bintang
Tel: 03-2143 7000
Fax: 03-2143 0000
www.capitol.com.my
Part of the Federal group, this 225-room hotel is smack in the middle of Bukit Bintang. Rooms are small but tastefully furnished; good restaurant and a café with gourmet sandwiches and coffee. **$$**

Hotel Grand Centrepoint
316 Jalan Tuanku Abdul Rahman
Tel: 03-2693 3988
A cheerful medium-budget hotel at the northern end of the Jalan TAR silk stretch and opposite the Maju Junction Mall, with an LRT station at its doorstep and Kampung Baru within walking distance. Rooms have solid sound-proofing from

the busy traffic. Offers tour arrangement, laundry services and transfers to the Duta Bus Station for airport-bound guests. **$$**

Hotel Malaya
Jalan Hang Lekir
Tel: 03-2072 7722
Fax: 03-2070 0980
www.hotelmalaya.com.my
In business since 1966, this 3-star hotel has been renovated several times, and the newly furnished rooms are warm and pleasant. A great location to experience the day and night rhythms of Petaling Street, which is right at its doorstep. Its Kafetien 1966 restaurant serves delicious Peranakan fare. **$$**

Quality Hotel City Centre
Jalan Raja Laut
Tel: 03-2693 9233
Fax: 03-2693 9634
www.quality.com.my
At the lower end of the medium-budget category; family friendly with large beds. Ask to inspect your room beforehand. Its coffee house serves a good buffet breakfast. Close to malls – particularly Pertama Complex with cheap and good leather products, and the Japanese department store Sogo. **$$**

The Royale Bintang
Jalan Bukit Bintang
Tel: 03-2143 9898
Fax: 03-2142 1807
www.royale-bintang-hotel.com.my
Located in the heart of the Bukit Bintang shopping area with 214 well-appointed rooms, plus a restaurant with international and local fare. **$$**

Swiss-Inn Kuala Lumpur
62 Jalan Sultan
Tel: 03-2072 3333
Fax: 03-2031 7799
www.swissgarden.com/hotel/sikl
Converted from an early 20th-century Chinese shophouse, this popular hotel fronts a street with great Chinese eateries, tea shops and souvenir outlets, while its back opens out directly to the Petaling Street bazaar. Cast in pastel shades, rooms are basic with small bathrooms, but they are clean and value for money. Internet rates are much lower

than published rates. **$$**

Backpackers Travellers Inn
2nd Floor, 60, Jalan Sultan
(opposite Furama Hotel)
Tel: 03-2032 1855
Fax: 03-2032 1988
Right in Chinatown, close to food and transport. Some rooms are air-conditioned with own bathrooms. Laundry, kitchen, left luggage facilities. **$**

Coliseum Café and Hotel
98-100 Jalan Tunku Abdul Rahman
Tel: 03-2692 6270
Tiny and very old 10-room hotel with shared baths, it is mentioned in every guidebook because of its historical importance. The café is popular for its good steaks and is infamously known for its cantankerous service; bar patrons are determined to keep up its colourful character. **$**

Heritage Station Hotel
Bangunan Stesen Keretapi
Jalan Sultan Hishamuddin
Tel: 03-2273 5588
Fax: 03-2273 2842
www.heritagehotelmalaysia.com
Sitting among the graceful cupolas of the old Kuala Lumpur Railway Station, this hotel has been extensively renovated. Although the rooms are smaller now, some of the old-style charm is retained in the furnishings and its restaurants. **$**

YWCA
12 Jalan Hang Jebat
Tel: 03-2070 1623
Fax: 03-2031 7753

e-mail: ywcakl@po.jaring.my
Small, clean, 12-room facility for women, couples and families only. It has a small restaurant, and is within walking distance of Chinatown. **$**

SELANGOR

The Mines Beach Resort
Jalan Dulang, Sri Kembangan
Tel: 03-8943 6688
Fax: 03-8943 5555
www.mines.com.my
Part of The Mines rehabilitated mining pond theme park and development, this classy 481-room hotel has an artificial beach, ferries to the Wonderland theme park, a spa, and a shopping and conference centre. It has four restaurants, and a rather stuffy lounge. **$$$$**

Palace of the Golden Horses
Jalan Kuda Emas, Mines Resort City, Sri Kembangan
Tel: 03-8943 2333
Fax: 03-8943 2666
www.palaceofthegoldenhorses.com.my
This opulent Moorish-influenced hotel at which heads of governments often reside and meet, has 480 rooms and seven restaurants, spacious gardens and good recreational facilities. **$$$$**

Eastin Hotel
13 Jalan 16/11, Pusat Dagang

Seksyen 16, Petaling Jaya
Tel: 03-7665 1111
Fax: 03-7665 9999
www.eastin.com
Good business hotel linked by a network of highways to suburbs like Bangsar, Mont Kiara and Damansara. Rooms are spacious and comfortable. The Chinese restaurant is good, particularly for dim sum. **$$$**

Hilton Petaling Jaya
2 Jalan Barat. Petaling Jaya
Tel: 03-7955 9122
Fax: 03-7955 3909
www.hilton.com
Located just off the Federal Highway, with airy rooms, delicious local cuisine, a popular pub that serves excellent steaks, and a Davidoff cigar store. Includes a spa and a gym. **$$$**

Shah's Village Hotel
3 & 5 Lorong Sultan, Seksyen 52, Petaling Jaya
Tel: 03-7956 9322
Fax: 03-7955 7715
www.shahsresorts.com
Family-run hotel with a tropical resort feel with swaying palm trees around the swimming pool. Rooms are individually furnished and offer endearing details such as batik sarongs for guests' use. A great local bar, Waikiki, next door, and the LRT station is a short walk away. **$$$**

Sunway Resort Hotel & Spa
Persiaran Lagoon, Bandar Sunway

Petaling Jaya
Tel: 03-7492 8000
Fax: 03-7492 8001
www.sunway.com.my/hotel
This plush hotel is next to the Sunway Lagoon theme park, the country's most successful rehabilitated mining pond, as well as the Egyptian-themed Sunway Pyramid shopping centre. The hotel has 439 rooms, a large and popular disco, and excellent Chinese, Japanese and American-Italian restaurants. **$$$**

Jungle Lodge
Alang Sedayu (Gombak)
Tel: 03-4252 9100 (Asian Overland)
Fax: 03-4252 9800
www.summercamp.com.my
About half an hour from KL, this large timber lodge sits in 2 hectares (5 acres) of green grounds with streams and ponds. Two river-fed swimming pools, treks, canoes, old war tunnels nearby and supervised outdoor activities. There is also a hostel for 60. **$$**

Kuala Selangor Nature Park
Jalan Klinik, Kuala Selangor
Tel: 03-3289 2294
Wake up to bird calls; these new budget chalets and dormitories at the park entrance have trails at the doorstep but may be fully booked on weekends. Delicious seafood in Kuala Selangor town is a short walk away. **$**

NORTHWESTERN PENINSULA

HILL STATIONS

Maxwell Hill (Bukit Larut)

All accommodation and transport come under the **Bukit Larut Hill Resort** (tel: 05-807 7241/3). Book in advance. The bungalows have to be booked in their entirety: Beringin (two rooms or eight people), Cendana (three rooms or eight people) and Tempinis (four rooms or 10 people, highest point). **$$**

Double rooms are available at the **Maxwell Hill Resthouse** and **Gunung Hijau** (four rooms each). **$**
Meals have to be pre-arranged. Dogs, pork, and unmarried Muslim couples sharing a room are not allowed.

Cameron Highlands

If you have to stay in Tapah for the night, you could try the **Rest House Tapah** (tel: 05-401 1190) or **N.H. Hotel** (tel: 05-401 7288). Both are close to the train station. **$**

Cameron Highlands Resort
Tel: 05-491 1100
Fax: 05-491 1800
www.cameronhighlandsresort.com
The former Merlin Inn has been renovated as a deluxe boutique hotel. The colonial ambience remains, while the most modern facilities satisfy the needs of discerning travellers. The spa specialises in tea-inspired treatments and Gonbei serves superb Japanese cuisine. **$$$$**

Heritage Hotel
Jalan Gereja, Tanah Rata
Tel: 05-491 3888
Fax: 05-491 5666

www.heritage.com.my
This boxy, 165-room hilltop hotel is the first you see when you reach Tanah Rata. Ask for a room with a view of the charming little garden. Cantonese restaurant, coffee house, bar and a health centre. **$$$**

The Lakehouse
30th Mile, Ringlet
Tel: 05-495 6152
Fax: 05-495 6123
www.lakehouse-cameron.com
The first hotel on the Cameron's road, 1 hour from the North-South Expressway, located opposite the Sultan Abu

Bakar lake. It features Tudor-style architecture, antique furnishings, 18 rooms and suites with four-poster beds, and a restaurant serving English-style cuisine, including Devonshire teas. **$$$**

The Smokehouse Hotel
Tanah Rata
Tel: 05-491 1215
Tel: 03-2163 3136 (KL)
Fax: 05-491 1214
Fax: 03-2161 2044 (KL)
www.thesmokehouse.com.my
Built in 1939, this is a beautiful replica of an English Tudor inn complete with a lush English country garden, log fires, antique furnishings, 13 family suites (most overlooking the golf course), dining and tea rooms, two bars and a restaurant; packed sandwiches and pies are available for your jungle walks. **$$$**

Strawberry Park Resort
Tanah Rata
Tel: 05-491 1166
Fax: 05-491 1949
www.malaysiahillresorts.com
Mock-Tudor blocks at the top of a steep, winding road, with great views from the 127 rooms and apartments (no cooking). It has a heated indoor pool, Chinese restaurant, coffee house, grill, bar, disco, racquet sports and travel service. Popular with locals and Singaporeans. **$$$**

Bala's Holiday Chalet
Lot 55, Tanah Rata
Tel: 05-491 1660
Fax: 05-491 4500
e-mail: balasch@hotmail.com
Former backpackers' hotel in an English cottage that has gone upmarket. The hotel is set in a delightful forested location 10 minutes from Tanah Rata (free shuttles), close to walks. It has 33 rooms – some with balconies – a lounge, restaurant, laundry service and tours. Book at least one week in advance. **$$**

Rosa Pasadena
Brinchang town
Tel: 05-491 2288
Fax: 05-491 2688/902
Right in town next to the bank and bakery. This is a

no-frills hotel with 120 rooms, a restaurant with big-city prices, karaoke, lounge, laundry, tours, babysitting by arrangement, basement parking and sports facilities. **$$**

Father's Guesthouse
Jalan Gereja, Tanah Rata
Tel: 05-491 2484
e-mail: fathersonline@hotmail.com
Basic but very popular 25-year-old backpackers' outfit with a variety of twin-sharing rooms and dorms and a lovely garden; tucked a little away from town. Local and Western breakfast and dinner available. **$**

Twin Pines Chalet
2 Jalan Mentigi, Tanah Rata
Tel: 05-491 2169
Fax: 05-491 5007
e-mail: firhill@tm.net.my
Friendly and clean backpackers' hotel located behind the new town development, offering hot showers, laundry, tours, travel arrangements, telephones, Internet access and free use of kitchen facilities. Also has a spacious lounge area with TV and videos, a restaurant, travellers' notebooks, free book exchange, indoor games, and a safe for valuables; free pickup. **$**

Fraser's Hill

The Smokehouse Hotel
Tel: 09-362 2226
Fax: 09-362 2035
www.thesmokehouse.com.my
Tudor-style hotel with beautiful gardens, antique-filled interiors, famous Devonshire teas. Very pricey, but very atmospheric; a great retreat. **$$$**

Highland Resthouse Holdings Bungalows
Tel: 03-2164 8937
Fax: 03-2163 2815
www.hrhbungalows.com
These beautifully renovated colonial bungalows provide contemporary comfort with old-world charm. Complete with dining and living rooms as well as English-style gardens, the three 3-roomed bungalows and two 4-roomed ones are only available for rent whole, whereas the six Temerloh Chalets and Pekan Bunga-

low rooms (8 rooms) can be rented individually. **$$–$$$**

Genting Highlands

Awana Golf and Country Resort
Tel: 03-2718 1118
Toll free: 1800-881 328
Fax: 03-2718 1888
www.awana.com.my
Offers much quieter surroundings, 10 km (6 miles) down the hill from Genting Highlands Resort, with an 18-hole golf course, nice views, full room facilities including jacuzzis, and outdoor activities. Packages include rides and use of facilities. **$$$**

Genting Highlands Resort
Tel: 03-2718 1118
Toll free: 1800-888 228
Fax: 03-2718 1888
www.genting.com.my
Six hotels in this resort: the 5-star **Genting Hotel** and **Highlands Hotel** (where the casino is); the 4-star **Resort Hotel**; the 3-star **Theme Park Hotel** (where the indoor theme park sits) and **First World Hotel** (the world's largest hotel); and the **Awana Genting Highlands Golf & Country Resort** (*see above*). Rooms are cheap, especially off peak. Excellent Western fare at The Olive. Health centre with jacuzzi and sauna, bowling alley, disco. Packages include rides and use of facilities. **$–$$$**

Gunung Jerai Resort
Gunung Jerai
Tel: 04-423 4345/0599
Fax: 04-423 2957
This 1920s building has 30 rooms, including two-bedroom chalets with cooking facilities. Good views, landscaped gardens. **$**

PERAK

Ipoh

Impiana Casuarina Hotel
18 Jalan Gopeng
Tel: 05-255 5555
Fax: 05-255 8177
www.impiana.com
A little out of town, this is Ipoh's swankiest hotel with 200 deluxe rooms, full

room facilities and an Italian restaurant. **$$$**

The Syuen
88 Jalan Sultan Abdul Jalil
Tel: 05-253 8889
Fax: 05-253 3335
e-mail: syuenht@tm.net.my
Central hotel, reminiscent of an enormous white wedding cake, with 290 rooms, Cantonese restaurant, spa facilities and Shiatsu massages, popular disco and poolside bar. **$$$**

Heritage Hotel
Jalan Raja Dihilir
Tel: 05-242 8888
Fax: 05-242 4959
www.heritage.com.my
Pleasant hotel, overlooking the Turf Club, with 265 rooms, Continental grill, a branch of a famous Chinese restaurant chain, and a health club. **$$**

Hotel Excelsior
43 Jalan Sultan Abdul Jalil
Tel: 05-253 6666
Fax: 05-253 6912
www.hotelexcelsior.com.my
Ipoh's first international hotel, and still popular with business travellers because of its central location. The management has been renovating the hotel floor by floor. Good Cantonese restaurant, and affordable buffets. **$$**

Majestic Hotel
Ipoh Railway Station
Tel: 05-255 4242
Fax: 05-255 4217
www.majesticstationhotel.com
Famous colonial hotel in the best tradition of railway station hotels, with huge verandahs. Many original fittings are retained, but the rooms, while spacious, are slightly worse for wear. **$$**

Rega Lodge
131 Jalan Raja Ekram
Tel: 05-242 5555
Fax: 05-241 1555
On the fringe of the town centre, but secluded. It has 93 rooms, a restaurant-cum-pub with Italian and local cuisine, and air-conditioned rooms with ensuite baths. **$**

YMCA
311 Jalan Raja Musa Aziz
Tel: 05-254 0809
Fax: 05-241 2093
On the fringe of town next to a park. Clean budget-class rooms with air condi-

tioning and ensuite baths and hot showers; basic canteen. **$**

Pulau Pangkor

Accommodation is on the west coast, with clusters at Pasir Bogak and Teluk Nipah. Tour companies and taxi drivers get a commission for recommending accommodation, so unless it is peak period, the best bet is to pick a beach, be dropped off on the main road and walk around until something catches your fancy. However, some tour agents can offer better prices – select from their photograph albums. At Teluk Nipah, the chalets are virtually identical and so are the prices; many do not offer food during the low season. During the busy periods, go for a room further back from the beach – it's quieter.

Pangkor Island Beach Resort
Teluk Belanga (Golden Sands)
Tel: 05-685 1091
Tel: 03-2287 6868 (KL)
Fax: 05-685 1852
Fax: 03-2287 6869 (KL)
www.pangkorislandbeach.com
Isolated hotel with great private beach and lush forest, and its own ferry from Lumut. With 240 rooms (top floors offer nice views), bungalows and chalets, watersports, restaurants, bars, barbecue on beach, children's activities, traditional massage, tours. Day-trippers are allowed to use the beach and facilities. **$$$**

Teluk Dalam Resort
Pulau Pangkor
Tel: 05-685 5000
Fax: 05-685 4000
www.tdr.com.my
Lovely setting, with 163 chalets, bungalows and luxury villas sprawled over 16 hectares (40 acres) of beach and forested land. Restaurants, pubs, special jungle trails, and tours. The beach is only suitable for swimming at high tide. **$$$**

Pangkor Holiday Resort
Lot 41, Pasir Bogak
Tel: 05-685 3321/685 3626
Fax: 05-685 3627

Unassuming but clean, with a beautiful jungle and orchard backdrop, 54 air-conditioned chalets, 108 rooms and 15 quads; no beach. Cafeteria offers local fare and DIY BBQ. Popular for group retreats, especially churches. **$$**

Pulau Pangkor Laut

Pangkor Laut Resort
Tel: 05-699 1100
Tel: 03-2145 9000 (KL)
Fax: 05-699 1200
Fax: 03-2418 7397 (KL)
www.pangkorlautresort.com
One of the country's most luxurious resorts sits on its own island and has its own ferry from Lumut. It has the gorgeous Emerald Bay beach to itself. With 178 luxurious rooms in hillside or beachfront Malay-style villas as well as suites on stilts over the sea. Swimming pools, six restaurants, a library of books and CDs, and a watersports centre complete the offerings. On the other side of the island is Pangkor Laut Estates, 8 secluded, walled estates with their own pool, outdoor jacuzzi, bedrooms and living and dining rooms. Built of stone and wood in the virgin forest or facing a private beach, each has its own chef and butler – all at a price of course. **$$$$**

Lumut

Orient Star Resort
Lot 203 & 366, Jalan Iskandar Shah
Tel: 05-683 4199
Fax: 05-683 4223
e-mail: tosrlso@po.jaring.my
Lumbering facility at the edge of town with a traditional Malay house entrance; 150 recently upgraded rooms (odd numbers are sea-facing), restaurants, lounge, swimming pool with bar. Also manages the Lumut International Yacht Club with five small but fully equipped cabins ($). **$$$**

Swiss-Garden Resort
Jalan Damai Laut
off Jalan Telok Senangin
Tel: 05-618 3333
Fax: 05-618 3388

www.swissgarden.com
Isolated in enormous grounds with ocean, mangrove, river, rainforest and oil palm surrounds, the resort is 20 minutes by ferry from Lumut, or over 1 hour by road. It features a beautiful pool overlooking the sea, 300 rooms, 18-hole golf course, disco, karaoke, and every sort of resort facility, including children's activities. Ask about a golf package with unlimited rounds; day-trippers are allowed use of facilities. **$$**

Blue Bay Resort
Lot 4, Jalan Titi Panjang
Tel: 05-683 6939
Fax: 05-683 6239
Block-ish accommodation with 66 decent rooms, swimming pool, garden and esplanade at the back, seafood restaurant. **$**

Lumut Country Resort
331, Jalan Titi Panjang
Tel: 05-683 5109
Fax: 05-683 5396
Built in the 1980s with colonial-inspired architecture and now fraying at the edges, but still decent. The 44 motel-style rooms surround the swimming pool. A bistro serves so-called "country fare" such as Beef Stroganoff and Chicken Maryland. **$**

Kuala Kangsar

Seri Temenggong Resthouse
Jalan Bukit Kerajaan
Tel/Fax: 05-776 3872
One of Malaysia's prettiest resthouses, with views of the Perak River and 17 rooms of various sizes with ensuite baths and hot water. An open-air restaurant, serving local and Western meals, overlooks the lake. The resthouse is within walking distance of attractions, so it is very popular; make sure you book ahead. **$**

Temenggor/Belum

Banding Island Resort
36 km (22 miles)
Grik East-West Highway
Tel: 05-792 1791
Fax: 05-792 1793

Lakeside motel that is very quiet unless there's a fishing competition. With 28 spacious rooms, a restaurant overlooking the lake, karaoke, fishing, boating, and jungle trekking; camping permitted. **$$**

Rumah Rehat Gerik
682 Jalan Haji Meor Yahya
Tel: 05-791 1454/791 2305
Fax: 05-791 2288
Basic and old hotel, but with clean and spacious rooms, some air-conditioned, for 50 guests. Restaurant serves traditional Malay, Thai and Western fare. **$**

Taiping

Legend Inn
2 Jalan Long Jaafar
Tel: 05-806 0000
Fax: 05-806 6666
Close to the bus station, this is the best hotel in town, set against Bukit Larut, with 88 rooms with bathrooms, hot showers and TV, and a café with a view. **$**

Hotel Panorama
61–79 Jalan Kota
Tel: 05-808 4111
Centrally located, next to a large supermarket, with 70 rooms, baths and hot showers; car rental. **$**

PENANG

The city's powerful preservation lobby has seen some of Penang's older buildings preserved as "nostalgia" and boutique hotels. Georgetown's bigger hotels cater to the business sector, while budget and backpackers' accommodation is along Lebuh Leith and Lebuh Chulia.

The beach hotels in Penang are among the country's oldest seaside resorts. Sea-view rooms are pricey during peak season; otherwise stiff competition makes them affordable.

E & O (Eastern & Oriental) Hotel
10 Lebuh Farquhar
Tel: 04-222 2000
Fax: 04-261 6333

www.e-o-hotel.com

Situated at the best site in Georgetown overlooking the sea, this extensively renovated hotel still retains the ambience of its former self. The "premier hotel east of the Suez" was patronised by Noel Coward, Douglas Fairbanks, Rudyard Kipling, Somerset Maugham and Herman Hesse during its early years. Sea-view suites are the best. Enjoy Devonshire tea in The Conservatory and steaks in the 1885 Grill. Also has a gym and a pool overlooking the sea. **$$$$**

Equatorial Penang
1 Jalan Bukit Jambul, Bayan Lepas
Tel: 04-643 8111
Fax: 04-644 8000
www.equatorial.com

Catering to the Free Trade Zone industrialists, this beautiful hotel with its impressive high-ceilinged lobby and lovely landscaping has 655 guestrooms and suites, 22 apartments, as well as restaurants and sports facilities including an 18-hole golf course. **$$$$**

The Northam
55 Jalan Sultan Ahmad Shah
Tel: 04-370 1111
Fax: 04-370 2222
www.northam-hotel.com.my

The town's fanciest business hotel with a resort feel, towering 38 floors high. Its 233 suites (96 of which are presidential suites) have all the business and non-business mod cons, such as jacuzzis with ocean views and in-suite massage service. There's fine dining in Italian, Indian and Chinese restaurants. Aptly situated on "Millionaires' Row", it assumes the colonial road name. Small swimming pool, gymnasium, spa. **$$$$**

Shangri-La Hotel
Jalan Magazine
Tel: 04-262 2622
Fax: 04-262 6526
www.shangri-la.com

Next to KOMTAR; its top floors offer great views of Georgetown rooftops. This business hotel has 442 rooms, a decent Chinese

restaurant, disco, car rental. **$$$$**

Shangri-La Rasa Sayang Resort and Spa
Batu Ferringhi
Tel: 04-881 1811
Fax: 04-881 1984
www.shangri-la.com

Reopened in 2006 after extensive and lavish renovations. Its signature Chi Spa has treatments inspired by traditional Tibetan principles. Rates have moved up accordingly. **$$$$**

Cheong Fatt Tze Mansion
14 Lebuh Leith
Tel: 04-262 0006
Fax: 04-262 5289
www.cheongfatttzemansion.com

This 19th-century landmark mansion famed for its architecture and *feng shui* offers an unforgettable place to stay. Each of the 16 unique rooms with ensuite bathrooms contains period furniture and antiques. A personal valet service completes the experience at this boutique hotel. **$$$**

Evergreen Laurel
53 Persiaran Gurney
Tel: 04-226 9988
Fax: 04-226 9989
www.evergreen-hotels.com

Located right on Gurney Drive and within walking distance of the food areas, this Taiwanese-owned five-star hotel has suites directly facing the bay – and therefore great ocean views. The hotel has a bright and cheerful atmosphere, and it is also handicap accessible. It has a nice swimming pool, a gymnasium, jacuzzi, great breakfasts and a fun lounge. **$$$**

The Gurney
18 Persiaran Gurney
Tel: 04-370 7000
www.gurney-hotel.com.my

Located at the end of Gurney Drive. Its selling point are its very large suites that have almost-ceiling-to-floor views of Gurney Drive; the best views are from the rooms closest to the sea. The spacious bathrooms are equipped with jacuzzi bathtubs. The hotel's Recreational Park is great for kids, and there is also a

popular club, a few cafés and some shops. **$$$**

Lone Pine Hotel
97 Jalan Batu Ferringhi
Tel: 04-881 1511/1512
Fax: 04-881 1282
www.lonepinehotel.com

Ferringhi's first hotel is now a boutique hotel, refurbished for a 1970s feel. There are verandahs for all 50 rooms, some of which have Balinese-style courtyards. **$$$**

Parkroyal
Jalan Batu Ferringhi
Tel: 04-881 1133
Fax: 04-881 2233
www.parkroyalhotels.com

Recently refurbished hotel with 330 large contemporary rooms and 30 suites, beautiful free-form swimming pool and right on the beach. Two restaurants, pool-side café and a bar. **$$$**

Sheraton Penang
3 Jalan Larut
Tel: 04-226 7888
Fax: 04-226 6615
www.sheraton.com/penang

Smack in the centre of the shopping district, with 295 rooms, coffee house, bars, swimming pool, health centre, disco. **$$$**

Bellevue Hotel
Penang Hill
Tel: 04-892 9600

Penang Hill's only hotel with fine views of Georgetown; built in colonial style with a garden terrace. Quiet and cool because of the altitude, with an aviary at the entrance. **$$**

Cititel Penang Hotel
66 Jalan Penang
Tel: 04-370 1188
Fax:04-370 2288
www.cititelpenang.com

In a great location on Penang Road with taxi and trishaw stations, and entertainment outlets at its doorstep, this four-star business hotel is popular with tourists. Although the rooms are not large, they are clean and afford lovely views from the top storeys. **$$**

City Bayview Hotel
25A Lebuh Farquhar
Tel: 04-263 3161
Fax: 04-263 4124/160
www.bayviewintl.com

Fringing the main shopping

area, within walking distance of Leith Street pubs, the hotel has a good Malay restaurant, a charming café serving hawker fare, and a revolving restaurant. **$$**

Copthorne Orchid
Jalan Tanjung Bungah
Tel: 04-890 3333
Fax:04-890 3303
www.millenniumhotels.com

One of the first hotels on the stretch, with 318 beautiful, breezy sea-view rooms with balconies. Cantonese and Szechuan restaurant; no beach. **$$**

Ferringhi Beach Hotel
Jalan Batu Ferringhi
Tel: 04-890 5999
Fax: 04-890 5100
www.ferringhi.com.my

For a no-frills hotel in a quiet location, look no further than across Ferringhi beach. Although there is a slightly dated feel, the rooms are a good size and clean. Overall, it offers a nice family environment. In addition, meals, including room service, are reasonably priced. **$$**

Holiday Inn Penang
Batu Ferringhi Beach
Tel: 04-881 1601
Fax: 04-881 1389
www.penang.holiday-inn.com

Beach hotel with 352 recently renovated rooms, good steakhouse. **$$**

Hotel 1926
Jalan Imigresen
Tel: 04-228 1926
Fax: 04-227 7926

Saved from demolition (and the erection of yet another modern shopping complex), this former government quarters has been conserved as a medium-budget boutique hotel with Penang's longest corridor, which also doubles as a sort of art gallery. The 94 rooms come in different sizes, but are all air-conditioned and have ensuite baths. Café, Malay restaurant, and lounge. **$$**

Malibest Resort
Pantai Cenang
Tel: 04-955 8222
e-mail: malibestlgk@yahoo.com

Five treetop chalets are the star attraction of this resort, which is located close to eateries and shops. Catering to medium-

and low-budget tourists, it also has 58 wooden chalets, two 20-person dormitories and even more accommodation across the road. Some rooms have air conditioning, hot water and a fridge. Reception is open from 7am–11pm. **$$**

Paradise Sandy Bay
527 Jalan Tanjung Bungah
Tel: 04-899 9999
Fax: 04-899 0000
www.paradisehotel.com
Pleasant all-suite hotel with 200 sea-facing rooms; popular nightspot, good Italian fare. **$$**

Shangri-La Golden Sands Resort
Batu Ferringhi Beach
Tel: 04-886 1911
Fax: 04-881 1880
www.shangri-la.com
Adjoining Rasa Sayang, an old hotel with renovated rooms and a large pool, 395 rooms, sea views, Italian restaurant. **$$**

Ali's Guest House & Restaurant
53 Batu Ferringhi
Tel: 04-881 1316
Friendly accommodation on the beachfront near Parkroyal. Nice restaurant/ pub in the garden. Fan and shared facilities; some rooms are air-conditioned with own bath. **$**

Shalini's Guesthouse
56 Batu Ferringhi
Tel: 04-881 1859
Budget accommodation with homestay feel. Shared bathrooms. Fans, good local meals, kitchen, self-service laundry. **$**

YMCA of Penang
211 Jalan Macalister
Tel: 04-228 8211
Fax: 04-229 5869
e-mail: ymcapg@streamyx.com
Clean hostel within walking distance of food stalls, hospitals and gardens. **$**

Butterworth

An uninteresting place, stay the night only if you're stuck here. Try **Butterworth Travel Lodge**, 1 Lorong Bagan Luar, tel: 04-333 3399 (**$$**) or **Sunway Hotel Seberang Jaya**, 11 Lebuh Tenggiri 2, tel: 04-370 7788, fax: 04-370 0555, www.sh.com.my (**$**)

KEDAH

Alor Star

Grand Continental Hotel
134–141 Jalan Sultan Badlishah
Tel: 04-733 5917
Fax: 04-733 5161
The town's fanciest hotel, central, with 130 rooms. Restaurant serves good local fare. **$$**

Hotel Grand Crystal
40 Jalan Kampung Perak
Tel: 04-731 3333
Fax: 04-731 6368
www.grandcontinental.com.my
Good value in central location, 145 rooms, swimming pool, sauna and coffee house. **$**

Sungai Petani

Swiss-Inn Sungai Petani
1 Jalan Pahlawan
Tel: 04-422 3333
Tel: 03-2141 5333 (KL)
Fax: 04-422 3423
www.swissgarden.com
Lovely hotel with 101 rooms. Restaurant overlooks nice landscaped pool. **$**

Pulau Langkawi

Everything is here, from some of the most impressive hotels in the country to budget accommodation. The beach hotels are certainly more pleasant, but Kuah town has more eateries and shops. Book ahead during the peak season.

The Andaman
Jalan Teluk Datai
Tel: 04-959 1088
Fax: 04-959 1168
www.ghmhotels.com
Exclusive luxury resort in rainforest surroundings, shares beautiful beach and views of Thailand's islands with the Datai *(see below)*. Both resorts, managed by GHM Hotels, have excellent spas and restaurants in both beach and forest settings. The Andaman has 186 rooms with three restaurants, including Malaysian/Indian and Japanese cuisine. Gulai House restaurant is located within coastal forest and accessible from the beach

on a forest trail. Close to 18-hole golf course; children's activities. **$$$$**

The Datai
Jalan Teluk Datai
Tel: 04-959 2500
Fax: 04-959 2600
www.ghmhotels.com
Award-winning Balinese-inspired luxury resort in isolated lush surroundings, with a beautiful private beach. It has 106 villas and rooms, a spa, three restaurants, and an adjacent 18-hole golf course. **$$$$**

Casa del Mar
Pantai Cenang
Tel: 04-955 2388
Fax : 04-955 2228
www.casadelmar-langkawi.com
The Spanish-influenced Casa del Mar (meaning "home by the sea" in Spanish) has 34 rooms and suites, all with floor-to-ceiling sliding picture windows that open to patios for stunning beach views. Its spa offers massages and body wraps. **$$$**

Four Seasons Resort
Jalan Tanjung Rhu
Tel: 04-950 8888
Fax: 04-950 8899
www.fourseasons.com/langkawi
Lovely hideaway set against beautiful virgin rainforest and limestone hills and with mangroves at its doorstep. The 91 Moorish-style pavilions and villas provide the ultimate in luxury pampering, hospitality and personal services. Its spa offers Asian-inspired treatments possible. The nature tours are worth taking. **$$$$**

Langkawi Lagoon
Lot 78, Jalan Kuala Muda, Padang Matsirat
Tel: 04-955 8181
Tel: 03-2283 1122 (KL)
Fax: 04-955 8881
Fax: 03-2283 6622 (KL)
www.langkawilagoonresort.com
An upscale resort, with charming wooden villas built over the sea and spacious hotel suites in a more conventional hotel building. **$$$$**

Meritus Pelangi Beach Resort
Pantai Cenang
Tel: 04-952 8888
Fax: 04-952 8899

www.pelangibeachresort.com
Set on a splendid curve of the beach with a gracious lobby, these traditional-style bungalows and chalets with 350 rooms are best known for having housed the Commonwealth heads of government, including Britain's Queen Elizabeth. Its kids' club has extensive activities from 9am to 9pm, while its spa's signature treatments draw on Malay/Indonesian and Thai traditions. **$$$$**

Sheraton Langkawi Beach Resort
Teluk Nibong
Tel: 04-955 1901
Fax: 04-955 1968
www.starwoodhotels.com
Luxury wooden resort set in rainforest surrounds with 231 rooms, including chalets with ocean views. A cascade of stairs lead down to the swimming pool. The sea-facing Captain's Grill serves seafood; popular disco. **$$$$**

Tanjung Rhu Resort
Tanjung Rhu
Tel: 04-959 1033
Fax: 04-959 1899
www.tanjungrhu.com.my
This luxury resort is peacefully situated on a secluded northern beach amid a lush mangrove forest. Beautiful landscaping and intelligent use of its sprawling grounds. Tasteful rooms featuring lots of wood and simple lines are huge. There is a 2½-km (1½-mile) private beach. Three restaurants, two swimming pools and spa. **$$$$**

Westin Langkawi
Jalan Pantai Dato' Syed Omar, Kuah
Tel: 04-960 8888
Fax: 04-966 6414
www.starwoodhotels.com
Formerly the Sheraton Perdana, the resort is isolated from other hotels, situated just past the yacht club and within walking distance of the jetty. There are 200 rooms. Although there is not much of a beach, the sports facilities are excellent, including salt- and freshwater swimming pools, watersports, jogging track, bicycles, a top-class gym, and squash. **$$$$**

Awana Porto Malai
Langkawi
Tanjung Malai
Tel: 04-955 5111
Fax: 04-955 5222
www.awana.com.my
Built on reclaimed land
with a marina, the hotel
has 175 sea-facing rooms,
a nice boardwalk café and
casual fine dining. Star
Cruise vessels moor at the
large ocean wharf here.
$$$
Bon Ton Resort
200 Pantai Cenang
Tel: 04-955 3463/6787
Fax: 04-955 4791
www.bontonresort.com.my
Bon Ton simply oozes
style. Authentic thatched
Malay-style village houses
with verandahs and
contemporary facilities.
Has a superb restaurant
and a good shop selling
stylish Asian products. $$$
Mutiara Burau Bay Resort
Pantai Kok
Tel: 04-959 1061
Fax: 04-959 1172
www.mutiarahotels.com
On one of the island's
loveliest beaches, the
resort has 150 cabanas
located in the forest.

These are small, simply
decorated but functional.
The restaurant, however,
is uninspiring. $$$
Beach Garden Resort
Pantai Cenang
Tel: 04-955 1363
Fax: 04-955 1221
www.beachgardenresort.com
An intimate German-run
resort. Its 12 rooms are
sparse and have no phone
or TV. The swimming pool
is also tiny, but the land-
scaping of lush greenery is
lovely and the beautiful
beach is right on the
resort's doorstep. Excellent
beachside bistro serves
great margaritas and
pizzas, and the breakfasts
are sumptuous. $$
The City Bayview Hotel
Jalan Pandak Mayah 1, Kuah
Tel: 04-966 1818
Fax: 04-966 3888
www.bayviewintl.com
Like a white monolith,
this 250-room city hotel
rises from among the
roofs of the market. Great
value rooms; ask for
promotional rates. The
top floors have sea views,
a swimming pool, sauna,
and gym. $$

The Frangipani Langkawi
Resort & Spa
Jalan Teluk Baru, Pantai Tengah
Tel: 04-952 0000
Fax: 04-952 0001
www.frangipanilangkawi.com
Formerly the Langkawi
Village Resort, this resort
was extensively renovated
in 2006. The free-standing
chalets are located along
400 metres (440 yards) of
beautiful coconut-tree-lined
beachfront. $$
Tanjung Sanctuary
Jalan Pantai Kok
Tel: 04-955 2977
Fax: 04-955 3978
www.tanjungsanctuary.com.my
Has 32 all-suite wooden
chalets with balconies, with
some fronting the beach.
Restaurant has 270-degree
view of the sea. $$
AB Motel
Pantai Cenang
Tel: 04-955 1300
Fax: 04-955 1466
e-mail: abmotel@hotmail.com
This 52-chalet resort is a
step away from the long
sandy Pantai Cenang.
Rooms are either air
conditioned and cooled by
fan. The restaurant serves
local food. Internet access,

bike hire, tours and water-
sports are available. $
Charlie Motel and
Restaurant
Pantai Tengah
Tel: 04-995 1200
Fax: 04-995 1316
Charlie has a great location
right on the beachfront.
While the place is a little
old, its value-for-money
chalets are ideal for those
travelling on a budget. $
Sandy Beach Resort
Pantai Cenang
Tel: 04-955 1308
Fax: 04-955 1762
One of Langkawi's original
budget resorts. The
A-framed chalets are air-
conditioned and the new
wing, away from the beach,
offers modern rooms. $

Perlis

Putra Palace Hotel
135 Persiaran Jubli Emas Kangar
Tel: 04-976 7755
Fax: 04-976 1049
e-mail: putrapalace@netscape.net
The state's fanciest hotel
with 146 rooms and
standard facilities; Asian
and Continental restaurant
featuring buffets. $$$

SOUTHERN PENINSULA

MELAKA

Melaka City

Room prices are lower by 30
percent on weekdays. Hotels
are located in a "hotel zone"
in the Jalan Bendahara area,
just outside the historic hub,
and in the Old Town across
the bridge.
   Backpackers' accommo-
dation is on Jalan Para-
meswara and the Taman
Melaka Raya, but be care-
ful about these, especially
if there are girls hanging
around downstairs. You'll
also find some lovely renovated accommodation
options that successfully
maintains a degree of old-
world charm.
Renaissance Melaka Hotel
Jalan Bendahara
Tel: 06-284 8888

Fax: 06-283 5351
www.marriott.com
Towering over the city, this
294-room luxury hotel is
beautifully furnished,
centrally located and has
great views of the town,
Melaka River and the sea.
Swimming pool on the 9th
floor, Chinese restaurant,
coffee house, lounge-cum-
library, disco. $$$$
City Bayview Hotel
Jalan Bendahara
Tel: 06-283 9888
Fax: 06-283 6699
www.bayviewintl.com
Situated near St Peter's
Church, this hotel has good
views, 182 rooms, a
swimming pool, Chinese
restaurant and coffee
house. $$$
Equatorial Hotel
Jalan Bandar Hilir
Tel: 06-282 8333
Fax: 06-282 9333
www.equatorial.com

High-rise luxury hotel, with
496 rooms, totally out of
scale with Melaka's
heritage surroundings but
in a good location. With
swimming pool and several
restaurants. $$$
Hotel Puri
118 Jalan Tun Tan Cheng Lock
Tel: 06-282 5588
Fax: 06-281 5588
www.hotelpuri.com
Carefully restored 1819
Peranakan house in the
quaint "Millionaires' Row",
which belonged to an
eminent philanthropist.
Marble and wood abound.
There are 50 rooms, a
decorated original airwell,
leafy beer garden and
L-shaped new wing; near
the Kochee Café. $$$
Mahkota Hotel
Jalan Merdeka
Tel: 06-281 2828
Fax: 06-281 2323
Sitting on reclaimed

coastal land near the
historic centre and the
Mahkota Parade shopping
mall, this massive 590-
room hotel has landscaped
swimming pools and a host
of activities. Rooms, in
contrast, are uninspiring
and dull. Appeals to mainly
tour groups. $$$
Emperor Hotel
123 Jalan Munshi Abdullah
Tel: 06-284 0777
Fax: 06-284 0787
e-mail: empehtl@tm.net.my
Decent and central, the
hotel has 235 rooms,
some with views of the
sea, a Chinese restaurant
with good dim sum, coffee
house, swimming pool and
sauna. $$
Heeren House
1 Jalan Tun Tan Cheng Lock
Tel: 06-281 4241
Fax: 06-281 4239
www.melaka.net/heerenhouse
Lovely, cosy six-room

restored shophouse in the Old Town overlooking the Melaka River and facing the historic centre. It has air-conditioned rooms with ensuite baths, and a café offering Peranakan and Portuguese fare. **$$**

Straits Heritage Lodge
591-A Taman Melaka Raya
Tel: 06-282 3950
Fax: 06-282 3957
Beautifully renovated Peranakan interior that belies its uninspiring facade; 20 minutes' walk from the historic hub. There is a lovely open-air fountain courtyard which serves as a reading area. Rooms are air-conditioned with ensuite baths. The Portuguese pub downstairs serves food and wine. **$$**

Baba House
125–7 Jalan Tun Tan Cheng Lock
Tel: 06-281 1216
Fax: 06-281 1217
Delightful Peranakan house in the old town. Popular backpackers' accommodation with clean simple rooms, some with air conditioning and ensuite baths, few with views. **$$**

Hotel Portugis
12–20 Jalan Melaka Raya 20
Tel: 06-292 4100
Fax: 06-292 9300
Loud and heavy on the kitsch, but decent standard rooms and wonderfully decorated VIP rooms which are nonetheless still affordable. Portuguese restaurant, 24-hour food court, karaoke. **$–$$**

Discovery Guesthouse
3 Jalan Bunga Raya
Tel: 06-292 5606
e-mail: dicovery-cafe@hotmail.com
Single, double and triple fan-cooled and air-conditioned rooms in a restored shophouse by the Melaka River, close to the main historic sights. Rooftop terrace offers scenic views and there's good Peranakan and Portuguese food in the café. **$**

Melaka Coast

Riviera Bay Resort
10km Jalan Tanjung Kling
Tel: 06-315 1111
Fax: 06-315 3333
Showy Roman gateway,

450 sea-facing suites, three restaurants, pub, swimming pool that is a better bet than the sea, and lots of facilities. **$$$**

Shah's Beach Resort
9km Jalan Tanjung Kling
Tel: 06-315 3121
www.shahsresorts.com
Famous old motel overlooking the Straits of Melaka. Fifty wooden chalets, pool and good restaurant. Very popular with Singaporeans and expats on the weekends and holidays when booking ahead is essential. **$$**

Ayer Keroh

A' Famosa Resort
Alor Gajah
Tel: 06-552 0888
www.afamosa.com
Sprawling theme-park hotel with Cowboy Town, Animal World Safari and Water World. Comfortable bungalows and condos. Golf course nearby. **$$**

Air Keroh Country Resort
Tel: 06-232 5211
Fax: 06-232 0422
A green and secluded chalet resort next door to Mini Malaysia, with swimming pool and restaurant; jungle-trekking and car hire can be arranged. **$$**

Air Keroh d'Village Melaka
Tel: 06-232 8000
Fax: 06-232 7541
e-mail: village@tm.net.my
Oldish resort with 274 rooms/chalets, seafood restaurant, coffee house, pool, terrace, sports facilities, bicycle hire. **$$**

NEGERI SEMBILAN

Seremban

Allson Klana Resort
Jalan Penghulu Cantik
Taman Tasik Seremban
Tel: 06-762 7888
Fax: 06-767 7788
www.allsonklana.com.my
Facing the pretty lake, this upmarket hotel has 228 rooms, full room facilities and service, Japanese and Chinese restaurants, coffee house, bars, business centre, fitness centre, swimming pool. **$$$**

Royal Adelphi
Jalan Dato AS Dawood
Tel: 06-766 6666
Fax: 06-766 6000
www.royaladelphi.com
Luxury hotel which offers the usual comforts with a good Chinese restaurant, swimming pool and outdoor jacuzzi. **$$$**

Carlton Star Hotel
47 Jalan Dato' Sheikh Ahmad
Tel: 06-763 6663
Fax: 06-762 0040
Central location near the bus and taxi station as well as food stalls, with 34 rooms, air conditioning, Chinese restaurant, coffee house. **$$**

JOHOR

Johor Bahru

Hyatt Regency
Jalan Sungai Chat
Tel: 07-222 1234
Fax: 07-222 9234
www.johorbahru.regency.hyatt.com
Luxurious hotel with 406 rooms, some with views of the Straits of Johor and Singapore, two-tier swimming pool, Roman spa. Within walking distance of town. **$$$$**

Mutiara Johor Bahru
Jalan Dato' Sulaiman
Tel: 07-332 3800
Fax: 07-331 8884
www.mutiarahotels.com
Within walking distance of large malls, this luxury hotel targets families with its junior club suite featuring double-decker beds, Playstation and games and soft toys. **$$$**

Puteri Pan Pacific
Jalan Abdullah Ibrahim
Tel: 07-223 3333
Fax: 07-223 6622
www.panpacific.com
Massive, central hotel, close to shopping malls. With 476 rooms, some with views of the straits and Singapore. Also has an Italian restaurant. **$$$**

Straits View Hotel
1-D Jalan Skudai
Tel: 07-224 1400
Fax: 07-224 2698
Out-of-town hotel with upstairs rooms overlooking the straits; 30 air-condi-

tioned rooms, open-air seafood restaurant. **$**

Endau-Rompin National Park

Staging Point and Campsites
Tel: 07-223 7471 (Johor Park Corporation in Johor Bahru)
Fax: 07-223 7472
The Staging Point at Endau-Rompin National Park has chalets (20 people) and dormitories (100 people – men and women separate); otherwise there are campsites: Kuala Jasin, Kuala Marong, Upih Guling, and Batu Hampar (maximum 200 visitors) with some shelters and basic toilets. Booking ahead is imperative. Bring everything, including food and cooking gas. Limited equipment may be hired. (*See page 234*)

Nature Education and Research Centre (NERC)
Tel: 03-2287 9422 (Malaysian Nature Society in Kuala Lumpur)
Fax: 03-2287 8773
www.mns.org.my
Offers 4-day/3-night nature courses (minimum groups of 10, maximum 40), including full board and excellent meals (student concessions available).

Kota Tinggi

Kota Tinggi Resort
16 Jalan Lombong
Tel: 07-883 6222
Fax: 07-883 1146
Resort comprising 63 chalets and rooms by the waterfalls with air conditioning and ensuite baths; mostly Singaporean clientele. Weekday rate 20 percent cheaper, also much quieter. **$$**

Desaru

Accommodation options here are more expensive because of the mostly Singaporean clientele. Weekend rates are about 20 percent higher. Eateries are in the hotels or in the coastal villages a drive away. Sea-view rooms are premium. All resorts have swimming pools, sea-sport facilities and bicycles.

Desaru Impian Resort
Tanjung Penawar
Tel: 07-2240 827
Fax: 07-2228 306
www.leisureholidays.com.my
This gigantic theme-park hotel at the entrance to Desaru has staff dressed as pirates, a water park surrounded by 16 blocks of 356 well-furnished all-suite family apartments (cooking allowed), two swimming pools – one in a Taj Mahal clubhouse on the beach –

mini zoo and sports facilities. Day use allowed. **$$$**
Sebana Cove Golf and Marina Resort
Tanjung Penawar
Tel: 07-826 6688
Fax: 07-826 6677
www.sebanacove.com
The approach road winds through an 18-hole golf course, past the yacht clubhouse and the beautiful marina which is overlooked by the resort's tavern. Sixty rather small rooms, some

with marina views. Pub lunches at the bar, nominal fee for recreational facilities, river cruises. **$$$**
Desaru Golden Beach Resort
Tanjung Penawar
Tel: 07-822 1101
Fax: 07-822 1480
www.desaruresort.com
An old resort with a 1970s feel, but still decent. There are 100 rooms in chalets, including newer sea-fronting villas. The famous

golf course is just down the road. **$$**
Tanjung Balau Fishing Village
Tanjung Balau
Tel: 07-822 1601
Fax: 07-822 1600
This government venture has 115 family and double rooms and 20 triple-share dorms, and a local restaurant. Traditional fishing is seasonal only, but there's a good fishing museum and a nice, uncrowded beach. **$**

PENINSULA'S EAST COAST

MERSING & ISLANDS

Accommodation on the islands is divided into what are termed as resorts – the bigger air-conditioned operations with hot showers – and chalets, which can be dormitory style. All have restaurants and snorkelling facilities, while some are diver-friendly. Some have their own offices or agents in town, but tour agencies can book you into any of the resorts – they receive a commission, so be firm. Ask to see their photo albums of resorts and boats. Enquire about 3-day/2-night packages, which include boat transfers, accommodation, all meals and a snorkelling trip.

Mersing

Hotel Timotel
839 Jalan Endau
Tel: 07-799 5888
Fax: 07-799 5333
www.timotel.com.my
Situated past the bridge north but within walking distance of the jetty, the 44-room hotel is clean, and has a coffee house serving local and Western food. **$$**
Mersing Inn
38 Jalan Ismail
Tel/fax: 07-799 1919
Next to a supermarket in a central location with clean, air-conditioned rooms, ensuite baths and hot water. **$**

Omar's Backpackers' Hostel
Jalan Abu Bakar
Tel: 07-799 5096
Mobile tel: 019-774 4268
Opposite the post office is Mersing's arguably best-established backpackers' hostel. Situated on the first floor with dormitories for 10 only; kitchen, tours, walking distance of jetty. **$**

Pulau Besar

Aseania Resort
Tel: 07-799 4152
Fax: 07-799 1413
Smartest hotel with 50 beach-fronting (premium) and hill-view coconut-framed chalets arranged in clusters for a village feel. With hot showers, lush grounds, 24-hour electricity, bar, sea sports, a 45-minute cross-isle jungle trek from back of huts; no TV or dive shop. **$$**
D'Coconut Island Resort
Tel: 03-4296 5753
Fax: 03-4291 1808
www.dcoconut.com
Village environment with 20 air-conditioned chalets with ensuite baths, satellite TV and mini fridge, mountain bikes, watersports, dive shop. **$$**
Nirwana Beach Resort
Tel: 07-799 1606
Fax: 07-799 5294
Basic chalets, some air-conditioned, all with ensuite baths, dormitories for 6–10 people, bar. **$$**
White Sand Beach Resort
Tel: 07-799 4955/2582
Fax: 07-799 2572

Established outfit with beach-fronting chalets, dive packages. **$$**

Pulau Rawa

Rawa Safaris Island Resort
Tel: 07-799 1204
Fax: 07-799 3848
www.rawasfr.com
With 53 wood-and-attap A-frames, chalets and bungalows on beach and hill, some with air conditioning and ensuite bathroom. A quiet spot with a lovely beach, electricity until midnight (lanterns provided), bar, sea sports, scuba gear for hire but no dive master. **$$**

Pulau Tinggi

Tinggi Island Resort
Tel: 07-224 0063
Mobile tel: 019-7433 252
Fax: 07-861 2005
Twenty-five no-frills twin-sharing rooms on hillside and beach next to the Marine Parks museum; with air conditioning and attached baths. Resort offers snorkelling and fishing trips. Both room-only and packages with meals are available. **$$**

Pulau Pemanggil

Basic accommodation and only packages are available, usually for groups of 10 or more. Enquire at travel agencies. The biggest operation is **Pemanggil Holiday Heaven**, tel: 07-799 4360 with 13

chalets and a 10-room longhouse; **Ranting Resort** is fairly big; other smaller operators with chalets and dormitories like **Pemanggil Baru Chalet**, tel: 07-799 2363 and **Pulau Pemanggil Mini Resort**, tel: 07-799 2660.

Pulau Aur/Dayang

Another packages-only destination. The prettiest beaches are on Pulau Dayang. Chalets and long-houses available at **Blue Water Holiday Resort**, tel: 07-799 4027; **Dayang Blues**, tel: 07-799 4558. On Aur, **Mahmood's Chalet**, tel: 07-799 4217. Enquire about the smaller operations at tour agencies; packages.

Pulau Tioman

Air Batang (ABC) and Juara beaches have backpacker and A-frame accommodation. Salang also has budget accommodation as does Mukut, while Paya and Genting cater to locals and Singaporeans and have more upmarket accommodation.
    There are dive shops at Tekek (Tioman Reef Divers and Scuba Point), ABC (B&J Dive Centre), Salang (Dive Asia and Fishermen Dive Centre), Penuba (Bali Hai Divers).
Japamala Resort
Tel: 09-419 6001/03-4256 6100
Fax: 09-419 6002
www.japamalaresorts.com

An exclusive and intimate resort offering a unique Asian resort experience. The luxurious accommodation includes treetop chalets, which are either located in the jungle or come with a plunge pool. The Tamarind Terrace Restaurant serves Thai and Indochinese cuisine. **$$$$**

Berjaya Tioman Beach Golf and Spa Resort
Tel: 09-419 1000
Fax: 09-419 1718
www.berjayaresorts.com
The island's largest resort with 361 rooms decorated in tropical tones. There's a coastal links-style golf course, spa and an extensive selection of water sports and land-based recreational activities. **$$$**

Pulau Sibu Besar

There is plenty of basic accommodation, mainly A-frames and huts, in Sibu Besar. **Sibu Coconut Village Resort** (tel: 010-761 2761) and **Junansa Villa** (www.sibuisland.com.my) offers village-style hospitality; **Twin Beach Resort** (www.sibuisland.com.my) commanders the middle of the island, and therefore two beaches. **Sea Gypsy Village Resort and Dive Base**
Tel: 07-222 8642
Fax: 07-221 0048
www.siburesort.com
Lovely resort set in a 2-hectare (5-acre) coconut-fringed site with 23 sea-facing Malay-style chalets with ensuite baths and verandahs. Bar, barbeque on Saturdays, dive shop, full-board. **$$**
Sibu Island Cabanas
Tel: 07-331 7216/1920
www.sibuislandcabanas.com
Comfortable, 18 fan-cooled chalets with king-sized beds, ensuite baths, dive shop; full board. **$$**

Pulau Sibu Tengah

Sibu Island Resort
Tel: 07-223 1188
Fax: 07-223 1199
www5.jaring.my/sir
Fancy resort and the island's only one with 171

air-conditioned chalets and a host of facilities and activities including batik-making classes, tennis courts, sunken pool bar; teh tarik stall in the shape of a boat, selling Indian breads and tea at night. **$$$**

PAHANG

Kuantan

M.S. Garden Hotel
Lot 5, P Lorong Gambut, off Jalan Beserah
Tel: 09-555 5899
Fax: 09-555 4558
This 202-room hotel is located in downtown Kuantan. It has a pool and a fitness centre and the beach is just 5 km (3 miles) away. Dine in the M.S. Coffee Garden or try the Chinese cuisine in Yuen Yuen Chinese Restaurant. **$$**
Hotel Pacific
60–62 Jalan Bukit Ubi
Tel: 09-514 1980
This six-storey budget hotel is located near the bus station. While the rooms are large, they are basic although air-conditioned. **$**

Teluk Chempedak Beach

Hyatt Regency Kuantan
Tel: 09-566 1234
Fax: 09-567 7577
www.kuantan.regency.hyatt.com
Grand old lady of the beach, with 330 rooms, restaurant with commanding views of the South China Sea, pizzas by the pool or on the beach, fun pub, tours. A range of watersports activities including catamaran sailing, kayaking and wind surfing. **$$$$**
Hotel Kuantan
Tel/fax: 09-517 7899
Distinct 1960s feel with high ceilings, colonial-style fan-cooled restaurant and bar. Some rooms come with air conditioning and hot showers, but bathrooms are tiny. Rooms upstairs rooms have

balconies. Friendly, family-owned. **$**

Beserah

Le Village Beach Resort
Lot 1260 Sungai Karang
Tel: 09-544 7900
Tel: 03-983 2268 (KL)
Fax: 09-544 7899
e-mail: fal@tm.net.my
Well-established resort 14 km (9 miles) north of Kuantan, with wooden chalets and blocks of rooms amid lush foliage. Water sports, tours and car rental available. **$$**
Swiss-Garden Resort
2656–7 Sungai Karang, Balok
Tel: 09-544 7333
Fax: 09-544 9555
www.swissgarden.com
This 304-room hotel 13 km (8 miles) from the Kuantan airport has a beautifully breezy lounge area and lovely garden terrace. **$$**
De Rhu Beach Resort
152 Sungai Karang
Tel: 09-557 9000
Fax: 09-557 9002
www.derhu.com
Oldish hotel that has changed hands several times, with a beautiful beach beneath the casuarina trees, large grounds, huge pool with sundeck, disco. **$**

Cherating

Club Med
Batu 29, Jalan Kuantan/Kemaman
Tel: 09-581 9133/03-2161 4599
Fax: 09-581 9172/03-2161 7229
www.clubmed.com.my
Just north of Kampung Cherating is Asia's first Club Med, spread out in carefully preserved forested surroundings, with a lovely private beach, the usual organised activities, including racquet sports, circus acts, rock-climbing, archery and watersports in non-monsoon period. Wide range of international food from Japanese to French, Rio-type carnival with live band every weekend. Day visitors from 10am to 12pm, 2 to 6pm. **$$$$**
Impiana Resort Cherating
32km Jalan Kuantan-Kemaman
Tel: 09-581 9000

Fax: 09-581 9090
www.impiana.com
Situated just beyond Cukai, this is a graceful and tasteful adaptation of traditional Malay architecture, with an interesting pond design merging into a lounge and 120 rooms. Outdoor jacuzzi, lessons on arts and craft, full sports facilities. **$$$**
Legend Resort
Lot 1290, Sungai Karang
Tel: 09-581 9818
Fax: 09-581 9400
www.legendsgroup.com
Average beachfront hotel whose brochures are much more impressive than the reality. With 152 rooms, two swimming pools, karaoke and live entertainment at its lounge. **$$$**
Holiday Villa Cherating
Lot 1303 Sungai Karang
Tel: 09-581 9500
Fax: 09-581 9178
www.holidayvilla.com.my
The first resort north from Beserah to Cherating. Lovely ambience with 130 rooms, including a unique kampung (village) section with a chalet cluster based on architecture from each state, two open-air jacuzzis, steak house, full watersports facilities. **$$**

Kampung Cherating

There is a host of accommodation here, now also called Cherating Lama ("old Cherating"). Many are still backpackers' hostels and budget-class hotels, but upmarket developers are gradually moving in.
Cherating Cottage
Tel: 09-581 9273
Fax: 09-581 9279
Classy chalets and double-storey block around a lotus pond. Some rooms with air conditioning and TV, open-air bar. **$**
The Shadow of the Moon
Tel: 09-581 9186
At the northern entrance, this is an established backpackers' hostel with attitude. Rustic fan-cooled and, imperatively, mosquito-netted, chalets are set amid much greenery on a hillside, all with baths. There is a wonderful restaurant/bar/reading

TRANSPORT
ACCOMMODATION
EATING OUT
ACTIVITIES
A – Z
LANGUAGE

area that is completely open – bring insect repellent. **$**

TERENGGANU

Kuala Terengganu

Permai Park Inn
Jalan Sultan Mahmud
Tel: 09-622 2122
Fax: 09-622 2121
Within walking distance of Batu Buruk beach, comfortable, pleasant hotel with 130 rooms, and a nice pool. **$$$**
Primula Beach Resort
Jalan Persinggahan
Tel: 09-622 2100/623 3722
Fax: 09-623 3360
www.primulabeachresort.com
Located about 1 km (½ mile) from the Kuala Terengganu city centre, this is the fanciest hotel around here, along a sandy beach; 248 rooms, some with sea view; grill, cosy Italian restaurant, tours. **$$$**
Pura Tanjung Sabtu
Kampung Tanjung Sabtu
Tel/Fax: 09-615 3655
Mobile tel: 019 983 3365
www.puratanjungsabtu.com
A beautiful complex of traditional old wooden palaces have been re-created in an orchard upriver from Kuala Terengganu. Run by the famous songket-weaving prince, Tengku Ismail Tengku Su, it offers package deals with transfers, accommodation, home-cooked meals and sightseeing trips. **$$$**
Grand Continental
Jalan Sultan Zainal Abidin
Tel: 09-615 1888
Fax: 09-625 1999
Beachside but close to the town centre, 200 pleasant rooms, swimming pool, pastries and cakes, live bands. **$$**
Hotel YT Midtown
Jalan Tok Lam
Tel: 09-623 5288
Fax: 09-623 4399
Right in the heart of town, a decent new hotel with 141 air-conditioned rooms with ensuite baths, good value set lunch and dinner; supper special of local

bread, *roti jala*, with curry. **$$**
KT Mutiara
67 Jalan Sultan Ismail
Tel: 09-622 2655
Fax: 03-623 6895
Centrally located with 51 clean, decent-sized rooms arranged around a central airwell with koi pond that looks better at night; hot water. **$**
Ping Anchorage
77A Jalan Sultan Sulaiman
Tel: 09-626 2020
Fax: 09-626 2022
www.pinganchorage.com.my
Central, small, clean backpackers' hostel with rooms and dorms atop the town's best travel agency; sunny rooftop café and bar. **$**

Dungun

Tanjong Jara Resort
8th Mile off Jalan Dungun
Tel: 09-845 1100
Fax: 09-845 1200
www.tanjongjararesort.com
Award-winning traditional Malay all-timber resort located 13 km (8 miles) north of Dungun on a 17-hectare (42-acre) site. There are 100 beach cottages and sea-facing hotel rooms (great views from second floor rooms) with 1½ km (1 mile) of private beach. Restaurants, two swimming pools, hot spa, library, "well-being" centre with stress-release programmes, massages. **$$$$**
Awana Kijal Golf & Beach Resort
Km 28, Jalan Kemaman-Dungun
Tel: 09-864 1188
Fax: 09-864 1688
www.awana.com.my
The resort is a prominent feature on the beach. There are 343 rooms, nine food and beverage outlets, a massive swimming pool and nine holes of golf fairways on either side. Cruise ships ocassionally unload passengers here for daily sightseeing trips. **$$$**

Rantau Abang

Prices are higher by about 30 percent during the turtle season of May–September. However, sightings can be

rare these days. While the turtles rarely come on to the beach to lay their eggs, the beach and the beautiful lagoon behind it are still worth a stay though.
Awang's Beach Bungalows & Restaurant
Tel: 09-844 3500
Long-time "turtle tourism" resort near Turtle Information Centre, it has 37 bungalows with terraces, and dormitories, and a self-service laundry. **$**
Dahimah's Guest House & Restaurant
Tel: 09-983 5057/09-845 2843
Clean, different-sized village-style chalets with verandahs, a little away from the beach. The river-fronting huts are nice. Restaurant open only during turtle season. **$**
Ismail Beach Resort
Tel: 09-844 1054
Right in front of the Turtle Museum, with choice of fan-cooled or air-conditioned. **$**
Rantau Abang Visitor's Centre
Batu 13 Jalan Dungun
Tel: 09-844 1533
Fax: 09-844 2653
Minimum quad-share traditional huts and chalets overlooking the lagoon, some air-conditioned. **$**

Marang

Anguilla Beach House Resort
Kampung Tanjung Rhu
Tel/fax: 09-618 1322
Opposite beach with 34 clean chalets in 2 hectares (5 acres) of well-kept grounds facing Pulau Kapas. Garden shelters, set meals, laundry, boat service. **$$**
Kamal's
Kampung Tanjung Rhu
Tel: 09-618 2181
Facing the lagoon is the original backpackers' hostel and therefore entrenched as the place to stay; dormitories and chalets in a pleasant garden. **$**

Pulau Gemia

Gem Isles Resort
As there are no scheduled boats and the resort takes

people booked on packages only, book through a travel agent such as Ping Anchorage, tel: 09-626 2020. The 52 air-conditioned chalets have views of the alcove and Pulau Kapas. Snorkelling, diving, non-motorised watersports, deep-sea fishing and squid fishing all available. Small turtle hatchery. **$$$**

Merang

Aryani Resort
Jalan Rhu Tapai-Merang
Tel: 09-653 2111
Fax: 09-653 1007
www.thearyani.com
Wonderful, and very exclusive heritage Terengganu house-suites by the same architect who designed the Floating Mosque; each house has a courtyard and an outside bath. **$$$$**
Sutra Beach Resort
Kampung Rhu Tapai, Setiu
Tel: 09-653 1111
Fax: 09-669 6410
www.sutrabeachresort.com
Traditional-style chalets gathered together in village clusters overlooking the islands; nice gardens. **$$**

Pulau Redang

There are no scheduled boats to Redang, so resorts offer packages, including boat transfers from Marang jetty, accommodation, meals and snorkelling trips and gear. Dive packages are available. Pickups from mainland airports can be arranged. Berjaya Air flies daily from Kuala Lumpur (*see page 348*). Resorts listed are in Pasir Panjang unless stated otherwise.
Berjaya Redang Beach Resort
Tel: 09-697 3988
Fax: 09-697 3899
Toll-free: 1800-88 8818
www.berjayaresorts.com
Luxury hotel in Teluk Dalam set on a stunning, pure-white sand beach washed by crystal-clear, turquoise waters. It has 273 rooms and suites in Malaysian-style chalets and a Ayura

spa with interesting body wrap treatments. **$$$**

Coral Redang Island Resort
Tel: 09-630 7110/7111
Fax: 09-623 6300/690 2112
www.coralredang.com.my
The nicest hotel on Pasir Panjang, with 40 chalets and standard rooms with air conditioning and hot water, around a swimming pool with bar. Local and continental dishes, dive shop. **$$$**

Redang Beach Resort
Tel: 09-623 8188
Tel: 09-2031 5079 (KL)
Fax: 09-623 0225,
Fax: 03-2026 2013 (KL)
www.redang.com.my
Rooms in a two-storey wooden block, good breakfasts, deck chairs, daily batik activity, jungle trekking, fishing and candat sotong (squid fishing), dive shop. **$$$**

Redang Kalong Resort
Tel: 09-622 1591
Fax: 09-622 8186
www.redangkalong.com
Thirty-eight beach-facing rooms in a longhouse with air-conditioning, hot showers and ensuite baths. Lots of sea and beach activities. But this beach is rather corally. Dive shop. **$$$**

Redang Reef Resort
Tel: 09-626 2020
Fax: 09-622 8093
Perched on rocks, this hotel has 24 air-conditioned rooms in a two-storey block with ensuite baths. Large wooden deck for dining overlooks the bay, also used for karaoke. Dive shop. **$$$**

Redang Pelangi Resort
Tel: 09-624 2158, 626 1189
Fax: 09-623 5202
www.redangpelangi.com
One of the better resorts, located at the centre of Pasir Panjang beach between Coral Redang and Ayu Mayang, Redang Pelangi offers air-conditioned twin- (4 units) or quad-sharing (37 units) rooms with attached bathrooms; dive shop. Activities include snorkeling, scuba diving, fishing, jungle-trekking, squid fishing and beach volleyball. **$$–$$$**

Pulau Lang Tengah

Lang Sari Resort
Tel: 09-623 5333
Tel: 03-2166 1380 (KL)
Fax: 09-623 9533
www.langsari.com
Peaceful and basic, this resort has 56 rooms in longhouses, all air conditioned and with ensuite baths; snorkelling, house reef good at high tide. Dive shop. **$$$**

Blue Coral Island Resort
Tel: 09-622 0851
Tel: 03-4257 8582 (KL)
Fax: 04-4257 4103 (KL)
www.aseaniaresortsgroup.com.my
Facing a lovely quiet beach are 55 rooms with air conditioning and hot water. Also has a swimming pool, library, movies, karaoke and grocery shop. Fishing and diving tours and instruction available; house reef good for snorkelling. **$$**

Pulau Perhentian

Facilities notwithstanding, these islands have not outgrown their original backpacker mentality. The smaller outfits have no proper reception area or management. Don't be surprised when faced with grumpy and/or ignorant staff. Water is also a problem during the dry months.
For information and bookings, try these tour operators:
Ping Anchorage
77A Jalan Sultan Sulaiman, Kuala Terengganu
Tel: 09-626 2020
www.pinganchorage.com.my
Paradise Tropical Discovery
2981-G, 1st Floor, Jalan Padang Garong, Kota Bharu
www.paradise.com.my
Anjung Holidays
S1A, Terminal Pelancongan, Kuala Besut
Tel: 09-697 4095
www.pulauperhentian.com.my

Perhentian Besar

Coral View Island Resort
Tel: 09-697 4943
Fax: 09-690 2600
The next upmarket resort to Perhentian Island

Resort, this dive operation pioneer has 71 pretty chalets on two beaches, of which only the rockier one is good for swimming. Some chalets are air-conditioned. Breezy restaurant. **$$$**

Perhentian Island Resort
Tel: 09-697 7562
Tel: 03-2144 8530 (KL)
Fax: 09-697 7199
The island's only three-star resort with 104 beautifully furnished chalets and bungalows with ensuite bath and air conditioning, some on the private beach. Excellent fresh grilled fish and dinner buffet, but food here is on the pricey side; dive shop, non-motorised sea sports, tennis and swimming pool, circular jungle trek behind the resort, tours. Cheaper rates from tour agencies. **$$$**

Flora Bay Resort
Tel: 09-697 7266
www.florabayresort.com
There are 80 free-standing chalets in two-storey wooden blocks. The resort fronts a good beach and diving is the big attraction here. Rooms are either air-conditioned or fan cooled. **$$**

Watercolours Resort
Pulau Perhentian
Mobile tel: 019-981 1852
www.watercoursworld.com
The resort offers twin-sharing chalets at its Impiana Resort and the Paradise Resort. Those at Impiana are more upmarket and more expensive (**$$**), while those at Paradise are older and cheaper. (**$**)

Perhentian Kecil

Perhentian Kecil is a backpackers' haven, with budget accommodation at Teluk Aur and Pasir Panjang. Around the jetty at Teluk Aur, where the best picture-perfect sunset scenes are, sit six chalet operators, including **Rajawali's** (mobile tel: 010-980 5244) in the headland in the north, with A-frame accommodation and great views of the bay.

Bubu Long Beach
Tel: 03-2142 6688 (KL)
Fax: 03-2141 0080 (KL)
www.buburesort.com.my
Fancy resort that signals the upmarket direction in which this backpacker stretch is heading; 39 sea-fronting rooms with balconies, air conditioning and hot showers; restaurant with local and Western cuisine; karaoke and dive centre; packages available. **$$$**

Mohsin Chalet
Tel/fax: 010-333 8897
e-mail: marhms@pc.jaring.my
Newer accommodation, set back from the beach with 30 hillside chalets with ensuite baths. Great views from the restaurant which serves local and Western fare. Use of telephones and Internet, friendly staff. **$**

KELANTAN

Kota Bharu

Budget accommodation in Kota Bharu, in the form of dormitories and rooms, are offered by: **City**, 2nd Floor, Jalan Pintu Pong; **Ideal Traveller's Guest House**, Jalan Padang Garong, tel: 09-744 2246 (52 rooms); **Rebana Hostel**, 1218, Jalan Sultanah Zainab (40 rooms).

Diamond Puteri Hotel
Jalan Post Office Lama
Tel: 09-743 9988
Fax: 09-743 8388
New high-rise with great river views in centre of town. Ask for promotion package deals, which includes dinner and breakfast. Great deals during Ramadan. Popular buffets at the riverview café. **$$$**

Renaissance Kota Bharu
Jalan Yahya Petra
Tel: 09-746 2233
Fax: 09-746 1122
www.marriott.com
The city's only international hotel is within reach of the State Museum. There are 298 rooms and suites, a business centre, swimming pool and Chinese restaurant. **$$$**

Juita Inn
Jalan Pintu Pong
Tel: 09-744 6888
Fax: 09-744 5777
Popular moderately priced
small hotel with 70 rooms
and a good café. In a
central location. **$$**

Perdana Resort
Pantai Cahaya Bulan
Tel: 09-774 4000
Fax: 09-774 4980
www.perdanaresort.com.my
Situated on the famous
Pantai Cahaya Bulan
(Moonlight Beach), about
a half-hour's drive from
Kota Bharu. The chalets
are well spread out along
the beach, and there are
decent Chinese and
Western restaurants.
Great sunsets. **$$**

EASTERN INTERIOR

Tasik Kenyir

For a visit to Tasik Kenyir, it
is more convenient to book
a package with a tour
agency in Kuala Terengganu
or directly with a resort at
Lake Kenyir. A package
includes accommodation,
meals, boat transfers,
trekking and a visit to a
waterfall. Each resort is
usually located close to a
waterfall and trek routes
and is pretty much isolated
from the others. Most are
very basic floating chalets
moored to the mainland,
which means that if a group
comes along and decides
to make merry, there isn't
much you can do about
claiming back peace and
quiet on the deck or in your
room. Otherwise, the
setting is truly tranquil.
Meals are Chinese style
and buffets. Generators
are usually switched on
only at night.

Kenyir Lake Resort
Tel: 09-514 6002
Fax: 09-513 5687
Chalets with ensuite
bathrooms and hot water
in an upmarket setup,
with animal viewing hides.
A free-form swimming pool
is fed by continuously
flowing natural springs;
there is a fish farm for

anglers and many
activities. **$$$**

Kenyir Lakeview Resort
Tel: 09-666 8888
Tel: 03-2052 8441/2/3 (KL)
Fax: 09-666 8343
A secluded retreat amid
lush greenery ideal for
those who love the great
outdoors. Stay in one of the
150 rustic timber chalets
and enjoy fishing, nature
walks, picnics beside
waterfalls, and breathtak-
ing views. The resort has a
restaurant serving
Western/Malaysian fare,
and also a poolside
restaurant. **$$$**

Lake Land Resort
Tel: 03-6273 2213 (KL)
Tel: 019-278 2939
Recently upgraded, this
remote resort comprises
20 green-roofed chalets
(4–6 people per chalet)
on an island. There is basic
accommodation on a float-
ing deck, 24-hour electricity, satellite TV, karaoke,
3-hour trail to
Ulu Terang. Camping is
sometimes available.
Two dining halls and a
bar. **$$$**

Uncle John's Resort
Tel: 09-622 9564
Fax: 09-622 9596
e-mail: ujohnresort@yahoo.com
Small floating concern
close to Lasir Waterfall,
with lovely design of
varnished split bamboo
and open deck, 12 rooms,
karaoke, videos, accessible
from main dam jetty. **$$**

Tasik Cini

Kijang Mas Gumum Resort
Kampung Orang Asli Gumum
Tel: 09-422 1448
Basic lakeside chalet outfit
run by the Aborigines
Affairs Department, set
within the modern village of
Kampung Gumum and
accessible by road and
boat. There are 10 chalets
and dormitories for 32;
shared facilities, tours. **$**

Rimba Resort Tasik Cini
Tel: 09-477 8037
Fax: 09-477 8036
Rather run-down govern-
ment-owned, 13-year-old
resort on the banks of a
lake that is lotus-covered
from June to September.

Decent-sized chalets with
balconies, some with air
conditioning; dormitories
and campsite. Jungle-
trekking (two guides) and
boat trips by arrangement.
Decent restaurant,
karaoke, TV in lounge.
Walkway leads to jetty of
private boat operators. **$**

Tasik Bera

Persona Lake Resort
Kompleks Pelancungan Tasik Bera
Tel/Fax: 09-276 2505
Set in the wilderness of
oil palms, this simple
lakeside resort has 50
rooms, dormitories for 40,
and a campsite for 200,
including eight riverine
huts. Interesting Orang Asli
homestay programme is
among the numerous tours
led by trained guides. **$$$**

TAMAN NEGARA

Kuala Tahan

**Mutiara Taman
Negara Resort**
Tel: 09-266 3500
Tel: 03-2145 1601 (KL)
Toll free: 1800-883 838
Fax: 09-266 1500
Fax: 03-2142 9822 (KL)
www.mutiarahotels.com
The best resort here but
needs a little maintenance.
Malaysian-style wooden
chalets with balconies, 110
rooms, dormitories, nice
camping ground with
limited equipment for hire,
pricey restaurant and
caféteria, tours, guides,
helpful information desk.
The lodges upriver at
Keniam and Terengganu
are currently closed and
their future is unsure. **$$**

Nusa Camp
Tel: 09-266 2369
Fax: 09-266 4369
e-mail: spkg@tm.net.my
Comprising 36 hectares
(90 acres) of park buffer
zone across the river;
located upriver, with its own
trails. Basic accommoda-
tion at 20 chalets and
A-frames, dormitories for
40, and a camping ground
(tents supplied).
Restaurant with a great

view of the river, and
guided tours. **$**

Kampung Kuala Tahan

Ekotone Chalet
Kuala Tahan
Mobile tel: 010-988 8932
Fax: 09-277 6652
A small complex of eight
chalets with air conditioning
and bathrooms. There is
also a larger fan-cooled
hostel. The location is quiet
and away from the river. **$**

**Liana Hostel and Floating
Restaurant**
Kuala Tahan
Tel: 09-266 9322
This is a no-frills hostel of
10 rooms, each sleeping
up to four people. The
rooms are fan cooled and
the adjoining floating
restaurant serves good
local food. **$**

Jerantut

Jerantut Rest House
Jalan Benta
Tel: 09-266 6200
Fax: 09-266 6200
This basic motel, which
also has dormitories, sits
500 metres (550 yds) from
the bus/taxi station, and
operates free pick-ups
within town. It also handles
Taman Negara bookings.
Food is available from
7am to 11pm. **$**

Hotel Sri Emas Jerantut
Bangunan MUIP, Jalan Besar
Tel: 09-266 4499/88/77
Fax: 09-266 4801
e-mail: tamannegara.8m.com
Doubles as pro-active travel
agency offering nightly
briefings on Taman Negara;
agent for some resorts in
the village. Dormitories and
restaurant. **$**

Kenong

Persona Rimba Resort
Kenong Rimba Park
Tel: 09-312 5032
Fax: 09-312 1421
Basic chalets on stilts
among trees accommodat-
ing 32 people. Activities
include jungle trekking,
mountain climbing, river
activities, cave exploration;
guides available; packages
only. **$$**

SARAWAK

KUCHING

Hilton Kuching
Jalan Tunku Abdul Rahman
Tel: 082-248 200
Fax: 082-428 984
www.hilton.com
Kuching's best hotel looks out across the Sarawak River and magnificent sunsets over the old trading town. Considered to offer to best dining of any major Kuching hotel. Facilities and service are as good as expected. **$$$$**

Crowne Plaza Riverside Kuching
Jalan Tunku Abdul Rahman
Tel: 082-247 777
Fax: 082-425 858
www.ichotelsgroup.com
Established hotel situated in town, 20 minutes from the airport, with views of the Sarawak River. Leisure and shopping options close by in the adjacent multi-storey shopping complex with cinemas and a bowling alley. **$$$**

Grand Continental Hotel Kuching
Jalan Ban Hock
Tel: 082-230 399
Fax: 082-255 099
Situated a little out of the old town centre, this 4-star hotel with a swimming pool, fitness centre and good business facilities is popular with local businessmen. **$$$**

Holiday Inn Kuching
Jalan Tunku Abdul Rahman
Tel: 082-423 111
Fax: 082-426 169
www.ichotelsgroup.com
The first 5-star hotel in Kuching, this has remained popular and is the only hotel set right on the edge of the Sarawak River. Contemporary-style rooms plus good facilities including one of Kuching's best bookshops. **$$$**

Borneo Hotel
Jalan Tabuan
Tel: 082-244 122
Fax: 082-254 848
Kuching's oldest established hotel with friendly staff but small rooms. A short walk from Chinatown, the river and Main Bazaar. **$$**

Harbour View Hotel
Lorong Temple
Tel: 082-274 666
Fax: 082-274 777
www.harbourview.com.my
New, good-value hotel in a great position overlooking the river and Chinatown. Excellent buffet breakfast included in room rate. **$$**

Singgahsana Lodge
1 Temple Street
Tel: 082-429 277
Fax: 082-429 267
www.singgahsana.com
This unique guesthouse offers decidedly homey and stylishly furnished with local artefacts. Just off Main Bazaar, and offering everything from bicycle rentals to broadband Internet. Breakfast is included in the price of accommodation. This is the choice of travellers looking for affordable luxury. Dormitory beds and private rooms; popular so book in advance. **$$**

Telang Usan Hotel
Jalan Ban Hock
Tel: 082-415 588, 425 316
Fax: 082-254 848
www.telangusan.com
A small, comfortable hotel owned by a well-known Kenyah family from the Baram district, this has traditional Kenyah decor as well as friendly and knowledgeable staff. A 10-minute walk from the Kuching Waterfront and Main Bazaar. **$$**

Green Mountain Lodging House
Jalan Green Hill
Tel: 082-416 320
Fax: 082-246 342
Popular with backpackers and travellers, this guesthouse is situated in a convenient location a short walk from Main Bazaar. Rooms are air conditioned. **$**

DAMAI BEACH

Holiday Inn Resort Damai Beach
Teluk Bandung Santubong
Tel: 082-846 999
Fax: 082-846 777
www.ichotelsgroup.com
Arguably the most attractive resort in Damai, with a comfortable atmosphere. Accommodation near the beach as well as hilltop rooms and suites overlook panoramas of the sea and mountains. A separate hilltop pool offers scenic vistas of the surroundings. **$$$**

Holiday Inn Resort Damai Lagoon
Teluk Penyu Santubong
Tel: 082-846 900
Fax: 082-846 901
www.holidayinn-sarawak.com
Rooms are located in multi-storey blocks with a few chalets near the vast lagoon-style pool and the beach. A full range of watersports and facilities are available. An easy walk from the Sarawak Cultural Village. **$$$**

Santubong Kuching Resort
Tel: 082-846 888
Fax: 082-846 666
e-mail: skresort@po.jaring.my
A smaller family-style resort without a beachfront but within 5 minutes' walk from the Damai Golf & Country Club. Watersports and activities including cycling. **$$**

Permal Rainforest Resort
Pantai Damai Santubong
Tel: 082-846 490
An outdoor activity centre not far from the Holiday Inn Resort Damai Beach, with log cabins, luxurious tree houses complete with air conditioning and bathroom, camping facilities and a rainforest location. Popular mostly with locals. **$-$$**

LUNDU

Hilton Batang Ai Resort
Batang Ai Dam
Tel: 083-584 388
Fax: 083-584 399
www.hilton.com
A longhouse-style resort with standard Hilton facilities, 4½ hours from Kuching, this is set on a promontory jutting out into a huge lake formed when the Batang Ai was dammed to provide hydro-electricity. It offers a gentle introduction to longhouse living. Close enough to real longhouses for excursions. **$$$**

Bukit Saban Tropical Resort
Paku River, Betong
Tel: 083-477 145
Fax: 083-477 103
www.sedctourism.com/hotel_saban.html
About 4½ hours from Kuching, this resort offers excursions to local plantations, longhouses and nature treks. It is popular with groups for human resource training and adventure activities. **$$**

Lundu Gading Hotel
Lundu Bazaar
Tel: 082-735 199
Fax: 082-735 299
Small hotel with air-conditioned rooms and bathrooms – a fine base to explore the Lundu area. **$$**

SIBU

Kingwood Hotel
12 Lorong Lanang 4
Tel: 084-335 888
Fax: 084-334 559
Sibu's biggest and perhaps grandest hotel complete with plush granite tiles, views of the Rejang River and a fitness centre with gym and sauna. **$$$**

Tanahmas Hotel
Jalan Kampung Nyabor
Tel: 084-333 188
Fax: 084-333 288
www.tanahmas.com.my
One of Sibu's best hotels with 120 rooms and suites, and a winner of awards for both accommodation and service. This is popular with local businessmen; offers river views, a good Chinese restaurant and a swimming pool. **$$$**

Hotel Capitol 88
19 Jalan Wong Nai Siong
Tel: 084-336 444
Fax: 084-311 706
Clean, comfortable rooms with air conditioning, and a 10-minute walk from the

express boat jetty. Good value and convenient for early morning departures upriver. **$**

KAPIT

Regency Pelagus Resort
Rejang River
Tel: 084-799 050
Fax: 084-799 060
www.theregencyhotel.com.my/pelagus
An Iban-longhouse-inspired resort situated just below the treacherous Pelagus Rapids in an untouched area of longhouses. A great place to simply relax, surrounded by rainforest. Has a small swimming pool, and activities include river safaris, nature excursions and trips to the nearby Iban longhouse, Rumah George. **$$$**

Ark Hill Inn
Lot 451 Jalan Penghulu Geridang
Tel: 084-796 168
Fax: 084-797 168
Just 19 rooms in this friendly hotel. Clean and reasonably priced, they come with air conditioning, TV, fridge and hot showers. Also organises river trips and longhouse visits. **$**

Greenland Inn
463 Jalan Teo Chow Beng
Tel: 084-796 388
Fax: 084-796 708
This small 1-star hotel has clean, comfortable rooms, air conditioning, TV, fridge and ensuite bathrooms – especially welcome after a journey upriver. **$**

BELAGA

Bee Lian Inn
Belaga Bazaar
Tel: 085-461 416
This is a small hotel in the middle of the town, with air-conditioned rooms of an adequate standard. **$**

Belaga Hotel
Tel: 086-461 244
A friendly hotel with restaurant downstairs and some air-conditioned rooms, TV, hot showers and a laundry service that is particularly welcome after a longhouse visit. **$**

MUKAH

Kingwood Resort Mukah
Jalan Mukah Balingian
Sungei Penian
Tel: 084-873 450
Fax: 084-872 288
A 4-star beachside resort with swimming pool and bicycles for rental. All accommodation is currently in the one building, but chalets are planned for 2007. **$$**

King Ing Hotel
2 Jalan Panggung
Tel: 084-871 400
Fax: 084-871 429
Located near the town's colourful old bazaar and a Chinese temple, overlooking the Mukah river. For character and local flavour it is the best place to stay. **$**

Lamin Dana
Kampung Tellian, Mukah
Tel/fax: 082-241 735
e-mail: info@lamindana.com
Has an excellent homestay programme that enables guests to experience authentic Melanau culture. Located near the river, it is the ideal base from which to take part in the local festivals, the biggest being Pesta Kaul in April. **$**

BINTULU

Plaza Regency Hotel Bintulu
Jalan Abang Galau
Tel: 086-335 111
Fax: 086-332 742
Bintulu's best hotel with a rooftop swimming pool, nice restaurant with Western food and elegantly furnished rooms. The bar with live entertainment is a popular spot to unwind. **$$**

Hoover Hotel
Jalan Keppel
Tel: 086-337 166
Fax: 086-332 742
A popular and moderately priced hotel in the centre of the old town. **$**

My House Inn
Jalan Taman Sri Dagong
Tel: 086-336 339
Fax: 086-332 050
One of the many inexpensive hotels in the city centre, this small, friendly place has clean rooms and air conditioning.

MIRI

Mega Hotel
Lot 907, Jalan Merbau
Tel: 085-432 432
Fax: 085-433 433
www.megahotel.net
A centrally located 4-star hotel with spacious rooms, good facilities including a pool, business centre and a popular Chinese restaurant. **$$$**

Miri Marriot Resort & Spa
Jalan Temenggong Datuk Oyong Lawai
Tel: 085-421 121
Fax: 085-421 099
http://marriott.com/property/property page/myymc
Once known as the Rihga Royal, this hotel has good facilities, including what is said to be the largest swimming pool in Malaysia next to the sea, and a full-service Mandara spa. **$$$**

Parkcity Everly Hotel
Jalan Temenggong Datuk Oyong Lawai
Tel: 085-418 888
Fax: 085-419 999
www.vhhotels.com
Located along the Miri river and facing the new Marina Bay development, this was the first 5-star hotel in Miri, opening as a Holiday Inn. Now under new management, this business hotel still offers spacious rooms and good food. **$$$**

Brooke Inn
Jalan Brooke
Tel: 085-412 881
Fax: 085-420 899
This old stalwart is a good location for budget travellers, close to the old town, bus station, Visitor's Information Centre and almost next door to Taman Seroja food stalls; friendly staff. **$**

MARUDI

Grand Hotel
Lot 350 Backlane, Marudi
Tel: 085-755 711/755 712
Fax: 085-755 293
Probably the best hotel in town, with some air-conditioned rooms, close to the boat jetty. Useful source of information for upriver journeys. **$–$$**

MULU

Royal Mulu Resort
Gunung Mulu National Park
Tel: 085-790 100
Fax: 085-790 101
www.royalmuluresort.com
Located by the river just outside the boundary of the national park, close to all the rainforest attractions. A comfortable resort with friendly staff, it offers a wide range of amenities and activities, including a bolted wall for rock climbing, a spa offering aromatherapy, massages and scrubs, as well as ATV quad bike safari tours. **$$**

BA KELALAN

Apple Lodge
Tel: 085-285 385
This little lodging house near the airport is clean and simple, providing adequate and friendly accommodation. **$**

BARIO

This highland valley has the perfect climate for trekking. Because of the lack of telephones, it is best to decide on your accommodation when your flight arrives; many guest houses have representatives waiting at the airport.

Tarawe's Lodge
Mobile tel: 019-438 1777
This small lodge, run by well-known local John Tarawe, is close to the airport and the main bazaar. Provides friendly service and big older-style rooms with two or three beds. Owners can assist with trekking advice and guides. **$**

SABAH

KOTA KINABALU

Shangri-La's Tanjung Aru Resort
Tanjung Aru
Tel: 088-225 800
Fax: 088-217 155
www.shangri-la.com
A very popular and well-regarded resort on a small headland, now grown to include two wings, the original Tanjung and the taller Kinabalu wings. Beautiful and spacious gardens; ferry serice to nearby islands. Heavily booked during peak season. **$$$$**

Sutera Harbour Resort
Tel: 088-318 888
Fax: 088-317 777 (Pacific Sutera)
Fax: 088-312 020 (Magellan Sutera)
www.suteraharbour.com
Comprising two hotels, the Pacific Sutera and Magellan Sutera, this sprawling resort sits on 156 hectares (384 acres) of reclaimed land overlooking a bay of islands, five minutes from downtown Kota Kinabalu. With an excellent Mandara Spa, a pool, tennis courts, signing facilities at adjacent golf and yacht club, and access to over a dozen restaurants. **$$$$**

Hyatt Regency Kinabalu
Jalan Datuk Saleh Sulong
Tel: 088-221 234
Fax: 088-225 972
www.kinabalu.regency.hyatt.com
This is a long-established, always pleasant hotel. Rooms enjoy magnificent sunset views over the waterfront and out to the nearby islands, and come with marble baths and balconies. **$$$**

The Jesselton Hotel
69 Jalan Gaya
Tel: 088-223 333
Fax: 088-241 401
www.jesseltonhotel.com
KK's oldest hotel has been delightfully restored but still retains a nostalgic air and the same gracious service. The popular coffeeshop is now run as an Italian restaurant, although some of the old local favourites are still available here at lunchtime. **$$$**

Layang Layang Island Resort
Pulau Layang Layang
Tel: 03-2162 2877
Fax: 03-2162 2980
www.layanglayang.com
Luxury resort on coral atoll 300 km (185 miles) from Kota Kinabalu surrounded by some of Malaysia's most dramatic dive sites. Offers comfortable rooms, a swimming pool, and fully serviced Padi dive centre. **$$$**

Le Meridien
Jalan Tun Fuad Stephens
Tel: 088-322 222
Fax: 088-322 223
http://kotakinabalu.lemeridien.com
The capital's newest 5-star hotel, Le Meridien faces the South China Sea. Some rooms come with sea views. The hotel offers the usual mod cons expected of an international-class hotel; within easy walking distance of the business and entertainment districts. **$$$**

Beverly Hotel
Lorong Kemajuan
Tel: 088-258 998
Fax: 088-258 778
www.vhhotels.com
This conveniently located 4-star hotel offers rooms with good views of Mount Kinabalu, a small free-form swimming pool and friendly service. **$$**

Backpacker Lodge ("Lucy's Homestay")
Lorong Dewan, Australia Place
Tel: 088-261 495
Fax: 088-261 495
A basic backpackers' lodge with dormitories, in a convenient location in the city, close to everything you need before heading into the interior. Lucy's has spawned many imitations, but no one matches her genuine warmth and friendliness. **$**

City Inn
41 Jalan Pantai
Tel: 088-218 933
Fax: 088-218 937
An budget hotel with 33 rooms, right in the heart of town. Good value and often full. **$**

Trekkers Lodge Kota Kinabalu
30 Jalan Haji Saman (opposite Wisma Merdeka)
Tel: 088-252 263
Fax: 088-258 263
www.trekkerslodge.com
Its ideal location in the heart of town is one of the reasons this clean and friendly spot is one of KK's favourite budget places. Also provides free transport from KK airport. Single and double rooms as well as air-conditioned and fan-cooled dormitories. Internet and laundry services. **$**

Town Inn
31–33 Jalan Pantai
Tel: 088-225 823
Fax: 088-217 762
Even smaller than the nearby City Inn, this hotel offers 24 rooms with good facilities; good value. **$**

Kinabalu Park

Kinabalu Park HQ (Sutera Sanctuary Lodges)
Reservations office: Lot G15, Ground Floor, Wisma Sabah, Kota Kinabalu
Tel: 088-243 629
Fax: 088-259 552
www.suterasanctuarylodges.com
Book in advance for accommodation at the park headquarters. Options range from dormitories to twin-bed cabins to comfortable self-contained lodges. Accommodation at Laban Rata higher up the mountain (Waras and Panar Laban huts, Gunting Lagadan Hostel and Laban Rata Resthouse) should also be booked here. **$–$$$$**

Mesilau Nature Resort
Reservations office: Lot G15, Ground Floor, Wisma Sabah, Kota Kinabalu
Tel: 088-243 629
Fax: 088-259 552
www.suterasanctuarylodges.com
Located at the foot of Mount Kinabalu, in the beautiful wild eastern portion of the park, Mesilau offers a range of attractive lodges. A challenging 5½-km (3-mile) trail up Mount Kinabalu starts from here. **$–$$$$**

Poring Hot Springs
Reservations office: Lot G15, Ground Floor, Wisma Sabah, Kota Kinabalu
Tel: 088-243 629
Fax: 088-259 552
www.suterasanctuarylodges.com
Accommodation in the hot springs region of the park include a hostel and 4 lodges. **$–$$$**

Kundasang

Kinabalu Pine Resort
Kundasang
Tel: 088-889 388
Fax: 088-889 288
e-mail: k_pine2002@yahoo.com.sg
The most attractive accommodation outside Kinabalu Park, with chalets facing Mount Kinabalu; the resort offers a pleasant open-air bar decorated with native orchids and an adequate restaurant. Very busy during local school holidays. **$$**

Perkasa Hotel Mt Kinabalu
Kundasang
Tel: 088-889 511
Fax: 088-889 101
e-mail: hpmk@tm.net.my
www.perkasahotel.com.my
Most rooms enjoy great views of Mount Kinabalu. Good facilities including tennis (bring your own racket), reflexology centre and a small shop. The hotel, just 5 km (3 miles) from the entrance to Kinabalu Park, is also a 20-minute drive from Mt Kinabalu Golf Course. Room rates include breakfast and dinner. **$$**

Kinabalu Rose Cabin
Kundasang
Tel: 088-886 233
Fax: 088-889 800
e-mail: kkrc@streamyx.com
Just 2 km (1¼ miles) from Kinabalu Park HQ and facing the mountain, this hotel offers basic rooms with bathroom plus backpackers' dormitories. The gardens are considerably more beautiful than the hotel interior, however. **$–$$**

PANTAI DALIT

Shangri-La's Rasa Ria Resort
Pantai Dalit, Tuaran
Tel: 088-792 888
Fax: 088-792 777/792 000
www.shangri-la.com
Fronting a 3-km (1¾-mile) powder-white beach, this luxurious modern holiday resort has a 18-hole championship golf course, a spa and a nature reserve with orangutans and long-tail macaques. Activities include nature treks, crabbing, fishing and horseriding as well as watersports and beach activities. **$$$$**

KARAMBUNAI

Nexus Resort Karambunai
Menggatal
Tel: 088-411 222
Fax: 088-411 028
www.nexusresort.com
This luxurious resort is about 30 minutes from Kota Kinabalu by road, situated on a pristine beach adjacent to an 18-hole golf course designed by Ronald Fream. There is a watersports centre on the nearby lagoon. The Borneo Spa features treatments inspired by traditional Bornean practices. **$$$$**

TUNKU ABDUL RAHMAN PARK

Pulau Manukan
Reservations office: Lot G15, Ground Floor, Wisma Sabah
Tel: 088-243 629
Fax: 088-259 552
www.suterasanctuarylodges.com
Twenty chalets near the beach or on the hillside of the largest island in this marine park, with a restaurant serving continental and Asian dishes. Activities include snorkelling, diving, trekking, and fish feeding. **$$$**
Gayana Resort
Pulau Gaya
Tel: 088-264 461
Fax: 088-264 460

e-mail: gayana@tm.net.my
Located on the border of the park on Gaya Island, the resort has stilted chalets built over the sea, backed by the rainforest. Watersports facilities and jungle walks available. **$$**

TENOM

Asrama
Agricultural Research Station
Tel: 087-737 952
Fax: 087-737 571
Camping facilities are available with the Sabah Agricultural Park, near an attractive lake. **$**
Perkasa Hotel Tenom
Tel: 087-735 811/736 166
Fax: 087-736 134
Overlooking Tenom town, on top of a hill, the seven-storey hotel has full facilities and great views. You can call to be picked up from the railway station and staff are eager to help with local knowledge. **$**

LABUAN

Hotel Sheraton Labuan
462 Jalan Merdeka
Tel: 087-422 000
Fax: 087-422 222
www.sheraton.com/labuan
Situated opposite the financial park, the Sheraton offers the best in service and cuisine. With 178 rooms with balconies looking out to great views. **$$$**
Hotel Global
Jalan okk Aawang Besar
Tel: 087-425 201
Fax: 087-425 180
A hotel with good facilities; good value. **$$**

SANDAKAN

Sandakan is the base for visitors embarking on tours to east Sabah. Many people choose to stay outside the town itself, at Sepilok, where it is quieter and probably safer.

Hotel City View
Block 23, Lebuh Tiga (3rd Avenue)
Tel: 089-271 122
Fax: 089-273112
Located in the centre of downtown Sandakan, this hotel is popular with budget travellers. **$$**
Hotel Sandakan
Block 83, Lebuh Empat (4th Avenue)
Tel: 089-221 122
Fax: 089-221 100
www.hotelsandakan.com.my
The newest hotel here conveniently located in town, popular with local businessmen. Its 105 rooms and suites offer wireless Internet access and satellite TV. There's also a good range of F&B outlets, including a Chinese restaurant offering dim sum for breakfast and lunch. **$$**
Pulau Selingan
Tour operators offer package tours to Pulau Selingan in the Turtle Islands Park. Alternatively, book directly with Crystal Quest (Tel: 089-212 711; Fax: 089-212 712; e-mail: cquest@tm.net.my). A speed-boat departs from the Sabah Parks jetty on Jalan Buli Sim Sim in Sandakan for Selingan at 9.30am daily, and leaves the island for Sandakan at 7am daily. **$$$**
Sabah Hotel
Jalan Utara Km 1
Tel: 089-213 299
Fax: 089-271 271
e-mail: shsdkfm@tm.net.my
Standing on the site of a former colonial governor's house, this modern hotel is located slightly out of town but in a pleasant hilly environment. It has a swimming pool backed by forest. **$$$**

PULAU LANKAYAN

Lankayan Island Dive Resort
Langkayan Island
Tel: 089-765 200
Fax: 089-763 575/763 563
www.lankayan-island.com
A luxurious resort on its own coral island in the Sulu Sea north of Sandakan.

There are good wreck dives and corals nearby, as well as a well-equipped dive centre located at the end of a jetty that is particularly favoured for sunset viewing. **$$$**

SEPILOK

Sepilok Nature Resort
2½km (1½ miles), Jalan Sepilok
Tel: 089-535 001
Fax: 089-535 002
www.sepilok.com
An upmarket resort adjacent to the Orang-utan Rehabilitation Centre, in a garden setting. Offering all the necessary creature comforts that you will appreciate after a day of trekking. It has timber air-conditioned chalets with private verandahs overlooking a natural lake. **$$$**
Sepilok Jungle Resort
Jalan Sepilok
Tel: 089-533 031
Fax: 089-533 029
www.sepilokjungleresort.com
The lodge is the handiwork of owners Datuk John and Datin Judy Lim. It offers a range of accommodation options, from campsites to air-conditioned chalets set amid beautifully land-scaped gardens filled with native birds and butterflies. **$–$$**
Sepilok Bed & Breakfast
Jalan Aboretum, off Jalan Sepilok
Tel: 089-534 050
Fax: 089-675 109
www.sepilokbednbreakfast.com
Located 1 km (½ mile) from the Orang-utan Rehabilitation Centre, this long-established B & B has greatly improved since a change in ownership. Clean, airy and in an attractive garden setting, it offers double and family rooms as well as a dormitory. **$**

KINABATANGAN RIVER

The major concentration of wildlife lodges along the Kinabatangan is near the village of Sukau, although a number of tour operators are now establishing lodges at Kampung Bilit, with a forest lodge further upriver at Danau Girang. All tour operators are able to offer package tours including transport, tours, accommodation and food.

Sukau Rainforest Lodge
Tel: 088-438 300
Fax: 088-438 307
www.borneoecotours.com
A comfortable lodge operated by Borneo Eco Tours, this has expanded considerably since it was established over a decade ago. It has a riverside dining/fishing deck and wildlife viewing decks; elephants regularly migrate along a traditional passage behind the lodge. **$$$**

Sukau River Lodge
Tel: 088-246 000
Fax: 088-231 758
www.wildlife-expeditions.com
The pioneer in the Sukau region, Wildlife Expeditions now offers two riverside lodges here; the original lodge is right at the junction of the Menanggol and the Kinabatangan rivers. **$$**

Sukau Tomanggong
Riverside Lodge
Tel: 089-534 900, 534 300, 013-856 0969
Fax: 089-534 900
e-mail: nbsafari@streamyx.com
A couple of kilometres by road downriver from Sukau, this lodge is in a beautiful location facing a limestone outcrop, with a riverside restaurant and simple twin rooms. **$$**

Bilit

Nature Lodge Kinabatangan
Kampung Bilit
Tel: 088-230 534
Fax: 088-258 263
www.trekkerslodge.com
Set on the bank of the Kinabatangan River facing the tiny Orang Sungei village of Kampung Bilit, this friendly budget lodge with twin rooms and dormitories is in an ideal spot for viewing wildlife such as long-tail macaques, gibbons and orangutans. A trail behind

leads to an oxbow lake. Guided treks available. **$**

Danau Girang

Uncle Tan's Wildlife Camp
Tel: 089-531 639
Mobile tel: 016-8244 749
www.uncletan.com
Basic accommodation, good food and a friendly atmosphere make this lakeside lodge set in the forest very popular with serious wildlife enthusiasts and budget travellers. Its 3-day/2-night package includes lodging, meals, transfers and jungle and river safaris. **$$**

Lahad Datu

The Executive Hotel
Jalan Teratai
Tel: 089-881 333
Fax: 089-881 777
e-mail: tehotel@tm.net.my
This hotel, regarded as the best in town, is fine if you're just looking for an overnight stop. **$$**

Danum Valley

Borneo Rainforest Lodge
Danum Valley
Tel: 088-251 634
Fax: 088-267 637
www.borneorainforestlodge.net
Inspired by Tiger Tops in Nepal, this pleasant nature resort is located beside the Segama River facing a misty and untrammelled jungle. Built on elevated plankwalks, the 24 chalets are comfortable with private bathrooms and hot showers. The resort also specialises in birding and wildlife excursions. Guides and talks are available for visitors. **$$$**

Tawau

Belmont Marco Polo Hotel
Jalan Kelinik
Tel: 089-777 988
Fax: 089-763 739
e-mail: bmph@tm.net.my
The premier hotel in Tawau,

this is popular with tourists as well as businessmen. Cantonese, Continental, Italian and local food is available, and there is a good lounge bar with live music. **$$**

Pan Sabah Hotel
Jalan Stephen Tan
Tel: 089-762 488
Fax: 089-763 878
This 24-room budget hotel offers good value and has a convenient location close to the bus station. **$**

Semporna

Seafest Hotel
Jalan Kastam (Seafest Jetty)
Tel: 089-782 333
Fax: 089-782 555
e-mail: seafest@tm.net.my
The best and newest hotel in town, right on the jetty where dive boats depart. **$$**

Pulau Sipadan

All accommodation on this world-class dive site were closed by the government in December 2004 in order to protect the environment. Most dive operators previously based on Sipadan now have accommodation on the nearby islands of Mabul and Kapalai, and organise day trips to Sipadan.

Pulau Kapalai

Sipadan-Kapalai Dive Resort
Tel: 089-765 200
Fax: 089-763 575
www.sipadan-kapalai.com
Built as an upmarket "water village" with comfortable chalets on stilts over a reef. These are linked by wooden walkways and have verandahs looking towards a distant horizon of the sea and sky. The resort organises dives around Kapalai, as well as day trips to Pulau Sipadan, only 15–20 minutes away.

Pulau Mabul

This small, flat island, about 20 minutes from Sipadan, has a very basic fishing village. It is now packed with resorts, some of which transferred here when all Sipadan accommodation was closed. Most offer dive packages with lodgings, transfers and meals included. Rates differ for divers and non-divers, and vary depending on whether air transport – from Kota Kinabalu to Tawau – is included.

Borneo Divers Mabul Resort
Tel: 088-222 226
Fax: 088-221 550
www.borneodivers.info
The pioneer operator on Sipadan now has 30 simply appointed chalets on a stretch of white, sandy beach on Mabul, all with views of the beach, plus a new swimming pool.

Mabul & Smart Divers Resort
Tel: 088-230 006/7
Fax: 088-242 003
www.sipadan-mabul.com.my
This resort consists of 45 beach chalets nestled under coconut trees and looking across to Sipadan Island. There's a lovely beach in front plus a small swimming pool.

Mabul Water Bungalows
Tel: 088-230 006
Fax: 088-242 003
www.mabulwaterbungalows.com
Fourteen luxurious water bungalows on stilts over the sea. The resort offers a host of sea sports activities, from diving to ocean kayaking.

Sipadan Water Village Resort
Tel: 089-752 996/751 777
Fax: 089-752 997
www.swvresort.com
A stylish water village built on stilts, which reaches out over shallow reefs from the main island. Comfortable and quiet with few distractions, a good restaurant and dive shop.

E ATING OUT

RECOMMENDED RESTAURANTS

WHERE TO EAT

Peninsular Malaysia

All of Malaysia's medium- and top-class hotels have decent restaurants, with some of the nation's best found in five-star hotels. Hotels at the very top of the range will probably have at least one Western outlet.

Hotels also usually offer high tea on weekends, and their coffee houses serve buffet breakfast, lunch and sometimes dinner. Western quick-service concepts such as McDonald's, KFC and Burger King are everywhere for those who need a break from local food. Coffee house chains like Dome, Coffee Bean, Starbucks and Gloria Jean are found in all the big cities.

Otherwise, try the local fare, which is not only different according to where you are, but sub-divides into ethnic and regional varieties too. For instance, Peranakan cuisine, which combines Chinese and Malay ingredients and cooking styles, is best enjoyed in Melaka and Penang, while the east coast states of Kelantan and Terengganu offer authentic Malay cuisine with a variety of unique dishes such as nasi dagang (long-grain and glutinous rice cooked in coconut milk and eaten with tuna curry), ayam percik (barbecued chicken) and nasi kerabu (rice salad with herbs). (See cuisine feature pages 93–7)

The best local food is often served in hawker stalls, sold on the streets or in coffee shops, although sometimes you can get authentic preparations in restaurants.

Breakfast is usually served 6–10.30am, lunch 11.30am–2.30pm, and dinner 6.30–11pm, although some places open until 2am or even later. Note that large restaurants charge a 10 percent government tax and 5 percent service tax.

Alcohol is expensive in Malaysia compared to some other Asian destinations. While it is forbidden for Muslims, it is freely available in pubs, hotels, Western restaurants and Chinese eateries, as well as in supermarkets in towns. It is however not as freely available in the traditionally Islamic states of Terengganu and Kelantan in the east coast. Duty-free wine, beer and other liquor are readily available on the islands of Langkawi, Labuan and Tioman.

Local coffee and tea pack a punch, and may be too sweet for unsuspecting drinkers as they are sometimes served with condensed milk and sugar. Ipoh white coffee has won a wide following because of its creamy smooth taste and strong flavour. It is widely available in coffee shops.

Sarawak

Other than typical Malaysian favourites such as roti canai (Indian flaky bread) and chicken rice, and the usual Western fare often found in the big hotels, Kuching has its own specialities as well. These offer influences derived from Malay, Indian, Chinese and Dayak heritages. The spicy Sarawak laksa is a big favourite, a noodle dish cooked in chicken stock with coconut cream and spices, as is umei – a Melanau dish of raw, marinated fish blended with limes, chilli and shallots. There are jungle vegetables like midin and paku – baby fern served boiled or fried with the spicy addition of belacan (prawn paste) and garlic and perhaps a hint of oyster sauce. Fresh seafood, venison, wild boar, pansoh manok – an Iban chicken dish cooked in bamboo tubes with rice wine – are not to be missed.

Kuching has some very good hawker centres offering Chinese and Malay food at reasonable prices. A favourite is the Open-Air Market, which is actually covered with a roof and located off Jalan Khoo Hun Yeang near Electra House. For those who prefer dining in air-conditioned environments, try the wide selection of local favourites at the Food Court in Medan Pelita, just off Main Bazaar.

Sabah

Dining in Sabah tends to be just as casual as the general lifestyle, with open-fronted restaurants, food stalls and simple coffee shops being very popular. Excellent and relatively inexpensive seafood is particularly popular with visitors and at least one meal in one of the main seafood restaurants is a must for tour groups, especially from Hong Kong, Taiwan and China. Sabah has its own specialties, especially vegetable dishes. Best of all is sayur manis, a green leafy vegetable with a slightly crunchy stem and sweet green leaves. Try it in oyster sauce, or for the Asiaphile, in a spicy sauce of sambal belacan (chilli with prawn paste), which has a heady, fishy tang that takes time to get used to.

PRICE CATEGORIES

Prices of meals for two people, including drinks, but excluding alcohol such as wine.

$$$$	more than RM200
$$$	RM100–200
$$	RM50–100
$	less than RM50

RESTAURANT LISTINGS

KUALA LUMPUR AND ENVIRONS

KUALA LUMPUR

Chinese

Chef Choi
159 Jalan Ampang
Tel: 03-2163 5866
Cantonese cuisine with modern twists. The foie gras in a caramelised superior stock is sublime, but it's the superlative "Buddha Jumps Over the Wall" soup, rich with morsels of abalone, dried scallops and black chicken, that truly steals the thunder. Other popular favourites include prawns in wine and saffron sauce, and fragrant duck wrapped in pancakes. Open daily for lunch and dinner. **$$$**

Hakka Restaurant
6 Jalan Kia Peng
Tel: 03-2143 1908
With a heritage of over 40 years and solid Hakka culinary traditions, this family-run restaurant is the best place for authentic Hakka food. Unmissable are the Hakka noodles with minced pork sauce, *mui choy kau yuk* (braised pork belly layered with preserved vegetables) and the unique stewed fish head with fermented red rice. Open daily for lunch and dinner. **$$**

Restoran Oversea
84-88 Jalan Imbi
Tel: 03-2144 9911
It's been around 30 years and has a loyal following for its Chinese cuisine with contemporary twists. Think butter-fried crab claws, black pepper lamb ribs and crispy cod with pork belly. The classic favourites are excellent too; try the steamed marbled goby, chaa siu (barbecued pork) and roast suckling pig. Open daily for lunch and dinner. **$$$**

Restoran Teochew
270–272 Jalan Changkat Thambi Dollah, off Jalan Pudu
Tel: 03-2141 4704

An all-day dim sum place, serving 30 to 40 varieties every day from Mon to Sat, and a whopping 100 types on Sun. There are also other Teochew favourites such as braised goose and fish paste noodles. Open daily 7.30am–3pm, 6pm–midnight. **$$$**

Soo Kee Restaurant
14 Medan Imbi, off Jalan Imbi
Tel: 03-2148 1234
Simple Chinese restaurant that has been here for over 50 years. Serves excellent beef *kway teow* (flat rice noodles), *saang ha min* (egg noodles with huge prawns), fried Hong Kong *kailan* (Chinese kale) and various Cantonese dishes. **$**

Soong Kee Beef Noodles
3 Jalan Tun Tan Siew Sin
Tel: 03-2078 1484
The best beef balls in the city are here at Soong Kee. Enjoy them in soup, accompanied by springy egg noodles tossed in a soy-based sauce with minced beef and garlic. These Hakka specialties are wonderful dipped in the own-made hot and sour garlic-chilli sauce. Open Mon–Sat 11am–midnight. **$**

Sun Hong Muk Koot Teh
35, 37, 39 & 41 Medan Imbi
Tel: 03-2141 4064
A good stop for *bak kut teh*, a hearty herbal broth with pork ribs, organ meat and bean curd puffs, eaten with *you tiao* (Chinese crullers) and yam rice. Try the sweet-sourish pig's trotters in black vinegar and chicken in rice wine too. Open daily 5am–midnight. **$**

French

Frangipani
25 Changkat Bukit Bintang
Tel: 03-2144 3001
This chic French fine-dining outlet, with tables set artfully around a pool, offers a lovely intimate atmosphere. Must-haves are the tea-smoked salmon with coffee-flavoured mash, roasted duck confit with

mustard cream, and its wicked signature dessert, chocolate ganache with candied almond meringue. Open Tues–Sun for dinner. **$$$–$$$$**

Le Bouchon
14 & 16 Changkat Bukit Bintang
Tel: 03-2142 7633
Le Table d'Hôte's more refined sister restaurant with cosy interiors. Classic French dishes such as garlicky spinach escargots, goose liver terrine, braised ox tongue with gherkins, mushrooms and Madeira sauce. An extensive wine list with a French bias supports the food. Open Tues–Fri for lunch and dinner, Sat and Sun for dinner. **$$$**

Le Table d'Hôte
38 Jalan Bidara (behind Hotel Istana)
Tel: 03-2145 4964
A casual bistro-style restaurant that opens out to the street. Try the braised pork knuckle in apple sauce, coq au vin and *boeuf bourgignon*. Drink French and New World wines supplied by the adjoining Tastevin Cellars at near retail prices. The Sunday brunch is popular with French expats. Open Tues–Sat for lunch and dinner, Sun 9am–5pm. **$$–$$$**

German

Deutsches Bierhaus
46 Changkat Bukit Bintang
Tel: 03-2143 2268
This wood-clad, country pub-like German restaurant dishes up hearty platters of home-made pork sausages and a superb pork knuckle, which you can wash down with a range of German lagers. Popular with expats. Open daily for lunch and dinner. **$$$–$$$**

Indian

Bangles Restaurant
270 Jalan Ampang
Tel: 03-4252 4100

Objets d'art and some 30,000 glass bangles dripping from the ceiling adorn this restaurant in a grand old mansion. The cuisine is northern Indian: *dum bryani* (rice cooked with spiced meat), *shish kebab*, fish *tikka masala* and butter chicken Mughlai. Alfresco seating in the garden with a barbecue. Open daily for lunch and dinner. **$$–$$$**

Bombay Palace
215 Jalan Tun Razak
Tel: 03-2145 4241/7220
Fine Indian food in a beautiful setting; with large variety of spicy and non-spicy meat and vegetable dishes, including northern Indian breads. **$$$**

Passage Thru India
4A Jalan Delima, off Jalan Bukit Bintang (behind the Indonesian Embassy)
Tel: 03-2145 0366
Cosy interior decorated with Indian collectibles. Best for tandoori prawns, chicken *tikka*, naan breads and delicious, creamy *lassi* (yoghurt drink). Live traditional music played in the evening. **$$$**

Saravanaa Bhavan
1007 Selangor Mansion, Jalan Masjid India
Tel: 03-2287 1228
Outstanding Indian vegetarian food. Have a banana leaf meal – rice served on a banana leaf with an assortment of sides, from pumpkin mash and chilli *paneer* (fried cottage cheese with chillies and onions), to cauliflower Manchuria and mushroom *roghan josh* (mushrooms cooked in yoghurt and spices). Open daily 8am–10.30pm. **$**

Sithique Nasi Kandar Pulau Pinang
233 Jalan Tuanku Abdul Rahman
Mobile tel: 016-382 4867
As with the many *nasi kandar* stalls in the city, it is curry galore here. Take your pick from fish-head, squid, beef, lamb and other

curries, to be splashed over fluffy white rice or to go with Indian breads like *roti canai* (flaky bread) and *thosai* (a paper-thin pancake). Open Wed–Mon 7am–7.30pm, Tues 7am–4pm. **$**

Vishalachirs Restoran
19 Jalan Travers, Brickfields
Tel: 03-2274 6819
This simple Chettiar family-run restaurant serves excellent traditional meals that are subtle blends of sweet, sour and lightly spicy. A typical meal offers rice on banana leaf with dhal and condiments such as *sambar* (stew made from pulses), *puli kulambu* (tamarind curry), and *rasam* (spicy soup), ending with sweet *payasam* (pudding). Open daily 11am–10.45pm. **$**

International

Alexis Bistro
Lot f15a, 1st Floor, Bangsar Shopping Centre, 285 Jalan Maarof
Tel: 03-2287 1388
Alexis serves fine examples from various cuisines: Italian (Napoletana and Margherita pizzas), English (fish and chips) and Malaysian (Sarawak laksa). Order the flavoursome herbed rice *nasi ulam*, with a spread of Malay-style dishes such as prawns on lemongrass skewers and jungle fern in chilli paste. Open daily 9am–midnight. **$$**

Coliseum Café
98–100 Jalan Tunku Abdul Rahman
Tel: 03-2692 6270
A colonial setting so real it is easy to imagine bushy-moustached white planters at the bar complaining about the heat. Try a gunner or a gin sling – then have a sizzling ribeye, baked crab-meat, or an English potpie from the wood-fired oven. Chinese and Malay dishes are on the menu too. Open Mon–Sat 10am–10pm, Sun 9am–10pm. **$$**

Peter Hoe Beyond
2nd Floor, Lee Rubber Building, 145 Jalan Tun H.S. Lee
Tel: 03-2026 9788
After shopping at Peter Hoe's ambience-filled

homeware store, head for his café. Order the broccoli–carrot quiche or chicken burger on homemade bread. The eclectic menu also features a tofu and orange salad and oven-roasted pumpkin soup. Scones and cupcakes for tea. Open daily 10am–7pm. **$–$$**

Shook!
Feast Floor, Starhill Gallery, 181 Jalan Bukit Bintang
Tel: 03-2716 8535
Adjoins JW Marriott Hotel, this chic inclusion into KL's eating scene has four kitchens: Chinese, Japanese, Italian and Grill. It's spacious and contemporary and you can choose food from all the kitchens. **$$$**

Telawi Street Bistro
1 Jalan Telawi 2, Bangsar
Tel: 03-2284 3168
In the heart of Bangsar's famous nightlife hub, this restaurant serves a wide array of international dishes based on a pan-global concept. The usual local favourites are served, along with Thai, Japanese, Italian and fine French fare. Very modern, minimalist setting with good ambience. **$$**

Top Hat
7 Jalan Kia Peng
Tel: 03-2142 8611
A gorgeous old bungalow behind the nightspots, with excellent Malay, Peranakan and Western fusion fare such as the Peranakan "top hats" – pastry cups filled with shredded yam bean, chicken and mushroom pie, and grilled rack of lamb. Set meals are good; book ahead. **$$$**

Japanese

Benkay Japanese Restaurant
Nikko Hotel, 165 Jalan Ampang
Tel: 03-2161 1111
Very elegant and authentic Japanese restaurant where the food style follows the decor. The sushi bar is especially popular for lunch. A great dessert is the green tea ice cream. **$$$**

Still Waters
Hotel Maya, 138 Jalan Ampang
Tel: 03-2711 8866
Exquisite *sosaku* (creative)

cuisine, combining Japanese and Western ingredients. There are delicately balanced dishes such as *den miso*-gratinated lamb, beef *wasabi* and pan-fried foie gras with daikon. For dessert, try the pandan *chawan mushi* (steamed egg custard with screwpine juice). Open daily for lunch and dinner. **$$$**

Malay

Bijan
3 Jalan Ceylon
Tel: 03-2031 3575
A cosy contemporary setting decorated with Malay artefacts, contemporary paintings and heritage textiles. Sumptuous Malay cuisine; try *masak lemak udang tempoyak* (prawns in fermented durian curry), chargrilled short beef ribs with *sambal* (chilli paste), and *kerabu pucuk paku* (jungle fern salad). **$$**

Enak
LG2, Feast Floor, Starhill Gallery, 181 Jalan Bukit Bintang
Tel: 03-2141 8973
Time-honoured family recipes are on the menu: Acehnese grilled prawns with a piquant fruit salad, slow-cooked beef with spices and herbs, steamed squid stuffed with mushrooms and more. The young coconut custard meringue is not to be missed. Open daily noon–midnight. **$$$**

The Gulai House
Carcosa Seri Negara
Tel: 03-2282 1888
Malay specialities, including satay and spicy curries in colonial setting. The restaurant is open daily for dinner only, but also serves a popular curry tiffin lunch on Sundays from noon to 2.30pm. **$$**

Rebung
4-2 Lorong Maarof, Bangsar Park
Tel: 03-2283 2119
Authentic dishes from the state of Negri Sembilan, such as aromatic *tempoyak daun kayu* (tapioca leaves in fermented durian curry) and spicy *rendang tok* (beef curry) topped with sweet young coconut slices, are served for buffet lunch and

dinner. Open daily noon–10.30pm. **$$**

Malaysian

CT Rose
Jalan Datuk Abdul Razak (opposite Sekolah Kebangsaan Kampung Baru)
Mobile tel: 016-997 8701
When the craving strikes, droves head for this biggest *nasi lemak* (coconut rice) stall in the city, complete with a stunning view of the Twin Towers. The *nasi lemak* is served with *sambal* (chilli paste) and a variety of sides, such as deep-fried anchovies, quail eggs and fried chicken. Open daily 6.30pm–5.30am. **$**

Kedai Ayam Panggang Wong Ah Wah
1, 3, 5, 7 & 9 Jalan Alor, off Jalan Bukit Bintang
Tel: 03-2144 2462
Local street food at its best here, down a bustling lane. Grilled chicken wings are the main draw, but equally lip-smacking are the grilled fish (such as stingray and mackerel), oyster omelette, and chilli-fried cockles. There's also satay from the stall in front. Open daily 5pm–3.45am, except alternate Mon. **$**

Little Penang Kafe
Lot F001 & F100, Mid Valley Megamall, Lingkaran Syed Putra
Tel: 03-2282 0215
Well regarded for its Penang-style noodles, from *char kway teow* (fried flat rice noodles) to the hot and sour *asam laksa* with a spicy tamarind fish gravy, to Hokkien prawn noodles. Order the multi-coloured ice *kacang*, a sweet shaved ice treat. Another branch at Suria KLCC (tel: 03-2163 0215). Open daily for lunch and dinner. **$–$$**

Madam Kwan's
F052, 1st Floor, Mid Valley Megamall, Lingkaran Syed Putra
Tel: 03-2287 2297
One of the three popular Madam Kwan's *nasi lemak* (coconut rice) restaurants in KL – the other two in KLCC (tel: 03-2026 2297) and Bangsar (tel: 03-2284 2297). The fragrant rice is served with chicken curry,

anchovy chilli paste, egg and more. There's also the well-loved *nasi bojari* – colourful fried rice paired with beef *rendang* (dry beef curry), fried chicken and *asam* (tamarind) prawns. Open daily 11am–11pm. **$–$$**

Sakura Café & Cuisine
Jalan Imbi
Tel: 03-2142 2319
Hawker fare in a restaurant setting, although the air conditioning is at sub-zero temperatures. Good *nasi lemak* (coconut rice), *laksa* (noodles in spicy gravy) and desserts; also steaks and other Western fare. **$$**

Sin Seng Nam Restaurant
2 Medan Pasar
Never mind the surly elderly waitstaff and old decor. This Hainanese coffeeshop has fabulous Hainanese chicken rice and chicken chops. Other must-tries include fish curry, *mee rebus* (noodles in a spicy gravy) and Indian *rojak* (salad). For breakfast, don't miss the local-style breakfast of toast with *kaya* (coconut jam), soft-boiled eggs and coffee. Open Mon–Fri 7am–2pm. **$**

Modern European/ Mediterranean

Cilantro Restaurant and Wine Bar
MiCasa All-Suite Hotel, 368B Jalan 1/68F, off Jalan Tun Razak
Tel: 03-2179 8000
Exquisite dishes that combine French and Japanese cooking styles and ingredients. Try the *wasabi*-crusted wagyu cheek, a creamy, zingy affair, and the *anago* risotto featuring saltwater eel fried as well as braised in a port reduction with sake and soy sauce. Friday set lunches, matched with wines, are popular. Open Mon–Sat for dinner, Fri for lunch only. **$$$$**

Med@Mgrohé
Rennaisance Kuala Lumpur
Jalan Sultan Ismail/Jalan Ampang
Tel: 03-2162 2233
With a welcoming interior and professional staff. The cuisine is Mediterranean-inspired and nurtured by a creative kitchen crew. Try the roasted rack of lamb, baked halibut and chocolate *tortino*. **$$$$**

Peranakan

Old China Café
11 Jalan Balai Polis
Tel: 03-2072 5915
Best time-trip café in KL, where the old-world ambience, vintage photos and memorabilia and marble-topped tables provide the perfect location for just as memorable Peranakan cuisine. Specialities include *laksa* (noodles in spicy gravy) and fish head in tamarind sauce. Try the delicious sago dessert called *gula melaka*. **$$**

Precious Old China Restaurant & Bar
Lot 2, Mezzanine Floor, Central Market, Jalan Hang Kasturi
Tel: 03-2273 7372
Perennial Peranakan favourites served here: "top hats" (pastry cups) filled with shredded yam bean, fish-head curry with salted fish, *kapitan* chicken (Peranakan-style chicken curry), and beef *rendang* (dry beef curry). Open daily for lunch and dinner. **$$–$$$**

Southeast Asian

Sao Nam
25 Tengkat Tong Shin
Tel: 03-2144 1225
Featuring a contemporary approach to traditional Vietnamese cuisine. The mangosteen salad is unique and so popular that regulars ring to pre-order. Reservations are essential. A well-priced wine list complements the superb food. **$$$**

Tamarind Springs
Jalan 1, Taman Tun Abdul Razak, Ampang Jaya
Tel: 03-4256 9300
Like its sister restaurant Tamarind Hill (1 Jalan Kerja Air Lama, Ampang; tel: 03-4256 9100), this atmospheric, open-concept outlet specialises in Indochinese cuisine – Thai, Laotian, Cambodian and Vietnamese. Has a complimentary shuttle bus service

from major hotels in KL. Open daily for lunch and dinner. **$$$**

Spanish

La Bodega
16 Jalan Telawi 2, Bangsar
Tel: 03-2287 8318
One of the longest-standing hangouts in Bangsar, and for good reason. Amid the Catalan ambience, enjoy authentic tapas like spicy prawns in Andalusia style, grilled lamb cutlets with garlic mayonnaise, and lobster and prawn croquettes. The drinks list focuses on Spanish and South American wines. Open Mon–Fri noon–1am, Sat and Sun 11am–1am. **$$$**

SELANGOR

Chinese

River View Seafood Restaurant
1 Jalan Besar, Pasir Penambang
Tel: 03-3289 6719
Very popular with tourists, this family-run eatery serves quality seafood dishes. It is breezy, and offers commanding views of the bridge, Bukit Melawati and the village. You won't go wrong with dishes such as buttered prawns, and fish in black pepper sauce. Open daily 11am–10pm. **$$**

Seafood Sin Kee
8 Jalan SG1/10, Pusat Penjaja, Taman Industri Bolton, Batu Caves
Tel: 03-6189 7972
Order the crabs with a spicy-sweet sauce, best mopped up with deep-fried bread rolls. Try also mussels in superior stock and wine, prawns tossed in cheese, and belly pork in soy sauce. Open daily for lunch and dinner. **$$**

Malay/Indian

Rahmaniah Mini Market
80 Jalan Sultan Ibrahim, Kuala Selangor
Tel: 03-3289 7723
Near Bukit Melawati in Kuala Selangor, this simple food outlet has excellent breads like *roti canai* (flaky

bread), with curries. It also serves *roti jala* (lacy pancakes) with chicken curry, *murtabak* (flaky bread with minced meat filling) as well as *mee goreng* (fried noodles). Open daily 5.30am–10.30pm. **$**

Sri Baratha Matha Vilas Restaurant
34 Jalan Tengku Kelana, Klang
Tel: 03-3372 9657
This is the place to have *mee goreng*, spicy fried noodles that even the late sultan of Selangor used to order to bring with him to London. S. Govindasamy has prepared this dish for half a century. It is served on a banana leaf, with slices of crispy battered prawn cakes. Open daily 7am–10.30pm. **$**

Western

Avanti
Sunway Lagoon Resort Hotel & Spa, Persiaran Lagoon, Bandar Sunway, Petaling Jaya
Tel: 03-7492 8000
The cuisine is described as Italian-American but expect traditional Italian favourites with a creative twist. The tenderloin with pan-seared goose liver and slipper lobster with pasta are recommended. With a good Italian and New World wine list. Try Sunday brunch with the 'singing chefs and waiters'. **$$$$**

Restoran Waterfall Café
88 Jalan Stesen, Kuala Selangor
Tel: 03-3289 2388
This family-owned café offers Western dishes like sandwiches and spaghetti bolognaise. But like every eatery in town, its specialties are Chinese seafood dishes. Open daily 10am–10pm. **$**

Uncle Chilli's
Hilton Petaling Jaya, 2 Jalan Barat, Petaling Jaya
Tel: 03-7955 9122
This has some of the best American-style New Zealand steaks in PJ. Of note are its BBQ ribs and sirloin steaks, but its pizzas and pastas are not bad either. A live band belts out current hits and requests from 9.30pm nightly except Sunday. Open daily noon–1am. **$$$$**

NORTHWESTERN PENINSULA

CAMERON HIGHLANDS

Tanah Rata's famous Indian fare outlets sit in a row opposite the bus station. Try **Suria**'s banana leaf rice and Indian breads. Opposite are Malay hawker stalls. Western set lunches are at **Café Downtown** and the **Highlander's Grill**. Brinchang's hawker fare is found at the bus terminal, and there are stalls throughout town selling Indian breads and curry. Good Chinese food can be found at **Kowloon Hotel**.
Bala's Holiday Chalet
Lot 55 Tanah Rata
Tel: 05-491 1660
Old English cottage restaurant, well known for its home-style cooking, especially its Indian curries; Western fare also available. **$$**
Gonbei
Cameron Highlands Resort
Tel: 05-491 1100
Excellent Japanese cuisine is served in a Zen-like setting that opens out to the rainforest. Has a *sake* bar with a range of traditional Japanese rice wines and whiskies. **$$$**
Kafe Palm Leaf
Brinchang
In front of Rosa Pasadena, dishes up good Thai, Western and local dishes at reasonable prices. **$**
The Smokehouse Hotel
Tanah Rata
Tel: 05-491 1215
Delectable cream teas, lunch and afternoon teas on the terrace, which on a fine day offers a view of the peaceful hills. English fare includes steaks, pies, seafood; light meals all day long in the conservatory. **$$$$**

FRASER'S HILL

The Smokehouse Hotel
Jalan Jeriau
Tel: 03-362 2226
Excellent high tea with scones and apple pie on the garden patio or in the cosy tea room. Dine in an elegant candlelit room on superb English pot roast with Yorkshire pudding, beef Wellington and home-made pies. Dress code applies. **$$$**

IPOH

FMS Bar
2 Jalan Sultan Idris Shah
Tel: 05-254 0591
This rather worn-down colonial gem by the Padang serves Western-style meals; its bar has hardly changed since British administrators sipped drinks at its counters. **$$**
Indulgence Restaurant and Jazz Room
15 Lorong Cecil Rae,
Taman Canning
Tel: 05-549 6941
In a city known for its Chinese hawker food, Indulgence stands out with its Modern European culinary direction. Local spices are paired with the best of the West in dishes like ginger-marinated rib-eye in miso soup and braised smoked duck in coconut. With a private dining room and a courtyard café. Open Thur–Sun. **$$$**
Ipoh Tandoori House
135F Jalan Dato Lau Pak Kuan
Tel: 05-548 0806
Opposite Fatimah Hospital in the Ipoh Garden suburb; good North Indian fare in an air-conditioned restaurant; try the breads. **$**
Lucky Seafood
266 Jalan Pasir Puteh
Tel: 05-255 7330
This is a very popular restaurant where the seafood is fresh and of excellent value. It is really popular; bookings are recommended. Most of the locals come for the steamed fish. **$$**
Ming Court
36 Jalan Leong Sin Nam
Tel: 05-255 7134
This popular and good dim sum venue near Excelsior Hotel is packed during breakfast. **$**
Restoran Yum Yum
5 Persiaran Green Hill
Tel: 05-253 7686
Eateries on Ipoh's gourmet lane, which is perpendicular to Excelsior Hotel, are more upmarket than those along Jalan Leech. Among them is this excellent outlet with great Chinese-Nyonya ambience; it serves an excellent grouper in basil, and Yum Yum fried chicken. **$$**
Sin Yoon Loong
Jalan Bandar Timah
(near Jalan Silang)
This is the original Ipoh coffee shop, where a fragrant local coffee brew tastes its best. Try the excellent home-made coconut jam (*kaya*) and toast for breakfast. **$**

PULAU PANGKOR

Guan Guan
Pangkor town (near jetty)
Chinese seafood eatery that is good but pricey. **$$**
Pangkor Island Beach Resort
Teluk Belanga
Tel: 05-685 1091
Enjoy Western dinners at the Pacific Terrace, happy-hour cocktails at the bar, seafood BBQ on Wednesday and Saturday, buffet with daily themes at the poolside Hornbill Terrace Restaurant. You can also dine and watch the sunset on a beautiful beach (upon request). **$$$$**
Yee Lin Seafood Garden
Pasir Bogak
Next to Coral Bay Hotel, this established seafood restaurant has typical Chinese decor; serves fresh fish, shellfish and crabs. **$**

TAIPING

Bismillah Restoran
(opposite the Town Market)
Enjoy fresh *roti canai* (flaky bread) with tea for breakfast. For lunch, try Indian briyani istimewa (rice and curries). **$**
Jalan Kota
A number of Chinese seafood restaurants line this road, with fresh produce from the Kuala Sepetang fishing area. **$**
Jalan Panggung Wayang
There's a multi-ethnic food centre beneath Fajar Supermarket, serving local delicacies such as popiah, satay, *rojak sotong* (squid salad with peanut sauce) and fresh ginger tea. **$**

PENANG

Chinese

The Bungalow
Lone Pine Hotel
97 Jalan Batu Ferringhi
Tel: 04-881 1511
Facing the hotel pool and the casuarina-lined beach, this restaurant housed in a colonial-era building has indoor and outdoor seating. At night, the atmosphere is very romantic. The menu concentrates on Hainanese dishes, but includes dishes such as fish curry, chicken rice and *filet* mignon. All-day dining. **$$$**
Goh Huat Seng
59A Lebuh Kimberly
Tel: 04-261 5646
This long-established restaurant is known for its Teochew cuisine and steamboat with a fish soup base. It also serves a large variety of meats, seafood and vegetables, as well as dim sum and sweet Teochew desserts. Open for lunch and dinner; closed on alternate Mon. **$**

Indian

Hameediyah Restaurant
164A Lebuh Campbell
Six generations of an Indian-Muslim family have run Hameediyah's. Famous for its chicken curry, *murtabak* (flat bread filled with minced meat) and mutton *briyani* (rice cooked with spices and ghee). **$**

Kapitan's
93 Lebuh Chulia
Tel: 04-264 1191
Open round the clock, this eatery serves up northern Indian fare. The fresh naan and sweet or mint chutneys best accompany the mild tandoori chicken, marinated in the signature spice mix and cooked in ovens. An iced fruit *lassi* (yoghurt drink) is the perfect complement to the spicy food. **$**

Tajuddin Hussain
49 & 51 Lebuh Queen
Tel: 04-262 5367
Having been around for 45 years, Tajuddin Hussain has perfected its *nasi kandar* (Penang-style rice and curries). The huge dining area is simply furnished, with wooden tables and plastic chairs. While the outlet specialises in tomato rice and roast chicken, the *nasi briyani* is also worth trying. **$**

Malaysian

Gurney Drive has the most famous of Penang's hawker stalls, selling favourites from spicy prawn-based Hokkien noodles to *jiu hoo eng chai* (squid with water spinach). Hawker food is also good at the **New World Park** food court at **Swatow Lane**, the **coffee shops** at **Jalan Penang** and **Jalan Macalister**, **Pengkalan Weld**, and **Jalan Burma**, up to **Pulau Tikus**. The **Chowrasta** stalls are a must for *nasi kandar*. The **Esplanade** in downtown Georgetown is great for night dining. Try the Indian-Muslim-style rojak *pasembur*, a salad with fried seafood covered in peanut sauce. **$**

Peranakan

Hot Wok
3H Jalan Pantai Molek, off Jalan Tanjung Tokong
Tel: 04-890 7858
Hot Wok is set in a bungalow adorned with antiques and Peranakan artefacts. Specialties are favourites like *otak-otak* (steamed spicy fish mousse), *kapitan* chicken curry and pork *cincalok*

(prawn paste). Open daily for lunch and dinner. **$$**

Nyonya Baba Cuisine
44 Jalan Nagore
Tel: 04-227 8035
This restaurant in a restored shophouse serves what is probably the best Peranakan food in town. Must-try dishes are *chun piah* (spring rolls), *kerabu moknee* (fungus salad), *kari kapitan* (chicken curry), and sea coconut dessert. Open Thur–Tues for lunch and dinner. **$$**

Vegetarian

Kek Lok Si Vegetarian Restaurant
Kek Lok Si, Ayer Itam
Tel: 04-828 8142
Located at Kek Lok Si Temple, this Chinese vegetarian restaurant has been around for some 14 years. Its menu is extensive; specialties include roasted mock chicken in Szechuan spicy sauce, a Thai *tom yam* soup, tofu dishes and noodle soups. Alternatively, order a set meal (rice with several dishes) or try a steamboat. **$$**

Western

Edelweiss Café
38 Lebuh Armenian
Tel: 04-261 8935
Set in a beautiful 1890s shophouse, this café is a hangout for local artists. The diverse menu includes sandwiches, salads, macaroni and cheese, and local dishes like fried rice and *mee soto* (noodle soup with chicken). Affordable three-course set lunch menus and bottled beer available. Closed on Mon. **$$**

Sigi's By the Sea
Shangri-La's Golden Sands Resort
Batu Ferringhi
Tel: 04-886 1191
Bright Mediterranean colours and a delightful menu at this bistro. Signature dishes include Moroccan roasted rack of lamb, lamb shank stew and a seafood combination called Fishing Bird. Barbecues on weekends and a Latin band performs every night. The

wine list centres on Australian vintages. **$$$**

PULAU LANGKAWI

Chinese

Asia Restaurant
3A & 4A Persiaran Putra, Kuah
Tel: 04-966 6788
Hearty home-cooked vegetarian dishes here, including steamed oyster mushrooms and *sambal* (chilli paste) tofu. This 1970s-style Chinese restaurant is part of the family-owned Asia Hotel. Chinese-style seafood is also on the menu. **$**

Wonderland
Jalan Mutiara 2, Kuah
Mobile tel: 012-494 6555
A no-frills eatery popular for its good-value Cantonese food. Try the home-style tofu, stir-fried fresh greens with garlic, *kung pao* chicken, squid stir-fried with dried chilli, and shrimp in batter cooked in a spicy tamarind sauce. **$**

Malay/Indian

Gulai House
The Andaman, Jalan Teluk Datai
Tel: 04-959 1088
Gulai House has a very unique coastal rainforest setting accessed via a beachfront trail. The local Malay and Indian dishes are excellent and the service polished and discreet. Fine wines are available to ensure a magical night. **$$$**

Matahari Malay Restaurant
Sunvillage, Jalan Teluk Baru, Pantai Tengah
Tel: 04-955 6200
A charming Balinese-influenced ambience at this restaurant. Meals are as good as homemade as they are prepared by cooks from the local village. Sit cross-legged in a cabana or dine by a landscaped pond, and feast on village-style *nasi campur*, a platter of 11 dishes including satay, local *rendang tok* (dry curry) and chicken curry. Dinner 6–11pm. **$$$**

Western

Beach Garden Resort
Pantai Cenang
Tel: 04-955 1363
Tables on the beach offer great sunset views. Excellent steaks, buttered potatoes, herbed salad, waffles and cream, and coffee, not to mention the fabulous margaritas, possibly the best on the island. The menu changes nightly. **$$**

Bon Ton Restaurant and Resort
Pantai Cenang
Tel: 04-955 6787
Bon Ton's Nam Restaurant has a menu featuring tantalising "West-meets-spice" cuisine, featuring dishes like pita bread with parmesan and harissa, and duo of baked Asian fish wrapped in banana leaf and pandan leaf with herbs. Enjoy pre-dinner sunset drinks by the pool with tapas served from 5 to 7pm. After dinner, sip drinks and liqueur-flavoured coffee at the Chin Chin bar. **$$$**

Mentari Beachfront Grill
The Frangipani Langkawi Resort & Spa, Pantai Tengah
Tel: 04-952 0000
The beachfront setting under shady coconut trees is superb. Start with sunset cocktails and then enjoy fine local and Western dishes under the stars. **$$**

Red Tomato Garden Café
Pantai Cenang
Tel: 04-4955 3088
Bright, cheery and laid-back beachside café with great breakfasts (eggs, pancakes, fresh rolls and bruschetta), superb Lavazza coffee and delicious herbal teas and fresh fruit juices. Breakfast until 2pm. Jazz plays on the stereo. **$$**

Sun Café
No. 8, Sun Mall, Jalan Teluk Baru, Pantai Tengah
Tel: 04-955 8300
Meals, at very reasonable prices belying the café's classy European look, are prepared with organic ingredients. The menu features hearty sandwiches, thin-crust pizzas, vegetarian meals and spicy local fare. The *creme brulee* and milkshakes are delightful. **$$**

SOUTHERN PENINSULA

MELAKA

Chinese

Hoe Kee Chicken Rice
4 Jalan Hang Jebat
Located near the bridge and open only from mid-morning to lunch, this has remained low key despite the fame won by its delicious Hainanese chicken and billiard-ball-sized rice balls; good home-made barley drink. **$**

Peranakan

Heeren House
1 Jalan Tun Tan Cheng Lock
Tel: 06-281 4241
Set lunches in a cosy and old-world environment, with Western, Peranakan and Portuguese dishes, and delicious cakes. **$**
Nancy's Kitchen
15 Jalan Hang Lekir
Tel: 06-283 6099
Nancy's serves authentic Peranakan cuisine. The *ayam buah keras* (chicken in candlenut curry) is a classic. Open for lunch only; closed on Wed. **$$**

Ole Sayang Restaurant
198/199 Taman Melaka Raya
Tel: 06-283 1966
Excellent authentic Peranakan cooking and great traditional decor; just ignore the morose staff. It is popular with large groups, so go early for lunch or dinner. **$$**
Restoran Peranakan Town House
107 Jalan Tun Tan Cheng Lock
Tel: 06-284 5001
A gorgeous Peranakan showpiece. All the well-known Nyonya dishes are on the menu and there is a nightly cultural show. **$$**

Western

Coconut House
128 Jalan Tun Tan Cheng Lock
Tel: 06-282 9128
A restaurant, art gallery, bookshop and art-film venue in a beautiful Peranakan house. Specialities are wood-fired pizzas and freshly baked cakes. **$$**
Discovery Café
3 Jalan Bunga Raya
Tel: 06-292 5606
Adorned with antique curios and vintage photos, this cosy café in a pre-war shop-house also has shady outdoor seating under palm trees. Offers excellent dishes like Devil's Curry and Portuguese baked fish topped with *sambal* (chilli). Handy Internet facilities and library of travel guidebooks.
Geographer's Café
83 Jalan Hang Jebat
Tel: 06-281 6813
Located in an ambience-filled corner shophouse. Bright and airy, this café is a nice place to chill out at and partake of local specialities and Western dishes. Live performances at night. **$$**

JOHOR BAHRU

Indian

Briyani House
Jalan Kebun Teh
Dishes up the Johor speciality of *briyani gam*, rice served with spicy mutton or chicken and pickles. **$**
Capati Corner
Jalan Kolam Air
Homemade *chapati* (flat Indian bread, served with *dhal* (lentil) or curries and vegetables of your choice. **$**

Malaysian

Tepian Tebrau Food Centre
Jalan Skudai
A favourite among locals for its seafood steamboat, *nasi briyani* (rice with mutton or chicken) and *ikan bakar* (grilled fish). **$**

Seafood

Eden Floating Palace
Johor Bahru Duty Free Zone
Jalan Ibrahim Sultan
Tel: 07-221 8000
A converted passenger ferry with three restaurants on four air-conditioned decks, seating 600 diners and serving duty-free wines. A Chinese seafood/Western menu. **$$$**
Jaws 5
Straits View Hotel, Jalan Skudai
Tel: 07-223 6062
Excellent Chinese-style seafood in a glitzy, overlit environment – try the drunken prawns and chilli crabs. **$$**
Prawn House
Jalan Kebun Teh
This seafood joint serves fresh fish cooked in various styles; a speciality is the yam cake dessert. **$**

PENINSULA'S EAST COAST

PULAU TIOMAN

Babura Sea View Chinese Restaurant
Babura Sea View Resort,
Kampung Tekek
Breezy beachside Chinese restaurant with excellent seafood and good beers. **$**
Liza Restaurant
Kampung Tekek
Good selection of Malay and Western dishes. **$**
Mekong Restaurant
Kampung Paya
Good Chinese-style seafood. **$**
Sunset Boulevard
Kampung Salang
Built on stilts over the sea. You can jump off your boat onto the restaurant itself. Good seafood. **$**

KUANTAN

Kampung Restaurant
Hyatt Regency Kuantan
Teluk Cempedak
Tel: 09-566 1234
A casual restaurant with teakwood chairs and tables. Enjoy good Malay and Continental food and excellent pizzas in this restaurant built on stilts over the sea. Features an open kitchen and ravishing views of the South China Sea. **$$**
Pak Su Seafood Restaurant
Batu 6 (6th mile)
Kuantan-Beserah Road
About half an hour north of Kuantan, just before De Rhu Beach Resort, sits this breezy Chinese restaurant overlooking the sea. It is well known for its stuffed crabs, salad lobster and spicy-sour *asam* (tamarind) steamed fish. Air conditioned. **$$**

KUALA TERENGGANU

Nils Restaurant
Pantai Batu Buruk
Renowned Malay seafood restaurant, famous for its *ikan bakar* (grilled fish with sambal sauce), right on the beach. Favourite dining spot with locals including royalty. **$–$$**

Good Luck Restaurant
11Y & Z Jalan Kota Lama
Tel: 09-622 7573
Popularly known as Lucky Restaurant, it is centrally located, next to a *bak kut teh* (herbal pork ribs soup) eatery, and serves seafood specialities and Cantonese-style frog legs, as well as one-dish noodle and rice meals. Air conditioned upstairs. **$**
Restoran Meka
66/16 Taman Seri Intan
Tel: 09-623 1831
Traditional Terengganu-style Malay cooking with mainly fish dishes in various spicy coconut concoctions, and *ulam*, traditional salads eaten with a prawn paste-based chilli condiment called *sambal belacan*.

The dishes are laid out in trays. **$**

KOTA BHARU

Azam
Jalan Padang Garong
North Indian fare,

including breads and *dhal* (lentil curry). **$**
Central Market
The bustling first floor is packed with food stalls selling local Malay rice and curries – try the *nasi kunyit*, yellow-colour, turmeric-flavoured glutinous rice concoction. There is

also a large variety of local *kuih* (cakes) that cannot be found outside Kelantan. **$**
Kedai Kopi White House
Jalan Sultanah Zainab
Located opposite the State Mosque, this is the best place to enjoy *nasi dagang* – long-grain rice

and glutinous rice cooked with coconut milk and eaten with tuna curry and vegetables. **$**
Kow Lun
Jalan Kebun Sultan
Chinese set-up with meat and vegetable dishes; piping-hot noodles, as well as beer. **$**

SARAWAK

KUCHING

Chinese

The old streets of Chinatown are lined with *kedai kopi* (coffee shops) serving fresh Chinese noodle dishes and specialties like laksa, *kolok mee* (tossed noodles with pork), and *kway chap* (wide silky rice noodles in soup with various pieces of pork including organ meat), and roast chicken and pork rice. Look around until you see a restaurant that looks attractive, find a seat and order up.
Li Garden
1st Floor, Hock Lee Centre,
Jalan Datuk Abang Abdul Rahim
Tel: 082-340 785
A local favourite for refined Cantonese cuisine, this is open for both lunch and dinner. If you yearn for a good Peking duck, this is the place to come to, even though the restaurant's location will mean a taxi ride. Booking is essential for dinner. **$$**
Lok Thian
1st Floor, Bangunan Bee San
Jalan Padungan
Tel: 082-331 310
This highly recommended restaurant is rather curious in that it also offers Thai and Japanese cuisines. The main attraction, however, is refined Cantonese fare. The service is efficient, the surroundings pleasant even if not elegant. Open for lunch and dinner. **$$**
Ting Noodle House
117B, Lot 132, Jalan Ban Hock
Located not far from the

end of Jalan Soon Thian Cheok, this air-conditioned and moderately priced restaurant is packed at lunch time. Open from 8am to 8.30pm, this is the place to come for all kinds of noodle dishes (the Taiwanese beef noodles are recommended) and interesting dumplings, as well as rice-based dishes. **$**
Toh Yuen
Hilton Hotel, Kuching
Tel: 082-248 200
This is one of Kuching's top places for excellent Chinese cuisine in elegant and air-conditioned surroundings. Dim sum is served at lunch, while in the evening, gourmet Szechuan and Cantonese cuisine star. **$$–$$$**

Indian

Bollywood Café
66 Lebuh Ewe Hai
Despite the trendy name, this conveniently located spot is decidedly simple, offering a good range of typical Indian food from 7am until about 6.30pm. Specialties are *briyani* – curries with rice, *chapati* (flat, unleavened bread), *roti canai* (flaky bread) and Indian sweetmeats. **$**
Lyn's Tandoori
Lot 62, No 10G, Lorong 4,
Nanas Road
Somewhat old fashioned but still popular, this restaurant is just a short taxi ride from town. Serves authentic northern Indian tandoori dishes and naan. **$**
Sri Shan
Lot 383, Jalan Ban Hock
Tel: 082-244 118

Run by a dynamic Chinese couple who offer authentic "curry and such" without any artificial additives, this spacious, brightly painted restaurant is spotlessly clean. Open from 7am to 10pm, the restaurant serves aromatic southern Indian cuisine, sometimes with a twist. Be sure to try the cheese-filled *roti canai* (flaky bread) and fish-head curry. **$**

Japanese

Minoru
Lot 493G, Section 10, Rubber Road
Tel: 082-251 021
Regarded by many as Sarawak's best Japanese restaurant, Minoru offers a selection of fine Japanese cuisine for both lunch and dinner, and is known for its attentive service. **$$–$$$**

Malaysian

Hornbill's Corner Café
Jalan Ban Hock
Tel: 082-252 670
Both a bar and a restaurant, the Hornbill has the best barbecue steamboat in town with an inexpensive all-you-can-eat buffet. The bar has a friendly clientele; cold draught beer and satellite-TV soccer attract many foreign visitors. **$**
Waterfront Café
Hilton Kuching
Jalan Tunku Abdul Rahman
Tel: 082-428 200
Gaze out across the Kuching River in air-conditioned comfort as you enjoy excellent espresso, freshly baked bread, salads and sumptuous buffets, as well as à la carte Japanese dishes. The café features

different food promotions each day. **$$**

Seafood

Benson's Seafood
49 Jalan Abell
Popular spot by the river for fresh seafood, this relaxed place is just past the Holiday Inn. Simply point to the vegetables and fish, crabs, prawns of your choice and say how you'd like them cooked. **$–$$**
See Good Food Centre
53 Jalan Ban Hock
Excellent seafood, fresh and affordable, served in a simple, open-sided eatery with some tables outside. Don't missed the curried bamboo clams if they're available. Delicious noodle dishes are served between main meal times. **$–$$**
Top Spot Food Centre
5th Floor, Jalan Bukit Mata Kuching
An open-air seafood plaza where half a dozen eating outlets vie for business with tempting displays of fresh seafood on ice. **$**

Western

Jambu
32 Jalan Crookshank
Tel: 082-235 292
Housed in a pleasant converted colonial-era bungalow with a patio and a lounge with TV screen, this restaurant-cum-tapas bar is a firm favourite with locals and visitors alike. The tapas bar has live jazz on Friday nights, while the restaurant offers a mix of Western and fusion Borneo cuisine. **$–$$**
Magenta
32, Lot 141, Jalan Nanas
Tel: 082-237 878

TRANSPORT

ACCOMMODATION

EATING OUT

ACTIVITIES

A – Z

LANGUAGE

Magenta is an elegant, good-looking restaurant set in a beautifully converted old Malay wooden bungalow just 5 minutes from downtown Kuching. Adorned with marble-top tables and Asian-inspired furnishings, it is popular for its Western dishes with Asian twists. Fine examples are seafood bouillabaisse, and grilled salmon with salsa and potato ragout – all artfully presented and served in generous portions. **$$**

The San Francisco Grill
Jalan Ban Hock
Although rather old fashioned, this is a long-time favourite. Offers good service and good steaks at reasonable prices. **$–$$**

The Steak House
Hilton Hotel, Kuching
Tel: 082-248 200
Although this place has the best steaks in town, it is even more popular for its sophisticated international cuisine served in elegant surroundings. Try the set meal for really good value. Dinner only. **$$–$$$**

SIBU

Chinese

Blue Splendour
5th Floor, Wisma Sanyan
Jalan Sukan
Tel: 084-323 366
A budget-priced place in an air-conditioned shopping complex, serving a range of ready-cooked Chinese dishes with rice at lunch time. A set dinner for two is excellent value at only RM30. **$**

Golden Palace
Tanahhas Hotel
Jalan Kampung Nyabor
Tel: 084-33 188
Cantonese and Szechuan dishes and plenty of seafood. Favourite dishes include king prawns in spicy sauce and local river fish, steamed or fried and served with a Thai-style sauce. **$$**

Hock Cho Lau Restaurant
Jalan Blacksmith
Tel: 084-316 523
A popular Chinese restaurant specialising in Foochow dishes; particularly popular for its duck and fried noodle dishes. **$–$$**

Malaysian

Central Market
1st Floor, Sibu Central Market
Jalan Channel
A wide range of stalls with local food available for breakfast, lunch and dinner. Chinese, Indian, Malay and simple Western food, plus fresh tropical fruits and fruit juices. **$**

Gerai Makanan Muslim
Jalan Khoo Peng Loong
Conveniently located by the river close to the express boat wharf, this simple wooden restaurant offers delicious Malay dishes.

Western

Esplanade Seafood & Café
Rejang Esplanade, Jalan Maju
This friendly, open-air eatery on the esplanade offers local dishes such as steamed river fish and stir-fried jungle fern, as well as Western food. Open in the evening only. **$**

Pepper's Café
Tanahhas Hotel
Jalan Kampung Nyabor
Tel: 084-333 188
Casual dining in one of Sibu's top hotels. Both Western and local dishes are available à la carte or in the buffet. **$–$$**

MIRI

Malaysian

Taman Seroja
Jalan Brooke
This collection of simple food stalls, which come into full swing at night, offers some of the best home-style Muslim food in Sarawak. A few stalls also open for breakfast and lunch. **$**

Jalan North Yu Seng
Tables and chairs are set up along a broad, leafy pavement in the evening. Food stalls here offer a wide range of Malay and Chinese dishes. **$**

Western

Al Fresco Sidewalk Café
Ground Floor, Pelita Commercial Centre, Jalan Bulan Sabit
Tel: 085-428 928
One of a cluster of casual restaurants in a popular district a short taxi ride from downtown. This friendly spot has fish and chips, pizzas, and grilled dishes. **$$**

Café Miri
Taman Yakin Shopping Centre
Jalan Bulan Sabit
Tel: 085-425 122
A few kilometres from the town centre, this relaxed café run by a local Chinese and his Australian wife serves a great array of drinks and Western dishes. Closed on Tues. **$$**

Seafood

Ocean Seafood Village
Luak Bay
Located by the beach about 10 minutes south of the town centre, this big open-concept restaurant is regarded as one of the best places to enjoy seafood in Miri. **$$–$$$**

Yi Hah Hai
Jalan Bandahara
Tel: 085-433 401
Sprawling over several adjacent shophouses along the Miri riverbank, this place is enormously popular in the evenings for its fresh, diverse and reasonably priced seafood. **$$**

SABAH

KOTA KINABALU

Chinese

Canton House
70 Jalan Gaya
(opposite The Jesselton)
Tel: 088-269 399
Bright and bustling, this air-conditioned restaurant specialises in all kinds of noodles, roast meat and poultry, and dim sum; there are also some good desserts and drinks. Very busy at lunch time and Sunday morning. **$**

Supertanker
Grand Industrial Estate, Jalan Bundusan (off Jalan Penampang)
Tel: 088-717 889
This large and popular restaurant, located about 10 to 15 minutes by taxi from the city centre, serves some of the best Chinese food in town. **$$**

Indian

Jothy's Restaurant
Block 1, Lot 9, Api Api Centre (near McDonald's, facing Coastal Highway)
The southern Indian food here, both vegetarian as well as meat, poultry and fish curries, is deliciously spicy. This simple restaurant is air-conditioned and spotlessly clean. **$–$$**

Kohinoor North Indian Restaurant
Lot 4, The Waterfront
Tel: 088-235 160
The only northern Indian restaurant in the city, this offers air-conditioned dining as well as tables on a seaside boardwalk. An extensive menu with plenty of vegetarian options, with inexpensive yet generous set lunches and lavish set dinners for four. Good food in unprepossessing surroundings. **$$**

Naan
Shangri-La's Rasa Ria Resort
Pantai Dalit
Tel: 088-792 888
Refined Indian food is prepared and served with a delightful modern touch in

this out-of-town restaurant. Well worth the drive for top quality Indian food; evenings only. **$$$**

Japanese

Nagisa Japanese Restaurant
Hyatt Regency Kinabalu,
Jalan Datuk Salleh Sulong
Tel: 088-221 234
Reputed to be the finest Japanese restaurant in the city offering Japanese favourites. It is tastefully furnished and has a separate sushi bar and teppanyaki counters. With views of the sea and Gaya Island. **$$–$$$**

Malay

Sri Rahmat
Ruang Tiong Hwa
Segama Complex
Right in the centre of Segama Complex in downtown Kota Kinabalu, and a minute or so from the Hyatt, this is a good place for lunch, with an air-conditioned dining section. *Nasi campur*, rice served with ready-cooked dishes of your choice, is very good here. **$–$$**

Sri Sempeleng
Block C Asia City (facing Centre-point Shopping Complex)
Open 24 hours a day, 7 days a week, this is one of the most popular Malay/Indonesian restaurants in town. Branches in Wisma Merdeka and Sinsuron Shopping Complex. **$**

Malaysian

Borneo 1945 Museum Kopi Tiam
24 Jalan Dewan
Tel: 088 272945
An atmospheric coffee shop where coffee is served in old-style cups, and charcoal-toasted bread is slathered with rich coconut jam (*kaya*). Lunch-time specials are as flavourful as they are nostalgic. Located on the site used by the Australian Armed Forces during the rebuilding of Sabah after WWII, the coffee shop displays many historic photos. **$**

Wisma Merdeka Food Court
2nd floor, Wisma Merdeka, Phase 1
Jalan Haji Saman
Always busy, this collection of food stalls offers an amazing variety of Malaysian food, plus a few Western favourites such as pastas, pizzas and hamburgers. The large Malay stall near the exit offers some of the best Malay and Indonesian food in town. Some stalls open for breakfast; closes around 9pm. **$**

Seafood

Garden Seafood Restaurant
Off Jalan Mat Salleh, Tanjung Aru
Tel: 088-442 222
This huge, open-sided restaurant has an extensive range of seafood, and also sells exotica such as ostrich and venison. The very clear menu helps in ordering either Thai or Chinese-style dishes. **$$$**

Port View Seafood
The Waterfront
Jalan Tun Fuad Stephens
Tel: 088-538178
The longest-established and most popular seafood restaurant in town with a huge selection of fresh seafood. Dine in the air-conditioned section if you wish to avoid the noise of the cultural show between 7 and 8pm. **$$$**

Suang Tain Seafood Restaurant
SEDCO Square, Kampung Air
Open daily from 5pm to 2.30am, this seafood restaurant dominates a popular open-air evening eatery. A large range of fresh seafood is available and the restaurant known for its reasonable prices. **$$–$$$**

Thai

Tham Nak Thai
Api Api Centre
Tel: 088-257 328
Part of a chain of Thai restaurants, this has all the usual Thai favourites, well presented in pleasant surroundings by attractively dressed staff. **$$–$$$**

Western

@mosphere
Menara Tun Mustapha, Likas Bay
Tel: 088-425 100
An elegant revolving restaurant and bar on the 18th floor of a tower, this offers spectacular views and modern Western cuisine with an Asian accent. **$$$**

Gunther's Gasthaus
9/11 Taman Sinar, off, Jalan Tuaran (opposite Kian Kok School)
Tel: 088-217 249
Located in a converted house less than 4 km (2½ miles) from the city, this overly decorated German–Swiss restaurant is popular for its steaks, sausages and braised pork knuckle. **$$**

Little Italy Pasta & Pizza Corner
Ground Floor, Hotel Capital
Jalan Haji Saman
Tel: 088-232 231
Located in the heart of town, this offers Italian favourites (with emphasis on pastas and pizzas) at reasonable prices. Outdoor and air-conditioned indoor dining available. **$–$$**

Luna Rossa
Lot 5, Tanjung Lipat, Jalan Gaya
Tel: 088-266882
Located at the end of a converted warehouse, this has a decor that is "Bali meets Borneo". Expect excellent pizzas, pastas and a range of other dishes. The long bar is particularly popular. Dining is either in air-conditioned comfort or out in the garden. **$$**

Peppino's
Shangri-La's Tanjung Aru Resort
Tel: 088-225 800
Casual, elegant restaurant in the city's premier resort. This serves Italian favourites, including plenty of seafood and vegetarian dishes. **$$$**

SANDAKAN

Sandakan has numerous coffee shops and simple restaurants serving excellent noodle and seafood dishes. The seafood is particularly good and generally less expensive than in KK.

The English Tea House and Restaurant
Jalan Istana
Tel: 089-222 544
This beautifully restored colonial-era bungalow overlooks Sandakan and the bay. English favourites, including bangers and mash, and selected Asian cuisine. You can even play croquet. **$$–$$$**

Ocean King Seafood Restaurant
Jalan Batu Sapi (4½ km), Pasir Putih
Tel: 089-618 111/616 048
A large open-sided restaurant built on stilts over the bay. There is a vague menu/price list written on a board in the verandah, but basically, if it swims, you can order it. Fish, crabs, prawns, lobster, squid and various shellfish are all available, and the bean curd and vegetable dishes are good. **$$**

Penang Curry House
Lebuh Dua (Second Avenue), next to the AM Finance
Featuring southern Indian cuisine, including curries, murtabak, *roti canai* (flaky bread) and *thosai* (rice flour and lentil pancakes) and plenty of vegetarian options in a busy, open-fronted restaurant. **$**

Restoran Habeeb
There are at least eight restaurants in this chain featuring Indian and local Muslim cuisine. One of the most convenient is located directly in front of Wisma Sandakan on Lebuh Empat (Fourth Avenue). **$**

TAWAU

Seafood

Kam Ling Seafood
24 Sabindo Open-Air Food Stall
Tel: 089-756 457
A simple restaurant that is a Sabah legend with its wide range of live fish, crustaceans and other seafood. Despite the unprepossessing surroundings, eager diners flock here for seafood at its best – and for the very reasonable prices. Menu in English. **$$**

ACTIVITIES

THE ARTS, NIGHTLIFE, FESTIVALS, SHOPPING, OUTDOOR ACTIVITIES AND SIGHTSEEING TOURS

THE ARTS

Art Galleries

Malaysia's serious art gained credence only in the 1960s after independence. Art is becoming a popular collectible locally, particularly in Kuala Lumpur with the number of exhibitions and galleries on the rise.

The diversity is staggering, from Chinese brush painting to abstract art and sculpture. However, it is hard to define what Malaysian art really is. Batik art comes closest to being a unique Malaysian visual artform. The artist who pioneered it, Chuah Thean Teng, has a gallery in Penang.

Newer artists are featured in smaller galleries throughout the country, with many congregating in the trendy Bangsar suburb in Kuala Lumpur. Check dailies for exhibition listings and art spaces.

Kuala Lumpur

Galeri Petronas
Lot 341–343, Level 3, Suria KLCC
Tel: 03-2051 7770
www.galeripetronas.com.my
Funded by the national oil company, this is the city's most accessible, located within the busy Suria KLCC shopping mall. An elegant space for traditional and contemporary art. Open Tues–Sun 10am–8pm.
Galeri Seni Maya
12, 1st Floor, Jalan Telawi 3,
Bangsar Baru
Tel: 03-2282 2069
www.mayagallery.com.my
Promotes Malaysian contemporary artists, especially young talented ones. Open Tues–Fri 10am–7pm, Sat and Sun noon–6pm.

Galeri Tangsi
PAM Centre, 4–6 Jalan Tangsi
Tel: 03-2691 0805
Focused on contemporary art, it has a network of over 100 professional artists. Also offers fine art services including consultation, conservation and evaluation of artworks. Open Mon–Fri 10am–6pm, Sat 10am–2pm.
National Art Gallery
2 Jalan Temerloh, off Jalan Tun Razak
Tel: 03-4025 4990
www.artgallery.gov.my
A striking purpose-built gallery housing a permanent collection of over 2,500 works by local and international artists, including ceramics, textiles and sculptures. Open daily 10am–6pm.
Valentine Willie Fine Art
1st Floor, 17 Jalan Telawi 3,
Bangsar Baru
Tel: 03-2284 2348
www.vwfa.net
With a busy calendar of exhibitions, this contemporary art gallery has an extensive selection of Malaysian and Southeast Asian paintings, sculptures and drawings. Open Mon–Fri 12–8pm, Sat 12–6pm.

Penang

The Art Gallery
368 Jalan Burma
Belisa Row, Pulau Tikas Penang
Tel: 04-229 8219
This gallery specialises in the works of pioneer Malaysian artists. Also features some works by artists from Singapore and Indonesia. New exhibitions are held every two months. Open Tues–Sun 11am–6pm.
Yahong Art Gallery
58D Batu Ferringhi
Tel: 04-881 1251
Home to the works of Chuah Thean Teng and his sons. Chuah pioneered the use of traditional batik

techniques in modern works in the 1930s. Open daily 9.30am–10pm.

Kuching

Artrageously Ramsey Ong
94 Main Bazaar
Tel: 082-424 346
www.artrageouslyasia.com
Featuring the works of flamboyant Sarawakian artist Ramsey Ong, as well as those of other local artists. Prints, cards and handicrafts are also on sale. Open Mon–Sat 9.30am–6.30pm, Sun 9.30am–5.30pm. Another Artrageously gallery in Kuala Lumpur (43 & 45 Changkat Bukit Bintang, tel: 03-2141 2566).
Galleria
Suite 1-3, Wesberley House
Lot 2812, Rubber Road West
Tel: 082-429 361
www.wesberly.com.my
A short taxi ride from the heart of Kuching, this spacious gallery has contemporary paintings by local artists, including those of the talented Iban artist, Melton Kais.

Kota Kinabalu

Sabah Art Gallery
Sabah Museum Complex
Tel: 088-253 199
www.sabah.gov.my/artgallery
Set adjacent to the main museum building, but with free entry, the Sabah Art Gallery houses a collection of paintings and 3D works by local artists.
Borneo Trading Post
Lot 16, The Waterfront
Jalan Tun Fuad Stephens
Tel: 088-232 655
www.borneotradingpost.com
The mezannine level of this quality souvenir store offers original artworks from around Southeast Asia at reasonable prices.

Performing Arts

Chinese

Traditional Chinese opera is staged on temporary platforms in the suburbs during special Buddhist or Taoist festivals. Based on Chinese myths and old tales, this sees the use of traditional Chinese costumes and heavy make-up.

Chinese dances are performed only during official functions, but there are many dance groups who use traditional dance as a base for modern works.

There are a few classical Chinese orchestras, with **Dama Orchestra** (tel: 03-6201 9108; www.damaorchestra.com) being the most professional and creative. Its repertoire is wide, although it specialises in popular Chinese music from the first half of the 20th century, usually featuring the sublime talent of soprano Tan Soo Suan. Dama performs in various venues in Kuala Lumpur, including the KL Performing Arts Centre and The Actors Studio (*see below*), and has an active tour schedule around Malaysia.

Contemporary Arts

The contemporary arts scene is centred in Kuala Lumpur, with some productions in Penang and Ipoh. Contemporary dancers have small companies and some are quite good, training and performing internationally. The most popular contemporary theatre is the comedy revue, attracting trendy urbanites, although drama, some locally written, is also staged.

For listings, check the dailies and the website www.kakiseni.com for theatre events and www.mydance alliance.org for dance performances.

The Actors Studio, Malaysia
T116, Level 3, West Wing,
Bangsar Shopping Centre,
Jalan Maarof, Kuala Lumpur
Tel: 03-2094 0400
www.theactorsstudio.com.my
A small, contemporary performing arts space run by the country's top theatre company, featuring mainly local productions; scheduled performances are held almost every week. It also has a training academy. Open daily 10.30am–6.30pm or till 8.30pm when there is a show. A branch in Penang (Ground Floor, Zhong Zheng School Memorial Centre, 32 Lebuh Light, tel: 04-263 5400).

Kuala Lumpur Performing Arts Centre (KLPAC)
Sentul Park, Jalan Strachan
Tel: 03-4047 9000
www.klpac.com
A beautiful, award-winning space

managed by The Actors Studio, with a 500-seat main theatre and various other performing spaces; about 60 percent of its productions are local; however it's tricky to get there by public transport. Daily 10.30am–6.30pm or till 8.30pm when there is a show.

Indian

Classical Indian artforms are well and truly alive, with dance, vocal and instrumental performances held regularly, particularly in temples. The most famous troupe is the Kuala Lumpur-based Temple of Fine Arts, known for its epic productions. It also incorporates contemporary and Malaysian elements in its shows.

Sutra House
12 Persiaran Titiwangsa 3,
Kuala Lumpur
Tel: 03-4022 9669
www.sutradancetheatre.com
Owned by classical Indian dance guru and odissi exponent, Ramli Ibrahim, Sutra House has a landscaped outdoor stage where Indian dance and music recitals are held under the stars; there is also an indoor art gallery.

Temple of Fine Arts
116 Jalan Berhala, Brickfields,
Kuala Lumpur
Tel: 03-2274 3709
Non-profit cultural organisation with centres in Malaysia, India, Singapore, Australia and Sri Lanka. It hosts classical Indian art forms. You can also learn dance, music, song and yoga here.

Music

Dewan Filharmonik Petronas
Ground Floor, Tower 2,
Petronas Twin Towers, Kuala Lumpur
Tel: 03-2051 7007
www.malaysianphilharmonic.com
This purpose-built classical concert hall has a full programme of classical music all year round performed by the resident Malaysian Philharmonic Orchestra (MPO) as well as by guest orchestras and soloists from all over the world, including renowned jazz and world music exponents. A dress code is imposed for evening performances. The MPO's performance calendar is available on the website. Sunday matinees are good value for money. Open Mon–Fri 10am–6pm.

Istana Budaya (National Theatre)
Jalan Tun Razak, Kuala Lumpur
Tel: 03-4026 5558
www.istanabudaya.gov.my
Modelled after betel leaves, the country's largest theatre stages big local and international acts including broadway musicals and symphonic orchestra performances. Open Mon–Fri 9am–6pm, Sat 9am–1pm.

Traditional Culture

Authentic cultural performances are difficult to catch these days. National Day and other colourful parades, such as that which kicks off the tourism event Colours of Malaysia (*Citrawarna Malaysia*), a month-long promotion of Malaysian cultural events and food in Kuala Lumpur, offer some glimpses. A handful of hotels also stage performances, as does KL's Central Market.

For traditional Bornean-Malaysian native performances, the Sarawak Cultural Village in Kuching has regular shows, as does the Monsopiad Cultural Village in Kota Kinabalu. The best performances are however in longhouses, the further into the interior the better; the local people are always ready for an excuse to break into song and dance. Likewise in the more remote areas in Sabah. The Harvest Festival in June is the best time to catch the action.

Kuala Lumpur
Central Market (Pasar Seni)
Jalan Hang Kasturi
Tel: 03-2272 9966
Cultural performances are regularly hosted in the main foyer area and on the outdoor stage, while alternative music performances are occasionally held in its annexe. Open daily 10am–10pm.

Kota Bharu
Gelanggang Seni (Cultural Centre)
Jalan Mahmud
Tel: 09-747 7554
Kelantan's traditional pastimes such as *gasing* (top) spinning and *silat* (Malay martial arts) performances are staged regularly. Open Thur–Sun 8.30am–4.45pm.

Sarawak
Sarawak Cultural Village
Pantai Damai, Santubong
Tel: 082-846 411
www.scv.com.my
Billed as a living museum, this award-winning cultural village is located in the foothills of Mount Santubong, 45 minutes from Kuching and close to the resorts of Damai Beach. Sarawak's ethnic diversity is highlighted in traditional homes and a cultural show at 11.30am and 4.30pm daily.

Sabah
Monsopiad Cultural Village
Kampung Kuai Kandazon, Penampang
Tel: 088-774 337
www.monsopiad.com
Although most famous for its House of Skulls, with trophies taken by the infamous head-hunter Monsopiad,

this excellent cultural village aims to highlight and preserve the indigenous Kadazan culture. Traditional games, food, a cultural show (11am, 2pm and 4pm daily) and a guided tour are included. Open daily 9am–6pm.

Cinemas

Cinemas in major cities are air conditioned and comfortable, with some offering THX sound system and luxury halls. Tickets are cheap. Cinemas screen mainly mainstream offerings from Hollywood, Bollywood and Hong Kong, as well as a scattering of local Malay-language films, Southeast Asian fare and arthouse releases. Blockbusters often get released the same day – in order to foil DVD pirates – as in the US, UK and Hong Kong, and queues can be long. Non-Malay-language movies have subtitles in Bahasa Malaysia and Chinese. English-language films rarely make it to the small towns. For listings, check the dailies or www.cinemaonline.com.my.

In deference to the official religion of the country, Islam, nude, semi-nude and even kissing scenes between unmarried people are edited diligently, but not always professionally, censored – so sometimes, vital dialogue disappears too.

There are two main cinema operators, whose halls are located in malls in major cities and screen mainly mainstream flicks. **Golden Screen Cinema** (tel: 03-8312 3456; www.gsc.com.my) theatres in Kuala Lumpur are located in the Mid Valley Megamall, Berjaya Times Square and 1 Utama, Petaling Jaya. The other operator is **Tanjung Golden Village** (tel: 03-7492 2929; www.tgv.com.my), whose Kuala Lumpur theatres are in 1 Utama, Suria KLCC, and Sunway Pyramid, Petaling Jaya. Berjaya Times Square also has a 3D IMAX Theater (tel: 03-2117 3046).

There are occasional short or independent film festivals, usually held at the HELP Institute theatrette (tel: 03-2094 2000) in Petaling Jaya, and the Kuala Lumpur Performing Arts Centre (see page 385).

NIGHTLIFE

Pubs, discos and karaoke lounges are where Malaysians party at night. The best nightlife is in the capital. Elsewhere, the action concentrates in hotel lounges and discos. Other than in Kuala Lumpur, people tend not to dress up, but shorts and sandals are definite no-nos.

Kuala Lumpur

Nightlife in the capital tends to congregate in specific areas; the main ones are **Jalan Sultan Ismail/Jalan Ampang**, **Asian Heritage Row** around Jalan Doraisamy, **Bukit Bintang**, **Bangsar**, and **Sri Hartamas**.

Generally, club crowds swell after 11pm. Clubs charge an entry fee from 10pm or 11pm, which includes one drink. Wednesday is ladies' night in most places, which means free drinks for women. Happy hour is usually 5.30–9pm, when drinks are at half price, which should be taken advantage of since alcohol is very expensive in Malaysia. Beers start at RM10 a glass and RM40 a jug, alcohol RM15, and wine about RM20–25 a glass and RM80 a bottle. Wines have become very popular, and a wide range is available, especially in wine and cigar bars. You can keep a tab going till you leave. Waiters generally expect a tip.

KL-ites tend to dress up to go the fancier clubs and some places enforce a dress code which, for men, stipulates at the minimum, a collared T-shirt, long trousers and covered shoes, while other places have a "no jeans, shorts and sandals" rule. Most clubs adhere to the 21-year-old age limit (the legal drinking age in Malaysia) but there are cases where this is openly flouted.

Live bands are popular and almost all the larger hotels have bars featuring live music, which usually begins at around 10pm. This is usually broad-appeal, middle-of-the-road music.

Bars and Pubs

Alexis The Bar Upstairs
29A Jalan Telawi 3, Bangsar Baru
Tel: 03-2284 2881
Alexis exudes chic and class with its trendy design and purple-hued bar. Acid jazz plays in the background. Go early if you want a seat at its famous balcony overlooking the Telawi street action.
Bar Savanh
62–64 Jalan Doraisamy,
Asian Heritage Row
Tel: 03-2697 1180
With long opium-den-style sofas, Buddhist sculptures, a fish pond, candles and incense, this place is hauntingly beautiful.
Karma Hartamas
1 Jalan 22A/70A,
Desa Sri Hartamas
Tel: 03-6203 2111
The decor features cascading water, wooden floors and luxurious drapes. Music is R&B and 1990s retro, and there's a great dance floor.

Little Havana
2 & 4 Lorong Sahabat
(along Changkat Bukit Bintang)
Tel: 03-2144 7170
See Cuban culture in action here. With Latin music, great wines, fine cigars, good food and hot salsa dancing.
Luna Bar
Pacific Regency Hotel
Apartments, Jalan Punchak
Tel: 03-2332 7777
A rooftop, outdoor lounge bar with a pool in the middle and views to die for. An exclusive chill-out venue.
The Poppy Collection
18-1 Jalan P Ramlee
Tel: 03-2141 8888
Several sexy bars share this boutique entertainment space with floor-to-ceiling glass windows and alfresco balconies and gardens. Upstairs is the small and sensual lounge, Passion, while Bar Mandalay and the Havanita Cigar Lounge are for serious unwinding.
The Pub
Shangri-La Hotel,
Jalan Sultan Ismail
Tel: 03-2074 3905
A traditional English pub tucked away in a corner, with pub grub, darts, pool and sports action on TV. A great place to drink, chat and relax. Happy hour (5–8pm) should not be missed.
Souled Out
20 Jalan 30/70A,
Desa Sri Hartamas
Tel: 03-2300 1955
Chill out in a large airy area outside – the dance floor is upstairs. A favourite with soccer fans; packed on weekends.
Telawi Street Bistro
1 Jalan Telawi 3, Bangsar Baru
Tel: 03-2284 3168
This slinky contemporary bistro and wine bar is intimate, with a great balcony for people watching. Enjoy tapas with a nice selection of red and white wines. Run by Spanish tapas specialist La Bodega, which also runs a bistro and wine lounge down the road.

Clubs

The Beach Club Café
97 Jalan P Ramlee
Tel: 03-2166 9919
A popular tropical-themed hotspot featuring live bands on Sunday and rave parties nightly till the wee hours. Plays all kinds of pop music. Also serves Asian food. Animal-rights people might be upset by the tanks of baby sharks amid the loud music. Can be a bit of a meat market with working girls gathering late at night.

Espanda
97 Jalan Sultan Ismail
Tel: 03-2142 6666
Hugging a prime corner location is this double-storey club with drapes, comfy divans and a large dance floor. Music offerings range from live Latin beats to R&B and house. When you've had enough of the bumping and grinding, retire to the lounge or cool down in the garden outside.

Hard Rock Café
Ground Floor, Wisma Concorde, Jalan Sultan Ismail
Tel: 03-2715 5555
This oldie-but-goldie international chain keeps them coming with live local and regional bands playing mainstream music. Attracts a mainly young crowd. Good American-style fare in large portions served in the café.

The Loft - Upstairs
28-40 Jalan Doraisamy
Tel: 03-2691 5668
Spread across four shoplots, clubbers dance till late to DJ-spun music at this large, open club. Has a steady, loyal clientele, mostly large groups of friends, mainly Chinese. Also houses Cynna, which has an extensive menu of vodka shots.

Nouvo
5 Jalan Sultan Ismail
Tel: 03-2170 6666
One of the best clubs in town featuring music mixed by local celebrity DJs and many international guest spinners. The action here starts very late.

Qba
Westin Kuala Lumpur,
Jalan Bukit Bintang
Tel: 03-2731 8333
Samba, cha cha and salsa to a live Latin band at this Havana-style club. Cigars and boutique wines are the other attractions of this classy two-storey place. Be sure to try its rum-based mojitos and caipirinhas.

Rum Jungle
1 Jalan Pinang
Tel: 03-2148 0282
Percussive drumming, reggae, Latin, Spanish and ethnic tunes are played at this tropical-themed club. Decor comes complete with water features, flaming torches and even a trapeze. Seating is on two levels and the dance floor is huge.

Zeta Bar
Hilton Kuala Lumpur,
3 Jalan Stesen Sentral
Tel: 03-2264 2501
Styled after the Hilton London's namesake nightclub, this sophisticated place is patronised by the who's who of Kuala Lumpur. DJs spinning rock and 1980s tracks alternate with a live band.

Zouk
113 Jalan Ampang
Tel: 03-2171 1997
This dome-shaped, Singapore-owned club strikes all the right chords. Velvet Underground's popular Wednesday Mambo Jambo nights draw the crowds with 1980s music, while the Loft's ever-changing line-up of local and international DJs keep electronic music fans happy.

Live Music/Jazz

Alexis Ampang
Lot 10, Ground Floor, Great Eastern Mall, 303 Jalan Ampang
Tel: 03-4260 2288
Hosting local and international singers and groups, including jazz acts, this sophisticated space also offers food and a choice of 300-plus wines. Showtime is 8.30pm; cover charge includes one drink.

Bangkok Jazz
Lot B1, Chulan Square, 92 Jalan Raja Chulan (Bukit Bintang)
Tel: 03-2145 8708
This Thai-accented bar with yummy tapas has live jazz by local groups Wed–Thur 9pm–1am, Fri–Sat 10pm–2am. Thursday is jam night.

No Black Tie
17 Jalan Mesui (Bukit Bintang)
Tel: 03-2142 3737
This pioneering space for local musicians/songwriters features quality acts ranging from jazz to Western classical music. Enjoy the music downstairs, or upstairs in its cosy and contemporary all-wood setting while you nibble on Japanese food. Showtime is 8.30pm and sometimes includes a cover charge.

Planet Hollywood, Kuala Lumpur
Ground Floor, Kuala Lumpur Plaza, Jalan Bukit Bintang
Tel: 03-2144 6602
Sunday Nite Live features great local acts, including some famous names. Packed on weekends, the American chain also offers burgers and other American-style grub.

Gay & Lesbian Venues

Blue Boy
50 Jalan Sultan Ismail
Tel: 03-2142 1067
Malaysia's oldest gay club which is almost 20 years old now. Packed on weekends, especially after midnight, it's friendly but smoky. Mainly Malay crowd. Good house dance tracks.

Frangipani
25 Changkat Bukit Bintang
Tel: 03-2144 3001
A seductive gay bar that attracts a stylish crowd. Offers a large selection of cocktails and shooters. DJs spin house music. Fancy couches and chairs add to its ambience.

KL's Nightlife Listings

Besides newspapers, you can get information from local magazines like *Faces* (www.faces.com.my), *Juice* (www.juiceonline.com) and *KLue* (www.klue.com.my), which are available free at Dome, Starbucks and Coffee Bean and Tea Leaf outlets; and *PM* (www.pmmag. com.my), from hotels and restaurants. Another good magazine which you have to buy is *Vision KL* (www.visionkl.com). For jazz listings, go to www.alldatjazz.com, and local independent or underground music, www.mentharas.com.

Liquid
Mezzanine, 2.04 Central Market Annex, Jalan Hang Kasturi
Tel: 03-2026 5041
Newly renovated with bead curtains, box lounges and interesting bathrooms, this sophisticated gay venue draws people especially on Wednesday, Friday and Saturday. The music is a mix of different strains of house.

Rahsia Restaurant & Bar
13 Jalan Damai
Tel: 03-2142 5555
Housed in a 1960s bungalow surrounded by greenery, the ambience is peaceful and stylish with jazz in the background. Complimentary cocktails plus 50 percent off beers and spirits daily from 4–8pm.

Shook!
Starhill Gallery, Jalan Bukit Bintang
Tel: 03-2719 8535
This classy gay-friendly hangout, which is spread over half the basement, has a circular cocktail bar where you can chill while listening to live jazz. An enormous array of food choices here and in the surrounding restaurants.

Penang

Most of the action in Georgetown tends to centre at The Garage, such as in the ever-trendy Slippery Senoritas along the waterfront also has numerous bistro-type pubs that open till the early hours.

Bars and Pubs

Cubar Club
75 Gurney Drive
Tel: 04-227 9823
This popular multiple-outlet nightspot comprises a wine and cigar bar on the ground floor, a lounge on the first floor, a barbecue restaurant on the second floor, and karaoke rooms at the top. Its selling point is its beer garden with wooden decks and fairy

lights, where you can sip Italian wine and shoot some pool. Open daily 5pm–3am.

Hong Kong Bar
371 Lebuh Chulia
Tel: 04-261 9796
Opened in 1920, this institution was a regular hangout for military personnel based in Butterworth. Today, it still attracts an assortment of prominent characters, many of whose photographs, medals and plaques plaster the walls and whose stories fill the guest book.

Shamrock Irish Pub
Ground Floor, MWE Plaza,
8 Lebuh Farquhar
Tel: 04-264 4748
This history-filled corner of Penang is home to an Irish pub, although the traditional cosy pub feel is sacrificed for a more open, breezier atmosphere. Tables spill outdoors onto the pavement. Thursday is ladies' night.

Slippery Senoritas
The Garage
Tel: 04-263 6868
A salsa club and Mexican restaurant. DJs spin a combination of R&B, house and current hits until 10pm when a live band takes over. Its cocktail menu offers 69 variations, which bartenders will deliver to you with an impressive stunt or two. Ladies' night is Wednesday.

Soho Free House Pub
50 Jalan Penang
Tel: 04-263 3331
A British tavern with a pool table, football on the telly and hearty pub grub, this tiny place draws local professionals as well as Britons and Australians. Happy hour is 5–9pm, when beer is a steal at RM5.50. Guinness on tap is RM14 a pint.

Clubs

ChillOut Club
The Gurney, Gurney Drive
Tel: 04-370 7000
This club is actually a complex of four bars and clubs, each playing a different style of music, including funk and R&B. The place is packed on weekends and on Wednesdays, when it is ladies' night. Post-partying, chill out at any of the cafés or 24-hour local eating outlets right on the doorstep of the complex.

Pulau Langkawi

The nightlife here is a little more laid-back. While there are many free-standing and resort bars, nightlife concentrates in Pantai Cenang and Pantai Tengah in restaurants such as Beach Garden and Bon Ton. These offer places for quiet drinks and good food and conversation.

Beach Garden Bistro
Pantai Cenang
Tel: 04-955 1363
One of the most popular nightspots in Langkawi. Sip margaritas under the stars after a dinner of steaks and pizzas.

Chin Chin Bar
Bon Ton Restaurant and Resort
Pantai Cenang
Tel: 04-955 6787
Enjoy cocktails or wine from an extensive wine list in this bar in a restored Chinese shophouse. Liqueur-flavoured coffee is its signature.

Sea Shell Beach Café
Mutiara Burau Bay Resort
Pantai Kok
Tel: 04-959 1061
Groove to live music under swaying palms. Café snacks and main courses are also served. Open noon–midnight.

Kuching

Kuching's nightlife centres on a few areas, such as **Jalan Padungan** and **Jalan Bukit Mata Kuching**. There are also bars and nightlife outlets in the hotels and resorts.

Jambu Tapas Bar
32 Jalan Crookshank
Tel: 082-235 292
A popular place to hang out at, especially on Friday nights when there is live jazz from 8.30pm onwards. Open Tues–Sun 5.30pm–12.30am.

Soho
64 Jalan Padungan
Tel: 082-247 069
Considered the chicest bar in Kuching, Soho is packed to the rafters at the weekend. Plays a mix of jazz, Latin and dance tunes. Serves good bar food and its restaurant caters to patrons looking for a more substantial meal as well.

Eagle's Nest
Jalan Bukit Mata Kuching
Another popular place for both pub grub and drinks at reasonable prices, as well as pool and darts. Open daily from 4pm till late. Happy hour ends at 9.30pm.

The Victoria Arms
Merdeka Palace Hotel,
Jalan Tun Abang Haji Openg
Tel: 082-258 000
Upmarket English pub with a restaurant and a wine bar. Friday is ladies' nights, and happy hour is 4–9pm. Open Sun–Fri noon–1am, Sat noon–2am.

Kota Kinabalu

A range of bars and pubs in the downtown area known as **The Water-**front offers drinks and entertainment both indoors and on the boardwalk.

Cock and Bull Bistro
The Waterfront
Popular pub with a live band performing every night. Pool table, wide-screen TV broadcasting football, and free WiFi Internet access. Open Sun–Thur 4pm–1am, Fri–Sat 4pm–2am. Happy hour is 4–9pm.

Shenanigan's Fun Pub
Hyatt Regency Kinabalu
Jalan Datuk Saleh Sulong
Tel: 088-221 234
Irish pub Shenanigan's remains a firm favourite, especially late at night, for its creative drinks and live performances by international acts.

Cocoon
Jalan Tun Razak Segama
Tel: 088-211 252
Located opposite the Hyatt, Cocoon entertains with live bands and DJ-spun R&B tunes.

SHOPPING

From international brands to hand-crafted ethnic artworks, Malaysia offers variety and choice for shoppers of every budget. The best times to shop are during the annual six-week Malaysia Mega Sale Carnival that starts in July when prices are slashed up to 70 percent. Throughout the year, sales are also held by the large departmental stores.

Shopping malls are found in every city and usually comprise a supermarket, departmental store, lots of smaller stores including fashion boutiques and shops selling shoes, watches, electrical goods, computers, mobile phones, books and more. Some also come with money changers, tour agencies, cineplexes and video game arcades. They usually have eateries, including food courts selling hawker fare, Western fast-food chains, and restaurants.

Open-air **night markets** (*pasar malam*) are good for soaking up local atmosphere and finding bargain-priced items, including clothes (which you try on in the open), shoes, trinkets, CDs, VCDs and DVDs (mostly pirated), and household items. There is also fresh produce, including fruit, and street food. The traders are itinerant, so check locations in the local press or at your hotel.

Kuala Lumpur

Shopping Malls

Avenue K
156 Jalan Ampang
Tel: 03-2168 7888

This spacious French-designed trapezoidal mall exudes luxury with arty video installations and fashion retrospectives alongside an Oriental Bazaar and boutiques selling international brands.

Bangsar Shopping Centre
285 Jalan Maarof, Bangsar Baru
Tel: 03-2094 7700
A favourite with expatriates. It has trendy shops, expensive restaurants and bars, designer boutiques and a Cold Storage supermarket stocking goodies from different countries. Holds a Saturday flea market.

Bangsar Village
1 Jalan Telawi 1, Bangsar Baru
Tel: 03-2288 1800
Another upmarket shopping centre catering to the neighbourhood with anchors like the Village Grocer, which carries international food items. Its new five-storey wing caters to lifestyle and fashion shoppers.

Berjaya Times Square
1 Jalan Imbi, Kuala Lumpur
Tel: 03-2144 9821
www.timessquarekl.com/home.html
A massive 900-outlet mall selling mainly medium-priced and lower-end goods, with leisure attractions like a cineplex (including an IMAX theatre) and a large indoor theme park.

Bukit Bintang Plaza
111 Jalan Bukit Bintang
Tel: 03-2148 7411
Adjacent to Sungei Wang Plaza, shops and boutiques here offer an astounding variety of audio-visual equipment, cameras, watches, clothes, leather goods, books and just about anything you can imagine.

Lot 10
50 Jalan Sultan Ismail
Tel: 03-2141 0500
www.ytlcommunity.com/lot10/index.asp
This green giant has a curvilinear atrium around which walkways go past upmarket shops selling the gamut from art books to club wear. The basement has a fancy hawker centre and supermarket. Anchor tenant Isetan offers a good variety of clothes.

Mid Valley Megamall
Lingkaran Syed Putra
Tel: 03-2938 3333
www.midvalley.com.my/store
Spacious walkways link over 430 outlets, including eateries, an 18-screen cineplex, and a Pets Wonderland and an entertainment centre for children, in a well-laid-out format. Anchor tenants are Metrojaya and Carrefour. A shuttle operates to the Bangsar LRT station and a walkway connects the KTM station to the mall.

Starhill Gallery
181 Jalan Bukit Bintang
Tel: 03-2148 1000

www.starhillgallery.com
A glitzy, exclusive mall for high-end fashion labels, often patronised by the rich and famous. Be sure to check out the Louis Vuitton Global Store. There are seven themed floors, covering food, art and health and beauty.

Sungei Wang Plaza
Jalan Sultan Ismail
Tel: 03-2144 9988
www.sungeiwang.com
This popular mall has 500-odd retail shops with moderately priced products and services. A good place for bargains. Check out Malaysian *haute couture* on the first floor. Adjoins Bukit Bintang Plaza.

Suria KLCC
Petronas Twin Towers, Jalan Ampang
Tel: 03-2382 3359
www.suriaklcc.com.my
This spacious and classy shopping venue has large departmental stores, including Isetan, Parkson Grand and Marks & Spencer, and over 270 specialty shops and food outlets. For ethnic goods, check out the Pucuk Rebung Museum Gallery and Aseana. Aseana's sarong section is excellent, as are its range of Straits Chinese embroidered *kebaya* blouses.

Handicrafts/Souvenirs/Markets

Central Market
Jalan Hang Kasturi
Tel: 03-2272 9966
Probably the best place for souvenirs, with its two levels offering Malaysian and Asian artworks and handicrafts.

Jalan Tuanku Abdul Rahman/Jalan Masjid India
Small interesting shops along **Jalan Tuanku Abdul Rahman** sell Asian wares such as Chinese embroidery and antiques. The Globe Silk Store along this road has affordable clothes and textiles. **Lorong Tuanku Abdul Rahman** is closed to traffic every Saturday 5–10pm and transformed into a *pasar malam* (night market) with stalls selling bargain goods. Jewellery, Indian saris and comfy cotton pyjamas are found in **Jalan Masjid India**.

Laman Seni (Art Market)
National Art Gallery, 2 Jalan Temerloh, off Jalan Tun Razak
Tel: 03-4025 4990
Held every first Saturday of the month from 8am to 5pm. The National Art Gallery's grounds are converted into a lively bazaar with paintings, sculptures and handicrafts by local artists. Workshops also take place.

Petaling Street Bazaar
The famous and crowded Petaling Street *pasar malam* comes to life

from 5pm to 11pm every evening, with a variety of stalls offering clothes, leather goods and copy watches.

Royal Selangor International
4 Jalan Usahawan 6, Setapak Jaya
Tel: 03-4145 6122
www.visitorcentre.royalselangor.com
Drop by the visitor centre of this successful home-grown label for a fine range of stylish pewter gifts and tableware, jewellery and sterling silverware. Don't miss the interesting (and free) factory tour.

Penang

Georgetown's maze of little shops around **Jalan Penang** are great for antiques and curios such as antique clocks, old bronze- and brassware, Dutch ceiling lamps, old phonographs, Chinese embroidery and porcelain, and Malaysian batik. **Saw Joo Aun** at 139 Jalan Pintai Tali has a large range of antique furniture.

Elsewhere in Penang, Little India on **Lebuh King** and **Lebuh Queen** has brightly coloured saris and *kurta* (mens' shirts), brassware and jewellery. **Lebuh Chulia** has good second-hand bookshops.

Chowrasta Market specialises in all kinds of cotton, silk and other materials, as well as dried local foods such as nutmeg and preserved fruits.

More bargain-priced Chinese souvenirs are at the **Kek Lok Si Temple** in Ayer Itam. **Batu Ferringhi** and **Teluk Bahang** offer brightly coloured, hand-painted batik sarongs and T-shirt souvenirs; the night market at the former sells fake but decent quality designer clothes and watches.

Modern **shopping malls** are at KOMTAR, Parkson and Gama on Jalan Penang, the Midlands Shopping Mall on Jalan Kelawei, the suburban Sunshine Square in Bayan Baru and Bukit Jambul Complex, which also has an ice-skating rink.

Melaka

Jalan Hang Jebat, formerly known as Jonker Street and once *the* place to shop in Melaka, has been a victim of money-driven urbanisation in recent years. Traditional craftsmen have been evicted and several historic shophouses have been demolished or else subjected to sham restoration projects where only the facades are kept while the interiors been modified beyond recognition. Still, antique collectors and bargain hunters will find what they want if they search hard enough. Authentic artefacts and relics, some over 300 years old, can be found along with a host of other more recent collectibles. Amid shops selling traditional crafts are trendy modern and creative handicraft shops.

There are more handicraft stalls are in **Taman Merdeka**, and a *pasar malam* (night market) takes place on Sunday at Jalan Parameswara.

Mahkota Parade
Jalan Merdeka
The city's biggest shopping mall, which also has an Asian antique and handicraft centre.

Orang Utan House
59 Jalan Hang Jebat
Run by local artist Charles Cham, whose humorous T-shirts and artworks make great souvenirs.

Wah Aik Shoemaker
103 Jalan Kubu
Located outside the main conservation area, this is famous for its tiny shoes made for Chinese women with bound feet, an ancient Chinese tradition of beauty that has long since died out.

Terengganu

In Kuala Terengganu, the **Central Market** on Jalan Sultan Zainal Abidin is the place to go to for batik and local handicrafts. Outside of town, the **Chendering** industrial estate offers handicrafts and batik, and along the beachfront to Marang, at Rusila, are numerous batik and basketware shops as well as vendors of the area's famous salted fish.

Teratai Arts and Craft
151 Jalan Bandar
Tel: 09-625 2157
A lovely gallery/shop owned by renowned artist Chang Fee Ming. It showcases his depictions of local life, as well as curios from all over Asia, including coconut-shell crafts and textiles.

Noor Arfa Batek House
Chendering
Tel: 09-617 5700
www.noor-arfa.com
Out at the Chendering industrial area is the Noor Arfa Batek House, Malaysia's largest, which welcomes visitors to watch and even participate in batik production. There is an excellent showroom as well.

Kelantan

Kelantan is an excellent place to purchase truly unique Malaysian gifts. The ultimate handicraft heaven is the road to PCB Beach (Pantai Cahaya Bulan), along which certain *kampung* (villages) are renowned for their particular handicrafts – contact Tourism Malaysia for more information.

Central Market
Kota Bharu
The Central Market has copious amounts of arts and crafts and batik items on the second level and produce stalls on the first.

Bazaar Buluh
Opposite the Central Market
Four floors of tiny shops display the best array of batiks in the peninsula. There's everything from hand-painted lengths of silk to hand-stamped sarongs, tablecloths, and cushion covers.

Kuching

Antiques, Iban textiles, handicrafts, and quality collectibles as well as pretty and interesting handcrafted souvenirs are readily available in Kuching.

Walking down the Main Bazaar can take all day for a shopping enthusiast. Old trading houses and shophouses have been converted and restored into galleries and shops selling a range of goods.

Anggun Collection
157E Jalan Satok
Tel: 082-422 495
It's well worth a short taxi ride from downtown if you're looking for exclusive fabrics and ready-made garments with Sarawakian motifs. Beautiful embroidered *kebaya* (some in organza), men's silk shirts, sarong and long scarf (*selendang*) sets as well as embroidered handbags and accessories are available.

Atelier Gallery
104 Main Bazaar
Tel: 082-243 492
Lucas Goh's atelier opposite the Chinese History Museum is filled with ethnic and primitive arts, furniture and tasteful accessories.

Nelson's Gallery
84 Main Bazaar
Tel: 082-411 066
Nelson Tan's gallery is so well known, it has no shop name displayed. It offers an eclectic collection with some very fine pieces of tribal art and ceramics tucked away under reproductions from Kalimantan.

Sarawak Handicraft Centre
Round Tower, Sarawak Tourism Complex
Watch crafts being fashioned by hand and buy the results; a good range of authentic, high-quality handicrafts.

Sarawak Plaza
Jalan Abell (next to Holiday Inn)
Kuching's oldest shopping complex still offers some interesting goods, plus a Coffee Bean outlet.

Sunday Market
Jalan Satok
Despite the name, this street market

starts at noon on Saturday and runs until Sunday afternoon. The market is filled with Dayak vegetable sellers, Chinese and Malay stalls selling all manner of handicrafts, jungle products, wild honey, pets, and plants, including gorgeous orchids.

Kota Kinabalu

Borneo Books
Ground and 2nd Floors, Wisma Merdeka, Jalan Haji Saman
The ground-floor shop has a range of souvenirs as well as books, while Borneo Books 2 upstairs has an unbeatable selection of books on Asia, particularly Borneo, plus a book exchange. Open daily 10am–8pm, except Sun until 5pm.

Borneo Trading Post
Lot 16, The Waterfront
Tel: 088-232 655
For quality handicrafts, jewellery, homewares, souvenirs and paintings from Borneo and the rest of Southeast Asia, this attractive, spacious shop is unrivalled. Open 11.30am–9pm.

Centrepoint Shopping Complex
Jalan Centrepoint
This is the largest shopping complex in town. Higher-quality branded goods are available on the 4th level in Palm Square, while food outlets can be found in the basement. Open daily 10am–9pm.

Handicraft Market
Jalan Tun Fuad Stephens
A rabbit-warren of tiny stalls filled with handicrafts from the Philippines (hence its local name of Filipino Market), Indonesia, Sabah and Sarawak. Take care of your bag, and be sure to bargain. Open daily 9am–6pm.

Wisma Merdeka
Jalan Haji Saman
Sabah's first shopping centre still offers a wide range of goods, particularly clothing (most of the cheap and cheerful variety) and shoes. Shops open at 9am or 10am and close around 9pm.

OUTDOOR ACTIVITIES

Nature Excursions

The **Malaysian Nature Society** (MNS) has chapters in many states, and a very active Selangor branch, which organises trips for members in caving, hiking, etc. MNS also runs nature education courses in Kuala Lumpur, Cameron Highlands, Kuala Selangor and Endau-Rompin in Johor. Tel: 03-

2287 9422, fax: 03-2287 8773; Sabah tel: 088-320 000; Sarawak tel: 082-682 185; www.mns.org.my.

Sport

The country's national sport is football (soccer), but favourites include badminton, basketball, hockey, netball, table-tennis, tennis, squash, *sepak takraw* (a local game), fishing, bowling, volleyball, martial arts and golf. In regional and international competitions, Malaysia has tended to shine in badminton and bowling, with squash being a rising star. Sports development falls under voluntary organisations, many affiliated to the Olympic Council of Malaysia.

Fishing

Malaysia offers good fishing but the sport is not regulated or organised. Boats range from bare basics to converted trawlers, and unless you go with a tour, you have to bring your own equipment. Shops stock the range, but do not rent. Malaysia is a manufacturer of rods and reels and is, in fact, a good and relatively cheap place to buy fishing equipment. Fishing tackle shops are found in all major towns.

Freshwater Fishing

Malaysia's fast-flowing rivers offer good fishing of smaller fish upstream. Many of these are found in pristine rainforest environments, usually accessible via four-wheel drive and some walking. Good spots include upper Sungai Endau in Johor, and the higher reaches of rivers that flow into Kenyir (Terengganu) and Temenggor (Perak). Here, you get the *kelah* (Malaysia Mahseer), a good fighter with which locals usually practise catch-and-release, and *tengas*, which also make fun fishing. Bigger-sized *kelah* are found in the middle river, as are *kaloi* (giant gouramey), *belida* (giant featherback) and the powerful *toman* (giant snakehead), the so-called shark of Malaysian freshwater fish.

Rivers in Sarawak and Sabah are excellent fishing grounds, particularly near the Kalimantan border, but the distances are great, and they are difficult to get to.

Lakes and reservoirs are where the other big freshwater fishing opportunities are. Since Malaysia has few natural ponds, anglers head for dammed lakes such as Kenyir and Temenggor. The natural lakes of Cini and Bera in Pahang are shallow, but good for *toman*.

Saltwater Fishing

Deep-sea bottom fishing is expensive, but compared to other countries in the region, relatively affordable. This involves going out with a rod and line with one or two hooks, using bait such as small fish and prawns, and fishing at depths of 50–100 metres (150–300 ft).

There are plenty of boats for hire on the coast. Most are basic, but a handful offer reasonable facilities. Nonetheless, some anglers find this primitiveness an attraction. Minimum numbers are needed before a boat will set off.

Some locations could be up to 4 hours away. A 2-day/1-night trip can be arranged, including boat, ice and bait. Meals can also be arranged.

Anywhere along the peninsula's west coast is good for fishing all year round, including Bagan Datoh and Pangkor (Perak), and Langkawi (Kedah). Table fish are the norm, including *kerapu* (grouper) and *ikan merah* (red snapper). Sarawakian locations include Miri and Tanjung Datu near Kuching.

The peninsula's east coast is good for blue-water game fishing. A popular centre is Mersing, the jumping-off point to the islands of Aur, Dayang and Pemanggil. Here you get black marlin, mackerel, sailfish, baraccuda, and giant trevally. Redang is another good location. In Sarawak, Miri is a centre; in Sabah, Labuan is good for bill fish, and Semporna and Sipadan are the spots for yellow fin tuna, great fighters that go up to 100 kg (220 lb). The best times for this sport are March–September.

Angling operators providing full facilities:

Cherry Bird Travel & Tours, 31A, 1st Floor, Jalan Barat, off Jalan Imbi, tel: 03-2141 1399, fax: 03-2141 3610; e-mail: cherryb@streamyx.com.
Hook, Line & Sinker, 44 Jalan Thamby Abdullah, off Jalan Tun Sambanthan, Kuala Lumpur, tel: 03-7725 2551; www.hook-line-sinker.net. It's also worth checking out the *Malay Mail* and angling magazines. Remember to ask about group sizes and facilities.

Golf

Malaysia is a golfer's paradise, especially on the peninsula's west and south coasts. The courses are designed to exploit the natural landscape and offer something for all levels of golfers, experienced and beginners, amateur or professional.

Generally, clubs are private. However, the so-called "resort clubs" are open to anyone, especially in holiday destinations. Courses are generally of international standard and are well-maintained; equal care is taken in the design and facilities of club houses. Equipment can be hired, and bought at affordable prices. Updated lists of golf clubs and resorts plus descriptions can be found in the monthly Pargolf magazine (www.pargolfmagazine.com), sold throughout the country and with listings of major golf courses.

Peninsular Malaysia

Awana Genting Highlands Golf and Country Resort, Pahang, tel: 09-211 3015; www.awana.com.my. At a cool 1,000 metres (3,000 ft) up in the Genting Highlands, this scenic 18-hole course is fairly demanding but enjoyable. Bunkers, ponds and streams add to the challenge. There is a three-tiered driving range.
Damai Laut Golf and Country Club, Perak, tel: 05-618 1020; www.swiss garden.com. This 18-holer is a challenging course on an isolated landscaped coast, designed by the golf course architect Ronald Fream. There is a club house, and a professional golf trainer is available. The club has links with the adjoining Swiss Garden Resort, across from Pulau Pangkor.
Datai Bay Golf Club, Langkawi, tel: 04-959 2700; www.dataigolf.com. A scenic, but tight 18-hole course between the Andaman Sea and the lush rainforest of Gunung Mat Cincang. The course lies uphill and downhill with some flat terrain. There is a club house and accommodations are available in the adjoining resorts The Andaman and The Datai.
Desaru Golf and Country Resort, Johor, tel: 07-822 2333; www.desaru golfclub.com.my. Famous old 18-hole course designed by Robert Trent Jones Jr, sitting in 120 hectares (300 acres) of forest along the coast; lovely all-wood club house with good views. It is linked to the Desaru Golden Beach Resort.
Kuala Lumpur Golf and Country Club, 10 Jalan 1/70D, off Jalan Bukit Kiara, tel: 03-253 1111. A 36-hole course and a fully automated computerised driving range. Visitors must produce their handicap cards upon registration. Fees for non-members are RM120 for 9-hole and RM180 for 18-hole during weekdays; and RM165 for 9-hole, RM250 for 18-hole during weekends.
Staffield Country Resort, Negeri Sembilan, tel: 03-8766 6177. Regarded as one of the country's best, this 27-hole course sits on 136 hectares (335 acres) of transformed rubber estate, with 82 bunkers and seven lakes. The Tudor-style club

house offers food and a wide range of sports facilities.

Sarawak

Eastwood Valley Golf and Country Club, Jalan Miri-Pujut By Pass, Miri, tel: 085-472 515. A new 18-hole course carved from a forest setting, with a driving range, timber chalets for rent and a restaurant.
Damai Golf Course, Santubong, tel: 082-846 088. A popular and accessible course with full facilities adjacent to Damai beach and the resort hotels.
Kelab Golf Sarawak, Kuching, tel: 082-440 966; www.kgswak.com. This championship 18-hole course is situated on converted secondary forest and swampland in Kuching, with ponds, sand traps and water hazards around the course's total of 36 undulating holes. The club house's terrace bar has a fine view of the course.

Sabah

Borneo Golf & Country Club, Km 69, Papar-Beaufort Highway, tel: 087-861 888. An 18-hole course designed by Jack Nicklaus, this is located about 1 hour's drive south of Kota Kinabalu. Apart from the restaurant, there are chalets for overnight accommodation.
Dalit Bay Golf and Country Club, tel: 088-791 188. Near Shangri-La's Rasa Ria Resort, about 45 minutes' drive from Kota Kinabalu. Offers smooth greens, sea views and a luxurious clubhouse.
Kinabalu Golf Club, Kota Kinabalu, tel: 088-251 615; www.borneo-online.com.my/kgc. The 18-hole course is set high on the slopes of Mt Kinabalu with magnificent views and the greater comfort of cooler air.
Sabah Golf and Country Club, Kota Kinabalu, tel: 088-247 533. A tricky 18-hole course with wide fairways and fast greens. The wind makes play even more interesting, especially during the monsoon months. Facilities include a swimming pool, gym and karaoke lounge.
Sutera Harbour Marina, Golf and Country Club, Kota Kinabalu, tel: 088-318 888; www.suteraharbour.com. Features a 27-hole Graham Marsh-designed course looking out to sweeping views of the South China Sea. Night golfing facility until 11pm.

Sport Diving

Dive operators are divided into on-site operators and those which arrange scheduled trips.
BSAC is offered by East Marine (tel: 04-966 5805; www.eastmarine.com.my) in Langkawi and Lang Tengah, a professionally outfit with multilingual dive masters and instructors.

Most operations are dive shops with dive masters and instructors; a few are certified dive centres offering the full range, from retail to rental and equipment servicing. Retail outlets are usually in the city rather than on the beach.

Peninsular Malaysia

Kembara Station, tel: 03-5635 2015; e-mail: enquiries@kembarastation.com. Focuses on diving in West Malaysia.
Dive Connection, tel: 03-2141 0031; e-mail: simrr@pd.jaring.my. Operates anywhere in Malaysia. It has a dive shop in Redang.
Pacific Dome, tel: 03-2770 5771; www.pacificdome.com.my. Reputable company that offers tours and dive instruction anywhere in Malaysia, including Mabul, and to Manado, Indonesia.

Sarawak

Although diving is not a sport normally associated with Sarawak, there is interesting diving off the coast of Miri.
Seridan Mulu Tours and Travel, Parkcity Everly Hotel, tel: 085-414 300; www.seridanmulu.com. This award-winning tour operator has a scuba diving division offering dives on the reefs within an hour or less of Miri; wreck dives and night dives also available.

Sabah

Among operators for scheduled trips, including instruction, are:
Borneo Divers, tel: 088-222 226; www.borneodivers.info. Dive pioneer specialising in Sipadan, nearby Pulau Mabul and the Labuan wrecks. It maintains a training centre on Mamutik island in Kota Kinabalu, where dive courses are given.
Layang Layang Island Resort, tel: 03-2162 2877; www.layanglayang.com. The sole resort on an island 1 hour's flight west of Kota Kinabalu. World-class diving and a luxurious resort.
Pulau Sipadan Resort and Tours, tel: 089-765 200; www.sipadan-resort.com. These resorts run their own excellent dive centres on Sipadan, Pulau Kalapai (close to Sipadan) and on beautiful Pulau Lankayan situated to the northwest of Sandakan.
Scuba Paradise, tel: 088-266 695, mobile tel: 019-881 1012. A Kota Kinabalu-based operator that arranges day-trips to Pulau Mantanani, an island north of the capital and renowned for its resident dugong.

Mountain Biking

Sarawak

Trails around rural areas outside Kuching, and near Damai Beach, are increasingly popular with many locals. For inexpensive bicycle rental and off-road cycling, contact **WG Cycles**, 36A, 1st Floor, Nam Meng Building, Jalan Ban Hock, tel: 082-238 239.

Sabah

Popular trails include rural areas around Kota Kinabalu. A good route is to bike down from park headquarters on Mt Kinabalu to Tamparuli, passing through magnificent verdant vistas and undiscovered villages.
TYK Adventure Tours, tel: 088-720 826; www.thamyaukong.com.

Rock Climbing

Peninsular Malaysia

Nomad Adventure, tel: 03-8024 5152; www.nomadadventure.com. This indoor rock climbing gym at a shopping centre in Kuala Lumpur organises trips to popular sites, runs special classes for women, and offers equipment for rent and sale.
Tracks Outdoor, tel: 03-7957 8363; e-mail: Tracks@mol.net.my. This operator has a 12-metre (39-ft) featured wall at Kuala Kubu Bharu with a slight overhang, suitable for all levels. Abseiling is conducted from 20–40-metre (60–120 ft) cliffs around its whitewater centre. Equipment can be hired and mountain bike trips arranged, too.

Whitewater Rafting

Peninsular Malaysia

Minimum numbers are required for whitewater rafting trips. Some companies also arrange transport from the city.
Nomad Adventure, tel: 03-8024 5152; www.nomadadventure.com. Specialises in whitewater kayaking and rafting in Sungai Sungkai and Sungai Kampar, Perak.

Sabah

Sabah has some of the country's best white-water with trips available to the scenic Kiulu and wild Padas rivers.
Riverbug, tel: 088-260 501; www.traversetours.com.

Aerial Sightseeing

Peninsular Malaysia

Aerial Sports, Experimental Aircraft Association of Malaysia, Nusajaya Flight Park, tel: 07-387 7411, 012-799 2529; www.ultralight.bizland.com. Offers lessons in flying and recreational hire of four types of parachutes and winged aircraft, the largest variety of recreational flying machines in Malaysia. Also offers hangar space rentals and maintenance as well as introductory flight lessons. You can solo in a powered paraglider or parachute aircraft in as little as 6 hours.

Sabah

Sabah Air, tel: 088-256 733/252 372; www.sabahair.com.my. View Mount Kinabalu, Sandakan or other Sabah tourist destinations from a helicopter in unique half-to-one hour aerial sightseeing tours. Aerial tours are also available over Kuala Lumpur. **Touchdown Holidays**, tel: 088-249 276; e-mail: victoria@touchdown.co.uk. For helicopter tours around Kota Kinabalu and north to Kudat.

SIGHTSEEING TOURS

The whole gamut is available, from city and night tours to week-long packages that cover several destinations, and any combination of fly, drive and coach choices with accommodations and sometimes transfers and food. Ask at your hotel, the tourism information centre, or check newspapers for the latest listings.

KTM offers good value rail packages to various destinations in Malaysia, which include train tickets, transfers, accommodation, some meals and tours. Try the Langkawi, Penang, Perlis or the popular Hat Yai (Thailand) package, tel: 03-2267 1200; fax: 03-2710 5716.

The **Eastern & Oriental Express** is the ultimate in luxury rail travel, complete with mahogany marquetry and Burmese rosewood inspired by the 1932 Marlene Dietrich film Shanghai Express. The 132-passenger train travels 2,000 km (1,260 miles) over 2 nights from Singapore through Kuala Lumpur to Bangkok (or vice versa) and stops along the way in Penang. For reservations, tel: 65-6392 3500 (Singapore); www.orient-express.com.

MAS's subsidiary, **MAS Golden Holidays**, offers a range of holiday packages including flights, transfers, accommodations, meals, and guided tours. There are options of fly-drive and coach holiday packages, as well as golf, scuba diving, and adventure packages. Tel: 03-7846 3000.

Kuala Lumpur

City Tours

New on the scene is the **Kuala Lumpur Hop-on and Hop-off Bus**. Launched in 2007, this service offers a convenient way of visiting the city's tourist sights on a double-decker bus. Plying 22 stops around the city, the buses run 8.30am–8pm daily. Waiting time is roughly 30 minutes and you can board and alight from the bus at any of the designated stops along the way. Pre-recorded commentaries in 8 languages are available on headsets. One-day tickets at RM38 for adults and RM17 for children and senior citizens can be purchased on board the bus, at selected hotels and travel agents or online at www.myhoponhopoff.com. For enquiries, call Elang Wah at tel: 03-2691 1382.

Tour Operators

Anjung Holidays, S1A, Terminal Pelancongan, Kuala Besut, tel: 09-697 4095; www.pulauperhentian.com.my. Various packages to Kelantan and Terengganu. Go island-shopping, caving, diving or fishing. You can also experience the Malay village lifestyle through the homestay package.
Asian Overland Services, 39C & 40C Jalan Mamanda 9, Ampang Point, Kuala Lumpur, tel: 03-4252 9100; www.asianoverland.com.my. A nationwide pioneer, which started with nature/adventure tours 30 years ago. It has broadened its scope to incorporate leisure, sightseeing, and other tour packages. Solid philosophy, trained guides, innovative ideas, tailor-made itineraries covering the whole country, good for long-haul journeys.
Mudtrekker Adventure Travel, 96-2 Jalan SS15/4B, Subang Jaya, Selangor, tel: 03-5632 3118; www.mud trekker.com. Offers eco-tours and adventure tours. Also offers tailor-made programmes, covering various areas such as Endau-Rompin, Ulu Slim, Lata Kijang and Taman Negara.
Ping Anchorage, 77A Jalan Sultan Sulaiman, Kuala Terengganu, tel: 09-626 2020; www.pinganchorage.com.my. This is your best bet for the east coast, especially Terengganu.
Utan Bara Adventure Travel, tel: 03-4022 5124; www.ubat.com.my. Specialises in jungle adventure and eco-tourism in lesser-known areas such as the upper Tenor river system in Taman Negara, Ulu Yam and Ulu Kemansah forests in Selangor, Ulu Cheh and Ulu Terong forests in Perak, and the Kuala Gandah Elephant Sanctuary in Selangor.

Sarawak

In Sarawak, tour companies are very helpful when it comes to longhouse visits and trekking tours. Unless one speaks at least a little Malay, visiting a longhouse without a guide is not recommended.
Borneo Adventure, 55 Main Bazaar, Kuching, tel: 082-245 175; www.borneoadventure.com. Known for its eco-tourism specialities, although it handles almost every type of tour. Another office in Kota Kinabalu (Gaya Centre).
Borneo Transverse, 15 Ground Floor, Jalan Green Hill, Kuching, tel: 082-257 784; www.borneotransverse.com.my.
CPH Travel Agencies, 70 Jalan Padungan, tel: 082-243 708; www.cph travel.com.my. One of Sarawak's oldest travel agencies, and the first to offer boat trips spotting Irrawaddy dolphins in the Damai region (May–Oct).
Seridan Mulu, Lot 273 Brighton Centre, Jalan Temenggong Datuk Oyang, Miri, tel: 085-415 582; www.seridan mulu.com. Miri-based adventure tour outfit offering white water rafting, diving, rock climbing, tribal trekking and caving; Mulu Caves specialist.

Sabah

Many excursions in Sabah are difficult without the help of a tour company, or at least a guide.
Borneo Adventure, 5th Floor, Room 509-512 Gaya Centre, Kota Kinabalu, tel: 088-238 731/2; www.borneoadven ture.com. Winner of international eco-tourism awards, this company specialises in individually tailored tours.
Discovery Tours, Wisma Sabah, Jalan Tun Fuad Stephens, Kota Kinabalu, tel: 088-221 244; www.infosabah.com.my/discovery. An energetic company with many interesting tours. It also has offices at the Shangri-La's Tanjung Aru Resort and Shangri-La's Rasa Ria Resort.
Borneo Eco Tours, 2nd Floor, Shop Lot 12a, Lorong Bernam 3, Taman Soon Kiong, 88300 Kota Kinabalu, tel: 088-438 300; www.borneoecotours. com. Block J, 1st Floor, Lot 74, Bandar Pasar Raya, Jalan Utara Mile 4, Sandakan, tel: 089-220 210. This award-winning company specialises in environmentally oriented tourism, with trips focusing on the flora and fauna of Sabah. The company also runs an eco-friendly lodge at Sukau on the Kinabatangan River.
Traverse Tours, 2nd Floor, Gaya Centre, Jalan Tun Fuad Stephens, Kota Kinabalu, tel: 088-260 501; www.traversetours.com. Adventure tourism specialist, including Riverbug's white water rafting.
Wildlife Expeditions, Shangri-La's Tanjung Aru Resort, Kota Kinabalu, tel: 088-268 309; www.wildlife-expeditions.com. Room 903, 9th Floor, Wisma Khoo Siak Chiew, Sandakan, tel: 089-219 616. Tours to most Sabah destinations including Mount Kinabalu, Sepilok, Tenom Rafflesia Centre, Padas River rafting, Rungus longhouses, Turtle Islands, Danum Valley and Kinabatangan.

A – Z

A HANDY SUMMARY OF PRACTICAL INFORMATION, ARRANGED ALPHABETICALLY

A ccidents

In case of an accident or emergency, call the following numbers: **Police/ambulance** – 999 (112 from mobile phone); **Fire/rescue** – 994.

In East Malaysia, however, it is preferable to call a major hospital for an ambulance. In Kota Kinabalu, call Sabah Medical Centre (tel: 088-211 333) or Queen Elizabeth Hospital (tel: 088-218 166). In Sandakan, call Duchess of Kent Hospital (tel: 089-212 111); and in Tawau, Tawau Hospital (tel: 089-773 533).

In Kuching, call Normah Medical Centre (tel: 082-440 055); in Sibu, Sibu Specialist Hospital (tel: 084-343 333); and in Miri, Miri City Medical Centre (tel: 085-426 622).

B udgeting Your Trip

Travel to Malaysia is relatively cheap. Accommodation prices generally start from RM40 a night in budget places to RM700 a night in five-star hotels. Many hotels include breakfast with the room rate. For those who stay in three-star accommodation and are prepared to eat with the locals, expect to pay about RM300 per day for lodging, transport and meals.

National park accommodation in Sabah is more expensive than in Sarawak, where dormitory beds can cost as little as RM10.

Good food of excellent value can be found in hawker centres, coffee shops and food courts in shopping complexes, where RM4–5 can buy you a meal and a non-alcoholic drink. Alcoholic drinks are expensive; expect to pay at least RM6.50 for a beer in a coffee shop and up to around RM20 in luxury hotels and nightclubs.

Public transport is cheap. Taxi fares are moderate although meters are not widely used and bargaining may be required. In cities, taxis may charge double by insisting on a flat rate; in Kuala Lumpur, there is a 50 percent surcharge for taxi trips between midnight and 6am. Car hire is reasonably priced, but parking in city centres and 5-star hotels is very expensive.

Business Hours

In an Islamic nation with a British colonial past, the definition of the working week varies. It runs from Monday to Friday in all states except Terengganu, Kelantan, Kedah and Perlis. These four states with a stronger Islamic tradition retain the traditional half-day on Thursday and businesses are closed on Friday, not Sunday.

The working day begins at 8am and ends at 5pm, with time off on Friday from noon to 2.30pm for Muslim prayers. Most private businesses stick to the nine-to-five routine. Shops start to close at 6pm, but large supermarkets, department stores and shopping malls are open 10am–10pm.

Children

There are enough attractions to keep children occupied when travelling in Malaysia. However, children might be more susceptible to heat and food- and water-related ailments. Suitable food could be a problem off the beaten track. Malaysian infrastructure is not at all baby friendly, even in the cities. There are few mother's rooms or nappy-changing tables in toilets, and it may be difficult to buy infant products in rural areas. Public transport and public areas are unsympathetic to pushchairs. Yet Malaysians love children, so a helping hand is never far away.

Children under 12 travel for half-price on buses and boats. Four- and five-star hotels and resorts offer clubs with children's activities. Bigger malls and fast-food outlets have play areas, and there are enough attractions in the cities to keep the young ones happy.

Climate

Malaysia's weather is generally hot and sunny all year round, with temperatures averaging 32°C (90°F) during the day and 24°C (75°F) at night. Humidity is high at 80 percent. Temperatures in the highland areas, such as Cameron and Genting, are lower and much more tolerable.

The monsoon season of April/May brings heavy rain to the west coast of Peninsular Malaysia. The east coast of the peninsula and Sabah and Sarawak experience their monsoon

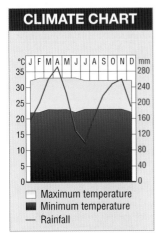

CLIMATE CHART

- ☐ Maximum temperature
- ■ Minimum temperature
- — Rainfall

season between November and February. The inter-monsoon periods can also be wet. Light showers come and go, helping to relieve the heat.

Thick haze has been recurrent from July to October, especially for the Klang Valley and East Malaysia, for some years. Most of the smoke and soot is blown in by the south-west monsoon from parts of Indonesia hit by forest fires, which have been worsened by the dry weather caused by the El Niño phenomenon.

Clothing

In Malaysia's tropical climate, think cotton and natural fibres. Sunglasses, sunblock and umbrellas or raincoats are advisable.

Malaysians are fairly informal but they do dress up for dinner or a night out, especially in the cities. In fact, the fancier establishments have a dress code. Moreover, since this is a predominantly Muslim and conservative country, observance of local customs is important. T-shirts and longish shorts are fine, except in rural areas and when you go off the beaten tourist track; in which case, keep your legs and upper arms covered. Shoes should be removed before entering temples and homes, so slip-ons are handy.

If you plan to visit the hill stations, bring along a light sweater for the cooler evenings.

Crime & Security

Like anywhere else, pickpockets and snatch thieves are your biggest worry. Snatch thieves tend to be two men on a motorcycle or men leaning out of moving cars to grab your bag. If your bag is snatched, give in, because many thieves carry knives which they do not hesitate to use. On pavements, always walk in the direction of oncoming traffic and make sure your bag is on the side away from the traffic.

Unless you are in a luxury hotel, do not leave valuables in your room, except in a safe. Carry your passport and money with you at all times – even while sunbathing – or keep them in the main hotel safe. Sling your camera around your body, and make sure your backpack is firmly strapped on. If you are going diving or snorkelling or taking part in any other adventure sport, put valuables in a small backpack which you can leave with the operators. Travelling on public transport is safe – just keep an eye on the luggage that is taken out whenever your coach stops. Walking around at night is generally

safe, especially in tourist areas, but keep to well-lit places.

Hitch-hiking is very uncommon and hence can be frustrating and even dangerous. Public transport, if slow and erratic in some places, is cheap and plentiful.

The **Tourist Police** (tel: 03-2149 6590) patrol tourist spots. Their uniforms feature a checkered hatband, dark-blue shirt and trousers, and a red-and-blue badge with the letter "I" (for information) on the breast pocket. They can help with the loss of passports and other documents as well as give general advice. Otherwise, do not hesitate to head to any police station or booth when you need help (tel: 999 or 112 from mobile phone).

Common Scams

Although Malaysians are friendly, they rarely approach foreigners or engage them in conversation. Always be on guard and walk away if they ask you to meet a "relative" who has "always wanted to visit your country", or to partake in a gambling session with "guaranteed winnings".

Be aware of people pretending to be police and demanding to see your ID. The police will not do so unless you have committed an offence or you are in a nightspot that is being raided.

Never buy anything from touts, whether bus, train or other tickets.

Women Travellers

Travelling alone is fairly safe for women, but Western women do have the image of being "easy", so a wedding ring helps, or a "Yes, I'm married" to the inevitable query. Ignore wolf whistles and catcalls. If you are approached, be polite but firm. Mostly people are just being friendly, even if some might be hoping for something more; if you start feeling uneasy, walk away. Be careful about being over-friendly with your tour guide.

Malaysians stare – both men and women – but wearing revealing clothes in areas that are newer to tourism will invite uncalled-for attention. In Malaysia's rural societies, young women rarely approach or speak to male strangers, and travel is virtually unheard of, let alone travelling alone. Topless and nude sunbathing is prohibited.

Customs Regulations

Import duties seldom affect the average traveller, who may bring in 250 g (½ lb) of tobacco, 50 cigars, or 200 cigarettes, and a 1-litre bottle of liquor duty-free as well as personal cameras, watches, cassette players, cosmetics, etc. The duty-free guidelines do not apply on domestic flights, or for Singaporeans.

On rare occasions, visitors may be asked to pay a deposit for temporary importation of dutiable goods (up to 30 percent of the value), which is refundable upon departure. Be sure to get an official receipt for any tax or deposit paid.

Pornography, firearms, ammunition and walkie-talkies are strictly prohibited. The export of antiques requires a licence from the Museum Department. Possession of narcotics and other illegal drugs carries the death sentence. For details, call Customs at tel: 03-8776 8055.

D isabled Travellers

Basic disabled-friendly facilities, like extra-wide parking bays, wheelchair ramps and toilets, can be found in major hotels, malls, theatres, fast-food chains and some government buildings in the bigger cities like Kuala Lumpur. The Kuala Lumpur International Airport and the Light Rail Transit (LRT) system in Kuala Lumpur are also disabled friendly. But in general, Malaysia falls short on accommodating the disabled. Urban streets are uneven and sometimes potholed and difficult to navigate, while ramps are not that common. Taxis will usually not transport people in wheelchairs.

E lectricity

Electrical outlets are rated at 220 volts, 50 cycles, and serve three-pin, flat-pronged plugs. Most supermarkets stock adapters for different voltages. Major hotels can supply adapters for 110–120 volt, 60 Hz appliances.

Embassies and Consulates

Embassies and consulates are located in Kuala Lumpur.
Australia, 6 Jalan Yap Kwan Seng, tel: 03-2146 5555; www.australia.org.my
Canada, 17th Floor, Menara Tan & Tan, 207 Jalan Tun Razak, tel: 03-2718 3333; www.dfait-maeci.gc.ca/kualalumpur
China, 229 Jalan Ampang, tel: 03-2142 8495
Denmark, 22nd Floor, Wisma Denmark, 86 Jalan Ampang, tel: 03-2032 2001; www.ambkualalumpur.um.dk
France, 196 Jalan Ampang, tel: 03-2053 5500; www.ambafrance-my.org
Germany, 26th Floor, Menara Tan & Tan, 207 Jalan Tun Razak, tel: 03-

2170 9666; www.german-embassy.org.my
India, Jalan Taman Duta, off Jalan Duta, tel: 03-2093 3510; www.indianhighcommission.com.my
Indonesia, 233 Jalan Tun Razak, tel: 03-2116 4000; www.kbrikl.org.my
Italy, 99 Jalan U Thant, tel: 03-4256 5122; www.ambkualalumpur.esteri.it
Japan, 11 Pessiaran Stonor, tel: 03-2142 7044; www.my.emb-japan.go.jp
Myanmar, 11A Jalan Aman, off Jalan Dama, tel: 03-2142 7954
Netherlands, 7th Floor, The Amp Walk, South Block, 218 Jalan Ampang, tel: 03-2168 6200; www.netherlands.org.my
New Zealand, Level 21 Menara IMC, Jalan Sultan Ismail, tel: 03-2078 2533; www.nzembassy.com
Norway, 53th Floor Empire Tower, Jalan Tun Razak, tel: 03-2175 0300; www.norway.org.my
Philippines, 1 Changkat Kia Peng, tel: 03-2148 9989; www.philembassykl.org.my
Singapore, 209 Jalan Tun Razak, tel: 03-2161 6277; www.mfa.gov.sg/kl
South Korea, 9 Jalan Nipah, off Jalan Ampang, tel: 03-4251 2336; www.malaysia.or.kr
Sri Lanka, 12 Jalan Keranji 2, Ampang Hilir, tel: 03-4256 8987; www.slhc.com.my
Sweden, 6th Floor, Wisma Angkasa Raya, 123 Jalan Ampang, tel: 03-2052 2550; www.swedenabroad.com
Switzerland, 16 Persiaran Madge, tel: 03-2148 0622
Thailand, 206 Jalan Ampang, tel: 03-2148 8222; www.mfa.go.th
United Kingdom, 185 Jalan Ampang, tel: 03-2170 2200; www.britain.org.my
United States, 376 Jalan Tun Razak, tel: 03-2168 5000; malaysia.usembassy.gov
Vietnam, 4 Persiaran Stonor, tel: 03-2148 4036; www.vietnamembassy.org.my

Entry Requirements
Passports & Visas

Passports must be valid for at least 6 months at the time of entry. Remember that Sabah and Sarawak are treated like separate countries, and you will have to go through customs and immigration with your passport again there, whether coming from Peninsular Malaysia or travelling between the two states.

A social single-entry visa valid for 3 months can be applied for at Malaysian diplomatic missions overseas. Check the Tourism Malaysia website (www.tourism.gov.my) or the **Immigration Department** website (www.imi.gov.my) for details about formalities and visa requirements. Citizens of Commonwealth countries (except Bangladesh, India, Nigeria, Pakistan and Sri Lanka),

ASEAN countries, the US, Switzerland, the Netherlands, San Marino and Liechtenstein do not need a visa. Citizens from some EU, South American and South African countries and Arab nationals do not need a visa for a visit not exceeding 3 months.

Extensions may be applied for at any immigration office:
Headquarters of the Department of Immigration Malaysia (Ministry of Home Affairs), Level 1-7 (Podium), Block 2G4, Precint 2, Federal Government Administration Centre, Putrajaya, tel: 03-8880 1000.
Kuala Lumpur, Aras 1-5, Blok 1, Jabatan Imigresen Wilayah Persekutuan, Pusat Bandar Damansara, tel: 03-2095 5077.
KLIA Immigration Office, Bangunan Airport Management Centre (AMC), tel: 03-8776 8001/3681.
Alor Star, Kedah, Wisma Persekutuan, Jalan Kampung Baru, tel: 04-733 3302.
Ipoh, Aras 2-4, Kompleks Pejabat, Kementerian Mal Ewal Dalam Negeri, Persiaran Meru Utama, Bandar Meru Raya, Jelapang, tel: 05-501 7100.
Johor Bahru, Johor, Wisma Persekutuan, Jalan Air Molek, tel: 07-224 4255.
Kangar, Perlis, Tingkat 1, Bangunan Persekutuan, Persiaran Jubli Emas, tel: 04-976 2636.
Kota Bharu, Kelantan, Wisma Persekutuan, Jalan Bayam, tel: 09-748 2120.
Kota Kinabalu, Sabah, Bangunan Wisma Dang Bandang, Jalan Tuanku Abdul Rahman, tel: 088-280 700.
Kuala Terengganu, Terengganu, Wisma Persekutuan, Jalan Sultan Ismail, tel: 09-622 1424.
Kuantan, Pahang, Jabatan Imigresen Negeri Pahang, Kompleks Imigresen, Bandar Indera Mahkota, tel: 09-573 2200.
Kuching, Sarawak, Bangunan Sultan Iskandar, Jalan Simpang Tiga, tel: 082-247 222.
Labuan, Kompleks Ujana Kewangan, Jalan Merdeka, tel: 087-412 298.
Melaka, Aras 1-3, Kompleks Kementerian Hal Enwal Dalam Negeri, Jalan Seri Negeri, Ayer Keroh, tel: 06-232 2662.
Penang, Jalan Kelasah, Seberang Jaya, tel: 04-397 3011.
Seremban, Negeri Sembilan, Wisma Persekutuan, Jalan Dato' Abdul Kadir, tel: 06-762 0000.
Shah Alam, Selangor, Kompleks PKNS, tel: 03-5519 0653.

Etiquette

Malaysians smile a lot, and are more often than not polite and helpful. They are remarkably tolerant and forgiving of foreigners' gaffes. In cities and tourist areas, they take a more liberal approach, but it helps to know a few local norms.

Greetings

Seniority is much respected. The oldest male member of a family is greeted first, often sits in the best and highest seat, and is consulted first on most matters. It is considered rude to address older people by their names. Unless you know your business associates well or you know otherwise, always use titles such as Mr (Encik), Madam (Mrs) or Miss (Cik). If you are a man, you must never offer to shake a Muslim lady's hand unless she offers it first. A simple nod or smile will suffice. Similar rules apply to women wanting to shake a Muslim man's hand. If you get what you think is a limp handshake, it is actually a Malay greeting (*salam*), which involves brushing the palm of the other person and placing the hand on one's heart. This signifies "I am pleased to meet you from the bottom of my heart".

Head and Feet

The Hindu religion regards the head as the wellspring of wisdom and the feet as unclean, so it is insulting to touch another adult's head, point one's feet at anything, or step over another person. Malays consider it rude to point the index finger at something, so when indicating direction, make a fist with the right hand with the thumb folded on top and then aim at the subject. Use the right hand to pass or accept anything. The left is traditionally "dirty" because of its washroom connections.

In Malaysian homes, it is rude, especially for women, to cross your legs in front of your host. If entering a Malaysian home, remove your shoes. It is courteous to come bearing a gift, no matter how small. Never refuse drinks or snacks served to you, even if it is to take a sip or bite. In a Malay home, when passing in front of someone, bow slightly while walking and point an arm down to indicate the path to be taken.

At Places of Worship

Remove your shoes before entering any place of worship. At the mosque, non-Muslims are prohibited from entering certain areas; signs are clearly displayed. Conservative clothing is advisable – meaning visitors, both men and women, must have their arms and legs covered. Some mosques, like the Putra Mosque in Putrajaya, provide robes as well as scarves for covering your hair.

Certain Hindu temples are not open to non-Hindus to keep the place "pure" from people who consume beef. If you enter a Sikh temple, be sure to cover your hair. Be sensitive about photographing worshippers in prayer.

Public Behaviour

While holding hands is common, displaying other forms of affection in public is considered bad form. The government is particular about upholding Islamic and Asian moral values, so such behaviour in public places is unacceptable, especially if you are with a local or look like one. Shouting and talking loudly, even outside a nightspot, is considered rude.

G ays & Lesbians

Like in many Asian societies, the gay scene in Malaysia is discreet although present. Homosexuality is illegal in Malaysia, although the society is generally tolerant. Gay visitors can travel safely and without fear of persecution in Malaysia, usually facing only minor harassment from the police if it happens at all. However, note that there are provisions in the Penal Code and for Muslims, Islamic Shar'iah laws that penalise same-sex sexual acts, sodomy, fellatio and cross-dressing.

Kuala Lumpur has a sizeable gay and lesbian community, unofficially estimated at 60,000. Comprehensive information and newsgroups are available on gay portal **Utopia** at www.utopia-asia.com/tipsmala.htm. For more information on the community, contact community rights and AIDS/HIV outreach organisation, **PT Foundation** (tel: 03-4044 4611; www.ptfmalaysia.org). For gay-friendly establishments, see page 387.

Government

Malaysia is a constitutional monarchy comprising 13 states and a federal territory. Independent from British colonial rule since 1957, the Malaysian government is regulated by the Parliament comprising the *yang di-pertuan agong* (king), who is elected for a five-year term from among the sultans of the states, and two houses: the House of Representatives, to which members are elected once every five years, and the Senate, to which members are nominated.

The executive functions of the government are carried out by the cabinet, led by the prime minister. The current prime minister in Malaysia is Datuk Seri Abdullah Ahmad Badawi, who came into office in October 2003. The political entity which has been in power since Independence is the Barisan Nasional (National Front) coalition representing numerous race-based parties.

H ealth & Insurance

Visitors entering Malaysia are not required to show evidence of vaccination for smallpox or cholera, but it is a good idea to immunise yourself against cholera, hepatitis A and B and tetanus. If you are visiting remote rainforest areas, it is advisable to take protection against malaria. See your doctor before leaving home. Malaria tablets are only available on prescription in Malaysia. To keep mosquitoes at bay, use insect repellents, mosquito coils and mosquito nets at night. There are also periodic outbreaks of dengue fever for which there is no immunisation, so take preventive measures like using insect repellent. If you suffer from a very high fever while (or shortly after) visiting Malaysia, consult a doctor immediately.

Treat open cuts and scratches immediately as infection in humid climates can delay healing, and at worst, cause tropical ulcers. It is advisable to read up on the rainforest and marine creatures to avoid.

Many first-time visitors to a tropical country take a while to adjust to the heat and humidity; make sure you drink at least 2 litres (8–10 glasses) of water to keep hydrated. Keep out of the sun during the hottest part of the day (11am–1pm). Tap water in the cities is potable but to be on the safe side, drink boiled or bottled water. Avoid ice cubes at streetside stalls and small coffee shops, as they are usually made using unboiled water. Refrain from eating peeled fruit at street stalls. Otherwise, food served in restaurants and hawker centres is clean.

Should you be in Malaysia during the haze period, be aware that the haze affects those with respiratory illnesses, especially asthmatics. Stay indoors or wear a mask when outdoors. Thankfully, the monsoon season right after helps clear the air. The risk of bird flu in Malaysia is believed to be very low. As precautions, avoid visiting live animal markets and poultry farms, and ensure poultry and egg dishes are thoroughly cooked. For more information, visit the **Department of Public Health** website www.dph.gov.my.

Hospitals & Medical Care

Hospitals & Medical Clinics

The World Health Organization's World Health Report 2006 ranked Malaysia in the global top 26 percent, according to various health-related indicators such as life expectancy and per-capita expenditure on health.

The country has some of the best doctors in the region, both locally and overseas trained and who speak good English. Advance medical care is available in both government and private hospitals, which are well equipped and have specialised clinics and good medical staff. Foreigners can seek treatment and get health screenings in Malaysia for fees much lower than in the West. Consultancy generally starts at RM20–30 for a GP and RM60 for a specialist. Government hospitals charge a fraction of what private ones charge, but there is usually a longer waiting period. See www.moh.gov.my for a hospital list.

For minor problems, there are smaller private medical clinics found all over the cities, with some open 24 hours. These dispense most generic medicines.

Kuala Lumpur
Hospital Kuala Lumpur
Jalan Pahang
Tel: 03-2615 5555
www.hkl.gov.my
The largest government hospital, it has 23 clinical departments, a large specialist team and good facilities.
Tung Shin Hospital
Jalan Pudu (near Puduraya)
Tel: 03-2072 1655
www.tungshinhospital.com.my
A good, medium-sized private hospital offering Western and traditional Chinese treatments.
Gleneagles Intan Medical Centre
Jalan Ampang
Tel: 03-4255 2786
www.gimc.com.my
A medium-sized private hospital with top-notch medical services. Favoured by expatriates, it offers special services for overseas patients, such as emergency airlift transfer arrangements.

Penang
Adventist Hospital
465 Jalan Burma, Georgetown
Tel: 04-222 7200
www.pah.com.my
Private, not-for-profit Christian hospital with various specialisations.
Gleneagles Medical Centre
Jalan Pangkor, Georgetown
Tel: 04-227 6111
www.gleneagles-penang.com

This private hospital has a wide range of specialisations and health screening packages.

Melaka
Mahkota Medical Centre
3 Mahkota Melaka, Jalan Merdeka
Tel: 06-285 2999
www.mahkotamedical.com
Various clinical specialisations are covered by Mahkota, which also offers a dental centre and a health screening centre.

Kota Kinabalu
Sabah Medical Centre
off Jalan Damai
Tel: 088-211 333
www.sabah.org.my/smc
The largest and best-equipped hospital in Sabah. A consultation with a general doctor here costs RM20, while specialists charge RM50–70.

Kuching
Normah Medical Centre
Jalan Datuk Patinggi
Tel: 082-440 055
One of Sarawak's best hospitals with a full range of services. A consultation will cost around RM15.

Dental Clinics

Dentists are called *doctor gigi* ("teeth doctors"). Many dentists have trained overseas so the services offered are of a high standard. Dental fees are substantially lower than those paid in the West.

Although major public hospitals in Sabah and Sarawak offer dental services, a higher standard of care is provided in private practice. Call first to make an appointment.

For a complete list of clinics, check the Malaysian Dental Association website at www.mda.org.my. Consultancy rates start at RM30.

Kuala Lumpur
Dentalpro Dental Specialist Centre
8 Lengkok Abdullah, Bangsar Utama
Tel: 03-2287 3333
Twin Towers Medical Centre KLCC
401 F&G, Level 4, Suria KLCC
Tel: 03-2382 3500

Kota Kinabalu
Lim Dental Surgery
1st Floor, Lot 20, Taman Fortuna,
Jalan Penampang
Tel: 088-256 788

Kuching
Dr Anthony Tan, G20 Jalan Borneo
Tel: 082-416 930

Pharmacies

Most towns, shopping centres and shopping malls have pharmacies often operated by chains like Watson's, Georgetown and Guardian. Usually, a licensed pharmacist is on duty on weekdays 10am–5pm. Many medicines are dispensed without prescription but controlled drugs require a doctor's prescription. Do check the expiry dates. Pharmacies also stock nutritional and personal-care products.

In Sabah and Sarawak, 24-hour polyclinics also provide medications. Prices are very reasonable, especially for Malaysian-manufactured drugs.

I nternet

Cybercafés with broadband Internet can be found in all the capitals and most towns and tourist areas. Many are in large shopping centres. Backpacker hotels seem to be more advanced in providing this service than some of the medium-class hotels. Major hotels offer an Internet service at a high cost in their business centres, and business-class international hotels offer it in the rooms for a fee.

Wireless broadband (WiFi) is also becoming quite widespread. In cafés, WiFi is usually free with the purchase of products; the cashier will give you a login name and a password. Rates start from RM2 per hour.

L eft Luggage

Hotels usually provide free left luggage services for their guests.
Kuala Lumpur International Airport (tel: 03-8787 4210) has locker rental services in the Satellite Building (RM5 per 2 hours) and counter storage services in the Main Building (RM10–30 a day). **KL Sentral** (tel: 03-8787 4210) has lockers on Level 1 and 2 (RM1 per item per day). There are also left luggage services at **Puduraya Bus Station** (tel: 03-2070 0145) at RM2 per item per day (8am–10pm).

There are no storage facilities at the airports in Sabah and Sarawak. Excess luggage can be stored at your hotel or tour operator's office if you are travelling to a longhouse or a jungle lodge. Kinabalu Park Headquarters has a luggage facility for those climbing Mount Kinabalu.

Lost Property

About all that can be done about lost property in Malaysia is making a police report and hoping that whoever finds it, is honest. Call the **Tourist Police** at 03-2149 6590 or lodge a report at the nearest police station. A police report will be important for making an insurance claim.

There is a Lost and Found service at **KLIA** (Main Building tel: 03-8776 4386; Satellite Building tel: 03-8776 2454) and **KL Sentral** (tel: 03-8787 4210). If you have left anything in a taxi or long-distance bus, try calling the relevant company as well.

M aps

Basic maps are available free at most hotels, Tourism Malaysia offices (*see pages 401–2*) and the Sabah and Sarawak Tourism Board offices. You can also purchase decent maps from any good bookshop or convenience store. The *Insight Fleximap Kuala Lumpur* and *Insight Fleximap Penang & Langkawi* are good ones to get. Also check out www.kuala-lumpur.ws/maps for a basic online map of the capital.

Media

Newspapers and Magazines

The main daily newspapers are in Bahasa Malaysia and English. There are also Chinese- and Tamil-language newspapers. The New Straits Times is sympathetic to government policy, while the city-based The Sun takes a more issues-based approach and champions more transparent government. The other big English-language national daily is The Star and the main business weekly is The Edge. The Malay Mail is an afternoon tabloid with a chattier, more local slant. Sabah and Sarawak have their own papers, including The New Sabah Times, Sabah Daily News, Daily Express, Sarawak Tribune and Borneo Post.

Most of these papers have online editions; The Star Online (www.thestar.com.my) is one of the most popular websites for Malaysian news. There is also a large number of local magazines, from leisure to entertainment to business. Foreign newspapers and magazines can be purchased in large cities.

To find out what is happening in the cities, look at the "What's On" sections of magazines like Juice, KL Lifestyle, KL Vision, KLue and Faces, which are some of the popular local lifestyle and entertainment magazines with news and listings. These are available free in cafés. For food and dining information, check out the Tatler Malaysia's Best Restaurants.

Sabah Tourism's informative monthly magazine (Malaysian Borneo Sabah) can be collected at its office in Kota Kinabalu. In Kuching, The Official Kuching Guide, updated

annually, is very helpful; also informative is the quarterly Kuching Talk. Both are available at the Kuching Airport and the Visitors Information Centre in the city.

Radio and Television

The radio can be heard everywhere, blaring a wild assortment of different sounds; a flick of the dial will tune you to Malay rock or heavy metal, Tamil numbers or Western classical music, Canto-pop or the latest hits from Britain or the United States. The main national English-language radio stations are: Hitz FM, Mix FM, Light & Easy (format radio stations which play a mix of local and international numbers), THR – which specialises in traffic updates – and the government-run Radio 4.

Television is the most popular medium in Malaysia, watched in both international hotel rooms and long-houses with the same enthusiasm. Programmes are cosmopolitan and American sit-coms and documentaries are shown alongside Indonesia's hottest films and Koran reading competitions. Sports are given generous amounts of air-time.

The government television stations are RTM1 and 2, the private operators are TV3, 8TV and NTV7, while the subscription-only satellite TV broadcaster, Astro, offers over 50 channels, including MTV, BBC World and CNN. The news in English is broadcast at 6.30pm on RTM1 (also known as TV1) and 12am on TV3 and NTV7. Some hotels offer an in-house cable station as well as selected Astro satellite channels. Check the local newspapers for programme details.

Money Matters

Malaysia uses ringgit and sen. RM1=100 sen. Coins come in denominations of 5, 10, 20, and 50 sen, and notes in RM1, RM2, RM5, RM10, RM50 and RM100.

Carry a combination of cash and traveller's cheques and/or a credit card. Cash is imperative in rural areas, but you can change travellers' cheques and use credit cards in urban areas and established tourist areas.

Changing money

Most currencies can be exchanged for ringgit, but the popular ones are US dollars, British sterling pounds, Euro and Singapore dollars. Licensed money changers (open from early morning until late at night) offer better rates than banks, while hotels and shopping centres levy a service

charge (usually 2–4 percent).

Local and international banks handle the gamut of transactions, and automated teller machines, from which you can use your credit card to withdraw cash, are widespread in cities, towns and transport hubs.

Banking Hours

In all states except Kelantan and Terengganu, banking hours are Mon–Fri 9.30am–4pm. Some open on the second and fourth Saturdays of the month 9.30am–noon. In Kelantan and Terengganu, banks open Sun–Thur 9.30am–4pm.

Credit Cards

The most widely used credit cards are Visa and MasterCard. Diners Club and American Express are less welcome, but accepted. Note that some retailers add a 2–3 percent surcharge for the privilege of using plastic – so ask first before paying. As with everywhere in the world, be watchful of credit card fraud. Make sure you have enough cash before you leave a city.
AMEX tel: 03-2031 7888
Diners Club tel: 03-2161 1055
Mastercard tel: 1800-804 594
Visa tel: 1800-802 997

Traveller's Cheques

All major brands of traveller's cheques and cash in major currencies are readily accepted in the major cities. Some big hotels exchange traveller's cheques for cash but their rates are not as good as banks, which have better rates.

P hotography

These days most photographers use digital cameras and there is an extensive selection of all the latest cameras and accessories for sale in Malaysia. Memory cards from a few megabytes to several gigabytes are also sold.

Most imaging shops have equipment to download images and can store them in CDs for between RM5 and RM10 a CD. It's also possible to print directly from memory cards.

Beware of the heat if using a conventional film-loaded camera. Exposure of film or camera equipment to hot sun causes changes in the chemical emulsions of the film, which detract from natural colour. Whenever possible, store your camera and film in a cool place; if not in an air-conditioned room, at least in the shade.

Get your films processed as soon as possible. You can do this everywhere in Malaysia. All outlets will process colour-print film, sometimes in as little as half an hour.

Be prepared for rain, even on sunny days – always have a plastic bag handy for your equipment. Note that rainforest excursions are damaging to cameras because of the humidity. Pack a dry, non-lint cloth to wipe your camera dry.

For rich colours, snap your shots before 10am or after 4pm. At noon, the light is too strong. Early morning or late afternoon sidelight produces softer contrasts and deeper colour density.

Most Malaysians are more than amiable about having their pictures taken. It usually takes a gang of schoolchildren about 15 seconds before they merrily begin jabbing peace signs in front of your camera. Mosques and temples are rightly more reserved about photographers posing their subjects in front of altars. Whatever the situation, it's best to ask for permission. This is imperative during religious ceremonies, when you should keep a respectful distance. Likewise with tribal people, ask your tour guide.

Population & Geography

Location: North of the equator, with the peninsula bordered by Singapore in the south and Thailand in the north. Sabah and Sarawak border Indonesia (Kalimantan).
Area: 329,000 sq. km (127,000 sq. miles) comprising Peninsular Malaysia, and Sabah and Sarawak on Borneo island.
Population: Over 26 million people. A blend of the great Asian cultures of the world, Malaysians comprise Malays and the indigenous tribes, which make up some 60 percent of the population, Chinese (fewer than 30 percent), Indians (fewer than 10 percent), and a potpourri of other ethnic groups.
Religion: The main and official religion is Islam, adopted by the Malays, but religious tolerance sees the open practice of Buddhism and Taoism among the Chinese, Hinduism among the Indians and Christianity among non-Malays. Some indigenous people retain their animist beliefs.

Postal & Courier Services

The **Malaysian postal service** (www.pos.com.my) is reliable, and there are post offices everywhere, generally open Mon–Fri 8am–5.30pm and Sat 8am–1pm. A handful in large housing estates are open until 10pm. The full range of services is available, including registered mail, parcels as well as the cashing of postal and money orders. PosLaju courier service, usually cheaper than private courier services, and overnight Pos Ekspres services are also offered.

Most large hotels provide postal services. Stamps and aerogrammes are often sold at small Indian sweet and tobacco stalls on street corners.

Courier services

International courier services include the following:
DHL
Tel: 1800-888 388 (within Malaysia)
www.dhl.com.my
Federal Express (FedEx)
Tel: 1800-886 363 (within Malaysia)
www.fedex.com
United Parcel Services (UPS)
Tel: 03-7784 2311 (Kuala Lumpur), 1800-180 088 (Penang), 06-284 5440 (Melaka), 082-233 150 (Sarawak), 088-726 876 (Sabah)
www.ups.com

Public Holidays

Many of Malaysia's public holidays relate to cultural festivals, the dates of which are not fixed but follow the lunar or Muslim calendar. These include Hari Raya Puasa, the main Muslim festival, a 2-day holiday celebrating the end of the Muslim fasting month of Ramadan; Hari Raya Haji, celebrating the annual Muslim pilgrimage season; Awal Muharam, the Muslim New Year; and the Birthday of Prophet Muhammad, during which prayers and Quran recitals are held at mosques.

Some festivals are observed only in certain states; for example, the birthday of the respective state sultans. If a public holiday falls on a Saturday or Sunday, the following Monday is a holiday; likewise, if a holiday falls on a Thursday or Friday in the states that follow the Muslim week, the following Saturday is a holiday. Check dates with **Tourism Malaysia** (tel: 1300-885 050 within Malaysia; www.tourism.gov.my).
January New Year's Day (1st); Thaipusam, the Hindu festival of penance, celebrated colourfully in Kuala Lumpur (Batu Caves) and Penang.
January/February Chinese New Year, a 2-day holiday for the main Chinese festival celebrated over a 15-day period. Make sure to visit Kuala Lumpur's Chinatown during this period.
April Mukah Kaul, a Melanau festival celebrated in the fishing communities around Mukah on Sarawak's north coast (thanks giving festival of this sea faring community).
May Labour Day (1st); Vesak Day, temple celebrations to mark Buddha's birth, death and enlightenment; Harvest Festival, a 2-day holiday, the main festival for the different groups of the state of Sabah.
June Gawai, a 2-day holiday that is the main official festival for the different tribal groups of Sarawak; Birthday of the Yang Di-pertuan Agung (king) (5th).
August National Day (31st), celebrated with parades.
October/November Deepavali, Hindu festival of lights.
December Christmas (25th), midnight mass, celebrated in churches throughout the country.

For more information on Malaysian festivals and events, see page 71.

School Holidays

When planning your holiday, note that school holidays occur during the months of March, May/June, August, November/December. During these times, attractions will be packed with families and school children. For exact dates, check www.moe.gov.my/tayang.php?laman=kalendar_sekolah&bhs=en. For Singapore school holiday dates, check www.moe.gov.sg/schapp/frames.htm.

Public Toilets

Public restrooms can generally be found near markets, parks and transport terminals, as well as in shopping complexes. Many still have squat toilets which visitors may not be familiar with. Toilet paper is not always available, although you can sometimes buy tissue paper at the entrance. Most malls charge a toilet entrance fee of 20–50 sen. If you are very particular, use hotel toilets.

R eligious Services

As the majority of the population are Muslim, mosques proliferate and all public buildings have at least one *surau* (prayer room). There are also ample places of worship for Buddhists, Taoists, Hindus, Sikhs and followers of other faiths. However, churches might be difficult to locate outside urban centres and in the predominantly Muslim east coast of Peninsular Malaysia. Check with your hotel.

The following churches offer English-language services.

Kuala Lumpur

St Mary's Cathedral (Anglican)
Jalan Raja
Tel: 03-2692 8672

Sun services 7am, 8.30am,
10.30am, 6pm.
Cathedral of St John (Catholic)
5 Jalan Bukit Nanas
Tel: 03-2078 1876
Sat mass (and Novena) 6pm, Sun
masses 8am, 10.30am, 6pm.
Church of the Holy Rosary (Catholic)
10 Jalan Tun Sambanthan,
Brickfields
Tel: 03-2274 2747
Sat mass 5pm, Sun mass 8.30am.
**Church of Our Lady of Fatima
(Catholic)**
Jalan Sultan Abdul Samad,
Brickfields
Tel: 03-2274 1631
Sun masses 7am, 10.30am,
Tues–Sat masses 6.30am.

Penang
Trinity Methodist Church
16 Jalan Masjid Negeri, Georgetown
Tel: 04-828 7445
Sun services 9am, 11am.
George Town Baptist Church
14 Jalan Larut, Georgetown
Tel: 04-229 7757
Sun services 9am, 11am.

Kuching
St Thomas Cathedral (Anglican)
Jalan Haji Openg
Tel: 082-240 187
Sun services 6.45am, 8.15am,
5.30pm.
St Joseph's Cathedral (Catholic)
Jalan Tun Haji Openg
Tel: 082-423 424
Sun masses 6.30am, 5.30pm.

Kota Kinabalu
All Saints Cathedral (Anglican)
Jalan Mat Salleh
Tel: 088-231 824
Sun services 7.30am, 10am.
Sacred Heart Cathedral (Catholic)
Jalan Menteri (off Jalan Mat Salleh)
Tel: 088-224 741
Sat mass 6pm, Sun mass 9am.

Taxes & Tipping

There is no general sales tax on
purchases, but there is a service
charge of 10 percent and a 5 percent
government tax in most large
establishments. Hotels and
restaurants usually separate the cost
and various taxes, which may be
written as "++".
　Tipping is not obligatory, although
it is appreciated and is common in
the cities and major tourist spots. In
large hotels, bellboys and porters
usually receive tips from RM2 to RM5
depending on the service rendered.
In smart restaurants you can just
leave behind the loose change.
Tour guides expect a tip, although a

simple "thank you" (*terima kasih*)
and a smile may be sufficient.

Telecommunications
International Calls
Most of the rooms in larger hotels
have phones with **International
Direct Dialling** (IDD) facility, but
charges are high. To call overseas,
dial 00 followed by the country code,
area code and phone number.
　The **country code** for Malaysia is
60. To call a Malaysian fixed-line
number from abroad, dial 60
followed by the local area code,
omitting the initial zero, then the
number you want.

Area Codes
Johor 07
Kedah 04
Kelanan 09
Kota Kinabalu 088
Kuala Lumpur 03
Kuching 082
Labuan 087
Melaka 06
Miri 085
Negeri Sembilan 06
Pahang 09
Penang 04
Perak 05
Perlis 04
Selangor 03
Terengganu 09
　Calls to Singapore do not require
IDD; simply dial the access code 02,
followed by the Singapore number.
　For local and international
telephone directory assistance, dial
103 (20 sen per call), and for
operator-assisted calls, dial 101
(RM1.50 per local call, RM5 per
international call).
　You can also buy **prepaid cards**
which offer cheaper rates for
international calls to certain
destinations. These use Voice-Over-
Internet-Protocol (VOIP) and the
connection may not be as clear.

Local Calls
To make a call to a number within a
state, simply dial the number without
the area code. For a call to another
state, dial the area code (with the
initial zero) and the number you want.
Note that phone numbers in Kuala
Lumpur and Selangor are eight digits
instead of the usual seven for those
in other states.

Mobile Phones
Malaysian mobile phones – the
numbers for which have the prefixes
010, 012, 013, 016, 017, 018, 019
– use the GSM network. If your mobile
phone has a roaming facility with
your home service provider, it will

automatically hook up to one of
Malaysia's digital networks (like
Celcom, DiGi, Maxis and TMNet).
Otherwise, prepaid local SIM cards,
with which you get a local mobile
number, are very affordable, starting
at RM20 for registration and air-time.
These allow you to call locally and
overseas, and can be topped up
at phone shops, newsagents and
petrol stations.
　To call a Malaysian mobile number
from overseas, dial 60 followed by
the prefix, dropping the initial zero,
then the number you want.

Public Phones
Local calls from a public phone cost
30 sen per 3 minutes. These can
also be used for calls to numbers in
other states and for international
calls (look out for phones marked
"international"). Booths are either
coin-operated or use phone cards.
Phone cards in denominations from
RM5 to RM50 are available at phone
shops, newsstands and petrol stations. In cities and towns, there are
also shops providing IDD services.

Time Zone
Malaysia's standard time is 8 hours
ahead of Greenwich Mean Time and
16 hours ahead of US Pacific
Standard Time.

Tourist Information
Tourism Malaysia (www.tourism.gov.my)
has offices in every state. The
amount of travel literature available
in TM offices varies, but there are
usually comprehensive brochures on
each state and sometimes on local
places of interest. The officers are
also informed and helpful. The
regional offices can also be
contacted for information on reliable
tour and travel operators, who have
to be registered with them.
　In addition, both Sarawak and
Sabah have their own state-run
tourism offices.

Tourist Offices
TM – Head Office, 24–27th & 30th
Floor, Menara Dato' Onn, Putra World
Trade Centre, 45 Jalan Tun Ismail,
KL, tel: 03-2615 8188; e-mail:
enquiries@tourism.gov.my;
www.tourism.gov.my.
Malaysia Tourism Centre (MTC),
109 Jalan Ampang, KL, tel: 03-2164
3929; e-mail: ticmtc@tourism.gov.my.
TM – East Coast Region, 5th Floor,
Menara Yayasan Islam Terengganu,
Jalan Sultan Omar, Kuala
Terengganu, tel: 09-622 1893;
e-mail: mtpbkt@tourism.gov.my.

TRANSPORT
ACCOMMODATION
EATING OUT
ACTIVITIES
A – Z
LANGUAGE

TM – Northern Region, Level 56, KOMTAR, Penang, tel: 04-264 3494; e-mail: mtpbpen@tourism.gov.my.
TM – Southern Region, L3–26, Level 3, Bangunan JOTIC, 2 Jalan Ayer Molek, Johor Bahru, tel: 07-222 3591; e-mail: mtpbjhb@tourism.gov.my.
TM – Sabah, Ground Floor, Uni Asia Building, 1 Jalan Sagunting, Kota Kinabalu, tel: 088-248 698; e-mail: mtpbbki@tourism.gov.my.
Sabah Tourism Board, 51 Jalan Gaya, Kota Kinabalu, tel: 088-212 121; e-mail: info@sabahtourism.com; www.sabahtourism.com.
TM – Sarawak, 2nd Floor, Rugayah Building, Jalan Song Thian Cheok, Kuching, tel: 082-246 575; e-mail: mtpbkch@tourism.gov.my.
Sarawak Tourism Board, 6th Floor Bangunan Yayasan Sarawak, Jalan Masjid, Kuching, tel: 082-423 600; e-mail: stb@sarawaktourism.com; www.sarawaktourism.com.

Tourist Offices (Overseas)

Tourism Malaysia has a network of overseas offices.
Australia (Sydney), Level 2, 171 Clarence Street, Sydney, NSW 2000, tel: 02-9299 4441, fax: 02-9262 2026; www.tourismmalaysia.com.au.
Canada (Vancouver), 1590-1111, West Georgia Street, Vancouver, BC, Canada V6E 4M3, tel: 604-689 8899, fax: 604-689 8804; e-mail: mtpb.vancouver@tourism.gov.my; www.tourism-malaysia.ca.
Germany (Frankfurt), Weissfrauenstrasse 12–16, D-60311 Frankfurt Am Main, tel: 069-4609 23420, fax: 069-4609 23499; e-mail: mtpb.frankfurt@arcormailo.de.
Singapore, #01-01B/C/D, 80 Robinson Road, Singapore 068898, tel: 6532 6321/51, fax: 6535 6650; e-mail: mtpb.singapore@tourism.gov.my.
Thailand (Bangkok), Unit 1001, Liberty Square, 287 Silom Road, Bangkok 10500, tel: 0662-631 1994/5/6, fax: 0662-631 1998.
United Kingdom, 57 Trafalgar Square, London WC2N 5DU, tel: 020-7930 7932, fax: 020-7930 9015; e-mail: mtpb.london@tourism.gov.my.
United States (New York), 120 East 56th Street, Suite 810, New York, NY 10022, tel: 212-754 1114/5, fax: 212-754 1116; e-mail: mtpb.ny@tourism.gov.my; www.visitmalaysia.com.
United States (Los Angeles), Suite 970, 9th Floor, 818 West Seventh Street, Los Angeles, CA 90017 U.S.A., tel: 213-689 9702, fax: 213-689 1530; e-mail: mtpb.la@tourism.gov.my.

Websites

A selection of useful news and travel sites on Malaysia.
www.airasia.com Malaysia's largest budget airline offers the cheapest flights within the country and to regional destinations. Book and pay for these flights online.
www.allmalaysia.info General site on all things Malaysian with content from leading English newspaper, *The Star*.
www.asianoverlandservices.com Malaysia's largest in-bound travel operator has tours to the nation's leading travel destinations at competitive prices.
www.friedchillies.com Honest reviews of and guide to food in Kuala Lumpur and Malaysia.
www.journeymalaysia.com Comprehensive information related to travel.
www.kakiseni.com E-zine featuring contemporary arts in Malaysia.
www.ktmb.com.my This website provides timetables and fares for trains within Malaysia as well as those to Singapore and Thailand.
www.malaysiaairlines.com Malaysia's international airline with connections to many domestic destinations and flies to six continents.
www.smarttravelasia.com/sabah.htm A coverage of the main places of interest, with listings of restaurants and hotels, and links to the latter.
www.sabahtravelguide.com Endorsed by Sabah Tourism, this award-winning website is a useful guide to the history, culture and destinations of Sabah, with star ratings for places of interest, online reservations for accommodation and tours, and links to other useful websites.
www.virtualmalaysia.com Both a travel magazine and a website, Virtual Malaysia highlights the country's best travel destinations.
www.wildasia.com A website concerned with conservation and responsible tourism, particularly eco-tourism. Plenty of practical travel information, articles and a photo library.

Weights & Measures

Malaysia follows the metric system, but people in rural areas might still use miles (*batu*) rather than kilometres for distance.

What to Bring

There is very little need to worry about leaving something important behind when you visit Malaysia. Toiletries, medicines, clothes, film, suntan lotion and straw hats are all readily available in most towns, and definitely in the large cities. So, travel lightly.

In more remote areas, you may not have the luxury of a shaving point, but disposable razors are widely available, or you can buy a battery-operated razor. Sanitary products for women are also available, but tampons are not easily obtainable in small towns.

Toilet paper is still not widely used, even in cities, so unless you are familiar with the local pail or hose-and-water method, pack a roll, or carry tissue paper with you.

What to Read

The major bookstore chains in Malaysia are Times, MPH, Kinokunuya and Popular, while some specialist bookstores are found mainly in Kuala Lumpur.

A rich repository of Sarawakian, Bornean and Asian published work is the Sarawak Museum shop in Kuching. An even bigger range is found in Kota Kinabalu at Borneo Books 2, on the second floor of Wisma Merdeka (they also have a book exchange). Small but good collections of nature books, including specialist titles, can be found at the Kuala Lumpur headquarters of the Malaysian Nature Society (MNS) (tel: 03-2287 9422) and the World Wildlife Fund for Nature (WWF) Malaysia (tel: 03-7803 3772).

History/Political

A History of Malaya, by Barbara Watson Andaya and Leonard Andaya, Macmillan London (1982). Non-colonial objective interpretation of the country's development.
The Golden Chersonese: the Malayan Travels of Victorian Lady, by Isabella Bird, Oxford University Press Singapore (1883), reprinted. Lyrical 19th-century impressions of the experiences of this intrepid traveller.
Government and Society In Malaysia, by Harold Crouch, Allen & Unwin Australia (1996). An insider's view from an outsider on Malaysian politics, founding his analysis on the fact that Malaysian politics and society operates essentially on the basis of a "moving equilibrium".
The Malay Dilemma, by Mahathir Mohamad, Malaysia (1970). Important text that outlines the prime minister's thoughts on the country's racial politics and economics; recent books by him have been compilations of his speeches and policies.

Malaysia's Political Economy, by Edmund Terence Gomez & Jomo K.S., Cambridge University Press (1997). An insightful and accessible analysis of contemporary Malaysian business and politics, examining through detailed case studies political patronage on wealth accumulation, and policies and their consequences.
Malaysian Journey, by Rehman Rashid, Malaysia (1993). A witty, sharp treatise on contemporary Malaysia, though somewhat dogmatic.
Malay Society: Transformation and Democratisation, by Khoo Kay Kim, Malaysia (1992). The study of Malay society from the Melaka Sultanate to the 1990s, by one of the country's most prominent historians.
Paradoxes of Mahathirism: An Intellectual Biography of Mahathir Mohamad, by Khoo Boo Teik, Oxford University Press (1995). Like all books on the prime minister, this takes an academic approach to his ideas on nationalism, capitalism, Islam, populism, and authoritarianism – the core of Mahathirism.

General

The Crafts of Malaysia, Dato' Haji Sulaiman Othman, Yeoh Jin Leng, etc, Archipelago Press, Singapore (1994). A beautiful documentary of the development of the Malay arts in a changing society, with pictures of the best craft from museums and private collections.
Culture Shock! Malaysia, by Heidi Munan, Graphic Arts Center Pub Co. (1991). A witty and invaluable treatise on Malaysian customs, can-do's and absolutely-nots.
Cuzinhia Cristang: A Malacca-Portuguese Cookbook, by Celine J. Marbeck, Tropical Press, Malaysia. A lovely collection of six centuries of the food of the Melaka-Portuguese Cristang people.
An Eastern Port and Other Stories:More Recollections of Singapore and Malaya, by Julian Davison, Topographica (2004). A second collection of sketches and anecdotes drawn from the memory of an English expatriate who grew up in Singapore and Malaysia in the 1950s and 1960s.
The Encyclopedia of Malaysia, Editions Didier Millet, Malaysia (1998). A highly-illustrative topic-categorised presentation of Malaysiana from early history and architecture to plants, literature and economics.
The Food of Malaysia, edited by Wendy Hutton, Periplus Editions, Singapore (1995). Handy-sized

collection of local recipes with nice background information and lovely colour photographs.
Kuala Lumpur – A Sketchbook, by Chin Kon Yit, and Chen Voon Fee, Archipelago Press, Singapore (1998). Beautiful watercolour paintings of old Kuala Lumpur with suitably brief captions.
Lat, Malaysia, Times Publishing. Compilations of the work of the country's sharpest and funniest cartoonist; hilarious depictions of Malaysian life and psyche.
One for the Road and Other Stories: Recollections of Singapore and Malaya by Julian Davison, Topographica (2001). Autobiographical vignettes based on the life of an English child during the bygone era of Singapore and Malaysia in the 1950s and 1960s.
Rasa Malaysia, by Betty Yew, Times Publishing, Malaysia. A collection of Malaysia's best-loved recipes by a leading chef and writer of cookbooks.

Natural History

A Diver's Guide to Underwater Malaysia Macrolife, by Andrea Ferrari and Antonella Ferrari, Nautilus (2003). This volume is illustrated with more than 800 colour photographs and describes in full detail 600 different Indo-Pacific marine species, focusing on those found in the South China, Sulu and Sulawesi seas.
National Parks of Malaysia, by WWF Malaysia, New Holland, UK (1998). Pictorial, tourist-market coffee-table book, with an excellent bibliography.
Photographic Guide to the Birds of Peninsular Malaysia and Singapore, by M. Strange, and A. Jeyarajasingham, Malaysia (1993).
Pocket Guide to the Birds of Borneo, by Sabah Society with WWF Malaysia, Malaysia (1995).
Visitor's Guide to Taman Negara, New Holland, UK (2005). The definitive guide for exploring Malaysia's largest national park. Excellent trail notes, maps and photos for the intrepid rainforest explorer.
Wild Malaysia: The Wildlife and Scenery of Peninsular Malaysia, Sarawak and Sabah, by Junaidi Payne, Gerald Cubitt (photographer), New Holland Press, UK (1990), World Wildlife Fund for Nature. A pictorial introduction containing 400 colour photographs of animals and habitats. The text, by a leading Malaysian environmentalist, examines conservation and development, as well as peoples and natural history.

Fiction/Biography

Among the White Moon Faces: An Asian-American Memoir of Home-

lands (Cross-Cultural Memoir Series) by Shirley Geok-Lin Lim, Feminist Press (1996). A biographical recount of a Malaysian childhood and later life in the United States; the author has also published short stories.
Lord Jim, by Joseph Conrad, Penguin, London (1900). The tale of an Englishman who abandons his ship and hides in Malaya eventually becoming a Lord. Conrad set many other stories in the Malay Archipelago, including Victory: an Island Tale and The Rescue.
Maugham's Malaysian Stories, by Somerset Maugham (1933, reprinted 1986). Masterful story-telling of British colonial life in the country.

Travel

Into The Heart Of Borneo, by Redmond O' Hanlon, The Salamander Press (1984). A heartwarmingly and laugh-aloud treatise on O'Hanlon's hilarious expedition to Borneo, told with great sympathy and style.
Stranger In The Forest, by Eric Hanson (out of print). A gripping and sometimes chilling tale of one man's adventures as he learns the ways of the tribal folk during his solitary wander through the forest.
World Within, by Tom Harrisson, Oxford University Press Singapore (1986). A classic story by the man who later became curator of Sarawak Museum tells of Bario's Kelabit Highlands during the Japanese occupation years of World War II.

Culture

Enchanted Gardens of Kinabalu, by Susan M. Phillipps, Natural History Publications (Borneo), Malaysia (1995). A beautiful book of botanical paintings that include coral gardens, too.
The Malay Archipelago, by Alfred Russel Wallace (1869). A classic tale of a Victorian naturalist who spent several years wandering through the archipelago. He was also instrumental in assisting in the setting up of Sarawak Museum and his theories on evolution coincided with those of Darwin.
Natural Man, by Charles Hose, Oxford University Press Singapore (1988). A reprint of a 1912 study by one of Sarawak's colonial administrators under Rajah Charles Brooke.
Sarawak Crafts – Methods and Motifs, by Heidi Munan, Oxford University Press (1989). Written by a Sarawak expert, this small book is filled with a wealth of information.
Sarawak Style, by Edric Ong, Times Editions Singapore (1996). Well-photographed book examining style in the Sarawak way.

LANGUAGE

UNDERSTANDING THE LANGUAGE

General

The official language is Bahasa Malaysia (Malay), but English is the language of business and technology. The Chinese also use Mandarin and various Chinese dialects, while the Indians use Tamil and other Indian languages. The indigenous people retain their own languages.

Bahasa Malaysia

Bahasa Malaysia is an Austronesian language also spoken in Indonesia, Singapore, Brunei, the Philippines and southern Thailand. Although there is a standard Bahasa Malaysia taught in schools and used formally, there are actually many regional Malay dialects that are not mutually intelligible. This is in addition to a simplified form of Bahasa Malaysia known as "bahasa pasar" or "bazaar Malay".

Bahasa Malaysia is also known as Bahasa Melayu and popularly abbreviated as BM. Since it is the official language, all signboards and public displays of writing are in Bahasa Malaysia, so it is useful to learn some words. It is written in the Latin alphabet, and is an easy language to learn.

The language is polysyllabic, with variations in syllables to convey changes in meaning. Words are pronounced as they are spelt. However, spelling can be tricky, for despite standardisation efforts, place and street names, for example, still follow different spellings. For instance, *baru* (new) is standard but also appears as *bahru*, *bharu* and *baharu*. Another example is *cangkat* (hillock), which is sometimes spelt *changkat* and *tingkat* (lane) as *tengkat*.

Root words are either nouns or verbs and prefixes and/or suffixes are added to change the meaning. Therefore, while *makan* is "to eat", *makanan* is "food" and *memakan* is "eating". The adjective always comes after the noun, so "my husband" is *suami saya*. To indicate plural, you often just repeat the noun, so "many rooms" are *bilik-bilik*.

When constructing a sentence, the order is subject-verb-subject: *Dia* (he) *makan* (eats) *nasi* (rice) *goreng* (fried). *Dia makan nasi goreng* = He eats fried rice.

Pronunciation Tips

In general the pronunciation is the same as in English, with some exceptions. The "a" is pronounced "ar" as in "tar" when it appears in the middle of a word. But when it ends a word, it is pronounced with an "er" sound as in "observe". Therefore *apa* (what) is pronounced as "arper". The "e" also has an "er" sound as in "observe".

"I" is pronounced with an "ee" sound unless it ends as an "-ik" or "-ih", in which case it is pronounced like the "a" in "agent", so *bilik* (room) is pronounced "bee-lake". The "u" has an "oo" sound unless it ends as an "-uk", "-up", "-uh" or "-ur", in which case it has an "oh" sound. Therefore *sepuluh* (ten) is pronounced "sir-poo-loh". "C" is pronounced "ch" as in "chair"; "sy" is pronounced "sh"; and "ai" is pronounced "i". A tricky one involving "ai", which you are likely to use, is *air* (water) which is pronounced "i-yeah".

"G" is always hard, as in "gun"; the "h" is always pronounced and you may come across "ny" and "ng" sounds which may not be common in your native language.

Although nearly all syllables are given equal stress, sometimes the final syllable of a word is emphasised, especially the last word in an utterance. This has led to the widespread use of the appendage -*lah* to the important word, whose purpose is purely emphatic. However, -*lah* is also liberally used in English; for instance, you could get thrown a "*Cannot-lah!*", when you are trying to bargain.

Forms of Address

When addressing someone formally, the form for men is *encik* (sir), which can be used on its own, or to precede a person's name, eg. *Encik* Razak. The female equivalent for married or older women are *puan* (Madam) and *Puan* Miriam (Mrs Miriam), and for single or younger women, *Cik* (Miss) and *Cik* Ros (Miss Ros). For men and women who are the same age, you may use "comrade" as in *saudara* (men) and *saudari* (women).

The informal form for older men of your father's age, is *pakcik* (literally "uncle") and *abang* (literally "older brother") for men slightly older than you. For women the equivalent is *makcik* (literally "aunty") and *kakak* (literally "older sister"). Meanwhile the gender-free informal form for younger men and women as well as children is *adik* ("younger brother/sister").

Regardless of formal or informal use, the word for "you" (*anda*, etc) is rarely used as it is considered rude. Instead replace it with the form of address or name, for example, *Encik dari mana*? or *Encik Razak dari mana*? ("Where are you from?") Note that other than for older people, the English pronoun "you" has become common, for example, "You *dari mana*?"

Vocabulary

You will find Sanskrit, Arabic, Tamil, Portuguese, Dutch, Chinese and English words in Bahasa Malaysia. English words are also increasingly being incorporated into the language, particularly in relation to business and technology. In spoken Bahasa Malaysia, short forms are usually used, and these are indicated within [ ] below too. Here are some useful words and phrases to get you going.

Useful Words and Phrases

General

How do you do? *Apa khabar?*
Fine/good *Baik*
Good morning *Selamat pagi*
Good afternoon *Selamat tengah hari*
Good evening *Selamat petang*
Goodbye *Selamat tinggal*
Bon voyage *Selamat jalan*
Yes *Ya*
No *Tidak*
Thank you *Terima kasih*
You're welcome *Sama-sama*
Please *Tolong/sila*
Excuse me *Maafkan saya [Maaf]*
May I ask you a question? *Tumpang tanya?*
Can you help me? *Bolehkah cik tolong saya?*
I am sorry *Minta maaf [Maaf]*
Please come in *Sila masuk*
Please sit down *Sila duduk*
Thank you very much *Terima kasih banyak-banyak*
You're welcome *Sama-sama*
Where do you come from? *Asal dari mana?*
I come from...... *Saya datang dari......*
What is your name? *Siapa nama anda?*
My name is...... *Nama saya......*
Can you speak Bahasa Malaysia? *Boleh anda bercakap Bahasa Malaysia?*
Only a little *Sedikit sahaja*
Wait a minute *Tunggu sekejap*
How much? *Berapa harga?*
That's too expensive *Mahal sangat*
Can you reduce the price? *Boleh kurang?*
Too big *Besar sangat*
Too small *Kecil sangat*
Any other colour? *Ada warna lain?*
I would like to change money *Saya hendak tukar duit*
Where is the toilet? *Di mana tandas?*
In the back *Di belakang*
What time does the bus leave? *Pukul berapa bas bertolak?*

Pronouns

I *saya*
you (to someone the same age or younger) *awak, anda* or *kita* (in Borneo Malaysia only)
you (formal) *encik*
he, she *dia*
we *kami* (excluding the speaker), *kita* (including the speaker)
they *mereka*

Directions

Right *kanan*
Left *kiri*
Turn *belok*
Go *pergi*
Stop *berhenti*
Follow *ikut*
Near *dekat*
Inside *dalam*
Outside *luar*
Front *hadapan* or *depan*
Behind *belakang*
Here *dini*
There *sana*
Where are you going? (*Pergi*) *ke mana?*
I want to go to... *Saya hendak pergi ke...*
Turn right *Belok (ke) kanan*
Turn left *Belok (ke) kiri*
Go straight *Jalan terus*
Please stop here *Sila berhenti di sini*
Where is this place? *Di mana tempat ini?*
How far? *Berapa jauh?*

Driving

Road *jalan*
Lane *lorong*
Street *lebuh*
Highway *lebuhraya*
Bridge *jambatan*
Junction *simpang*
Danger *awas* or *merbahaya*
No overtaking *dilarang memotong*
Slow down *kurangkan laju*
Speed limit *had laju*
Enter *masuk*
Exit *keluar*
Keep left/right *ikut kiri/kanan*
One-way street *jalan sehala*
North *utara*
South *aelatan*
East *timur*
West *barat*

Food and Drink

Eat *makan*
Drink *minum*
Bread *roti*
Beef *daging lembu*
Chicken *Ayam* (pronounced "ah- yarm")
Fish *Ikan* (pronounced "ee-karn")
Vegetables *Sayur*
Fried noodles *mee goreng*
Fried rice *nasi goreng*
Salt *garam*
Spicy *pedas*
Delicious *sedap*
A cup of coffee *kopi satu*
A cup of tea *teh satu*
Water *air* (pronounced "i-yeah")
Less sweet *kurang manis*
Without sugar *tanpa gula*
Without milk *tanpa susu*
Without ice *tanpa ais* (pronounced "ice")
Not enough *tak cukup*
Not hot/cold enough *tak cukup panas/sejuk*
Add *tambah*
A little *sedikit [sikit]*
A lot *banyak*

Numbers

1 *satu*
2 *dua*
3 *tiga*
4 *empat*
5 *lima*
6 *enam*
7 *tujuh*
8 *lapan*
9 *sembilan*
10 *sepuluh*
11 *sebelas*
12 *dua belas*
13 *tiga belas*
20 *dua puluh*
21 *dua puluh satu*
22 *dua puluh dua*
30 *tiga puluh*
40 *empat puluh*
100 *seratus*
263 *dua ratus enam puluh tiga*
1,000 *seribu*

Time and Days of the Week

minute *minit*
hour *jam*
day *hari*
week *minggu*
Monday *Isnin*
Tuesday *Selasa*
Wednesday *Rabu*
Thursday *Khamis*
Friday *Jumaat*
Saturday *Sabtu*
Sunday *Ahad*
What time is it? *Jam berapa?*

Other Useful Words

what? *apa?*
who? *siapa?*
where (place) *di mana?*
where (direction) *ke mana?*
when? *bila?*
how? *bagaimana?*
why? *mengapa?*
which? *yang mana?*
sleep *tidur*
bathe *mandi*
come *datang*
buy *beli (membeli)*
sell *jual (menjual)*
road, walk *jalan*
airport *lapangan terbang*
post office *pejabat pos*
shop *kedai*
coffeeshop *kedai kopi*
money *wang, duit*

ART & PHOTO CREDITS

S.T. Amerasinghe 226
Amri/HBL Network 75
H. Berbar/HBL Network back cover
left top and bottom, 6, 31, 37, 46,
85, 87, 89, 90/91, 110, 114, 150,
174, 215, 217L/R, 221, 223, 224,
225T, 299, 300, 306, 333
Dr Hans-Ulrich Bernard 267
David Bowden 71, 331
Marcus Brooke 173, 189,
236/237, 238, 242, 246, 249,
252, 258, 321
A. Buu/HBL Network 58
Frank Castle 24
C.L. Chan 326T
Wendy Chan 93, 279, 280, 283,
283T
Tommy Chang 335T
Alain Compost 52/53, 56, 167,
326
Robert Condrum 77
V. Couarraze/HBL 126/127
Alain Evrard 10/11, 57, 61, 66L,
200, 210/211
E. Fearn/HBL Network 14
K. Fletcher 270
Flyright Air-Sport 241
Jill Gocher front flap bottom, back
cover right bottom, spine bottom, 1,
2/3, 2B, 66R, 72/73, 104R, 111,
166, 180/181, 187, 192, 193,
194L, 205L, 217T, 255, 262, 268,
274, 281T, 282, 285, 286, 287,
288, 292, 293, 296, 297, 298,
298T, 301, 302, 304, 305L/R,
307, 315, 315T, 316, 317T, 318,
322T, 329, 332, 336, 338, 339,
341, 342, 343
Manfred Gottschalk 7, 95, 135,
171L, 197, 202
Grunau/HBL Network 244
Francisco Guerrero 231
Hans Hayden 228
HBL Network 48, 97, 219T
Dallas & John Heaton 190R
Hendrick/HBL Network 122
Hans Höfer 5B, 6/7, 21, 23, 27,
29, 30, 62/63, 69, 169, 172T,
178, 277, 281, 290, 320, 322,
324
Jack Hollingsworth 68, 78L/R,
329T
J. Houyvet/HBL Network 108/109

Wendy Hutton 319T
Jati/HBL Network 19, 50, 51
Ingo Jezierski 79, 88, 135T, 179T,
186T, 188T, 190T, 193T, 196T,
198T, 202T, 204T, 220, 221T,
222T, 225, 231T, 252T
Jungle War in Malaya 41, 42
Yap Piang Kian 120/121, 170,
203, 204
Anthea Lamb 162, 325
David Lane 255T
Max Lawrence 45, 152
Alan Lee 191
R. Lendrum 284
Philip Little 8, 32R, 59, 185, 188,
190L, 194R, 205R, 229, 245, 313
Joseph Lynch 9, 74, 76, 84,
100/101, 156, 209T, 232, 253,
257, 266, 323
Malaysian Industrial Development
Authority 47
Malaysian Nature Society 7, 235
R. Margaillan/HBL Network back
flap top, 60, 115, 243, 251, 335,
340
Nickt Wong/APA 7, 132, 133,
134T, 134, 136, 137T, 137, 138T,
138, 139, 140L, 140R, 141T, 141,
142, 143T, 143, 144T, 144, 145T,
145L, 145R, 146, 147L, 147R,
148, 149, 152T, 152, 153T
Richard Maschmeyer 247
Gloria Maschmeyer 105, 248
R. Mohd. Noh 4BR, 20, 22, 28, 81,
103, 106, 107L/R, 151, 163,
177T, 201, 207, 207T, 222, 230,
233, 249T, 264, 344
Reg Monison 96
Museu Militar, Lisbon 26
Muzium Negara, Malaysia 16/17,
18, 25, 34L/R, 35L, 38, 40, 43
National Archives, Singapore 33
Navaro/HBL Network 208, 263,
310, 337
Frank Newman 244T
Helen Newman 340T
R.C.A. Nichols 172
Private Archives 35R, 44
Photobank Singapore 9, 32L, 55,
80, 92, 94, 214, 259
Picture Library/KL 64, 128
G.P. Reichelt 8/9, 65, 70, 291
D. Saulnier/HBL Network 160

Ruth Seitz 199
Hugh Sitton/Tony Stone Images
cover, 3B
S. Sreedharan 334
The Straits Times, Singapore 39
Morten Strange 269, 272/273,
289, 303
Larry Tackelt 330
Arthur Teng front flap top, back
cover right top, back cover centre
top, 4/5, 6, 8, 12/13, 49, 67,
82/83, 86, 102, 104L, 116/117,
118/119, 137, 153, 154/155,
161T, 164, 165, 170T, 175, 195,
196, 209, 212, 219, 227, 254,
278T, 291T, 308/309, 317, 319,
327
Albert Teo 304T
Trade Development Corp. of
Malaysia 159
Gorazd Vilhar 165T
Bill Wassman 8, 146T, 168, 171R,
250, 256
Westfries Museum, Hoorn 36
S.L. Wong back cover centre
bottom, 4BL, 113, 176, 177, 179,
198, 234, 235T, 258T, 265L/R,
268T, 271, 301T
Yeoh Thean Yeow 161
Joseph Yogerst 54
Chan Yuen-Li 112, 328

Photo Features

Pages 98/99
All pictures by: R. Mohd. Noh.
Pages 182/183
All pictures by: R. Mohd. Noh.
Pages 260/261
All pictures by: R. Mohd. Noh.
Pages 294/295
All pictures by: Jill Gocher.

Cartographic Editor: Zoë Goodwin
Map Production: Colourmap
Scanning Ltd, James Macdonald

©2007 Apa Publications GmbH & Co.
Verlag KG, Singapore Branch

INDEX

Numbers in italics refer to photographs

A
B
C
D
E
F
G
I
J
a
b
c
d
f
g
h
i
j
k
l

INSIGHT GUIDES

The classic series that puts you in the picture

Alaska
Amazon Wildlife
American Southwest
Amsterdam
Argentina
Arizona & Grand Canyon
Asia's Best Hotels & Resorts
Asia, East
Asia, Southeast
Australia
Austria
Bahamas
Bali & Lombok
Baltic States
Bangkok
Barbados
Barcelona
Beijing
Belgium
Belize
Berlin
Bermuda
Boston
Brazil
Brittany
Bruges, Ghent & Antwerp
Brussels
Buenos Aires
Burgundy
Burma (Myanmar)
Cairo
California
California, Southern
Canada
Cape Town
Caribbean
Caribbean Cruises
Channel Islands
Chicago
Chile
China
Colorado
Continental Europe
Corsica
Costa Rica
Crete
Croatia
Cuba
Cyprus
Czech & Slovak Republic
Delhi, Jaipur & Agra
Denmark

Dominican Rep. & Haiti
Dublin
East African Wildlife
Eastern Europe
Ecuador
Edinburgh
Egypt
England
Finland
Florence
Florida
France
France, Southwest
French Riviera
Gambia & Senegal
Germany
Glasgow
Gran Canaria
Great Britain
Great Gardens of Britain
  & Ireland
Great Railway Journeys
  of Europe
Great River Cruises:
  Europe & the Nile
Greece
Greek Islands
Guatemala, Belize
  & Yucatán
Hawaii
Hong Kong
Hungary
Iceland
India
India, South
Indonesia
Ireland
Israel
Istanbul
Italy
Italy, Northern
Italy, Southern
Jamaica
Japan
Jerusalem
Jordan
Kenya
Korea
Laos & Cambodia
Las Vegas
Lisbon
London

Los Angeles
Madeira
Madrid
Malaysia
Mallorca & Ibiza
Malta
Mauritius Réunion
  & Seychelles
Mediterranean Cruises
Melbourne
Mexico
Miami
Montreal
Morocco
Moscow
Namibia
Nepal
Netherlands
New England
New Mexico
New Orleans
New York City
New York State
New Zealand
Nile
Normandy
North American &
  Alaskan Cruises
Norway
Oman & The UAE
Oxford
Pacific Northwest
Pakistan
Paris
Peru
Philadelphia
Philippines
Poland
Portugal
Prague
Provence
Puerto Rico
Rajasthan
Rio de Janeiro
Rome

Russia
St Petersburg
San Francisco
Sardinia
Scandinavia
Scotland
Seattle
Shanghai
Sicily
Singapore
South Africa
South America
Spain
Spain, Northern
Spain, Southern
Sri Lanka
Sweden
Switzerland
Sydney
Syria & Lebanon
Taipei
Taiwan
Tanzania & Zanzibar
Tenerife
Texas
Thailand
Tokyo
Toronto
Trinidad & Tobago
Tunisia
Turkey
Tuscany
Umbria
USA: The New South
USA: On The Road
USA: Western States
US National Parks: West
Utah
Venezuela
Venice
Vienna
Vietnam
Wales
Walt Disney World/Orlando
Washington, DC

The world's largest collection of visual travel guides & maps